T0373718

TRUE TO THEIR SALT

ROB JOHNSON

True to Their Salt

Indigenous Personnel in Western Armed Forces

HURST & COMPANY, LONDON

First published in the United Kingdom in 2017 by
C. Hurst & Co. (Publishers) Ltd.,
41 Great Russell Street, London, WC1B 3PL
© Rob Johnson, 2017
All rights reserved.
Printed in India

The right of Rob Johnson to be identified as the author of
this publication is asserted by him in accordance with the
Copyright, Designs and Patents Act, 1988.

A Cataloguing-in-Publication data record for this book
is available from the British Library.

ISBN: 9781849044257

This book is printed using paper from registered sustainable
and managed sources.

www.hurstpublishers.com

This book is dedicated to my mother, Pam, who knows how to advise, mentor and nurture, and who has always been true to her salt.

CONTENTS

PREFACE

This book seeks to address the problems, risks and benefits of recruiting and managing local personnel in the armed forces of Great Britain, France and the United States from the mid-eighteenth to the early twenty-first centuries. Recruitment of indigenous forces, outside national armies, has long been practised in the West and seems to have returned in recent years in a new form with the creation of armies in Iraq and Afghanistan, and interventions using Western air power in support of local militias. Historically, despite the growth of nationalism, or notions of a 'nation in arms', two concepts which still dominate the scholarship of Western armies, the Europeans often established local forces to augment their manpower, using a variety of justifications for them, some ideological and others pragmatic. In the twenty-first century, Western armies talk of partnering and mentoring local forces, created in their own image, as part of a strategy of state stabilisation or as the means to advance their national interests. Similar tactics are used by other powers, most notably Russia and the Syrian government in the Syrian civil war, which may be eroding norms of international affairs, but which are also re-establishing a much older practice. This book investigates the issues, the challenges and some of the solutions in a wide range of contexts, covering different historical time periods and geographical settings in order to show the distinctiveness of changes as well as thematic similarities. This book contains an inherent warning. The collision of local expectations and Western ideas, of clan politics and Weberian bureaucracy, and cultural norms with new opportunities for wealth and status caused considerable distortion as well as development in the societies Westerners encountered, yet today there are confident predictions about the value of using indigenous or proxy forces which may not take full account of the problems or the consequences.

The book raises a number of questions: How were local forces recruited? How were Western standards and local expectations managed? How was 'loyalty' created and maintained? How were personnel retained during the transition to post-colonial independent states? What special ideas and practices prevailed during the Cold War, in Vietnam and during decolonisation when Western forces were not in permanent occupation, as they had been during the colonial era? How exactly did these forces perform: were they, ultimately, an asset or just a destabilizing force and a liability? The book examines the themes of cohesion, motivation in conflicts where local troops were serving foreign masters, and the implications of failures in discipline. The book addresses the murder of Western officers and NCOs, what happened when it all went wrong, and, conversely, why some personnel performed so well, even when serving a foreign interest. There is also coverage of armies of newly independent post-colonial states and their interventions in civil politics. The book provides a basis for a fuller understanding of the emerging issues surrounding contract personnel, security forces' assistance and the role of local forces in stabilisation missions.

In essence, this work examines how Western armies and governments tried to utilise or exploit local human resources. In existing studies of armies and empires, it is often assumed that Western colonial authorities were adept at raising and using local assets, that loyalty was easily 'transferred' and there was almost an automatic aspect to the phenomenon, but this assumption should be questioned and tested. What is clear is that indigenous auxiliaries have always been important tools in the projection of Western power and influence, if not always reliable ones, and they were equally important as the West withdrew its direct involvement in the Caribbean, Africa, the Middle East, Asia and the Pacific. A number of scholars have made detailed studies of selected forces over the years, and some have made syntheses of these, particularly Ashley Jackson, David Killingray and John Lynn. What emerges from these studies is the critical role that armies played in the creation of states, in the expansion of empires, in the process of decolonisation, and in the success or failure of efforts to stabilise states after 1945. From the 1990s, Western military interventions in the Balkans, North Africa, the Middle East and Afghanistan nevertheless pose unsettling questions about the re-establishment of security and who, precisely, benefits. Military personnel are eager to develop indigenous armies as part of a more positive and benign process of stabilisation and transition, and new doctrine has emerged in NATO nations on mentoring, advising and partnering, which gives this book significant contemporary resonance. Unfortunately, much of the existing work in this regard is based on very limited experiences, with no theoretical underpinnings and inadequate historical perspective.

The purpose of this book is to establish a clearer understanding of how non-Western service personnel were recruited and managed; an assessment of the appeal, value, effectiveness and results of this service; an evaluation of where and why the systems failed and where they succeeded, particularly in insurgency and unconventional conflicts; and how our understanding of these issues could affect current and future recruitment and management patterns. In essence the book attempts to offer a more enriched understanding of the successes and failures of the past, the tools and levers by which men had been brought into Western-controlled forces, and some understanding of the risks and benefits of such practices as were adopted in Iraq and Afghanistan, and elsewhere.

The Contemporary Context

The decision to establish a Sons of Iraq, or Awakening movement, among the Sunni population of Iraq, and simultaneously to incorporate, through institutions and power-sharing, the Shias of that country, was regarded as the turning point in the Iraqi Insurgency of 2004–10.[1] In 2008, in Afghanistan, the US Army announced its decision to replicate the recruitment of local forces, the Sons of the Shura, as a measure to bring the Taliban insurgency there to an end.[2] In both cases, the US forces also led on the creation of an Iraqi regular army and an Afghan national army entirely from scratch. The raising of new armies is always problematic, and is especially so during an insurgency. The recruitment of former insurgents, for example, or the arming of local fighters may actually make the situation worse, although invariably these men have made the best fighters on either side. Quality and reliability lie at the heart of the concerns. The creation of a vast, volunteer citizen army at great speed may not ensure the cohesion necessary to withstand the very shocks the army is designed to tackle. Moreover, the current predilection for drawing conclusions only from the experience in Iraq and Afghanistan lacks depth, and it is clear that a more comprehensive analysis is required.[3] The historical record is rich with examples of the raising and maintenance of indigenous forces and how such forces succeeded or failed. The recruitment of local auxiliaries was an essential component of the European colonial experience, and, in the transfer of power and security at the end of that colonial era, the raising of local forces using existing models became the norm. The period of colonial rule and decolonisation is remarkably instructive on how stabilised states and their armies can be transferred, and the unforeseen consequences. Here, the West's insights need to be understood in the context of their own points of reference and how, by contrast, local expectations can alter their plans. An understanding of the structures and dynamics of clan leadership and loyalty, of social networks, patronage and power relationships, and of identities in indigenous societies that have not been exposed to, or have specifically rejected, the model of a bureaucratic state is often salutary.[4]

This book considers how Western authorities recruited collaborating personnel as local troops, paramilitaries and peripheral irregulars within their own lands (including individual actors, clans, militias, gangs and countergangs). It examines the appeal for non-European personnel, when the nationality, ethnicity, culture, religion, value systems and beliefs of the Europeans were so alien.[5] It looks at the link between time and cohesion, asking: did the longevity of European colonial rule make a difference, or was financial and military power more influential? This raises the important question of whether longer occupations are ultimately more successful than expeditionary warfare favoured by some leading authorities.[6] It is also a reminder of the agency of local personnel themselves.

This work examines how Britain, France and the United States used local forces to defeat their enemies in the Americas, Asia, the Middle East and Africa. All three countries were involved in the struggle for North America in the late eighteenth century, but their fortunes were significantly different thereafter. This book analyses why, after a prolonged period of colonial success, the British failed to achieve the same results in India after 1945 or Aden in 1967; why the system failed for France in Indochina and Algeria; and why it went wrong for the United States in Vietnam.[7] There is a particular examination of the Montagnards of the central highlands of Vietnam and the parallels for France and its use of the Harkis in Algeria, but also how local forces were used in counter-insurgency operations, then and since.[8] Although not specifically addressed, the examples used throughout the book raise the question of how national preferences influenced the style of forces raised, and whether some states, like South Africa, the Netherlands in Indonesia, and the Soviet Union in Afghanistan had different approaches from the model used by France, the United Kingdom or the United States.[9]

By interrogating the past, critically examining the failures as well as the successes, it is possible to draw out the practices that were largely hidden by

PREFACE

national histories, which sought to play down the contribution made by the collaborative personnel to their empires.[10] Taking a broader look at the Western experience also opens up new questions of comparability, and reduces the risk of adopting a single conclusion. There are interesting opportunities, in making the comparison between the British and French experiences of decolonisation, in considering North American units operating in remote peripheries, or in the performance of paramilitary police units and gendarmerie in the face of political violence and intimidation. The book considers how similar target groups were recruited either into armies or into unconventional organisations, although the latter are only briefly dealt with in this book because of the limitations of space. Indeed, in the research for this book and the process of editing, I was painfully aware how much was being left out, and how many more case examples ought to have been included, such as the covert American operations to enlist or support local forces in Central America, the use of local proxies in Angola, or, further back in time, the partnership with the forces of the Philippines. My only defence is that I could not include everything and had to be selective, incorporating only sufficient numbers of cases to illustrate a particular set of themes. Critics may disagree with the choices.

Historical examples invariably yield some instructive and useful ideas about how local forces were used. These are all especially pertinent for examination particularly when the Western powers extracted themselves from Iraq and Afghanistan in the early twenty-first century on the basis of creating effective and resilient security forces. After the end of combat operations, when insurgents appeared to have remained resilient, the United States and its NATO allies gave further consideration to the raising of local auxiliaries, operating with proxy forces and how to maximise the benefits of 'training teams' as part of a broader new approach to waging war or stabilising states with limited liability.

This book has been several years in the making. A personal disquiet with the Western-centricism of strategic and military studies demanded a more thorough examination of the global and local aspects of the management of armies. A single volume cannot do justice to this theme, and while there have been various study days, workshops and conferences dedicated to the subject, it has been necessary to produce at least a short and preliminary study that others can criticise and develop. I hope this volume can contribute to the debate on military intervention, counter-insurgency and the development of local security forces beyond the fields of military and cultural history.

PREFACE

All scholars stand on the shoulders of those that come before them, and I have been dependent on the vast literature created by so many others. At the Oxford Changing Character of War Programme, which I have had the privilege to serve as Director, a great wealth of exchange has helped me formulate this work. I am particularly grateful to Professor Sir Hew Strachan, now at St Andrews and also Emeritus Professor at All Souls, Oxford; and the colleagues that I have worked with at Oxford either as faculty or visiting professors on this subject, especially Professor Doug Porch, Professor Tony King, Professor Patrick Porter, Professor David Parrott, Dr Adrian Gregory, Dr Annette Idler, Dr Sarah Percy, Dr Robert Fletcher, Dr Daniel Spence and Dr Mike Finch. I have been indebted to Professor Ashley Jackson, the leading light in this subject who has written an outstanding work on local forces in the Second World War; Dr Tim Winegard whose doctoral study was on indigenous communities of the British Empire in the First World War; Dr Chris Tripodi, Dr Geraint Hughes and Dr Jeff Michaels of King's College London; Professor David Anderson at Warwick; Professor Jeremy Black at Exeter; Professor Erik-Jan Zurcher at Amsterdam, who led the outstanding project called 'Fighting for a Living' to which I was attached; and Dr Kaushik Roy at Kolkata and PRIO. In France, I am indebted to the enigmatic and brilliant Raphaelle Branche and the erudite Thomas Flichy. I was given access to materials that would otherwise have eluded me by a number of scholars. I would like to thank Professor Natalie Zemon Davies for giving me the work on black regiments in the American Civil War. In the United States there are many I need to thank, including the hugely experienced Austin Long and Dave Philips.

There are some colleagues who consistently develop one intellectually, and also provoke that fellowship that is as precious as it is intangible. Dr Iain R. Smith, the brilliant historian of South Africa, has long been my inspiration. His work on the siege of Mafeking was particularly useful to me, but his support goes far beyond that. He is the 'beau ideal' of a scholar and teacher.

I derived great insights from the work of my former doctoral students, each of whom has advanced academic work in this much-neglected field, and therefore I should like to thank Dr Steven Wagner, Dr Jacob Stoil, Dr Ahmad Siddiqi, Dr Nate Pulliam, Dr Todd Greentree, and (soon to join them, my current student in this field) Melissa Skorka. I was also assisted by my MPhil students, especially Alex Neads, who went on to produce an excellent doctorate in this subject. The work they have completed is helping to open up this area of significant interest.

I have been privileged to be able to work with personnel of the British Army, the United States Army and United States Marine Corps over the last decade, and to listen to their insights and experiences in the training and mentoring role for local forces. I am immensely grateful to have been able to join the National Training Mission Afghanistan and advise on and assist in the training process, particularly in leadership development. I have been involved in discussing and helping with this subject at the Defence Academy of the United Kingdom, the United States Army War College, the Allied Rapid Reaction Corps, the NATO Defence College and the Supreme Headquarters Allied Powers Europe. It is impossible to mention all those in uniform who helped me, but my gratitude is boundless. I have shared platforms with General Graham Lamb, whose critical insights are as invaluable as they are engaging. I have learned much from good friends who served as mentors and advisers, men and women who understand far better than I how to make the system work.

I would, however, like to single out two comrades for special mention. Brigadier Ian Rigden shared with me anecdotes of life with the Gurkhas, composed partnering doctrine and then went to Qargha to assist in the further development of the Officers Academy in Afghanistan. Fearless, generous, selfless, devoted, and full of cheer, he epitomises the ethos and spirit of both the Gurkhas and the British Army. The other is Dr Duncan Anderson, from the War Studies Department at the Royal Military Academy Sandhurst, who helped in the establishment of the Officers Academy in Afghanistan, designing its curriculum and finding the time and immense energy to continue all his other work in supporting military personnel, despite the near misses in that country. His insights merit far more attention, and, like many civilians who worked in Afghanistan, his service deserves far more recognition than it ever received.

I am immensely grateful for the extra time and unceasing support, not to mention immense patience, given me by Michael Dwyer and Jon de Peyer of Hurst. Sorry I was so late with the manuscript. Inevitably, my apologies are also due to my family, especially my children, for missing out on life to pursue the research for this book.

The final thank-you is to the officers and men of 22 SAS. You know why. Thank you for sharing the pilgrimage.

Rob Johnson   June 2017

1

INTRODUCTION

PARTNERING WITH INDIGENOUS FORCES

In 2015, the Syrian town of Kobane, near the Turkish border, became the centre of an intense struggle between fighters belonging to the so-called Islamic State and Syrian Kurdish militia. The Jihadist fighters advanced against the town on several axes, their tanks preceded by handfuls of black-clad suicide bombers on foot or in commandeered vehicles. These men would detonate their explosives at the threshold of defended barricades and buildings. The defending Syrian Kurds would try to suppress their attackers with improvised mines and heavy machine guns mounted on 'technicals' (converted pickup trucks), while the United States air force screamed in overhead, dropping devastating munitions on the parts of the town that had fallen. Behind this Dantean landscape, and beyond the spectating Kurds on the Turkish border, a potentially even more significant transformation was under way, namely a 'train and assist' mission by American personnel. This was designed to enhance the effectiveness of the anti-Islamic State resistance and, by default, the chances of success of those factions that oppose the Syrian dictatorship of Bashar al-Assad. Nevertheless, within months, the Russians announced their own intervention in support of Assad's Syrian army and air force, while Turkey made an incursion against Syrian Kurds. The response of the weakened Daesh jihadists was to increase its output of social media videos, complete with drone footage, and to extend their terrorist attacks beyond

Syria into Europe, most notoriously by murdering dozens of unarmed civilians in Paris and Brussels.

There have been a number of claims that the character of war in the early twenty-first century changed so profoundly from its historical antecedents that its very nature had also been altered. Claims have been advanced that 'new wars', fought primarily by dispossessed non-state actors on issues of identity or political and economic disenfranchisement require entirely new solutions, indeed, a completely new conception of war.[1] Western observers draw attention to the rapid transformations wrought by new technology and by an increase in the preference of violent non-state actors for terrorism or insurgency which, by their nature, are inherently difficult to combat.[2] The two issues of new technology and methods of insurgency are closely related. It is widely understood that it was the technological prowess of the West that made it impossible for weaker states and actors to mount an effective challenge in conventional terms.

To circumvent Western military power and to resist occupation, opposition groups turned to guerrilla warfare and more radical ideological justifications for violence. Concealed in plain clothes and hidden in the backstreets of cities or in remote rural peripheries, popular resistance was mobilised with the express intention of rendering any occupation costly in both lives and treasure. Keeping the flame of resistance alive, serving local political, sectarian or economic interests, and directing their violence at foreign domination or collaboration, these resistance fighters waged unrelenting hit-and-run warfare but, at the same time, disciplined their own populations, asserted factional supremacy, and settled old scores, often with a murderous sectarian or communal edge. In Iraq, some groups, believing in unlimited violence and subscribing to the ideology of al-Qaeda, waged a brutal campaign of terror, largely against the Iraqi population. Exploiting the collapse of order, several criminal syndicates and small-time militia leaders also tried to assert themselves, creating what David Kilcullen called a complex and multi-layered 'insurgent eco-system'.[3] Foreign personnel operating in Iraq and in similar conditions in Afghanistan acknowledged the difficulty of identifying the true adversary, understanding the operating environment and contending with differences in culture, language and perception among indigenous populations. Inevitably there were errors. Local expertise was needed desperately.

Foreign intervention forces are particularly prone to making errors among a local populace, fuelling a dislike of heavy-handed and alien occupation. Air strikes, a necessary tool for swiftly neutralising enemy fighters and protecting relatively small numbers of Western personnel, were capable of turning entire communities against the very troops that had come to assist them. Commanders attempting to conduct counter-insurgency in Afghanistan and Iraq were frequently confronted with the problem of protecting the population and securing routes or large areas of territory with their limited manpower. While the insurgent has the ability to strike anywhere, the counter-insurgent forces cannot be strong everywhere.[4]

The logic of the dilemma appeared to be the recruitment of local personnel to provide insight and understanding, to participate in their own defence, and to augment the security forces. This fulfilled the goal of winning hearts and minds, not to earn gratitude or affection, but to compel a population to choose sides. Thus, in essence, they would be obliged to commit either to the government, and its foreign backers, or resistance groups which were dedicated to continuing the conflict and therefore the destabilisation of the state. Robert Thompson, the author of a seminal book on anti-communist guerrilla operations in the 1960s, concluded: 'The government should formulate long-term political aims, backed by political and economic initiatives; these in turn will be supported by a counter-insurgency plan involving the police, the armed forces and any locally raised militias, home guards and other auxiliary forces.'[5] The detail and emphasis on the types of local forces revealed just how important Thompson believed these local forces to be to the success of the counter-terrorism or counter-insurgency plan.

The wars in Iraq and Afghanistan were dominated, at least in Western circles, by two debates: one, the legitimacy of intervention, and, two, the relative merits of counter-insurgency as the method for defeating resistance. These discussions were entirely understandable, but the solutions to the conflicts lay in establishing legitimate authority in government, at every level, from district to the national, and in re-establishing security. Local forces were the critical component in both. Creating national security forces helped to constrain insurgency and re-establish order, which, in turn, enabled the government to actually function. Moreover, local security forces indicated that the state was beginning to restore its sovereignty and independence. Local military and police units were the physical manifestation of the government's power, and this put them at the centre of the controversy.

The Changing Character of War and Fighting Forces

In the 1990s, Mary Kaldor posited that a 'new type of organized violence' had developed, especially in Africa and Eastern Europe, stating: 'New wars involve a blurring of the distinctions between war (usually defined as violence between states or organized political groups for political motives), organized crime (violence undertaken by privately organized groups for private purposes, usually financial gain) and large-scale violations of human rights (violence undertaken by states or political groups against individuals).'6 At the end of the Cold War, it was understandable that conflicts occurring outside the old zones of confrontation might be seen as new, particularly when the bipolar constraints that had contained violence were released. Such sentiments were reinforced by awe at new technologies and speculation about their implications.

Critics have argued that too much emphasis is placed on this perception that everything about warfare in the 1990s and early twenty-first century was somehow 'new' or defined by the rise of the 'non-state actor'. The historian Hew Strachan demonstrated that apparently 'new' actors in war do not alone constitute change in war; war is more multidimensional and complex than that.7 Nor is it the case that ways of conducting war are somehow culturally immutable throughout history. Attempts to identify an enduring Western way of war from ancient epochs to the present tend to be too reductionist in order to retain distinction. To reach the verdict of an unchanging Western approach, there is a conflation of styles and glossing of contexts, attributed to regional characteristics. If there is a distinctive character about the way particular groups fight, at certain periods, then that should be clarified, not obscured. Techniques and technologies change, opportunities and constraints arise, and groups adapt to new situations.

It is the essence of war, its *Natur* as the Prussian writer Carl von Clausewitz put it, that has remained unchanged through history. His vivid description of the fear and confusion of battle would be as recognisable in the street fighting in Syria after 2011 as it was in the early nineteenth century. Indeed, the unchanging nature of killing and destruction described as long ago as Thucydides evokes the essentially human experience of war across the centuries, even when the technologies change radically. Many theorists have, of course, tried to capture the various elements of war and harness them into principles that might assist in producing victory. Clausewitz himself emphasised the importance of particular features that would avoid the sort of protracted people's war which he had witnessed and which, he felt, conventional armies were ill equipped to deal with. He was nevertheless reacting to the innate conservatism of his homeland and appealing for recognition of the sheer power of a total mobilisation of the people against an occupation. Clausewitz himself served for a time in a foreign army, against the wishes of his countrymen, in order to sustain resistance to Napoleon. The paradox was that he fought against Napoleon's multinational and multi-ethnic Grande Armée during its invasion of Russia in 1812, a force that contained a large number of his fellow Prussians. The ability to transfer loyalty appeared to be relatively easy.

Since the terrorist outrage of 9/11 in 2001 the world has grown accustomed to the unconventional methods of terrorist organisations and insurgents, often fought by 'foreign fighters' drawn from countries well beyond the zone of operations, and it is tempting to describe this as an entirely new phenomenon well beyond the historical world of Clausewitz. Yet this focus on the identity and particular fighting methods of irregulars masks much more significant changes as well as continuities. Guerrilla warfare—the hit-and-run attack, the raid, the use of terror—has existed since prehistory and was clearly identified by generations of scholars of war, but, in the early decades of the twenty-first century, one is witness to four important trends which have created a new and distinctive prominence: the privatisation of violence, the increasing importance of stealth or dispersal, the miniaturisation of combat power, the devolution or distribution of command, and the dispersal of forces.

All of these have very significant implications for the Western states. Not every future conflict will be an insurgency or one of the 'wars among the people' because the character of war changes with every conflict, so these themes of privatisation, stealth, miniaturisation, devolution and distribution will apply as much to conventional as to irregular wars and will form what Clausewitz called the 'grammar of war' in this age. The manner in which insurgent groups and terrorist cells operate appears to confirm that these themes are important, and the response of states has been to rely perhaps far more on clandestine operatives, private security contractors, smaller numbers of multiuse military platforms, and devolution of security responsibilities to 'host nations' and local military forces.

Since 2001, there has been a polarisation in the use of military technologies. On the one hand, the sophistication and cost of high-tech weapons and systems mean that 'platforms', be they ships, aircraft or vehicles, need to be able to tackle a wide range of tasks, from surveillance to strike. Yet, at the other end of the spectrum, a vast number of low-tech, cheap weapon systems are flooding the battle space. Impoverished and weak armed groups, equipped with assault rifles, rocket-propelled grenades and improvised explosive devices, are a common feature in the conflict zones of the world. One naval officer remarked in 2012 that it seemed absurd that multi-billion dollar warships were being tasked to patrol the waters off Somalia against pirates in flimsy motor boats armed with Kalashnikovs.[8] The implication of this is that states need to develop cheaper and more appropriate systems for dealing with lower-level threats while retaining their high-tech capabilities for more serious challenges. States will continue to protect their global interests, project power and respond to confrontations with conventional force, but there is considerable pressure to develop cheaper, agile and more appropriate force structures to defeat insurgency and terrorism. After expensive technologies, manpower represents a considerable cost to Western nations, and it is not surprising that, in labour-intensive missions to restore stability, they should look to local military forces.

There is often a difference between what lessons a conflict has taught and which ones are learned. Each generation will derive different conclusions about a war, and the military interventions in Afghanistan, Iraq, Libya and Mali in the early 2000s are no different in that regard. The most important lesson appeared to be the urgent need for a coherent Western strategy that aligned policy to the appropriate use of force. Too much of the planning in the conflict in Afghanistan was hasty, not based on understanding of the country, and barely consultative of the Afghan viewpoint. Western Coalition efforts lacked coherence and were subject to particularistic national agendas. Grotesquely, government officials were prevented from deploying outside secure bases, and military units themselves were subject to more and more restrictions to avoid 'risk'. A British training team in Iraq was prevented from leaving their base in 2016 on similar grounds, which diminished their ability to achieve their 'advise and assist' mission. Crucially, in the Afghanistan and Iraq conflicts of the early 2000s, too little time was allocated to training local forces, and the outcomes were disappointing, which resulted in frustrations on both sides.[9] The Iraqi Army, after millions of dollars spent on it, almost collapsed when attacked by the more determined and smaller bands of the Islamic State movement. A proportion of Iraqi Sunni officers and men actually joined Daesh because of their anger with an unpopular sectarian government in Baghdad.

All wars require adaptation in planning, in ways of operating and in their means. Clausewitz famously observed that the very first and most important decision was to ascertain what type of war one was in, and then the imperative was to transform and adapt faster and more effectively than the enemy. All war is a dynamic and an iterative process. But what Western powers may have learned from the wars of the early twenty-first century was that the overall objective, the ends, must be clear, consistent and united, and that there must be planning for the long term, even if the desire is to have short, rapid and decisive operations. There were significant adaptations in Western forces during the stabilisation campaign in Afghanistan, but the political objectives were woefully inadequate, under-resourced and lacked commitment. Crucially, like the operations in Iraq, there was little acknowledgement of the local divisions within the respective societies: political rivalry, fear of other factions, sectarianism, ethnic conflict, criminal opportunism and deep-seated fissures that widened once an authoritarian system of government had been swept away by Western military force. When it came to the development of local security forces, it was evident that there was a constant change in targets, too few qualified trainers, and too much haste to create numbers without ensuring quality, which necessitated retraining. This led to a great deal of detrimental political interference from the host nation government.

What was required before deployment on expeditionary warfare, or for missions to stabilise fragile states, was a comprehensive study of each country and its region, a greater effort to understand the dynamics and the aspirations of the people, and the fulfilment of political and economic agendas that did not alienate but assisted them. The chief problem, however, was time. There was an urgency to create security forces quickly, not only to end the interventions as rapidly as possible for political reasons at home, but as the means to generate sufficient numbers of local forces to swamp the insurgencies that had developed. In Afghanistan, the objective was to establish democratic, bureaucratic institutions, but this threatened every vested interest in a patrimonial clan system that had endured for hundreds of years, and a sense of ethnic difference which had been reinforced by the experience of thirty years of civil war. Many local leaders were eager to retain their own private military forces or to ensure national security forces protected their factional interests.

The conflict in Afghanistan taught the West of the need for parallel 'lines of operation', that is to say, to combine political, economic and military efforts to achieve specific, feasible objectives in partnership with local sources of power and influence in order to benefit and protect the people. And here was the crux. War is ultimately about politics, and can only be resolved by politics.

The aspirations and optimism after the rapid Coalition victory in Afghanistan in 2001 obscured the need for a more appropriate and gradualist transition in the country's political economy. It was also a reminder that, while the West might have preferred a short, decisive campaign, it could not guarantee that it would get one. Moreover, despite the aspiration to intervene against failing or failed states, and the consequent demand for reconstruction and other stability operations, the military forces of the West were really only configured for the expeditionary offensive and not for the critical periods which followed. For the rebuilding of armies, the West needed cadres of personnel able to train not only new military personnel but also border guards and police officers, and to advise ministries on how to develop criminal justice systems, complete with prisons, courts and detention staff.

Every war requires the urgent strategic correlation of ends, ways and means. Every war demonstrates the enduring importance of command and leadership; the need to bolster morale among one's own forces while eroding that of the enemy; the difficulties of sustaining resistance amid heavy losses: wars within countries highlight the thorny political problems of suppressing internal revolts, and the common asymmetry of civil war. To this one must add the critical importance of domestic political will and public morale. The West's experiences since the 1990s in the Balkans, the Caucasus, Iraq, Afghanistan and the conflicts following the so-called Arab Spring of North Africa and the Middle East indicated that the fundamental issues of insurrection, insurgency and war were not new at all, and that solutions to them were also familiar, if, as always, difficult to calibrate and implement. Clausewitz articulated the common problems of 'friction' and warned that, in the face of popular insurgency, normal military operations become far more difficult and often inappropriate. To the immense frustration of Western military personnel, there was a corresponding expectation that Western armies would only apply lethal force with the same care and diligence as a police officer in a peacetime domestic environment. This, they believed, threatened the licence of military commanders to fulfil their missions. It not only had profound implications for how Western forces operate, but it shaped expectations about how their partner or mentored forces would operate too.

The degrading of Western military advantages by insurgency in the early 2000s led to a search for solutions in a number of areas. At the policy level, there was some faith in the idea that democratisation would give a voice to the people and remove the need for resistance. This gave rise to the establishment of representative institutions and elections, although this was often derailed by a great deal of manipulation by local factions. In Iraq, the Shia-dominated government began to consolidate an exclusive hold on power the moment the Americans withdrew.

At the same time, there were attempts to reach negotiated settlements with various insurgent groups, while programmes of reconciliation and reintegration were developed in both Iraq and Afghanistan. Projects designed to offer enhancements to the economic well-being of the population, and thus demonstrate that the offer of the government and its foreign backers was better than that of the insurgents, were established as part of a multi-agency, comprehensive approach. For the Western military forces, new doctrine was developed to facilitate the reorientation of training, structures and procedures for counter-insurgency, with greater constraints in the rules of engagement, demands for the prioritisation of medical evacuation of the wounded over the achievement of the mission, and greater precision in the use of heavy weapons or air power.

While 'surge' troops augmented the existing garrisons to engage insurgents, pursue them and eventually dampen down the violence, the critical factor was to build up local military and police forces in this window of opportunity. The process, which is the focus of this book, was not a smooth one. In the transition of power to local government control, the need to have Western troops embedded, partnered and training local forces led to friction and periodic murders of Westerners by disgruntled indigenous soldiers and police. The 'green on blue' problem was, again, hardly a new phenomenon, and had been a recurrent issue for those Europeans who led less committed local forces in the past. T.E. Lawrence, the British facilitator of the Arab revolt in 1916–18, famously described the task of the counter-insurgent as messy, like 'learning to eat soup with a knife'.[10]

The difficulties of the campaigns in Iraq and Afghanistan between 2001 and 2014 reinforced the desire in the West to disengage from costly ground-holding in favour of precision air power and the 'light footprint' of Special Forces who could be used not only to carry out the capture or killing of insurgents, but to support local irregular forces. These methods, it was assumed, could avoid the need for a large-scale and long-term campaign commitment. The outcomes of such campaigns were nevertheless unsatisfactory. In Libya, assistance to local militias around Benghazi evolved into a more sustained campaign against regime forces under President Gaddafi. The collapse of the regime was supposed to herald the formation of a new, more accountable and democratic polity. It did not. The militias began a contest to control the economy of the country and Jihadist organisations regarded the region as the springboard for further international operations. In Syria and northern Iraq, there was initially more success in using air power and local Kurdish forces, but Sunni militias proved less reliable. Once again, extremist groups began to profit from disorder and Russian military intervention further complicated the Syrian campaign.

Subsequently, the idea of using local forces and perhaps training and developing them before their states faced a crisis of insurgency or civil war had much appeal. The development of local, indigenous forces reduced the need for 'boots on the ground', avoiding the need for American or NATO military personnel who might be in harm's way. The commensurate reduction in casualties, it was argued, would appeal to the voting public, and the lower profile of such forces would attract less negative media attention. The assistance offered by military and security forces would constitute 'upstream influence' and build capable forces which would, indirectly, serve the West's interests. The cost-effective nature of a small and timely commitment would also satisfy the political leadership, who were always eager to reduce expenditure. Moreover, the relatively small number of personnel for these missions would nevertheless offer an ideal outlet for the battle-seasoned troops of Afghanistan and Iraq, reinvesting their experience to benefit the West's allies. Many of these factors would also apply to European countries where legal and constitutional constraints overlay the deployments to combat operations outside the home continent. Making commitments to states not actually at war or plagued by domestic insurgency helped Europeans avoid the unpopular risks of Iraq and Afghanistan.

While there seemed to be an overwhelmingly positive appeal to the partnering and development of armies outside the West, there were particular requirements for success and intrinsic constraints. The most obvious perhaps was the fact that host nations would insist on having the lead in the development of their own security forces, restricting where and to whom assistance could be given. This 'agency' of host governments might not accord with Western interests, particularly if non-Western governments wanted to train sectarian or communal elements, sought to focus on draconian internal security, or refused to accept international standards in the treatment of their own populations. There would be further complication in cultural sensitivities, a problem familiar to those who trained Iraqi and Afghan forces. More fundamentally, shifting to training local security forces would require mastery of indigenous languages and highly developed skills in mentoring, which in turn implies a long-term commitment in terms of careers and training in Western armies. Evidently, where the West might like to be to exercise influence might not always accord with the areas to which states would be prepared to grant access. Somalia, Yemen and Syria were hardly permissive in the early 2000s, except for a handful of Special Operations Forces deployed there clandestinely. Indeed, the most successful experiments in training local forces occurred in states where peace had already been established, such as Sierra Leone.

Perhaps of even greater importance are Western expectations of time and results. To train any local national requires a long-term programme, but this fundamental fact is at odds with the desire for a short-term 'expeditionary' posture, limited liabilities and minimal manpower commitments.

The United Kingdom's National Security Strategy (2010 and 2015) placed a particular emphasis on 'influence' rather than military force, describing it as a phenomenon of 'soft power'. Influence does not always equate to power. Influence is neither the same as an alliance with local forces nor is it a form of control. Influence is only persuasion, and this may fail at precisely the time when it is needed most, such as during a crisis, if it cannot be demonstrated as having credible power behind it.[11] Stathis Kalyvas observed that, in civil wars, local populations will flock to sources of power.[12] It is not only communities that will do this, but political leaders too. It was noticeable that, once the Americans sent their Marines in 2009 to Helmand, where British troops had previously enjoyed a monopoly, the local provincial governor spent considerably more time with the Americans than the British. He was clearly aware that his survival and his opportunities lay with the stronger Americans, regardless of all the British attempts to exercise a benign and supportive influence over him hitherto. Thus the problem is how to convert one's influence into actual power. It seems the use of local indigenous forces provides one such avenue.

Armed Forces and the State: Local Forces and the Non-State

The role of armed forces might seem obvious. They are the executive arm of the state, legally sanctioned to use lethal force against external enemies. Yet the origin of armies was just as much to preserve the governing elite against internal enemies as against 'foreign' ones. Personal bodyguards and retainers, trained in military skills, might be augmented with local auxiliaries in times of crisis through some established system of obligation, tribute or slavery. State laws gave the executive greater legitimacy in the use of force. The development of state armies, navies and eventually air and missile forces was accompanied by the establishment of international recognition of state sovereignty. The bureaucratisation of state power, armed forces and international relations turned the legitimation of armed forces into a norm. Naturally it follows that a challenge to that state power, to authority and legitimacy, will also be a challenge to the law and the position of armed forces as agents of the executive. Internally, that challenge can manifest itself as a revolution or insurgency, or, if the military itself is involved, as a *coup d'état*. Against a foreign occupation and the shoring up of a state's power, an insurgency or guerrilla war, or, if a state is very weak, a terrorist and subversion campaign, will invariably be the methods of resistance. These forms of armed opposition defy attempts to limit irregular resistance to particular periods of the past and illustrate instead that they are situational and can be understood in a theoretical and comparative context. Armed forces will adapt to new threats, both internal and external, to new technologies, to the techniques used by allies or adversaries, and to their available resources. It follows that armies can be examined through the various roles they fulfil, taking full account of many variables that have an impact upon them.

There have been attempts to create a typology of military styles, but the tendency has been to see developments as dependent solely on historical context. Arguably the most significant observations in this regard revolve around the military revolution debates and the system of categorisation offered by John Lynn. From the outset it is worth noting that these discussions have focused primarily, and often exclusively, on the West. There have been subsequent efforts to extend definitions to a global setting, with varying degrees of success, but developing a taxonomy that is not rooted in assumptions of linear development is long overdue. To make comparative judgements and to understand what features of the past might still have relevance in the present century requires a more comprehensive approach.

In the 1950s, Michael Roberts, the historian of early modern Europe, posited that a military revolution had taken place between 1560 and 1660 as a result of the technological development of gunpowder weapons.[13] These new weapon systems required specialist training and a resource chain quite unlike the traditional reliance on bows or bladed arms and the metallurgy that existed before. Acknowledging the limitations of early experimentation, Roberts argued that there was a turning point with the reforms of Maurice of Orange and Gustavus Adolphus of Sweden. Under the command of trained officers, the ranks of their armies learned to fire by volleys, each line retiring to the rear to reload while the next gave fire. This continuous rolling fire required nerve when under the threat of a charge by opposing forces, and that in turn led to the imposition of strict discipline. The establishment of regular formations, where pikemen could provide a hedge of spikes to deter enemy horsemen, allowed both protection and the maximum effect of fire to front or flanks. To manoeuvre efficiently and rapidly itself required drill—regular movements co-ordinated by simple words of command and the beat of drum or trumpet calls. For Roberts, this was the period in which regular, modern armies were being forged.

Roberts nevertheless acknowledged that most forces in Europe were unable to fulfil the necessary requirements of the new technologies and techniques. Militia was raised in an emergency, but lacked the time for the requisite training. The core of the army might therefore consist of mercenaries and proficient bodyguards. The mercenary, derived from the Latin '*mercenarius*', was simply a paid soldier as opposed to a citizen volunteer or conscript, but in the sixteenth and seventeenth centuries these mercenary troops were clustered in certain locations. Surplus and trained manpower from marginal economies in Switzerland and the German states provided large numbers, but the conflicts in the Italian states proved to be an attractive and lucrative location for operations. The inability to sustain payments, particularly over the winter when campaigning was suspended (largely because of the absence of grazing and shortages of foodstocks), could induce mercenary forces to change sides, to abandon a particular ruler or to take the law into their own hands to secure funds and supplies, but it is a myth that mercenaries were combat-averse. Dynasts, faced with the threat of unruly hirelings, paid mercenaries throughout the year, which in turn required a more thorough system of revenue collection and accounting. Thus, following Roberts's thesis, mercenary service and the new gunpowder armies were the catalysts for the bureaucratisation, and therefore modernisation, of the state.

Geoffrey Parker challenged Roberts's conclusions, suggesting that sieges had been more important than battles in the early modern period, and it was here, in fortification design and in its destruction by gunpowder weapons, that the true innovation had occurred.[14] The sheer cost of siege and defence placed enormous premiums on dynastic states, but it also meant that a variety of military forces were retained, from cheap militias to specialist artificers. Relatively small numbers of men could hold fortresses, but the logistical lines of communication, gathering of supplies and other tasks required substantial amounts of casual labour.

David Parrott noted that the demands for mercenary service and fortification, which had begun decades before Roberts's estimates, had created a military-fiscal crisis in the mid-sixteenth century. This prompted an increase in outsourcing of military labour, shifting the liability to 'mercenary captains' who, as contractors, started to take on larger and larger forces. To pay for the enormous costs, officers like Albrecht von Wallenstein would contract out, acquire lump sums and extract plunder or ransoms from defeated enemies. They were so successful they could offer loans and financial services. Mercenary captains were not so much 'employees' of a state as 'creditors' and contractors.

The system was successful in its time and elements of it survived until the 1850s, but dynastic leaders, whose sovereignty over their domains was acknowledged formally in the Treaty of Westphalia of 1648, set about incorporating the mercenary professional into their states. Made members of a royal court, granted ownership of land, and subject to internal laws, the new mercenary now owed his rank and title to a political system. His financial return came from land revenue and a share of the royal wealth allocated for manpower and supplies. In time, the relationship was institutionalised and portrayed as part of an older European heritage of fealty to a monarch under the system of chivalry. Aristocratic noblemen invariably embraced the arrangement which gave them added security and legal recognition of their status, wealth and authority. The regularisation of armed forces was extended more slowly to navies. Entrepreneurial sea captains would engage in privateering on behalf of the state, gathering personal wealth through 'prize money', and this too lasted until the mid-nineteenth century.

The relationship of a regular force to a nation came much later. Personal loyalty to a ruler was often more important until the twentieth century. In the seventeenth and eighteenth century, regiments were frequently named after their colonels or members of the royal family. When Napoleon invaded Russia in 1812, he did so with an army that consisted of a million 'foreigners'. Regular regiments were made up of Polish, Swiss, Irish, Portuguese, Dutch and Prussians, some of whom had been prisoners of the French just a few years before. In 1831, in Algeria, on the periphery of French dominions, a variety of nationalities served in the Foreign Legion. The first foreigners were Polish exiles of the 67th Regiment, but battalions were later formed by nationality: the 1st was Swiss; 2nd and 3rd German; 4th Spaniard; 5th Italian; 6th Walloon and Dutch; and 7th Polish.

For a state in Europe, gaining control over the private military forces of aristocrats was a slow and gradual process, and not always successful. Nevertheless, accepted articles of war gradually emerged which tended to dissuade some forces from excessive behaviour. As dynastic rulers asserted themselves over their states, larger standing armies, under the permanent command of the monarch, emerged as the new norm. On the periphery, however, irregular and auxiliary forces continue to survive. The Cossacks, for example, emerged as a regular organisation around 1575, and famously, at the Battle of Poltava in 1708, they changed sides. They subsequently went into the service of the Khan of the Crimea, and revolted against both Peter and Catherine the Great of Russia. It was Catherine who established her own regular corps of

INTRODUCTION

Cossacks as a counter-force, and, with little sympathy for ethnic Russians, the Cossacks eventually filled the ranks of 900 squadrons and were often deployed on internal security duties inside the Russian Empire, or operated on its frontiers in the Caucasus and Central Asia. Indeed, the existence of irregular units, employed by some distant figure, tended to mark the very limits of state and imperial power.

These were the European origins, but from the first colonial encounters in Africa, Asia and the Americas, the Western powers had begun to employ local labour, casually at first and sometimes only as local allies. Gradually, the recruitment of local military personnel became more regularised, more comprehensive and more widespread. These forces are the main focus of this book.

Partnering

There has been a long historical precedent for the Europeans' use of local forces across the globe. Indigenous troops were always used to compensate for the lack of their own manpower, and to create the effect of 'mass' in land operations. On the whole, these local forces were more effective when organised like the European armies themselves, and they were less effective when they remained as untrained militias, which drove a trend towards regularised, professional military personnel. Nevertheless, there were exceptions to the rule. In the nineteenth century, some local forces that were retained as light infantry or light cavalry excelled because they remained more flexible and more fluid and could operate in traditional ways as skirmishers, raiders and scouts. Moreover, some Asian armies that adopted the outward forms of European regular forces, with infantry, cavalry and artillery units in Western-style uniforms, but failed to transform themselves doctrinally, institutionally and in their approach to fighting, often failed when tested in war. Forces which looked like the European model, but which did not adhere to the requirements of internal cohesion, prowess through training, and the willingness to sustain losses in the pursuit of their military objectives, among other factors, were unsuccessful.

This raises an interesting point about the assumptions made historically and in the present about the motivation of troops in war. One approach is to assume that all men are, essentially, the same in terms of their reactions to fear, the risk of death or injury, and their psychology. Many studies indicate that, under fire, inexperienced men will tend to go to ground and 'herd' together. Groups of demoralised men can break and run collectively as well as individually. Conversely, acts of inspirational courage can drive others, despite their doubts about their chances of survival, to similar acts of selfless courage. Groups whose situation appears to be hopeless can occasionally rouse themselves to sacrificial defiance. History is replete with examples like these, providing us with a rich and varied catalogue of humans at war, but with common characteristics across time and space.

Another approach is to assume that all men are culturally conditioned and therefore groups at war are distinct and dependent on their specific contexts. This might include an aversion to casualties, views about fighting and which causes are acceptable, and the influence of class and status on their willingness to wage war and under what terms. These culturally specific criteria can also be self-fulfilling. The 'martial races' theory propagated by the British in South Asia and Africa in the nineteenth century held that certain groups from pastoral settings, like the Madrassis, were less warlike than the mountain peoples of the north, such as the Gurkhas, or the peoples with long military traditions in their families and faith, such as the Sikhs of the Punjab. These views tended to prevent Madrassis being sent on overseas expeditions where they might gain military experience and thus their performance tended to deteriorate in relative terms to the Sikhs and Gurkhas, whose deployments were far more frequent. There was also a psychological dimension: the martial races were constantly reminded of their elite status, which created its own dynamic of wishing to retain their reputation.[15]

The history of partnering indigenous forces in the colonial period can obscure the difficulties and comparative value of raising and managing local forces in the post-colonial era. Nationalism and other liberationist ideologies have altered perceptions and global political consciousness significantly. In the colonial era, it was easier to justify the recruitment and training of local forces and there was an ideological confidence in categorising the colonial subject as an apolitical manpower resource. This reached its nadir with the Social Darwinian theories of the late nineteenth century. Previously, in the late eighteenth century, there had been considerable faith in the transformative effects of modernisation and progressive politics, regardless of race, and so this volume contains examples from that earlier era for the sake of comparison. By the 1850s, pessimism had set in among Europeans as the gap between their own modernity and their observations about primitive, pre-modern societies grew wider. Racial categorisations were associated with qualitative values, including the degree of martial prowess different groups possessed. In broad terms, select mountain dwellers and rural stock from marginal environments were considered more warlike than the pastoral plains-dwelling agriculturists who had become accustomed to the tranquillity of colonial rule.

There were exceptions: persistent resistance was condemned by the categorisation of 'criminal tribes'. Recent scholarship on this issue, which is voluminous and impossible to summarise successfully here, suggests that the Europeans favoured ethnic groups that consistently exhibited traits closest to their own, and they embraced ideal types. This emphasis on certain groups became self-reinforcing. Treating selected ethnic clans as martial, and elevating their status accordingly, tended to reinforce their own self-perception and make them more willing sub-imperialists. Entire groups were labelled in ways that suited European tastes and preferences. Thus, 'martial' clans from West Africa were collectively called Hausa, even when this title obscured a great diversity of separate communities. In South Asia, various Nepalese clans were grouped under the title of Gurkhas, and recalcitrant *qawmi* from the North West Frontier of India were all called Pathans (a Hindu corruption of the local term Pashtuns) or subdivided according to districts, regardless of their patrimonial connections. Each group was associated with particular values. Interestingly, not all British military or civilian personnel accepted the categorisation of the races and some instead worked to create national armies that overcame racial prejudices, in the expectation this would create an imperial identity and loyalty over old, clan-based and ethnic rivalries.

The British and the French were pragmatic rulers and they made use of a variety of cultural factors within indigenous societies to draw the people into the imperial system. The costs of European manpower to ensure the security of their possessions was offset by the vast reserves of India and Africa, but both the British and the French were eager to select distinct groups, or to create distinction, to ensure loyalty. Their recruitment policy was an amalgam of race theory imported from the West, combined with a practical desire to exploit existing prejudices, and a juxtaposed desire to maintain balance in the composition of their regiments and corps.

Regimental loyalty was constructed carefully, emphasising the importance of selfless, courageous and exemplary Western leadership, *esprit de corps*, ideology, pay and conditions, and distinctiveness. Even the detail of uniforms, locality, elite status, the position of depots, training regimes and eating arrangements could enhance differences and fuel a healthy competition without creating serious divisions. The British made great efforts to encourage customs and rituals, such that observance of religious ceremonies was in some ways fossilised and protected in a far more 'pure' form than in civilian life.

Rites and ceremonies, colours and standards, and even the threads on a uniform could enhance separateness, and the British combined different ethnic or class groups into each unit to foster competitiveness within single regimental identities. French methods were similar, but they were careful to station regiments that consisted of one ethnic group in areas quite distinct in identity to avoid fraternisation.

The 'martial race' theory was not entirely a Western invention, as it owed its origins to indigenous ideas about status and hierarchy. Martial race theory was, in essence, designed to select various communities, often on the margins of imperial rule, who were thought to possess militarily useful characteristics. As an idea it was absorbed and reshaped by the selected communities of South Asia, the Caribbean and Africa under colonial rule. Various myths were invented or existing histories enhanced in order to create distinctions that would bolster regimental pride and loyalty to the Empire. In India, this helped to overcome the problems that had plagued the army before the Mutiny of 1857. The chosen communities were, in part, self-selecting, and sometimes elements within the army did their best to exclude those they deemed rivals or unfit. The Gurkhas, for example, worked hard to prevent rival clans joining the Indian Army, and established a monopoly of employment for their exclusive groups. As a lucrative source of income and regular employment, it was in the interests of certain communities to keep other groups out.

The organisational or bureaucratic approach to the recruitment and management of the imperial army enabled the British to overcome customs and caste prejudices that impaired military efficiency. There were essentially three elements to this: the welfare system, which provided incentives to enlistment and long service; regimental organisation, which absorbed the clan and caste ethos of various communities and created new identities; and the courts martial system, which imposed a moderate system of coercion to assist with the cohesion and integrity of the individual units. It is interesting to note that, in recent decades, the bureaucratisation of the Western militaries has continued to the exclusion of cultural diversity or accommodation in the recruitment of local forces. David Omissi points out that the old colonial armies emphasised rewards, making military service in the Empire a lucrative pursuit compared with the vagaries of civilian life.[16] It was also a system that depended to a large extent on local elites 'buying into' the colonial state. Their patronage networks meant it was relatively easy to acquire labour for military service. However, the transformation of society through the twentieth century, and the growth of the ideology of nationalism, rendered these systems increasingly redundant.

INTRODUCTION

While racial theories in recruitment seem reassuringly distant from the recruitment policies of Iraq and Afghanistan, it is worth reflecting that 'levels of development' have replaced the categorisation of race. It is difficult to believe that the Western powers would have felt as confident in constructing armies for counter-insurgency in Bosnia in the way in which they did in Afghanistan. The approach to building capacity and stabilisation was influenced very directly by assumptions about the level of development and education across Afghanistan. Little consideration was given to Afghan regional agendas or aspirations. Too often they were assumed to be a resource to be managed, won over, coerced or 'developed'. Less developed peoples are still viewed by Western militaries as resources that are problematised and essentialised, requiring direction and leadership.

Because of Western assumptions and expectations, there can sometimes be local opportunities in the building of armies that are overlooked. Local rituals and beliefs can be reinforced, creating pride, a vested interest and stability. Combining regional and national identities can, for example, develop a sense of civic pride. In all armies, promotions, rewards and honours can motivate individuals. Power and responsibility can be developed through careful mentoring. There are foreign concepts and expectations against which local forces will fail, particularly if literacy levels are lower, but appropriate levels of training, equipment and procedures can be invaluable.

History is often a guide in this respect. The regular, professional armies built up by the British in India provide an instructive example. In 1941–3, Indian troops under British command were able to endure intense fighting, heavy losses and a series of significant defeats. With established traditions, the gradual Indianisation of the officer corps, effective morale building welfare measures, investment in new equipment, and tact over the soldiers' aspirations for national independence, the British led them to victory in North Africa, Italy and Burma in 1945.[17] Successful regular and professional forces could also be found outside South Asia, in the King's African Rifles, the West India Regiment and the Malay Scouts. Dozens of other units, of varying degrees of regular or irregular status, were formed to carry out covert operations, border patrols and internal security, and protect lines of communication.

Nevertheless, there were failures too. The greatest mutiny against the British occurred in 1857 in India, necessitating the entire reconstruction of the old East India Company Army into a more regularised state structure under the British Crown. Indian soldiers mutinied again in Singapore in 1915, and the South Persia Rifles mutinied in 1916 during operations in the First World War.

There were mutinies in the Second World War, and the Indian Navy strikes in 1946 marked the end of British rule in India. The Aden Police mutinied in 1967, causing significant political changes and the eventual relinquishing of colonial rule in southern Arabia. Jewish troops that had served with the Allies in the Second World War, many of them as commandos, turned their weapons against the British in 1946 when they perceived a reluctance to grant them a homeland, and the end of the mandate in Palestine followed soon after. Military unrest was a significant catalyst for political change.

The idea of stabilising states by recruiting and training state security forces or, perhaps, training rebel armed groups to overthrow another malign state that sponsors terrorism offers many opportunities for Western powers, but it also imposes constraints. Men, and sometimes women, enlist for a variety of reasons, which we might broadly characterise as 'push' factors (such as poverty or local threats) and 'pull' factors (allegiances, opportunism, socio-economic or cultural advancement, or a route to survival). These individual factors are often interpreted through the Western concept of the 'nation in arms', that is a collective citizenly obligation to serve the greater good of the state and its people. Since the French Revolution, service in an army has been seen as the means to develop state cohesion, even if the historical reality was rather different.[18] European empires were also willing to incorporate men of fighting age from troublesome territories adjacent to their possessions in order to absorb and neutralise the threat. In the early nineteenth century, Tharu and Madhesi in the Terai of India and Nepal were recruited successfully by the British into their armed forces to prevent them from raiding other areas. In Afghanistan, a report produced by Oxfam cited the verdicts of local people that unemployment made the perpetuation of civil war more likely. One Kandahari man noted: 'If people are employed, the fighting will end.' A Kabuli woman explained: 'We thank God that the fighting we saw during Taliban does not exist now, even though still they do suicide attacks. The main harm of the current conflict is poverty and unemployment. If there are employment opportunities for the people, there won't be killings.' A Parwani man concluded that unemployment and conflict were linked proportionally: 'If the people are jobless, they are capable of anything.'[19]

Historically, the use of indigenous forces by Europeans was common, whether as mercenaries, as partnered forces in Europe and North America, in colonial armies, or as levies and auxiliaries in the peripheries. These practices withered as states sought to control or assert an ideological coherence through national identity. Relics lingered, but the standard model was towards national

INTRODUCTION

armed forces. Armies and navies reflect the societies from which they are drawn, including its stratifications of class and region. They are influenced by paradigmatic armies, adopting and adapting to new methods, technologies, cultures and appearances. Nevertheless, there are some more general consistent themes that armies and navies must master in order to increase their chances of success: cohesion, discipline, motivation, commitment, good quality leadership, acceptance of casualties and sustained high morale. Military forces need technical support, not just in the weapons, equipment and transport they use but also in logistics, support, welfare, training and competence skills. Troops must also be willing and able to manage internal threats as proficiently as external ones, and be able to operate alongside other arms and services, as well as civil police forces, and with those in political authority in accordance with accepted laws and customs.

There are evident advantages in the recruitment of local personnel. Local forces may free up regular forces for manoeuvre operations by providing fixed-site security or protecting routes. Indigenous forces often enjoy better relations with the civilian population, sharing the language, customs and values. They invariably know the local terrain, both human and physical. In some cases their fighting style of locally recruited irregulars matches that of the enemy forces and may in any case fit with regional expectations about service in defence of their community. Indigenous troops working for a government may prevent or even reverse the process of recruitment of marginalised groups by insurgents or rival armies. Local security forces can have a vested interest in defending a nation, city, town, village, a valley or a development project that brings benefit directly to them, and employment alone can represent a significant investment in a community through a soldier's wages. Local forces can assist in governance building from the bottom up and in the administration of justice and, ultimately, contribute to national security.

There are nevertheless significant risks and objections to the use of indigenous forces. There is always a chance that arming men in stabilisation missions against insurgency may lead them to change sides and become criminal or guerrilla forces. Any military alliances with selected local groups risk stirring rivalries and internal power struggles in areas outside central government control, undermining the fundamental objective of stabilisation. While governments may be willing to raise forces and pay for them, there is no guarantee they will be willing to fight if called upon to do so. Indeed, the lower the level of training, interests and investment, the less likely it is the local forces will prove to be reliable. There is a further risk of local forces becoming lawless, seizing property or killing beyond the limits prescribed by a government. Moreover, local forces may pursue their own agendas even while serving under a foreign or government remit. The result may be a *coup d'état*, or episodes of turning their weapons on their former employers when the situation is perceived to have changed, to settle scores or to seize opportunities for short-term gain.

Methodology

In his influential assessment of army styles, John Lynn looked for explanations of variation and dynamics of change over the *longue durée*.[20] He narrowed his focus to armies of the Western world, rather than navies and air forces, on the basis that it is land forces that provide the tools of internal control and *coup d'état* as well as external defence. Assessing armies in the West nevertheless neglected the colonial state models, which retained a great deal of what Lynn considered obsolete, and his emphasis on technological change and innovation tended to obscure the manner in which protracted guerrilla warfare and insurgency could blunt the technological and organisational superiority of Western forces. Yet Lynn's idea was to assert the relative importance of institutional development over purely tactical and technological advantages, to assess the convergence or divergence of styles and the different paces of change. He acknowledged that there were distinctively Western features of warfare, without going as far as John Keegan or Victor Davis Hanson, who had argued that the West had a unique approach to fighting that was traceable through time.[21] The West, for example, had not made use of slave-soldiers or migratory cavalry armies in the way that Central and East Asian armies had.

It is unlikely that there could be a fixed method of fighting, a way of war, that remained unchanged for so long, given the political, social and military transformations that have taken place in human history. That said, there are characteristics of conflict for some societies that do endure, sometimes dictated by human and physical geography, and those with deeply ingrained cultural markers have often interpreted events through a lens that is distinct, leavened, of course, by functionalism and experience. Hence, impoverished desert communities living a marginal existence were forced to fight in a manner which made use of distance, the environment and concealment, evolving tactics of raiding as a result. Their emphasis would be on possession of resources rather than necessarily killing large numbers of their enemies. On the other hand, groups who feared reprisals from more organised enemies or for whom it was impossible to carry away all the spoils of war, including slaves, might conduct a form of warfare that emphasised annihilation. The problem we have is that so many accounts of combat are no more than partisan national or cultural histories designed to fit a set of expectations and cultural norms within a particular society: experiences are reshaped and defined according to accepted terms, narratives and standards.[22]

The variation with the rest of the world, or Western 'style' as Lynn termed it, could be identified through a certain number of factors, and these were so pervasive as to encourage non-Western forces to attempt to adopt the style of Europeans and North Americans as they emulated their success.[23] In those attempts, they were rarely successful because emulation, rather than genuine adaptation, failed to get to the root of the Western method.[24] The outward adoption of uniforms, formations and even military institutions could not convert the society and economy from which the Western methods had sprung. The failure of adopted styles was a strong indicator that armies are in many ways the product of the societies from which they are drawn, while retaining their own distinctive internal and hierarchical cultures.[25]

Lynn argued that technology had had a significant impact on types of armies, but he was not deterministic about its influence, arguing instead that new technology and organisation offered a 'menu of possibilities'. This would be manifest in selecting forces that had greater mobility (such as light cavalry or light infantry) or greater resilience ('heavy' forces), and of course the best option is the combination of such forces and attributes for the most efficient and beneficial effect. What Lynn omitted to mention here was the equalising effect of geography: mountains, deserts, jungles, steppes and vast distances could compel forces to adapt and create a variation in style, while at the same time neutralising certain technologies. In the Algerian desert in the early nineteenth century, the French army found that its European structures and technological superiority in artillery had little impact on the local resistance and their raiding parties. The French were forced to establish a defensive perimeter and to garrison their possessions, but when this method failed they had to adapt to light forces with greater mobility in order to conduct raiding deeper into the interior. The American armed forces faced similar challenges in the opening up of the western states, where mobile mounted units operating between secure forts were more important than the deployment of batteries of artillery or the massed infantry formations that characterised the campaigns of the Civil War.

Lynn also made the case for paradigm armies in which a force became a model for others of its age, an effect enhanced by partnering or loaning officers to other armies, or by the subordination of armies within an alliance. Lynn argued that 'victory chose the paradigm' until the twentieth century, suggesting that successful methods were transferred and successful Western armies 'acted as a magnet' that pulled armies 'towards a common pattern of military development'.[26] Citing the classic shift from the French to the Prussian model in the late nineteenth century in Europe, Lynn could be forgiven for downplaying the less voluntary adoption of either American or Soviet systems in the Cold War in their respective European partners or, indeed, in other parts of the world. Moreover, armies were compelled to react to the style of warfare of others in the colonies, even when their preferences lay in other directions. The British Army had made a virtue of close-order tactics and disciplined control of fire, but was compelled to adopt light infantry for skirmishing after setbacks in North America, while continuous fighting along the North West Frontier of India made loose skirmishing formations, the adoption of khaki and new tactics essential for survival and success.

Lynn nevertheless hinted at another reason why these paradigms change, aside from defeat or technological developments, and that was because of their tendency to fossilise, that is, to lose their relevance as the context changes. Lynn would attribute change to the fortunes of particular wars, but he put less emphasis on political changes which could also alter a particular style. Thus, if we proceed beyond Lynn's foundational theory, we would perhaps deduce that, outside the West, armies that were part of an imperial apparatus or an unequal alliance would be shaped by the hegemonic power, and these armies could easily 'fossilise' if the environment and the threats against them failed to necessitate significant change. However, political dynamics could orchestrate changes, while leaving 'relics' in place.

At the tactical level, there were other considerations which changed the way in which armies were constituted and operated over time. Recruitment and training began the process of creating cohesion, and the socialising of soldiers reinforced the early bonds. Equally, competitive behaviour between subgroups, emphasised by the conferring of new identities, could be generated. The most obvious distinctions developed between soldiers and civilians, but tribal rivalries between regiments and companies were common. As conflict approached, these bonds could be tested and developed. In the immediate anticipation of combat, the effects of discipline and prior training would be most manifest. The natural increase of anxiety, around the prospect of either death or injury, was invariably tempered by concerns about performance in action: soldiers have often expressed a desire not to let the side down by showing fear. The effect of a strong cohesion can also produce higher morale, that is, the desire to endure hardships, take losses and still fulfil a mission. Once combat is under way, the dynamics change again, as soldiers contend with the shock of first impressions (how fear and disorientation are overcome), closing with the enemy (coping with the sights, sounds, confusion, and acts of killing), and the immediate post-combat experience (where men come to terms with the loss of comrades and commanders, confront fatigue, and manage a combination of guilt, relief, euphoria and anticlimax). These dynamics illustrate the complexity of the fundamental question of why men fight.

In summary, men fight as the result of a complex array of factors, including solidarity with comrades, the higher cause, a desire to fulfil a mission, attachment to a leader, religious or ideological motivations, a desire for revenge and the will to protect or survive. War produces an ugly array of atrocities and brutal behaviours, but soldiers testify to corresponding acts of compassion such as succour to the wounded, selflessness to the point of sacrifice, and moments of inspirational courage and endurance. For obvious reasons, all armies have wanted to know how to motivate men in combat and how to maximise their efficiency, particularly to overcome the paralysing effects of fear.[27] Our assessments must reflect the complexity of the subject but seek an accurate and clear method for better understanding.

The Research Method

How can one compare forces recruited from indigenous personnel into foreign armies across different periods and continents with any degree of scientific accuracy? The solution would appear to be, first, some intellectual honesty about distinctiveness: difference and variation are to be expected, not least because the contexts and dynamics, frequencies of conflict, and numbers of variables were wide-ranging. Nevertheless, to offer some evaluation with deductions that are objective, it seems sensible to offer a matrix of types, matched against a set of influencing factors. This gives us a comparable assessment of influences (such as pay and conditions, leadership, training, discipline), types (based on levels of professional training descending to untrained, armed civilians) and a range of other factors (armaments, situation, scale and experience, among others). We know, from previous studies, that cohesion and motivation in groups are based on training, discipline, the ethos of the forces they belong to, exemplary junior officers, their time in combat, the conditions they face and a number of external influences. These differences are most easily discerned between 'professional' and 'citizen' soldiers, or 'seasoned' and 'raw' fighters.[28] The development offered by this volume is to attempt to outline these variations and their effects.

In other words, rather than a period-dependent system of categorisation, it is suggested that instead there is an analysis of armed forces by type against a list of factors that induce variations, namely their character. For types, there are essentially nine categories, reflecting levels of training or appropriate experience:

1. Untrained personnel
2. Local levies
3. Militia
4. Scouts
5. Inexperienced regulars
6. Experienced regulars
7. Veteran regulars
8. Officers and elite forces
9. Mercenaries and others

The character of each of the forces is assessed by twenty criteria:

1. Initial motivation on recruitment
2. Status
3. Terms and conditions of service, once established
4. Size of force to which they belong
5. Loyalty and reliability
6. Training and experience
7. Cohesion
8. Discipline
9. Resilience, morale, including the willingness to take casualties
10. The compulsion to change and the survival of relics
11. Technologies with which they are equipped
12. Tactics preferred
13. Command and civil–military relations
14. Common use of their force
15. Cultural influences and their manifestations
16. Socio-economic background
17. Political system, civil control and relationship with military authorities
18. State stabilisation role and view of internal security

19. Quality of the officer corps
20. Prevalence of war and exposure to it, including tempo of operations and casualty rates.

The net result is a more comprehensive and realistic assessment of performance. The use of case studies ensures that there is no loss of the important detail of the context. Examining the variables in more detail reveals some well-established deductions, but also valuable insights into the nuances of certain cases. It allows us, for example, to determine why two apparently similar armies could perform so very differently in their own situations, which professional doctrine manuals or a superficial study might obscure.

It is well known that, under ordinary circumstances, the less well-trained or inexperienced a force is, the less successful its performance will be. Poorly trained men, in attack, frequently herd together and present a bigger target, or hit the ground at the first shot and refuse to move forward.[29] Nevertheless, the presence of certain characteristics can change the outcome significantly. So, for example, while untrained personnel may be expected to fail through lack of cohesion, competence and experience, there are occasions when a sense of purpose, charismatic leadership and significant numbers, as well as other variables, will change the situation. This variation would also apply to local levies, who might have a modicum of experience in military skills, or militia, whose level of competence might be marginally greater. The increasing levels of training or experience in combat for regulars might also be expected to produce a more definite result, but, once again, variations and character will play a crucial role in producing certain outcomes. Veteran regulars, for example, may perceive a reputation is to be upheld if they fight in the presence of inferiors, but, equally, previous adverse experiences or poor leadership can degrade their performance. The best achievement might be anticipated among officers and elite units, such as Guards regiments, or Special Operational Forces, while the most variable might conceivably be found in modern mercenaries.

The initial motivation for recruitment can consist of a variety of factors, but financial return, advancement and opportunism characterise voluntarism, while threats of varying severity epitomise the situation of the conscripted serviceman. Religion, patriotism, notions of the defence of hearth and home, and ideological justifications may also be expressed. Men might enlist for a 'cause', Captain Robert Graves noted in the First World War, but while ideas motivated men, 'patriotism in the trenches was too remote a sentiment, and at once rejected as only fit for civilians or prisoners'.[30] Ideology was therefore invariably merely the basis or justification for going to fight, and might even create, in part, the bonds of cohesion, but it was not always the main motivation when men faced the trial of combat.[31] For the state, the manner in which troops are initially raised and organised reflects the values of the socio-political system. If regular troops are desirable, then recruitment will reflect that emphasis, and training regimes will be extensive as a result. Political concerns about training potentially rebellious citizens will preclude regular training, and smaller forces raised under a compulsory system with minimal proficiency may be the result. Full conscription may only be possible in highly centralised and bureaucratised states, and ones where a sense of national identity is strong. Equally, the existence of a long-service professional force can also be a strong incentive to voluntary enlistment, as young men aspire to become part of an organisation with status.

Status is a tremendously important aspect of military service of all types. Status and authority matter to even the most ill-trained forces, and are often the most cited attraction for those that consider themselves 'elite'. A reputation for success, the opportunity to command, rich experience in actual combat operations, reinforced by decorations, the possession of icons, flags, war booty, accoutrements and badges of high status, have an effect out of proportion to their size and measurable worth. Famously, during the Roman invasion of Britain in AD 54 when the soldiers appeared reluctant to jump into the surf in the face of local hordes, the standard-bearer of the X Legion is alleged to have declared: 'Leap, fellow soldiers, unless you wish to betray your eagle to the enemy. I, for my part, will perform my duty to the republic and to my general.'[32] The defence of those items imbued with status, be they colours, artillery or a particular leader, could inspire acts of immense courage. Religious motifs and ideas were invoked in such a way as to compel individuals and groups to kill without the consequences of some sacred condemnation or psychological guilt. For many pre-modern societies, individual acts of courage in close combat were the means to achieve adulthood, transition into a form of citizenship by proving their worth, and eligibility for marriage and leadership. The transformative process was marked by ritual or the collection of a talisman, trophies or even body parts of the enemy.

At a more prosaic level, the terms and conditions of service, once men were established in the armed forces, could have either a positive or negative effect. Failure to pay troops or to provide supplies or accommodation could result in low motivation or even mutiny. By contrast, the prospect of better pay, the spoils of war or promotion could generate greater devotion to duty and inspire enterprise or risk-taking. For the state, finances or a reluctance to pay military personnel in favour of other priorities might delay reforms, lead to inadequate weapons and equipment, or fossilise armed forces, but excessive spending on armed forces could also lead to bankruptcy and unpopular reforms that could inspire civil resistance. In the 1770s, it was this dilemma that led to reduced spending on Britain's Royal Navy, but compelled the British government to raise taxation to pay for the expensive Seven Years War, which, in turn, produced popular protests in the American colonies.

The size of force to which the service personnel belonged could affect their performance. Island nations tended to have smaller armies, and commensurately more spending on navies, but the size of a force could act on the confidence levels of the troops. A small force, believing itself to possess high status through training and other measures of exclusivity, might fight determinedly regardless of the odds against it. Less well-trained forces might feel that there was security in numbers or overwhelming firepower. The momentum of numbers going forward could also provide a measure of confidence, while retreating armies, gradually diminished in numbers compared with an enemy, might steadily lose confidence. Ardant du Picq once identified the collective desire to move forward in order to get out of a killing zone as 'flight to the front'.[33] On the other hand, the sudden defeat of a portion of less well-trained force could induce flight in the rest, causing a catastrophic collapse of morale, discipline and order.

Loyalty and reliability were frequently debated when employing 'foreign' elements in another force, the question being what other allegiances a fighter might possess which could, under the wrong circumstances, persuade him to change sides or turn on his employers. There were specific rites and rituals designed to create bonds with the employer, from the special recognition of a monarch, the conferring of titles, oaths, religious ceremonies, parades and uniforms. If loyalty was offered by the employed, then the employer expected reliability, and there were severe punishments for disloyalty or indiscipline.

Training and experience, or the equivalent seasoning of battlefield inoculation, could make a significant difference to the performance of military personnel. Where raw recruits could be expected to experience a degree of paralysis in the shock of coming under attack for the first time, more seasoned fighters knew how to distinguish various levels of threat and to continue to function.

Cohesion is a critical bond for military organisations, which enables them to carry out essential tasks under conditions of intense stress and take casualties yet still remain operational. US Army Historical Teams during the Second

World War realised that men tend to fight for their immediate comrades rather than any higher cause, and they were eager to discover how small groups remained cohesive. Edward A. Shils and Morris Janowitz, in examining German troops of that war, concluded:

> It appears that a soldier's ability to resist is a function of the capacity of his immediate primary group (his squad or section) to avoid social disintegration. When the individual's immediate group, and its supporting formations, met his basic needs, offered him affection and esteem from both officers and comrades, supplied him with a sense of power and adequately regulated his relations with authority, the element of self-concern in battle, which would lead to disruption of the effective functioning of his primary group, was minimized.[34]

Sam Stouffer, who conducted thousands of interviews and questionnaires in the 1940s, suggested that individuals' actions defined and were defined by their primary groups and the context of their society, noting that status could be enhanced or diminished by their combat experience in a phenomenon of 'relative deprivation'.[35] The very combat experiences that encourage bonding also bring casualties, followed by a stream of replacements that lack primary group ties, and thus the cohesion of the group is eroded.[36] Nevertheless, even replacements can be rapidly assimilated. Filtering into existing units with which they have yet to establish the close bonds, they will share some identities (language, regiment, region and training experience) with the men they had joined. For seasoned troops, group cohesion reinforces confidence and even appears to help veterans through personal and individual reflexes to killing.[37] The question of loyalty and contract has nevertheless always been tested to the extremes in the crucible of combat. As Ben Shephard noted in his work on the psychology of soldiers, ultimately the 'soldiers' dilemma' is to decide who comes first—his comrades or the government and its mission for which he fights.[38] In some wars, soldiers have resorted to a form of bargaining, believing they had shouldered their 'fair share' of casualties and effort relative to others.

A combination of loyalty, identity and an individual's spirited response to the prospect of danger sometimes rallied entire units and exemplified the concept of cohesion. William Slim (later Field Marshal) was in an attack that stalled in the First World War:

> As we wavered, a private soldier beside me, whom one would have thought untouched by imagination, ran forward. In a voice of brass he roared 'Heads up the Warwicks! Show the Blighters your cap badges!' Above the din, half a dozen men each side of him heard. Their heads came up. They had no cap badges—they were wearing steel helmets—but they had remembered their regiment.[39]

INTRODUCTION

This may be dismissed as a sentimental interpretation, but it reminds us that bonds of loyalty and allegiance may overlap from the individual, to small groups and up to larger associations. The cohesive effect of identity is not limited to small groups, and associations of up to two hundred appear to have particular strength.

Discipline, and the constant communication of it, according to sociologist Tony King, has a part to play in determining performance.[40] Flight out of the combat zone carries penalties, either 'official' ones imposed by the authority of the armed force which might include punishments for cowardice, or 'social' ones that involve fear of peer judgement. Stephen Wesbrook argued there are three primary methods of obtaining the compliance of troops necessary in preserving unit cohesion and preventing military disintegration: physically coercing alienated individuals, remunerating those who engage in battle in order to achieve tangible rewards, and the use of normative power to bind morally involved individuals.[41] Combat motivation may be reinforced by the presence of battlefield police.[42] Provosts behind the firing line were permitted to shoot stragglers or deserters to discourage flight.[43] Nevertheless, battlefield conditions tend to eliminate coercion as the principle means of control at the front line. It is by normative control of morally involved individuals that armies ensure compliance. This could exhibit itself in episodes of self-sacrifice in which individuals or whole units would opt to die fighting rather than surrender or make good their escape. In these cases an honour code could assert itself over the rational choice of self-preservation.

Resilience, including the willingness to take casualties and endure the conditions of war, was another important requirement of armed forces, and Western leaders sought this characteristic in their local forces. The (in)ability to endure minor losses or the privations of campaigning was often used as 'evidence' of racial categorisation, with, for example, much praise for hardy and courageous Gurkhas, and condemnation of 'soft' Madrassi Indian troops or 'effeminate' Chinese. Such deductions were based on misunderstanding of the context. In the mid-nineteenth century, some Chinese musketeers carried parasols to keep off the sun, thus appearing to emulate women, and, as a result, John Crawfurd, writing for the Royal United Services Institute in 1858, concluded the Chinese regarded war as 'an idle and profitless employment'.[44] Yet, Chinese inefficiency against Indian and European forces owed more to their experience of maintaining internal security with long periods spent garrisoning fortifications. Faced with overwhelming firepower, Chinese troops would break and run, but were capable of re-forming readily once they

31

were out of immediate danger. What the Chinese lacked was the training, discipline, leadership and unit motivation to wage war against Europeans and Indians effectively.

This brings us to the next characteristic via a question: what compels change? Moreover, what compels the survival of relics in armed forces? John Lynn was particularly interested in the dynamics of change and the existence of continuities, the latter 'lag' effect having a profound influence on the way that armies entered war with inappropriate tactics. To explain change in army style in the period after 1789, Lynn cited developments in the political systems such as underlying changes to the demography, industrialisation and increasingly representative institutions. At the macro level, and for Great Britain or the United States, this broad trend appears to be valid, but it falters when examining the modernisation of the contemporary Prussian Army or the Russian Army in the later nineteenth century. Moreover, for the purposes of this book, it does not offer a sufficient explanation for the development of local forces under Western control. For this, Lynn instead referred to the paradigm army concept, in which client states or independent polities looked to emulate the Westerners success.

According to Lynn, the style of the early nineteenth century gave way to a new system in the 1860s, when the cost of vast conscript armies was offset by the emergence of reservists. For the British and Americans, however, small volunteer forces had always been the preference. In Britain's case, there was also greater reliance on locally raised forces to augment much-needed manpower for imperial garrisons.

For the survival of relics, Lynn referred to the survival in European armies of an aristocratic officer corps, and to the fact that mass conscription was limited to wartime, but a more detailed survey would reveal that a great number of relics and rites from previous epochs were present in armed forces. The notion of a chivalric code that governed the conduct of officers, the treatment of civilians (especially women and children), and religious iconography remained strong and transferred itself successfully from the British colonial era in America, through independence and into the present. The ethical foundations were subsequently codified by a legal system with national and international recognition. In the case of the British Indian Army, the survival of relics was so successful that the ceremonies and rituals of an earlier period were fossilised within the armed forces, and some British traditions can still be found within the modern Indian and Pakistan armies.

Technologies with which the armed forces are equipped can affect the performance of the troops. Forces armed with obsolete weapons, compared with their enemies, can become demoralised once losses mount. By contrast, units re-equipped with better technologies gain greater confidence and may believe in their innate superiority. Technologies could influence the tactics that personnel preferred, but there could be a variety of background factors at work, such as the willingness to devolve control to subordinates and thus adopt skirmishing techniques and more adherence to 'fieldcraft'. Men accustomed to mounted operations, to manoeuvre in mountainous terrain or to fighting at sea were sought out by the Western forces as their auxiliaries, and very often their tactical preferences were retained.

Command and civil–military relations could have a profound influence on military performance. At the tactical level, the competence and degree of exemplary leadership in combat, supply and administration could create fighting units intensely loyal to their commander. Equally, leaders able to produce an optimum span of command, that is, not trying to orchestrate too many trained subordinates by devolving responsibilities, were often rewarded by men willing to use their initiative or innovate. On the other hand, untrained personnel were much more dependent on charismatic and personal leadership. In all cases, the competence of commanders could make a significant difference in the performance of the troops and therefore their cohesion, which might itself be bound up with accumulated achievements. The literature of military history is full of anecdotes of successful commanders able to inspire their subordinates, and many examples of failure which led to disaster.

John Lynn identified that the use of forces in war could have the effect of not only defining an army style but accounting for a change. Lynn stopped at the observation that, in the nineteenth and twentieth centuries, mass armies could strike deep into their enemies' territories, but this tended to subside after the era of total war, and was replaced by an emphasis on skill and mobility over mass. To this one might add that the common use of force could have a profound impact on the levels of competence, the willingness to use force given the relative faith in its ability to produce satisfactory political results, and a resilience based on a habituated acceptance of violence. These additions were important in societies that Europeans encountered in the colonial period. The British, for example, often encountered what they assumed were 'warrior peoples'. Naturally, in search of competent manpower, the British were drawn to these peoples and did their best to recruit them.

Cultural influences, and their manifestation, characterise military forces to a large extent. While a term that is over-used, culture can be defined as consisting of three aspects.[45] The first is that influences, derived from many sources, act on any group or individual, and these include history, language, geography, religion, social norms, notions of political values, guiding philosophies, education, and economic conditions. The second aspect is the cultural variation with whatever system is encountered and can take the form of the relative importance of individualism, the sense of where power lies, the degree of formality and informality in social relations, attitudes to uncertainty and risk, preferences for the long or short term view, perspectives of time, the preference for concluding a bond or keeping open relationships, and priorities. The third aspect is the manifestation of culture, which, in military terms, may occur as a particular approach to planning, an attitude towards authority, negotiation techniques, willingness to compromise, risk-taking and timekeeping.

Closely related to the idea of culture is the socio-economic background to the individuals and formed units that make up military forces, but also the context of the nation and international economic relations in which an armed force operates. Impoverished nations can rarely afford the very best technologies and struggle to resist the overwhelming conventional power of a stronger army, navy or air force. This would compel the local forces to adopt tactics that ensured survival or maximised the asymmetrical advantages afforded by other factors such as terrain, environment or popular support. Developed economies can generate mass technological uniformity, but also specialist education, surplus arms and munitions, and sophisticated logistics in the support of partners and allies.

Moreover, the political system that the armed forces serve can have an effect on their performance and character. Imperial British forces emphasised loyalty to a monarch rather than a specific government, which gave the armed forces a continuity in allegiance within an increasingly democratic political system in which government policies could oscillate every few years. It also ensured a unity between British personnel and their local partners, while, at the same time, created a mystique of distance and reverence. The British political system also reinforced a sense of class difference, and the hierarchy of the armed forces had its parallels in the social class system. Both the British and highly democratised American political economies nevertheless maintained civil primacy through their constitutions, which other European powers did not always achieve.

The colonial era for Britain and America was, in global terms, extensive but also relatively short. Lynn noted that the experiment with colonial forces occurred under a very peculiar political and economic setting, and that after 1945 the British employment of colonial forces began to ebb away quickly. Nevertheless, the employment of colonial forces was replaced with the desire for military manpower in state stabilisation missions, during conflicts of decolonisation or, for the United States, in Korea and Vietnam. These requirements produced particular views of internal security and military aid to the civil authority which spanned the period and, arguably, became more important after 1945. In the British case, it was the reluctance to use Indian or other colonial forces in the internal security role, based on their historical experience, which hastened the end of the British Empire.

The quality of the officer corps, already hinted at earlier, can prove vital to the performance of military personnel. Lynn noted that the trend in the West was for the aristocratic officer corps to be replaced in the nineteenth century with more middle-class candidates and better standards of education. The emergence of specialist war colleges and academies increased the competence levels and sense of professional identity of the officers that passed through them. General, air and naval staffs reinforced that trend still further. Selection has further enhanced this process of creating highly motivated elites.

Finally, there is the prevalence of war and exposure to it, which inoculate, habituate and develop the experience necessary for success in armed conflict. Men used to war tend to be more resilient, if losses are tolerably low, and this would also account for the selection preferences of certain armed forces through history. There are limits of course. Units or individuals that have experienced catastrophic defeat may be less willing to return to conflict, however attractive the terms or conditions might seem.

Combat itself seems to be an unchanging experience with common characteristics, although group responses can alter the individual's reactions, and these group responses are dependent on very specific contexts, such as levels of training, degree of cohesiveness, or leadership. Small, self-directed professional soldiers react very differently to untrained, uncertain and mass formations of militia when under fire and subject to the intense stresses of close combat. Individuals are so profoundly affected by the group they belong to that it affects their endurance, their willingness to take risks, and their eagerness to kill. Individuals in cohesive groups can be inspired to behave more courageously in front of their comrades, although internal cohesion in wavering groups can seemingly induce mass flight. The experience of combat can produce much more reliable and competent personnel, but it can also generate recklessness, reluctance and fatalism. It is nevertheless a factor which can affect the character of a military force.

With these characteristics now established, there are certain questions that might be addressed to any case study of local military forces in foreign employment.

Research Questions

This book is founded on several questions. The first is a curiosity as to why, having been lavished with training programmes and modern military equipment, the Iraqi security forces practically collapsed in a matter of weeks in 2014 when confronted by a virulent insurgent organisation that shared only a sectarian affinity. This demands further questions about the resilience of armies, their identity, their part in politics, and their cohesiveness. It throws into sharp relief the difference between a force that has been trained to fight and one that is actually willing to fight. It suggests that armies are not just, to paraphrase T.E. Lawrence, the business of algebra and bionomics—the numbers and sustainment of forces—but diathetics too; that is, the desire to fight, the morale and willpower to endure, take losses and continue to function as a corporate body. War is not just a question of bodies and bullets; war is fought in the minds of men.

Why do men enlist, co-operate and remain in foreign armies? What is the relative importance of the 'push' and 'pull' factors for individual men from indigenous communities when considering enlistment in an alien army? Many factors appear to be common to all men and women who join a military force, but there are also significant variations. How are the forces of local men ideally structured? Some armies have permitted a great deal of local cultural influence; others have done their best to eradicate it altogether. The results have been equally mixed. How were the purpose and role of local military forces tailored to their specific context, and what happened when they were transferred to an entirely unexpected theatre of operations? How were morale and cohesion maintained? And what assessments can be made of the variable quality of leadership, especially where Western powers treated the local troops with little respect or, conversely, elevated them to a status far beyond that of their original socio-economic background?

Raising local forces requires time and investment, but one of the research questions is: how long? And how long should the relationship last once an army has been raised? The Iraqi Army had been trained from 2003, but failed after eleven years; a stark contrast with its ability to confront and defeat Iran in ten years of intense fighting in the 1980s. What are the essentials? To what standard should an army be expected to operate? Several fundamental conditions are required. Relatively benign base areas are obligatory and newly formed units have to be tested, inoculated and trained progressively. Furthermore, they require more than the outward trappings of close-quarter combat training so favoured by Western militaries, and they need more profound development than the provision of precise or heavy weapons. National armies will reflect the society from which they are drawn and will require a deep improvement in the values identified in the typology and characteristics listed in this chapter. Lest they become brigands preying on their own people or those of neighbouring states, they need to embrace certain values, restraints and forms of professionalism. These are not easily imported, but must be established from within their own cultural terms of reference. In the history of many national and colonial armies, loyalty and allegiance were as important as effectiveness, but so too were a variety of factors that have been identified in this book.

Should training and development be focused at the policy level or the tactical? Does it matter more getting the organisation and funding right or should the emphasis be on training the individual? In recent decades there has been a strong emphasis on the individual's experience in war. Taking only individual emotional responses to fighting, one could be forgiven for assuming that the 'face of battle' is entirely randomised and unstructured. If that were so, we would still have to account for the larger group, formation, political and even societal responses to military service and to war. The conclusion we might draw is that individual emotional reactions possess similarities in psychology but can be shaped by, as well as shaping, group responses. In turn, group cohesion, while exhibiting some universal characteristics, is context-specific and shaped by a range of influencing factors. Small, self-directed, highly trained and well-motivated groups appear to manage the stresses of combat and killing with greater composure than a mass of inadequately trained, badly led and poorly motivated groups. Well-trained, seasoned and professional troops exhibit different reactions to taking or inflicting casualties from raw, citizen soldiers. The boundary, though, is blurred and dynamic. Individuals can take on the collective conscience of a crowd, but single soldiers can sometimes behave more bravely in front of groups and, in turn, inspire others to act collectively. In the past, armies have expressed such reactions under the universal theme of morale, but scholars identify a greater complexity than this term would imply. This book of those in 'foreign service' allows us to strip away some of the veneer of national history or other assumptions about 'ways of war' in order to examine cases with greater rigour.

The recruitment of local forces, both proxy actors and regular units, also raises the question of consequences. Was the model of armed forces the West promoted between 2001 and 2016 acceptable, and to whom? What is the likelihood that a force raised and trained by the West might inflict casualties on the civilian population or pursue its own agenda against its rivals, including its own political leadership? What will critics concentrate on: human rights abuses; 'green on blue' incidents; or the fuelling of internal conflict and the consequent undermining of a mission of stabilisation? Even more fundamental is the question of understanding: has the West allocated sufficient numbers of trained personnel, fluent in local languages, with the requisite skills of tact, mentoring and personal development? There are inherent risks, and this book attempts to trace both the benefits and the drawbacks of partnering with a variety of local forces, using history and social scientific research as a guide to understanding the issues of the present.

In chapter 2, there is an examination of the raising of local forces in the late eighteenth century, contrasting the cases of the three nations that form the basis of this volume—the United States, France and the United Kingdom—in the context of fighting in North America, with France and Britain in South Asia. In chapter 3, there is a more detailed study of the themes of motivation, loyalty and rejection of military service in the nineteenth and twentieth century, with brief comparisons with other nations. In chapter 4, the reconstruction of armies after unrest and the development of a penal system are analysed. Chapter 5 and 6 illustrate the complexities of raising and maintaining regiments in the West Indies and United States, contrasting voluntarism and the most extreme form of conscription, namely slavery, with varying quality in performance from the soldiers and their European officers.

Chapters 7 and 8 examine the methods of generating imperial forces in Asia and in Africa, illustrating the successes and failures. Chapter 9 analyses irregulars and auxiliaries in foreign service, comparing ethos, skills, discipline and performance. Chapter 10 examines the various contingents that served in the First World War, including labouring units. It also examines T.E. Lawrence and his advisory work among Arab irregulars. His unabridged '27 Articles' on how to deal with local partners appears in an appendix at the end of this volume.

Chapter 11 illustrates the variety of forces raised during the Second World War, their value and their limits, but also the profound consequences of military service in a war fought for liberation. Chapter 12 evaluates local and partnered forces during the period of decolonisation, with sections that compare the British in southern Arabia, the American use of Montagnards in Vietnam, and the French use of local forces in Algeria. Chapter 13 discusses the role of auxiliary and partnered forces in counter-insurgency, especially in Iraq after 2003 and Afghanistan after 2001. Finally, in the concluding chapters, all the themes are brought together and some reflections are made on 'defence engagement' and future directions.

2

RAISING ARMIES

NORTH AMERICAN AND SOUTH ASIAN PERSONNEL IN BRITISH, AMERICAN AND FRENCH SERVICE, 1746–1783

In North America, since European personnel were relatively few in number, the rival powers of Great Britain and France were compelled to augment their strength either with indigenous allies or with a trained cadre of local men.[1] First Nation fighters were employed, partnered or allied by both sides. In the French and Indian War (1756–63) and in the subsequent Revolutionary War (1775–83), there was no attempt to train indigenous warriors, as their skills in fighting in the forested terrain of North America were considered superior to those of the colonists. By contrast, in the Indian subcontinent, South Asian personnel were critically important to the British and French military effort in the Carnatic Wars (1746–8; 1749–54; 1757–63). Native forces were employed with an emphasis on the steady improvement of their efficiency and cost-effectiveness although quality was linked to the tasks they were to perform. Levels of training were also aligned to their role: irregular forces were thought to possess certain inherent qualities that required only British leadership, but the majority of South Asian men who were employed were trained along European lines as regular troops.

Drawing on the British and American experiences of the eighteenth century in North America, and the British campaigns in South Asia, this chapter analyses the types, recruitment patterns and uses of military labour, offering a comparison between the two theatres, including the assessments made by contemporaries. Archival records suggest the French, British and Americans were eminently pragmatic in their decisions about manpower. The French were outnumbered by their British adversaries, and the vast territories of North America militated against the concentration of force. The solution was to make use of First Nation allies and partners, encouraging them in the belief that the British intended to take their lands. The British faced the same challenge of manpower, and mobilised their own North American partners, both colonial militia and First Nation fighters. In the Revolutionary War, the Patriots initially lacked any regular forces of their own and they appealed to certain First Nation groups. Despite trying to preserve their neutrality, a far larger proportion of First Nation fighters fought on the British side, not least because the British insisted it was they who were eager to preserve land in the hands of the indigenes and it was the Patriot colonists who were likely to expropriate territory.

The British were just as pragmatic in India. The French had enjoyed some success with their employment of South Asian men in trained, regular units. Short of manpower, the British had adopted the French model and raised their own trained companies. They interpreted conditions in South Asia through their own experiences, looking for particular 'types' of men, but they also borrowed from local practices and in some cases worked with local irregulars, particularly when the sheer demand for trained manpower in the 1750s outweighed any ideological considerations. The British were aware of the need to acknowledge cultural sensitivities, and the East India Company Army was not converted entirely to a 'European' model.

In order to assist in making wider comparative judgements about local forces in this period, it is possible to identify here certain trends. In North America, the British tended to rely on barely trained militia consisting of European colonists and highly proficient local irregulars. The French possessed a small regular force, the Troupes de Marine, and a militia, some of whom were very experienced in fighting in forests. They also had large numbers of local and highly competent First Nation allies. The army of the East India Company in South Asia was a force consisting of European regulars with a handful of local militia and irregulars, led by an officer corps that was only in part 'professional'. By the end of the Third Carnatic War, roughly equivalent to the Seven Years War in Europe, the troops of the East India Company consisted of experienced regulars, augmented by auxiliaries who might still be categorised as irregulars, thus constituting a 'mixed force'. The

European contingent, raised by a combination of voluntaryism and 'crimping' (impressment), were inexperienced regulars, with relatively low levels of competence, but some were veterans, especially those who had served for a long period in India or those with specialist skills, such as gunners. This chapter examines these types comparatively.

Assessments of the Raising of Local Forces

Over the last thirty years, a great deal of attention has been paid to interpretations of the colonial period in the light of post-colonial studies.[2] There has been a comprehensive search for the ideological assumptions and constructions of the colonisers and the subsequent reactions of the colonised. The approach itself has been scrutinised and critiqued, with detractors arguing that the colonised were not simply passive victims of colonising 'discourses' and power relationships, but active agents in the dynamic processes at work. Subsequently some scholars have tried to show that the European empires and their colonial subjects were engaged in 'dialogues' of power, with more nuanced interpretations of class and race.[3] Commentators nevertheless insist that the European empires were inherently violent, stripped peoples of power and dignity, which, at times, altered their behaviour so profoundly that, even after independence, a sense of inferiority persisted. With a deeply moralised agenda in keeping with late-twentieth-century ideas of social justice and equality, the colonial period has been condemned as fundamentally unjust, often cruel and irredeemably corrupt. The collaboration of local people in the colonial enterprise, their engagement in commerce, enlistment in military forces, alliances and partnerships problematise this simple condemnation. Whatever the interpretation one places on the past today, it is evident that there were many more sentiments at work for contemporaries. Whatever one's position, these debates are particularly important in any consideration of the British and European employment of local forces in the eighteenth century.

Far from simply being solely a system of violence, the British used their army, in keeping with mid-eighteenth-century ideas about the state and public order, to confront external threats from France and establish pacified regions more conducive to commerce. As the wars in North America indicated, the British were frequently engaged in partnerships and alliances. It was the fighting power of the First Nation tribes that ensured the British could match the French and their allies in the hinterland, while concerns not to alienate colonist opinions prevented the conversion of militia into regular forces. In the subsequent Revolutionary War (1775–83), Congress initially struggled to convert its patriotic militia into regular regiments, while First Nation fighters in British service were a significant threat. However, in the major engagements of the war, the British relied on their regular troops, and when the Patriot cause could raise its own continental army and benefit from the arrival of French regulars, it enjoyed success.

The recruitment of an effective, trained and disciplined army was also a crucial element of the British success in South Asia. Despite numerous attempts to identify ideological reasons for the expansion of Company rule in India, the conduct of its officers and the raising or use of armies, the British displayed a practical approach to the problems they confronted. Their points of reference were, unsurprisingly, entirely European, but they applied no rigid systems and responded in a way that took account of local conditions to establish their own local supremacy, encourage the free flow of trade, minimise costs, and maximise profit. Moreover, the colonial army was crucial to the way that the East India Company developed: faced with a great threat from French forces and local instability, the Company employed a greater proportion of trained Indian personnel and engaged in a series of significant military operations. While the British adopted European standards in selection, training and tactics, they were also conscious of the limitations of British personnel in terms of health, quality and availability.

It is generally accepted that the British learned from the French model both in North America and South Asia, namely, that use of local manpower, some trained in the European modes of warfare, was crucial to winning the campaigns. After years of setbacks, it was the assistance of the First American fighters to the British that provided the only tactical successes of the French Indian War. In South Asia, trained sepoys were vital in augmenting the limited British manpower, thus providing forces that could outmanoeuvre and defeat the French.

North American Militias and Partners in the Seven Years War

From the establishment of New France, and as enshrined in royal ordinance in 1627, the French regarded the First Nation inhabitants as their equals and partners. Intermarriage was frequent, and there was some blending of local and French customs. Both sides learned their respective languages, and, at arranged meetings, a combination of French and First Nation rituals were observed. Unsurprisingly, when conflicts occurred with the British in 1754, the French colonists turned to their 'natural Frenchmen' partners. It was two years before the Seven Years War (la Guerre de la conqûete) broke out, but this brought an escalation to the fighting in North America and began to turn the tide against France. Until then, the combination of French Troupe de Marine regulars and the irregular First Nation fighters had inflicted a succession of defeats on the British.

The fighting began with a series of skirmishes around Fort Duquesne over disputed claims at the Forks of the Ohio.[4] At Jumonville Glen, a French patrol was ambushed and defeated by the Virginia militia (May 1754). General Edward Braddock attempted to take the French settlement with an offensive approaching on multiple axes, but the assaults were defeated and Braddock's command was routed at the Battle of Monongahela (9 July 1755). The French officer Daniel Liénard de Beaujeu had led his First Nation allies into battle bare-chested and covered in traditional war paints as a mark of his solidarity with his partners. By contrast, Braddock had rejected the use of native auxiliaries, believing his 2,000-strong force of two regular battalions from Ireland and a large number of local militia companies gave him superiority over the French. He had far too few guides, just eight, for the scale of the operation, and the requirement to move cannons along the inadequate roads forced Braddock to split his column in two.

The French garrison was reinforced sufficiently to allow an attempt to delay the British as they approached. The 200 French regulars and their Canadian militia would have been too weak to resist the British, but some 600 Indian fighters tipped the balance in their favour. In the initial engagement, the British fire was effective and killed Beaujeu, sending the Canadian militia into flight. The First Nation fighters dispersed, engaging the British with musket fire and traditional weapons from the forest. Small groups sent against them were wiped out and their scalps nailed to trees.

At this point the French forces rallied and returned to the fight, and the Indians scouted on the flanks of the British. The militia fell back or themselves took to the forest, but the British regulars, unused to the environment and shocked by casualties inflicted by an enemy they could not see, began to retreat in disorder.[5] With the greatest difficulty, Braddock rallied his men and they re-formed, firing volleys into the trees. In the smoke and confusion, some of this fire was directed against their own militia. When Braddock was fatally wounded, his entire force began to fall back again. At Monongahela, the cohesion of the British regulars collapsed and the Indian fighters began to pick off the retreating parties of redcoats. The victors did not pursue the remnants after dark but set about looting the column's baggage and scalping the dead and the wounded. Most of the 50 women accompanying the British had been killed or captured, and more than half of Braddock's column had been killed and wounded. The disaster led to consideration of new tactics, including the deployment of light infantry that could fight in the forests on the Indians' terms rather than depending on close-order formations and volley fire.

Intermittent war continued over the next two years, and invariably the French had the upper hand through their First Nation auxiliaries. The situation was serious enough to persuade the British to expel all Acadians, including those that had been nominally loyal to the Crown, after 1755. The expulsions were resisted with protracted guerrilla war, and after the Seven Years War some were permitted to resettle, but British colonists had by then taken a substantial portion of the land.

In 1757, however, the French under Louis-Joseph de Montcalm succeeded in taking Fort William Henry on Lake George. The 6,000 French regulars and militia were accompanied by almost 2,000 First Nation fighters, who, failing to comprehend the Europeans' agreement that the British should capitulate and withdraw 'with the honours of war', set upon the retreating column and massacred some of the troops and their families, and the wounded. Montcalm had endeavoured to prevent the killings, but had been unable to stop an initial raid into the fort after its surrender, where the sick and wounded had been killed and scalped. The multiple groups of Indians had no authority over each other, and tended to be drawn to the prospect of loot and enhanced status through taking scalps. Some of the French officers refused to heed the British appeals for support, and the massacre became somewhat exaggerated in its subsequent reporting. Nevertheless, the theft of the baggage, clothing and weapons was sufficient to persuade many First Nation fighters that the war was over and they left Montcalm's side. This may have persuaded Montcalm to abandon any further pursuit of the British forces. Undisciplined irregular allies were therefore an asset when there was a prospect of material and moral gain for the fighters, but the episode demonstrated that Montcalm could not exercise control over them or sustain their effort for a larger operational or strategic purpose.

The First Nation groups in French service in the north of the theatre of operations were the Abenaki and the Mi'kmaq, while in the Great Lakes area the French drew upon the Huron, Mississauga, Ojibwa, Winnebago and Potawatomi. The British relied on their own native allies as the war developed, particularly the Iroquois, Six Nations and, until the outbreak of a local conflict in 1758, the Cherokee. Despite the apparent clarity of division, there were countless local arrangements in which tribal chieftains allied to or resisted the British and the French and rival tribesmen. Much depended on the allegiance of the tribal leadership and the advantages they believed they possessed at a local level. Respect for individual European figures could also determine loyalty. When fighting began in upstate New York, the Iroquois sought out William Johnson, the superintendent of Indian Affairs, who had a long-standing and friendly relationship with them. His position as colonel of the New York State Militia made a military partnership with the Iroquois a given. On the other hand, the Creek and Cherokee, while ostensibly neutral, were subjected to diplomatic overtures and assurances from both the British and the French. The Pennsylvania authorities had rather more success in arranging First Nation neutrality in their state by the terms of the Treaty of Easton in 1758, and the British were able to seize Fort Frontenac (August 1758), which cut off French supplies to Ohio. The decimation of tribal groups by a smallpox epidemic also led to a catastrophic reduction in trade. More First Nation tribes made their peace with the British as a result, which cleared the way for a major British attack on Quebec.

The British had initially expected more from their colonial militias, and while there were undoubtedly some successes, it was clear that the war in North America could only be won with the arrival of regular troops. For the siege of Quebec, General James Wolfe commanded 7,000 British regulars and 400 gunners, and was supported by a strong naval flotilla. Establishing a base of operations on the St Lawrence, Wolfe's troops laid siege. The French distributed their garrison of 12,000 to cover all possible landing sites and repulsed the first attack at Montmorency. To draw the defenders out, Wolfe destroyed settlements along the St Lawrence, deploying some of his Rangers in the task. These militiamen had developed 'Indian tactics' over many decades, initially as parties that could avenge atrocities and raids by tribesmen. By the time of the siege of Quebec, there were fourteen companies, totalling 1,400 men, under the nominal command of the enigmatic Major Robert Rogers. The Rangers had been involved in a number of encounters as an independent corps, and had not always been successful, but their triumph was in the siege of Fort Louisbourg where they captured a number of French and their militia allies singlehandedly. The Rangers also carried out the raid on St Francis near Quebec and during their withdrawal they were forced to live off the land in precarious conditions, and possibly half the force of 200 became casualties.

Wolfe's troops had been adversely affected by disease throughout the three-month siege, and, with a sense of time running out, he famously ordered the scaling of the cliffs upstream of Quebec. The unexpected manoeuvre led directly to the battle of the Plains of Abraham, when Montcalm, with greater numbers, chose to confront the British in open battle. Montcalm could command over 13,000 'regulars', 200 cavalrymen, an array of 200 cannon, and an assortment of Canadian militia and 300 First Nation fighters. Wolfe had just 3,000 regulars, but his advantage was that his men were expecting a conventional, European-style action, while most of the French militia and irregulars were more comfortable in guerrilla operations. Moreover, although these troops engaged the British left from woodland on the periphery of the battle, Montcalm was relying on his regular troops to take the offensive and drive the British off before they could be reinforced or commence siege works. The French Troupes de Terre had been replenished over the preceding months by militia and were largely inexperienced men. The British regulars, exercising great nerve and discipline, held their fire despite two ragged French volleys, until the French were within thirty yards, and then they fired. Advancing a few paces, they discharged a second volley and the French fell back. The contagion of retreat spread rapidly and the entire French force retreated towards the defences of Quebec, the pursuit only being checked briefly by the gun batteries on the walls. The French garrison divided, and much of the force withdrew, leading to the capture of the strategic city. The following spring, a French counter-attack was a partial success but the city remained in British hands. Later, in 1760, Montreal was also taken by a force of 17,000 British regulars and colonial militia, which marked the end of significant French resistance.

First Nation and Militia Participation in the American Revolution

At the outbreak of the Revolution in 1775, the British government expected that colonial militia would form the bulk of the forces for its suppression, since this was, after all, considered an insignificant period of unrest. Yet it was clear to those with authority in the colonies that regular troops would be required. Although figures can only be approximate, about 20 per cent of the population could be considered loyalists, while twice that number was sufficiently angry to identify with the revolution, and the rest hoped to remain neutral. While some 25,000 were to serve the Crown as Loyalists, only a relatively small number were militia since the majority served in the Royal Navy. Those in the militia were often reluctant to make war on those they considered similar to themselves.

In the regular army there were also those with qualms about defeating the revolt. Guy Carleton, after his victory over the Patriots at the Battle of Valcour Island on Lake Champlain in 1776, discouraged his men from exhibiting any expressions of elation, since they had, as far as he was concerned, only defeated their own kinsmen. Carleton also released prisoners he had taken, taking them to the Americans at Fort Ticonderoga rather than having them interned far from their families in Canada.

The revolutionary cause was barely understood in the British government. It was a *sine qua non* that civic duty came before personal liberty, and there was a great deal of suspicion that the refusal to pay for the costs of the French Indian Wars and the taxation requirements for imported goods was the result of corrupt practice. The exaggerated commentary provided by the radicals was dismissed and it was expected that the colonists would have to accept the continuation of British government direction for the sake of good order and loyalty to the Crown. To the colonists, the Quebec Act, which confirmed the promises made in the Seven Years War to protect the land of the First Nations, seemed to be a denial of an opportunity for further development, and attempts to curtail widespread smuggling also threatened illicit livelihoods. The first response of the radicals was to demand that militias be placed under their control, and some began drilling in expectation of conflict soon after. Disorder had broken out in Boston when seven soldiers, surrounded by a mob of 200, opened fire to drive back the crowd, but the incident was seized upon by radicals as a 'massacre'. The Tea Party was another orchestrated event, almost certainly carried out by those who had made their fortunes through smuggling during the Seven Years War, and those that donned disguises as First Nation warriors had made a weak attempt to disguise their crime or deflect retribution. The so-called Sons of Liberty used Indian names, but this was equally ineffective. The fact that the habeas corpus legislation was being debated in Britain, which could lead to the abolition of slavery, also produced fear in a particular section of the colonial population that the British government would favour Indian and former slave interests over their own.

First Nation tribes were divided over their allegiances, but the preference was for neutrality. Nevertheless, for many, concerns that the colonists would take their lands meant that there were rather more who supported the British. The Iroquois fielded a contingent of 1,500 and, together, about 13,000 First Nation fighters fought for King George III. Large numbers of the Seneca, Onondaga and Cayuga fought alongside the British, but the Mohawks were divided and took part in the fighting on both sides. The Tuscarora and

Oneida, sensing better opportunities with the new dispensation, backed the Patriot colonists.[6] In Georgia and South Carolina, Creeks and Seminoles carried out raids on behalf of the British. The result was the destruction of settlements along the Broad River. Hundreds of Chickasaws and Choctaws also fought alongside the British in the south, although they remained bitter rivals to each other.

The initial offensive by the Patriots, towards Quebec and Montreal, failed to meet their expectations. In the defence of Quebec, Sir Guy Carleton could muster only 70 regulars, 35 Marines, 300 sailors and 800 Canadian militia, but he was aided by local deception plans and an intelligence network that informed him of the precise nature of the attack. When Benedict Arnold's offensive faltered, he tried to sustain the siege by recruiting local French-speaking militiamen. The siege was broken after an epic relief effort by the Royal Navy at the height of winter, and Arnold's broken forces were pursued back to Fort Ticonderoga on Lake Champlain. A second Patriot invasion of Canada was repulsed in 1777 thanks to Loyalist militia, the ranks of which were swelled by refugees seeking to avoid intimidation and property seizures in the colonies to the south.

The process of intimidation and condemnation, with corresponding exemplary punishment of 'Tories', persuaded some colonists to join the revolution somewhat reluctantly. The First Nation auxiliaries accompanying Lieutenant General Burgoyne from Canada in 1777 also deterred many potential Loyalists. About 400 fighters tended to prey on isolated farmsteads, destroying property and killing or assaulting those they found there. The infamous murder and scalping of Jane McCrea and Mrs McNeil, the partners of serving Loyalist officers, acted as a strong deterrent.[7] There was little sympathy for Burgoyne for his employment of German mercenaries either, for they had little in common with the population. The 'Hessians', like the 650-strong militia, were useful militarily, but were too few to defeat the strengthening resistance that Burgoyne encountered en route to Saratoga. General William Howe was expected to march towards Burgoyne, but Howe felt inclined to remain in a position to threaten the revolutionary capital at Philadelphia, for which he was subsequently criticised. Aside from his strategic situation, Howe's chief dilemma was manpower. Although he proved able to defeat George Washington's militia forces, he could not replace his casualties and his dwindling force could not prevail against the numbers of rebels he faced.

Washington had similar problems. In the winter of 1777, the Patriots were in danger of having almost no force at all. With supplies dwindling to a critical level, Washington pleaded with Congress to provide food, clothing and shoes to his nascent army as a matter of urgency. He wrote: 'unless some great and capital change suddenly takes place, ... this army must inevitably ... starve, dissolve or disperse, in order to obtain subsistence in the best manner they can'. In the previous winters, men had drifted away from their militia units in such numbers that it was almost impossible to maintain a front against the British. Without sustained training they lacked competence and cohesion. Time and again they were driven from the field because they lacked the ability to function effectively as formed units, and efforts to fight from prepared positions could only provide a temporary tactical solution.

In their new permanent winter encampment at Valley Forge, the chief problem was supply. Food was scarce and soldiers were sometimes forced to depend on 'firecake', a mash of flour and water. Animal fodder was also intermittently supplied and many of the cavalry mounts and draught horses died in the cold weather. Militia uniforms, such as they were, were not replenished and some of the troops were dressed in rags. In damp, fetid huts, inadequately fed and without winter clothing to keep out the cold, many men were incapacitated by disease. Typhoid, dysentery and pneumonia killed perhaps as many as 2,000, with a further 4,000 reported as unfit for duty. Inevitably, under such circumstances, many men began to desert.

In December, Johann Dekalb had written:

Our men are infected with the Itch, a matter which attracts very little attention either in the hospitals or in the camp. I have seen poor fellows covered over and over with scab ... We are already suffering from want of everything. The men have neither meat nor bread for four days, and our horses are often left without any fodder.' A surgeon of the camp listed the problems in his private journal: 'Poor food—hard lodgings—cold weather—fatigue—nasty clothes—nasty cooking—smoked out of my sense—the devil's in it—I can't endure it—why are we sent here to starve and freeze? ... here, all confusion—smoke and cold—hunger and filthiness ...

He noted with bitterness that 'yesterday upwards of fifty officers resigned their commission'. Officers who left took their servants with them. Some commissary officers sold the camp's flour to the citizens of Philadelphia or perhaps to the British. Soldiers simply abandoned their posts and used guard duty as an opportunity to run away from military service. Drunkenness and indiscipline were serious problems.

Camp indiscipline extended to bad hygiene and the mishandling of supplies. In the orders of 13 March 1778, there was a note that 'the carcasses of dead horses are lying in and near the camp, and that the offals near many of the commissaries stalls still lie unburied, that much filth and nastiness is spread amongst the huts, which are, or soon will be reduced to a state of putrefaction'. Criticisms began to extend to Washington himself. While some blamed Congress, others, like the veteran fighter General Charles Lee, felt Washington was 'not fit to command a Sergeant's Guard'. But quarrels between all the leading officers were not uncommon and several duels took place that winter.

Nevertheless, what made Valley Forge so significant was Washington's ability to retain a significant portion of his force and to improve it throughout the first six months of 1778. By doing so, Washington kept resistance alive. Indeed, his efforts made it possible to put the American cause on a more solid foundation. Two elements in particular were crucial to his success: the involvement of patriotic citizens, particularly the women of the army, and the training programme implemented by Baron Friedrich Wilhelm von Steuben.

The camp followers of any eighteenth-century army were vitally important. In the absence of formal military services and logistics, women often acted as the victuallers, nurses, seamstresses and labourers of the force. These regimental camp followers were crucial to sustaining Washington's army at Valley Forge, not only providing the rations and repairs that were necessary but bolstering the faltering morale of the troops. By being co-located with the men, this little army of women and children prevented wholesale collapse.

The greatest contribution to the development of the army came from Baron von Steuben. A former Prussian army officer who had served under Frederick the Great, this volunteer was quickly appointed by Washington with the duties of acting inspector general. Although he spoke almost no English, he realised that each American unit was using its own variation in drill, musketry and manoeuvre. Soon after his arrival in February 1778, Steuben therefore drew up his own drill and training manual, cutting corners in the formal and long-winded European methods, to standardise all practices. His staff translated the manual from Steuben's French version and began to disseminate the work. Steuben himself worked with individual units, often demonstrating drills and, through translators, taking time to explain the processes. The approach was considered revolutionary even by some American officers, since drill and manoeuvre was never a subject soldiers were expected to understand, only to obey. Nevertheless, Steuben was no saint: his faltering English led to misunderstandings and frustrations, and Steuben often exploded in rage. This so amused the troops that, in time, Steuben learned almost to caricature himself, using a mixture of threat and humour to win over the men.

The training was relentless. Parades began at six o'clock in the morning and continued for two hours. At nine, the parades began again for three hours. At noon, NCOs were trained, and drilling for the men ran again all afternoon. Specialist training in tactics and leadership was given to the officers. A particular emphasis was placed on officers getting to know their men by name and character. There were lectures on camp hygiene, kitchen maintenance, changing bedding, and washing. There were sessions set aside for the manufacture of weapons and gunpowder, for the repair of tools and arms, and for the construction of earthworks under French engineers led by Brigadier General Louis Duportail.

With sub-units mastering the individual skills of marching in line and column, loading and firing and responding to commands, Steuben turned to the movements and direction of larger formations. Companies, regiments and then brigades eventually learned the business of battlefield manoeuvre. Steuben also recognised that the Americans had hitherto feared the British bayonet charge, even when they occupied entrenched positions. He therefore introduced measures to build confidence and instil aggression in making their own attacks with the bayonet. Steuben was responsible for the creation of a regular American army that could fight the British on their own terms and retain the field. Although the Patriots would continue to rely on irregular tactics and elements of guerrilla warfare, there was an understanding that victory could only be achieved by taking the fight to the British and going onto the offensive.

When France allied with the American revolutionaries in May 1778, this new regular force would be augmented by European professionals on land and sea, greatly adding to their strength. The French alliance also had the effect of changing the British strategy completely. London could not afford to view the American colonies as the main theatre of operations when France posed a threat much closer to home. Moreover, Britain was more concerned with protecting the West Indies and its colonial possessions in India, and was forced to divert naval and land resources to these other regions.

The return of better weather and the existence of the core of the new army at Valley Forge also drew back men who had deserted over the winter. New volunteers appeared, provided with uniforms, and then integrated into the established formations. A spirit and pride had evolved which could not be easily extinguished. By the summer, the new army was able to take the field with confidence.

The British, led by their new commander Sir Henry Clinton, decided to quit Philadelphia in the light of the French alliance and to fall back on New

York. Unable to load the men aboard ships in the Delaware because of a lack of transports, Clinton had to march the army overland. The column of troops and supply wagons extended over twelve miles, which made it vulnerable, and Washington felt the time had come to test the new Continental Army. In stifling heat, the Americans tried to concentrate their forces and catch Clinton at Monmouth County courthouse in the village of Freehold. The two sides clashed on 28 June and, through Lee's hesitation, the Patriots were bundled back by British Grenadiers. Clinton escaped, but the American army had been inoculated in battle and it was only a matter of time before they made use of the training and experience to better effect. The result of the American alliance with France was the arrival of French regulars, and a significant reduction in the British naval presence off the coast of the colonies. At Yorktown, an isolated British garrison under General Cornwallis was forced to capitulate in 1781, indicating the direction the war would now take.

African Americans also participated in the war on both sides. The Patriots created all-black units in Rhode Island and Massachusetts. The British raised an estimated 5,000 African American militia, recruited from slaves who were promised their freedom after the war. In addition, thousands of escaping slaves sought refuge in British territory, especially those who had worked on Loyalist plantations. The British defeat meant not all were granted the freedom they had expected. Some fugitives were resold in the West Indies, although a substantial number were freed and resettled in the northern states. Many black men who had fought or actively assisted the British were, like white Loyalists, treated with contempt and, in places, subjected to severe retribution.

South Asian Sepoys in the Carnatic Wars

The historian Philip Mason suggested that, once the British learned the value of the Indian sepoy, they possessed the means to conquer the South Asian subcontinent.[8] Channa Wickremesekera disagreed, pointing to the widespread contempt for Indian soldiers and their secondary roles in all their campaigns.[9] He argued that the Europeans felt the Indians were incapable of effective leadership or initiative. Indians were therefore used only as factory guards or garrison troops. Where units were raised, they were Europeanised, that is trained, drilled and even clothed on European lines, under British officers. He argued that Indian troops were rarely used against French units and tended to be deployed only to guard the baggage and lines of communication. If they performed well, the British attributed this to their own officers or the inspiration of the British soldiers who accompanied them. In the key engagements of the Seven Years War (1756–63, contemporaneous with the Third Carnatic War), European troops invariably led in the assault. The only significant changes, he argued, were in the numbers actually employed (which was a consequence of extended commitments) and an equalisation in weaponry between British and Indian forces (after 1760, both were armed with flintlocks).

It is easy to assume that racial stereotypes, which were to become so prominent in the nineteenth century, determined ideas in this earlier period. In fact, calculations about the need for, and costs of, military manpower, regardless of ethnicity, were more important. The East India Company was eager to find those that would work with it and, in peacetime, to simply keep labour costs to a minimum. Manpower demands in wartime could overcome peacetime prejudices very rapidly. Furthermore, while it is easy to find episodes where Indians were not trusted to make independent judgements without the direction of European officers, this would also apply in exactly the same way to European infantrymen. Men with rural backgrounds, lacking education, characterised both European and Indian foot soldiers. Discipline was harsh for both but was proven, time after time, to be necessary to drill men to overcome their instinctive desire to save themselves in a close-quarter battle. The forging of a collective solidarity and sense of purpose, often through the moniker of the regiment or the willingness to follow a particular leader, applied equally to British and Indian troops. The environment and human health also had a part to play. Gerald Bryant argued that the need to garrison India and to provide internal security, in an environment that Europeans found debilitating and even lethal, but for which Indian troops were better suited, meant that Indians were preferred.[10] Moreover, some European officers were critical of the poor performance of bad-quality European soldiers compared with the sepoys.

In the 1740s, the British had been content to use casually employed local armed men for the protection of their caravans, goods and quarters.[11] From the outset, control of territory brought with it the obligation of security of the population although the Company's priority was to avoid this sort of commitment in favour of commercial activity. Initially, the only reliable military forces were European troops shipped from the British Isles. The first were the King's troops, four companies of which landed in Bombay in 1662 and who were invited to take up their arms in 1668 as regulars of the East India Company. In 1664, two companies of 'Rajputs' had been enlisted, but they got neither British officers nor training. They used their own weapons, possessed no uniforms, and their pay was often in arrears. They were accordingly described by the Governor of Bombay as 'more like bandits in the woods than military men'. In response he organised a militia of all freemen and landholders. The officers were English but the ranks were filled with Indians who had largely converted to Christianity. Nevertheless, in 1706, six companies of 'Gentoos' (Hindus) were disbanded because they were so unreliable. By the 1740s, garrisons were held by Europeans and elderly or infirm mestees (men of mixed Portuguese and Indian descent, sometimes described as 'Portuguese'), topasses and peons (Christian Indians, the latter being the term used in Madras), and 'seapoys' (men armed with their own weapons, fit only for guard duty).[12] In February 1747, Madras was protected by 3,000 peons, but only 900 had muskets and these were all matchlocks. The verdict that one must draw is that the Indian troops in the Company's employment before 1750 were cheap, were attracted by financial reward but were of a very low quality indeed; all of which was the result of peacetime parsimony.

As in North America, the British use of local forces was transformed by encounters with the French. The Nawab of the Carnatic had been defeated by a French force made up of Europeans and sepoys under Captain Paradis, while the fleet under Bertrand-François de La Bourdonnais had taken Madras in 1746. By contrast, the British, despite having a strong fleet, failed to capture Pondicherry, simply because they lacked the resources and manpower for a land campaign. Although Madras was returned on the conclusion of peace two years later, the seriousness of the threat and the French alliances with local rulers had revealed the precarious position of the East India Company in the subcontinent. The 'unofficial war' between British and French forces in India in fact continued, with each unable to maintain a fleet off the east coast of India for long, and with both sides plagued by the steady loss of European troops who died of disease. The French and particularly the British had too few Europeans to take and hold all the hill fortifications that lay between their territories or those of their allies. Garrisoning the settlements that were captured used up precious manpower. The solution was therefore entirely pragmatic: recruit more Indian personnel who could cope better with the climate, survive local diseases and augment the dwindling numbers of trained Europeans.

The British position was weakened further when Joseph–François, Marquis Dupleix, the Governor General of the French possessions in India, allied himself with the new Nizam of the Deccan, and earned the Mughal title of 'Commander of the Seven Thousand' from the Emperor. At Arcot, the French had gained another ally, Chanda Sahib, the new Nawab of the Carnatic. This put several thousand Indian troops at the disposal of France. The British had backed Chanda Sahib's rival, Mohammed Ali Khan Wallajah, at Trichinopoly and provided a garrison of 600 men, but the city was besieged in 1751. At Fort St George in Madras and Fort St David, there were barely 350 British personnel available—too few for a relief force. Nevertheless, Robert Clive, who had been appointed originally as commissary of supply, was permitted to march out with 200 European and 300 Indian troops, and three small field guns, to make an audacious attack on Chanda Sahib's capital at Arcot. After the surprise capture of the town, Clive put the settlement, with its mile-long perimeter, into a state of defence. Clive possessed only 120 British and 200 Indians fit for duty at the commencement of the siege. After a bombardment, a series of sorties and a major attack on a breach in the walls, this garrison had been reduced to 80 British soldiers and 120 sepoys. Nevertheless, reinforced, and then relieved at Arcot by additional indigenous troops, Clive pursued the French and Indian armies and inflicted a major defeat on them at Arni.

Clive's successes helped turn the tide of the war: Chanda Sahib's forces were drawn off from Trichinopoly, Mysore and a portion of Marathas joined Mohammed Ali. Dupleix tried to restore the situation by advancing towards Madras with 400 Frenchmen and 2,000 sepoys. This force ambushed Clive at Kaveripak (1752), when the British had force-marched to intercept him. Clive defeated the ambush with his own outnumbered brigade. Indian men employed by the Company went on to fight against the French and their allies, describing themselves as the 'veterans of Arcot', which, given there had been only 120 survivors and the new force numbered 600, might refer to French-trained sepoys who had changed sides.[13] There are other possible explanations. They may have been sick soldiers who had recovered, or new recruits who had joined the core of the old formation, although changing sides was not so unusual in the fluid arrangements of southern India.

What was clear, from the emergence of the French as a more significant rival to the East India Company in the Indian subcontinent after 1750, was that the British were deficient in trained manpower. Indian personnel were therefore trained by Clive and others on the French model, and, by the end of the fighting in 1753, it was clear that organisation, improved discipline and the toughening experience of campaigning had improved the quality of the British Indian forces. The fact was that European personnel in India were not available in sufficient numbers. Part of the problem was the supply: there was considerable competition for recruits with the regular army back in Britain. The outbreak of the Seven Years War in North America and Europe therefore necessitated that regular regiments were sent out to India. This immediately raised questions about whether the Company or the Army should exercise command and jurisdiction, but with 63 per cent of the Company's forces being made up of regular units, the issue of manpower and who was to provide it became a critical and much-debated issue.[14] In Britain, potential recruits sought to avoid all of the tropical destinations as deathtraps, and that included India.[15] The regular army, which needed to fill its own ranks, pressured its parliamentary allies to limit Company recruitment quotas. These pressures meant that the Company was compelled to release more funds to raise local personnel.

The Recruitment of the Company Sepoys

In 1757, Robert Clive had recruited the first Bengal native regiment, the Lal Paltan, as a selected, 515-strong unit serving under British officers, thus expanding the Company Army from its companies in Madras and its garrison at Bombay. According to a return of the Bengal troops dated 10 April 1757, Clive commanded some 1,914 'seapoys', of which 1,400 were, in fact, from Madras. In addition, the return listed 257 topasses, 157 of whom were drawn from Bombay and the rest from Madras, but all of these were confined to garrison and guard duty.

The new Bengal sepoys were picked using the standard British criteria of the day. Many British soldiers were enlisted in rural Scotland as well as the English countryside because of a preference for rural workers. Tall and physically robust men were selected because of the endurance required in military service. Agricultural labourers were considered tougher, more used to the outdoors, able to move longer distances, and more biddable than urban folk. The Indian recruits had to stand 5'7" tall and meet the same physical standards as would any British enlisted man. There was little ideological about this, and the approach was universal.

There were, however, some other considerations. In 1750, Robert Orme drew up a categorisation of 'martial races' based on the dietary habits and climatic zones of the subcontinent.[16] In general terms, Orme believed that wheat-growing areas produced physically better and therefore more 'martial' types than the areas where rice was grown and where people were shorter. Accordingly, the Company confined its recruitment to villages in wheat zones and therefore largely within its own territories.[17] In 1757, immediately after the Battle of Plassey, the Company recruited in the Bengal Presidency because it was dissatisfied with the standards of recruits in the Nawab of Bengal's forces, but it found few men met the required height standard.[18] The rural men were thought to be 'undersized'. As a result, by the 1770s, recruitment had been extended into northern India, where, again, wheat-growing predominated. There, the British most often selected what they considered 'higher-caste Brahmins'. This was not just because of their physique, however, but of self-perceptions of 'warrior traditions' and their ability to influence the recruitment of other 'sturdy' peasants. This self-perception as a warrior caste was common in various parts of the world that had been plagued by persistent conflict in this period.

Another criterion for the recruitment of troops in the past had been the need to find employment for unskilled men who might otherwise foment disorder.[19] In the Terai areas of Bengal, Robert Brooke was charged with establishing a regiment to absorb selected hill raiders and to employ them in the pacification of their own homelands. Warren Hastings expressed the view that preserving the caste system in India would prevent the 'danger that they will soon be united and embodied as an armed nation after the example of the Sikhs'.[20] He was concerned that they might 'become too formidable for their rulers'. The Company therefore continued to co-opt potential, and even actual, enemies throughout the next seventy years, and, with the exception of the Bengal regiments, looked particularly for men from marginalised or peripheral rural communities who would have little sympathy for the majority of the population.

The effect of British concerns about rebellion and the raising of Indian regiments was to exaggerate the special status of caste privileges in Indian units, preserving their preference not to travel across the *Kala Pani* (the black sea), to eat only certain foods and to respect religious rituals. These enhanced the self-esteem of the troops but caused resentment among civilians of similar caste. These moves were designed to promote recruitment, separate the sepoy from any attachment to the people, and ensure continued loyalty to the Company above the local population. It was for these reasons also that the Company's military men opposed the ingress of Christian missionaries who might, reflected the subsequent Commander-in-Chief, Charles Cornwallis, 'endanger a government which owes its principal support to a native army composed of men of high caste whose fidelity and affections we have hitherto secured by an unremitted attention not to offend their religious scruples and superstitions'.[21]

The practice of recruitment, following British methods, was not entirely uniform. In Britain, recruiting sergeants would seek disaffected workers, enquiring as to those who felt their masters were unjust, their wages too low, or their lives too limited by their womenfolk. Pay and employment, especially when other options were constrained, were a strong incentive to enlist. Family size seems to have made a difference for some, as opportunities to inherit land or business were curtailed. A tradition of some sort of public service within the family, often military, could make the appeal stronger. Young men, regardless of their nationality, often express a desire to be tested as a rite of manhood or to experience adventure in such a way as to elevate their esteem with peers, family or clan. Some men were trying to escape issues at home (the 'push' factors), including getting girls pregnant, drudgery and petty crimes, but others felt the army had its own attractions (the 'pull' factors), including the ostentation of uniform or the appearance of young men returning on furlough who were better fed, taller and fitter and who often encouraged others to enlist.[22]

In Britain, there were also some sharp practices. Wealthy men hoping to advance themselves by the raising of a regiment for the government, such as the Duke of Atholl in 1778, were not above using the middlemen of local businesses and hired agents as 'human blood hounds' to pursue men and conscript them.[23] Officially, recruiting sergeants were permitted to raise groups of men 'by beat of drum', literally beating a tattoo to get the attention of young men and then regaling them with stories of immediate cash, generous wages, adventure and personal glory. At country fairs and taverns, alcohol and stirring military music sometimes encouraged men further. These tricks tended to attract a low quality of recruit, as recruiting sergeants themselves recognised. Many people had a low regard for the army and artisan families felt that enlistment was the act of the desperate. However, countless young men still regarded the army as a manly profession, with glamorous uniforms likely to seduce women.

In its search for European personnel, the Company was forced to hire 'crimps', agents who were paid on the basis of the number of recruits they ensnared.[24] Kidnapping was common, the victims being locked up until they could be placed on board ship and sent out to India. The only volunteers coming forward were those attempting to escape imprisonment or the gallows. There were no officers to escort them or depots in Britain, and consequently there was no attempt to instil any discipline or training. They were largely debtors, drunks and criminals and they were accused of carrying 'insolence, mutiny, profligacy, debauchery and disease into their Armies in India'.[25] To make matters worse, the Company did not have the powers of martial law over their recruits while they were still in Britain. Part of the reason for the draconian recruitment process was to prevent men simply escaping back to civilian life.

When the Seven Years War began, the numbers of men recruited for the Company actually fell as the Services at home took a larger share of the pool. In 1754–5, the Company had obtained 1,001 men, but a year later only 488 were procured. In 1759–60, only 202 men were found, and in 1761–2 this had fallen to 197.[26] The Company Army complained that too few were being sent to maintain their regiments and they had to turn to as many Europeans in Bengal as they could find to remain effective.[27] In 1759, the Court of Directors admitted it was 'impossible' to provide the 2,000 men required by the army in India because it was experiencing 'the greatest difficulties in raising recruits'. They directed that operations should be limited to the manpower available.[28]

After the war, gradually there were changes to the system. In 1769, the Company was permitted to raise recruits 'by beat of drum', that is, by officially advertising rather than by kidnapping, and was also empowered to raise a regiment in Britain, with commissioned officers. Complete units would be sent out, rather than 'trickle-posting' any arrivals. It was permitted that up to a third of the regiment could consist of 'foreign protestants', but there was a deep suspicion of enlisting Catholics or Germans.[29] Indeed, the Company directors were most concerned that the regiment might be answerable only to the British government and could, therefore, threaten the independence of the Company altogether. Another issue was cost: for all its faults, crimping was cheaper than regular army recruiting or paying vast bounties, and the Seven Years War cost the Company a fortune.

Regular officers in Britain were equally prejudicial on their side about the new arrangements. They argued that India was a drain on manpower which swallowed up men who should be deployed in the defence of Britain. One MP likened India to 'a sink'.[30] As a result, the reforms failed and the system reverted to crimps, only to collapse once more during the American War of Independence until it was decreed that Irishmen might be recruited from 1781 onwards. However, standards of recruits remained very low and some, having failed even the easiest tests, were actually sent back to Britain. Figures for the 1790s, which appear to be typical even earlier in the century, suggest a rejection rate of 10 per cent.[31] Some were 'particularly incapable of carrying the load of arms, ammunition, necessaries and provisions, and undergoing hardships and fatigues, to which soldiers to be of use to the public must necessarily submit'.[32] It was not until 1799 that the practice of crimping was brought to an end and recruitment put under the jurisdiction of the regular army.[33] However, the British Army remained short of manpower for each of the military operations of the period.

The Organisation, Management and Performance of the Company Army

In his account of the fall of Calcutta to Siraj ud-Daula, the Nawab of Bengal, in 1756, John Holwell noted that the defences were manned by a handful of gunners with 145 infantry of which, in total, only 60 were Europeans. The militia consisted of 100 'Armenians', who were 'entirely useless', and a further 100 Indian 'boys and slaves who were not capable of holding a musket'.[34] He estimated that, even with men drafted from the ships in port, the garrison numbered only 250, including officers. Predictably, when Siraj ud-Daula's forces came into view, the militia deserted and some Company officers fled to the ships. The standard interpretation of the war is that dramatic improvements were made to the quality of the Indian troops through the imposition of discipline and European drill. By increasing manpower and the quality, the British were able to turn events around. However, the improvement of the Indian troops was only part of the formula: the logistical expertise of Stringer Lawrence, Vice Admiral Watson's amphibious operations up the Hooghly River and Robert Clive's leadership, intrigues and personal courage were crucial, as was the Company's capacity, in contrast with the French Company, to fund the conflict.

The improvements had begun with Stringer Lawrence in Cuddalore in 1748. He imposed strict discipline on topasses and Europeans alike at Fort St David, mindful that Madras had fallen to the more effective French units. In December 1758, that new Company force was put to the test in a siege at Madras, and endured two months of bombardment and over a thousand casualties before it was relieved. But it was also the growing experience of the Company troops through the Carnatic Wars that made the greatest difference. New units could draw on the expertise of veterans, especially junior commanders, and apply this directly to their training. Clive's sepoys displayed remarkable endurance when besieged, on campaign marches and in battle. At the siege of Arcot, for example, their morale remained intact despite a steady attrition of their numbers, and in the march to intercept Dupleix in 1752, the sepoys made 50 miles in just 20 hours, covering a total of 66 miles in 36 hours and winning a night battle at Kaveripak against the odds. At Volconda (or Golkonda) on 29 May 1752, a force almost entirely made up of Indian personnel in British service charged a French battery and their supporting infantry. Despite taking heavy casualties, the sepoys pressed home with the bayonet and killed or captured the French, which suggests that their discipline, training and trust in their junior leadership were robust. The following year, Subadar Sheikh Ibrahim, without any British support, defended his battery position against a Franco-Indian force, and earned a significant reward from the Company for his devotion to duty.[35] With six years of fighting behind them, with improved discipline and the personalised and charismatic leadership of Lawrence, Watson and Clive, the Company had an effective sepoy army with naval support to rival the French.

After the Seven Years War, the level of improvement among Asian units was manifest in other ways. The standards of British recruits coming to India showed no sign of improvement, prompting the Governor General to write: 'what shall I say of the Company's Europeans [soldiers]? I would infinitely rather take the 73rd [Native] Regiment upon service with me than the six Company's [British] battalions'.[36] Such comments have to be seen in context: the sentiments may be exaggerated because of a sense of exasperation. Nevertheless, European officers were aware that Indian troops were cheaper, better adapted to cope with the demands of campaigning in the heat and humidity of South Asia, and, when trained in the European manner, capable of the same achievements.

Although there had been only companies in the 1740s, it was decided in 1759 to raise battalions of Indian troops to match the French threat. Two had in fact already been formed, but an additional five battalions were organised. By the end of the war, the Company Army's establishment was for ten battalions. Every battalion consisted of nine companies, each of 120 men, and one of these was a grenadier company.

In Clive's 'Return of 1757', the Indian troops are recorded as having various ranks: subadars, jamadars, havildars and naiks, colour (flag) men, tom-toms (drummers), trumpeters and 'seapoys'. It had been assumed in the 1740s that Indian ways were so strange that only Indian officers could command Asian troops at the company level. Indeed, the first Indian officers were really contractors who served as the recruiter for the men. Loyalty to the contractor was more important to the early recruits than to the Company. But new contracts in the 1750s changed this. Each man was made aware that he served the Company and was paid by the Company. In November 1755, regulations stipulated that there should be one subadar, four jamadars, eight havildars (sergeants) and eight naiks (corporals). At the end of the war, this establishment of Indian leaders was reduced (one subadar, two jamadars and six havil-dars per company) and each battalion was furnished with two commissioned officers, three sergeant majors (Europeans) and a 'black commandant'. However, Mason noted that these Europeans were in little more than a super-visory capacity or to maintain numbers. There was little chance of promotion as a commander in an Indian battalion, as progression could only be made in European units. They were to 'make them keep up a good command amongst the sepoys and to support them well in it'.[37] The sergeant majors were to have 'immediate direction of three of the companies' and were charged to take 'care of their discipline'. Mason suggested that the NCOs were the backbone of the Indian units and that the concept of gentlemanly officers had not yet manifest itself. He also argued that the survival of the 'black commandant' was testa-ment to the importance of the old 'reciprocal' chieftain system. In fact, it seems likely that the commandant was an adviser to the Europeans on cultural matters and the link to the recruiting base on which the battalion depended.

What was the appeal for Indian men to serve in the Company army? There was perhaps not the strong tradition of service that would come to character-ise the Rajputs in British formations from the mid-nineteenth century. What the British could offer was regular pay at six rupees a month.[38] Many Indian rulers rarely paid their men more than eight months a year, leading to wide-spread brigandage, but even this salary was often in arrears and siphoned off in ghost payrolling by intermediate commanders. The advantage of the small European formations was that it made corruption more difficult. The Company was also flexible in its arrangements. Sepoys of South India were permitted to bring their families along with them to stations, garrisons, and even on campaign. Pay advances were available, and, as early as 1762, sepoys on overseas service could opt to have a portion of their pay delivered directly to their families. Indians could pay for commissions from 1763, and these were still relatively cheap (a week's pay in 1763), making personal advance-ment possible within the Company Army.

Many European soldiers, enlisted either as conscripts or as volunteers, grumbled about having their pay held back because of costs they had to meet: 2d here and 2d there for blankets, boots, cleaning equipment, and additional or extraordinary rations. Some soldiers wrote about not being able to leave the service because of indebtedness. However, this was not always financial, but rather a matter of honour. The Indian expression 'having to remain "true to their salt"' seems to have pervaded British personnel in some cases and not just the sepoys of the Honourable East India Company. Such sentiments would have taken time to develop, but the shared isolation of India, regular pay and continuous employment, and the camaraderie of the ranks transformed an otherwise alienating experience into a positive one. In other words, recruits became regular soldiers with an *esprit de corps* and a professional indifference to outsiders. Oaths of loyalty were not introduced until 1766, but they appear to have underpinned some existing understanding about service in the Company Army and how it related to concepts of personal honour.[39] The creation of battalions led to the adoption of colours, and these were incorporated into a symbiosis of European and South Asian rituals to create a bond of loyalty and possession. Southern Indian troops, for example, thought of their leaders and their colours as distinctly and uniquely theirs.

Did the Indian infantry in Company service determine the outcome of the Carnatic Wars in South Asia? What assessment can be made of their effectiveness? It was once assumed that the British possessed technological superiority which gave them the edge in their engagements with the Indian states. In fact, matchlocks with which the Indian forces were armed had a higher rate of fire and a marginally greater range than the flintlock, although the flintlock, in trained hands, could sustain the same rate of fire. Moreover, the French forces in India were armed with the same weapon types as the British. Indeed, within a few years, all the armies in India were using flintlocks.

Certainly the British made extensive use of light, quick-firing, manoeuvrable artillery. At Trichinopoly in May 1754, three British six-pounder guns devastated French infantry with case-shot at close range. Roundshot ricocheting through dense cavalry also warded off large formations of mounted men. Artillery was widely available in South Asia, but many guns possessed by Indian rulers were fixed or difficult to move, and there was little standardisation in their ammunition or calibres. However, while Indian forces failed to produce guns that could be manoeuvred easily, many of the batteries of the southern rulers were staffed by European mercenary gunners. At Plassey, for example, the guns of Siraj ud-Daula were directed by French artillerymen.

The differences between European and Indian forces were really more regular organisation and better discipline, which in turn meant that, on the battlefield, sepoys and European troops could maintain a high rate of fire and sustain casualties without losing cohesion. These reflected a particular type of military labour organisation. Large numbers of ill-disciplined cavalry or poorly armed peasants, led by individuals who merely wished to demonstrate their personal courage, failed against the relentless machinery of European warfare. The point is that it did not matter whether the forces were Europeans or not; what mattered was their level of training, morale and discipline.[40] It is interesting to note that the Marathas adopted European methods to create a disciplined and cohesive army, built up with mercenary troops including Europeans in senior positions, and they too enjoyed some years of success against the British.[41]

In R.O. Cambridge's *Account of the War in India*, published in 1772, the key reason for the defeat of Indian armies by the Europeans and their sepoys was the former's neglect of infantry. While Indian cavalry was perfectly capable of charging against other horsemen, they tended to avoid the well-drilled Company infantry for fear of losing their horses on which their wealth depended. For the Company, raising and training infantry was cheaper than cavalry, and the infantry could hold ports, forts and garrisons as well as act as a strike force.[42] Moreover, if supported by light artillery, infantrymen could traverse all terrain in southern India. Certainly the labour categories in the 1757 Return for Plassey indicate that all the troops were dismounted.[43] The lack of cavalry put the Company at a disadvantage in terms of reconnaissance and therefore of intelligence gathering, but this, if anything, made them even more dependent on local sources of power, their Indian allies and intrigues against their adversaries.

Comparison of Forces

The two cases of North America and South Asia in the eighteenth century illustrate the many variables that determined the quality, scale and performance of the armies that were raised. They highlight the problems that each of the nations faced when trying to utilise untrained or indigenous military labour, especially when budgets were constrained and there were geographical and climatic challenges to confront as well. The examples indicate that Western nations made extensive use of local forces, especially semi-trained personnel, the militias or local irregulars, largely because of the pressing and urgent need for manpower. Garrisons and guard duties absorbed a significant proportion of men, leaving far too few for effective strike forces, particular when casualties, sickness and desertions took their toll. The British found themselves outnumbered in the French and Indian War, in the Revolutionary War and in South Asia. Local personnel were critical to their operations.

The local indigenous forces made a considerable impact on the campaigns and a great deal of effort was made to partner with them. Indeed, their contributions were strategically very important to the outcome of the various operations. Local fighting styles, in forests in North America or as mounted forces on the plains of India, were significant at the tactical level and enhanced the effectiveness of the European armies.

Discipline proved to be crucial to the success of the forces that were raised by the British, French and the Americans for their campaigns. Training, cohesion and the gradual accumulation of experience proved to be essential for success. A regular supply of money to pay the troops, and a reliable system of logistics, also proved to be critical to the survival and cohesiveness of the forces that were raised.

Local men enlisted for a variety of reasons, but the variables of personal prestige, better and more regular income, enhanced status, faith in a cause, a desire for adventure, a military tradition and other 'pull' factors could all be found in these forces in this period. For the indigenous forces that remained outside the European system of training, like the First Nation Americans, there were still sufficient incentives for them to preserve their military culture and yet benefit from the partnership with Europeans. The Europeans regarded the local personnel as essential, whether because of the relatively cheaper costs, because they could survive healthily in the climate or environment, or, in the case of the indigenous native population, because they might otherwise pose a threat if enlisted by a rival state.

Local forces were cost-effective and could be utilised easily to protect and guard routes or sites of importance, releasing regulars for more offensive operations. On the other hand, local troops tended to be of a lower standard in terms of nutrition and health, which could limit their endurance, and they were not always reliable. Indeed, the concern that they might revolt or change sides meant that the Europeans in South Asia tended to accept concessions towards dress, fighting style and dietary or ritual preferences far more readily. Moreover, local leadership proved to be essential. Where this was not available, the Europeans emphasised a personal connection, offering the same style of command as that to which the indigenous personnel had become habituated.

Yet local forces employed in this period also indicated the limits of European state power. The need to engage local labour marked the boundaries of imperial and colonial control, while the horizon of environmental limits was similarly imposed by certain diseases. The boundaries of allegiance and cohesion were exposed in the various alignments of surviving local polities in North America and South Asia. In the next chapter, it is the internal limits of cohesion that are exposed.

3

THE MERCENARY MOTIVE, CONTRACTS
AND MUTINY

Those who joined the British as colonial soldiers did so as free volunteers. Even those who felt under pressure from family or a recruiting officer were not conscripted. They enlisted for reasons that would be understood across time and cultures, specifically because of the appeal of a smart uniform, the attraction of certain accoutrements and adornments, and the status associated with bravery and strength that was, in the minds of the enlistee, as likely to impress a peer group as it was to appeal to women.[1] Certainly being in uniform conferred a distinction that set a man apart from the majority, and enabled younger men to enjoy a social position free of the usual restrictions imposed by caste, class or culture.

The life of a soldier also offered the chance to leave behind a familiar and pedestrian situation in favour of far-off locales, with all the connotations of the thrill and the mystery of adventure. Young men might also inherit a family tradition, and look upon themselves as acquiring the favour of family or clan, ancestors and relatives by continuing a service history. In rural and conservative societies, there had always been a strong sense of obligation. But young men themselves also sought some advancement, the chance to excel, earn promotion or special recognition.

Soldiers and NCOs already in the service might encourage young men from their own backgrounds to join up if they felt it strengthened the influence of a particular group within a regiment or corps. Family with relatives already serving would be conscious of the financial benefit of more members in the service. Community leaders too might wish to have men serving in order to gain a secondary influence of their own among their social group. If a local dignitary could show that a 'quota' had been met, he could expect some recognition from the authorities. If a young man showed reluctance to enlist, he might be given incentives or put into an awkward social position in order to change his mind. Recruiting officers might also offer a friendly word, which alone might be sufficient 'recognition' to persuade a young man he was of some worth and therefore entitled to enlist.

Economic factors might also push a man into military service, particularly in areas of rural overpopulation, where land and opportunities were scarce, or where there was a period of economic hardship. On the other hand, rising prosperity, the attraction of better jobs in growing urban centres, and alternative employment could just as easily threaten a steady stream of recruits. Nevertheless, all economic downturns produced a larger crop of rural manpower for the army. When food prices increased, some fathers preferred to keep their sons on their farms in order to capitalise on the profitable opportunity.

What was clear in the era before nationalism was widespread, was that young men rarely enlisted for patriotic ideals. Instead, with a tradition of having served whoever was in power, regardless of their background, race or religion, the colonial soldiers were mercenaries; yet, they would not switch allegiances easily. There was a contract, often vague and unspecified, that held the men in a bond. So long as the authorities did not break their side of the bargain, men in the ranks would generally remain true to their salt.

European forces held out the prospect of honours and privileges that would elevate a volunteer soldier over his peers. From the British, a range of honours were available, some of which reinforced an existing hierarchy, such as the number of guns fired in salute of Indian princes based on their accepted level of prestige, while others were far more democratised and available to all. In the case of the latter, the Order of British India, for example, could be bestowed in two classes. For the subedars and above, in the first class, recipients would be known thereafter as *Subedar Bahadur* (chief) but they would also receive an additional increment of pay of two rupees a month. The second class was awarded to Indian officers, who received a smaller increment but could also be known by the suffix of *bahadur*. Furthermore, the Indian Order of Merit could be earned by a man of any rank for acts of conspicuous courage in the face of the enemy. A single act would entitle the bearer to a third increase in pay and pension, while two acts would increase pay by two-thirds. A third act of such courage would lead to a doubling of pay and pension. This award was considered the 'Victoria Cross' of the Indian Army until 1912. After that date, Indian personnel were eligible for the same award as the British themselves, namely the Victoria Cross. Consequently, during the First World War, a number of VCs were earned by Indian troops alongside their British comrades. Recipients would sometimes be granted a commission on retirement as a special recognition of the leadership role they undoubtedly played.

Colonial soldiers were also entitled to periods of leave during which they could visit family and make checks on any land or property they might hold at home. Certain religious festivals, marriages and funerals might also demand a soldier return to his family. In the early years of the nineteenth century in India, the Bengal Army had no married quarters for its troops, so generous leave arrangements were made instead. The large distances in India and the absence of railway transport at that time made it imperative that extended periods were granted by the authorities. The routine of garrison life also included a considerable amount of time off. The intense heat made vigorous training inadvisable, except in the very early hours of the day. Consequently, duties tended to be curtailed by noon. In the cavalry, time was allocated for exercising the horses, but even here there was plenty of time set aside for festivals, social activities and sports, all of which bonded the unit together.

Another appeal of military life in European service was the 'wonder' of modern medicine. The Presidency armies of India had had their own medical services from the 1760s, but these eventually formed the unified Indian Medical Service (IMS) in 1896. Although it was a military service, its officers frequently served civilian needs too, which benefited populations far beyond soldiers and their immediate families. Within the units of the Indian Army, however, there was a dedicated medical officer, supported by a hinterland of staff and specialist officers. In the early years of the Indian service, most of the serious wounds required cleaning and amputation, but the climatic conditions made the death rate from injuries and their treatment far higher than in Europe. To assist the medical staff, who were often busy because of the range of diseases and infections in tropical locations, unofficial bearers and assistants were common. But these became the nucleus of an indigenous cadre of medical personnel, and encouraged the subsequent development of large civil medical services.

In action, recovery of the wounded and the dead was a point of pride for most units, especially when certain adversaries had a reputation for the torture of injured comrades or the mutilation of the dead. On the North West Frontier of India, the Pashtun practices towards the wounded or dead elicited the strongest reactions. In one incident, probably not uncommon, the troops retaliated by refusing to take prisoners.[2] By contrast, the British were prepared to offer battlefield medical treatment not only to their own men, but also to their enemies. Sir Henry Lawrence had encouraged the development of medical dispensaries close to the frontier, and, amid the frequent skirmishing in the hills, there would be requests from the local fighters to have access to treatment. Lieutenant General Daly stated: 'The consequence of this was many a strange scene of war and confidence: men wounded on the hill-side fighting against us were brought to our picquets, and shouts came across the rocks for permission to bring their wounded to our hospital—even while the fight was going on.'[3]

During the eighteenth and early nineteenth century, there were a number of ailments and diseases against which the West seemed powerless. Until the 1840s, British soldiers wore the uniforms in the tropics designed for a European climate. Deaths through 'sunstroke', caused by heat exhaustion or heat stroke, both of which involved overheating (though they could be exacerbated by dehydration) were commonplace. In southern Africa, the British were caricatured as lobster-red figures and referred to by Afrikaners with the derogatory term *rooinekke* (rednecks), which indicates just how unsuitably they were dressed. By the time of the Indian Mutiny, when some European troops still died from the effects of heat, most units took a more pragmatic approach to their uniforms. During the hot weather, one eyewitness noted that British troops marched 'in their short sleeves like a lot of insurrectionary haymakers'. The shako gave way to the light cap, complete with neck covering and peak to keep off the sun. The solar topee helmet also appeared, offering better ventilation to its wearer, and gradually lightweight, cotton tropical uniforms were introduced for British and colonial troops.

Cholera had been a significant killer of colonial forces in the nineteenth century. The disease, spread by infected water or by flies carrying the microbes, often from the waste of existing victims, was a mystery for decades. Outbreaks could devastate a unit in a short space of time. Various theories were put forward, but few cures were effective. The idea that the disease was connected to the functions of the bowels, not least because of the violence of its accompanying dysentery, led to the introduction of cholera belts and spine pads. The established solution was to march out of barracks into the countryside, stopping each night in a new 'cholera camp'.[4] Those suffering were left in place attended by orderlies, while the rest of the unit marched on. The remedy was crude and attributed to exercise and air, but, in fact, the unit was marching away from the source of the infection and effectively leaving in quarantine those already afflicted. What magnified the effects of the disease in camp was that victims, complaining of thirst, would be administered with more of the water that had been contaminated in the first place. The casualty would have to endure painful stomach cramps, and those in attendance would have to endure the alarming spectacle of seeing the victim, issuing abundant 'rice-water' stools, lose their strength and often dying in a short period of time. The infection could sweep through a regiment, taking the accompanying women and children with it. The frequent accounts of family loss, or of the sheer magnitude of numbers who died, are among the most pathetic of military history. The authorities did not know that clean, boiled water, and the addition of sugar and salt, were often sufficient to keep a patient alive.

Camp hygiene and disease control gradually improved towards the end of the nineteenth century, although on campaign it was often a struggle to ensure cleanliness when troops were accompanied by large numbers of transport animals and facilities for water and sanitation were rudimentary. Flies seemed to accompany every army, regardless of theatre of operations. The British insisted on improved camp discipline among their colonial troops, cultural preferences notwithstanding. One effective measure was to fill in pools of standing water in the vicinity of camps and barracks, an action which denied the rapid development of mosquito colonies and therefore reduced the incidence of malaria. Quinine, often taken with alcohol, reduced the outbreak of the disease too, which made having a gin and tonic, the latter containing the quinine, towards the end of the day something of an institution for the British. It was an Indian Army medical officer, Sir Ronald Ross, who made the link between the anopheles mosquito and malaria, and, like many of his peers, he made a significant contribution to knowledge of tropical medicine.

Sir Charles Napier made significant improvements to the design and construction of barracks for the troops, insisting on the generous allocation of space and double ceilings to encourage air flow. His reasoning was simple: 'such barracks are expensive no doubt, [but] so are sick soldiers; so are dead soldiers'.[5] He continued: 'The difference of these expenses is, that the first is once and done with, the second goes on increasing like compound interest and quickly outstrips the capital.' Napier also insisted in improvements in the provision of meals, especially for the sick. He condemned the excesses of luxury of young officers and insisted that officers in the infantry march with the men rather than riding, which otherwise created an enormous demand on fodder and logistics. Lord Roberts, when he became Commander-in-Chief of

India, continued making improvements, largely inspired by his own early career in the Indian Army. He had recalled that proper sanitation for Indian troops stationed at Peshawar had been considered 'unnecessary' because of cultural assumptions. But all of the measures that Roberts and his predecessors insisted on were always met with resistance from those who demanded efficiency and savings. The construction of new barracks by Napier in the decade between 1866 and 1877 cost £11 million. On top of this, in the same period, the Indian exchequer had to pay a capitation rate of £10 per head for each British soldier stationed in India. Pensions also had to be funded by the Indian taxpayer. This considerable expense therefore gave an impetus to the British civil administration in India to try to reduce costs whenever possible. The Second Anglo-Afghan War, for example, caused a significant spike in expenditure, and the pressure to bring the operation to a speedy end was, in part, due to the sheer cost of sustaining a large occupation force beyond India's frontiers. Moreover, the idea of further military reform, with associated costs, filled the Indian administration with anxiety.

Legitimacy and Local Military Forces

Whereas the British Empire sought to impose order in periods of popular unrest or resistance, the concern of the colonial power was to ensure an enduring stability and to create authority. This authority was manifest in three forms: as legal, political and moral. All these were designed to reinforce the idea of legitimacy, but each one carried inherent constraints. Legal authority was the focus for legitimising military intervention but also suppressing and punishing rebellion as an act of war 'against the Crown'.[6] Political authority was assessed to be the right to govern, either through the justifications of civilisation, guardianship and trusteeship, or even on behalf of a local surrogate ruler. Moral authority enabled the British security forces to concentrate on breaking the will of their armed adversaries and to justify doing so, but it also created a set of self-limiting measures in governance. Indeed, so strong was the habit of restraint that it was identified as a cultural characteristic of the British approach to countering unrest. Several historical studies have demonstrated that this was not always exercised in practice, but it reveals something of the British mentality in this regard. There is no claim to British exceptionalism here, merely the observation that the British case is rich with examples and archival resources to enable us to study the issues empirically.

Restoring British authority without resort to force was particularly favoured by colonial institutions since it represented the cheapest means by which they could achieve their governance objectives. Considerations of cost frequently asserted themselves in colonial decision-making and as a result there was a tendency to try to avoid major internal unrest. Lord Cromer noted:

> There is truth in the saying ... that the maintenance of the Empire depends on the sword; but so little does it depend on the sword alone that if once we have to draw the sword, not merely to suppress some local effervescence, but to overcome a general upheaval of subject races goaded to action either by deliberate oppression, which is highly improbable, or by unintentional misgovernment, which is far more conceivable, the sword will assuredly be powerless to defend us for long.[7]

Resorting to force was invariably a measure of last resort, and, when force was applied, the hope was that it should be overwhelming and decisive. The British knew that military force had its limits and the risk of a temporary military setback had the potential to damage prestige profoundly. In general terms, the British Empire favoured the promotion of commerce over war, surrogate rulers who recognised British suzerainty over expensive direct rule, and the issue of subsidies to local intermediaries if the costs and hazards of occupation seemed too great. Exceptions abound, of course, and where other European powers or indigenous polities posed a significant security threat, the British were willing to make military interventions.

If the strategic ends of pacification were to restore order and authority, and the ways included a willingness to use escalating degrees of force, there was nevertheless a consciousness of the limited nature of the means available. Britain could deploy only a relatively small number of troops into North America, Asia, the West Indies and Africa, relative to other Continental powers and this compelled the British Army to raise local auxiliary forces, such as the three Presidency components of the East India Company Army in India, and a variety of regular and irregular units. The governing doctrine for the use of these formations was to maintain a concentration of force, with a mobile reserve that could reinforce any threatened garrison, line or detachment. It was expected that local forces, trained as regulars, would be reliable if led by British officers, but there was anxiety that native troops might, if placed under strain and forced to serve alone, might fraternise with a rebellious population. Wherever possible, British troops were preferred for internal security, and if local auxiliaries were used, they were usually co-located with British units.

For a maritime empire like the British, the Royal Navy was absolutely essential: it was able to rush reinforcements to threatened colonial stations on a number of occasions and provided the much-needed augmentation of ethnically British manpower. For land forces, there was an emphasis on retaining the initiative by staying mobile, adopting an offensive posture and maximising firepower. However, the campaigns in African and Asian hinterlands put considerable strain on logistics and transport. Protection of lines of communication not only absorbed much-needed manpower but also required time-consuming operations to clear routes, to relieve beleaguered garrisons and to prevent or punish raiding. To carry out the immense number of guard duties, again auxiliaries and trained regular manpower were essential. Local irregulars were also immensely useful for reconnaissance in an age before air power.

Force had a very precise utility. In the event of rebellion or insurrection, the objective of the British military forces was to use force to bring about the re-establishment of government control either by the colonial authorities or by a local surrogate leadership at the earliest possible opportunity.[8] The military task was to fulfil this mission by breaking the will of the insurgents, and throughout British contemporary writing the emphasis was on 'decision', looking for a decisive result that would avoid protracted warfare. This could be achieved by inflicting casualties, and, where insurgents remained elusive, they were to be induced into a show of force by attacking the fabric of their economy, which might include the destruction of property and livestock. The aim was not to antagonise the population, but to draw fighters into a battle where the firepower and discipline of British forces and their trained auxiliaries could be brought to bear. There was a great deal of emphasis on acting without hesitation, which would be interpreted by local populations, it was argued, as a sign of British weakness. To bring about the decisive result, the exercise of bold leadership was thought to be the best method to ensure the continuation of military superiority and prestige, two components that would reinforce the idea of British governance.

Money, in the form of subsidies, was used frequently to augment the limited British military power as the cheaper alternative, and some of that could be used to raise local levies as rival forces to any rebels.[9] The chief problem was that cost also precluded the creation of larger civilian administration, and much work on the peripheries of the British Empire was still left to soldiers.[10] The interim solution, to use political officers and advisers, some of them actually soldiers on secondment, could cause a conflict of interest between military and political objectives.[11]

The alternative to the use of military power was the use of local rulers and chiefs to govern under British suzerainty. This had the advantage that existing structures, hierarchies and authority could simply be incorporated under the British flag, and their own local forces, paid for by their own rulers, could be used to provide the security of these domains. Subordinate leaders could also be dismissed and replaced if they failed to remain compliant, and the British could potentially exploit rivalries between sectarian or ethnic communities if deemed necessary.[12] The British imperial project frequently tried to bring together quite distinct entities in order to create economically and administratively viable groupings in the form of federations or states, like the Indian Empire or the Union of South Africa, and this too had a beneficial implication for regional security. The emphasis, then, was on the value of collaboration with the imperial project, and local military forces were an essential component of it.

The practice of employing one 'alien' group to govern another was long-established and predated European imperialism. Within Europe, there were countless examples of hiring or conscripting those that would not hesitate to enforce the writ of a dynast or state ruler. In the Russian Army, a large proportion of the officer corps was drawn from the Baltic German stock, while the rank and file had a profile that over-represented Bashkirs, Kalmucks, Ingush and Ossetians. The army was also the dumping ground for vagrants, criminals and political exiles. Military colonies on the frontiers were self-contained communities that developed their own exclusive and distinct identity. Ambitious men tried to redeem themselves in the eyes of the royal court by acts of bravery on the frontiers.

In France, in the 1830s, rising crime caused by rural overpopulation and scarcity persuaded the government to give criminals the option of imprisonment or military service in Algeria's Bataillon d'Afrique, but foreigners and some local Algerians were also swept up into formations of Zouaves, a name originally attributed to the fighters of the local Kabyle clans. Swiss personnel, who had served in the regiments of the French Army for decades, including that of both the *Ancien Régime* and Napoleon, were permitted to serve in their own formation of the French Foreign Legion. Napoleon had envisaged commanding a colonial army which, like the British, would consist of a core of European soldiers with wings of locally recruited forces. With his plans to dominate the Middle East, the recruits were to be drawn from Greek, Armenian and Arab populations. In Egypt, he established a Mameluke corps, made up of Copts and other Egyptians. Colonial operations in Africa in the nineteenth century continued the tradition, and by 1841 there were three battalions of Infanterie légère d'Afrique and three battalions of Tirailleurs indigènes, as well as three mounted regiments of Spahis. The French ensured a balance in the numbers of local communities that were rivals in each unit, particularly between Berbers and other Arabs. Locals were permitted to become officers, especially those of mixed race, but no artillery could be placed in the hands of local forces, and the proportion of French-born officers and NCOs was never less than half the strength of the unit.

The Breakdown of Legitimacy and Contract: The Vellore and Barrackpore Mutinies

The Mutiny of the Bengal Army of the East India Company has been interpreted in a number of ways, most recently as a proto-nationalist revolt. There is no doubt that the opportunities that arose when both military and political control were temporarily incapacitated were seized upon by a number of Bengali and northern Indian civilians, and there was certainly a great deal of anger and resentment, but to attribute the events of 1857 to a nationalist agenda is anachronistic. Where most historians and commentators do agree, however, is the extent of anxiety about the Company's expanding political control, Christian proselytising and the mistreatment or neglect of the Bengal sepoys. Allegedly, the outbreak of the Mutiny in 1857 was fuelled by the punishment of sepoys who refused to obey orders, particularly with reference to the use of new greased cartridges for the Enfield rifled musket. Herein lies a significant problem. The punishment of Sepoys had not changed for decades and was, in essence, little different from the disciplinary system of the British Army. If the accusation is that the British mistreated their Indian soldiers, one would have to acknowledge that, as John Keegan put it: 'Bondage, in a stronger or weaker form, is a common condition of military service.'[13]

At Vellore in May 1806, a handful of sepoys had mutinied because the relationship between employees and employers had grown progressively more distant over time, to the point of mutual incomprehension. Sir John Kaye, author of a contemporary work on the Mutiny, noted: 'And so, for a time, the Sipahi did not know his officer, nor the officer his men; they met almost as strangers on parade, and there was little or no communion between them. It was a transition period of most untoward occurrence, when so many other adverse influences were destroying the discipline of the army.'[14] The ringleaders were flogged but the mood only darkened among the rest of the garrison. Kaye recorded:

> Nor was it a mere local epidemic. At other military stations in the Karnatik there was similar excitement. Midnight meetings were being held in the Lines; oaths of secrecy were being administered to the Sipahis; threats of the most terrible vengeance were fulminated against any one daring to betray them. The native officers

took the lead, the men followed, some roused to feelings of resentment, others huddling together like sheep, under the influence of a vague fear. In the bungalows of the English captains there was but small knowledge of what was passing in the Sipahis' Lines, and if there had been more, discretion would probably have whispered that in such a case 'silence is gold'.[15]

On 10 July 1806, there was therefore a second and more serious mutiny in which sepoys complained of changes to their headdress, shaving regulations, and the prohibition of religious ornaments and caste marks. Local people began to treat the sepoys with contempt, arguing that their uniforms were part of a conspiracy to convert them to Christianity, from the cross belt, literally in the shape of the crucifix, to their round hats. If the humiliations of local civilians were not enough, the sepoys were also angry about their pay. The motives of the mutineers did not include any reference to national identity, but were full of understandable anxieties about their terms and conditions of service. The fact that a handful of local princes sided with and harboured the mutineers made the British concerned about a potential conspiracy. Their reaction was swift and severe: hundreds of the sepoys were killed in the fighting and the subsequent executions. Indeed, the reprisals were enough to deter any thought of further insurrection. What had been worrying was the level of discontent in other stations in the subcontinent. At Hyderabad, Nandidrug and Paliankotta there were signs of impending mutiny and local outbreaks of violence, but swift preparations or arrests had stemmed a full-scale insurrection. In most cases, aside from complaints about uniforms, it was the fear of forced conversion to Christianity which the sepoys cited as their primary grievance.[16]

Status was a critical component in the appeal of soldiering for Indian sepoys. When he became a soldier, he did not cease to be a civilian. He retained his family ties, and made frequent and regular visits to his home. He was not an outcast, but the main breadwinner in his community, and often in possession of favourable land holdings as a result. His esteem was enhanced by the notion of long and prestigious service, for 'It was a decorous boast in many families that generation after generation had eaten the Company's salt'.[17] Their land holdings naturally increased their social rank, and this in turn enhanced their ability to be heard before other suitors in civil courts; an important advantage when the legal system was otherwise remote and ponderous. Back in barracks, the British officer, while alien, was nevertheless the arbiter of minor annoyances and disputes. The frequency and regularity of respectful petitions made the officer their father, and they his *baba-log* (adored infants).

Environmental conditions could nevertheless upset this balance. When cholera broke out among Muslim cavalrymen at Arcot in 1822, the disease was attributed to divine displeasure because of the creeping advance of Christianity in southern India and the emanation of prayers deemed blasphemous to Islam. The grievances were answered without recourse to fighting, despite the existence of messages that called for Muslim *sowars* (troopers) to murder their British officers.[18]

Conditions of service and religious observance arose as the primary driver in the Barrackpore Mutiny of 1824 two years later. Once again, this unrest had all the hallmarks of misunderstanding rather than conspiracy. During the First Anglo-Burmese War, sepoys of the 47th Regiment, whose high-caste status prevented them from travelling by sea, were ordered to march to Chittagong by land. Their status also demanded that they had to transport their personal effects, under caste rules, but there were no bullocks to draw their carts because the Company had already exhausted its supply for the war effort. The men's complaints and petitions were ignored and largely dismissed as indiscipline.

Inactive in camp at the height of the monsoon, they were then exposed to some exaggerated rumours of alleged British setbacks in Burma. Sir John Kaye noted:

> It happened that ominous tidings of disaster came to them from the theatre of war. The British troops had sustained a disaster at Ramu, the proportions of which had been grossly exaggerated in the recital, and it was believed that the Burmese, having cut up our battalions, or driven them into the sea, were sweeping on to the invasion of Bengal. The native newspapers bristled with alarming announcements of how the Commander-in-Chief had been killed in action and the Governor-General had poisoned himself in despair; and there was a belief throughout all the lower provinces of India that the rule of the Company was coming to an end.[19]

The sepoys nevertheless grew angrier still when it was announced that their camp followers would receive higher pay than the troops themselves. The Sepoys therefore refused to march on to Burma. Colonel Cartwright, their commanding officer, offered to fund the purchase of bullocks from his own account, but the damage had by then been done. Sir Edward Paget, the Commander-in-Chief, ordered that the spread of this strike action and insubordinate behaviour, now verging on rioting, be met with decisive force. Swiftly surrounding the battalion in barracks, the punitive formation of British troops opened fire and the mutineers dispersed. In order to deter similar acts of defiance, the regiment was removed from the army's order of battle, the ringleaders were hanged, and many others were imprisoned. Nevertheless, the severity of the reaction drew significant criticism. Other sepoys of the Bengal Army were appalled. One old soldier noted bitterly: 'it is your own men whom you have been destroying'.[20]

In the next two decades there were further problems. Troops not on campaign were informed of the 'half-batta' order, whereby pay was reduced as a cost-saving measure. This true understandable criticism from soldiers sent a signal about their value in society and in the eyes of their British overlords. There was even disquiet when apparently concessionary measures were introduced. The imposition of corporal punishment, although rare in Indian regiments, was abolished for ten years and then reintroduced by Governor General Lord Hardinge. The measure was interpreted as a weakening of the will to govern and merely produced contempt. One old veteran warned that the Indian soldiers had *Fauj be-dar hogya*, that is, 'they had ceased to fear'.[21]

The concern about the British disregard for established practices was not confined to a single regiment like the 47th at Barrackpore. The Mutiny of 1857 involved one-fifth of the Bengal Army, some 35,000 men, and among the more frequently cited complaints was the affront to religious sensibilities, fear of Christianising influences and 'a succession of British interferences with Indian culture'.[22] Nevertheless, it was the mundane business of pay and allowances which drove the disputes in the twenty years before the Mutiny of 1857. The 34th Bengal Regiment had refused to march into Sind in February 1844 because the soldiers believed they should be entitled to an additional payment for what constituted an operational task, rather than garrison duty at home. While the senior officers contemplated whether to march the regiment back to a secure station in order to disband it, the 7th Bengal Cavalry also refused to march, and a succession of regiments en route to Sind looked equally unreliable. What made the issue more threatening was that the soldiers of at least one British line regiment was in sympathy with the sepoys and there were reports that they would refuse to act against any Bengali unit. Many of the officers offered their own pay to increase an allowance, but the Army's headquarters refused to increase pay for what was, effectively, garrison duty. The commanding officer of the 64th Bengal Regiment assured his men that the allowance permitted during the Afghan War, nicknamed 'General Pollock's batta', would be forthcoming, but this was subsequently refused. The result was that Bengali regiments had to be relieved of the deployment to Sind and replaced with Madras or Bombay regiments.[23]

Attempts to reduce costs prompted further trouble. The 6th Madras Cavalry, one of the regiments ordered up to replace the Bengal units, was

Muslim in composition and had large expenses to cover in order to preserve the strict purdah of their women and various traditions in lifestyle. They had accepted their posting to Sind on the understanding it was a temporary deployment, and had arrived without their families, but on arrival they learned the garrison duty would be prolonged and their pay would be less than they had expected. The result was another set of mutinous complaints. When ordered to train or parade there was widespread defiance and abuse, and the brigade commander intervened to call for their petitions to be submitted, via their troop commanders, to him. The allowances were then granted. Yet there was more confusion. When the 47th Madras Infantry embarked for Sind, they were assured that, since their particular posting lay outside the limits of the Presidential boundaries, including the Bombay Presidency, they would be entitled to extra allowances.[24] The Governor General, prompted by the Governor of Bombay, objected to this special treatment, which, they claimed, overstepped the limits of the authority of Madras. The result was that the sepoys paraded as normal, but refused to obey orders. For several days they refused to march, dismiss or assemble when ordered, but their commanding officer, having accepted soldierly and orderly representation, assured them of their pay and allowances and briefly imprisoned the ringleaders for insubordination. The incident highlighted that the sepoys felt that a loss in pay would affect their ability to provide for their families, and, in turn, diminish their honour among their peers.

Dealing with mutinous regiments ordinarily followed an accepted pattern. If the officers could not, after getting some insight into the grievances, address the complaints directly, or if the mutiny occurred within proximity of the enemy, as in the case of units close to the border with the Sikh Kingdom, then the East India Company would simply disband a unit and thereby cease to pay for the men and their families. Such a threat was often sufficient to deter any serious unrest. But in the 1840s, with Bombay and Madras regiments so far from their home stations, there were added dilemmas and risks. Sir John Kaye wrote that punishment of an entire regiment 'falls alike on the innocent and on the guilty'.[25] Of the 7th Madras Cavalry, at least half the regiment had remained loyal, and all the native officers. He added: '[Disbandment] fills the country with the materials of which rebellions are made, or sends hundreds of our best fighting-men, with all the lessons we have taught them, into the enemy's ranks.' Yet to march a regiment back to its home station, many weeks and even months later, with an uncertain fate hanging over every man, seemed unjust if not even more risky. Disbandment generally had to take place where

British regiments were co-located, in order to deter any possibility of violence. This left the Madras authorities in a difficult position.

What the civil authorities did not realise was that, even by averting violence by granting the pay that the sepoys had petitioned for through concessions, they had, in so doing, undermined their authority. Kaye believed that civil primacy and military authority were ultimately at stake: 'What the State ought to have learnt from this lesson was the paramount obligation which rested upon it of clearly explaining to its troops all regulations affecting their pay and allowances, and especially such as entailed upon them any loss of privileges antecedently enjoyed.'[26]

The Indian Mutiny of 1857

In the 1850s, much of the subcontinent was under Company rule or allied to it, and a long succession of wars had resulted in a significant military expansion. Together, the three Presidency armies could muster 233,000 men, with 45,000 British personnel.[27] There was also expansion of the numbers of British officers.[28] Inadvertently, this had served to weaken, rather than strengthen, regimental cohesion. Indian officers were relegated to matters of culture or welfare, becoming advisers rather than commanders, although irregular cavalry units were largely unaffected. Complacency, deteriorating supervision and the careerism of European officers widened the gap between officers and men.[29] Moreover, a breakdown of trust, fuelled in part by a British ideological drive for efficiency over cultural considerations, and coupled with a fear in India that the Company was intent on converting all Indians to Christianity, periodic disputes over pay, and the Europeanising of Company administration, all added to the gulf emerging between the sepoys and the British officer corps. This led, ultimately, to the Mutiny of May 1857.[30]

One observer noted that the deterioration of relations between officers and men, while not universal, was a developing problem: 'The sepoy is sworn at. He is spoken of as a n———r ... as a pig ... The younger men seem to regard it as an excellent joke and as a praiseworthy superiority over the sepoy to treat him as an inferior animal.'[31] William Henry Sleeman, a district commissioner in northern India, also warned about the growing gulf between British and Indian, a fact that was also remarked upon by other 'old hands' of the Company. Despite the sense of friction, few appeared willing or able to change the trend.[32] Sleeman wrote: 'I was concerned to find that there was no longer that sympathy between the people and the agents now employed in these regions by our government. The European officers no longer showed the courtesy towards the middle and higher classes and that kindness towards the humbler which characterised the officers of our day, while the native officers rather imitated or took advantage of this.'[33] In 1850, Major Hodson, the commander of Hodson's Horse, informed General Napier, the Commander-in-Chief, that he was 'frightened, as he well may be, at the fearful want of discipline in the native army'.[34]

Among British officers there was disdain for the 'gossip' of the locals, and European officers spent less time learning their military craft from the older Indian NCOs.[35] Officers no longer hosted nautch dancing for their men or took them hunting. Better communications with England meant that there was a longing for home news and more attention paid to English society and events. The old habits of cohabiting with Indian mistresses, or of marrying them, were dying out too in a climate of prejudice and contempt. In short, there was a withering of the connections between the Company Raj and their Indian subjects as British administration became ever more distant, hierarchical and less dependent on its roots of personalised leadership.

In contrast with the complacency of Anglo-Indian society, the Indian population were increasingly alarmed by the signals of impending unrest. Using their traditional networks of bazaars and news from itinerants, the people seemed conscious that trouble was brewing. There were plenty of signs: the demand for cash and the price of gold rose steeply in Oudh, merchants appeared to be anxious about the future, and sepoys asked repeatedly for news. In intercepted letters, Sir Robert Montgomery, the Chief Commissioner of Punjab, noted that coded phrases were being used to describe the apparent weaknesses of British military power, such as 'hats were hardly to be seen and turbans very plentiful'.[36] Less coded expressions of discontent were evident in the Indian press. The *Sadiq-ul-Akhbar* and *Delhi Urdu Akhbar* printed anti-British sentiments both before and during the Mutiny.[37] Despite the growing signs of unrest, many assumed that the Indian troops would simply carry out their orders and contain any disturbances. Major General Hearsey, the commander of the Presidency Division in Calcutta, refused to spy on his sepoys to obtain 'secret information' because he said 'it would not be proper for me to do it'.[38] Captain Richard Lawrence of the Thagi and Dakoiti Department nevertheless sent a Brahmin agent into the sepoy lines and received a typical report: they were 'full of *fissad* [sedition]'.[39]

Most enigmatic of all was the mysterious passage of chapattis from village to village in January 1857. Few actually understood what they were supposed to herald, and the British regarded them as evidence of some widespread conspiracy, but it seems likely that they belonged to a far older superstition of rural India whereby bad luck, disease or misfortune could be removed from a village by sending out food.[40] However, what made this occurrence so unusual was that they spread so far and wide. From a centre in Indore, they were transmitted through Gwalior, across the British North West Provinces, to Oudh and Rohilkhand, moving at an estimated 200 miles every night. Although cholera was prevalent at the time, they had not appeared in such abundance during previous outbreaks. British suspicions were fuelled when it was noted that the mutiny at Vellore in 1806 had been preceded by chapatti distribution.[41] British officials who interviewed Indians about the affair disagreed on their meanings, and it seems that the chapattis had a different significance in each district.[42]

Despite the growing anger, there is no evidence that the Mutiny was planned by a centralised group of conspirators. James Cracroft Williams, the Special Commissioner appointed after the Mutiny to punish the guilty and reward the loyalists, concluded that the sepoys had not known of any plans except that they should act as other regiments did in the event of trouble. Major G.W. Williams, another Special Commissioner, believed that the rapid spread of the Mutiny suggested that some co-ordination had taken place, but the large numbers involved only indicate that many were drawn in by the opportunities, financial or otherwise, that could arise through fear. Their anxieties were twofold: one, that their religion was about to be overthrown, and, two, that once their comrades or regiments had thrown in their lot with the mutiny there could be no going back or hope of leniency. The religious dimension was certainly mentioned time and again by participants, as were omens and 'signs'. British eyewitnesses noted that the mutineers often reverted to local styles of clothing adorned with beads, perhaps to reassert their religious identity. There is little doubt that each group in Indian society had some particular reason for joining or resisting the rebellion. All the sources agree that the trigger factor for the sepoys was the greased cartridges affair, but landowners and officials who had been displaced by British annexations, peasants unhappy about taxation, and the difficulty of getting grievances redressed through the British administration also played a part, and the sepoys' families could not have remained unaffected by such concerns.

It is well established that the outbreak of the Mutiny was sparked by the refusal of sepoys of the Bengal Presidency Army to accept a new rifle because its cartridges, which had to be bitten to be used, were greased in pig and cow fat that would cause ritual defilement to both Hindu and Muslim soldiers. Yet the uncertain British reaction may also have played a part. The first unit to refuse to obey orders, the 3rd Bengal Cavalry, had been angered by the punishment of 85 of their own sowars, and it was this breach of unit cohesion and solidarity that led them to mutiny. They killed their British officers. The British in Meerut, the seat of the unrest, believed this outbreak was isolated and could be contained, but it soon became apparent that the same anger and frustration had infected much of the Bengal Army. The mutineers marched off to Delhi, the capital of the old Mughal Empire, to appeal to Bahadur Shah II to be their leader and rouse the rest of the army against the hated *feringhees* (foreigners).

This decision to muster at Delhi revealed an absence of any strategic direction. There were no operations against Calcutta or the ports, which would have been essential. Instead, attacks were made on British garrison stations, where there were few to resist, while the strongest posts were avoided. After the initial outbreak, and some resolution in action, there was a rapid subsidence in determination. Mutinous units began to fragment.

At Delhi, there were no British regiments, just three battalions of Bengal infantry. On the morning of 11 May, the mutineers arrived quite suddenly and, despite the efforts of some British officers to close all the entrances to the city, the rebels secured the southern Rajghat Gate. Noisily proclaiming the hour of deliverance, mobs of citizens saw an opportunity to loot and to destroy the symbols of authority. British officers and their families were soon being cut down, murdered and mutilated in the streets. At the palace, the chaplain and two girls were butchered. When some tried to seek refuge in the Main Guard, a bastion on the northern walls, the sepoys of the garrison joined the mutineers and slaughtered the group holding this particular strongpoint. A handful of British officers then summoned two field guns and some sepoys not yet involved in the fighting, and recaptured the Main Guard in hand-to-hand fighting. Nevertheless, the main magazine of the garrison, protected by nine British officers and troops of doubtful loyalty, was confronted by hundreds of angry mutineers who began to scale the walls. For five hours, this group of officers kept at bay their assailants until their ammunition ran out. They knew their fate was sealed but they resolved that the ammunition and powder of the arsenal should not fall into the mutineers' hands. Thereupon they decided to sacrifice themselves: Lieutenant Willoughby set the fuse, and the entire building was engulfed in a gigantic explosion. The detonation tore down neighbouring buildings and killed some of their assailants, but, miraculously, six officers survived the blast, and, in all the confusion, they escaped the city.

Sensing that British authority had collapsed, the sepoys who had initially helped recapture the Main Guard now threw in their lot with the rest of the mutineers and the surviving British soldiers and civilians were forced to flee. Most made for the ridge to the north-west of the city where telegraph officers were sending urgent warnings to other garrisons about what had occurred.

The events in Delhi suggest that there was some doubt in the minds of the sepoys of the garrison until they could see which way events were unfolding. Outside the immediate vicinity of Delhi, there were similar decisions being made. At Meerut, Colonel John Finnis of the 11th Native Infantry had visited his soldiers' lines to reason with them, but he had been shot dead by a handful of sepoys, which committed the rest because they knew that collective punishment would follow. Indecision on the part of senior British officers at Meerut was also much cited as a reason whey events were permitted to get out of hand. Despite the entreaties of his officers, General Hewitt, in command at Meerut, refused to act promptly or pursue the mutineers as they made for Delhi, preferring to remain on the defensive. For those far removed from the seat of the unrest, one calculation could trump the grievances. Lawrence James summed it up: 'Money, or the prospect of it, commanded allegiance during the Mutiny.'[43] This may be putting it too strongly: soldiers, a disciplined and habitually loyal social group, can also feel a strong sense of obligation, which could, of course, determine allegiance to either side. This is reinforced when one assesses the casualties of the subsequent fighting on the British side: even at Delhi, some '82 per cent of the casualties among the other ranks were classified as "native"'.[44] This underscores the point that, even at the height of the Mutiny, the British were still able to call on a significant number of other Asian personnel who were willing to risk life and limb to serve the authorities.

Although the Delhi rebels outnumbered the British survivors, initially they made no move against them. Inside the city, the mutineers refused to co-operate with each other, and there was even disagreement over the execution of the 52 European civilians who had been captured alive earlier on the first day. Some of the rural population had joined the revolt, but others merely saw an opportunity to loot or extort from both sides and cared little for either liberation or loyalty.

By 17 May, the British survivors of Delhi were joined by the garrisons of Ambala and Meerut and, under the command of General Barnard, this small contingent managed to wrest the Delhi Ridge from a larger force of mutineers at the Battle of Badli-ki-Serai. The ridge lay just 1 km (0.75 mile) from the Kashmir Gate of the city, with a canal to its west. The British built a series of redoubts along the crest, and the centre of the position, known as Hindu Rao's House, was occupied by the loyal Gurkhas of the Sirmoor Battalion.

The Gurkhas had regarded the greased cartridges issue as irrelevant. They dismissed the complaints of the '*kala log* [black fellows]' and insisted on using the new Enfield rifles to demonstrate their superiority in military matters. The Sirmoor Battalion had been active in suppressing the rising from the outset, but in the early days of the Mutiny their arrival at Delhi was greeted with suspicion. Not knowing whom they could trust, the British placed them on the extreme flank of their position. But the defence of Hindu Rao's compound reassured the British troops that the Gurkhas were entirely dependable. When mutineers called on the Sirmoor men to 'join us', it is alleged the Gurkhas replied cheerfully: 'Oh yes, we are coming'; and then, when just twenty yards from the main body of the rebels, they opened fire and dispersed their enemies.

Unfortunately, the south of the ridge led into a labyrinth of village streets and gardens, providing much cover for the approach of their attackers. Yet the Sirmoor Battalion proved adept in the close-quarter fighting among the houses and gardens that lay in front of the British position, in which the kukri proved particularly effective.

From the ridge it was clear that Delhi was held too strongly to be taken by storm unless the British could muster greater numbers. However, over the days of May and June, more and more mutineers poured into the city from the south and east. By July, the rebels possessed ten cavalry regiments, fifteen infantry regiments and an unknown number of well-trained artillerymen. As the British lamented their lack of siege guns and transport, the result of earlier cost-cutting measures in peacetime, it became apparent that it was going to be the British who would be besieged, not the city of Delhi. However, by mid-July, about half of the original Sirmoor Battalion had been killed or wounded.[45] The 'line boys', that is, sons of those serving, volunteered to join the fighting.

As early as 19 June, the mutineers made a major attack on the ridge, pushing in from three directions. The British and their Gurkha allies were only just able to cling on and for a time contemplated evacuating the position altogether. Four days later, the mutineers tried again, and for a second time came within a breath of victory. The crisis came when a vast assault was made by the mutineers which fell onto the positions held by the surviving Sirmoor Gurkhas and the neighbouring 60th Rifles: waves of attacks were made, and each one was beaten off by the dwindling defenders. Much of the fighting was at close quarters. When the mutineers pulled back, bodies lay strewn across the ridge and its approaches. For days, these corpses putrefied and a serious risk of contamination and disease, especially cholera, added to the burdens on the exhausted British and Gurkha force. The heat grew intense and the only relief from the sun was the flimsy tents erected behind the ridge, just out of reach of the cannon fire. Periodic alarms from the picquets in front of the ridge roused the diminished force to stave off another attack, but each one caused their numbers to dwindle still further. In one week in July, twenty-five officers and 400 men were killed or wounded resisting raids.

Hope was lifted by the arrival of the Corps of Guides, an elite Muslim force led by British officers that had force-marched hundreds of miles from the Punjab in the broiling sun to support the troops on the ridge. Soon after Brigadier John Nicholson, a veteran of the Sikh wars, leading a force of 4,200 men and a siege train of guns, was within reach of the reinforced garrison. Nicholson gave the defenders of Delhi Ridge much-needed relief, which was as much moral as it was physical: many Sikhs on the ridge regarded Nicholson as a warrior saint, to the extent they referred to themselves as 'Nikalsenyi Faqirs'.

To prevent the British from mounting a bombardment with this new ordnance, the mutineers made a desperate sortie on 25 August at the height of the monsoon, but Nicholson had anticipated the move and routed the rebels at the Battle of Najafgarh. His technique was as much psychological as military: he had his guns open fire but ordered the infantry to march silently against the rebels until they were within just 110 yards (100 metres), whereupon they delivered a single, devastating volley and then charged, bayonets levelled, with an indescribable war-cry. The rebels bolted and most of the British force could concentrate on bayoneting and clubbing their way into a hastily built redoubt. The morale of the British on the ridge soared, but the mood among the mutineers was now one of bitterness and recrimination against their leaders for the lost opportunities.

The British redoubts were soon filled with guns: fifteen 24-pounders, twenty 18-pounders and twenty-five mortars and howitzers, supported by 600 cartloads of ammunition. By stages, new batteries were constructed closer to the walls of Delhi. Inside, the mutineers were daily more disillusioned. One officer wrote: 'guns and mortars were pouring shot and shell without a moment's interval on the doomed city. The din and roar were deafening; day and night salvoes of artillery were heard, roll following roll in endless succession, and striking terror into the hearts of those who felt that the day of retribution was at hand.' Every effort to overwhelm the British had failed and now their own supplies of food and ammunition were reduced. Rumours of defeat were being spread by Asian agents of the British inside the city. Nevertheless, the assaulting British force was little more than 5,000 strong against many thousands of rebels, both sepoys and citizens. The city itself was vast, and coordinating a major assault was a significant challenge.

For two days, the fighting went on in and around the breaches and gates. Some rebel Muslim troops, calling themselves Mujahideen, wanted to fight to the death, but many of the mutineers were dispirited by their losses and the sheer determination of the British to fight on. Gradually the British managed to extend the area under their control. They retook the magazine on 16 September and three days later recovered the palace. Bahadur Shah, the reluctant leader of the rebellion, had fled before they arrived, but he was captured by a detachment of cavalry under William Hodson soon after. Fearful that they might be trapped as the British took each bastion in turn, the majority of mutineers began to evacuate the city. On 21 September, after an epic battle lasting eight days, Delhi was back in British hands.

The British forces had numbered 10,000 British and loyal Indian troops, with an estimated 3,000 Sikh, Gurkha and Pathan allies. The Kumaon Battalion took part in the final attack on Delhi, which had involved a week of tough street fighting. In the final assault, over 5,700 men had been killed or wounded. The casualty figures of the original 42,000-strong force of mutineers are unknown, but their losses may have been of a similar magnitude. The willingness of the assaulting force to take heavy losses reflected the importance of the mission and anxiety about the consequences of failure. The British knew that their ability to govern rested on breaking both the capability and the will of the mutineers at their 'capital'. Indeed, the fall of Delhi proved a major psychological blow to the rebellion. By retaking the city, the British had signalled their determination to reassert exclusive rule. Angered by the massacre of British civilians, many advocated a punitive regime, but, despite isolated atrocities, both the British and the Indians were eager to restore peace and order.

The most significant and iconic event that determined the severity of the British reaction had been the massacre of civilians and captured troops at Cawnpore. The garrison town had been denuded of troops for campaigns overseas and only 300 Europeans were in residence, compared with over 3,000 Indian soldiers. The key determining factor, however, was not the imbalance of the strength of forces but the accumulation of grievances and their coincidence with the aspirations of Nana Sahib, the son of the last titular leader of the Maratha Confederacy who had recently been denied his inheritance by changes in the political administration of northern India.

The sepoys had initially shown no sign of joining the mutiny, but as soon as General Sir Hugh Wheeler, the local garrison commander, started to make preparations for a defensive position at an incomplete barracks outside the city, the locals expressed their resentment by refusing to assist. Wheeler, who had an Indian wife, placed his faith in the continued friendship of Nana Sahib. Mrs Emma Ewart, wife of the colonel of the 1st Bengal Native Infantry, had, like many others, doubted the seriousness of the threat. In one of the last letters she had written to her sister, she noted: 'We can never feel secure in the country. How fortunate for us that the people do not know how to combine sufficiently to subvert the empire. You see they have no leaders, no definite cause, no real patriotism; so that there is nothing likely to arise out of these disturbances but a great amount of mischief and temporary suspension of order.'[46] She continued that her husband had learned the sepoys were intent on 'destruction of the officers' but he had insisted on sleeping in their lines in order to demonstrate his trust in them. Neither she nor her husband survived the uprising.

When the Indian troops mutinied on 4–5 June, Nana Sahib joined the revolt, and the combined forces laid siege to the entrenchments of Cawnpore. An attempt was made to storm the British position after a prolonged bombardment of 17 days, but it was held off. The exhaustion of the small garrison, and the lack of remaining ammunition, food and water convinced Wheeler to accept Nana Sahib's offer of safe passage.

The capitulation was nevertheless betrayed when Nana Sahib opened fire on the surviving soldiers and civilians on the banks of the Ganges at Satti Chaura Ghat. The ambush was comprehensive, guns having been assembled on the banks and fires prepared to burn the boats on which the prisoners had embarked. No quarter was given, and the mutineers swept the whole group with musketry and cannons, before wading into the shallows to finish off the wounded. One boat with four survivors escaped and a handful of women and children threw themselves on the mercy of Nana Sahib. On 15 July, having been imprisoned at Bibighar, the survivors were butchered and their remains tossed into a well. General Henry Havelock's relieving force were appalled at the scenes of slaughter they encountered, and many officers swore they would avenge the murdered civilians. Brigadier General Neill was not alone in insisting that captured mutineers would be compelled to clean a portion of the desecrated spot and then face a hanging. Others advocated that the Mughal practice of executing captured mutineers by blowing them from the muzzle of cannon was the only appropriate retribution. William Forbes Mitchell of the

93rd Highlanders stated that the massacre of prisoners and civilians at Cawnpore turned the conflict into *guerre à la Mort*.

It was evident from the outset that, alongside resolute action by the British themselves, Indian allies would help to turn the tide. The Maharaja of Jodhpur immediately offered his troops to the British to crush the mutineers, and Maharaja Jayajirao Scindia of Gwalior did the same, although not all of the soldiers followed their instructions. Sikhs and Gurkhas, loyal remnants of the mutineer battalions and many of the Europeans' own servants also fought on the British side. The merchant classes of Delhi, both Hindu and Muslim, regarded the insurrection as a threat to the prosperity they had enjoyed under British rule. Many of them passed information to agents like Mohan Lal.[47] Mark Thornton was approached by the Seth family, who were influential bankers at Mathura, and they offered him their entire intelligence network and two cannons.[48] At the defence of Lucknow, 700 of the garrison holding out against the mutineers, a third of the force, were sepoys.

British reinforcements were brought to India from Malta, South Africa and Burma, and troops en route to China were diverted. All had been alerted by telegraph and the passage of steam shipping. Yet until they arrived, there were precious few men that could hold the isolated positions at Cawnpore, Lucknow and on the ridge outside Delhi. At this point, it was imperative to prevent the further spread of mutiny so as to concentrate the available manpower at the most threatened points. The difficulty to begin with was knowing who could be trusted.

To the south-west, the officers in the Bombay Army were taking precautions against insurrection, and, in so doing, secret correspondence between Bombay sepoys and the mutineers was discovered on 14 June.[49] Rumours were rife, and it was almost impossible to be sure of information. When a sepoy of the 13th Native Infantry warned his officers that the Lucknow garrison meant to join the mutiny, his information was ignored because it could not be verified.[50]

Elsewhere in India, however, there were very few disturbances at all. Kaye attributed this to the British practice of co-opting local rulers to govern autonomously, many of them possessing their own (albeit limited) military forces, in return for fealty towards the 'Paramount Power'. He wrote:

> I think, then, it will be generally conceded that the attitude of the principal protected chiefs throughout India, during the most terrible crisis to which English rule has ever been subjected, was of a character to justify generally the antecedent administration of the foreign overlord. The action of the native chiefs was, in fact, a barometer full of encouragement and yet not wanting in warning for the future.

It was gratifying to see that the indicator gave evidence of, in the great majority of cases, just and beneficent dealing. In fact, in those parts of India in which the British rule had been beneficent, for instance, in Rajputana, in central India, in western India (except the southern Maratha territory), in southern India, including Haidarabad and Maisur, the native chiefs were loyal, often as anxious and energetic on behalf of their overlord as though that cause had been their own. In other places where the natives had not appreciated the rule of their masters, in places for instance where these had displayed a hard and unsympathising resolution to graft western ideas on an eastern people—in, for example, the North-West Provinces of India, in the Sagar and Narbada territories, in Jhansi, in western Bihar, in the southern Maratha territories, in Oudh, the native chiefs and people, acting in concert, evinced a hatred to the British rule which led them to risk all they possessed in the world to shake off their yoke.[51]

The news of terror tactics by British troops who advanced to the relief of the besieged garrisons, itself a response to the widespread murders and mutilations of Europeans, confirmed the resolve of many mutineers that there could be no going back and no negotiation.[52]

Flying columns eventually reached Lucknow and relieved the garrison there, and reinforced the meagre numbers on the Delhi Ridge. In time, stronger columns converged on Oudh. Lucknow was actually relieved in two phases, after significant street fighting and a sustained artillery bombardment of the defending British garrison. It was noticeable that the relief marches encountered mutinous sepoy forces that selected to fight in the style in which they had been trained, namely in open formations or from defended positions such as the streets of Lucknow. Nevertheless, a portion elected to continue resistance in the more remote rural areas and adopted a guerrilla style. This final phase of the mutiny has attracted far less attention among scholars and yet was roundly disliked by contemporaries who had to conduct the 'mopping-up' operations. Sir Garnet Wolseley regarded this phase as the most 'derogatory to a soldier's profession' and yet still inherently full of risk.[53]

The immediate aftermath of the fighting led to an extensive inquiry into the causes of such a serious outbreak of unrest, the degree to which it had been premeditated or spontaneous, the value of the more seasoned troops stationed in the Punjab and their allies, compared with the 'petted' regiments of Bengal. The most debated theme of all, however, was trust. Several officers who went on to senior command never forgot their terrifying days in 1857, and the measures they imposed and the degree of trust placed in certain Indian units stemmed from their personal experience. Lord Frederick Roberts, for example, who won a Victoria Cross as a subaltern in the Mutiny and went on to become the Commander-in-Chief of India, was the champion of a system of recruitment and selection that specifically set out to avoid a repeat of the Mutiny. When there were tactical setbacks in various conflicts, officers like Roberts grew more anxious about potential unrest, and emphasised the need for bold and resolute action to re-establish British prestige and a sense of military superiority in the minds of the Indians.[54] Colonel Callwell, who catalogued the tactical lessons of the Mutiny, concluded that British successes were invariably due to the strong sense of resolution felt among all ranks of the outnumbered British forces, but also to the determination to make 'every successive victory as complete as possible'.[55]

Breakdown of the Contract

The Indian Mutiny has often been cited as a classic conflict between colonisers and colonised, in which it was clear that co-operation, or more accurately, the contract between employers and military employees had broken down. While the majority of the Bengal Army rejected British control and represented a very serious threat to the East India Company's rule, the British forces in India were supported throughout the 1857 rising by large numbers of Indian troops from the other Presidency armies and armed civilians. Crucially, in northern India, the British were supported by the Sikhs and Punjabi Muslims, who, while only recently enemies of the army of the East India Company, were eager to exact revenge for their defeats at the hands of the Hindus. In addition, much of the south and central parts of India remained quiet, and, perhaps crucially, there was no intervention by the Muslim tribesmen of the North West on the weakened Indian frontier. Indeed, there were many who came forward to assist the British rather than oppose them. The British were able to make use of the support provided by those Indians who were alarmed by the violence and high-handedness of the mob or by the possibility that a Muslim ruler might be restored over a land consisting of a majority of Hindus.

The unrest was made more serious by the thousands of civilians who joined the rising through opportunism, fear of forced conversion to Christianity, anxiety about losing their land, and anger about aspects of British rule, not least the rise of moneylenders and land speculators. Contemporary British accounts emphasised superstitions, such as the passing of chapattis from village to village and other coded signals, and the denuding of British troops for campaigns in other theatres as their own explanations, but Indian scholars of the period tended to explain the rebellion as a war of religion. The decision of the local landed elites to join the rising, caused by British annexations and dispossession of a few key figures, was crucial in determining the allegiance of many communities. For the sepoys, there was the short-term issue of contaminated cartridges, but there was also disaffection with their treatment, the gap between them and their British officers, and the lack of respect shown them on issues such as overseas service, which, in crossing the 'black water' of the Indian Ocean, meant pollution for high castes. The Bengal mutiny had provided the spark for a general rising, but it also deprived the British of the means to suppress the revolt, and was another reminder of the vulnerability of the British system of colonial governance. Unsurprisingly, contemporaries derived important lessons about widening the base of support for British rule, ensuring sufficient ratios of British and Indian forces were maintained as garrison troops, and cultivating their local leaders, namely the Indian princes, as military allies.

Since 1947, the nationalist agenda has, to a large extent, obscured the critical element in ensuring the survival of British colonial rule, namely the participation of a significant number in the Indian Army and constabularies. This gave rise to another interpretation, championed by Ranajit Guha and Frantz Fanon, that empires were ultimately systems of violence inflicted upon the civilian populations. This perspective did not acknowledge the contemporary view that the use of force against colonial subjects, even against native forces, was regarded as a failure of governance. Incorporation, assimilation and persuasion were more important, especially as they were generally cheaper and avoided disruptions to commerce. The British were convinced they were enemies of militarism, even though it evidently existed, and they preferred to rely on the authority of the Sahib or the Governor, rather than demonstrations of power. Ronald Hyam concluded that force was the basis of British rule, but it was tempered by ideals of justice and an unerring faith in the idea that the empire was beneficent.[56]

The mutinies of local forces are cases which demonstrate the way in which contracts between soldiers and foreign employers can break down. Cultural affronts are just one aspect of grievances that can develop over a long period, and pay and conditions seem to rank far higher in the reasons for unrest. Denial of privileges, prolonged hardship, the lack of rotation out of the most difficult duties, unsympathetic leadership, and accumulated misunderstandings can all contribute to the outbreak of a mutiny. Not all are violent and many were resolved by conciliation, but the general approach was to have mutinous units disbanded immediately, even if only a handful were involved.

While authorities might acknowledge that pay and conditions need to be supervised and carefully maintained, with allowances honoured, there has generally been little sympathy for those who are striking for higher pay.

The lethality of the British reaction in 1857–8 was proportional to their sense of betrayal and the violent nature of the outbreak. The murder of European women and children, all of whom were the families of serving military personnel, ranked even higher in their calculations than the desertions and disorder of the Indian sepoys. The retribution was so severe that the Governor General had to make direct appeals for it to be ended. The debate about the long-term response, and whether to retain local military personnel at all in India, began almost immediately and continued, in various forms, for the rest of the period of the Raj.

4

DISCIPLINE AND PUNISHMENT

Rebuilding the Indian Army after the Mutiny

There was considerable disagreement about the future of the army in India after the Mutiny. One proposal was to abolish Indian regiments and garrison the subcontinent entirely with British personnel. This was quickly dismissed on grounds of cost and recruiting problems, and no one was prepared to countenance conscription to fulfil the quotas required for imperial garrison duty. As it stood, it was necessary to withdraw several British units from the colonies of settlement to find the necessary manpower for India. The remaining Indian Army was to be rebalanced, with a higher proportion of British troops brigaded with Indian ones, and the overall size of the force was to be reduced. One-third of the complement of the army in India was to be British. The arrangement of three Presidency armies was retained, despite criticism from some quarters, on the grounds that unrest in one would be dealt with by either or both of the others. The Presidency armies survived until 1895 when a new centralised headquarters and four regional commands were introduced.

It was agreed, however, that Indian units were to be deprived of artillery. All field ordnance was manned by British personnel, and the exception was the small, low-calibre mountain artillery batteries. Given the level of destruction they had wrought on defended positions during the Mutiny, it was thought too great a risk to permit Indian troops to possess artillery in the future.

There was considerable attention to the drivers of the Mutiny and why it had occurred in the Bengal Army and not in the other two Presidency forces.

The conclusions were that the recruiting base of the Bengal regiments had been too narrow. Sir Henry Lawrence had warned a decade before the Mutiny that: 'Our [Bengal] Sepoys come too much from the same parts of the country. There is too much clanship amongst them.'[1] Of the 40,000 men of the Bengal Native Infantry, the majority came from Oudh, and most were high-caste men who guarded their rituals and rites jealously in order to keep out lower castes. The British officers, eager to avoid offence, tended to acquiesce in the system. By 1855, lower-caste men were officially excluded from the Bengal infantry, not least because the high-caste sepoys refused to take orders from low-caste men, and this prevented any promotion prospects and made the service of this group meaningless.

The threat to Bengali exclusivity had come after 1849 when Punjabi Sikhs, following the disbanding of the Sikh Kingdom's army, needed employment. To refuse their entry into Company service risked flooding the countryside with thousands of unemployed and experienced troops. As a result, the Punjab Irregular Force had been created, and the Company had absorbed some 30,000 men of the Punjab by the time of the Mutiny. A year after the outbreak that number had risen to 80,000, with a further 50,000 paramilitary constabulary.[2] The necessity of finding sufficient numbers to combat the Bengal Army mutineers had prompted Sir John Nicholson, the local commander, to embark on a rapid recruiting campaign. There was no shortage of volunteers. Their loyalty and resolute service meant that there could be no question of excluding these men in the future. Indeed, while subsequent generations have decried the evolution of a 'martial races' theory for recruitment in the latter decades of the nineteenth century, there can be no doubt that, in the period after the Mutiny, it was a simple pragmatism that dominated decision-making.

The Peel Commission, chaired by the Secretary of State for War, met in 1858, and heard contradictory testimony about the future of the Indian Army. Some favoured more reliance on Muslims and Sikhs, while others argued that to exclude Hindus carried a greater risk. Some decried the presence of high-caste men, others argued these made the best military material. The commission considered whether to recruit Africans and Malays as the garrison troops for India, but this was rejected as far too inflammatory.[3] The commission concluded that mixing Indian castes and communities throughout the army would provide the best guarantee of security and the highest quality of soldiers. It gave no specific direction on who should be recruited or to which formation, and so, in the immediate few years after the Mutiny, the only significant changes came in the Bengal Army, where the personnel of a number of regiments were replaced with Gurkhas, Sikhs and Punjabis, or with men raised in 1857–8 from low-caste Hindu groups. That said, no fewer than 18 infantry battalions were retained from the old Bengal Army. The historian David Omissi wrote that 'no defined principle guided British policy except that the high-caste sepoys of Awadh were widely discredited'.[4]

Nevertheless, the lesson of the Mutiny had been that, if the various communities of India remained as divided as they were, there was a stronger rationale for the continued leadership and direction of the British, which provided its own inherent security. Competition has been encouraged in every army, but identities were particularly strong in the Indian Army. The Gurkhas tended to look down on Hindus because they felt they did not meet their own standards of individual courage, while Sikhs despised Muslims, and the Muslim–Hindu antagonism was equally widespread. In the Madras and Bombay armies the rivalries were less acute because units tended to be mixed, although class companies, which consisted of a single ethnic or religious group, would compete with other companies within the same battalion as a point of honour.

By the 1860s, the pressure to save money led to calls for the reduction in the size of the Indian Army, and attention focused on the Madras Presidency because of accusations it was the least efficient and 'warlike'. The number of battalions of infantry was reduced from 52 to 40, but calls for further cuts were rejected on the grounds that it could jeopardise the internal security of the region. But it was not only domestic security that was at issue. There were new demands for expeditionary service in the second half of the nineteenth century, in China, Abyssinia, Afghanistan and Burma. There was also the looming threat of Russian expansion across Central Asia towards India, which several commentators predicted would one day conclude with an attack on Britain's frontiers. This posed a particular dilemma. The Indian Army was equipped below the standard of the British forces, in rifles and artillery, in order to reduce the risk of a powerful, mutinous force, but if it was to confront the Russians, a well-armed European adversary, it would require better weaponry and comprehensive training. Moreover, the primary operational function of many Indian regiments was counter-insurgency on the North West Frontier, or in Burma, against increasingly well-armed and determined irregulars. When Lord Roberts took over as Commander-in-Chief in India, he assessed the Indian regiments as 'not fit to take the field against a European enemy'.[5] He had also been alarmed by his experiences in the Second Anglo-Afghan War in which some Indian units had not performed well, and, in one instance, a Muslim battalion at Peiwar Kotal had warned the Afghans of the covert approach of a British force.[6]

The Martial Race Theory

The solution, according to Roberts, was to recruit men from the most 'martial races'. He did not believe the purpose of the Indian Army was to effectively police itself, that is, to provide troops that were there not only 'to act as a check on another soldier'.[7] Yet the policy that was devised represented a self-reinforcing prejudice against the southern Indians in favour of selected northern groups. The system worked, and was largely accepted, as long as the Indian Army was not called upon to provide more than a relatively small expeditionary force for a limited war. The world war would create all manner of difficulties for the idea of 'martial races'.

The Madras Army, long deprived of active military operations and staffed with older men, including in the British officer corps, could not have been expected to be at the peak of efficiency. Various explanations were nevertheless attributed to the Madras force which made the lower standard of performance more likely. Instead of improving and developing the Madras Army with rotations into combat roles, it was made to languish still further. This merely confirmed the suspicions and prejudices that existed. For the army that had won the wars in the Carnatic and much of central India, it was an unjust outcome.

What set the seal was the lacklustre performance of the Madras regiments in the Third Anglo-Burmese War of 1885–6. Roberts did not entirely write off the southern soldiers. He praised the Sappers, but he urged the Madras Army's commander, Sir Charles Arbuthnot, to replace the 'distinctly unwarlike material ... with the least possible delay'.[8] He requested that all Indian troops, include those of the Princely States, should be given modern firearms. Roberts therefore introduced the Martini-Henry breech-loaders into Indian regiments, although the latest models were retained in British units. The deterioration of the Madras Army seemed to be confirmed the following year when, against a trend of reduced numbers of punishments or courts martial across the Indian Army, the Madras Army's increased.[9] Madrassi soldiers were, like their northern counterparts, all long-service men, but the length of service in the south was the longest. In 1879, some 37 per cent had more than 15 years' service, compared with 11 per cent in Bengal and 23 per cent in Bombay. British officers too tended to be long-serving. Younger men were attracted to the prospect of higher allowances and more active service in northern regiments, with the result that posts normally held by junior officers were staffed by older men. Reductions in the numbers of regiments reallocated the older officers among the remaining battalions, which also closed vacancies to younger men. The proportion of subalterns and captains fell significantly, but colonels were over-represented.[10] It has been assumed that this ageing of the Madras officer corps impaired efficiency and vigour, but, examined the other way round, it actually endowed the Madras regiments with a great deal of experience and a deeper knowledge of the men under command.[11]

The assumption that the Madras regiments were less fit to take the field meant that there were further reductions in the scale of the force, and replacement with other 'martial' categories of troops.[12] Nevertheless, the fact that Madras was far removed from any seat of war or any violent frontier, and that civilian governors did not call on the Madras troops to maintain internal security, reduced the need for them in any case. In 1885, when war with Russia seemed imminent, eight Madras battalions were disbanded and replaced with Sikhs and Gurkhas. An army reserve was established that year but it was overwhelmingly drawn from northern soldiers. By 1900, there were only 25 Madras infantry battalions, half the number there had been forty years before. It was the accumulated effects of reductions, ageing, lack of active service opportunities, and the general disdain with which the Madras Presidency Army was treated that adversely affected morale, and thus its performance.

Between 1862 and 1914, there was a steady reduction in the numbers of men being drawn from Madras, equating to a quarter of the force that had been in existence at the time of the Mutiny. The numbers drawn from Bombay were halved, but the scale from Punjab and the North West Frontier Province doubled and the numbers of Gurkhas increased fourfold.[13] But there were experiments to find southern men with 'martial qualities' to augment the Madras Army, especially among Mappilas and Coorgs. The Mappilas of south-west India were a landless, mainly Muslim minority often engaged in small trades but whom the vagaries of the economy had left vulnerable to unemployment. They had a reputation for armed resistance because of their treatment, but the British envisaged their employment in the army not only as a solution to manpower requirements but also as the means to inject income into their community and thus reduce their predilection for violent disorder. The experiment, begun in 1900, failed within seven years. The soldiers were insubordinate and refused to accept the discipline required for military service. Their community leaders had long fostered an ideology opposed to authority and the landowning classes, but there were also economic factors at work. The most active men could find employment that carried more status and opportunity on the railways or in the plantations of Ceylon. The Coorgs had seemed to be in a similar situation, with a great deal of rural unemployment and what seemed like a warrior tradition. Their fair skin, lack of education and absence of rituals that might impair military effectiveness seemed to make them suitable for recruitment. In 1901 the first units were supposed to form up, but the close familial networks avoided service in the Indian Army. The attempt to raise forces here was abandoned in 1904, having failed to attract enough recruits.

By the time of Lord Kitchener's appointment as Commander-in-Chief, the preferential trend of recruiting men from Punjab and the mountain peripheries was well established, and represented about 60 per cent of the entire army. Even the Madras battalions were being reconstituted with northern men. By 1909, just 11 of the Madras infantry regiments were still recruited from the region, while the rest came from outside. By 1914, the proportion of northern and hill men in the Indian Army was therefore closer to 75 per cent. The Bombay Presidency, while being granted the right to draw recruits from Sind, Rajputana and central India, nevertheless also looked to the Punjab and the hills for their rank and file. While the presidencies established official recruiting depots, the old practice continued of enlisting men from villages and districts with a long-standing and established tradition of providing men for the army. This was the preference of the villages themselves because it guaranteed employment and elevated its status.

The consequence of this practice was that local communities embraced and endorsed the idea of 'martial races' for their own, largely economic purposes. Many of them spoke of a tradition, imagined or otherwise, that ranged into antiquity. Muslim men often invoked the past histories of conquest and religious obedience, while Sikhs referred to a more recent tradition of the military Gurus and the independent warrior state of Ranjit Singh, which was, by analogy, not unlike the Prussia of Frederick the Great. Mahrattas referred to the conflicts that had marked the end of the Mughal dynasty; Gurkhas believed their traditions had always been martial, but this was given empirical support by their determined resistance to the British in 1816. Rajputs, disdaining agriculture, thought of themselves as warriors through and through.

The British had their own views of what constituted a 'martial race'. The criteria were more closely related to military necessity than many scholars assume. While race has become the subject of intense study over many decades, the British were more interested in particular qualities and applied, in stereotyped form, these attributes to selected groups. The categories were assessed on the basis of location, physical or mental attributes, cultural characteristics and, above all, loyalty. Given the diversity and complexity within and between these groups, the simplified categorisation was an attempt to make the identification easier and therefore more useful from a military point of view. This process was not limited to Indian or other Asian and African groups, but was applied to the British and Dominion forces too. English infantrymen were considered obedient and reliable, but lacking in vigour at times; Irish soldiers and Scottish personnel were thought to be full of energy, fighting spirit and inspiration, but there was always a suspicion that they would get out of hand. British cavalry were seen as having the courage and resolution of Cromwellian Ironsides. Correspondingly, Jats were independent but offered 'more dogged courage than dash'; Gurkhas were thought timid with a wonderful sense of humour in peacetime, but utterly ferocious and courageous in battle; Sikhs were stately and reliable, and would endure all manner of hardships.[14]

There was generally a preference for men who were not so well educated that they would question their military service or demonstrate nationalist sentiments. City dwellers were not as attractive as recruits from agricultural areas because they did not seem so used to a life in remote rural regions and therefore not inured to the hardships of campaigning.[15] It was also more difficult to ascertain the origins of the urban inhabitants and therefore place them within the hierarchy of castes and classes in a regiment. By contrast, Dogras, a corrupted term used to encompass all Hindu groups recruited from Jammu, Kangra, Chamba and the neighbouring hill regions, were thought to possess 'a natural respect for authority' and as a result 'have ever been distinguished for their military fidelity and loyalty'.[16] Hill men were thought especially well suited to the most common theatre of war, the mountains of the North West Frontier, and better able to stand arduous marches, changes in the weather and the physical demands of the terrain. Martial race attributes in rural stock were also intended to make the connection between British officers and their Asian soldiers easier. If both officers and men embraced the specific qualities they were deemed to possess, it was more likely they would try to live up to that reputation. Rather like appending the title of elite to a military force, a degree of pride and status can, in time, inculcate a much greater willingness to endure, take casualties and remain cohesive in combat. This is the ultimate test of military efficiency.

British officers were also led to believe that Indians were incapable of inspired leadership, and so, regardless of the presence of experienced Indian officers, the British saw themselves as providing the education, resolve and control that the Indians naturally lacked. The assumption also created an air of self-confidence, an important element for young officers posted into an alien culture and expected to perform. Officers were also taught to guard against undue trust, a legacy of the Mutiny but also the experience of leading men from the North West Frontier where treachery against officers could be expected. Pathans were suspected of untrustworthiness, extending clan feuding from home, opportunistic theft and betrayal if the odds looked uncertain. Pathans also rarely co-operated and so, with the requisite knowledge of their origins and identity, they could be relied upon to perform well in operations against rival groupings. Knowledge of the various clans was thought to be important enough to merit detailed handbooks. There were similar guides to the Gurkha clans, some 800 in the case of the Magar and a further 300 clans of Gurung. Other ethnographic surveys proliferated in the late nineteenth century as the British sought to gain a better understanding and refine their grasp of South Asian groups.

The British drive for categorisation became infused with the assumptions of social Darwinism that were evolving in this period, although these deductions were not accepted by all, and some Indian Army officers rejected outright the alleged attributes of the various Indian communities. In some quarters, caste was assumed to be a form of race and social class combined, and there were attempts to trace the lineage between the Aryan invaders of South Asia in antiquity and the European racial branch. In maintaining the hierarchy of races, however, the theorists argued that generations of miscegenation had diluted the original Aryan stock. There was a preference for lighter-skinned Indians in this realm of thinking, and purity of race, whatever its position in the alleged hierarchy, was preferred over those that seemed to have mixed over time. Sikhs who had refrained from marrying into Hindu families, for example, were the preference of the British.[17] Racial groups that had remained in one area for generations seemed to have the best chance of maintaining this racial purity, and hence the regionalist preferences of the British recruiters were reinforced by their own theories.

There were repeated warnings from critics of the 'martial races' recruitment policy that such a narrow pool of soldiers might cause problems when social or political unrest developed in their homelands. In 1907, ex-soldiers featured among protesters in the Punjab and Sikh unrest in 1911, prompted by an outbreak of plague but fostered by the radical Tat Khalsa movement, which also affected areas from which soldiers were sourced.[18]

The Mahars from Maharashtra, who, as an Untouchable class, had been recruited until the advent of martial races theories took hold, petitioned the government of India as economic hardship began to take hold. Their appeal was not just on grounds of economy, however. They argued that their record of military service in the past deserved more distinguished treatment as it amounted to a form of imperial citizenship; their position in society they regarded as little different from the British working classes, who were, they pointed out, perfectly entitled to enlist.[19]

The petitioners and critics were unable to arrest the steady 'Punjabisation' of the rest of the Indian Army. In 1865, the 42nd Assamese Light Infantry of the Bengal Presidency had the standard eight companies: two consisted of Sikhs, the Gurkhas made up four companies (although a quarter of each company was of Jarwahs, the local hill clans), and two companies of Hindustanis, one Muslim and one Hindu. By 1880, the same regiment had been reconstituted entirely as the 42nd Gurkha Light Infantry and its manpower consisted entirely of Gurkha riflemen.[20]

Lord Lawrence had advocated as early as 1844 that Indians should be permitted to acquire officers' commissions in order to avoid a permanent state of subordination and where the 'energies and talents under the present system are too liable to be brought into the scale against us'.[21] Lord Napier of Magdala, a former Commander-in-Chief, also advocated Indian officers. Roberts disagreed, believing that Indians did not possess the qualities of British officers. Perhaps the real doubt was still loyalty: Roberts could not be certain, especially after his experiences in the Mutiny, that an Indian officer corps, more educated and in command of thousands of troops, would willingly remain under British rule. The existence of Indian officers in the Princely States was permitted as long as they continued to acknowledge the paramountcy of the British. Under Roberts's command, from 1885 to 1893, steps were taken to incorporate elements of these state forces into the Indian Army's order of battle, as Imperial Service Troops, under British direction.

Roberts, like other advocates of the 'martial race' doctrine, did not believe that the military prowess of particular groups was necessarily permanent. He was quite prepared to admit that southern Indians, without exposure to constant campaigning, had lost their keen edge. It implied the threat that any group, unless kept at a high pitch of trained excellence, might slip into the enervating routine of garrison life. The North West Frontier, and the operations in the

North East and Burma, provided one arena to keep the army in fighting condition. Another route was to continue to foster competitiveness between Presidency Army groups, regiments and even companies. In Roberts's defence, therefore, we might acknowledge that, while a man of his time when racial and other supremacist ideas were abroad, his main motivation was the improvement of the Indian Army. Indeed, it is this motivation that continued well after his time as Commander-in-Chief, and he was a champion of reform for the British Army after its performance in the South African War (1899–1902).

The problem with competitiveness within the Indian Army was the denigration of the Madras soldiers and the risk that it could impair discipline in any unit, although the troops themselves seemed to prefer to serve with their own kind.[22] What was effective, however, was the redefinition of identity. Military history is replete with illustrations of relatively small, well-defined and cohesive forces defeating larger, more amorphous masses, and being able to take higher casualties and yet remain combat-effective. The British Indian Army created the smaller unit identities it would require to operate not only against much larger numbers of mutineers, but also against large angry populations and, crucially, against more numerous Russian forces attempting to advance against India from the North West. In the hill fighting of the frontier districts, a strong sense of unit cohesion built resilience against the draining effect of constant vigilance, ambushes and the inevitable small but steady trickle of casualties.

Mountain warfare also kept soldiers up at a higher peak of physical fitness. The historian of the Indian Army T.A. Heathcote concluded: 'Hard countries breed hard men.'[23] There was suspicion that life down on the plains of India, subjected to the exhausting climate, softened all personnel. The anxiety was that, by the end of the nineteenth century, the primary threats to Indian security came from the hardy Russians and the merciless mountaineers of the Pashtun belt on the North West Frontier. This increased the motivation to select the best recruits, insist on the highest levels of efficiency and prepare the Indian troops for the most challenging environments and adversaries. Roberts hoped: 'when the time comes for us to meet a Russian army in the field, our own force will consist mainly of Europeans, Goorkhas, and the best kind of Sikhs and Dogras.'[24]

The Gurkhas' Sirmoor Battalion had distinguished itself during the Indian Mutiny at Delhi, and British officers were struck by the fighting spirit of the 5th Gurkhas during the Second Anglo-Afghan War. In 1879, the 72nd Highlanders developed a particularly strong bond with them during the campaign, and insisted on being photographed together in Kabul. The campaigns across the North West Frontier between 1863 and the end of the century gave further opportunities for the Gurkhas to demonstrate their fighting skills and their fidelity. The historian V.G. Kiernan argued that there was a simple explanation for the loyalty of the Gurkhas: 'they were accustomed to the authority of clan chiefs, [which they] easily exchanged for that of British captains'.[25] Yet there was far more to it than that. A culture of loyalty may be strong, but is not so easily transferred. The key factor was that of personalised leadership. The Gurkhas pride themselves in the motto 'I will keep faith', which could extend to the point where Gurkhas refused the orders of any officer other than their own. This level of faithfulness to particular officers, combined with evident military skill, appealed to the British, and the mutual affection increased as the years passed.

Indian soldiers tended to view British cultural habits with suspicion if not disdain, but the Nepalese were more open to change. While Indian soldiers rejected alcohol, the Gurkhas embraced the British habit of taking rum. The British response to the loyalty of their Gurkhas was naturally to reward them and elevate them. This could take prosaic forms. Subedar Major Sangbir Thapa of the 2nd Gurkhas, after years of loyal service, was given the reward of his own land in 1868.[26] Yet, for all the British initiatives and impositions elsewhere in the Indian Army, the Gurkhas themselves embraced a tradition of discipline and loyalism. In other words, the British did not invent the notion that the Gurkhas were the bravest and most loyal of their Indian troops; the Gurkhas were inherently predisposed to it. But there were penalties too: the Indians often resented the loyalty of these northern hill soldiers.[27]

The British authorities were naturally keen to acquire more Nepalese men, and in the early 1880s they aimed to increase the number of Gurkha battalions significantly. In Nepal itself there was growing anxiety that the British meant to annex the country and were using the recruitment of young men as a preliminary measure to reduce its defences. On the British side, there was also a moderate concern that returning or time-served Gurkha riflemen and NCOs might form the nucleus of a rival military force. The impasse was broken by rivalry and coups inside the Nepal government, the outcome of which was that the faction of Bir Shamsher permitted more recruitment in return for a free hand in the country's internal affairs. Yet even this arrangement was insufficient to find the numbers the British required, and efforts to offer inducements faltered when some new recruits, complaining of pressure to enlist, deserted. Indeed, the 3rd Gurkhas at Almora mutinied when they learned of a proposed reduction in allowances, which itself had been the result of a sudden correction in years of overpayment by a generous commanding officer. Further complaints emerged about the lack of promotion prospects compared with other Gurkha regiments that had a second battalion, but the British authorities were also rather critical of the 3rd for a higher–than–average incidence of venereal disease in their station. The solution was to encourage the men to get married, bringing up families and their descendants as 'line boys' to carry on the regimental traditions. The only concern was the potential for the loss of the 'wildness' that characterised the hill fighter.[28]

The experiment was a success. Moreover, after years of rather informal and often clandestine recruiting, a new formal arrangement was agreed in 1888 after improvements in diplomatic relations. The appointment of a sympathetic Resident, Colonel H. Wylie, further improved relations.

The Penal System

The Indian Mutiny had been a profound shock to the British authorities and it generated a furious debate about the future of the Indian Army and the balance between welfare and discipline.[29] In the immediate aftermath of the Mutiny, regimental officers insisted that it should be their prerogative to decide what level of discipline and punishment was appropriate in order to ensure that the sepoy's primary loyalty was to his regiment and his commanding officer. The most senior officers disagreed. They held that the bonds of loyalty should be created to the Indian Army as an institution and that a centralised disciplinary system would avoid the inconsistencies that might lead to jealousy or resentment and hence disorder in the ranks.

The debate had preceded the Mutiny, resulting in shifts in policy. In 1827, the Commander-in-Chief, Lord Combermere, had removed the commanding officers' authority to inflict corporal punishment or dismiss sepoys from the service. One of his successors, General Edward Barnes, restored the authority of the regimental officers in 1832. Commanding officers could therefore summon a court martial and execute the case, awarding punishments that fitted particular cases but gave the opportunity to take into consideration the previous conduct of the accused. In the mid-1830s, Governor General Lord Bentinck took an entirely different view. While he accepted that there was a need for a special bond between the sepoy and his British officers, not least because the British sahib had effectively replaced the traditional tribal chief in the minds of the troops, he nevertheless felt that there was a risk that commanding officers would exceed their powers.[30] Bentinck was convinced that the tribal relationship had been based on kindness and trust as much as discipline and power. Conscious that no tie of national loyalty could be used for Indian troops commanded by foreign officers, he argued that it became all the more important that the corporate loyalty towards the Company was emphasised and proper checks placed on the potential excesses of the regimental officers. Consequently, he removed much of their power and abolished flogging or summary dismissal.[31]

After the Mutiny, Bentinck's measures were regarded as responsible in part for the breakdown of discipline. One group of officers believed that the commanding officers' powers should be restored with the supervision of local brigadier generals and major generals, but not by some remote and unknown army headquarters.[32] They stressed the importance and distinctiveness of the Indian Army, which depended on the relationship between officers and men to a far greater degree than in the regular British Army. Critically, they argued, the Indian sepoy preferred the immediate exercise of power and authority of their own officers.[33] It was thought they could not comprehend the distant and bureaucratic powers of the army's headquarters. It was even said that the sepoys would grasp far more easily, and appreciate, even arbitrary punishment from a personalised authority rather than some obscure set of rights or written laws which they could not follow.[34] In essence, these officers advocated a personal, 'heroic' form of leadership that was based on an intimate knowledge of the men under their command and that allowed discipline to be administered appropriately to each individual sepoy.

The advocacy of this personalised form of leadership stemmed in part from its assumptions about the nature of the society from which sepoys were drawn. Unlike British soldiers who came from a country with a long tradition of liberty and a sense of common rights, the Indian, it was assumed, knew only Orientalism despotism. There could only be officers with absolute authority in the Indian Army because, it was argued, the men would expect it. Yet the assumption also reflected a growing impatience with the development of bureaucracy in government and in the army. Regimental officers wanted freedom of action, and, although there is no doubt about their sincerity in their arguments, to some extent the call for the full restoration of the powers of the commanding officer was an attempt to push back against all forms of impersonal and unwelcome interference. Another way of looking at this development, however, is that the British officers had begun to adopt what they perceived as 'Oriental' practices: in other words, they were tailoring their usual approach to a radically different set of local expectations.

Some of the concern about personal leadership had stemmed from a pre-Mutiny observation that, as the power and the authority of the commanding officers had been diminished, the sepoys spent less time trying to please their immediate superiors. Discipline had begun to deteriorate as a result.[35] One of the most egregious problems was the consequence of the decision to impose promotion by seniority among sepoys. Commanding officers resented this interference and the absence of promotion on merit.[36] General Charles Napier, the Commander-in-Chief in 1849, had applied the measure precisely because he felt the regimental officers possessed too much power, but we should also note that a similar conservative reaction was going on inside the British Army. In India, commanding officers were furious that sepoys would appeal to Army Headquarters if they felt that a more junior man was promoted ahead of them, and the upholding of their appeals left British officers exasperated by the diminution of their authority. Regimental officers were also prevented from denying furlough, awarding extra duties, 'busting' NCOs for bad conduct, imposing summary punishments including drilling with a trial, or ordering arrests. One example was presented as indicative of the malaise: in 1853, the 3rd Sikh Infantry had refused to construct their lines as directed by their commanding officer, but the individual lacked the authority, or indeed the personal charisma, to impose his will.[37]

Lord Bentinck had been influenced in his judgement about greater humanity by his own personal involvement in the Vellore Mutiny: it had been his order about dress and appearance that had provoked the unrest, and he had been recalled. His instinct for liberalisation had caused the British government deep embarrassment in 1815 when he was appointed to administer Sicily. His efforts to bring about a constitutional form of governance had ended in failure. He had angered military officers by cutting their salaries while Governor of Bengal, and he had offended conservatives with his insistence on tackling *suti* and refusing to accept 'unenlightened' Indian culture. On the specific question of military reform, he would have been influenced by cases such as the treatment of the mutineers of the 3rd Cavalry of the Hyderabad Contingent following an incident on 6 May 1827. The violence had been the result of objections to the habit of British officers to beat the sowars with a cane for minor infringements on parade. The difficulty was that such cases were the exception rather than the rule, but a new system had been imposed to prevent its recurrence. Yet there is no doubt that Bentinck was a relatively unpopular figure in conservative military circles.

Bentinck took the view that men who enlisted were, by default, loyal and therefore not in need of draconian punishments. His identification of high castes requiring greater respect seemed to reinforce his assessments, but the ideas were already popular with liberal reformers in Britain.[38] The Duke of Wellington, as Commander-in-Chief of the British Army, had little faith in such optimistic appraisals of human nature. Even though flogging was in decline from the 1790s, the senior officers insisted on retaining corporal punishment because of the quality of the recruit material and the habits of the rank and file. The British officers in Indian regiments pointed out that one could not abolish flogging for sepoys if it had not been ended in the British Army because of the way in which regiments of both forces were brigaded together in the subcontinent. Major General S. F. Whittingham warned that there would be 'dangerous feeling' in British regiments if the soldiers discovered they were 'still subject to a vile degradation from which his black comrade in arms has been so lately exempted'.[39] Bentinck more accurately made the observation that fines or threats of dismissal from the service were more likely to act as a guarantee of good conduct, since the sepoy's family was dependent on him and a sudden dismissal would prove catastrophic to their finances.

Bentinck's termination of corporal punishment was short-lived: by 1845 his successors had restored it for a number of reasons. The most immediate was that crime increased within the Bengal Army. Another was that officers objected to the sentencing of sepoys to hard labour alongside civilian criminals. They wanted a separate system which kept their men apart from the local population. In part this reflected their view that the Indian soldier was somehow better than his civilian counterpart, but it also served the practical side of keeping the sepoy in a more distinctive condition from those in civilian life, one in which separateness could foster a different identity. The sepoys, especially those of high caste, agreed. They objected to hard labour alongside criminals, not least because it meant digging or working alongside low-caste men. Where men had been subjected to the humiliating experience of road construction work, they tended not to come back to the service, so officers were keen to end a practice which deprived them of much-needed manpower.[40]

Hoping for compromise, the reformers of 1858 had asked that rather than full arbitrary powers, the commanding officers should come under supervision, and certain cases ought to be 'referred up'. For example, if a sepoy had more than five years' service, he ought not to be simply dismissed, but his case should be brought before the local brigadier general.[41] The chief advocates of the restoration of the powers of the commanding officers won the argument in 1859. Colonel E. Haythorne, the adjutant general at Army Headquarters, nevertheless remained a stern critic of the reform and continued to speak out against summary trials and the 'despotism' of the regimental officers. In 1864, noting that there had been a trial of sepoys for their use of vulgar language and disobedience on parade, without the required number of commissioned officers present, he threatened to revoke the authority of all commanding officers across the entire army.[42] The following year, the Commander-in-Chief had objected to the flogging of a sepoy who had been insubordinate to an officer. The cause of the imbroglio was nothing more serious than a request for the redress of a legitimate grievance, but the treatment of the sepoy had, according to General William Mansfield, been disproportionate and had been the result of a summary trial.[43] There was, however, no change to the system until 1895, when it was decided that permission for trials had to be sought from the staff officers of the brigades, districts and divisions concerned. Interpreters were also brought in, and evidence had to be produced, records kept and generally the entire apparatus made more deliberate rather than hasty.

There were further reductions in the power of commanding officers with regard to friction with local police. Instead of the regimental officers being permitted their own exclusive authority of courts martial, in such cases the civilian department's views also had to be taken into account, and if there were attacks on police posts, the commanding officers had to report to the local stations. Senior officers were also given sanction to intervene if necessary.

By the outbreak of the First World War there had been further curbs on the arbitrary powers of commanding officers. As in the British Army, flogging was abolished, although not until 1877 (compared with 1868 in British service). Already in decline after the Mutiny, its use had been exceptionally rare. There was just a single case between 1860 and 1865, but none by 1914.[44] Other punishments were reduced in severity by the end of the nineteenth century. The length of time an officer could impose a period of imprisonment was reduced from over thirty to just seven days.[45] Commanding officers also lost the ability to stop pay for a month in each year. In its place, sepoys or NCOs could be deprived of a day's pay or for the duration the offence had lasted. Senior officers could continue to intervene and change these punishments, an important clause designed to prevent vindictive penalties. Yet much store was placed on the commanding officers' knowledge of their men, particularly with regard to their character when they appeared before courts martial. Moreover, the regimental officers retained the power to demote NCOs or make the case for their dismissal. Furthermore, in serious cases the commanding officer could confine sepoys in their lines for a period up to 15 days, as long as he sought the approval of the adjutant general. Men who were caught as deserters could be charged under summary court martial and be detained within their regiment pending trial. For other breaches of discipline, officers could impose punishment drill, require some form of hard labour, and, if the individual 'refused to soldier', then he could be detained and placed on a restricted diet. These practices mirrored those of the British Army.

Punishments were only part of the mechanism for imposing discipline. The more potent effect was the shame the sentences carried in the eyes of the other ranks. The humiliation of being drilled at high speed or forced to work on some digging task in front of one's peers was in fact more effective than the nature of the punishment itself. Esteem could be restored, just as physical effectiveness was, and yet these carried less of the lasting damage that would have been inflicted by flogging or dismissal.

The more serious offences were still subject to courts martial. Other than the summary courts martial mentioned already, the Regimental Courts Martial were the lowest of the more serious forms, rising through District or Garrison Courts Martial and the General Courts Martial. The summary cases could impose financial punishments, such as forfeit of part of a pension, or, until its abolition, the lash. District courts could impose fines, demote individuals in rank or sentence a man to penal servitude for a limited period. The General Courts Martial could impose long-term imprisonment, including life terms, or the death penalty. The number of officers increased with the severity of the case or the seniority of the courts. In the aftermath of the Mutiny, the power of the lower courts martial were actually reduced while that of the General Courts Martial increased, which reflected the centralising tendency of the authorities in the early 1860s, but the sheer cost in terms of time and personnel meant that by the middle of that decade powers had been restored to the lower courts in order to prevent less serious cases being referred up. At the district level, a sepoy could be sentenced to two years' hard labour, subject to imprisonment with solitary confinement, or dismissed from the service, which was a strong deterrent.[46]

The entire system was based on the so-called Articles of War, which, prior to the Mutiny, were supposed to be read out to the sepoys four times a year. Many officers found the practice to be detrimental, perhaps because it was too frequent a reminder of the penal system and therefore a slight upon the otherwise assumed good character of a regiment. Brigadier Christie of the Dinapore Division held strong views on the subject, arguing that, particularly among the irregular cavalry, the troopers resented the bureaucratised system of the Articles and preferred their own, older *panchayati* system. The system involved the convening of a committee of at least five to hear evidence and pleas from an entire community, invariably dealing with breaches of custom or occasionally a more serious crime; fines or penalties were imposed through committee discussion and a degree of consensus. The solution that most Indian Army officers favoured was to have a separate system, based on the Articles of War, but tailored to the needs of Indian culture and preference, to enforce discipline.[47] Some officers, like Bartle Frere, the Commissioner of Sind, doubted that the Indian sepoys would understand the Articles and much confusion would result. Christie argued that the Articles actually undermined morale. Nevertheless, Army Headquarters continued to insist on the readings, even going so far as to order prisoners to attend the parades, and special arrangements were made to have the Articles read in the military hospitals too. The oral delivery was essential, the argument ran, in a society where literacy levels were so low. Even in their own vernacular languages, it is estimated that only 15 per cent of the cavalry could read the Articles and about 5 per cent of the Punjab Irregular Force. In other branches of the army the figure was even lower.

A further bone of contention that emerged after the Mutiny was the value of the initial oath on recruitment as a vehicle to ensure lasting loyalty.[48] An oath had been introduced by Army Headquarters in 1840, following a simple statement in order that even uneducated recruits could repeat it and understand it. In 1856, the oath had been altered to include the idea that each sepoy pledged himself to 'general service'. The change had fuelled the existing suspicions in the ranks of the Bengal Army and contributed to the Mutiny the following year, so its inclusion, wording and use were suddenly a subject of intense debate in 1858–9. The officers who commanded irregular cavalry had long ignored the idea of an oath until the army insisted on one being taken. Fortunately, older sowars were exempted because of the anticipated humiliation of experienced men having to take a mere recruit's oath of promised service. Most of the officers doubted its value for men who had served loyally for years in any case, not least because so few could actually remember its wording. Moreover, grievances that emerged during the course of one's service were hardly likely to be tempered by some obscure statement made in one's early career. Where the oaths could serve a purpose, however, was in the courts martial. Tailored to one's religious belief, as Hindu, Muslim or Christian, the oath carried a moral pressure to tell the truth.[49]

The prisoners who had fallen foul of military discipline had originally been held at the regimental level or placed in the work details to conduct hard labour, but by the last quarter of the nineteenth century there was a great deal more interest in the quality of prisons. To improve supervision and detention, a military prison was constructed at Poona, complete with penal staff and drill instructors. Detailed records were kept on the prisoners and their conduct, but also on soldiers who were convicted of lesser offences. These conduct or character sheets were designed to act as an incentive to good order and discipline within the army.

The longest-serving Indian personnel were often the Indian officers, but views about their value were contested. Some British officers felt that, while they had been a valuable source of knowledge and experience, they had failed to warn the British of the impending Mutiny in 1857. Most were prepared to acknowledge they had not actually led any unrest, but they had hardly had any positive effect either. Nevertheless, many had remained loyal and provided good service during the fighting. The question was therefore what degree of responsibility to give these long-serving Indian men. If promoted on merit, there was some concern that the patronage system might be eroded, or even a challenge created for less experienced British officers and therefore the entire legitimacy of British imperial control, based as it was on the assumption that Indians were incapable of modern military leadership and required the British to do so on their behalf. One area that all agreed on was that there should not be examinations or tests as had appeared in the British Army after 1871. Commanding officers wanted to retain the choice themselves of the men who were to become the guardians of the regiment's traditions and supervised the welfare of the younger sepoys. Moreover, their role was seen as specific enough to mean they could not be replaced by British NCOs entirely. The solution appeared to be one that had been adopted by the Punjab Irregular Force, namely a combination of seniority and merit which placed the decision in the hands of the commanding officers. This also meant that, from a disciplinary point of view, the Indian officers would remain subordinate and faithful to the decisions of the commanding officer when it came to punishments and courts martial.[50]

Nevertheless, the sepoys themselves were unhappy about being judged by Indian officers, as a result of which prejudices of family, class, caste, ethnicity or even place of origin would impose themselves. The British officers were regarded as alien and therefore neutral in such matters. But Indian officers were included as representatives in all courts martial after 1877, and in 1895 they were awarded an 'observer status' to ensure, perhaps by conscience alone, there were not excesses or abuses by commanding officers. More remarkably, all regiments permitted the Indian personnel to conduct their own *panchayati* system of justice as long as it covered matters that lay outside the business of the army. Commanding officers did not interfere either in its processes or in its outcomes. The most common punishment these hearings inflicted was a stoppage in pay or some other small financial redistribution.

If a sepoy fell foul of a civil court, the army rather generously stepped in to pay his costs, largely as a measure to demonstrate a reciprocal loyalty. If subject to a civil sentence, the army continued to pay a subsistence salary, not least to keep the sepoy's family alive during the period of punishment.

Even in the military context, sepoys were granted particular measures of leniency. Hard labour or punishment drill could not exceed six hours a day in the hot season, or seven hours in the cold weather. Each drill session could not exceed one hour or a work detail no more than four consecutive hours, with shade provided if the weather was hot. Meals had to be provided regularly and medical care could not be denied if the men fell sick. Even places of detention had to meet certain standards of cleanliness and ventilation, and be sufficiently spacious and safe. Even soldiers who had been subjected to a dietary restriction for their refusal to carry out their duties could not be made to do hard labour as a result. If a sepoy was aggrieved at his treatment by a British officer, the commanding officer could call a court of inquiry. But if the commanding officer was accused, then a sepoy was entitled to make an appeal to the Division. In a court martial, an accused sepoy was permitted to make his defence and to cross-examine witnesses.[51] All these measures amounted to a degree of protection for the Indian soldier.

Equally, the refusal of any sepoy to co-operate with the military judicial system would incur several penalties. After the Mutiny there had been a desire to remove the sepoy's ability to appeal to more senior officers, as it was thought to have undermined the authority of the regimental officers. In the irregular cavalry, since no regular system was ever imposed, there was no desire to have any such measures withdrawn. In regular units, however, commanding officers already had the ability to impose 'Article 70', which, by being an unspecified measure to cover breaches of discipline, could be used for almost any offence. In addition, Article 25 covered 'conduct unbecoming', while wasting the commanding officer's time with spurious or false appeals could carry its own penalties under Article 167. Once again, these measures were not unusual in any army and certainly characterised the regular British Army in the same period. Sepoys were given the choice whether, on having been found guilty of an offence, they wished to appeal or accept the verdict issued by their own officers. This was also the practice in the British Army. In an otherwise excellent study, one Indian historian considers the apparent contradiction of imposing a military judicial system against the sepoys and the desire to retain the powers of the commanding officers to be 'confused'. He deduced: 'On the one hand, they were ready to prevent the commanding officers from becoming too powerful; but on the other, they were afraid that if all the soldiers were backed to the full, it would jeopardise the structure of command.' This is not quite correct. The system that the British employed was not atypical and certainly reflected the discipline they demanded of their own men in the British Army. In this sense it was simply a system that preserved military discipline, creating the best guarantee of soldiers being treated fairly and officers' powers being curbed, while at the same time preventing soldiers from becoming their own 'barrack-room lawyers' and subverting the discipline of the army as a whole. Indeed, compared with other European forces in this period, and given the shock of the Mutiny with all its associated atrocities, what is perhaps more remarkable is how fair the system turned out to be. It is certainly a far cry from the usual accusations that the British Raj was programmed towards brutality and racial discrimination.

Punishment in British African Forces

The use of corporal punishment was gradually regulated in Britain's African forces during the late nineteenth and early twentieth century, reflecting the changes in values in Britain itself, but also the contrasting sense that African military personnel, drawn from a less 'civilised' society, required some forms of corrective discipline that were otherwise obsolete in the United Kingdom.[52] Crucially, however, the slow decline in the application of corporal punishment reflected views held by the British officers themselves that strict discipline was required to prevent excesses and opportunism by their soldiers, especially when on active service. Changes in manpower requirements, the outbreak of the world wars, and then the return to peace in 1945 caused fluctuations in the policy of punishments and sanctions against African soldiers.

Corporal punishment was a standard feature in British schools, colonial schools, prisons (until 1861) and in the African colonies during the nineteenth century. The justification was, in the case of Africans, that more primitive people needed a cheap and efficient form of discipline because they had not experienced the regulating effects of the industrial workplace in Britain, where time, one's location and one's income were controlled. It was widely believed that

Africans felt less pain than Europeans and so a more violent form of correction was more suitable, and there were frequent references to the brutal punishments that existed within African societies and which, therefore, would be understood by the population more readily than any long and confusing criminal justice system. Imprisonment would not be understood, it was argued, and in any case was impractical when commercial and military needs for labour required men to be in the workplace or on the march. As in India, gradual regulation and recording of cases, with medical staff, supervision and eventual abolition, characterised the official use of physical punishment in Africa, although there is anecdotal evidence that illustrates unofficial punishments continued. The changes were the result of pressures from the Colonial Office, which itself was subject to lobbyists calling for reform or abolition, but the War Office itself changed its position in the first half of the twentieth century. Educated West Africans also played their part in reporting cases of abuse, and the publicity of certain incidents elicited condemnation from the Colonial Office. British Army officers in Africa tended to regard this external interference as impractical: their experience was that men drawn from the rural peripheries of the colonies would not behave like Europeans, and that, where there was no supervision by their officers and NCOs, they would seize opportunities for criminal gain. Moreover, without the threat of physical punishment, the levels of desertion or misconduct tended to increase.[53] Accordingly, when physical punishments were reinstated, these levels fell dramatically.

British officers, as elsewhere in the Empire, tended to recruit from rural areas, especially in the peripheries, rather than urban centres, believing that the rural men were inherently more hardy, martial and unsullied by vices. This raw material was assumed to be more suitable for military training, as David Killingray noted: 'loyal aliens served the colonial purpose well, their usefulness often enhanced in official minds by a supposed martial origin'.[54] This was important when the quotas of former slaves and runaways had been used up after the abolition of slavery in the 1830s. The attraction of military service for African men was familiar: regular money, a uniform that conveyed authority and status, meals, and the possibility of illicit gains and the 'spoils of war' on active service. The British believed that raw recruits required between three and six months for basic training in order to make the physical and behavioural transformations that characterised regular soldiers. The new intakes were compelled to take an oath on enlistment, pledging their loyalty from tribe, chieftain and family to the corporate 'army' or an individual officer. Drill, inspections of turnout, 'skill at arms', and maintenance of equipment and vehicles were all orientated towards obedience, discipline and loyalty to a new identity. New medical arrangements and an emphasis on hygiene, reinforced by the African NCOs and their wives, added a social pressure to behave in a more disciplined manner. The wife of the most senior African NCO was herself granted powers to inflict punishment on soldiers' wives who did not conform to a sober and moral code of behaviour. Soldiers' slang, their own language, further reinforced the new identity alongside the badges, accoutrements and association they were given by the British. It is worth repeating that these devices were only coincidental to any construction of colonial power: these were standard approaches to creating any military force, and were the same practices used in the British regular forces. They were used because they were proven to be effective over many generations, and they combined, successfully, the bonds of small unit cohesion and a wider identification with the army, a body apart from the civilian, and the British government. Soldiers regarded themselves as trusted servants, rather more important than the civilians of their own society, and physically superior.

Nevertheless, things did go wrong. The drunken and abusive behaviour of nine men of the Gold Coast Constabulary in 1888 angered locals and led to severe punishment.[55] A march from Bambile to Krachi in West Africa in August 1914, in which British officers could not accompany every part of a long column, led unsupervised soldiers to loot villages and rape local women along the route.[56] The British established a regular pattern of punishments for misconduct, including fines, confinement to barracks, drilling, fatigue duties and imprisonment. Yet, on active service, it was impossible to impose many of these sanctions, and the extreme nature of the situation tended to produce a more severe reaction. Until its abolition in 1908, a decision taken by the West African Frontier Force and subsequently endorsed by the Colonial Office, African soldiers could be flogged (with the 'cat') or whipped with either a rattan cane or a hide whip. The punishments were conducted before the rest of the unit to make an example of the miscreant. During the Asante campaign of 1896, it was ordered that a maximum of 12 lashes could be administered with the 'cat'. It was further laid down that in West Africa soldiers in the Northern Territories of the Gold Coast could receive the maximum of 36 strokes with a whip or cane for stealing, 30 for looting, 25 for insubordination and sleeping on duty, and a minimum of 12 lashes for a number of offences that came under the general category of 'gross neglect'.[57] The Colonial Office nevertheless grew more concerned by the turn of the century with cases of severe punishment that occurred in peacetime. The beating of the nine Gold

Coast Constabulary men in 1888 by an officer known for his excessive temper led to his dismissal. In 1901 it emerged that a mutiny of the Gold Coast contingent of the West African Frontier Force was the result of excessive force. Private Bokara Bawkawa at the subsequent court martial noted of his commanding officer: 'he punish too much and flog plenty'.[58]

In peacetime, physical punishments were therefore tempered after 1908, but African soldiers and British NCOs had their own form of social discipline. If a soldier committed a misdemeanour, his preference was to have it dealt with swiftly and within the ranks if possible. Bringing matters to an officer would have far more serious consequences, physically or financially. As in the British Army, NCOs might take an offending soldier out of sight and give him a beating. This private correction was seen as something that got the issue over and done with more swiftly and lasted a far shorter time than the routine of orders, parades, drilling or possible imprisonment.

During the First World War, with manpower needs at a premium, there was concern in West Africa that the numbers available were falling through desertions, and officers blamed the abolition of physical punishments. By April that year, wartime conditions were imposed, flogging and whipping were reintroduced, and the desertion rate fell steeply.[59] The commanding officer of the Gold Coast Regiment argued that corporal punishment was essential: 'The greatest asset of this type of punishment is that it does not interfere with the training of the soldier ... In twelve weeks discipline is the hardest thing to teach them and this is all too short a period. Rough and ready methods, tempered with justice a native never resents, [contrast with] leniency [which] is a thing they cannot understand ... By no methods can I maintain and teach discipline in the short time at my disposal other than corporal punishment now instituted.'[60]

The return to peace in 1919 meant that the pressure returned for an abolition of all forms of corporal punishment. In the 1920s, hide whips were done away with and physical punishments were officially limited to awards made by courts martial. Unofficially, beatings and lashings continued. However, the outbreak of the Second World War placed all African units under the Army Act, which automatically banned all forms of corporal punishment. When cases occurred during the war, the War Office agreed with the Colonial Office that the practice must be stopped, not least because a fear of punishment was thought to deter recruitment and appeared to be little better than the methods of coercion being condemned as Nazism and Fascism. Even when courts martial in Africa issued instructions about when corrective measures could be used, it aroused strong criticism amongst lobbyists and MPs in Britain.

The advocates continued to point to episodes of indiscipline by African soldiers as reasons for its retention. General Nosworthy, the General Officer Commanding in West Africa, had agreed to end corporal punishment of African soldiers who served overseas, although he advocated its use within Africa to ensure that there were not abuses of the local population. He also noted in 1944, as he toured overseas to visit stations of troops, that he had 'witnessed manifestations of open disorder and indiscipline among West African troops' in the Middle East, which he was convinced would not have arisen 'if the application of corporal punishment had been available in the earlier stages of the trouble'.[61] There were further outbreaks of unrest involving West African soldiers in 1944 at Rabat, in Alexandria, and in Ranchi in India. Nosworthy was not alone in warning that more discipline would need to be imposed if trouble was to be avoided during a prolonged demobilisation, which had been a significant problem even among British troops at the end of the First World War.[62] When the war came to an end, there was clearly a new, more benign political climate about the treatment of Africa, but it was also evident that the end of the war meant there was no longer any need for the wartime measures of punishment that had existed. Therefore, all forms of physical punishment were firmly abolished in 1946.

Breakdown in Discipline: The Mauritius Regiment

In December 1943, discipline in the 1st Battalion, Mauritius Regiment, broke down as it marched into a training camp on Madagascar.[63] While the immediate causes were dissatisfaction with a long route march in hot weather and spartan accommodation, there had been a number of accumulated grievances that led the soldiers to refuse to obey orders. The King's African Rifles were called in to round out the mutinous troops and the battalion was disbanded a few months later. It provides an object lesson in how motivation, regardless of any other standard measures of military discipline, failed and could not be restored, with the consequence that the unit never achieved the status of a combat-worthy battalion.

Mauritius had provided its own Territorial Force before the Second World War and the number of personnel serving in this and other units expanded to over 12,000. Local men filled the ranks of the Coastal Defence Squadron, Home Guard, Mauritian RAF, Royal Pioneer Corps in North Africa and the Civil Labour Corps. The Mauritius Regiment was made up of men not only from the island of that name but of personnel drawn from Diego Garcia and the dependencies of the Indian Ocean. There was some resentment at the expansion and postings to other stations, but the troops were sent to Madagascar to give them some experience of a 'foreign' posting before any thought of further deployment perhaps to India or Burma. The East Africa Command verdict was that they should be given combat training as part of their 'toughening up'. There was some concern that the French elements in the battalion had Vichy sympathies, but the military training was designed to overcome the lingering affiliations held back at home and forge a more robust spirit. The presence of a battalion of the King's African Rifles was also assumed to be a stiffening force that would set a good example for the Mauritius men to follow. Nevertheless, it was the very idea of overseas service that created a mood of resistance among the soldiers. Many felt that only non-whites were being sent abroad to face danger. Others believed they had been tricked out of their Territorial Force or Constabulary status, which implied only home service.[64] Race was a prominent issue in the domestic politics of the island, and was naturally being played out in this recently raised force. The NCOs, for example, were drawn largely from the higher-status Creoles, who to some extent resented the British officers. They also kept themselves separate from Indian personnel in the regiment and regarded them as their inferiors. Worse still, the soldiers themselves were dissatisfied that the British officers received a generous salary while they were given only 'African pay', which, in Mauritian society, was regarded as a term of abuse and inferiority.

British officers and European settlers did not regard Mauritians as 'martial' peoples and there was some concern that arming a portion of the population would lead to trouble.[65] But the consequence was that few thought they were going to do anything useful in the war other than provide garrison troops. Major B.J. Landrock, the commanding officer of the 2nd Battalion, which would remain on the island as a depot or reserve element, admitted that it was hard to sustain morale.[66] Low morale led to acts of indiscipline. Soldiers refused to carry out fatigue work, arguing that they had not enlisted for such tasks. Absconding from barracks was common as well as inventing illnesses, malingering, in order to avoid duty. There was a rise in self-inflicted wounds to avoid being sent overseas. Among the techniques, men would induce eye infections, deliberately infect knee joints with faeces or lacerate the knees, or make numerous and invariably fake claims of backache.

The officers made matters worse. Those called up from civilian work on plantations tended to treat the soldiers with disdain. Local Franco-Mauritian officers were not trusted and relations broke down. The commanding officer of the 1st Battalion was described as a 'tyrant', although, to be fair to him, he was eager to get the soldiers up to a state of war readiness and recognised just how bad the morale and quality of the regiment was. He recognised that there were only six good officers and felt that only the better class of Creoles had any inclination to serve and carry out their duties.[67] Others attributed the feeling of the Mauritian population towards the conflict as the main reason for the lack of enthusiasm: this was, in their view, not their war. One officer believed there was some external propaganda at work too. There was a fear that, if they went overseas, East African men would rape their wives.[68] There seemed to be a widespread fear of the Japanese as ruthless and merciless enemies and the soldiers were afraid they would be used as cannon fodder for the benefit of others. When the 1st Battalion was ordered to embark for Madagascar, they were 'supervised' by the King's African Rifles, but it was evident to all the eyewitnesses that the men did not want to go and believed they were going to be pitched into action against the Japanese. The presence of the African soldiers just made the sentiments worse: there were memories of Zulus having been posted to Mauritius in the First World War, and they had looted shops and attacked islanders. Homesickness set in as the soldiers sailed away.

Morale and discipline collapsed soon after the battalion arrived in Madagascar. Men had fallen out of the march, there was a fire in some of the accommodation, and the men refused to obey orders. Some simply left the camp and set up on the nearest beach. More buildings were set alight and the men refused to parade for physical training the morning after. Some 500 of the 1,000 men present were arrested and were disarmed by the King's African Rifles. Most of the guilty were set to road building and at least 15 were court-martialled. The ringleaders had their death sentences commuted some months later and were given 15 years' imprisonment or a period of hard labour. After the mutiny, efforts were made to reform the regiment, but claims of ill health and low morale persisted. Standards of physical fitness remained low. Some men were transferred to the pioneer corps and new officers brought in from the King's African Rifles. There were significant improvements to accommodation and welfare. There was some improvement in relations between the officers, NCOs and men, and efforts were made to create a sense of purpose with lectures on the war, especially the South East Asian theatre. A group of about 150 men nevertheless remained unreconciled to their position, refusing to carry out their duties, claiming sicknesses and otherwise affecting the rest of the battalion badly. It was proposed that these men should be weeded out and sent home.[69] However, a more effective remedy proved to be sending men found not to have ailments on a succession of long marches, and, if they fell out, were simply ordered to join another one. Despite the measures, sick parades remained extraordinarily large.

To find a solution, it was thought that the regiment should not be considered a front line unit and instead either broken up or reallocated to less physically demanding tasks. It was disbanded in August 1944. Of its personnel, some were retained as a smaller nucleus of one company with a headquarters. There was an implicit threat that further unrest would attract only the strongest reprisals.

Despite all the standard measures for training and developing a battalion, from its highly motivated and understanding officer corps to the provision of regular meals, better-than-average pay and accommodation, the Mauritius Regiment was a failure. The men did not accept the rationale of their enlistment, were bitterly divided on racial grounds, and reluctant to serve overseas. They had made no threat of violence against their officers and NCOs, and had instead withdrawn their labour or exercised a protracted passive resistance. Their situation, on a distant island, was perhaps the only reason for the absence of large-scale desertion.

Discipline and Mutiny

Mutiny is usually associated with a dispute over pay and conditions or the deterioration of relations between the officers or government on one side and the troops on the other. But mutiny is a breakdown in the entire contract, not just as a bureaucratic and pragmatic issue, but as a social contract too.

Restoring a military force to order and discipline is not just a question of improving the terms and conditions of service, but it affects the status of both sides. Unrest exposes the limits of loyalty. The chance of disorder is invariably mitigated by troops that are experienced and engaged in long service, and a sense of cohesion across a unit or army can prevent unrest reaching violent proportions. There can be other cultural influences, including the prevailing social system, that can either enhance or diminish the chance of disorder and protest. Yet, historically, there could be only one remedy to a mutinous regiment and that was its disbandment, even if only a handful were involved. Pay and conditions need to be maintained to acceptable levels, and allowances honoured, but striking for higher pay cannot be tolerated.

After mutiny, states have invariably addressed the discipline of the army, developed the penal system to tackle indiscipline, and ensured that leading personnel were dismissed and punished. In the case of the Mauritius Regiment, clearly there were more significant issues at stake than simply the pay, status and accommodation of the troops. There was a profound sense of unfairness, a feeling that a contract had been imposed or broken from the outset, and a set of prejudices that led to enflamed reactions to even the most standard demands on troops training for war. The authorities' reaction was to call on other units to carry out the arrests of the mutinous troops and to ultimately disband the Mauritius Regiment. At other times authorities have also responded with a more selective recruitment programme, the replacement of officers that may have been the cause of the disputes, and the creation of new roles for the force concerned. It is a reminder that a much wider field of criteria for the assessment of military forces is required, and that some evaluation of the socio-political background, the state of civil–military relations, and the context of a particular conflict all have a part to play.

5

SLAVE SOLDIERS OF THE AMERICAS

The most extreme form of conscription is slavery. While it might seem obvious that such troops are forced to serve and might look to desert at the first opportunity, slave soldiers were a feature of several pre-modern armies and their regiments did not dissolve the moment they had the chance. Indeed, they were, in many cases, exceptional soldiers. The appearance of slave soldiers tells us a great deal about the importance of status, especially that which is generated internally by the troops themselves; it illustrates that status is a relative concept, which might persuade enslaved personnel that they could be in a better position than their non-military counterparts. The fact that their pay was not a critical issue enables us to assess the corresponding importance of discipline, professional pride, and group cohesion. It also gives us the chance to examine a distinct form of military culture and how individuals, in extreme circumstances, are assimilated into a social organisation with a much stronger identity. Military service conveys a sense of strength and solidarity, which would be denied slaves or even free civilians. This chapter illustrates these issues through two examples. The first is the West India Regiment of the British Army and the second is the black regiments of the American Civil War, who were either free volunteers or men in search of liberation.

The West India Regiments

The West India regiments of the British army had their origins in a handful of small corps composed of enslaved and emancipated black soldiers led by British officers. They had originally been formed in 1778 during the American Revolutionary War when, in South Carolina, regiments consisting of white loyalists and free blacks had been raised. When America became independent, the regiment was moved to Jamaica in December 1781 to garrisons at Fort Augusta in Kingston harbour until 1793. In that period white plantation owners viewed the black corps with suspicion and regarded it as a threat to their security, so the unit was moved to the Leeward Islands and formed into a composite formation known as the Black Corps of dragoons, pioneers and artificers. The total strength of the force was just 279 all ranks. The unit was moved again in 1789 to Granada, but, in 1793, when war broke out between Britain and France, the black Carolina Corps took part in a series of operations against the French on the islands of Martinique, St Lucia and Guadeloupe.

The first of the new units was raised in Martinique in 1795. Initially, they were titled with the names of their commanders and known as groups of four or Rangers. The units known as Malcolm's Rangers, Malcolm's Corps or the Royal Rangers participated in the fighting in St Lucia under General Abercrombie. A number of other smaller units were raised but served only so long as the danger existed and included the Carolina Rangers, Dominica Rangers, the Island Rangers (of Martinique), the Black Rangers of Granada, the Tobago Blacks and Angus Black Corps. Only the Carolina Corps, Malcolm's Rangers and St Vincent Rangers received government pay, the others being paid for locally. In 1795 the various corps were amalgamated into regiments of infantry named after their colonels, but they were already known collectively as the West India Regiments of Foot, and they were formed each of eight companies with a total of over 1,000 men per battalion. A troop of cavalry was also raised but this was disbanded again in 1797 because of concerns it would give undue power to black personnel. By 1799 the various corps had been formed into the West India regiments and consisted, at their greatest extent, of twelve separate battalions.[1]

They followed exactly the model of British line infantry regiments, the only difference being the composition of their rank and file. The personnel were initially made up of locally employed slave soldiers and some volunteers. It was decided that the slave soldiers were to be owned rather than leased by the government, mainly to preclude the problem of demobilised soldiers re-entering the labour market with military skills. Initially, local Creole blacks were the favoured personnel as it took imported slaves too long to learn English and basic infantry drill. The army was quite selective in its choice of slaves, choosing those of the best character and health. However, this proved impractical as local plantation owners were unwilling to release their best slaves for military service and there was soon a shortfall in recruits. The army therefore sought slaves from Sierra Leone and the Gold Coast for enlistment into the West India regiments, and these men became the mainstay of the force thereafter.

The purchase of slaves was not cheap and each man cost between £60 and £120. In 1804, some 204 slaves were imported to serve in the 2nd West India Regiment, and, in December that year, 72 slaves were purchased for the 5th West India Regiment in one day.[2] This represented a significant cost. However, despite the initial outlay, one observer noted that black soldiers were better value for money than whites, who tended to fall sick or die in a relatively short period of time. The officer commented: 'every white soldier sent this country [Haiti] cost nearly as much as the price of a Negro, the greater part of the soldiers are rendered unfit for service inside six months ... and must be replaced by others'.[3] The general assessment was that, with smaller pensions and fewer transport and pension costs, black slave soldiers cost only one-sixth of the price of white troops. Until the abolition of the slave trade in 1807, British officers could select the 'finest and best shaped' men to serve in the West India regiments. Each man enlisted was a member of the regular British Army and, as such, they were expected to perform the tasks of any front-line infantry regiment, from garrison duty to the suppression of slave revolts.

The primary advantage of black soldiers was that they were resistant to the diseases that affected white soldiers. They appeared not to suffer from heat in the same way that European soldiers did. One observer noted that 'the British, without the means of being recruited locally, are rapidly diminishing by sickness and mortality which prevails amongst them'.[4] The sickness rate in the Leeward Islands in 1796, without combat, was 33 per cent in British line regiments, but only 3 per cent among black slave soldiers. In Jamaica in 1807, the casualty rate among white regiments was between 8 and 33 per cent, but the corresponding rate for the 2nd West India Regiment was 6 per cent.[5] The contemporary view was that 'in the West Indies the African is in his element; the heat of the noon-day sun, which to the European soldier (clothed in warm regimentals, and burdened with musket and heavy accoutrements) is a source of great annoyance and painful bodily fatigue, is unfelt by him'.[6] It was therefore imperative to raise local troops or to import men more suited to a tropical climate.

In 1799 the Governor of Jamaica believed that 'no material assistance being expected from home, I see no other resource than the raising, in the first instance, a strong Regiment consisting of 1,200 slaves'.[7] The threats of French invasion or the possibility of a slave revolts was so great that 'however respectable the Militia may be ... in times like the present a proper establishment of regular troops is absolutely necessary for our safety'. Black soldiers also relieved white personnel of the unhealthiest missions and garrison duty. In areas prone to fevers or in locations where white soldiers could not be trusted, such as guard duty over rum stores, black soldiers proved more suitable. After the West India regiments had been raised, the death rate among white soldiers fell by 20 per cent, and the overall numbers of white soldiers in the Caribbean fell by 63 per cent, while the number of black soldiers had increased by 59 per cent. The death rate among black soldiers rose by a more modest 4 per cent. The overall strength of the garrison in the West Indies therefore increased with the establishment of the West India regiments.

In 1795 Port-au-Prince was defended entirely by black soldiers. Although the port was important strategically, it had been found that 'English troops are inadequate, for any length of time, the fatigues of long marches and other duties in the field, destructive to European constitutions in the West Indies, but necessary in the present state of the island, whilst, on the other hand, the native troops are better adapted to this mode of warfare than for Garrison service'.[8] General Sir John Moore advocated the use of black soldiers in the interior of the Caribbean islands not only because of their survivability but because of their use in the pursuit of rebel slaves and their ability to return runaways to their estates. As an advocate of light infantry, Moore believed the black soldiers should be considered elite regiments. He wrote: 'they possess, I think, many excellent qualities soldiers, many with proper attention become equal to anything. Even as they are at present they are to the West Indies invaluable.'[9] Other advocates were just as enthusiastic and claims were made that they even required less sleep than European troops and were, in the climate, 'more efficient, contented and healthy'.[10] One Caribbean historian imagined the West India Regiment soldiers to have been 'quite tall and athletic, with redcoats, and, in a line, bristling with steel, their ebony faces gave them a peculiarly warlike appearance'.[11] But the British were also realists and, quite simply, where the climate demanded and, critically, where the French had armed black soldiers, the British felt compelled to follow suit.[12]

Nevertheless, not all were so supportive of arming blacks, either from the perspective of local, internal security or from a strategic point of view. There was also simple prejudice against men who had been rendered into slaves. Vile criticisms made of black troops could also have been made of European soldiers, and the real test was their performance on active service. The 2nd West

India Regiment had been used to cover a retreat on St Vincent in 1796 when engaged by rebel forces. Despite taking heavy casualties, they held firm. In the same operation, alongside other units, they went on to take 700 prisoners.[13] Their real strength, however, was maintaining the numbers required to garrison islands against any potential threat. In 1799, when Honduras was threatened, a garrison of 108 men was available from the original strength of 112, which was considered 'strong additional proof of the excellence of a Corps of colour in the Tropical Climate'.[14]

The soldiers of the West India Regiment developed a strong sense of loyalty through association. Identification with the officers was one aspect of this phenomenon. In 1800, a ship carrying the 2nd West India Regiment foundered on rocks off the coast of Trinidad, and, according to the regiment's history, many officers' lives were saved because their men swam with them and supported them through the heavy surf.[15] According to the historian Roger Buckley, the British were successful in creating a regimental identity and overcoming ethnic and tribal divisions with a new set of loyalties.[16] When new recruits of the 2nd West India Regiment mutinied in 1808 and charged across a parade square to bayonet the officers, the trained soldiers remained fiercely loyal: 'The barrack guard, which had already killed some of the mutineers inside of the fort, was joined by a general rush of the Regiment, enraged by the deaths of their officers, attacked the recruits at once, and notwithstanding that every effort was made to restrain them by their officers, killed nine mutineers on the spot, one other dying shortly afterwards from the effect of wounds—17 in all being killed'.[17] The Commander-in-Chief presented a reward of £5 and a medal to several men for their loyalty. One private, Peter Tracey, although unable to save his officer's life, attacked and killed the assailant, and was himself wounded twice with a bayonet in the effort. In another incident, even verbal insubordination could elicit a fatal defence. When an officer of the 2nd West India Regiment was insulted by a black soldier, the soldiers rallied to the officer's defence and moved to bayonet the offender themselves.[18] Attachments to officers were therefore particularly strong.

Group loyalties, so strongly felt, could present their own difficulties. The corps of Colonial Marines, composed of black Americans, which was deployed against the United States in the War of 1812, refused to be transferred into the West India Regiment, because 'the strong ... prejudices of these men against the West Indian Corps and the high ideas of superiority which they attach to themselves over the African Negroes who chiefly compose these regiments, with which I am sure no inducements could tempt them to indiscriminately mix &

enlist themselves in the same corps'.[19] When a West India Regiment officer was brought in to teach the corps light infantry drill, the men were suspicious that this was another attempt to bring about an amalgamation.[20]

The strength of identity within the various elements of the West India Regiment was all the more remarkable when one considers that the personnel were formed by merging the original members of the black corps, each with its own strong sense of identity, and consisting of purchased local slaves, imported slaves and a handful of volunteers. Moreover, we know from courts martial records that many of the soldiers spoke French and some of their officers were French émigrés.[21] Many of these men had been enlisted in St Domingo (Haiti), had fought for the British against the slave uprising there, and were then formed into the 6th West India Regiment along with loyal French slaves.[22] Roger Buckley notes that the 5th West India Regiment had soldiers from 38 different social groups in the period 1798 to 1808, but because of the common practice of using generalised linguistic or ethnic categories to identify the personnel, it is likely that the men were drawn from an even wider number of communities.[23] It may have been the great diversity of backgrounds that paradoxically enabled the men of the West India regiments to form such strong new identities so readily. That said, racial co-operation appears to have been relatively straightforward. In the Jamaica militia, two-thirds of the force were white, a quarter were mulatto and some 10 per cent black, and the militia had no particular difficulties in terms of cohesion, command or performance.[24] Indeed, it represented the mixed nature of Jamaican society. Edward Braithwaite believes that this mixing, and a common practice of being accompanied by women, made the West India regiments an agent of creolisation that provided 'a not insignificant contribution to social integration'.[25]

The variety of backgrounds among the rank and file of the West India regiments was reflected in the number of languages that the soldiers used. Courts martial papers show that translators were used regularly and in at least one instance an officer could only communicate with his men by hand gestures.[26] Orders appeared in a number of languages and, in the early years, few of the soldiers could speak English. They responded to words of command by sounds, as they did not understand the meaning of the words used. Miscommunication and misunderstanding account for much of the discontent in the first years of the West India Regiment, not least in the difficulties of explaining the terms and conditions of service for the soldiers.[27] The frustration of being unable to communicate led to episodes of disorder and abuse. In 1812, a recruiting station was established on Bunce Island in Sierra Leone which greatly assisted homogenisation, since all those enlisted tended to be drawn from the same area. Within three years, some 700 soldiers were under training on the island. Nevertheless, the creation of a new, entirely military identity, with its rituals and icons, was still more important to the subsequent cohesion of the regiment.

The abolition of slavery meant a sudden transition in the status of the soldiers of the West India Regiment. This caused some confusion. In 1812, 20 men who rebelled against their indenture in Jamaica were sent to England to be impressed into the Royal Navy, but under British law they had to be considered free men and therefore could only be considered voluntary enlistees. Ten of the men subsequently volunteered for the navy and the other half volunteered for the West India Regiment. The naval captain sought clarification as to whether the men were truly volunteers or should be considered as paid 'bounty'.[28]

The new conditions for recruitment meant that, in common with other parts of the British Empire, there was a preference for rural recruits who were 'wholly unacquainted with and uncontaminated by the Vices which prevail among the slaves in the Towns and Plantations, having no acquaintance or connection of any sort, as such as they form in the regiment'.[29] There was an understandable desire to have the regiments drawn from a single background or, as one officer of the 11th West India Regiment put it, 'composed of a particular class or nation'.[30] From experience, officers concluded that certain groups were more suitable than others. Lieutenant Howard of the York Hussars concluded: 'The best Negroes, that is those who have most capacity and are willing to work and learn, are brought from Rada, Mozambique, Congo, Bambara, [and] Cotcolli while those from the Nago and Hibo were intractable and obstreperous.' He criticised the latter as 'extremely sulky on being brought over and those who come over [from Nago] seldom or ever get over it'.[31]

Cohesion was forged by strict discipline. The surgeon of the 11th West India Regiment on Demerara in 1796 observed the 'very rough treatment exhibited towards the recruits by despotic sergeants and corporals of their own colour'.[32] He described a drill session in some detail:

Often when stepping forward to the words 'left, right, left, right', a stout black sergeant suddenly seizes the leg of someone who does not put it forth to his mind, and jerks it on with a force that endangers the dislocation of his hip; when the poor fellow, forgetting that his body must maintain the military square, whatever becomes of his limbs, looks down to see that he steps out better next time; but another sergeant instantly lodges his coarse fist under his chin, and throws back his head with such violence as almost to break his neck ... Then, by some mistake, the right leg advances instead of the left, or the left instead of the right, the remedy for which is a hard kick, or a rough blow upon the shin ... Thus the poor black is beset on all quarters and at all points, and whether standing or moving, feels the weight of the cane, the fist, or some other weapon, upon either his head or his shoulders, his back, shins, knees or naked toes.[33]

The mutiny of the 2nd West India Regiment in 1808 occurred during just such a period of drill. The mutineers, all drawn from the Gold Coast, enjoyed an exceptional common identity. Feeling themselves attacked as a group, their reaction was understandable. Despite the outbreak of violence, many were pardoned and later became NCOs responsible for precisely the kind of training they had objected to while recruits.[34]

Despite the excellent record of loyalty and good service, British officers and white civilians never entirely trusted their black troops. In the Haiti uprising it was noted that mulattos had 'always broken their faith with both parties [rebel and loyalist] and they will ever do so the moment it suits their purpose'.[35] Similarly, black troops ordered to open fire on a rebel chief had refused to obey orders, arguing 'they would not fire on their brethren', and they had given themselves up to the rebels.[36] The French suffered similar acts of disloyalty. A mutinous unit at Port-au-Prince the year before had seized the fort there until overwhelmed by local French troops.[37] The presence of black soldiers did not fill local civilians with confidence. The raising of a new corps in Jamaica in 1795 was feared because the men appeared to have been drawn from Jamaican prisons, and their appearance, according to one eyewitness, 'made us tremble'.[38]

The possibility of mutiny or rebellion meant that limits were placed on the numbers of black troops in the Caribbean. It was decided that there should be no more than one black soldier to two white on any island. Even after the Napoleonic Wars it was felt that it was neither safe nor expedient to rely solely on African soldiers. There was unrest among the soldiers in 1798, 1802 and in 1808.[39] One of small detachments of the 6th West India Regiment was reported to be poorly disciplined because of a long period of isolation. Their offences included the sale of equipment, disobedience and theft. One soldier of the 1st West India Regiment was convicted of concealing women, held against their will, in his quarters. Passive disobedience could also occur. In 1847 one officer joining the West India Regiment was informed by his sergeant major: 'I fear you will have a good deal of trouble with some of the men unless you compromise with them.' In drilling the soldiers, the officer made an error and the men ridiculed him: 'The blacks all burst out laughing, said that this new captain, "he know nothing; he no good; you ride horse at home; let us go back to barracks." And away they all went, shouting with laughter, leaving me and some dozen new officers standing in the middle.'[40]

The quality of officers was a consistent problem for the regiment. Few wished to be posted to the West Indies because of the chance of ill health and the distance from Britain. The command of black soldiers was also unfashionable for many. Some regarded the West India Regiment only as a stepping stone to further promotion, with hopes to obtain a more senior commission through the West India Regiment by purchase before transferring to a line regiment elsewhere in the British Army. Some, having obtained a commission, did not even arrive to join the regiment. In July 1795, 1st West India Regiment had a full complement of officers on paper but few actually present on duty. In 1807, there were still 14 officers absent and this situation was common across other battalions. Those that did join took little interest in their soldiers. Those that stayed on were generally of low quality and unable to obtain a commission in the army elsewhere. Those who finished lowest at Sandhurst were the ones who went into the West India Regiment. In the Caribbean, some fell victim to drink, looked only to find a wife among the plantation community, or sought to otherwise enjoy themselves in the bordellos.[41] A captain found himself the commanding officer of 3rd West India Regiment because his colonel was acting as the brigadier and the only other major available was under arrest pending court martial. Drunkenness was a serious problem amongst the officers, largely through boredom, and at least one officer of 4th West India Regiment died through drinking too much rum.[42] Another officer of the 2nd West India Regiment was accused of withholding £21 from his soldiers. It was not uncommon for officers to be accused of scandalous and disorderly behaviour or for being in a state of extreme intoxication, using indecent language or being drunk on parade.[43] The situation in the militia was bad and sometimes worse. Many militiamen deserted because of a lack of confidence in their officers. Among the offences for which officers were courtmartialled were absence without leave, fighting, making false accusations, disobedience, obtaining property by deception, withholding pay, employing soldiers on private business without pay, attacking soldiers and levying unjust charges on their men.[44] In 1802 an officer of 12th West India Regiment even killed the quartermaster of the 14th Foot in a duel.

Faith in the officers was certainly misplaced during the War of 1812. The 5th West India Regiment took part in the campaign against New Orleans in January 1815. However, 'no attempt was made to furnish the men with warm clothing, and their sufferings from this cause, they being all natives of the tropics, can be better imagined than described'.[45] During the voyage 'the soldiers were obliged to sleep on the deck, exposed to the torrents of rain which fell by day and to the frosts that came on at night'. As a result, 'Many of the wretched Negroes, to who[m] frost and cold were altogether new, fell fast asleep and perished before morning.'[46] An officer of the 95th Rifles who was present noted that the black soldiers 'suffered in consequence of the severe cold ... having nothing but their light and thin West Indian dress to keep it out'.[47] The conditions in the campaign were, however, exceptional. Two white officers the 1st West India Regiment also died from the effects of exposure.

In the regular British Army, NCOs played a key role in enforcing discipline. In the West India regiments the NCOs tended to be the undesirable material that other regiments wished to get rid of. Africans were promoted as NCOs if they had the ability to speak some English rather than for demonstrating their professional competence.[48] Most of the NCOs of the regiment were illiterate.

In action, however, the officers and NCOs of the West India Regiment could exceed all expectations. The 2nd West India Regiment was congratulated for its enthusiasm in 1796 on St Vincent; one officer was presented with a sword of honour by local civilians and a sergeant was commended for courage.[49] The greater demands of leading the regiments of the West India Regiment, caused by the difficulties of language, cultural differences and the sensitivities of working with former slaves, paradoxically produced a better class of leader. Officers and NCOs had to work harder and exhibited 'a great deal of art and management to keep them in the right way'.[50] Fortunately for the officers and NCOs, fewer of the West India Regiment soldiers could desert because of the island nature of their postings. Desertion from military service, perhaps by joining the bands of rebellious slaves, could also produce far greater penalties.[51]

Episodes of misconduct by soldiers of the West India Regiment were far less serious than in the Indian Mutiny of 1857. Despite the fears of civilians, there were no attacks on the population when unrest did occur. Indeed, the soldiers could generally be relied upon to suppress disorder. In 1816 the 1st West India Regiment crushed a rebellion by slaves on Barbados known as Bussa's Revolt. They showed no sympathy with the rebels.[52]

Unlike many British soldiers, most of the men drank with moderation or exercised temperance. The Mandingo, for example, did not drink alcohol. Colonel Hislop regarded the 11th West India Regiment as 'the most orderly, clean and attentive soldiers'.[53] The mutiny of 1802 was the result of excessive provocation. The 8th West India Regiment under Colonel Johnstone, who also served as the Governor, suffered a great deal. Johnstone was guilty of defrauding his men. The soldiers had not been paid for some time. When ordered to drain the marshes on the approaches to the fort he occupied, Johnstone instead purchased the land and used his soldiers to clear it for a plantation. The men were not paid for this work, which Johnstone presented as if it was government duty. Rumours then circulated that the regiment was to be disbanded and the serving troops sold off as plantation slaves. The rumour seemed true when the men were employed as labourers without receiving the standard allowances. There were very few officers to explain the truth of the case. The sudden appearance of two warships in the harbour was widely interpreted as transport ships come to take them into slavery. As a result, the soldiers, fearing the worst, mutinied. In the fighting, some of the officers were killed and three were taken hostage. The fort fell into the hands of the mutineers. Johnstone declared martial law and laid siege to the fort. The mutineers, now realising their situation, agreed to surrender. When the gates were opened, Johnstone marched in with artillery and, instead of instantly disarming them, he berated the men. The mutineers, fearful of retribution, refused to surrender their weapons. This led to an exchange of fire. Some of the mutineers jumped from a cliff into the sea, but several were killed. In the inquiry following the mutiny, Johnstone tried to have his second-in-command court-martialled. When the second-in-command was acquitted, and made a counter-accusation, Johnstone himself stood trial. He too was acquitted, but his reputation was beyond redemption.[54]

The soldiers of the West India Regiment developed a strong sense of group cohesion and identity. Colonel Hislop wrote:

> The new African recruit becomes gradually initiated into the habits of military life, and 'ere long discovers the superiority of his situation above the slave, whose debased state he has never been subject to. He likewise feels himself proportionally elevated, from the rank which his officers hold in society, and the respect which he sees is paid to them.[55]

The black soldier was in one sense a challenge to the strict hierarchy of racial prejudices that existed in the West Indies. Within the regiment, black soldiers could converse with whites on a relatively equitable basis, and certainly in ways that they could not do in civilian life. This was also particularly the case in the Royal Navy. White and black sailors were 'ever on the most amicable terms'.[56] Braithwaite continued: 'This is evidenced in their dealings, and in the mutual confidence and familiarity that never subsist between the slaves and the resident whites. There is a feeling of independence in their intercourse with a sailor, that is otherwise bound up in the consciousness of a bitter restraint, that no kindness can overcome ... In the presence of a sailor, the Negro feels a man.'[57]

In the West India Regiment, one eyewitness observed that black soldiers 'carry themselves proudly, called themselves the "Queen's gentlemen", and looked down with contempt upon the n———s.'[58] Taking the Queen's or the King's shilling as volunteers immediately created a sense of contrast with those who remained slaves. Even when slavery was abolished in 1807, the sense of difference and separate identity remained. Black soldiers would address civilians with the expression: 'me no n———r; me Queen Man'.[59] In 1798, when a force of black pioneers was raised, the authorities were eager that this labouring unit should never be armed since 'it being a known fact that the negro is never of any use in the plantations after they have carried arms'.[60] In other words, being in military service made them feel that they were above hard labour. Military discipline, while strict, still conferred a higher status and was in a sense egalitarian. Ultimately, status was better in the army than as a plantation worker.

Soldiers of the West India Regiment were dressed in the same uniforms as their white counterparts, carried the same weapons and received the same benefits. They were paid according to standard British Army pay scales, although they did not receive the allowances for serving in the Caribbean. In 1797, the daily rate of pay was sixpence.[61] There were, however, problems. Apart from the usual stoppages for uniform and rations, their equipment and arms were often poorly maintained. There were deficiencies in pipe clay and in swords because they could not be exported from Britain. Nevertheless, financial awards could be earned for exemplary service. Provision was also available for the wives and families of men who were incapacitated and injured in service. After 1818, black soldiers of the West India Regiment were permitted to have Chelsea pensions as long as they had proven their good conduct.[62] The pensions represented a significant elevation of status among their contemporaries. The greatest appeal for military service is not merely the pension at the end of a career but the promise of liberty.[63] Unlike plantation workers who could not be sure that they would ever gain their freedom, black soldiers knew that they would receive their liberty as long as they maintained their good conduct record.[64]

It was this promise of liberty that acted as a threat to plantation owners, but there was another reason for their anxieties. Soldiers of the West India

Regiment formed associations with female workers and would often seek to marry them, whereupon they would be lost to the plantation. Nevertheless, some less scrupulous plantation owners would permit female workers to be used for prostitution. Military officers did their best to prevent liaisons that threatened the good conduct and discipline of their soldiers. In Jamaica, officers acquired the support of magistrates that women without signed passports from the masters could be sent to the workhouse.[65] Another solution was for black women to be purchased by the West India Regiment and allowed to marry the best soldiers. Their children would remain with the regiment and the boys became a source of recruitment. Marriage was seen as a reward for the better soldiers and there were severe punishments for adultery.[66] As many as six wives were permitted per company 'on the strength', and if men were dispatched on active service any additional women were left behind. The same practice was applied to the British regiments with white soldiers. Rifleman Harris of the 95th Rifles, embarking at Deal for service in Europe, remembered the 'terrible outcry there was amongst the women upon the beach on embarkation, for the allowance of wives was considerably curtailed on this occasion, and the distraction of the poor creatures on parting with their husbands was quite heartrending; some of them clinging to the men so resolutely, that the officers were obliged to give orders to have them separated by force'.[67] The separation from their wives and families was considered unavoidable when war broke out. It was the lot of military families to suffer isolation in wartime.

There was of course an enthusiasm among the soldiers to do their duty in wartime, not least because of the chance of higher pay, greater status and rewards. This mercenary motive tended to inoculate them from the Republican ideology espoused by the rebels on Haiti and raised by the French Revolution. Those units that started to become unreliable on Haiti were locally raised formations and not the regulars of the West India Regiment. The sense of difference from local plantation workers and slaves reinforced the distance between Republicanism and service to the Crown. The soldiers' primary loyalty remained with their regiment and with each other. This sense of internal cohesion was reinforced because black soldiers of the Jamaican militia were barred from becoming cavalry, could not attain ranks higher than that of sergeant, and were otherwise under-represented as NCOs.[68]

Yet the higher status of the West India Regiment rank and file can also be exaggerated. Black soldiers were invariably used on fatigues, placed in labour details or forced to drag heavy guns. They were also used as labourers on long-term military engineering projects. They rarely received the additional pay they would otherwise have got on fatigue duty. If, on campaign, labour battalions were absent, black soldiers were usually used instead. There is evidence to suggest that periodic beatings and the casual contempt of racism were normal. But not all accepted this casual abuse. Sir John Moore wrote: 'I saw no reason why a man should be treated harshly because he was black or of colour; all men were entitled to justice, and they should meet with it from me without distinction or partiality, whether white or black, Republican or royalist.'[69] Moore's education in the Scottish Enlightenment reinforced the view that even enemy soldiers, if 'regimented and in arms, of whatever colour, should be treated as prisoners of war'.[70] One must also place the condescending attitudes of the officer corps in their proper context. British officers regarded West Indian slavery as having little difference from the conditions of English rural workers and, as such, they felt it was perfectly acceptable.

Some forms of equality, especially before the law, were nevertheless beneficial to the troops. Before 1807 and the revision of the Mutiny Act, black soldiers were subjected not only to military law but to the slave laws. This created a legal problem in that a black soldier could not follow orders if it involved action against any white civilian. This was a direct contradiction for any soldier attempting to carry out his duties under orders. The reform of 1807 placed black soldiers on exactly the same legal status as white soldiers. There were objections from white slave owners of the plantations and fears of slave uprisings or unrest among plantation workers. These did not subside throughout the early years of the nineteenth century. The necessity for manpower, the prospect of French invasion, and the possibility of slave insurgencies were sufficient to require the stationing of black soldiers. When the Bahamas presented petitions to the United Kingdom to prevent a black garrison being stationed in the islands, they were ignored on the grounds of necessity.[71] This was mirrored in Jamaica where plantation owners similarly tried to prevent black soldiers becoming the garrison. The government threatened to withdraw all funding to the military in Jamaica, white or black, unless black soldiers were accepted. The Jamaican plantation owners continued to insist the black soldiers should remain subordinate to whites and contested the arming of black men for many years.[72]

Black Troops in the American Civil War

The Europeans constructed ideas about racial difference throughout the nineteenth century, attributing martial prowess to some, but finding contradiction in the desire for subordinate personnel or partners. At the end of the eighteenth century, the British and French had made use of slave soldiers, just as older imperial systems had done, but there were significant challenges to the concept from the beginning of the nineteenth century. While slavery was being discredited as an institution, racial differences were becoming institutionalised. In 1792 black men were barred from joining the United States Army.

If the American Civil War was not caused solely by disputes over slavery, it certainly became of the most seminal issues of the conflict. Some lobbyists in the North wanted to encourage slaves to abscond from the southern plantations to create the dual effect of humanitarian liberation and damage to the economy of the nascent Confederacy. Nevertheless, there were mixed reactions to the idea that black men might serve in the army of the Union. Free black men who formed the First Louisiana Native Guards in New Orleans were described as men of education and property, but there were expressions of disdain in Philadelphia. Recruits had to assemble after dark to avoid the criticism from some sections of the public. In the Confederacy, news that the North would raise black regiments was greeted with outrage. President Jefferson Davis ordered that Federal officers who recruited blacks, such as Major-General David Hunter and General Phelps, be considered outlaws. If captured, these men were not to be held as prisoners of war but detained pending execution. The order was made general on 1 May 1863 when the Confederate Congress passed a resolution on the issue.

The irony was that General Hunter, a long-standing advocate of black emancipation, had begun to recruit enslaved men direct from the plantations of South Carolina in April 1862 without official authorisation. His impatience to form a regiment of trained men led him to impress free blacks alongside the former slaves. He made a proclamation of May 1862 to the effect that, since Georgia, South Carolina and Florida flouted the laws of the Union through rebellion, it was incompatible to tolerate the continuation of their slavery policies with their status, and, as a result he unilaterally declared that slavery was therefore abolished. The proclamation was repudiated immediately by Washington, which was concerned about the need to respect property and retain for itself the sole capacity to make or repeal legislation. Regardless of the politics, Hunter's haste meant his experiment with black units was a failure. Fearful they would be sent as slaves to Cuba, the pressed men were afraid of the military discipline to which they were being subjected. Many deserted, and, when pay was not issued for five months, the remnant was disbanded.

Nevertheless, in 1863, following the passage of the Second Confiscation and Militia Act through Congress, the Federal Secretary for War, Edwin M. Stanton, gave his consent that volunteers of African descent could serve in their own separate corps, and recruiting stations were opened across the Union. The first units were to form were the 54th and 55th Massachusetts Infantry and the 5th Cavalry. There was some derision from white residents of Ohio and Maryland, and the 54th was hissed at by civilians as it marched through Boston. The opinion of the force was generally low, in part due to perceptions of its status as a regiment of slaves, but in fact only 247 had had this background out of a total of 700 men. They were all volunteers and almost half were of mixed descent. This was in contrast to the 1st South Carolina, a regiment entirely of former slaves.

Discipline was an issue that had particular sensitivity for the black regiments. Undue harshness could be seen as a mere extension of the treatment the men had endured as slaves, but the army expected that the black troops would be treated no differently from white soldiers. Colonel T.W. Higginson, who commanded the 1st South Carolina, exhibited a greater tolerance and did not inflict punitive measures. Colonel R.G. Shaw of the 54th Massachusetts took a different approach, insisting on exactly the same range of measures as for any other regiment, including flogging and execution. The soldiers themselves responded equally well to the training, each enjoying the fact that 'For the first time in his life he found himself respected, and entrusted with duties, the proper performance of which he would be held to strict accountability'.

The men clearly had a point to prove. There was a great deal of curiosity about them, and one supporter argued: 'It is not extravagant to say that thousands of strangers who visited the camp were instantly converted by what they saw.'[73] The 'Sunday morning inspections discovered a degree of perfection that received much praise from several regular as well as veteran volunteer officers'. The soldiers were eager to demonstrate that they were the equal of any other, and their dedication to drill and training was exemplary.

That dedication was put to the test in the attack on Fort Wagner. In early July 1863, the first attempt to capture the Confederate fortifications that protected Charleston had ended in failure. Fort Wagner on Morris Island was to be subjected to a second assault on 18 July. The task was particularly difficult because the only approach that could be made to the fort was across a narrow neck of land that was swept by entrenched artillery and rifle fire, and the frontage allowed only one regiment at a time to make an attack. Despite a preliminary bombardment, the Confederate garrison was protected by deep and revetted shelters and the 54th, which was selected to lead the attack, had to do so against a position unaffected by any covering fire. The Federal bombardment was delivered to within 200 yards of the first wave in the hope of keeping the Confederates pinned down, but the garrison held its fire until the 54th were within point-blank range. The result was carnage, but the survivors managed to reach the parapet, engaged in hand-to-hand fighting and held the south-east corner for an hour. The second and third wave of attackers met a similar fate, but they could not reinforce or relieve the now stranded first wave. The Confederates, desperate to recover the lost section of the fort, threw everything at the remnants of the 54th and the handful of troops from the 6th Connecticut that had lodged themselves. Improvised explosives, pikes, bayonets and volleys of rifle fire gradually killed off the remaining attackers. Colonel Shaw, who had been just 26 years old, was killed, and 13 other officers were either killed or wounded out of 22. Of the original 650 soldiers, 255 were killed or wounded. Some 20 men were taken prisoner in the fort. Shaw's body was buried without military honours by the Confederates in the same mass grave as the soldiers, which, although intended as a slight, was probably what Shaw himself would have preferred.

Despite proving their worth, the black soldiers were not granted the same pay as whites, contrary to assurances on enlistment. The rate for most troops was $13 a month, but the black soldiers were offered just half that amount.[74] The state authorities of Massachusetts agreed to make good the shortfall, but the troops refused, arguing that they were employed by the Union and not the state. It was a matter of principle, and the men showed a strong loyalty to each other in that not a single one accepted the additional cash on offer. The men refused all pay until the full amount was issued. The results were protracted and involved a great deal of hardship, especially for their families. The 55th Regiment went further one morning and piled arms, refusing to soldier. They appealed to their officers, arguing they would rather be marched out of camp and shot dead than endure further humiliation regarding their pay.[75] Similar tactics were adopted by the 3rd Carolina. Yet here, a sergeant who had ordered the men to lay down their arms, was court martialled under the articles of war, and shot. For months, the troops were paraded for pay and each time they refused. The 54th received no pay whatsoever for 18 months in total. Finally, the Federal authorities relented and paid the soldiers, but only if they swore an oath that they had been free on the date of enlistment. Those that had officially been slaves, but had escaped the plantations of the South, were not granted the concession.

The value of the black soldiers in the war was remarked upon by several sympathetic commentators. Contemporaries believed the black soldiers to be more timorous but as a result more biddable than the whites. They believed them 'less skilful' but suitable for siege operations. There was universal acceptance of the idea that 'the black will do a greater amount of work than the white soldier, because he labours more constantly'. While it was said they displayed less urgency, they could not be hurried in their work even when faced with danger. Sickness rates were also lower, with 13.9 per cent of black troops and 20 per cent for whites during the siege at Charleston.[76]

The verdict was that 'they have not the will, audacity, or fertility of excuse of the straggling white, and at the same time they have not the heroic nervous energy or vivid perception of the white, who stands firm or presses forward'. Instead, the black soldiers were praised for their ability to stick at a task or duty, however difficult: 'to stay, to endure, to resist, to follow, to work patiently, doggedly, to obey orders, never to skulk, or to desert their officers in trying moments'.[77] These qualities meant that 'engineers clamoured for details of black troops'. The willingness of the black regiments to take casualties, to prove their worth, was significant and not just in the siege of Charleston. At the Battle of Olustee (20 February 1864), the 8th Colored Infantry suffered losses of 310 killed, wounded and missing, which was among the highest losses of any regiment in the conflict.[78] At the Battle of the Crater (30 July 1864), another Federal setback, the Union attack was checked and the survivors were compelled to surrender. Although the white troops were spared, the black soldiers were summarily executed. Treatment of black prisoners was generally far worse than that of whites, but conditions for both were often appalling.[79]

Despite the losses and the constant engagements, there were some 145 regiments of infantry, 7 cavalry regiments, 12 heavy batteries, 1 light battery and 1 engineer unit which consisted of black and coloured soldiers. A third of these saw action, and the losses suffered totalled 143 white officers and 2,751 black men.

Towards the end of the war, the Confederacy, urged on by Robert E. Lee who desperately needed the manpower, authorised the conscription of black men to form regiments. They decided that no more than 25 per cent of eligible men between the ages of 18 and 45 should be called up, but the measure was so delayed that the war was concluded before the troops were mustered. The Southerners who advocated the measure hoped that this would create a sense of national unity for the Confederacy, but the vested interests against the scheme far outnumbered them. In the North, some 179,000 black men had served in the Federal forces during the war, equating to about 10 per cent of the entire army, with a further 19,000 in the US Navy. Some 40,000 died in the conflict, but three-quarters of these losses were from sickness and disease, a ratio equivalent to white personnel. About 80 black men were commissioned as officers, and 16 received the Medal of Honor.

After the war, black regiments became part of the permanent establishment of the United States Army. In 1866, there were six regiments, and in the scaling down of the entire army in 1869, two black infantry and two black cavalry regiments were retained, known later by their more familiar nickname of 'Buffalo Soldiers.'

Indigenous First American men also provided scouts for the army during the expansion into the West. Apache Amerindians served as scouts for General Crook in operations in Arizona in 1872 and 1873. He also used Crows in the pursuit of Sitting Bull after the defeat of General Custer in 1876.

The westward expansion continued across the Pacific. In Luzon in the Philippines, General Frederick Funston established the Headquarters Scouts, which were both an intelligence-gathering and strike force. They disguised themselves as peasants and ambushed insurgent roadblocks that had been set up to collect taxes, and they lost no opportunities to exact revenge against their rivals, the Tagalogs.[80] Nevertheless, the United States Army, which made use of the Macabebes, the local Philippine cavalry from the Ilocano population, were embarrassed by the brutal reputation of these forces against Tagalog prisoners and civilians.

Despite these experiences, there was generally an American aversion to the use of locals in scouting and intelligence work because it was so difficult to know who could be trusted if they were not subject to Western standards of discipline and training. On the other hand, enthusiasts like Crook believed that local scouts could sow dissent among the enemy. In the pursuit of Geronimo, he stated: 'It is not merely a question of catching them better with Indians, but of a broader and more enduring pain—their disintegration.'[81]

Compulsion and Motivation

Despite problems in leadership and management, the West India Regiment produced a relatively disciplined force which served its strategic purpose of defending the islands of the Caribbean. Under conditions which killed off large numbers of white troops through sickness, the employment of more resilient black labour was a purely practical response. Moreover, when the

French set about arming blacks as soldiers elsewhere in the Caribbean, the British were quick to adopt similar measures.

The officers were of a particularly low quality and the regiments were more dependent on the corps of NCOs to maintain discipline and effectiveness. There was a strong positive appeal in military service, despite the status of the troops, since life in a regiment was more benign and carried a greater esteem than the conditions facing the plantation workers. There were also opportunities for higher pay, rewards and recognition, and, of course, liberation on completion of service.

The selection of the soldiers was by race, and the penal-disciplinary system they were subjected to was severe, but this did not appear to have a detrimental effect on their status or morale. The soldiers enjoyed a cohesiveness, generated internally, and a sense of superior status over their civilian counterparts, regardless of strict discipline and the occasional abuses by their superiors. They possessed a strong sense of identity and military purpose which allowed them to absorb the worst of their treatment. They expressed little sympathy for their fellow blacks in the islands, particularly those in positions of slavery. Their primary loyalty was with each other and the regiments they belonged to. They followed their officers with loyalty because these officers were the symbols of their regiment and of their future good conduct. This could bring its rewards, but perhaps it is not an exaggeration to say that the greatest reward was the sense of identity and cohesiveness itself. This case suggests that conditions and appeal are relative to the social, economic and political situation around a group or an individual. Even conscripted personnel, subjected to tough conditions and fierce discipline, can emerge as competent and effective soldiers. They can even do so when the quality of officers is very low indeed.

The black regiments of the American Civil War create some parallels with the West India case, but also some distinctions. The soldiers generated a significant internal cohesion, enduring a prolonged period without pay in order to assert their equal status to the rest of the army. Their terms and conditions of service were relatively benign, compared with the position of civilians of the same age and background. The system of discipline and punishment was no different from their white counterparts, which was also the case for the West India Regiment. Black soldiers in the Civil War nevertheless developed a particular pride in their service, and it was this sense of mission, devotion and cohesiveness that permitted them to endure the very high casualties they suffered in actions such as the Battle of Fort Wagner. During the war, and indeed after it, they developed a new military culture of their own.

6

ARMIES OF EMPIRE

In 1896, Charles Edward Callwell published a handbook on colonial warfare entitled *Small Wars: Their Principles and Practice* and in it he identified seven types of adversaries that the British and other European powers had faced during the expansion of their empires between the 1830s and the 1890s. The first category was of those who had been 'trained as Europeans' and the second were organised troops from developed societies, such as China and Algeria. The third were organised forces armed with primitive weapons, which were exemplified by the Zulus. The fourth were styled as 'fanatics'. The fifth were actual European enemies, such as the Boers, while the sixth, using similar tactics to the Afrikaner-speaking fighters, were guerrillas, such as the Xhosa of southern Africa and the Maori of New Zealand. The final category was irregular cavalry, such as Mahrattas and Arab horsemen. Callwell's list reflected the diversity of the resistance the Europeans had faced, but his categories were inconsistent and unscientific. It was unclear whether he was really describing fighting methods, levels of development, regional variation, prejudices based on ethnicity, or tactics forced upon fighters by overwhelming European firepower.

European and American expansion had brought vast swathes of territory under control. From small bridgeheads on the coasts of Africa and Asia, and the eastern seaboard of North America, most regions of Africa, South and East Asia, and the Pacific were annexed by the Western powers. Russia extended its control of Central and East Asia, while the United States colonised the western territories and parts of the Pacific. The Western powers used their large oceanic fleets to transport their armies, their financial organisation to sustain their campaigns, and, by the late nineteenth century, their superior weapons technology to project their power.

But there were always two recurrent problems: an acute shortage of manpower and a constant need to minimise the costs of expansion. Most colonial campaigns in Africa and Asia were fought by Europeans who were accompanied by large numbers of local auxiliaries. In the British campaigns in India in the nineteenth century, Asian troops on the British side tended to outnumber European personnel. Manpower shortages remained acute for the British throughout the nineteenth century. In the period between 1819 and 1828 the British Army had just 47,000 men in the United Kingdom and 53,000 overseas. While the annual mortality in Britain among the troops was 1.5 per cent, overseas the death rate was 5.7 per cent and, as such, was twice as high as that of men of the same age in civilian employment.[1] To meet the demands for personnel and the challenges of the geography, specialist local units were raised, particularly where there were distinctive requirements caused by mountainous or forested terrain, or if there were large distances to navigate.

The costs of imperial expansion were important in determining the type of military forces that were selected. French taxpayers could be reassured that the cost of empire was reduced by employing cheap native troops. Colonial wars, while expensive, could be made less onerous when resources were available after conquest or, as in the case of China, the defeated power could be made to pay. Even so, limits were placed on the size of military forces by governments. The Indian Mutiny had cost £28.7 million; the Second Anglo-Afghan War of 1879–81 cost £23.4 million; Abyssinia, which had required a force of 12,000 troops in 1868, cost £9 million; the Sudan (1884–5) had required 26,000 men but cost £7.3 million. The Second China War, the occupation of Egypt, and the Zulu War had each cost around £4 million. The two Maori wars in the 1860s cost £700,000, while the Asante campaign of 1873 cost £661,000.[2] One cost-saving feature of the colonial wars of the late nineteenth century was technological superiority, which reduced manpower demands. However, forces that resisted the Europeans could also acquire better weapons by the end of the century. In the Pathan uprising of 1897, the hill fighters possessed breech-loading magazine rifles. The arms trade became an issue of strategic importance. The import of weapons into Somaliland, for example, was considered very serious from a security point of view.[3]

Bold, destructive campaigns that inflicted maximum casualties on any resistance at the outset were thought preferable, for the simple reason that Europeans wanted to avoid protracted guerrilla wars in which manpower demands were always higher, and, on the whole, there were few capital cities to capture to conclude the wars in a Western style. The Europeans were almost invariably on the offensive, but short-term defensive actions were accompanied by a great deal of anxiety and eagerness to return to the offensive so as to retain the initiative. Moreover, the presence of local forces frequently raised questions of their reliability, willingness to engage an adversary, and fighting prowess. Nevertheless, it was possible to raise local forces that were perhaps familiar with the tactics and fighting styles of those fighting the Europeans, and who knew the territory. While scouts were useful, they tended to be limited in number, and irregular auxiliaries always ran the risk of getting out of the Europeans' control.

A loss of control could prove operationally disastrous. Asian, African and North Americans could, at times, exploit tactical errors made by Western forces or neutralise the local levies the Europeans had employed. A largely conventional Afghan army defeated an outnumbered British brigade at Maiwand in 1880 by using local superiority in numbers, modern European artillery, and envelopment of a badly sited position that had not been reconnoitred. But locally raised troops accompanying the British broke and fled, which proved catastrophic to the entire defence. Local troops had proved to be very unreliable in a previous engagement on the Helmand River just a few days before, firing over the heads of their supposed enemies, while horsemen, ostensibly on the British side, tried to seize and ride off with a battery of British guns. Indeed, the British commander had embarked on his bold and offensive manoeuvre in part because he believed, as many contemporaries did, that bold action would steady and encourage his wavering local allies.

Abuse of civilians remained a particular concern when indigenous troops got out of control. Racial prejudice made the acquisition or rape of native women by Europeans gradually less likely in the nineteenth century, but Indian troops still regarded women as a form of booty. When Canton was overrun in 1842, local Chinese complained of the molestation of women by Indian troops.[4] The French nevertheless rewarded their Senegalese soldiers with captured women and nicknamed them *épouses libres* (free spouses).[5] Theft and looting were particularly prevalent among the camp followers accompanying the European armies and their auxiliaries, but when licence had not been given for such activity, the authorities did their best to control it by occasionally flogging or hanging the worst offenders.

In the interior of Africa, where railway networks did not exist and navigation by river was sometimes limited, the Europeans were confronted with all

147

the problems associated with moving their forces and their logistics (much of it wheeled and horse-drawn) across mountain, desert, or densely vegetated terrain with no infrastructure. In Indochina, artillery had to be dismantled and carried in parts on bamboo supports. These topographic obstacles and the great distances involved made it even more imperative to hire local labour either as auxiliary military forces or to porter loads of supplies. It also made decisive military operations imperative, because protraction was too expensive to sustain. Boldness and resolution by commanders of small detachments were considered crucial, and this explains the actions of officers such as Mikhail Skobelev in Russian Central Asia or General Custer at the Little Big Horn in 1876. Moreover, passive defence or hesitation was considered 'fateful to the morale of the troops', especially native forces.[6] Nevertheless, offensive spirit did not replace the importance of tactics in modern warfare. Officers in India, while encouraged to be on the offensive, would also attack economically, taking whatever cover was offered, advancing only in open, skirmish order, and placing the emphasis on winning a firefight. Volley fire was replaced with individual marksmanship and fieldcraft became the norm. Furthermore, while entrenchments were discouraged as fixing an army, it was standard practice to construct earthen defences even for temporary encampments on the North West Frontier of India and light field obstacles, such as *zaribas* of thorn hedge, were used to protect colonial forces in Sudan.

The reasons for local enlistment into these advanced Western forces are not difficult to ascertain, for, in general terms, they are universal. Regular pay, a system of rewards, and the possibility of health improvements, welfare benefits and better living conditions for oneself and one's family all featured in the appeal, but so too did the attachment to charismatic and highly competent officers, and there might be a variety of local push and pull factors, such as the encouragement of elders or elites, a background of misdemeanours in the community, or rivalry with others in the region of origin.

The pool of labour in India was so vast that the British were able to recruit entirely new levies even after the disaster of the Indian Mutiny. The ability to raise such a large force and to reconstruct the Indian Army so readily after the Mutiny gave rise to theories that the British, by race, must possess some special attributes that fitted them for the natural role of governance. The contemporary historian G.B. Malleson accounted for it all in simplistic terms: 'It was a question of race.'[7] Race and class were reflected in the construction of the Indian Army after 1859, however flawed their judgements may have been. Mixed-class regiments, with companies drawn from different communities, created unity of identity while retaining small-unit solidarity and cohesion; a blend of competitive spirit and regimental cohesion. The soldiers embraced many of the attributes with which they were associated. In seeking to explain why the small detachments of 36th Sikhs had held out at Saragarhi and had been killed in the defence of that post, a Sikh soldier concluded: 'Surrender is a word we do not know or use.'[8]

There was, however, no universal, 'one-size-fits-all' approach for success. The British struggled to replicate their Indian recruiting processes in Burma. The Burmese were divided by ethnicity, geography and culture, but the British had their own reasons for selecting, or not, particular communities. The Burmans were considered 'intelligent and attractive, but temperamentally unsuited to the strictness and regularity of army life'.[9] The British found them to be like many educated Bengalis: too problematic to serve quiescently in the army. The Shans were thought 'too simple and peaceable'.[10] The Christians of the south-east, near Rangoon, were unenthusiastic about military life. Some Karens were recruited, but the majority that were taken into service were Kachins and Western Chins, perhaps because they reminded the British of the Gurkhas. The fact that these men were drawn from the periphery gave greater confidence that they would be willing to enforce internal security. However, the pacification of Burma also relied on Indian troops. One officer mused: 'How long would it have taken to subjugate and pacify Burma if we had not been able to get the help of the fighting men from India, and what would have been the cost in men and money?'[11]

Men were selected from among indigenous populations if they already had a reputation for fighting prowess. In the Dutch East Indies, where climate and disease could take their toll on the small European forces available, native troops were essential. One French officer in Dutch service believed the Macassars and Boughis were the best fighting men. They were 'curious and often irresistible'. The Macassars coated their swords with poison and had a ruthless reputation. The Boughis were tall and muscular, with a reputation of mercenary service across East Asia, and were regarded as 'faithful as well as courageous'.[12]

There were similar approaches in the hiring of indigenous personnel in Africa. When General Wolseley was tasked to pacify the Asante in a punitive mission in 1873, his well-equipped British force was accompanied by local levies known as the Hausa, a peasant population that had been formerly subjugated by the Muslim Fulani Empire. Two native regiments in Wolseley's order of battle consisted of large numbers of Hausa; paradoxically, his enemies, the Asante, had also enlisted a Hausa corps. Nevertheless, the British found it difficult to acquire native forces where labour was more scarce in the south of the continent. A relatively small formation raised to fight in the Zulu War, the Natal Native Contingent, was hardly a front-line force. Many of the troopers enlisted in order to avoid tax, it had little equipment, the officers and NCOs were of low quality, and not all were British. In action some of its men deserted.

Belief and culture, as well as unit cohesion, could have a significant effect on the ability of an indigenous force to perform well in action or even to remain intact. Callwell, in his handbook of colonial warfare, remarked that night attacks by African and Asian forces were surprisingly rare.[13] He offered no explanation, but the darkness and the associated powers of evil were quite likely the cause. In East Africa, the Germans found it difficult to compel their soldiers to carry out night marches because the Askaris and porters were terrified of ghosts.

Religious belief both hindered and assisted European armies. Christian converts were accused of being a 'fifth column' by the Chinese Boxers in 1900, and Christian Indians sided with the British during the Mutiny of 1857. The Natal Native Horse in British service were Zulu or Swazi converts to Christianity. In the Dutch East Indies, the Amboinese were Christians and provided both soldiers and native police. Christian converts also assisted the French occupation of Indochina. On the other hand, it was widely believed in India that the presence of chaplains and priests had persuaded British officers to give up taking Indian wives and drove the British and Indians apart. Christians could also sustain resistance to imperial expansion.[14] Religious difference was a particular problem when more and more Muslim soldiers were employed by the Christian Europeans in their colonial armies. There was also the question of how this would affect the reliability and loyalty of troops if they faced a Muslim enemy. In Somaliland, the reputation of the mullah who led resistance at the turn of the century filled the British auxiliaries with 'a superstitious awe, [there was a] growing belief that the mullah was immortal'.[15] Religious rituals were therefore tolerated and even encouraged. Hindu priests would bless regimental colours in India with British officers present; and British officers would also preside over the animal sacrifices that were common in Gurkha regiments. Indian regiments were accompanied by Hindu, Muslim and Sikh holy men to encourage their martial ardour or to attend them in matters of welfare.[16]

The beliefs of the Zulus, while often misunderstood by European contemporaries, were thought in part to account for the courage of their warriors. Europeans looked upon them as not unlike the Highlanders of an earlier epoch and thought they had the potential to become 'among the bravest soldiers of the Empire'.[17] There were concerns, however, that indigenous populations, even in military service, might revert to their 'natural' state. This would include various forms of licentiousness and depravity, intrigue and treachery, and therefore represent a threat to settlers, especially women, and to the security and fabric of the Empire.[18] Indigenous adversaries had no knowledge of or respect for Western rules of engagement that had been developed in an entirely different context. Abuses of flags of truce, the murder of prisoners or the butchering of the wounded or of civilians were the usual subjects of condemnation.[19] Burmese guerrillas or bandits, for example, would frequently crucify captives and set them alight.[20] A long list of atrocities featured in the arguments to justify the use of Maxim machine guns, dum-dum ammunition and later air policing.[21] They had another effect. Atrocities convinced the European officers that native peoples needed firm government and, where necessary, coercion. When General Kitchener reconquered the Sudan in 1898 he made use of forced labour, while his insistence on flogging and occasional hanging were criticised in Cairo.[22] Yet, to Kitchener, these draconian measures seemed absolutely necessary to enforce discipline and ensure control.

European junior officers embarking on colonial service had impressed upon them the absolute importance of firmness, control and confident command. British authorities frequently referred to the importance of prestige and 'bearing'. Actions which might damage the esteem of whites were to be avoided, and could even extend to other European nationalities, so that, at least in some quarters, racial solidarity was supposed to be a higher priority than national interest. One observer wrote that, in the East, 'defeat—and everyone deserts'.[23] Britain's Governor General of India in 1847, Lord Hardinge, believed that any military setback would 'vibrate throughout India; aye, through Asia … Every skirmish against our arms with the Caffres is joyously proclaimed in the native press.'[24] Military officers were eager to avenge the death of General Gordon in 1885 because it was widely believed that Muslims would be celebrating 'in every bizarre from Cairo to Calcutta and central Asia'.[25] There was anxiety about bazaar gossip and rumours which might mobilise indigenous populations against European governments.[26]

The reputation of particular officers was thought not only to ensure a loyal following from native soldiers, but to enhance prestige to the point where local populations would be deterred from resistance. The Governor General of India, the Marquess of Dalhousie, believed the names of Hodson and Nicholson 'cowed whole provinces'.[27] After the First Anglo-Afghan War, the

Duke of Wellington had urged the authorities of India to avenge the retreat from Kabul in order to uphold British prestige in the East. On 31 March 1842, the Duke of Wellington had written to the Governor General: 'It is impossible to impress upon you too strongly the Notion of the importance of the Restoration of Reputation in the East.'[28] Callwell urged his readers that the way to handle Asiatics was to 'cow them by sheer force of will'.[29] All European officers were urged to act with resolution and not to hold back with military force in the early stages of the operation: 'uncivilised races attributed leniency to timidity', wrote Callwell, 'Fanatics and savages must be thoroughly brought to book and cowed' or they will rise again.[30] Sir Harry Johnston in Africa thought the Dutch and Germans had the measure of their native populations: 'On first contact with native races they are apt to be harsh and even brutal, but this wins them the respect of Asians and Africans, who admire rude strength.'[31]

Nevertheless, British officers were often at pains to prevent massacres and excessive actions, lest it 'exasperate' the local populations and generate protracted resistance. In 1893, when the fort at Nilt on the northern frontier of India was stormed and captured, the officers prevented Gurkha, Dogras and Pathan soldiers from killing the entire garrison in revenge for the own casualties. The storming of defended locations, such as forts and towns, had always been costlier, and, in the European context, it was an accepted principle that if a defended settlement or fortress refused to surrender, then it could expect to be sacked if overrun. The same principle was transferred to Asia and Africa. At Bougie in Algeria in 1832 three days of street fighting were concluded by indiscriminate slaughter at French hands. After suffering heavy casualties in the battles of the Anglo-Sikh wars, and seeing the European regiments exacting a fearful retaliation, the Indian troops joined in the retribution. The destruction of a fleeing adversary was not only the result of anger at having suffered heavy casualties in an advance to contact; it could also be a calculated decision to prevent a far more numerous enemy from rallying and becoming a threat in the future. Inflicting heavy casualties upon an enemy would act as a deterrent to future resistance. As a result, in the retribution after the Indian Mutiny in 1857, Sikh soldiers were given licence to make an example of Fatehpur.[32] In 1886, in Indochina, local auxiliaries, accompanied by some regular troops, were sent into the two provinces by the French authorities to subjugate resistance by merciless repression.[33] In southern Africa, the local Fingo (Mfengu) auxiliaries were eager to exact their own revenge against the Xhosa who had long oppressed them: British officers could not prevent them from murdering prisoners except by physically restraining them and placing a number under arrest.[34] The French found the hill men of central Vietnam, the Montagnards, content to make war on the people of the plains, a process they entitled the *politique des races*. The selection of one ethnic group or community as allies against the majority was an efficient form of governance for imperial authorities and was used by the British in Uganda after 1895, by the French in West Africa, and by the Americans in the Philippines. Gilbert Murray nevertheless criticised the 'continual employment of uniformed savages liable to lead British warfare, in various unmentionable details, rather too close to that of savages without uniform.'[35]

Once in the service of Europeans, there was another set of compelling features that tended to encourage retention among indigenous personnel. The cohesion wrought by training, or even by association with young men of the same background, could be enough to form bonds not easily broken. Fierce discipline in European-led armies was also common. Flogging for minor infractions was not uncommon in most armies, for European as well as local personnel.[36] Campaigning was the greatest test of cohesion and the most likely, if the unit endured, to create the strongest personal links. In the Second Sikh War, a British regiment passed through the camp of the 72nd Native Infantry, halted and 'gave lusty cheers', for, as one of the private soldiers recorded: 'This Regiment had fought gallantly by our side, and would face a forlorn hope cheerfully with us.'[37] In the storming of the heights at Charasiab near Kabul in 1879, the 72nd Highlanders and the 5th Gurkhas went into action together and there was mutual admiration for the physical courage shown against numerically superior numbers of Afghans.[38] General Roberts recorded: 'The 72nd and the 5th Gurkhas had been much associated from the commencement of the campaign, and a spirit of camaraderie had sprung up between them, resulting in the Highlanders now coming forward and insisting on making over their greatcoats to the little Gurkhas for the night—a very strong proof of their friendship, for in Kabul in October the nights are bitterly cold.'[39] The attachment of the hill soldiers of Nepal exemplifies the links between the Europeans and their Asian or African military forces.

The Gurkhas

The Gurkhas were a distinctive force within the British military system. Drawn from the independent Kingdom of Nepal, the troops were mercenaries in British service, but defenders of the Gurkhas are always quick to point out that, despite the rather brutal simplicity of the contract, there developed a long-standing affinity and mutual respect between the British and the Nepali riflemen. Critics argue that the Gurkha–British relationship owes a great deal more to sentimental myth than the hard financial reality of the case. Nevertheless, seeing it all as a simple labour contract fails to capture either the nature of the association or the reason for its longevity. Given the difficult beginnings of the link, the strength of the bond, contractual or otherwise, is even more remarkable.

The Anglo-Nepalese War of 1814–16, fought over territorial control of the borders between the Kingdom of Nepal and the East India Company, had been characterised by hard fighting. Deserters from the Company army had assisted the Nepalese with preparation and training prior to the war, but during the campaign Nepalese deserters had been formed into corps of irregulars to fight for the British. It was these, and the resistance the British had encountered, that persuaded Colonel (later Major General) David Ochterlony and the British Political Agent, William Fraser, to raise a unit on a permanent footing.

The Nepalese were, of course, not a united people at the time of the British expansion. There were ethnic and hierarchical divisions and the relative status of certain groups was disputed. The generally accepted explanation was that Rajput refugees displaced by Muslim invasions of South Asia around AD 1300 eventually intermarried with local hill clans, but there was some preservation of the Hindu caste divisions of Brahmans (priestly class), Kshatriyas (warriors), Vaishya (merchants) and Sudra (workers and outcaste). The warrior descendants were subdivided into Chhetris (nicknamed Khas), Tagadharis and Matwalis. The Rajah of Gorkha, an impoverished hill state chieftain, was successful in the eighteenth century in forming an army not confined to the strict caste divisions of his forebears, and he recruited from Gurungs and Magars, a middle group of yeomen, as well.[40] To motivate his army, every man was paid according to his land holding, which fuelled expansionism. The need to pay the troops resulted in more conquests, which in many ways mirrored the dilemma faced by the East India Company. Not only was the Kathmandu Valley sought after, but so was the Terai, the forested plain below the foothills of the Himalayas. Nevertheless, poverty was endemic in the rural areas of Nepal and those that fell on particular hardship looked to military service as a form of income. The alternative was to fall into a system of internal slavery.

The British had originally been called to halt the southern advance of the Gorkhas as early as 1767, but the small brigade under Captain Kinloch was decimated by malaria. The Nepalese were checked in their expansion by the

Chinese, which sent an army that almost reached Kathmandu in 1792, and then by the more determined efforts of the East India Company. The Nepalese tried to play both sides off against each other, and appealed to the Chinese for military assistance in 1816, but without effect. Political infighting made the Nepali state, such as it was, unstable. There was nevertheless considerable faith in the inviolate nature of the mountain state. For generations, the chieftains had raided those settled people for revenue, trusting to the remoteness of their hill fortresses to defy their enemies. The East India Company was not so easily deterred and it had dispatched four large columns, mainly of Indian personnel, into Nepal. The advantages for the Gorkhas were that they had over twenty years' experience of constant fighting to draw on and a wealth of knowledge of their own mountains.

The fighting ended in a series of setbacks for the British: three of the four columns were repulsed. In one episode at Jaithak, a desperate charge by 200 cornered Gorkhas actually broke the 3,000 irregulars sent in to pursue them. Legend has it that the British officer, Lieutenant Young, refused to run away and this earned the admiration of the dashing Gorkhas.[41] Young's conduct, if true at all, was in marked contrast with either the recklessness of some British officers or the pusillanimity of the rest. Major General Marley actually deserted his army. Several colonels had to be invalided out of the service because of their age and infirmity. Colonel David Ochterlony, the commander of the fourth column, was the exception. He felt the war against an established government in Nepal was an error, but he also believed that a reckoning between the British and the Nepalese was inevitable.[42] Ochterlony was also canny in his tactics. Realising that his Indian sepoys might not stand against Gorkha charges or close-quarter fighting that pitted his bayonets against the *kukri* knife, he tried to draw the Gorkhas into positions where he could bring his artillery to bear. He built, for example, small hill positions that would compel the Gorkhas to make the attack, thus utilizing the idea of strategic offence combined with tactical defence. At Dionthal, Ochterlony managed to divide two Gorkha forces with a fortified stockade on an important ridge. Despite a battle lasting several hours, the Gorkhas were unable to dislodge him. The death of a favoured leader, Bhakti Thapa, proved to be the turning point. Ochterlony, realising the significance, returned the body to the local capital and the Gorkhas, who ordinarily mutilated the enemy dead, returned intact a British officer who had been slain in single combat the day before.

The war came to end when the Nepalese troops began to desert, the Sikhs refused to join against the British, and Ochterlony's column and his artillery reached the regional capital at Malaun. Meanwhile, the setbacks to the other Company columns had prompted the Governor General to raise corps of irregulars. Lieutenant Colonel William Gardner, who had been a mercenary in service with the Marathas, raised levies among the hill men who opposed the Gorkhas and all the impositions they had made of their vassals. With Colonel Nicholls and a force of 2,000 additional Indian regulars, they seized Kumaon. The name for these and others who had deserted was the collective term Gurkha, but the levies the British raised differed from the apprenticeship system that characterised the main Gorkha warrior caste: here, slaves would be tutored while on campaign and might eventually take their place in the ranks of an auxiliary Gorkha force.[43] The system ensured a steady flow of highly trained and dedicated fighters, and the British would benefit enormously when many of these men eventually found their way into the Company army.

David Ochterlony and William Fraser were the leading advocates of Gurkhas being employed in Company service at the rate of six rupees a month, but there was some doubt that 'real Gorkhas' would serve outside their own state.[44] The first Gurkha battalion, the Nasiri Regiment, was established in April 1815 and soon two battalions existed, numbering 5,000 men, consisting of Gorkhas, Kumoanis and Garhwalis. The term Nasiri, according to one regimental historian, may have been derived from Nasir ud-Daula ('he who gives victory to the state'), and they had worked well during the operations on the Dionthal ridge, exhibiting a dedication and good humour despite all hardships. These were the attributes that would characterise all the Gurkha regiments that were to follow.

A second formation, later known as the Sirmoor Battalion, was established at the same time from those former Gorkhas who had fought at Jaithak and Kalunga. What seems to have appealed to them was the discipline and courage of the British regulars, as these were values which they themselves esteemed. They also appreciated the British habit of referring to past martial histories, and, while they tended to look down upon sepoys from the plains as inferior, they were eager to demonstrate to the British why they felt they were the better Asian soldiers. There was also a strong attachment to the British leaders who fought bravely, which, again, reflected qualities that they had admired in their own forces. A while later a third Kumaon Battalion was contracted, although not all were by any means Gorkhas.

After the war, it was considered 'prudent' not to discharge the men, who might simply rejoin the Nepalese, and the four battalions raised were first tasked to garrison the western hills in order to release British and Indian personnel for the Maratha wars. When a second war with Nepal broke out in 1816, the new units were not deployed. The British, using overwhelming numbers, were again deeply impressed by the Gorkhas' refusal to give ground, even when the fire directed against them was overwhelming, as at the Battle of Makwanpur. Even wounded Gorkhas insisted on returning to the fighting front and there were anecdotes of hard fighting and heavy casualties among the hill men who, despite the odds, simply refused to give in. The Treaty of Segauli (1816) ended a war that both sides were keen to conclude, but it also established a new competition for military manpower between the Nepalese, the Sikhs and the Company.[45]

These Gurkhas took part in the Sikh wars, but earned particular distinction during the Indian Mutiny. It was also noteworthy that the Nepalese Gorkhas assisted the British during the relief of Lucknow, where twelve regiments under the command of Jang Bahadur were much needed. Jang had made repeated offers of military assistance over the previous decade in order to win the approval of the Company and thus ensure his survival against an expansionist power, but he was also able to frustrate any attempts at internal interference in his own domains. He obstructed Company recruiting of Gurkhas wherever he could and the Honourable W.G. Osbourne, Military Secretary to Governor General Lord Auckland, complained that while the Sikhs had no difficulty in getting Gurkha recruits, 'we have found the greatest difficulty in keeping our own ... regiments complete, from the jealousy of the Nepaulese'. In fact, the Sikh ruler Ranjit Singh had filled the ranks of his mountain regiments with Kashmiris because he too could not get Gorkhas from the heart of Nepal.[46] The Nepalese threatened to execute anyone enlisting in foreign forces, and British recruiting officers in the western regions resorted to moving at night in order to find the manpower they required.

In 1850, when the Company made a direct approach to Jang Bahadur, his offers to make men available were insincere. An assembly of men in Kathmandu seemed encouraging at first but they were excused service on one pretext after another. Of the 52 that were finally eligible, 20 deserted immediately. A second attempt failed when the 'allocated' men turned out to be discharged Gorkhas who did not want to serve but for various reasons had been imprisoned and tortured. None wanted to leave Nepal. Jang added other disincentives. He refused to allow any man who had taken service with the British to return to Nepal, arguing that criminals had fled the country into the Company's army and they were not to be permitted back. Jang could also refer to the Treaty of Segauli: the terms did not permit him to recruit Europeans, since the British had been concerned about trained mercenaries assisting him; Jang felt that the British should not be permitted to recruit Nepalese who might pose a threat to his country in the future. The concern he felt was also manifest in the increased scale of the Gorkha army—from 10,000 in 1816 to 27,000 in 1854. This was not a standing force, but consisted of many *dhakres* (trained men in reserve).

The British could have interpreted the limitations on recruiting as hostility, but Jang resisted the demands of his countrymen to attack the Company in 1857 and join the muntineers. Although he believed the Nepalese could recover the Terai and raid the plains for a while, he anticipated that the British would fight back and Nepal would be overrun. Jang justified his actions as a demonstration of fidelity, that to oppose would lead to the ruination of Nepal and that he anticipated future good faith and an alliance by his support.[47] The British, while making use of the troops Jang had provided in the relief of Lucknow, were nevertheless concerned by Jang's unbridled ambitions to become the undisputed ruler of Nepal and by the widespread looting of the city after the relief. As they marched home, 'loaded with plunder', they struck one officer as resembling a 'rabble' rather than an army.[48] The British officers who had been attached to the formation were relieved to be released to return to their own forces. This, and the British refusal to recognise Jang as a monarch, did not bode well for an alliance, although the British returned portions of the Terai as recompense for Jang's assistance during the Mutiny. Jang responded by refusing to permit any recruitment of Nepalese into the Company's forces, with the death penalty for any infringement. The British persevered for a while but had to abandon the deployment of recruiting officers because the only men who would come forward were the desperate or criminals. In 1864, recruitment was changed to individual contacts—Gurkhas attracting other Nepalese to join up.[49]

While in British service, particular characteristics were reported by the officers who came into contact with the Gurkhas, and although some scholars are eager to explain these away as forms of 'Orientalism', the fact that they reappear with such regularity over a period of two hundred years cannot be dismissed as the fanciful notions of a colonial mindset. That is not to say that the British were not guilty of misunderstanding what they observed, and some of the attributes they identified were wide of the mark, but their assessments cannot simply be condemned: some had foundation in fact.

The Gurkhas were preferred for a number of reasons. One was that, unlike the Bengali sepoys who insisted on elaborate rituals for taking meals, the

Gurkhas could prepare and consume their food in half an hour. The Gurkhas 'laugh at the pharisaical rigour of our Sipahis, who must bathe from head to foot and make puja, 'ere they begin to dress their dinner, must eat nearly naked in the coldest weather, and cannot be in marching trim again in less than three hours'.[50] In other words, the British viewed the Gurkhas more favourably from a position of military efficiency.

Another observer tellingly described the Gurkhas as being 'the smartest and most European-like soldiery in India'.[51] It was that similarity which the British preferred, not least in a region where most local customs appeared to be an obstacle from a military point of view. After the Battle of Sobraon against the Sikhs, Sir Hugh Gough, who had commanded the British and Indian forces, praised

> the determined hardihood and bravery with which our two battalions of Goorkhas, the Sirmoor and Nusseree, met the Sikhs ... Soldiers of small stature but indomitable spirit, they vied in ardent courage in the charge with the Grenadiers of our own nation, and, armed with the short weapon of their mountains, were a terror to the Sikhs throughout this great combat.[52]

General Napier, who became Commander-in-Chief in India, believed that Gurkhas would accept less pay than Indian sepoys and could form a third force that would enable the British to rule without constantly worrying about causing offence to Indian culture or British political sensitivities at home. He wrote: 'The Gurkhas will be faithful, and ... we can enlist a large body of soldiers whom our best officers consider equal in courage to European troops.' While India might be held thanks to the presence of military forces under British control, it was expected that, if resistance was impossible, there would eventually be consent to foreign rule. Napier hoped to create an army of 30,000 Europeans with the same number of Gurkhas so that neither Hindu nor Muslim forces would be able to defeat them, either alone or in combination.

After the Mutiny, the Gurkhas continued to be recruited. The Sylhet Light Infantry in Assam, which had recruited Nepalese before 1857 and had fought against the mutineers, was joined by new units outside the army of Bengal: the 4th Battalion and the 5th, which was raised from the remnants of the Sikh Gurkhas under Ranjit Singh and was designated the 25th Punjab Infantry or Hazara Goorkha Battalion. After proving their value as soldiers on so many occasions in the nineteenth century, a formal arrangement was finally reached for the recruitment of Gurkhas into British service in 1888. By proclamation, the Nepalese authorities agreed to enlistment some seventy years after the process had been in place, and the system would endure.

The Gurkhas were regarded as brilliant light infantry, particularly in mountain warfare, and it was not surprising that they were often the most favoured troops for leading assaults against tribesmen and Afghans on the North West Frontier of India. They were accorded the honour of wearing rifle green uniforms with a Kilmarnock cap (later replaced by the slouch hat) to reflect their special status, but, on campaign, khaki became the standard camouflage dress from the 1880s. Their association with Highlanders meant their band featured drums and bagpipes as well as the bugles of light infantry formations. While Scottish regiments claim a special bond with their Gurkha counterparts, it is true to say that every British soldier has a close affinity with their ever-cheerful comrades from Nepal, and they have always been accorded a great deal of affection and respect.

The Sikhs

The appeal of the Sikhs as a military force was obvious to the British. Having been persecuted by a succession of Muslim rulers, especially the Mughal Emperor Aurangzeb, the Sikhs were forced to create a polity based on a military system. The Khalsa, or 'elect', was a military fraternity and each man was known as Singh (Lion). To maximise their constant military preparedness, they rejected alcohol, tobacco or other intoxicants. To increase their martial appearance, they refrained from shaving their hair or their beards. To generate the strength of their identity, they adopted five accoutrements to remind themselves of the Khalsa: the *kes, kaccha, kankan, kirpan* and *kangha* (long hair, pantaloons, comb, dagger and iron discus). After decades of conflict and having endured an existential threat for so long, the military traditions of the Sikhs were well established. With the decline of the Mughal Empire, the Sikhs then re-established themselves in the Punjab. In the nineteenth century, under Maharaja Ranjit Singh, the Sikhs were not so much a state with an army as, not unlike eighteenth-century Prussia, an army with a state.

During the British campaigns that annexed northern India, the authorities were particularly concerned by the Sikhs' resistance in the 1840s because they were better paid than the East India Company's sepoys. Some Bengali men in British service deserted during the campaign against the Sikhs, and a number fled rather than take part in more frontal assaults like those ordered by General Gough at Ferozeshah or Chillianwallah. The majority, however, stuck it out, despite heavy casualties. What the British noticed, however, was the determination and military skill of the Sikh forces.

After the death of Ranjit Singh, the government of the Punjab had been riven by faction and intrigue and the Sikh Army was at the centre of the various conspiracies. Despite British success in the First Sikh War (1845–6), tensions had remained, and the murder of two British officers in Multan in April 1848 led directly to the outbreak of war. The British besieged Multan, which, after a brief pause in operations, fell in early January 1849. Subsequently, an army under General Gough was assembled in order to pursue and defeat the main Sikh force. In December 1848, Gough attempted to envelop the Sikhs with a portion of his army, but they did not press home their attack and the Sikh army retreated to a stronger defensive position on the banks of the Jhelum. On 13 January 1849, in order to prevent a repeat of the situation in December, Gough advanced directly against the Sikh forces and this meant pushing through some densely vegetated country. At the village of Chillianwallah, a Sikh outpost was taken, but while Gough halted for the night he came under sustained artillery fire, and this compelled him to bring forward the attack. The frontal assault was costly, and casualties heavy among British and Indian troops. Nevertheless, even as the Sikh line was rolled up, the British observed that the Sikh gunners refused to abandon their guns. Eyewitnesses were impressed with the dedication of the Sikh troops.

The polities of Asia, which were bitterly divided or failed to co-operate in the face of British or French invasion, struggled to modernise their forces to confront the European incursions. Many of the rulers had long been dependent on mercenaries and therefore neglected the development of their own military formations. When these states were overthrown, the troops who were cast into unemployment looked to gain new positions with the British or the French. The Maratha soldiers, for example, were quickly enrolled into British service. However, in the early years of the operations in South Asia, there were often rumours that the sepoys would just as easily change sides again if the British were to meet with a single repulse.[53] When confronted by the Sikhs in 1845, the risk of a serious setback was increased significantly. The First Anglo-Sikh War was characterised by four major battles, the second of which, at Ferozeshah, was hard fought and described as 'the most bloody and obstinate contest ever fought by Anglo-Indian troops'.[54] The action lasted for 36 hours before the Sikh commander, perhaps prompted by the *paches* (the committees that represented the soldiers), withdrew from his field fortifications. On the British side, there had been a number of desertions by Indian troops. At the Battle of Aliwal in January 1846, there was again severe fighting until the Sikhs were driven off. At Sobraon on 10 February, the fighting was just as fierce, and much of it hand to hand. As the Sikhs started to retreat, they came under devastating fire as the British were eager to ensure that resistance was finally broken. The frontal collision of the Sikh and British Indian armies was repeated in the Second Anglo-Sikh War just two years later. The conditions of the campaign were made worse by the climate, long marches in hot weather and lack of water. Corporal Ryder of the 32nd Foot recorded that the intense heat caused a man next to him to drop dead and even the *bheestis*, the water-carriers, abandoned the army. When the British and Indian forces were on the brink of victory at Multan, and the city stormed, the hardships of the campaign and the heavy casualties released a flood of looting and brutality. One eyewitness wrote that the soldiers were 'brutish beyond everything ... Our native soldiers were much worse, and more brutish; but they were more to be excused, as they were natives.'[55] Despite the carnage, the British were impressed with Sikh resistance. Corporal Ryder noted that Sikh gunners 'stood and defended their guns to the last; they threw their arms around them, kissed them, and died'.[56] Another factor which had made the Sikh gunners more formidable was the presence of European advisers among the artillery train. Deserters from the Indian army not only reached the Sikh forces but also assisted in developing and training the Gurkha military forces of Nepal.

The opportunity to make use of the Sikhs, from all branches of the army, came soon after in the Indian Mutiny, when Sikh men enlisted readily, eager for revenge against the Hindus and for some shares of the spoils available in the taking of Delhi. Once again, the British were impressed with the fighting prowess of the Sikh soldiers.

The Sikhs won a number of accolades for their exemplary courage in action. Among the most celebrated of the nineteenth century was the last stand of the 36th Sikhs at Saragarhi on the North West Frontier in 1897. It took place during the largest and most serious outbreak of fighting on the North West Frontier during the colonial era, an uprising that engulfed the region of Swat, Tirah and the Khyber Pass. The revolt was actually a series of local insurrections involving over 50,000 fighters, including Afghan volunteers, and it required over 59,000 regular troops and 4,000 Imperial Service Troops to deal with it: the largest deployment in India since the Mutiny of 1857–8.[57] Its outbreak proved such an unexpected and significant shock to the British that they conducted detailed inquiries after the event. Various explanations were offered but it is generally accepted that recent encroachments into tribal territory, with fears that the British meant to occupy the region permanently as a prelude to the destruction of their independence and way of life, led to the initial fighting.

There were other contributory factors: a perception that the Amir of Afghanistan, Adbur Rahman Khan, would support an anti-British jihad; rumours that the Christian world was finally in retreat; and local conspiracy theories involving the British and women, moneylenders and road-building.[58]

The initial outbreak had occurred at Maizar, where a detachment of 1st Sikhs was accompanying a British political officer on a routine reassurance mission. While dining, the force was suddenly attacked and the Sikhs were almost overwhelmed. Nevertheless, their discipline and cohesion were such that they brought a small battery of mountain artillery into action. This held off their assailants for a time but eventually their ammunition ran out. The detachment therefore made a fighting retreat through the hills, closely pursued. However, they remained intact, bringing all their guns, wounded and surviving personnel with them, which, under the circumstances, was a remarkable achievement. It was this 'steadiness' under pressure that deeply impressed the British authorities, and an unprecedented nine of the leading Sikh soldiers won the Order of Merit, the highest award for courage, that day.

More clans joined the uprising. At the Malakand Fort at the head of the Swat Valley, several tribal confederations converged. It took four days to drive off a succession of attacks by several thousand fighters. As the British restored control in Malakand and Swat, more Pashtun groups further south joined the rising. On 26 August, the forts of the Khyber Pass were attacked and captured, despite the resistance of some Afridi levies.[59] Ammunition and rifles were seized in large quantities, adding to the considerable arsenal of modern weapons the fighters already possessed.[60]

There was an attack on the Samana forts by the Orakzais soon after, and raids towards the Settled Districts by smaller parties.[61] At Saragarhi, a detachment of 36th Sikhs defended their isolated post to the last man, earning a great deal of admiration, even from their enemies, who subsequently provided the details of the action. The offensive had begun in early September 1897 and General Yeatman-Biggs took a composite force to block the movement of a large number of Orakzai and Afridi Pathans through the Khanki Valley.[62] The manoeuvre was successful but, exhausted and short of water, his force withdrew. The large group of tribesmen then attempted to cross the Samana Ridge, which was held by a small garrison in three separate outposts. The stone structures, the smallest of which was Saragarhi, had not been designed to withstand a major siege, and its garrison of just 21 Sikhs was far too small to hold out against several thousand hill fighters. Yet the force managed to defend the post for seven and a half hours of continuous battle, beating off two rushes and enduring significant sniping. On the third assault, some of the fighters managed to threaten the gate, so the walls had to be abandoned to hold it. In doing so, the tribesmen were able to scale the tops of the walls and a hand-to-hand fight developed in the small courtyard. A signaller alerted the neighbouring posts that the position was about to fall, and finally, the sole survivor, one solitary Sikh, barricaded inside a tower but refusing to capitulate, was killed when the Afridis set fire to his strongpoint. The fighters then set about destroying the entire position, so that, when a relief force arrived, they found the site levelled and the bodies of the Sikhs badly mutilated.[63] One officer concluded 'there is perhaps no more touching instance of inflexible devotion to duty than this in the whole narrative of frontier fighting'.[64]

Not every commentator was prepared to see the episode in a positive light. Unlike smaller posts held by local levies, who tended to negotiate a way out or simply abandoned their position, the Sikhs knew that there would be no quarter for them. The small scale of the post made it vulnerable and one critic believed: 'there must be something very wrong in a system which thus makes the fate of a small party of soldiers a foregone conclusion'.[65] In the neighbouring post, Fort Gulistan, the garrison was large enough to make counterattacks. One section of the 36th Sikhs, commanded by Colour-Havildar Sunder Singh, used his initiative and made his sortie without waiting for orders in order to clear dead ground on the approaches to the position. The action was a great success and was sufficient to persuade the attacking tribesmen to fall back. Three men of the section went over the walls a second time to retrieve their wounded comrades, again with success. As night fell, the post was subjected to constant fire, and the tribesmen tried to work their forward in the dark, to pick off the defenders on the parapets. The garrison maintained their vigil and conserved their ammunition, and then assisted the relieving column to defeat and then drive off the final assaults of the hill fighters.[66]

There were some ambiguities about the Sikhs, despite the universal praise for their actions at Saragarhi. As the theory of martial races became more established in the 1880s, and codified in recruiting handbooks, a degree of stereotyping enveloped the definition of 'Sikh'.[67] This was manifest in religious observance. The British had respected and encouraged the veneration of the Guru Granth Sahib, the holiest book of Sikhism, and it was given a prominent place in any Sikh encampment on campaign.[68] Lapses in ritual by any individual soldier were frowned upon and the effect was rather to fossilise the faith within Sikh regiments. While in the Punjab itself, close attention was paid to the family origins and branches of the Sikhs, on the periphery of the

British Empire more flexible definitions were applied, and Punjabis and even Madrassis were sometimes labelled as Sikhs.[69]

Sikhs were used as auxiliary military police as well as conventional military forces in South East Asia and Africa. In Nyasaland in 1892, Sir Harry Johnston made a request to the government of India for a contingent of Sikhs, although it was clear that he had only a vague idea of the specific criteria of Sikhs and was really in need of the best 'martial material' available from India, which, like many contemporaries, he believed originated in the Punjab.[70] In South East Asia, similar assumptions were made. After the uprising of Chinese tin miners and their secret societies in 1875 in Perak, which had necessitated the deployment of units of the Indian Army, there was an urgent request for a police force that consisted of Indian personnel. As a result, Sikhs were employed as sentries at residences, staff for jails and in other constabulary duties. The Perak Armed Police was organised and disciplined on the lines of the Indian Army, and, despite the preference for Sikhs, a number of Punjabis of other backgrounds were employed. In the same period, the Hong Kong government also made requests for Indian personnel to serve in their police force.

One eyewitness described the Indian police as 'splendid looking men with long moustaches and whiskers, wearing large blue turbans, scarlet coats, and white trousers, which to all intents and purposes were soldiers, drilled and disciplined as such'.[71] Not all eyewitnesses were so impressed. Many European residents regarded the Sikhs as a useless extravagance and their arrogance provoked widespread critical comment. The Indian constabulary in Perak were considered overbearing with a rather high opinion of themselves. Nevertheless, in the Straits Settlements, a Sikh contingent of 165 men was established in 1881, and in 1883 the authorities decided to recruit a troop of cavalry, some 15 sowars, drawn from Fane's Horse (19th Bengal Lancers), in order to conduct night patrol work. At the same time, the 1st Battalion Perak Sikhs was expanded to consist of 701 Sikhs and 175 Malays. In 1889 a Sikh contingent was also deployed to the eastern state of Pahang. However, they did not perform well during an uprising of local Malays in 1891. Despite misgivings about the Indian police, they were preferred over the Chinese, who were distrusted because of their ties to secret societies and considered too dangerous to employ in any number. By the end of the century, of the entire force of 2,000 police, approximately 300 were Sikhs and the rest Malays.

In the 1890s, as British control extended into Africa, the demand for Indian police personnel once again increased. There was already a flow of Indian labourers, merchants and clerks into East Africa, so the requests were understandable in their context. But there were those who imagined a far more significant role for South Asians than mere migration. Sir Harry Johnston thought that the future of the African continent would properly depend on Indian colonisation.[72] Indians were soon recruited into the Imperial British East Africa Company, especially former sappers and miners to fulfil the multitude of local construction tasks. When the British East Africa Company faced bankruptcy in 1893, there was a desperate search for alternatives, but the verdict of Rennell Rodd, the Consul General in Zanzibar, was: 'I am at my wits end where to find men; the Arabic irregulars cannot be relied upon, while the Swahili troops are unseasoned and not very courageous.' He believed that 'a force of 100 Sepoys is more valuable than three or four times that number of Swahili's'.[73] Sir Harry Johnston similarly sought Indian personnel for the British protectorate of Nyasaland.

The Indian Army was nevertheless concerned that the highly paid employment on offer in Africa might 'weaken our military resources'.[74] The Indian Army therefore attempted to limit, if not exclude, Punjabis from service in Africa. In a reply to the enquiries of the War Office, the authorities in India recommended that, for the Hong Kong Police, Madrassis of the south should be used, while Hindustanis could be deployed in Central Africa.[75] There were soon objections to the use of Hindus for police work in Africa on the grounds that their culture, their diet and their preference for their own climate would prove them 'a lamentable failure'. The underperformance of South Indians in military operations in Burma was cited as evidence that they would also fail in Africa. Similar objections were raised about recruiting men from the Hyderabad Contingent.[76]

Johnston argued that Britain would only be able to maintain its supremacy in Africa if it deployed higher quality Indian troops.[77] As a result, 100 men were sent to Central Africa from the 35th Sikhs in February 1893. A second detachment, at company strength, from the 1st Sikhs was sent a few months later. Units such as these tended to be pitched straight into action and therefore there was a special need for trained and disciplined men, for there was little time for further training for military operations in the region. There was some tension between Johnston and the Indian Army because the Sikh soldiers deployed might be persuaded to join colonial police forces with their inducements of better pay. Johnston argued that Africa could not do without its Sikh detachments, believing that it was not only their demeanour towards the native, which was 'invariably conciliatory', but each man 'makes himself useful in road making, in the construction of bridges, and the organising of telegraphs, and all the work where acute intelligence is needed'.[78] On the other hand, those in favour of the scheme believed that the opportunities for Indian personnel might in fact 'enhance the popularity of the Indian Army by giving highly paid openings to well conducted men of adventurous spirit'.[79] The chief difficulty was the difference in pay. An Indian soldier was paid 7 rupees a month in this period but, after deductions, he possessed just 4 rupees. The African colonies offered 18 rupees a month, with free rations and a bonus of 100 rupees at the end of the three-year term of service. The Hong Kong Regiment offered 15 rupees and free rations. The Hong Kong Sikh police earned 32 rupees a month, while the police in Malaya and Perak between 18 and 22 rupees. There was also the concern that relatives of those who took up this service would not wish to join the Indian Army and would seek to get better employment in one or other of these constabulary forces. Even in 1895, when Indian sepoys' incomes rose to 9 rupees a month, they could still not compete. When the government of India conducted a survey to discover what manpower reserves they might draw from the Punjab, especially from Sikhs, it revealed that approximately one in ten of the Sikh male population was employed by the Indian Army, while among Punjabi Muslims some 2 per cent of eligible men were in military service. By contrast, in other forms of colonial service, in Hong Kong, Malaya, Central Africa and Uganda there were barely 5,000 men. This contrasted with 40,006 and 21,000 Punjabis in the Indian Army. Indian personnel were also recruited into the King's African Rifles when it was established in 1902, but their numbers too were very small.[80] In the British Central African Rifles, in Nyasaland, one company was made up of Sikhs and the other six, totalling 800 men, were made up of the local Atonga, Yao and Marimba. This was in addition to the Indian Army contingents that were deployed for emergencies, as in Uganda in 1898 and Somaliland in 1905, but, in sum, the number of Indians serving in Africa at the turn of the century was far fewer than the authorities in India had feared.

When the British authorities made enquiries, they learned that Indian personnel were being employed privately across South East Asia as watchmen and guards, often for commercial organisations eager to protect their goods. Lord Curzon as Viceroy in 1903 was concerned that Indians could end up in Dutch, Siamese or, worse, French and Russian service. He wrote: 'We may have at any time to fight one or other of these powers, perhaps more than one in combination. I think it is a most serious thing that we should possibly be confronted by our Indian subjects whose brothers and cousins and kinsmen are in the ranks of the Indian Army.'[81] Nevertheless, it proved impossible to control the flow of labour to police and other civil opportunities overseas, and, in 1909, the Indian government gave up attempting to regulate recruitment of the local colonial police forces of South East Asia.

Sikhs and other Indians were seeking employment across the globe, including sizeable populations in South Africa, the United States and, although the attempt failed in 1914, Canada. There was evidence that those who had joined the police services were also developing a consciousness of their enhanced bargaining position. In September 1906, half of the Indian constables in Shanghai went on strike for higher wages. The British responded by reducing the number of Indian personnel in police forces in Shanghai and Beijing. But what put a halt to further Indian recruitment was the outbreak of the First World War. Such were the demands for manpower that it proved impossible for Indians to continue to seek work in colonial service. But, even before the war, the fashion of recruiting Indians in African military formations was coming to an end. By 1912, Indians were no longer being employed in East African military units. The last contingent in Uganda, for example, left Africa in February 1913 and was replaced by local Baganda. The mutiny of Indian troops in Singapore in 1915 also had a profound effect on the preference for Indian recruits in that colony. The Malay States Guides, which had been made up of Sikhs, was abolished in 1919. Local Malays were encouraged into the police and military forces to replace Indian personnel. Changes were slower in Hong Kong and the Chinese treaty ports, but even here the process of employing more local personnel had begun.

Modernisation of Army Management

The standardisation and regularisation of the management of armies was an important advantage the Europeans possessed over the polities they confronted across the Global South. In contrast with relatively impoverished states that paid their soldiers intermittent low wages and relied on a personalised style of governance, which was open to corruption by middle-ranking officials and hence embezzlement of soldiers' pay, a system that offered regular employment, guaranteed salary payments and a higher rate of pay had a distinct advantage. Across Africa and Asia, it was this modernised and regularised approach that won the Europeans the willing recruits and sustained the numbers in their military and police forces. Moreover, it was the certainty of payment that made a difference in largely agrarian economies that were subject to the vagaries of climate, weather and the performance of harvests. Seasonal employment, the high prospect of unemployment, and dramatic variations in income could be avoided in military service. The bureaucratisation of pay and conditions created a new set of loyalties. At the risk of oversimplification, clan chieftains found it harder to compete with European paymasters for the affiliation of their manpower.

Europeans were able to source the personnel they required because they could pay consistently above the market rates for any comparable employment. In Calcutta, for example, in 1831, a skilled civilian metalworker or carpenter would earn on average 10 rupees (£1) a month; unskilled artisans would earn half that amount, while labourers got 3.8 rupees and agricultural workers between 2 and 6 rupees. In small towns and rural districts, the rates were lower. A ploughman or a labourer would not earn even 1 rupee a month in outlying areas. Imagine, then, the effect of an infantryman in the Indian Army earning 7 rupees a month, after deductions for uniform and rations, while gunners and cavalrymen earned 8 or 9 rupees. These rates continued to be higher than civilian employment throughout the nineteenth century. While civilian wages remained low, by the 1890s a cavalry trooper would be earning 31 rupees a month before deductions. A senior subedar, or NCO, would earn 100 rupees. It was this generous salary scale that maintained the appeal of military service under the Europeans.

There were other financial benefits. Soldiers in European service were given accommodation. In the early nineteenth century, sepoys of the East India Company Army were simply allotted land to construct their own huts, but these tended to be built without regard to sanitation. Health problems multiplied in these flimsy constructions. Consequently, the Indian Army insisted on the construction of barracks, usually containing four man rooms and separate blocks for ablutions and latrines. In time, entire military cantonments developed, complete with their own bazaars and services.

Medical support had a strong appeal and conveyed European influence beyond the areas it controlled directly. Medical aid had traditionally been given to the enemy as well as to Europeans in battle. Sikh survivors of the Battle of Chillianwallah were treated in a British hospital and given 'the greatest care'.[82] Similarly, at the Battle of Bharatpur in 1825, hundreds of the enemy wounded were given medical aid by British medics.[83] In the First 'Opium War' in China, after the bombardment of Chapo in 1842, significant efforts were made to treat both enemy forces and the British wounded. One surgeon wrote: 'The Chinese cannot understand and say—"yours is a curious kind of warfare; you come and fire upon us and wound us, and then pet us and cure us"'.[84] Among those that served in European colonial forces, the knowledge that one might be saved from death or wounds by trained medical staff made a significant difference to morale and consequently to their willingness to hazard their lives.

Pensions could be earned by the soldiers too. In India, inheriting an older Mughal tradition, pensions could be in cash or in the form of land grants, or *jagir*, for the produce or revenue of a particular estate. In the early nineteenth century, land was available, but this became harder to acquire by 1900. Pensions tended to be paid out in three instalments: the first and most generous on leaving the service, the second instalment after three years, for a period of two years, and then a smaller amount for life. The gradations represented the anticipated higher outlays required to buy a house or land on entering civilian life. After 1886, pensions were granted to any servicemen who had completed 21 years in the army. Those who were invalided out received a full year's pay, but those who had suffered wounds that required them to leave the service gained a pension for life. Dependants would receive a full pension if a soldier was killed in action or died on campaign.

Bounties in enlistment were also a standard feature of European service. In the Indian Army in 1880, a man would receive 50 rupees in two instalments: half for enlistment and the other half if he completed three years' service. Field service allowances, known as *batta* in India, were also much sought after. Soldiers might also be offered free carriage of their property, good conduct pay of varying scales depending on length of time served, or extra payments for volunteering to serve overseas in other theatres. To this list one must also add the important psychological factor of the prospect of further reward and recognition that could lead to promotion. The chance that one might excel on campaign and prove oneself worthy of additional rewards was a significant spur to action, and one which was reinforced by the collective willingness of the formation to which a soldier belonged.

Imperial Forces

The expansion of the European empires increased manpower demands dramatically, and it would not be an exaggeration to say that local indigenous personnel were crucial to the process of colonialism. The relative cost of local forces could influence the type of fighting units that were raised, although factors such as social organisation, climate, terrain and environment could also play a part.

The overriding concern of the Europeans, in terms of security, was the extent to which any local forces could be considered reliable. A full programme of training and regularisation was one method to ensure that local troops could be relied upon, but often the requirement for cheap labour, raised in haste, possessing certain skills or ready to provide some rudimentary security, prevented the development of large-scale local formations. The Europeans therefore remained concerned that local personnel might either lack the discipline to stand and fight against native adversaries or get out of hand, advance impetuously to secure material goods, and commit atrocities against their rivals. There were times when rivalry between indigenous peoples could be useful to the Europeans. Nevertheless, in some regions the Europeans found that locals were simply unwilling to serve them, regardless of the inducements. Religion, for example, could sometimes work in the Europeans' favour, but could just as easily be the basis for sustained resistance or mutiny.

Selection for efficiency was by far the most reliable method for creating dependable soldiers. The Gurkhas, for example, proved invaluable to the British when carefully selected, but the process by which they came into service was far from straightforward. Indeed, it was really the result of a unique situation. What the British recognised was that the Nepalese had a proven track record and considerable experience in close combat. The absence of various prejudices and constraints which had characterised the Indian troops in British service also had a strong appeal. The Sikhs too had long experience of conflict and their entire social apparatus had been shaped by repeated existential wars with their neighbours. This made them a perfect group for the British, who found them to be highly disciplined, faithful, cohesive and courageous in combat. They proved so popular as soldiers they not only were employed in South Asia, but spread across South East Asia and parts of Africa.

The management of armies became increasingly bureaucratised through the nineteenth century, which was part of a process taking place across all sectors of European industry and society. A more scientific approach developed in officer education, in procurement, ordnance, munitions and military organisation. Contemporaries realised there was far more to developing local forces than personal, charismatic leadership and tactical training, and attention had to be paid to the development of depots and barracks, logistics, pay and finance, manufacturing, engineering, nutrition and medicine. Arguably, nowhere was this more important than in the African continent, to which we now turn.

7

IMPERIAL ARMIES IN AFRICA

The expansion of the British Empire increased the numbers and variety of local military formations across the globe. Among the white settler populations, it was anticipated that Western men would form the basis of local volunteer corps, modelled on the British system. In Canada, for example, the 1st American Regiment, the title conferred by the King in 1779 as a mark of appreciation of its services, could trace its origins back to 1755. It had been raised in New Hampshire as a company of scouts under the command of Captain Robert Rogers, and, as the demand for its services grew, it was expanded to 11 companies and known as Rogers's Corps of Rangers. These were the forerunners of British light infantry and rifle regiments. Almost every large force of regulars operating in North America had an attachment of Rogers's Rangers. They served alongside British units in campaigns against the French, against Pontiac's Indian Rebellion of 1763 and in the American Revolution. They acted as vanguard and rearguard units, protected the main body of the army, and gathered vital information about their adversaries. They were specialists in guerrilla warfare, raids, long-range reconnaissance and sabotage. In one example, near Lake George in 1759, they marched 50 miles in extremely low temperatures and deep snow, and fought two engagements, all in just one day. Subsequently, on the way to St Francis to punish Indian allies of the French for committing atrocities, including the scalping of 600 civilians, they marched for nine gruelling days through marshy territory to fulfil their mission. By the end of the eighteenth century, the 1st American Regiment had its own infantry, cavalry and artillery. During long periods of peace, it was temporarily disbanded, but it was raised again whenever war threatened, before finally establishing a permanent headquarters at Fort York, Toronto.

On the other side of the world, in Australia, and inspired by the volunteer movement in the mid-nineteenth century in Britain, a number of white part-time units were established. Each state of Australia provided for its own defence, and, in Sydney, a strategic port, there were 20 companies of infantry, a troop of mounted rifles, and three batteries of artillery by 1860. The government of Australia gave encouragement to voluntary service in defence of their country, and a law passed in New South Wales in 1867 gave grants of land to those who had attended training regularly and passed their efficiency tests.

Yet in the African continent the situation in the 'settler colonies' was more complicated. In the Cape Colony there were white volunteer units: in 1860 there were no less than 37 in existence. Most of the units were very small since the entire volunteer force of the Cape Colony was numbered at only 600 men, and many of them appear to have been no more than bodyguards for officials and administrators, such as the Cape Town Cavalry, a formation that existed from 1857 to 1889, but whose duties consisted entirely of ceremonial appearances. In contrast, the Northern Rhodesia Police, which consisted of men from the Awemba, Angoni, Baila and other black communities, led by British officers and NCOs, was able to operate not only in Rhodesia but also in other parts of Africa. The Northern Rhodesia Regiment and Rhodesian African Rifles were placed into the Central Africa command in order to facilitate cross-border operations. Their motto, which says much about their ethos, was 'Differing in race, equal in fidelity', and in the Second World War they formed eight battalions which served in Africa, the Middle East and Burma. In addition, the Royal Rhodesia Regiment was a volunteer force raised briefly during the South African War and again in the First World War until more firmly established from 1926.

In Western Africa there were a number of more indigenous military and constabulary units. The Gold Coast Constabulary dated from 1844 and was restyled the Lagos Hausas in 1865 before being retitled the Gold Coast Armed Police in 1873. Its military and policing roles were more clearly defined by 1879 when it was given its final title, the Gold Coast Constabulary. Like many other imperial police forces, it was led by British officers and NCOs on similar lines to an infantry regiment. In 1901, the units became the Gold Coast Regiment, part of the West African Frontier Force. Dressed in a blue cotton shirt and long shorts, the men carried a Martini Carbine on long foot patrols, often through difficult terrain, in order to investigate crimes, apprehend criminals and establish a presence to deter cattle raiders, women stealers or uprisings. Local knowledge was vital in order to discern the truth in a society dominated by faith in magic, diviners and secret societies. In essence, the Gold Coast Constabulary was much more than a police force, and was capable of military operations when required. Similarly, the Nigeria Regiment, formed in 1899, formed part of the Western African Frontier Force alongside the Gold Coast Regiment, the Sierra Leone Battalion and the Gambia Company. All were regular soldiers who, aside from dealing with internal security issues, could be sent on service to any part of the West African colonies. The men were drawn from a variety of communities, were led by British officers and NCOs, and were versatile enough to take part in a number of operations around the turn of the century, including the Kano expedition of 1903, Sokoto in 1903, Hadejia in 1906 and the last Asante campaign in 1900. During the First World War, the Nigeria Regiment expanded to five battalions, and in the Second World War it numbered no less than thirteen battalions. Two West African divisions, the 81st and 82nd, eventually served in Burma.

The Kings African Rifles (KAR) was formed in 1902 from an amalgamation of the Central Africa Regiment, the Uganda Rifles and the East Africa Rifles. It was a regular regiment, enlisting men from many tribes and races, including Somalis, Congolese, Sudanese and South Asians. It possessed its own supply and transport units and formed a number of infantry battalions that were stationed in Kenya, Uganda, Nyasaland, Tanganyika and Somaliland. Its British officers and NCOs were seconded from the British Army, and all KAR regiments were liable for overseas service. While the principal function of the regiment was conventional military operations, it could be called upon to support armed police and local irregular defence forces that were made up of Europeans. In 1903, when a detachment of the King's African Rifles was sent to Somaliland, a proportion of them were formed into a Camel Corps, proving their versatility. In the First World War, the King's African Rifles formed 22 battalions.

By comparison, in the Pacific, there were also military police forces, including the Fiji Constabulary. This, unlike the Africa models, was composed of Fijians, Indians and a number of British personnel. The Fiji Defence Force, a small military detachment which was expanded during the Second World War, consisted of four infantry battalions, artillery batteries, engineers, signals, medical, ordinance, and Army Service Corps units. It also had its own labour battalions and home guards. It should also be noted that Fijians served with the Americans in the Pacific. Fijian commandos took part in operations during the island-hopping campaign, including the hard-fought efforts to liberate the Solomon Islands. These contrasting examples raise questions about the specificity of the African case: how distinctive and important was the situation in Africa, and how far did race have a part to play in the treatment and consequent performance of the local African units?

Black Units in the South African War

The South African War of 1899–1902 was of particular interest to European armies at the turn of the century. Here, forces of European descent, namely the Afrikaners, armed with European weapons (often German-made rifles, machine guns and artillery), were pitted against the regular, professional soldiers of the British Army. It was a surprise to many observers that the Afrikaners launched an immediate offensive and invested three settlements, the largest being Kimberley and Ladysmith, with the westernmost, Mafeking, nearer the border of Bechuanaland. The investments were the result of a second surprise: British forces being defeated in the field. The Europeans concluded that the British had been spoiled by a succession of easy victories against colonial African enemies and were ill prepared for the conflict. 'Black Week', when British forces suffered three setbacks in a matter of a few days in December 1899, was a humiliation. It was clear that the numbers available to restore the situation were limited, since Britain had only a small volunteer army. Yet there was an understanding, from the outset, that this was to be a 'white man's war', given the ethnicity of the Afrikaners, which ruled out the use of black troops.

The Afrikaner strategy of sitting out the sieges rather than pursuing an offensive towards the ports of the Cape Colony was a mistake, but the 'Boers', as the Afrikaners were known to contemporaries, had calculated that the British would capitulate and reach a political settlement, as they had done after a defeat in 1881 at Majuba Hill, rather than fight an expensive colonial war. In fact, the British were determined to reassert their control of southern Africa and avenge their defeats. The orthodox account of the war illustrated this in a specifically selective narrative: reinforced by forces from the United Kingdom and other garrisons, the British 'steamroller' bypassed each of the Boers' positions and set out to relieve the besieged settlements. The conventional phase of the conflict ended with the completion of these relief missions, the capture of Pretoria and Bloemfontein (the capitals of the two Afrikaner republics) and a decisive defeat of the Afrikaners at Paardeberg in 1900. A core of the Afrikaner fighters nevertheless refused to accept defeat and waged a guerrilla war for a further two years until food, ammunition and, crucially, horses ran out. The British established cordons across South Africa and combed the countryside looking for guerrillas. To prevent the insurgents getting supplies from the sympathetic population, farms were burned, livestock seized, and civilians moved into internment camps, which became known as concentration camps. Deprived of their mobility by their own losses and by extensive British field defences, the 'bitter-enders' finally capitulated in May 1902.

The war was also explicated through certain iconic incidents. During the siege at Mafeking, Colonel Robert Baden-Powell had, with a small garrison, managed to withstand periodic artillery bombardments and one or two more determined assaults. His defence of the town was a celebrated aspect of the war because Baden-Powell appeared to have upheld British honour with his determination and grit at a time of military setbacks. But he had also depended on a contingent of armed black men to assist the garrison, not only of the small 'white' town of Mafeking, but also the extensive black settlement of the Barolong and other communities.

During the war, despite the claim that it was a white man's affair, both the British and the Afrikaners made extensive use of black noncombatants and, occasionally, of armed men too. Accurate numbers are not available but estimates had been made by the historian Peter Warwick about the military and civil tasks of the war in which black labour was essential, including digging trenches, repairing railway bridges and tracks, building dams, road construction or the portering of equipment and supplies.[1] Black men were also employed in providing transport, driving cattle, horse-management and other labouring associated with the provision of supplies. By 1902, there were some 20,000 African workers on the railways providing manual labour. It is estimated at least 14,000 worked as transport drivers. In total, the British Army may have employed as many as 100,000 black men in labouring tasks during the conflict. In addition, there were thousands of workers recruited for the war industries. Despite higher wages, there were more men conscripted into forced labour for the mines and the railways. The Afrikaners too employed black labour, and some 10,000 were conscripted to serve the commandos in the field. This labour was available because the gold mines in the Transvaal were closed at the beginning of the war and the majority of the black workers on the Rand had been sent home, causing severe hardship. Men were therefore willing to take up some employment, however hazardous, in return for wages.

Black men were also used as combatants. The Afrikaners claimed that they had no armed blacks on their side, except at Mafeking, because it was there that the British had chosen to arm blacks on a large scale. This claim seems to have been generally true, but local men were used as scouts, guides and spies, and some Afrikaners had personal retainers who carried their master's gun into battle and supported them in the field. The Boers claimed that the British had broken the rules of civilised warfare by arming large numbers of Africans to fight against them. The British government denied arming blacks at all, except the African irregulars who needed weapons for the defence of their own territories on the periphery of southern Africa, in Zululand, the Transkei and Bechuanaland (Botswana). Gradually, it emerged that, during the period of guerrilla war that developed after 1900, the British had provided arms for 10,053 blacks inside the old and new colonies and employed these men in a variety of roles. These included scouts, guides, cattle guards and, crucially, watchmen on the lines of blockhouses that criss-crossed the country in an attempt to prevent the movement of insurgents. The British authorities argued that it was essential to arm them for their own safety. During the war, the Afrikaners had made it their policy to shoot armed or unarmed Africans caught serving with the British. Executions of prisoners were not uncommon, although there are few records. The British government estimated that between November 1901 and January 1902 there were 235 reported murders of unarmed Africans by Afrikaner guerrillas in the field. The deaths, the government claimed, vindicated their decision to arm the blacks for their own protection.

African scouts were vital in defeating the guerrillas and ending the war, since it was the intelligence they provided on the locations and movements of the Afrikaner commando bands that enabled the British counter-insurgency commander, General Kitchener, to interdict them or corral them into particular locations before combing them out in extensive 'drives'. The Afrikaners were ruthless in their treatment of blacks whom they suspected of assisting the British for precisely this reason. There was also growing anxiety amongst Afrikaners about the assertiveness of blacks in areas they controlled. Some groups reasserted their independence between 1900 and 1902 in the Rustenburg–Marico district, the Pedi heartland and the south-east Transvaal bordering Zululand. Anxious Afrikaners began to consider capitulation in order to preserve their control of the lands they possessed, hoping for a negotiated settlement with the British before they lost out entirely to black resistance. In the third resolution of the Vereeniging peace terms advanced by

Afrikaner delegates in 1902, it was stated that 'the Kaffir tribes, both within and without the territories of the two Republics, are mostly armed and are taking part in the war against us, and through the committing of murders and all sorts of cruelties have caused an unbearable condition of affairs in many districts of both republics'. On 5 May 1902, a desperate commando, led by General Louis Botha, stole cattle from the Qulusi near Vryheid. In a reprisal, unauthorised by the British, the Zulus attacked the commando and killed 56 Boers at Holkrans. Nevertheless, the deterioration of the Afrikaners' ability to resist also played a decisive role in bringing the war to an end. While it was reported that Africans were troublesome when 'used by the British', black populations continued to supply the commandos with food. Grain, bought or commandeered from African kraals, was vital for the survival of the resistance. The eventual exhaustion of supplies, lack of horses, larger numbers of Afrikaners joining the British against the 'bitter-enders' and relentless military pressure brought the war to its conclusion.

In the war, the blacks suffered higher casualties than the whites and there was some bitterness that loyal service had not produced a better outcome for the majority population, especially the extension of the franchise to black people. Silas Molema, a Mafeking veteran, wrote in 1920: 'It is a fact—the position of the Bantu after the South African War was worse than before it.' Sol Plaatje, another who had endured at Mafeking and wrote his memoirs years later, concluded: 'What must be the feelings of these people ... now that it is decreed that their sons and daughters can no longer have any claim to the country for which they bled?'

Black Levies at the Siege of Mafeking

For most contemporaries, the defence of Mafeking was a purely white affair which exemplified the stoicism of the British character. However, as the diary of Sol Plaatje reveals, black personnel played a far more significant role in the siege than once realised. Blacks at Mafeking were not merely victims of white policies, either getting shelled and shot at by the Afrikaners or deprived of resources by the British. Instead they played a role in the defence of the perimeter of Mafeking and provided important labour. The motives for choosing to join the defence were undoubtedly, in part, the result of long-standing land disputes with the Afrikaners and, in part, rivalry with other black African communities.

The black population of Mafeking was larger than the white and they occupied a separate settlement to the south-west of the railway junction, known locally as the Stadt. The majority of the population were Barolong, placed there by their chief Montshiwa in 1857 as part of a ring of settlements that would prevent Boer colonisation.[2] Many of the Barolong had taken up employment in the white town from 1885, especially when rinderpest devastated the cattle population on which they depended for their livelihood. The Barolong had no sympathy for the Afrikaners, not least because they had been subjected to at least six violent campaigns against them in the previous thirty years. With this background, they felt able to defend themselves and consequently the town against any besiegers.

In the Stadt there were also several hundred Mfengu (Fingo). They had moved from the Eastern Cape and settled at Mafeking some years before. There was also a community of Cape Coloureds (creole people) and these provided many of the craftsmen, artisans, railway workers and police in the town. There were a few Indians, mainly engaged in commerce, and a handful of Chinese who worked in market gardens and provided foodstuffs. The largest group were refugees, an influx of several thousand Africans from all over the region looking for protection after the outbreak of war in 1899. Although the British had considered razing the Stadt in order to provide clear fields of fire and a shorter perimeter, it was an easy decision to retain the black African township in order to augment the garrison, the labour force and, most importantly, the sympathy of the local population. The blacks already had a quantity of their own firearms and limited supplies of ammunition. When they made an appeal to the British to be provided with more, initially they received limited stocks.

The Barolong were, at first, not entirely convinced that the British would be able to hold the town against large numbers of Afrikaners.[3] Baden-Powell, as the commander of the garrison at Mafeking, approved of armed blacks in defence of the town but was compelled to keep a low profile in order to avoid antagonising white opinion. Sol Plaatje noted: 'The European inhabitants of the besieged town had a repugnance to the idea of armed natives shooting at a white enemy; but the business-like method of General Cronje in effecting the investment had a sobering effect upon the whole of the beleaguered garrison; the Dutch 100 pounder Creusot [artillery] especially thundered some sense into them and completely altered their views.'[4]

When the siege began on 13 October 1899, there were 400 chosen black men with arms were tasked to defend the south-western approaches to the town. Of this force, approximately 70 were made up of Cape Coloureds commanded by Captain Charles Goodyear of the Cape Police. The Mfengu also formed their own detachment under Sergeant Daniel Webster. The refugee contingent, approximately 300 strong, were nicknamed the 'Black Watch', and one of the areas they were designated to protect was known as the brickfields. This area was to become a scene of some determined actions, and developed into maze of trenches and dugouts. Finally, some of the Indians and other Asians were incorporated into the Town Guard, which was a mixed force of white and black volunteers.

The Afrikaners believed that the most vulnerable section of the defences was held by the black contingents, but their first attack, which sought to exploit this avenue of approach on 25 October 1899, was repulsed. Encouraged by their resolution, the British issued more rifles and ammunition to the black contingents, and this attracted more volunteers so that there were soon 500 in their ranks. They gave themselves military titles including field marshal and general, while smaller groups were led by men who styled themselves as NCOs. There was particular respect for Sergeant Abrahams, a white NCO embedded in their ranks, because of his personal bravery and example, and his instructions were heeded readily.[5]

The brickfields area soon became the focus of further attention because the broken ground conferred a relatively protected line of attack for the Afrikaners to reach the town. The British offered higher pay for those who were prepared to man the defences of the brickfields. It soon became a warren of trenches and revetted positions. The second major attack on Mafeking was made here in March 1900, but the Cape Police, who held the positions that day, did not give way. The only setback was the death of Sergeant Major William Taylor, who was widely regarded as the bravest man of the garrison, but who died from head wounds caused by a shell fragment.

The refugees provided, in return for much-needed pay, essential labour, preparing defensive positions, dugouts and trenches around the perimeter. At the end of three months' work, the contingents of 200 to 300 men who had worked shifts day and night, had created extensive fortifications. The Barolong, noting the willingness of the whites to pay, believed they should be entitled to higher pay than any other group, but Baden-Powell insisted that for such a privilege they would have to join the labouring gangs. This they declined; some even went on strike, believing their pay was to be reduced, but the threat did not materialise. It was a reminder that contractual terms were far more important to the black workers than the 'cause' of defending a settlement in someone else's war.

Nevertheless, black personnel were provided for the dangerous tasks of spies and dispatch runners that kept the British abreast of developments in the

Boer lines. Runners also penetrated the Afrikaner cordon and got information in and out. Messages were hidden in cartridge cases or the soles of shoes, while carriers were instructed to conceal or throw away messages if their capture was imminent. One woman smuggled messages into Mafeking by having them sewn into the hem of her dress. However, Afrikaner sentries would shoot and kill those they suspected of carrying information which would be of value to the garrison. Captives were interrogated and occasionally executed on the basis that all blacks leaving Mafeking ought to be considered combatants.[6]

One of the most valuable contributions made by blacks at Mafeking was cattle raiding. Small groups would cautiously approach Afrikaner stocks and stealthily edge a handful of animals away from the main herd—then, at last moment, rush them as fast as they could into the garrison. On one occasion, in a period of just four days, they stole 56 oxen.[7] One raiding party of Barolong under the leadership of Mathakgong slipped out of Mafeking, moved deep into the countryside, and attacked farmsteads in surrounding districts and killed a number of Boers whom they found. They then commandeered livestock, property and weapons. The attacks had a deep psychological effect. The Afrikaners ambushed his party on two occasions, killing the cattle and many of his men; although Mathakgong escaped, the Afrikaners killed off the wounded that fell into their hands. Unable to catch the raiders, the Afrikaners turned to using blacks themselves to draw the Mafeking fighters into ambushes. In April 1900, during a cattle raid into the Transvaal, a mixed group were betrayed by those in the employment of the Afrikaners and wiped out.[8]

By January 1900 food supply was becoming critical and some of the garrison began to die from the effects of starvation.[9] Baden-Powell asked the Barolong chiefs to encourage the black refugees to leave, so the remainder would have enough to eat. But then the situation in the rest of the war had its own detrimental impact: in early February, the British authorities further south asked the garrison to hold out until the end of May. Baden-Powell had to find the means to supply his force and the rest of the population of the Stadt. There was therefore a new urgency to eject as many black refugees as he could.[10] Small groups of refugees did try to escape but had to run the gauntlet of Afrikaner snipers and, while already malnourished, the long treks in the countryside. This was especially hard when the veld was already stripped of resources by both sides. In late February, a group of 300 refugees managed to pass through the Afrikaner lines. However, a week later, an attempt to get a group of several hundred out of the town failed when the Afrikaners opened fire upon it. British threats to withhold food, in order to encourage more to leave, did not, in the end, materialise. Rations had to be reduced to feed everyone. For those unable to pay for their food, special soup kitchens provided some sustenance for free, but the system was often badly managed. Those who did get away but who were captured by the Boers resembled walking skeletons.[11] Some of the Afrikaners also deliberately shot blacks trying to escape Mafeking in order to put pressure on the garrison's remaining supplies and hasten its capitulation. By mid-April, only half of the original population of 7,500 was left in the Stadt, but the armed force remained at its previous strength.

On 12 May 1900, Commandant Eloff and his commando made a final attempt to break into Mafeking via the Stadt. Although the Afrikaners were able to capture one of the forts, they were then surrounded and trapped. The Barolong had played a significant role in stopping this final offensive although their success was played down at the time. Mafeking was relieved just five days later on 17 May and this brought the siege to an end. Some of the black contingents immediately set off in pursuit of those Africans who had sided with the Boers during the fighting, and there was a settling of scores.[12] After the siege the British authorities congratulated the Africans who had participated in the defence and issued certificates of appreciation to their leaders. The Africans then asked Baden-Powell if he would convey to the relevant authorities their desire to acquire lands to the south-east of Mafeking which they might consider their own. However, the requirement to come to terms with the Afrikaners two years later at Vereeniging meant that no such agreement was forthcoming. Land reform therefore remained at the heart of the agenda of black aspirations, but the African contribution to the British military success at Mafeking and in the wider war was long forgotten by the time the black majority in South Africa were able to enjoy political equality in the country.

French Colonial Troops

In its initial operations in North Africa, the French had used their own personnel. Soon after the occupation of Algeria, France established an *armée coloniale*, initially finding recruits from less desirable parts of French society.[13] Criminals were given the option of joining the battalion being sent out as a military labour unit, or face imprisonment, hard labour or execution. Foreigners were soon able to enrol in the formation known as the Zouaves of Algeria, and by 1840 the rank and file of the Zouaves were drawn from across the world. This was also the case with the French Foreign Legion, established in 1831. In the 1850s, the Swiss company was established, part of a long tradition of mercenary service from Switzerland, followed by other 'national' contingents. It was no surprise that the headquarters of the Legion was established at Sidi Bel Abbés, south of Oran.

Despite the existence of the *armée coloniale*, the French believed that Algeria would become a source of military labour for its colonial armies, and some authorities believed that North Africa, and indeed the entire Near East, would become as important to France as India was to Britain.[14] In 1832 the French established three battalions of light infantry (Infanterie légère d'Afrique), the penal battalions known as Joyeux, and three battalions of locally recruited *tirailleurs indigènes*.[15] By 1841, there were four regiments of Chasseurs d'Afrique and three cavalry regiments known as Spahis. By 1873, the collective Armée d'Afrique became an established part of the order of battle of the metropolitan French Army, and was titled XIX Corps. Units containing indigenous personnel were known by their origin, as *tirailleurs sénégalais, tirailleurs malgaches* or, in the case of South East Asia, *tirailleurs indochinois*, but the exception was that all West African forces were known by the collective title *tirailleurs sénégalais* to reflect the seniority of the original French colonial forces that were drawn from Senegal.[16]

The officers of the mounted Spahis were French, but Arabs could easily rise to the rank of lieutenant. Some were even promoted to more senior positions. General Yussuf, for example, was born in Italy, had been enslaved and converted to Islam while in Algeria, but, when liberated by the French, he enlisted and rose to divisional command. Similarly, General Alfred Dodds, who led an invasion force into Dahomey with 4,000 legionnaires, African *tirailleurs* and French specialists, had been born in Senegal and was a mulatto. Despite this apparently enlightened approach, trust was limited: in colonial French units, it was decreed that half of the NCOs and all artillery should be in French hands.[17] As a further precaution, Berbers constituted a part of any force as a counterweight to Arab personnel. In West Africa, certain groups were enlisted, or men selected from particular areas, to ensure loyalty to the French rather than the majority population. In remote locations, however, garrisons were made up of local personnel under French command. This mirrored the situation for other European countries. The troops under Spanish command in the Philippines, for example, were recruited entirely from local areas.

Colonial campaigns required the support of large numbers of transport animals, porters and mule drivers. In 1894, French planners believed that, to conquer Madagascar, they would require between 18,000 and 20,000 porters and mule drivers in support of an expeditionary force of just 12,000 men. In the event, the introduction of lightweight carts reduced the numbers required to 7,000, but it still created a vulnerable caravan 'tail' for the army. Management of the logistics and transport system also proved a far greater challenge. When the French requisitioned 35,000 camels to supply the Tuat Expedition of 1901–2, some 25,000 died because the French troops did not know how to manage this livestock, and locals had not been employed in order to reduce costs.

The problems of stamina, mobility, logistics and cost in colonial campaigning were offset by the use of locally recruited soldiers. Critics argued that irregular levies could prove more trouble than they were worth, not least because of their indiscipline. Irregulars were not prepared to use the same direct tactics of frontal assaults or decisive blows favoured by the Europeans, and many indigenous forces regarded the possession of territory as transitory. Battles were merely an opportunity to demonstrate personal courage by flirting with danger. The objective was to stay alive in order to collect trophies such as women, livestock or possessions. Local warriors who co-operated with Europeans and became auxiliaries frequently saw their better-armed partners as the means to exact revenge against rival groups or to take the land of a long-standing enemy. In other words, they rarely shared the same objectives as the Europeans.

The use of local forces could create confusion on campaign. In 1881 in the southern Oran region of Algeria during the Bouamama revolts, a French force lost 72 soldiers killed and wounded and most of their baggage and transport, when Arab horsemen, mistaken for French-led *goum* mounted auxiliaries, were not engaged as they approached. In the Western Sudan, the French dependence on tribal levies or badly disciplined Senegalese, led to far greater devastation than anticipated. French colonial soldiers were quick to abandon the firing line to obtain loot or female slaves. Of the French column which captured Ségou in 1890, only 50 were European, since there were 500 regular native soldiers and the remaining 3,000 men in the column were porters and auxiliaries provided by their African partners. In 1898, the Voulet-Chanoine expedition ended with significant destruction and a mutiny, which caused a scandal in France. There were therefore serious doubts about the reliability of local military labour.

A far greater problem was the loyalty of auxiliaries, particularly those that were irregulars. In their conquest of South-West Africa, the Germans complained about their Herero levies during the Nama revolt in 1904. The Germans were forced to disarm the Nama contingent and deport them to Togo because they had participated in the uprising. During the Italian expedition in Tripolitania in 1915, local levies also turned against the European troops. More often, locally hired irregulars would simply desert. The Natal Africans in the Zulu War abandoned the British rather than face highly disciplined and ruthless Zulu warriors at the Battle of Isandhlwana in 1879. In 1890 the French established a battalion of *tirailleurs soudanais*. African porters who were conscripted to support their operations had to be chained together on the march to prevent desertion.

There was always the fear, even when using indigenous personnel in trained regiments, that the locals would lose the rusticity, spontaneity and resilience that supplied the edge which the Europeans required for mobile operations and which had characterised these troops in the first place. To obtain the best results from local forces required an officer corps with a command of local languages and customs, prepared to endure a low standard of living in the most testing of environments. French officers serving with Saharan troops had to endure sandstorms, difficult camel transport, high temperatures and all the demands of campaigning on a diet of water, dates and couscous.

After the Franco-Prussian war, the French colonial army consisted of 15,300 white and 7,420 indigenous troops. The conquest of Tunisia had required 35,000 troops from France in 1881, but casualties from disease meant that these were soon replaced by Algerian units. The original invasion force of Tonkin in Indochina in 1883 was 4,000, but the force required to subjugate the region grew to 40,000 within two years. The conquest of Dahomey had required just 3,400 men in 1892. By 1914, the French colonial army had grown to 42,100 white and 88,108 native troops. The Algerian garrison was equivalent of two army corps before the First World War. This was important when there was such anxiety about the demographic growth of Germany, which, potentially, could give them additional reservists to overwhelm the French Army. In his book *Force noire* in 1910, General Mangin had urged his countrymen to draw more manpower from the colonies, but Georges Clemenceau disagreed and believed that colonial expansion wasted the critical resources required to develop an army to confront Germany on the north-eastern frontier of the country. In France, resistance to colonial expansion was magnified by even minor setbacks in the field. In 1894, at Timbuktu, a French camp was attacked by the Tuaregs. The position was overrun and 13 French officers and NCOs and 68 native soldiers were killed. The reaction in France was protest at the ugly realities of the so-called civilising mission, and, ultimately, military administration in West Africa was replaced by civil governance.[18]

In May 1913, selective conscription was applied to the Muslim population of Algeria in order to scour the colony for recruits. But, from an eligible annual cohort of 45,000, only 2,000 conscripts a year were obtained and it remained overwhelmingly a volunteer force. In 1914, the Army of Africa in Algeria and Tunisia comprised nine regiments of Algerian *tirailleurs*, four of Zouaves, six of Chasseurs d'Afrique, four of Spahis and two of the Foreign Legion. In Morocco, there were a further nineteen battalions of *tirailleurs* and nine of Zouaves, along with detachments of the Foreign Legion and the African Light Infantry. A large proportion of these troops were sent immediately to serve in France in the First World War. Some 33,000 Muslim Algerians served as the Spahis, *tirailleurs* and other units of the Army of Africa. During the course of the war, a further 137,000 enlisted, either as volunteers (57,000) or as conscripts (80,000).

The French also raised local forces in South East Asia. During the campaign in Tonkin in 1883, several irregular units of Tonkinese militiamen were raised from amongst the Christian population who felt little loyalty to the regime of Tu Duc. These units were established as temporary levies, and were disbanded when the French withdrew from Tonkin in early 1874, but it had proved the potential for the recruitment of local auxiliary soldiers in the region. A more permanent arrangement was made in Cochin-China, where a regiment of Annamese riflemen, known variously as *tirailleurs annamites*, *tirailleurs saigonais* and *tirailleurs cochinchinois*, was established in 1879.

In 1883 French forces were pitted against the Black Flag Army, and their supporting Vietnamese and Chinese forces in Tonkin, and manpower demands increased exponentially. General Bouët and Admiral Courbet repeated the raising of local levies, and in August 1883 the Yellow Flag units were used extensively as auxiliaries.[19] They had originally been established by Georges Vlavianos, a European mercenary, in 1873, and they were a competent formation when used as skirmishers at the Battle of Phu Hoai (15 August 1883) and the Battle of Palan (1 September 1883). Nevertheless, their indiscipline compelled the French to disband them again soon after. To ensure more reliability and discipline, the French established their own regular regiments of *tirailleurs tonkinois* in 1884.[20]

As a result, the column commanded by Admiral Courbet in the Son Tay Campaign included four companies of Annamese riflemen from Cochin-China, and each one was attached to a marine infantry battalion to ensure it was sufficiently 'stiffened'. Some 800 local auxiliaries were nevertheless retained, led by Bertaux-Levillain, and it was clear that many of them had previously served in the Yellow Flag formations, but they played almost no part in the fighting at Phu Sa on 14 December or Son Tay on 16 December.

By contrast, the regulars of the *tirailleurs annamites*, with their French officers, captured the trenches of their enemies at the Battle of Phu Sa. General Charles-Théodore Millot, who replaced Admiral Courbet as commander of the Tonkin Expeditionary Corps in February 1884, was an enthusiast for native auxiliaries. Millot believed that, if they were led by an appropriate number of French officers and NCOs, the inefficiencies and indiscipline of the previous experiments could be avoided. Consequently, he reorganised the Tonkinese levies into regular companies, each under the command of a Marine infantry captain. Subsequently, several of these companies of riflemen took part in the Bac Ninh campaign in March 1884 and the Hung Hoa expedition in April 1884, and they numbered 1,500 in strength.

Millot, impressed by their performance, gained further authorisation to raise two regular regiments of Tonkinese *tirailleurs*, each of 3,000 men, organised into three battalions, with four large companies of 250 men each. They were known as the 1st and 2nd Tonkinese Rifle Regiments and were commanded, as before, by experienced Marine officers. The two commanding officers, Lieutenant Colonel de Maussion and Lieutenant Colonel Berger, had an experienced track record in operations the previous year in Indochina. Obtaining officers with sufficient experience took time, but by the summer of 1884 the full complement of troops, NCOs and officers had been established.

Millot was also prepared to contemplate the enlistment of his former enemies. When several hundred Black Flag fighters surrendered after the fall of Hung Hoa and Tuyen Quang in July 1884, Millot created a separate company of Tonkinese Riflemen, and dispatched them to an isolated post on the Day River. They were to be trained and disciplined by Lieutenant Bohin, but there was considerable disquiet about the concept and about the vulnerability of this post. Bohin was even nicknamed *le condamné à mort* by his fellow officers. For some months the experiment appeared to work. The new company was prepared to operate against local insurgents, but in December 1884 they deserted en masse, killed a Tonkinese sergeant and made their way to rejoin the Black Flag Army to the north. To everyone's surprise, Bohin was left unharmed. The prospect of an imminent Chinese victory, which seemed likely in Tonkin, had prompted their calculation to rejoin the winning side. There were no further attempts to enlist those that had been in enemy employment, and instead a third regular Tonkinese Rifle regiment was raised by General de Courcy in 1885, with a fourth in 1886.

At the turn of the century, the *tirailleurs* were used for frontier security against criminal gangs but, because of fears of fraternisation, the Tonkinese rifles were invariably accompanied by detachments of French colonial infantry or Foreign Legionnaires. To meet the demands along the borders, a fifth regiment of Tonkinese Rifles was raised in 1902 but it was disbanded in 1908 when the requirements had subsided. In 1914, the more experienced Marine infantry officers could not be spared and many of the French officers and NCOs of the *tirailleurs tonkinois* and *tirailleurs annamites* returned to France. Nevertheless, one battalion of 6th Tonkinese riflemen served on the Western Front near Verdun. In 1915, a battalion of the 3rd Regiment was ordered to China to garrison Shanghai, while in 1917 the *tirailleurs* in Indochina were needed to suppress a mutiny of the Garde indigène in Thai Nguen. Towards the end of the war, in August 1918, three companies of *tirailleurs tonkinois* formed part of a composite battalion of colonial troops sent to Siberia as part of the Allied intervention force. These operations had vindicated the faith of the original architects of an auxiliary force in Indochina, and they provided the basis of a more modernised force to follow.

African troops in British Service

Africans were used by all the European powers to augment their imperial forces, in every variety from irregular levies to trained regulars. Whether mounted on camels and horses, or jogging on foot; and whether armed with traditional weapons or the latest rifles, the indigenous African was an integral element of colonial warfare. Even private companies would employ armed black labour. In 1889, Cecil Rhodes, the southern African mining magnate, established a corps of Mashonaland Pioneers in order to conquer territories further north in the interior. It consisted of a variety of nationalities, all mounted, and included 300 hand-picked natives.[21] As Cecil Rhodes's force became more successful, resistance from local clans increased, including that of the Matabele (Ndebele). But Rhodes not only possessed more firepower, he could also employ more auxiliaries, including a force from Bechuanaland led by its chief, Khama. The combined effect of his mobile manpower and machine guns devastated the Matabele impis.

In East Africa, the British East Africa Company made even greater use of native troops. Frederick Lugard, the son of the army chaplain in India who had served in the Second Anglo-Afghan War, in the Sudan and Burma, employed 3,000 men from the Sudan for his operations until, in 1897, they mutinied.

Auxiliary forces were also used in suppression of revolts. When, in 1900, the Nandi rose in revolt in Uganda, a British protectorate, a contingent of 400

Punjabis led by six officers were brought in to suppress it. Zulus were thought such good fighters that, in 1898, the British considered bringing a force of 2,000 enlisted Zulu warriors to the Sudan, not only to provide a formidable force for internal security, but also to prevent French incursions, as had occurred at Fashoda that year.[22] Increasingly, consideration was given to the utility of Africans to release European troops for service against rival Great Powers.

Africans were also important in conventional operations against the large and well-organised African polities that stood in the way of European expansion. While the French employed North African and West African troops against the kingdoms and empires of the western interior, such as the Fulani, the British employed Egyptians and Sudanese against the caliphate of the Mahdi and his successor, the Khalifa, in Sudan. The British had decided to reoccupy the Sudan, a former Egyptian colony, in 1896 when other European powers seemed to threaten the security of the region. Major-General Herbert Horatio Kitchener prepared the reconquest in meticulous detail. He began with the recapture of the Dongola province, defeating a Sudanese force at Firket (7 June 1896). He then set about the construction of a railway across the desert to avoid having to stretch his communications along the Nile. British troops reinforced his regular Egyptian army in January 1898 and on 8 April Kitchener attacked the entrenched camp of Uthman Diqna (or Osman Digna) at Atbara. The war correspondent G.W. Steevens accompanied General Kitchener during his advance southwards into the Khalifa's territories, and observed at first hand the battle of Atbara. Having described the successful attack made by the British soldiers, which ended in a close-quarter fight inside the Dervishes' encampment, Steevens narrated the attack made by the Sudanese:

> Meanwhile, all the right hand part of the zariba was alive with blacks. They had been seen from the British line as it advanced, ambling and scrambling over rise and dip, firing heavily, as they were ordered to, and then charging with the cold bayonet, as they lusted to. They were in first, there cannot be a doubt. Their line formation turned out a far better one for charging the defences than the British columns, which were founded on an exaggerated expectation of the difficulty of the zariba, and turned out a trifle unhandy. And if the zariba had been as high and thick as the Bank of England, the blacks and their brigaded Egyptians would have slicked through it and picked out the thorns after the cease fire. As against that, they lost more men than the British, for their advance was speedy and their volleys less deadly than the Camerons pelting destruction that drove through every skull raised an inch to aim.[23]

Steevens appeared to answer the common criticism that African soldiers could not be kept under control, which would squander their military value:

But never think that blacks were out of hand. They attacked fast, but they attacked steadily, and kept their formation to the last moment there was anything to form against. The battle of the Atbara has definitely placed blacks—yes, and the once condemned Egyptians—in the ranks of the very best in the world. When it was over their officers were ready to cry with joy and pride. And the blacks, every one of whom would beamingly charge the bottomless pit after his Bey [officer], were just as joyous and proud of their offices. They stood about amongst the dead, their faces cleft with smiles, shaking and shaking each other's hands. A short shake, then a salute, another shake and another salute, again and again and again, with the head carving smile never narrowed for an instant. Then up to the Bey and the bimbashis—mounted now, but they had charged afoot and clear ahead, as is the recognised wont of all chiefs of the fighting Sudan when they intend to conquer or die with their men. And more handshakes and more salutes: 'dushman quaiss kitir', ran round from grin to grin; 'very good fight, very good fight'.[24]

Clearing the position at Atbara in just two hours, Kitchener paused for more reinforcements, bringing his Anglo-Egyptian army to 26,000 men. On 1 September, Kitchener arranged his forces in a defensive square, supported by gunboats on the Nile, within sight of the Khalifa's base at Omdurman. The next morning, the Dervishes attacked but were unable to get to close quarters, being mown down by British rifle, artillery and machine-gun fire. The British were firing at ranges above a thousand yards, yet inflicted 10,000 casualties. When Kitchener advanced, two 'flags' (wings) of the Khalifa's army, which had remained in reserve, then attacked but they were cut down, mainly by Sudanese soldiers in British service. Steevens again narrated the performance of the Sudanese and Egyptian troops, illustrating first the scale of the threat to the Egyptian and Sudanese brigades:

The blacks of the 13th Battalion were storming Gebel Surgham. Lewis and McDonald [British brigade commanders], facing west and south, had formed a right angle. They were receiving the fire of the Khalifa's division, and the charge of the Khalifa's Horseman; behind these the Khalifa's huge black standard was flapping raven-like. The Baggara Horseman were few and ill-mounted—perhaps 200 altogether—but they rode to get home or die. They died ... The fellaheen stood like a wall, and aimed steadily at the word; the chargers swerved toward McDonald's. The blacks, as cool as any Scotsmen, stood and aimed likewise; the last Baggara fell at the muzzles of the rifles. Our fire went on, steady, remorseless. The Remington bullets piped more and more rarely overhead, and the black heads thinned out in front. A second time the attack guttered and flickered out. It was just past 10 ... Then once more the howling storm rushed down upon us; once more crashed forth the answering tempest. This time it burst upon McDonald's line—from the North West upon his right flank, spreading and gathering to his right rear. For all their sudden swiftness of movement the Dervishes throughout this day never lost their formation; their lines drove on as rigidly as ours, regiment alongside regiment in lines of six and eight and a dozen ranks, 'til you might have fancied the Macedonian phalanx was alive again. Left and front and right and rear the masses ate up the desert—12,000 unbroken fast and fearless warriors leaping 'round 3,000.[25]

The critical moment had arrived, and it required some nerve to withstand the scale of the attack against them:

[Macdonald's] blacks of the 9th, 10th, and 11th, the historic fighting regiments of the Egyptian army, were worthy of their chief. The 2nd Egyptian, brigaded with them and fighting in the line, were worthy of their comrades, and of their own reputation, as the best disciplined battalion in the world. A few had feared that the blacks would be too forward, the yellows too backward: except that the blacks, as always, looked happier, there was no difference at all between them. The Egyptians sprang to the advance at the bugle; the Sudanese ceased fire in an instant silence at the whistle. They were losing men, too, although eyes were clamped on the Dervishes charges; Dervish fire was brisk. Man after man dropped out behind the firing line. Here was a white officer with red-lathered charger; there a black stretched straight, bare-headed in the sun, dry lips, uncomplaining, a bullet through his liver; two yards away a dead driver by a dead battery mule, his whip still glued in his hand. The table of loss topped 100–150—neared 200. Still they stood, fired, advanced, fired, changed front, fired—firing, firing always, death in the din, blind in the smarting smoke, hot, dry, bleeding, thirsty, enduring the devilish fights to the end.[26]

Steevens concluded his account of Omdurman with an assessment of the Sudanese and Egyptian soldiers' performance. He wrote:

The native troops vindicated their courage, discipline and endurance most nobly. The sudden, unforeseen charges might well have shaken the nerve of the Egyptians and overexcited the blacks; both were absolutely cool. The only fault was in shooting. At almost every volley you saw a bullet kick the sand within 50 yards of the firing line. Others flew almost perpendicular into the air. Still, given steadiness, the mechanical art of shooting can be taught with time and patience. When you consider that less than six months ago the equivalent of one company in each black battalion were raw dervishes, utterly untrained in the use of firearms, the wonder is they shot as well as they did. Anyhow they shot well enough, and in trying circumstances they shot as well as they knew how. That is the heart of the matter.'[27]

Contemporaries of the Battle of Omdurman, the German authorities, eager to create their own imperial dominion, wanted to emulate the British and European colonial practice of raising local armed forces. In the Cameroons the Germans made use of military police drawn from outside the colony, particularly Nigeria, Togo, Dahomey and Sudan. In 1895 the Germans went further in copying the colonial model and established a regular military force known as the Schutztruppe. Although a law in 1896 limited the number of native troops that could be armed to police each territory, in East Africa the German colonists, anticipating that they might have to defend the territory against other European powers, made more extensive use of native manpower. German officers were selected on the basis of experience, and an excellent service record, and their NCOs were expected to learn the local language.[28] The German colonial troops, the askaris, were initially recruited from Sudan as the British had done, but, in time, local men were also enlisted. Every effort was made, through the provision of privileges and by creating the impression of elite status, to inculcate loyalty to the Kaiser and to Germany. The troops responded by demanding servants, women and groups of camp followers in emulation of the Europeans. As a result, for each company (5 Europeans and 150 soldiers), they were accompanied by 500 noncombatants. The model was to prove a great success in German East Africa in the First World War.

African Armies

Africans served in the military forces of the European empires for similar reasons to the men in Asia, the Pacific and the Caribbean. A combination of push and pull factors motivated young men to enlist, some of them external and others internal. Once in the service, a combination of discipline, enhanced status, internal cohesion, and attachment to local leaders sustained them. Pay was far higher in relative terms than that of their peers and the main limiting factor on their numbers was the amount of resources the Europeans were prepared to commit to African security. Before the First World War, African contingents tended to be quite small, and the largest forces were to be found in North Africa and Sudan.

The North Africans in French service were used across the French African colonies and indeed beyond the continent. West Africans in British service tended to be limited to their own region, but elements of the King's African Rifles, established at the turn of the century, were drawn from a wide area of Central and eastern Africa and the British looked upon them as a force that could be deployed in any part of the Empire, like the Gurkhas or the Sikhs.

The Sudanese and Egyptian troops who fought in the Sudan in the 1890s were regulars, trained and disciplined to the same standard as British troops, and expected to fight using the standard tactics of the Europeans, although their weapons were of a moderately lower standard. By contrast, the Africans enlisted to assist in the South African War were militia and irregulars.

Although the arming of blacks was officially denied in that war, local arrangements had led to the widespread use of scouts, armed levies and partnerships
with local tribes. In sieges and other operations requiring the construction of
field fortifications and trenches, African labour was indispensable, but the use
of black troops, even as militia, was an important if deliberately neglected
aspect of the conflict. The Africans had strong motives to fight the Afrikaners,
but they lacked the armaments, training and organisation to succeed in any
struggle for liberation. Under the conditions of the siege at Mafeking, they
displayed remarkable endurance.

Manpower needs had driven the Europeans to seek local forces and, of
course, large numbers of labourers. In the South African War, significant numbers of black men had been used to assist the British in the construction of
field fortifications and railways. Local men had also been enlisted in larger
numbers as armed personnel as the number of security tasks increased exponentially. They were invaluable as scouts, couriers and spies, being able to pass
themselves off as civilians and blending into the population. Their reasons for
co-operating followed a pattern of employment income and relative security
but also, in cases like the Barolong at Mafeking, because of a coincidence of
aims. Nevertheless, despite their important contribution, their efforts went
largely unappreciated, obscured by a combination of needing to reach an
acceptable settlement with the Afrikaners and imperial prestige.

For the British and for the French, the issue of trust was critical to the success or failure of their local forces. The careful selection of certain African
groups, particularly where the absence of native sympathy with a majority
population could be guaranteed, was a well-established method, but there
were limits to how far the Europeans were prepared to put their faith in armed
local security forces. Reliability was always being questioned, a point that the
correspondent G.W. Steevens felt compelled to emphasise in positive terms in
his reports on the fighting conducted by local forces in the Sudan. Local forces
were thought to be useful in terms of acclimatisation, endurance and cost, but
there were frequent alarms about the potential for indiscipline. It was assumed
that, without European regular soldier training, local auxiliaries would revert
to a form of ruthless, unlimited and even bestial warfare. Local objectives
could easily be misunderstood: rival communities represented an existential
threat in some cases, and war was an opportunity for the acquisition of certain
goods, women and land, but also for survival by the elimination of enemy
personnel. Betrayals, changing sides and desertions could also influence
European perceptions not only of individual local fighters, but of entire
groups, clans and communities.

Campaigning before 1914 in Africa, where infrastructure was limited and the environmental conditions often severe, placed enormous demands on both local and European personnel. The requirements expected of French officers commanding local troops in isolated and alien landscapes, for example, were particularly tough. Under these conditions, it is hardly a surprise that many of them developed an equally hard attitude towards those that resisted them. Indeed, colonial campaigning was an experience that demanded discipline and endurance in large measure. Europeans were expected to perform to high standards in the presence of local personnel but, for some individual officers, there was a degree of freedom that would otherwise be denied them in a standard European regiment. The greatest opportunities lay with irregular and frontier units, and it is on these examples that we must now focus our attention.

8

IRREGULARS AND ADVISERS
IN COLONIAL SERVICE

Indian Irregular Cavalry

Alongside the regular army of the East India Company, the British in the sub-continent employed irregular forces. Frequently, these forces were raised because of some urgent necessity when there was insufficient time to set about the training of a regular formation. In South Asia in the early nineteenth century, the abundance of relatively trained military manpower made this process far easier for any power with sufficient funds to employ them. In the war against Nepal, some 4,000 experienced Rohillas accompanied the British and were used as a skirmishing line ahead of the main force, and, after the war, the Gurkhas were also incorporated in this fashion. Indian light irregular cavalry also augmented the British order of battle on the plains of the subcontinent. To defeat the Tipu Sultan of Mysore, thousands of Maratha horsemen were enlisted; their mobility enabled them to raid, harass and pursue their enemies. Their success was also to divert the Tipu Sultan's forces and deprive him of critical resources. Based on these expedient uses, the British therefore increased the numbers of their own irregular light cavalry under the command of British officers and kept them on a permanent establishment. The aim was to retain the mounted skills of selected men, while inculcating an elite ethos. Armed with several weapons and with a reputation for dash and courage, 'They are reckoned,' one eyewitness noted, 'by all the English in this part of the country, the most useful and trusty, as well as the boldest body of men in India.'[1]

Skinner's Horse was the most senior regiment of Indian cavalry of this stamp. It had been raised in 1803 during the Maratha Wars from men first enlisted by the French adventurer and adviser Pierre-Cuillier Perron while in the service of Daulat Scindia of Gwalior. When General Gerard Lake fought the Marathas, one of their officers, James Skinner, a man of mixed descent, temporarily withdrew from the regiment he had hitherto served, but when Lake won his victory at Delhi and the cavalry force enlisted in its entirety with the British, Skinner rejoined them. When Skinner was offered a commission by the East India Company, he became the commanding officer of the regiment. The unit was nicknamed the 'yellow boys' from the colour of their uniform but was thought to be one of the most militarily efficient forces in the entire Company Army.

In 1857, at the outbreak of the Indian Mutiny, they were known as the 1st Bengal Irregular Cavalry, and they were stationed at Multan under the command of Captain Neville Chamberlain. The regiment at that time consisted of Hindustani Muslims, Rajputs and Jats, as well Asanghars, that is, Muslims who were of Rajput descent. The regiment had a larger complement of native officers than most regiments of the Company Army and only three British officers: there was therefore considerable doubt about their loyalty when the unrest began that year. The situation at Multan was worsened by the presence of two regiments of Bengal Native Infantry and a battery of native horse artillery. As tensions increased, one of the native officers approached Chamberlain to complain that they were not being trusted by the British. Chamberlain handed him a jewelled sword, known to the regiment for its great value, with the statement: 'Give me this back when this war is over.' It was said that the risaldar, Shaidad Khan, was so moved that, full of tears, he knelt before his commanding officer and pledged his allegiance. Critically, of course, both men had exhibited trust in each other. Skinner's Horse proved loyal during the Indian Mutiny and fought throughout the campaign with distinction. Chamberlain's gesture, 'livid, emotional, generous', had been sufficient to 'turn the scale'.[2]

All irregular cavalry in the Indian Army had just three British officers. This system had survived on the recommendation of Brigadier-General John Jacob, who had commanded an irregular cavalry regiment himself, initially known as the Scinde Irregular Horse but later given his name. Apart from a prolific administrative career and the transformation of thousands of acres of desert into productive land in upper Sind, he wrote a number of pamphlets, letters to the press and professional journal articles, extolling the value of light irregular cavalry. His argument was that there should be a minimum presence of British officers and that those chosen should be carefully selected for their qualities. He believed that only five or six officers were needed for cavalry regiments consisting of 1,600 Indians, which implied that native officers were given real responsibility and thoroughly trusted by their British counterparts. In due course, Indian cavalry officers found themselves in command of outposts hundreds of miles away from the responsibility of the British. Jacob believed their experience made them better than junior British officers, but they too were carefully selected for their energy and efficiency, and Jacob rejected entirely the principle of promotion by seniority that existed in the rest of the army at that time.[3]

Jacob's system had been proven to be essential during the Mutiny. Although Jacob himself was in Persia, serving under Sir James Outram, his two regiments, the 1st and 2nd Scinde Irregular Horse, were stationed in their home province. The men, most of whom were drawn from Delhi and the western part of what later became the United Provinces, and who shared the same background—indeed were sometimes related to—those who participated in the Mutiny, did not betray their British officers. There were entreaties by the mutineers for them to abandon the British and desert, but they refused to do so. The secret was simply mutual respect. Jacob had stated: 'You should show all the men that you respect and regard them as men; you should get them to respect themselves and feel proud of themselves—and then you will be loved, respected, almost adored.'[4] Yet the system also relied on all power being in the hands of the commanding officer, who could recruit, promote and punish. There were no courts martial; a committee of five native officers would inquire into any case and report on it with their own recommendations, but the final decision was for the commanding officer alone. The threat of dismissal often precluded the need for severe punishment, because dishonour had a greater currency. No records were kept, no formal committees were established and there were no rules of evidence. Appeals were made directly to the commanding officer. It was the ultimate in personalised command, but could not suit lesser men.

This system had been possible because the irregular cavalry was not under the Commander-in-Chief of either the Bombay or the Bengal Presidency Army. They came directly under the control of the Chief Commissioner for Sind, Sir Bartle Frere, and he was a firm believer in devolving responsibility. It is often the case that giving full responsibility earlier than superiors are comfortable with will produce more resourceful, more loyal and more willing subordinates. Moreover, by being given responsibility, younger personnel invariably live up to it.

The Scinde Irregular Horse was a first-class frontier regiment whose excellence derived from their constant readiness for action and ability to conduct an immediate pursuit against raiding forces from the mountains. Rather like the reputation of the Canadian Mounties, who would 'always get their man', the Scinde Irregular Horse prided themselves on their willingness to pursue any tribal war party, regardless of either its size or its invariably almost inaccessible location. In one incident, when a group of Baluch tribesman had stolen camels, the native officer, Durga Singh, commenced an immediate pursuit with just 15 troopers. By the time he had made contact with the 40-strong war party, having dispatched the sowars in the search, the native officer had just three companions with him; but he refused to turn back, and wasted no time in making his assault, because he believed that Major Jacob would consider him unfit to command if he did not engage the enemy immediately: it was a matter of honour.[5] He and two troopers carried out their attack, killed and wounded 15 of the enemy, but were themselves killed in the action. Only their guide escaped. Such willingness to fulfil their duty not only inspired the admiration of the regiment, it also acted as a cumulative deterrent against the raiding parties.

As with other so-called irregular regiments, the title 'irregular' referred only to their administrative reporting line and the fact that each man owned his own horse. It did not refer to their state of discipline. Indeed, the irregular cavalry were among the most highly disciplined of the Indian Army. Although they were dressed in loose uniforms, because of the climate, they were nevertheless armed with the best weapons available. These they also owned themselves. Unlike most regiments, which required a period of notice before they could move, the irregular cavalry would move immediately when ordered. The ethos of the cavalry was to be in a constant pitch of combat preparedness.

The origin of the Indian light cavalry was based on the *silladar* system, which originally had referred to an officer commanding groups of mounted men, 50 or more, as retainers, who also operated as tenants of the land that he owned. It was the commander's responsibility to provide the horses and arms for his own mounted force. They were known as his *bargirs*. By the mid-nineteenth century, the term '*silladar*' had changed its meaning. Formerly, a ruler had paid for an *asami*, or place, in a mounted force, which was a fixed amount. This payment might be drawn by a serving horseman, a retired cavalryman, a widow, or indeed a moneylender to whom the place had been sold. The holder of the place would pay a man to occupy a position in the cavalry force; in other words, he would pay a *bargir*, and would provide him with a horse and weapons, while keeping a small profit for himself. A wealthy man serving in a horse unit of this type might pay for several places and fill them with sons, nephews or other relatives. John Jacob modified this system. He stopped places being owned by those outside the regiment. Any serving man who died would have his horse and weapons sold and the proceeds passed on to a relative. But no man was permitted to be in debt. He did, however, encourage a man to own three or four places in the regiment for relatives to serve. This also allowed a horseman to afford to keep a groom, a grass cutter and perhaps a camel or ponies for baggage. Irregular cavalry possessed no wheeled vehicles or hired animals. The ethos of the unit was to be completely independent and self-reliant. There was some government support. If a horse was killed in action, the government would pay for compensation. If a horse died of natural causes, compensation was paid from a regimental fund. Yet everything was done to encourage the horseman to take care and act with responsibility. If a horse had a sore back, for example, the rider would walk until it was fit and pay a fine for having neglected his mount.

When the Indian Army was re-formed after the Mutiny, the eight Bengal Army cavalry regiments were disbanded, but the eight irregular regiments survived and, in 1861, became the first eight regiments of the reformed Bengal Cavalry. Probyn's Horse, another unit named after its commander, had been known as the 1st Sikh Irregular Cavalry and had been raised in the Punjab on the orders of Sir John Lawrence in 1857. Its first commander, Captain Frederick Wale, had been killed in action and so Dighton M. Probyn took over. In 1858, promoted to major, his commission and appointment was a reward for his courage in the Mutiny, in which he had won a Victoria Cross at Agra. Although the naming of regiments after their commanding officers had been ended in the British Army in 1751, in India the tradition continued. Among them were Gardner's, Gordon's, Jacob's, Fane's, Cureton's, Lumsden's, Sam Browne's and Murray's in the cavalry, while in the infantry there were Rattray's, Lumsden's, Wilde's, Vaughan's, Russell's, and Outram's. Regional titles and the conferment of the names of members of the Royal Family were also common.

The Punjab Irregular Force (the Piffers)

When the British annexed Sind and the Punjab, it placed their possessions alongside the mountainous region subsequently known as the North West

Frontier. It was a region inhabited by a variety of clans, ethnic groups and polities who had invariably defied monarchical systems imposed from either Central Asia or the subcontinent. This defiance was made manifest in their habit of raiding the more settled districts that lay adjacent to them, not least because the mountain fastnesses on which they depended for their security and independence could barely provide even a viable subsistence. Raiding, for material gain, murder of rivals or to acquire women, became an established part of the frontier, but the security demands represented a drain on the exchequer of the Kingdom of Punjab and then, after 1846, on the British. Sir Henry Daly noted, 'for a thousand years and more, the valley of the Indus under the Suleyman range had been studded with a line of forts and towers—ruins of which still remain—as positions and outposts against the ceaseless raids of mountain marauders'.[6] Despite their strength, estimated to be over 100,000 men, they were bitterly divided, and only rarely combined in the face of a common threat. The broken nature of the country, with countless defiles and valleys, would have required many thousands to conquer, and this made permanent occupation by a conventional force almost impossible. Consequently, the British sought cheaper alternatives, including the enlistment of a select corps that, using speed and the same mountain warfare tactics as the raiders, could intercept and defeat their enemies.

Soon after the First Anglo-Sikh War in 1846, the Governor General, Sir Henry Lawrence, established the Frontier Brigade consisting of four infantry regiments and a handful of irregular horsemen. The mainstay of these infantry regiments were Sikhs, recently demobilised but ready to serve as military professionals, and for the cause of defending the Punjab plains on which their peoples depended. To differentiate them from the rest of the Company Army, they were styled the 1st to 4th Sikh Local Infantry Regiments. Meanwhile, in Peshawar, Lieutenant (later Sir) Harry Burnett Lumsden, an intrepid officer with an acute understanding of the nature of irregular warfare, established the Guides cavalry. From the outset this force was regarded as the elite element of the Indian Army, and they were the first formation to appear in khaki as an acknowledgement of the importance of camouflage in the tactical fieldcraft in which they excelled. After the Second Anglo-Sikh War in 1849, another force was created to augment the Frontier Brigade. Consisting of the 1st to 5th Punjab Infantry, the second formation was entitled the Transfrontier Brigade. Four years later, the Scind Camel Corps, which had been raised in 1843 at Karachi on the orders of General Charles Napier, became the 6th Punjab Infantry. The two brigades were known as the Punjab Irregular Force, nicknamed the Piffers, from 1865, and its members took immense pride in their selection and in their disdain for parade-ground drill or other conventional military routines. Theirs was a more fluid if purposeful approach to their duties: their emphasis was on swift tactical manoeuvres, carried out by small groups. There was a great deal of emphasis on using their initiative, personal courage and an absence of formal orders or control. The free, high-risk and dynamic nature of the force was a magnet for the most enterprising men, and British officers who served in the Piffers were practically venerated.

Sir Henry Lawrence, who modelled the Piffers on the original small corps of Guides, had been struck by the difficulties that the Army of the Indus had faced in its campaign in Baluchistan and Afghanistan. The absence of knowledgeable men to guide the army, with a command of the local languages, had caused immense problems in supplies and increased the level of local resistance. The Guides were established to have 'hardy men accustomed to every region and accident of service, and familiar with every village dialect'.[7] The original force, a single troop of cavalry and two companies of infantry, was insufficient for the task, so there had to be expansion.

The selection process was an important strength of the Guides. Each man was carefully screened and Lumsden made it his business to get to know well the individuals under his command. Care was taken to select men from a range of groups, including Afridis, Waziris and other Pashtuns; Gurkhas, Sikhs, the Shia Hazaras and 'even Kaffirs' (referring to the pagans of the Kalasha and Nuristani districts astride what became the Afghan–British Indian border). This gave Lumsden men who could speak every language of the frontier, including often 'dialects unknown to the men of the plains'.[8] Aside from languages, Lumsden deliberately sought out men who had a reputation: 'men notorious for desperate deeds, [and the] leaders in forays'. The appeal was regular pay but also the spirit of enterprise and adventure that accompanied a 'special' force. Lumsden benefited from the means by which reputations and ideas were spread: word soon travelled across the valleys and hills, and the stories grew with the telling. The attraction of money and adventure, licensed by a man with authority, seemingly unlimited funds and modern firearms, proved irresistible to the most daring and entrepreneurial.

Among the Yusufzai, a Pashtun clan close to the Khyber Pass, there was a strong sense of independence. Dilawur Khan was infamous, even in this tough community, for his raids, kidnapping and ruthlessness. He made excellent use of the hills to launch his attacks and then quickly withdraw, never occupying a single, central base but constantly moving. He had been schooled in religious doctrine by clan mullahs, but he had rejected a similar career in favour of material gain and found that holding wealthy men to ransom was the most lucrative life. Lumsden, with characteristic 'neck', invited this well-known criminal to his camp, and, much to everyone's astonishment, Dilawur Khan accepted. Lumsden pointed out to him that the British were gradually establishing their presence in the region and that Dilawur Khan's days of plunder was numbered. He therefore offered him a place in his corps of Guides. Dilawur Khan burst out laughing and returned to the hills but, within six weeks, he returned and offered to enlist on certain terms. These included a refusal to do the 'goose step' which would be degrading in the eyes of his peers. Lumsden patiently persisted, arguing that, in order to join the Guides, Dilawur Khan would have to learn the entire 'art of war'. In time, the man relented: Dilawur Khan learned foot drill and became another established figure in the unit.

Not every member of the Guides was a former hill raider. At least half of the force were sons or relations of notable chiefs, an important means to ensure good conduct among them but also to guarantee all the clans knew the Guides and would accept their presence. There developed some competition between local leaders to have their sons in the Guides. Before long, there was a long line of young men awaiting their chance to enter Lumsden's service, which only added to its exclusive appeal. Shooting competitions, with rewards of a place in the corps, became the scene of great enthusiasm, as clans felt there was much esteem at stake. In contrast with the way in which the Sikh Kingdom had approached the region, as fit only for conquest and subjugation, Lumsden had made a virtue of its lawlessness. The base he established at Mardan, in Yusufzai territory, became an influential hub and the centre of recruitment.

The affection that developed for Lumsden as a man who turned a blind eye to some of the practices of local populations and made no demands for taxation, in contrast with the settled areas to the east, was evident. When Sir John Lawrence visited the Guides' headquarters, he was nevertheless eager to make enquiries into the management and administration of the district around Mardan. One of the Guides' Afridi troopers, noting that Lumsden seemed burdened by the presence of the Governor General, offered to provide a decisive solution. He stated: 'Since the great Lawrence came, you have been worried and depressed; many have observed this, and that he is always looking at papers, asking questions, and overhauling your accounts. Has he said anything to pain you? Is he interfering with you? He starts for Peshawar to-morrow morning; and there is no reason why he should reach it.'[9] Lumsden naturally declined this lethal option.

During the Second Anglo-Sikh War in 1848, the Guides were frequently in action and suffered significant losses, but there was always a steady stream of volunteers to fill the gaps. Pay was correspondingly higher than in the rest of the army, and the losses necessitated double the number of local officers and NCOs to ensure continuity in command, although it also suited the more independently minded troops within the force.

The Punjab Force which developed from the Guides, was, by the mid-century, made up of five infantry and five cavalry regiments. The mounted element consisted of a commandant and just three British officers, but had 18 native officers with 588 troopers. The Infantry also had just 4 British personnel, 18 native officers and 896 in the rank and file. As in the Guides, the native officers and NCOs consisted of relations of prominent nobles and chiefs, including Afghans. The forces were kept at a constant state of readiness, with their own ponies and mules to carry supplies across any type of terrain. Fire support was provided by three batteries of horse artillery, manned by Sikhs and officered by subalterns of the Bengal Horse Artillery. Outposts were held by veteran Sikhs, most of whom had seen plenty of active service. The guns in their posts were held in almost sacred awe, a tradition they had inherited from the times of Ranjit Singh. They swore to sacrifice themselves rather than see these weapons fall into the hands of their enemies. By 1852, the Punjab Frontier Force numbered 11,000 men with 64 guns, but its real strength lay in its willingness to chance all and endure every hardship rather than in numbers.

The mettle of the force was tested in over fifty significant engagements in its first decade, and perhaps one of the most prominent missions was the expedition of 1860 against the Mahsud Waziris. In it, the 'irregular' title of the force was demonstrated to be a misleading epithet that referred only to its administrative status as outside the normal Presidency system of India: the Piffers reported directly to the Governor General. On operations, while the men retained the enterprising spirit of taking the initiative and being self-reliant individuals, the British were keen to praise their discipline, which provided an example to other formations in the Indian Army and the fact that, in effect, the Piffers were really like every other regiment of the Indian Army: 'Discipline and military science being maintained, experience has proved that the State enjoys special advantages from having this border force at its disposal. On all expeditions, while serving with corps of the line, the Punjab regiments are subject to the same rules and regulations as others, and no distinction exists between them. There is no jealousy; for the officers are drawn from the army at large, and appointments to the force are prizes which many seek. With the men, transfers and exchanges are also frequent.'[10]

General Sir Neville Chamberlain noted that, while the rest of the region was generally at peace, he was inundated by petitions from the districts adjacent to the Waziris to stop the constant raiding and plundering of farms and settlements. In 1859, one of the raiding forces had numbered 5,000 strong, which swept away any local efforts at resistance. Families were left destitute, menfolk murdered and property destroyed in their wake. The force dispatched to bring the raiders to heel consisted entirely of local forces under British command. Some 5,200 troops, with 64 British personnel, had to scale the mountains and precipitous valleys, entirely supplied from their own resources, in the teeth of Waziri resistance. The area to be traversed was unsurveyed, while the Waziris knew their own country well. The tactics that Chamberlain adopted had been learned from previous campaigns in the mountains of the frontier and Afghanistan. The heights were scaled and 'crowned' with strong detachments, while encampments on the valley floors were held with equally strong picquets, and at least half the force was ready to move instantly. After several days' advance into Waziri territory, the clans made a sudden attack, with about 3,000 fighters, and overwhelmed the perimeter. About 500 penetrated the camp where a close-quarter battle developed, but when half had been killed and wounded, they withdrew. Negotiations stalled and the Waziris put their faith in being able to hold the Kani Goram gorge, which had been prepared for defence.

Chamberlain's guns had little effect on the stone sangars and defences that had been constructed, and could not reach the bulk of the 6,000 fighters entrenched behind them. When the first storming party approached, they were showered with rocks as well as musket fire, and then subjected to a counter-attack that threatened to engulf the entire force. The 1st Punjab Infantry, hurrying up to position themselves alongside the guns, checked the huge onrush of fighters. They inflicted severe losses and the Waziris lost heart; they were chased back into their original positions and resistance collapsed soon after. The Punjab force was praised for having stood its ground against such a significant and large-scale attack, while it was noted how other, less well-trained or resolute forces might have broken and endangered the entire force.

Camp Followers and Logistics

The greatest suffering of Asian personnel on campaign occurred among the camp followers rather than the troops. Traders, kiosk- and stall-holders accompanied the Indian armies in the hope of making a small profit from the troops. Garrisons were surrounded by these small businesses but, even on campaign, the forces were followed by a large caravan of men and women offering a range of services. Some regiments became so accustomed to their presence that they had recognised 'regimental bazaars', and the stall-holders would transport themselves wherever the force went. Cooks, personal servants, bearers, grooms, barbers and the rest would march along behind the army in the field, sharing the hardships of the troops but with a great deal less protection. During the First Anglo-Afghan War, one British officer recorded: 'On the march today [I] saw a great number of Bengal native followers lying by the road side, in some cases singly and in others in groups, quite worn out with fatigue starvation or disease—some of them reduced to perfect skeletons and unable even to stand. A few of the most helpless I had brought in on the Dhoolies and Hackeries appropriated for any of the soldiers who might be taken ill—those that were able to walk were urged on and I believe reached our camp—but what is to become of them is easy to foresee—poor creatures.'[11]

In the infamous retreat from Kabul in January 1842, the majority of those who perished were civilians and camp followers, most of whom had joined the Army of the Indus when it settled in the Afghan capital. It was their presence, and commercial success, that angered the Kabulis, although the orthodox historiography has tended to concentrate only on the romantic liaisons of the British troops or the religious divide between the occupiers and the occupied.[12] Supported only by limited finances, the camp followers made themselves indispensable to the troops. The 'lascars' were an organised body of labourers, often tasked with the erection of tents, camp facilities and road construction. Sweepers dealt with latrines and waste. The syces cared for the animals, and the grass cutters provided the forage. Cutlers, one of whom accompanied each troop of cavalry, maintained the bladed weapons of sword, sabre and lance. It was the *bheesti* of the Indian Army, the water-carrier, who was immortalised for his service by an observant Rudyard Kipling in the fictional character of Gunga Din. Nevertheless, Itarsi, a sweeper with the 125th Napier's Rifles who accompanied his regiment to Mesopotamia in the First World War, won the respect of his comrades when, as the men around him were killed and wounded at the Battle of the Sanniyat during the attempt to relieve Kut in 1916, he joined the firing line with a rifle and bandolier.[13] Thereafter, although still a civilian, he was regarded as an 'officer' among his peers in the sweeper classes. It was an indication that even men considered to be of the lowest possible social status could earn elevation through military service and their preparedness to place themselves in the greatest hazard.

The British would also make full use of local systems of transport and supply to maintain their army's logistics. It was therefore not unusual to find the Company Army on campaign attended by thousands of camels, bullocks, mules, horses and porters. In 1840, for operations in the Punjab, there were 20,000 camels in Company service. The enormous Army of the Indus which invaded Afghanistan was similarly burdened with thousands of animals, and the 4,500-strong force which attempted to retreat from Kabul was dwarfed by a mass of over 12,000 civilians, camp followers, and thousands more baggage animals. In Burma, in the 1824–5 operations, elephants became the main means to move artillery through the forested uplands of Arakan, but the snail's pace of the Indian Army's logistics was a constant complaint into the early twentieth century. However, the business relationship that such transport and employment needs created also fostered closer ties with the banking families, traders and commercial households of India. These relationships, and the military and diplomatic power the Company developed, became the system by which the British acquired resources, information and intelligence. The latter became a vital component of Wellington's success against the Marathas, and subsequently during the Mutiny. In contrast, the rulers of the subcontinent and other Asian states failed to adapt to the arrival of European methods or, more accurately, the synthesis of Asian and European approaches to war. In a seminal article, Kaushik Roy concluded: 'the Indian princes failed to integrate the imported Western art of war with the traditional Indian method of conducting warfare'.[14] The same would also be true of other polities that, while assuming the outward trappings of the West, failed to transform and adapt to the Western onslaught.

Imperial Service Troops and Imperial State Forces of India

In the late nineteenth century, the British gave consideration to the idea that the Indian Princely States, which possessed their own military forces or armed retainers, might play a part in the defence of the subcontinent or even serve as auxiliaries in support of the Indian Army in overseas operations. In the summer of 1885, when war with Russia seemed imminent, several state rulers had offered money and men.[15] General Sir Frederick Roberts, the Commander-in-Chief of India, therefore examined how the great variety of state forces might be brought up to the same standard as the regular army and how they might be incorporated into the order of battle. It was also a political move: a military contribution from the Princely States would bind them more firmly into the fabric of the Raj and create a strong base of loyalty among the South Asian elites.

In 1798, the Governor General, Richard Wellesley, had adopted the Mughal principle of subsidiary alliances with selected rulers, which meant the stationing of troops of the Indian Army in the domains of the Princely States, paid for by those states, either with the submission of land for revenue purposes or with a financial tribute. Theoretically, these forces were positioned to protect the states against internal unrest, but they had the effect of keeping the states under British jurisdiction. But the Company also permitted the existence of Contingent forces, smaller states' armies, which could be used for internal security, and which could act as auxiliaries or allies alongside the British if they were compelled to take the field against another state.

Contingent troops were unreliable and were maintained at a poor state of military efficiency. Many of them joined the Mutiny in 1857 and were therefore disbanded soon after, but a handful were retained and became the basis of regiments that were incorporated into the Indian Army.[16] The Sikhs of the Bhopal Contingent later formed the core of the Central India Horse, and the Bhopal Levy, raised from the Bhopal, Gwalior and United Malwa Contingents, was retitled the Bhopal Battalion in March 1865, became 9th Bhopal Infantry in 1903 and was later incorporated into 16th Punjab Regiment as 4th Battalion (Bhopal), and nicknamed 'the Bo-Peeps' when they served on the Western Front in 1914.

The state's retained their own private armies after the Mutiny, but there was some concern among British authorities about the scale of these contingents, not because they posed any great threat, given their relatively outmoded levels of efficiency, but because they cost the Princely States a considerable sum to maintain and there was a chance they could attempt to overthrow their rulers and therefore create disorder. This would necessitate the deployment of British troops of the Army in India, but these were always in short supply. Moreover, the disbandment of the Contingent forces meant that the states were making no real contribution to the defence of India.

In 1873, Major Owen Tudor Burne submitted a damning report on the forces of the Princely States. His verdict was that they were a liability and could not be incorporated. The Governor General concurred on the 'the impracticability, under present conditions, of working out a scheme for associating the troops of the Native States with the Imperial Army'. He concluded that since they could not contribute effectively to the defence of India, 'it follows that, if they are in excess of internal requirements, they ought to be reduced'.[17] However, in the 1880s, Colonel George Chesney, Military Secretary to the government of India, proposed that elements of the state armies should be trained and brought up to 'first line' standards so that, on operations, if required, they could be called up from their function of guarding the lines of communication. Major Melliss, Bombay Staff Corps, conducted a tour of the state armies to assess their actual and potential capabilities. He reported that elements, but not all, could be equipped and trained for active service. Meanwhile, the Princely States themselves had made offers to have some of their contingents trained to Indian Army standards so that they could make an active contribution. This was a cost-effective way to enhance their prestige and to assert their loyalty, competitively, among their peers. In 1888, a scheme was therefore developed by Sir Frederick Roberts, the Commander-in-Chief; George Chesney; Sir Mortimer Durand, Foreign Secretary to the government of India; and Sir James Lyall, the Lieutenant Governor of the Punjab. On their recommendations, the Viceroy, Lord Dufferin, confirmed the terms of service: No state would be asked to maintain a larger force than it could support financially; British officers would act as advisers and inspectors, while drill instructors would come from the Indian Army; and the troops would be armed with breech-loading rifles paid for and supplied by the British government.

The Imperial Service Troops (IST) consisted of regiments of cavalry, infantry, companies of sappers, mule and pony transport units, and more specialist contingents such as the Bikaner Camel Corps. British officers had to ensure that the levels of training and equipment were inspected on a regular basis. They were usually majors and captains, entitled inspecting officers and assistant inspecting officers. They were seconded on fixed tours and were selected on the basis on suitability and experience. Later, their titles were changed to the more diplomatic military adviser and assistant military adviser. However, if deployed for war, it was widely accepted that the British inspectors/military advisers would accompany the units they had trained, be designated as special service officers or, if required, assume command of the unit outright. The most senior officer of the scheme was the Inspector General, later known as Military Adviser-in-Chief, who was either a major general or brigadier general. The chief concern was readiness for war and he required regular assessments of the strength, morale, quality of native officers, and proficiency of the men. His power lay in being able to recommend the formation of new units or the disbandment of those that consistently failed to meet the standards required. However, in practice, this proved much more difficult to enforce. The native officers were regarded as Indian gentlemen, and many of them were members of the families of the rulers. Given that the forces were paid for by these rulers, it was extremely difficult to enforce the same standards as in the Indian Army. British officers had to use a great deal of tact and diplomacy, not least because the rulers were sensitive to their status and position vis-à-vis other rulers. Criticism of their forces was taken as criticism of their regime as a whole. It was therefore unsurprising that, when the world war broke out in 1914, the state contingents of the IST were not of the standard that had been envisaged. Such was the demand for effective fighting manpower that Lord Roberts had written to George Chesney and asked: 'What do you think of making enquiries as to whether we could get Zulus or some other good fighting men in Africa to enlist as soldiers for service in India at a reasonable cost?'[18]

Despite the criticism, the Indian Imperial Service Troops did participate in frontier operations. In 1892, during the campaign to secure the northern border by incorporating the hill states of Gilgit, Hunza and Nagar, a significant number of the personnel were Imperial Service Troops of Kashmir. Kashmiri soldiers also took part in the Chitral relief expedition of 1895, as did transport units from Gwalior and Jaipur. In the suppression of the Mohmands during the Pathan Revolt in 1897, the cavalry units of Patiala and Jodhpur earned praise for their reconnaissance work. In the Mittai and Swan valleys, the Patiala Regiment formed the rearguard which saw action. Imperial Service Troops participated voluntarily in overseas operations in China in 1900, South Africa in 1900–2, and the Somaliland expedition of 1902–3. In Somaliland an officer of 4th Gurkha Rifles serving with the Bikaner Camel Corps earned the Victoria Cross, while his Bikaner comrade, Subadar Kishen Singh, who was wounded in the same incident, won the Indian Order of Merit.[19]

The Princely States retained their own military forces, although few were of a high standard and certainly not in a position to conduct expeditionary operations. In total, there were 93,000 troops, broken down into 16,000 cavalry, 7,000 artillery, and 70,000 infantry. The only forces of any value were Imperial Service Troops and some of the contingents of Gwalior, Hyderabad, Kashmir, and the Sikh and Rajputana states that had begun modelling their units on the IST or the regular Indian Army. When the world war broke out in 1914, the IST scheme appeared to have fallen short of its original conception. Most units were not at their full strength, and their armaments were obsolete or worn out and had to be replaced. None of the units had machine guns. The performance of some units left much to be desired in action, but they did provide a vital addition of 18,000 men to the Indian Army, especially in the early stages of the war when manpower demands were acute. Moreover, the troops were maintained in the field at the expense of their rulers.[20] Casualties were replaced by men from their own states. As planned, two or three British 'special service officers' accompanied the units that were deployed but when criticism of the Indian commandants mounted, more special service officers were appointed and many were simply placed in command.

Several IST units were brigaded together. The 15th (Imperial Service) Cavalry Brigade, for example, was made up of the 1st Hyderabad Lancers, Mysore Lancers and the Patiala Lancers, with the Bikaner Camel Corps acting as an administrative formation. It was raised in October 1914 at Deolali, India, and was deployed to Egypt in November. Its first role was in providing reconnaissance in the defence of the Suez Canal against the Ottoman offensives. In early 1916 the brigade was then tasked to secure the railway and the Sweet Water Canal. In May 1916, the Patiala Lancers were transferred to Mesopotamia, but the brigade was reinforced by the Jodhpur Lancers in early 1918. In February 1918 the brigade fought in Palestine and in July 1918 it formed part of 2nd Mounted Division as 15th (Imperial Service) Cavalry Brigade. On 23 September 1918 the Jodhpur and Mysore Lancers assisted in the capture of Haifa. On 26 October 1918 the Mysore Lancers and two squadrons of the Jodhpur Lancers charged the enemy at Aleppo, which led to its capture. The brigade was finally disbanded in January 1920.

The Princely States also assisted by providing manpower for the regulars of the Indian Army. The Indian Army had always been permitted to recruit from within the states, but with the greater demands caused by the world war, the states provided manpower and were permitted to have units known by the name of the state, creating, for example, the 3rd (Kolhapur) Battalion, 103rd Mahratta Light Infantry; the 1st Battalion, 140th Patiala Infantry, the Kathiawar Company, 125th Napier's Rifles, and the 51st (Patiala) Mule Company of the Transport Corps.[21]

After the war it was clear that improvements were needed in the training of states' officers and the standardisation of establishments to match their equivalents in the Indian Army. The result was that a new level of efficiency was expected and, to make the change, the IST were retitled the Indian State Forces (ISF). The best units would, after a short period of re-equipment and additional field training, have to be prepared for operational duty. They could not, however, be used for internal security in British India and there were financial limits on whether they could serve overseas for any length of time. But they continued to be maintained at the expense of the Princely States, the only exception being the issue of arms and equipment by the government of India. State troops, retained by the rulers, were not of the same standard but could provide a form of internal security forces within the states. In terms of performance and role, there were three categories. Class A units were those organised according to the Indian Army system and they could be deployed alongside the regulars on active service overseas. Class B units were not up to the same standard in arms, training and discipline, and they were not considered for active service. Nevertheless, they could, in time, be brought up to a higher standard of efficiency and transferred into Class A. Class C were part-time militia, and they were of an inferior standard in all areas.

In the inter-war years, paradoxically while the numbers of men serving in the ISF increased, the arms available declined. In 1932, as a result of the Great Depression, the government announced that it could no longer meet its commitments towards the State Forces. Instead, states were permitted to purchase arms at their own expense. Nevertheless, in May 1939, when another war seemed likely, the government of India decided to bring the state forces back up to the required standards and refunded the states for arms they had purchased. New terms were announced too. Minor units of no significant military value were to be dropped. Bodyguard cavalry were redesignated as irregular troops. A new category of Field Service Units (FSU), at battalion strength and conforming to adequate standards of efficiency, replaced the Class A scheme; General Service Units (GSU) could be offered for service overseas after a period of further training; and State Service Units (SSU), smaller units of a squadron or company strength, were to be retained for internal security duties. FSUs were issued with arms and equipment. State rulers had to pay for the arms and equipment of GSUs and SSUs. As before, British officers could accept or refuse a unit into the system or transfer a unit from one category to another. The government of India also agreed to the supply of horses from Indian cavalry regiments, to permit state forces' officers to attend Kitchener College, Nowgong, and Staff College, Quetta, and, during the war, allocated spaces at officer training establishments, such as the Officers' training schools at Mhow and Belgaum, and the junior commanders' course at Poona.

By November 1939, 33 states had joined the scheme. By 1945, state forces had served in every theatre of the war, with 50,290 having been raised or deployed. They included the 34th Indian States Forces Brigade in East Africa, the 150th Infantry Brigade in Hong Kong; and Force 281 in the Mediterranean.

Nevertheless, war service was not without its problems. Some state forces personnel joined the Japanese-led Indian National Army and the states were affected like the rest of India by the wartime unrest. On the other hand, several state forces personnel were decorated for courage in action, and the majority served without hindrance alongside their comrades in the Indian Army.

Smaller states, as well as the larger ones, also found a role in the provision of service support units. Transport companies, medical units and garrison forces were in high demand, and the states created formations such as the Dewas (Senior) Medical Section of the Indian Army Medical Corps. The Indian Army was also able to form six battalions of infantry, four engineering companies and twelve transport companies from the recruits drawn from the states, and hundreds of individuals volunteered separately for enlistment and were absorbed into the rest of the army.

When the British announced they would leave India, the Instruments of Accession did not include the Indian state forces, so the question of what would happen to the 75,000 ISF troops was left unresolved. The Bahawalpur State Army was integrated into the Pakistan Army as 6th Bahawalpur Division, but in India the new government tried to absorb the state forces with some difficulty. Travancore, Cochin, Mysore, Baroda and Kolhapur were taken in, but the Indian Army could not take on all the personnel. So, for a time, state forces were permitted to remain on the same terms of service as had been established by Britain. The exception was Hyderabad, which had refused to accede on Independence and which had the largest state army. Exasperated by the protracted talks, the government of India invaded Hyderabad on 13 September 1948. The state forces initially resisted, but the sheer scale of the Indian Army made the outcome inevitable. The government gradually ran down the size of the remaining state formations until 1950, when they were brought under their direct control. The only relic of these units was their names, which, for many years, survived India's independence.

The Indian state forces and the IST and ISF schemes had exemplified a curious political arrangement, whereby a hegemonic power could permit, even encourage, small military contingents to exist, equipping and arming them where necessary, in order to create loyalty and an augmentation to its own military capacity. The system is not unique to empires, and can be a recognisable feature of military alliances in which one partner is dominant. It also illustrates the importance of interoperability, the standardisation of processes, arms and munitions, without which the smaller forces are an expensive extravagance, born of pride rather than military utility. The system also depended on excellent military advisers and inspectors, who, with sufficient tact, could improve and direct a local military force. The difficulty of this task can be illustrated with two examples of military advisory work.

Military Adviser: Captain Charles Christie

Captain Charles Christie of the 5th Bombay Native Infantry had been sent to western Afghanistan in 1810 to gather intelligence. His mission was to gather information on the local tribes, their leaders and the numbers of fighting men they could command, and the defensive possibilities of the terrain in the region. This intelligence was considered vital if, as many analysts believed, Russia began an advance through Central Asia as part of a threat against British India. To fulfil his clandestine mission, Christie disguised himself as a Tartar from the Caucasus operating as a horse dealer.[22] When his cover was blown several weeks into his journey, Christie pretended to be a hajji Muslim on his return from Mecca. After four months of hazardous travel from Bombay, Christie arrived at Herat and resumed his disguise as a horse trader. He took every opportunity to survey the fortifications and defences of the city and its environs. He decided to return to India via Persia and travelled on to Meshed. Once in Persia he could take advantage of the protection offered by the Shah to British subjects. Yet, while in Persia General Malcolm, the British military attaché, asked Captain Christie to stay on and help train the Shah's troops against Russian aggression in the Caucasus.

Consequently, in 1812, Christie found himself leading some of the Persian infantry he had trained against a Cossack force in the southern Caucasus. The Russians had crossed the River Aras to confront a Persian force under the heir to the Persian throne Abbas Mirza. In a previous encounter with a weak Russian detachment, the Persians had been successful and had driven the Russians back, but, conscious that a much larger and stronger force was en route, Captain Christie and his fellow adviser, Lieutenant Henry Lindsay, an artillery officer, urged them to withdraw. General Malcolm, who was aware that Britain and Russia were de facto allies against Napoleon, ordered the British officers to leave the Persian units behind in order to avoid the risk of diplomatic embarrassment. But Christie and Lindsay could not consider the dishonour of abandoning the men they had trained. When the Russians attacked, the two British officers led, rallied and encouraged their Persian troops.

The Russians were held, briefly, and at one point even driven back. The Russians then made a counter-attack at night, and, in the confusion, the

Persians opened fire on their own ranks by mistake. The Persian commander decided to break clean and abandon the position. Christie still refused, believing that a precipitate withdrawal now, in the face of the enemy, would lead to a rout and certain disaster. This only provoked the Persian commander, Abbas, to demand, in person, that Christie and his troops fall back, and he seized the staff of the colours of the regiment that Christie was accompanying. At that precise moment Christie was shot through the neck and mortally wounded. Many of the Persian soldiers, inspired by this British officer, risked their lives to bring their wounded commander safely from the battlefield. Many were killed and wounded in the attempt and the stricken Christie had to be left behind. When approached by a Russian party, Christie lifted himself to fight on, and shot at least one of those who attempted to capture him. The Russian commander, Kotlyarevsky, ordered that the wounded British officer must be disarmed and taken prisoner, but Christie was not prepared to be paraded like a petty felon by the Russians and forced to apologise: he resolved he would not be taken alive, and, although by now bleeding his last, he killed and wounded several more of those of his would-be captors. He was finally shot dead by a Cossack.[23]

Christie's efforts, while courageous and loyal to those under his command, proved to be in vain. Persian casualties in the battle numbered in the thousands, far higher than the Russian losses, and they lost a dozen guns. Indeed, they were driven back to within a few leagues of Tehran until the casualties they inflicted on the Russian invaders forced a pause in the operations. Within a few years, the frontier stabilised with the Caucasus firmly in Russian hands. Christie may have felt his personal honour to have been at stake, but he had exceeded his mission, and refused to obey the orders not only of his own military attaché, but also of the local commander of the Persian forces. His self-sacrifice may have prevented the collapse of the Persian forces at a particular juncture in the action, but he might also have avoided the defeat they subsequently suffered if he had remained in command to effect a fighting withdrawal. Clearly, his situation was difficult either way, not least because his role was really that of a trainer and adviser, not a fighting command. Yet it is a salutary reminder of what can go wrong in a 'train and advise' mission.

Military Adviser: Charles Gordon

There were limits in how indigenous populations and their states could confront European advantages in warfare. One approach was to adopt European tactical methods and discipline, and to modernise their forces, although *adopting* the outward appearances of the West was rarely a sufficient substitute for *adaptation* to the new threats they faced and to their own distinct context and culture. Some of the Indian states in the early nineteenth century imitated the European models and employed European mercenaries or men of mixed descent who possessed proficiency and competence in training or in operational command. However, as many other polities found, it proved difficult to alter their semi-feudalised social structure in order to create a modern force that truly resembled and operated on Western lines. Moreover, it proved far harder to create a trained officer corps separate from the social system, with all its privileges, status and rank, that already existed. In the Sikh Kingdom, for example, some of the *sidars* (noblemen) refused to allow the Sikh Army to adapt entirely to the European style.[24]

A deep-seated reluctance to change also characterised the Chinese army, but the innate sense of Chinese superiority over Europeans proved the biggest obstacle in the adoption of Western methods. Chinese officials, particularly those in the civil service, distrusted military men with ambition; they considered a more effective army to be a threat to the foundation of the regime from which they benefited.

Following the defeats of the Opium Wars, the destabilisation of Chinese society was manifest in the outbreak of the Taiping Rebellion. The rebels, inspired by a form of pseudo-Christianity and propelled by a desire for profound social reorganisation, could muster some 120,000 fighters by 1852. They seized the ancient capital of Nanking and posed a direct threat to Beijing and Shanghai. Other revolts broke out in central China, including Muslim rebellions in Yunnan province, the Miao tribal rising, the Kwangtung rebellion around Canton, Islamic revolts in Kansu, and the Nian revolt in Chi'hi province. The Nian were a particularly powerful alliance of peasant militia, salt smugglers and tax protesters who united into a mounted army that evaded all attempts by the Imperial Chinese authorities to crush them.

The Chinese government, realising that its traditional army was inadequate in Hunan, hired mercenaries with higher pay in battalion-sized units, supported by local militia. By 1860, the Chinese Army was beginning to resemble a more Westernised model with regiments, divisions and corps. Commanders were given responsibility for recruiting their own soldiers and ensuring they reached an adequate level of performance. Secret society groups and others which threatened loyalty and cohesion were gradually weeded out. In 1862, this branch of the Imperial forces became known as the Anhwei Army and received the instruction of 140 Western advisers, including Major Charles Gordon. It was equipped with 15,000 modern rifles and artillery, as well as paddle steamers with their own guns.

Charles Gordon had arrived in China at the end of the Second China War in 1860. As a Royal Engineer, his task was to build barracks for the Europeans at Shanghai, but during his time there the Taiping Rebellion broke out, which quickly engulfed much of the region. Gordon found himself caught up in the unrest, and was selected to command an untrained and polyglot brigade to suppress the rebellion.[25]

The leader of the Taiping movement was Hung Sen-tsuen who believed himself to be the son of God and the younger brother of Jesus Christ. Claiming to have visions during sustained trances, he proclaimed a new kingdom of heaven on earth. His vision for the future was far from benign, however: his new religion envisaged elements of Chinese culture but demanded a savage eradication of the existing Imperial Chinese hierarchy. The appeal to ordinary Chinese citizens was his reform agenda, such as the fight against corruption and the awarding of land to the peasantry. Those that resisted the Taiping were driven out and tortured, beheaded, crucified and, in some cases, buried alive. The subordinate leaders of the Taiping movement, known as *wangs*, were eager to demonstrate their loyalty by their ruthlessness. Central China was in the grip of terror.

The Taiping approached Shanghai and intended to capture it because of its lucrative commercial possibilities. They were prepared to do business with Europeans who might sell them arms, and they were looking to recruit gunners and other military experts from among the foreign sailors or mercenaries who could be found in each of the so-called treaty ports. The success of the Taiping was attributed to the fear they induced rather than a true military capability. Gordon wrote: 'Their chief condition to success is to strike terror, first by numbers, and secondly by the tawdry harlequin garb worn by them which has such a strange effect on the minds of all classes of people. Their long, shaggy black hair adds to the wildness of their look, and when this fantastic appearance is accompanied by a certain show of fury and madness, it is really little to be wondered at that the mild Chinese will either take to flight or submit.'[26]

The British were eager to protect the port of Shanghai and were willing to work with the Imperial Chinese government to protect the city. The Imperial government was just as eager to protect their customs revenue which they could gather from foreign officials and the population, particularly the wealthy merchant classes. The Shanghai merchants themselves were quite prepared to raise and pay for their own private army, known by its somewhat exaggerated title, the Ever Victorious Army (EVA). The EVA was initially commanded by two American mercenaries, Frederick Ward and Henry Burgevine. Ward was killed in action soon after his appointment and so Burgevine, an abrasive figure, assumed the leadership of the force. His heavy drinking, lack of tact and misconduct alienated all those who served under his command. Nevertheless, the Chinese government, under the influence of the Dowager Empress, sent 9,000 Imperial troops to co-operate with the EVA. The British, along with the French, agreed to take military action against the Taiping rebels close to Shanghai, but insisted that the liberated area came under the jurisdiction of the Imperial Chinese government. The Europeans were eager to protect their commercial interests but did not want to assume responsibility for territorial administration. The British sent two battalions and artillery to Shanghai in 1862, and Major Charles Gordon carried out reconnaissance for this force.

Despite holding the city, the outbreaks of malaria, dysentery and cholera began to affect the European troops badly. Moreover, the Imperial Chinese forces were incapable of holding the locations that had been cleared on the approaches to the city. If the Chinese regulars took a district, they were soon thrown out by the Taiping. As a result, the countryside was filled with burning villages and the roads lined with corpses, with no end to the conflict in sight. Nevertheless, the attention of Taiping rebels was temporarily diverted to Nanking when the Imperial Chinese moved against that city. The lull gave the EVA the opportunity to recruit more men and expand to a strength of 5,000. A more streamlined command structure was worked out and the EVA soldiers were paid on a regular basis. The provincial governor appointed General Ching to be the overall commander, even though Ching had been a former Taiping rebel who had changed sides. When Ching complained of the behaviour of EVA soldiers towards local people, the financiers of the project reduced their payments, which only worsened the looting and misconduct of the EVA troops. The Shanghai population, predictably, blamed the foreigners for the situation.

The relationship between Ching and Burgevine soon became so bad that the American had to be replaced, and Gordon was selected for the post. The British government agreed that Gordon could carry the Chinese rank of colonel. He made a good impression from the outset, for within two hours of his appointment he began training the EVA troops and changing their routine. Gordon was under no illusion about the quality of the force at his disposal, and initially described the EVA in dismissive terms. He concluded: 'You never saw such a rabble.'[27] The rank and file were mainly local peasants and the only foreigners were mounted as officers, operating the guns or acting as NCOs. The Chinese soldiers avoided alcohol and expected only the occasional benefits of prize money or the opportunity for some looting. Despite an official uniform the men were mostly in rags, but their simple battle drill, which relied on speed of movement and the ability to shoot, made up for their shortcomings in appearance.

The only members who had professional training, other than Gordon, were five British regulars whom he had brought in as brigade staff or as trainers. The rest of the European contingent were good fighters but poorly disciplined, given to quarrelling and broadly described as 'compulsive drinkers, gamblers and brawlers'.[28] They brought to the EVA the 'habits of the California gold mining camps' and 'they were touchy over rank and precedence, apt to become worked up over imaginary grievances, and riddled with jealousies'.[29] Gordon soon recognised that the Taiping rebels were more determined fighters than those that could be found in the ranks of the Imperial Army or much of the EVA. He therefore turned his attention to enlisting as many prisoners from the Taiping into the EVA as possible.

Gordon did his best to set a professional example. He worked long hours, day and night, and he carried no weapon—he went into action smoking a cigar and carrying only a light cane. His uniform was plain and unadorned. He dealt with all matters, administrative and operational, with a simplicity and professionalism that commanded respect. When fifty of his officers signed a letter of protest at the dismissal of their former American commander and complained of the regulations Gordon was insisting upon, he assured them he would not dismiss any of them. Yet he stuck to his demands, and won them over by leading them to a series of victories. By indirect methods and avoiding frontal assaults, Gordon gave them military success at Fuzhou, a fortified town south-west of Shanghai. The Imperial authorities were so delighted they promoted him to *tsung-ping* (brigadier).

When an Imperial Chinese force was defeated at Taitsan, 30 miles north-west of Shanghai, it was Gordon who was ordered to take the town. He made use of a small flotilla of gunboats to pound the walls of the fortress and effected a breach. He then led a storming party of 2,000 against a garrison of 10,000. When the first two assaults faltered, he personally led the third and final attempt to carry the breach, stopping only to encourage or cajole his EVA soldiers in the action. Casualties in the EVA force were nevertheless high. Of

105 officers, some 35 were killed and 54 wounded. A large number of other ranks had also become casualties.

Men will serve for money, but it cannot make them brave. The devotion of his troops cannot be explained solely by a salary which they frequently disputed anyway. There must be another ingredient, perhaps a diligence Gordon had shown towards his soldiers. He was, according to one biographer, 'exhilarated by danger, fascinated by the problems of command, [and saw] battle as the supreme challenge'.[30] He was also a strict disciplinarian with a flaring temper. When angry, he would sometimes delegate the administration of a rebuke or punishment in order to maintain his self-control. Yet he shared genuine tears for the suffering of his own wounded men and treated his soldiers as individual human beings rather than as cannon fodder. This mutual attachment was all the more remarkable when one considers Gordon knew only a few words and phrases of Chinese.

Some 700 former Taiping prisoners joined Gordon's force after the storming of Taitsan, and 100 of these eventually became his personal bodyguard, such were his winning ways. Although the Chinese authorities wanted Gordon to go on immediately with his offensive, Gordon knew that the EVA still needed training, discipline and more ordnance. The rank and file and many of the officers wanted to return to Shanghai in order to spend the loot they had acquired, but Gordon insisted they go into further training. Many of the officers threatened to resign and Gordon responded by explaining he would accept their resignations with immediate effect, but was prepared to wait until the following morning. The next morning all the officers reported for duty.[31]

Gordon's reputation assisted in the capture of Quinsan, his next objective. After bombardments by the flotilla of river gunboats, a portion of the garrison of Taiping rebels began to retreat. The gunboats pursued them, firing into the retreating rebels for a distance of several miles before returning. The remaining garrison of 7,000 attacked the screening force Gordon had left in place, but the gunboats returned in the nick of time and their firepower turned the tide. As the EVA prepared for a final attack the following morning, the town capitulated. Gordon's losses were just two killed and five wounded, but the Taiping casualties were estimated to be upwards of 4,000, with 2,000 taken prisoner and a huge arsenal of arms, artillery and ammunition that fell into Gordon's hands.

Despite the victory, a number of Chinese NCOs in the EVA mutinied, claiming they were being deprived of the opportunity for plunder. Gordon dealt with the problem by threatening to shoot one in five until they revealed the ringleader of the conspiracy, but with the group beginning to stir angrily, Gordon suddenly ordered the shooting of one corporal—and he was killed instantly. The shock effect was overwhelming: the entire group was so cowed that they received impassively the news that they were all to be imprisoned until an answer was forthcoming about the ringleader of the plot. After just one hour in the cells, the mutinous NCOs gave Gordon the information he required: the name of the man who had been shot, or so they claimed. The important point was that the NCOs returned to duty.[32] The incident revealed Gordon to be a realist and, when necessary, a ruthless leader of men. He had no legal grounds for the actions he had taken, but any hesitation and he and his escort might have been overwhelmed and possibly killed. Strikes and desertions remained a distinctive problem of the EVA, but fear of Gordon improved discipline and stanched the flow. Ultimately, the soldiers admired Gordon for his courage, resolution and determination to have his own way and he had given them success.

The Taiping rebels eventually lost Suzhou and their forces were divided between Nanking in the North and Hangzhou in the south. Gordon therefore seized the initiative and drove the EVA between the two regions in the depths of winter. He and his men endured bitter snowstorms and they passed through a landscape devastated by war and full of the gruesome victims of atrocities. There was some skirmishing, but Gordon was becoming tired of the jealous quarrels of his officers and NCOs. His final objective was Hangzhou, and before the final assault on 11 May 1861 there was prolonged bombardment. Imperial Chinese troops began an attack on one breach in the walls of the city, but were driven back, which gave Gordon the chance to lead the Ever Victorious Army in a second wave. At the breach, he once again led his men from the front as they scrambled through the gap. Soon after, the city surrendered. Gordon then marched his EVA back to Shanghai for its disbandment, concluding: 'A more turbulent set of men than formed the officers [of the EVA] have not often been collected together, or a more dangerous lot if they had been headed by one of their own style'.[33]

Irregulars and Advisers

The case of irregulars illustrates a number of the themes that appear throughout this volume. While discipline varied across irregular units, and was a cause of anxiety for European authorities, there seemed to be more scope for personalised command, a greater emphasis on honour, and a more pressing requirement for mutual respect or equality between European officers and local men than was the case with many regular local units. It seemed that many irregular forces benefited from fewer, if selected and experienced, European officers and NCOs: the minimised presence of Europeans and the greater opportunities this afforded local personnel to become leaders in their own right seemed to pay dividends. There was, in common with other units, a strong appeal in an elite or specialised status. This was further reinforced by selection and hard training. Irregular units performed better in small-unit actions, while regulars were more easily co-ordinated in higher-formation manoeuvres. Irregulars were, by definition, potentially less reliable, but generous funding and the preservation of their own military culture could easily act as a remedy. Irregulars nevertheless suffered from weaker logistics in most cases, unless, of course, they could rely on the local population to support them.

Armed forces have political as well as military purpose. The Indian Imperial Service Scheme had not only acted as a mechanism to augment the mass of military forces under British command, but also served to create loyalties across political divisions, like junior partners or allies under the leadership and supervision of a paramount power. Working as a mentor and supervisor to such forces required tact and diplomacy, particularly when it came to pointing out faults and requirements. The British supplied weapons and equipment to these auxiliaries, although neither could guarantee improvements in efficiency or effectiveness. Indeed, the British found there was a difficult balance to be struck between efficiency and cost, a familiar problem faced by regular Western forces. Moreover, there was an equilibrium to be established between expeditionary readiness and garrison work for irregular as well as regular forces. The solution was to create specialised units for particular tasks. Nevertheless, another decision was whether to try to preserve the original characteristics of irregular military culture and specialism that had made the irregulars appealing in the first place, or whether they should be adapted into a more standardised system in order to supply them with weapons, equipment, pay, pensions and other aspects of a bureaucratised, modern army.

The irregulars and auxiliaries also raise the question of appropriate leadership styles, especially for trainers and mentors. There are clearly limits for those confined to being a trainer compared with those that have the expectation and opportunity to exercise direct command. Sharing the hardships and hazards of local forces is a faster route to establishing trust and rapport than a trainer who never deploys alongside the troops. Historical cases indicate that commanding officers who possessed significant powers were more effective, even though there was a greater risk of arbitrariness if such men were not carefully selected. For local men selected for command, indigenous cultures had to be respected and incorporated: local leaders did not expect to be trained alongside their men, but wanted to be treated with greater deference and respect, and accorded more privileges appropriate to their rank. For European officers, there was a similar expectation: only the best officer trainees would expect to be sent to a colonial unit; they would have to learn their duties in a European unit first, then in a local force in order to master languages and certain skills, before being sent, experienced and prepared, to the unit to which they had been originally destined.

The formula for leadership, selection and small unit operations had worked well in the later nineteenth century, but in 1914, with the outbreak of a world war, this system would face its greatest test.

9

COLONIAL ARMIES AND IRREGULARS
IN THE FIRST WORLD WAR, 1914–1918

The use of native troops against Europeans in the First World War was condemned in the strongest terms in Germany. The German view was at least consistent. They believed that the French introduction of Algerian Turcos from Africa into the Italian War of 1859 and the Franco-Prussian War of 1870 was 'a retrogression from civilised to barbarous warfare'.[1] Nevertheless, in France, given the concerns that their main adversary, Germany, had a larger population, it was simply regarded as pragmatic and realistic to consider the use of augmenting domestic manpower with colonial soldiers from the metropolitan departments of North Africa and possibly elsewhere in the continent. Colonel (later General) Mangin was a leading advocate in 1910 for the use of West African soldiers, volunteer or conscripted, in the French Army in the defence of the homeland. Part of Germany's objection to increasing French influence in Morocco in the 1910s had been that the country offered the French 'excellent raw materials in the soldiers and therefore additional divisions with which to fight Germany in the future'.[2] The anxiety goes some way to explaining the aggressive response of Germany to the Morocco crisis of 1911. The German Kaiser's close association with the Ottoman Empire and Germany's expansionist plans across the Middle East were also driven in part by the desire to acquire additional manpower and offset the strength of the Entente powers and their colonial forces. It was for this reason that the Kaiser called for the Germanisation of the Ottoman Army when General Otto Liman von Sanders was appointed as its most senior adviser.[3]

In the First World War, such was the demand for manpower in Britain that the recruitment of colonial personnel was extended. In India, despite its providing 1.3 million volunteer soldiers, towards the end of the war conscription was being considered. The prospect of conscription in the traditional recruiting grounds in Punjab and the insistence on meeting unofficial quotas led to increasing unrest. In Egypt, a voluntary system was also retained, but labourers were conscripted from rural areas along with their animals, which generated resentment and fuelled unrest in 1919. The War Cabinets considered the use of Japanese troops in India in order to release more soldiers from garrison duty in the subcontinent, while China was encouraged to contribute more labouring manpower.[4] The Chinese labour issue divided opinion among the Allies and was only partially resolved. In 1916, the War Office also looked to employ more black troops. Commander J.C. Wedgwood, who had served at Gallipoli and compiled a report on the Mesopotamia campaign for Parliament, noted: 'I am only too anxious to get all I can and have been scouring the world to find out where they can be raised.'[5] The government of South Africa strenuously resisted the endless demands for more manpower, fearing the effects on the economy of the country, but also the political implications.[6]

France faced an acute manpower crisis, particularly when, at the end of 1914, it had already suffered a million casualties. Of all the French troops in the First World War, some 9 per cent were non-French. This represented 500,000 men from the colonies, with a further quarter of a million labourers. Some 160,000 men came from West Africa alone, but to obtain this number had required considerable coercion.[7] A combination of taxation, forced labour and recruitment efforts for the army led to unrest in Dahomey and other areas; paradoxically, this required French forces to suppress the unrest.[8] New methods were therefore required to raise manpower. In Senegal, chiefs were paid for each man they could bring in, which replicated the system of acquiring slaves of a former era. Approximately 100,000 labourers were found from Indochina, largely by force, which led to lingering resentment and ultimately political mobilisation against France in subsequent generations. Another tactic was to encourage voluntary enlistment through the example of men already serving. One Senegalese sub lieutenant, decorated for courage, announced to all new recruits: 'You are the first among the blacks, for the French, first among the whites, have conferred this distinction upon you.'[9] General Mangin, the enthusiast for colonial soldiers, believed that black troops, given their innate warlike qualities, could accomplish more than French soldiers on the Western Front in offensive operations.[10] Colonial troops were particularly prominent in the offensive on the Chemin des Dames in 1917.

The 2nd Colonial Corps of General Mangin's 6th Army on the Chemin des Dames attacked the sector between Cerny and the Ferme d'Hurtebise on 16 April 1917. The Ferme d'Hurtebise was a known strongpoint and the 2nd Colonial Corps had been instructed to take it, before advancing across a plateau, through the Vauclerc Wood, across a valley known as the Ailette, before finally reaching their last objective, the Bièvres valley. The French commanders expected all these objectives to be taken in just seven hours, reflecting General Nivelle's concept of speed and penetration as the new operational 'edge' of 1917. It was calculated that the troops would advance 100 metres every three minutes, and artillery was timed to keep up the pace behind which the infantry would be protected. The offensive began at 5.45 a.m., and the Senegalese soldiers, who had been suffering from the cold, were eager to get moving. They scrambled uphill through the first German outpost line, taking a number of prisoners, and reached the plateau at 7 a.m. Here, the flat terrain gave the German machine gunners a perfect field of fire, and the tiring Senegalese troops were cut down. Three of the four French colonels were killed and the troops were soon pinned to the ground, with any movement attracting intense fire. The second and third waves, advancing in accordance with the strict artillery timetable, caught up with the survivors of the first line, but, as they crowded behind the inadequate cover available, they also suffered heavy casualties. The artillery barrage was now far ahead, and so the troops were exposed without fire support. The 15th Colonial Division, on the left, had been tasked with taking Cerny, but they were checked by intense fire. Attempts to get forward became suicidal. They lost 280 officers and it proved impossible to get the men moving again. The 10th Colonial Division, on their right, could not get much further forward than a road that ran across the edge of the plateau.

Urgent requests were made to General Mangin to redirect the artillery and recommence the barrage on objectives that had already been passed. The headquarters staff believed the artillery would have done its job in neutralising the German defences and therefore it was assumed the only explanation for the stalled attack must be the reluctance of the North African troops to engage and advance. Consequently, the formations were ordered to continue the attack through the gaps between the remaining points of resistance. When one battalion of Senegalese attempted to do so, near the village of Ailles, they were cut to pieces. The surviving officers were concerned that the losses were so heavy that there was a significant risk the men would run if they were counter-attacked. There was little they could do but consolidate their positions. It was, of course, a not untypical outcome given the character of war on the Western Front in 1917.

France had embraced the colonial troops that were brought to Europe. Among the French public, the arrival of Indian soldiers from the Lahore and Meerut divisions in Marseilles in 1914 was greeted with particular curiosity and enthusiasm.[11] There was more of a sense of relief amongst the British authorities when it was found that Indian troops were able to stand against a European adversary. One officer, H.V. Lewis, attached to the 129th Baluchis, commented: 'Our men are very cool under fire, [and] don't seem to mind a bit, I think.' He praised particularly their skills in night patrolling.[12] Another officer was more concerned by press sensationalism which had raised expectations about 'the marvels of night scouting, surprise attacks and *kukuri* work which would be performed by Indians'. He did not think that they could be considered equals of the British soldier, for if they were, 'India would not be a British dependency'.[13] As V.G. Kiernan put it: 'Britain wanted to think its native troops good enough to help win the war, but not good enough to be able to break away from the Empire.'[14] Lewis noted: 'The general opinion was that an Indian victory over white troops would have a bad effect on India.'[15]

Some sections of the German authorities hoped to weaken the Entente powers by fomenting mutiny or colonial revolts. They funded the Ghadr conspirators, tried to ship arms to India, attempted to transmit Indian revolutionaries via Afghanistan into the subcontinent, and encouraged uprisings in Persia and the Gulf.[16] The British were successful in thwarting these plots through a combination of intelligence and timely military intervention, although there was considerable unrest in Persia. There was even more concern about desertions from the Indian Army by Muslim soldiers who may have been affected by the Caliph's call to jihad in November 1914. There were isolated incidents. One group of the 10th Baluchis en route to Mesopotamia shot their officer and were subsequently redirected for service in Burma. The Germans and the Ottomans attempted to distribute propaganda leaflets into Egypt as well as to Senegalese Muslim troops in French service in Gallipoli.

In Singapore in 1915, the Indian 5th Light Infantry mutinied. These Punjabi Muslims, on their way to garrison duty in Hong Kong, wrongly believed they were being sent to fight their co-religionists in Mesopotamia. They were radicalised by an *Alam* in a local mosque, which, according to the court of inquiry, played on the soldiers' 'gullibility and credulity, which were almost beyond belief'.[17] Singapore was also the safe haven of a number of

Indian nationalists and it remains unclear what influence they had in orchestrating the mutiny. On 15 February, in the early morning, the mutineers killed some of their officers and spread out throughout the city, releasing some German internees along the way. The only security forces available were armed police, many of them Sikhs, and civilian volunteers, both European and Chinese. French sailors and the crew of the gunboat *Cadmus* also came to the assistance of the authorities. In the emergency, Japanese inhabitants were enrolled as special constables. A machine gun, hastily mounted on a lorry, was also brought into action. Against these combined forces the mutineers quickly lost resolution and cohesion, and resistance began to fail the moment their barracks came under attack on the 16th.[18] Although 47 of the mutineers were sentenced to death, many of the men had their sentences commuted to transportation. The regiment was then reorganised and sent to the Cameroons.

In the Cameroons, the small German garrison had armed some local indigenous fighters in order to have them operate as snipers, but the guerrilla strategy they planned was not enough to prevent the colony from being overrun. The Germans were more successful in East Africa thanks largely to their native soldiers, the askaris. In response, the British created a larger Rhodesian force made up of 10,000 white soldiers and 14,000 black troops. These were given regular army training and as a result they performed better than the Portuguese of Mozambique, who were criticised as having generally 'bad commanders and ill-trained troops'. When the Germans approached the border of Mozambique, the demoralised Portuguese officials and police abandoned their posts.[19]

The British net that closed around German East Africa represented a wide cross-section of Imperial forces. One column was made up of British, Nigerian and Kashmiri soldiers. In 1915, the Germans could muster some 2,200 Germans, 11,000 African regulars and 3,000 irregular warriors. Most of the native forces were sustained by the German assurance that they were fighting as Muslims against the Sultan's enemies.[20] However, the Germans used considerable coercion to maintain their war effort in East Africa: they roped together men to act as carriers, and sometimes used women in this role. Hundreds perished, and those that attempted to escape were often shot.[21] By contrast, the Allies could draw on a much larger pool of labour and therefore did not have to resort to such extreme methods

British officers believed, after initial setbacks, that their Indian troops thrived in the environment of East Africa. One officer remarked his Pathans were 'having the time of their lives', especially in the cat-and-mouse patrolling in the bush.[22] There were still concerns about the long-term effects of native soldiers being encouraged to kill European adversaries. One war correspondent wrote: 'The white man cannot teach the blacks of Africa how to kill his brother white man without breaking down many of the ethical principles upon which European rule in Africa is based.'[23] General Molitor of the Belgian contingent condemned the German mistreatment of European prisoners as 'vile, unspeakable regulations ... that destroyed the prestige of the white man in the native's eyes.'[24] It was widely anticipated that the social transformation wrought by the war could be far-reaching. African women, for example, supported auxiliary forces not only as camp followers: if they came from traditions where women had participated more actively in war, as in Dahomey or Asante, they might become auxiliary fighters in their own right.[25] The sense of expectation from such service during the war could have been considerable.

The Indian Army in the First World War

In 1903, after significant debate about the efficiency of the forces in the subcontinent with its search for 'martial races', the old Presidency armies system was abolished and a single Indian Army was created by Lord Kitchener, then Commander-in-Chief of India. Old Presidency titles were, in theory, abolished, but various names and nicknames survived. Crucially, units retained traditions and customs to reinforce their identity and regimental *esprit de corps*, including their religious observance, selective diets or eating rituals. To 'stiffen' and supervise the reformed Indian Army, and provide it with heavy and field artillery, British regiments were brigaded with two or more Indian ones. The arrangement was known by the name 'the Army in India'. Its proportions of British and Indian troops, and the long-standing article of faith that Indian troops should be equipped only with light mountain guns, were legacies of the Indian Mutiny. In order to ease the administration of this large force, in 1908 the Indian Army was divided into a northern and southern army.

The strength of the force was in its ability to garrison every part of the subcontinent, dispatch troops to pacify the frontiers, and, if necessary, deploy independent brigades overseas. Before the Great War, there were 39 regiments of cavalry (not including contingents of bodyguards), 95 single-battalion regiments of infantry, 12 single-battalion Pioneer regiments, and 11 double-battalion regiments (39th Garhwals and the ten Gurkha regiments).[26] There were three units of sappers and miners (for engineer operations), mountain artillery, ordnance units, logistics teams, medical units and administrators. There were also the Imperial Service Troops, militias, levies and scouts, who provided some regional and frontier security, especially to British political officers and the various Indian constabularies. There was also a pool of European and Anglo-Indian Volunteers who could be called on to protect installations such as the railways, and there were still sizeable private armies controlled by the Princely States under British supervision, such as the Hyderabad Contingents, the Central India Horse or the local units of the other Princely States such as Malwa, Erinpura and Deoli, where the quality varied from anachronistic retainers to more modernised troops.

The legacy of the nineteenth century was not limited to titles and organisation, but extended to the source of manpower, which still favoured certain 'martial races'. Punjab and the mountainous north seemed to produce especially warlike groups, and the Indian Army recruited from them extensively. Thus, while there were just 5,588 Madrassis and 3,000 Tamils from the south in the army in 1904, there were 31,000 Sikhs, 32,000 Punjabis, 14,000 Gurkhas and 11,000 Rajputs.[27]

The Indian Army had built up an expertise in the leadership of local forces over many decades. In 1914, each infantry battalion had 12 European officers, and subordinated to them, regardless of experience, were 17 Indian officers carrying the Viceroy's commission. Together they commanded 729 ranks and 42 civilian 'commissariat' followers. In the cavalry, the proportions were the same. There were obvious cultural differences between British and Indian Army units, and they were also evident among the officer corps.[28] In the Indian cavalry, the legacy of being 'irregular' and under the personal command of pioneering individuals gave rise to an attitude that praised initiative, carried disdain for the rest of the army, and cherished the horses above all else. The fact that sowars (troopers) owned their own mounts made the men particularly attentive to the endurance of their animals.

In the Indian infantry, Claude Auchinleck, who saw action in defence of the Suez Canal and in Mesopotamia during the war, described an atmosphere of respectful relations between officers and men. He wrote: 'there was no question of ordering them about—they were yeomen really and that made all the difference'.[29] The more senior and experienced Indian leaders known as Viceroy's commissioned officers, despite their subordination, were the most respected of all, and guided young British subalterns in their role. They were referred to as 'God's own gentlemen'. In contrast to most European armies which expected their 'native' soldiers to learn the Europeans' language, in the Indian Army every officer had to learn to speak to his soldiers in their vernacular, not least because he was regarded as the neutral arbiter in any local disputes.[30] The emphasis on personal leadership led to a tendency to lead from the front in combat, but that had its own attractions for young British officers. The appeal of command in the Indian Army was so high that, in 1913, of the top 25 cadets at the Royal Military Academy Sandhurst, 20 of them opted to join the Indian Army.[31]

In 1914, the motivation of the Indian Army was not in doubt. A hierarchy of prestige, based on 'fighting quality' and physique, ran through the different ethnic groups that constituted the army, and each was eager to assert its martial prowess.[32] This competitiveness existed between units recruited on the basis of territorial demarcation as much as on ethnicity, and it was common in 'mixed' units where companies were made up of a particular 'class'. The 6th Bengal Lancers, for example, consisted of one Muslim squadron, one Hindu and one Sikh, with the Headquarters Squadron made up of troops from all three 'classes'.[33] Half of the regular army was drawn from the Punjab, and even regiments designated with particular regional titles might actually contain a cross-section of more competitive groups.[34] However, there was also a trait among some groups to enlist for the 'fight' rather than identity per se.

At the tactical level, certain experienced regiments of the Indian Army, such as the Frontier Force and the various battalions of the Gurkhas, were highly accomplished, able to use fieldcraft to great effect and skilled in the precise use of fire to defeat guerrilla fighters on the frontiers. However, units with little experience of mountain warfare were often unsuited to the modern conditions of combat.

At the higher command level, a General Staff was created in 1903 to manage the complexities of training, military policy, operations, plans, intelligence, and deployments. However, while relieving the Commander-in-Chief India of many tasks, the General Headquarters had still to manage a high volume of minor administrative matters, and there was no clear chain of command to the divisional level. Moreover, the Commander-in-Chief had to combine the duties of military member of the Viceroy's Council (1906) and responsibility for military supply (1909). Divisional commanders were burdened with administering not only their three infantry brigades, a cavalry regiment and their artillery and pioneers, but also all the additional formations in their area of responsibility, including militias and volunteers, even though these would not be the units under their command in wartime. Indeed, when a divisional headquarters was deployed, these other militia and volunteer units were simply abandoned, with no plan for continuity in such an eventuality. Moreover, while there was a surplus of this additional man-power, there was a paucity of vital ancillary services, including medical and administrative staff.

Worst of all, there were far too few staff in each headquarters. In 1906, 'A' staff of the General Branch, directed by the Chief of Staff, were concerned with training, discipline and personnel; while 'Q' staff were concerned with equipment and supply. The following year, a staff college was established at Quetta, ending older systems of patronage or dependence on the British staff college at Camberley. The only tragedy of this excellent reform was that it was too late to produce senior staff-trained officers before the outbreak of war in 1914.

The Indian Army of 1914 was a long-service professional force, but one of its fundamental flaws was that it lacked sufficient trained reserves to be able to regenerate itself in the event of significant casualties. Frontier fighting had required well-trained units with the cohesion to withstand demoralising insurgency, but casualties had, on the whole, been light.[35] The fighting had offered sufficient hazard to reinforce one's personal *izzat* (honour) or sense of fate, demonstrate attachment to one's officer and unit, and earn decorations and promotion without a high probability of death. The Afghan and Pashtun tribes' habit of murdering the wounded and mutilating the dead meant that heroic efforts were always made to recover casualties, which again reinforced cohesion. Service in Indian regiments tended to deter the rapid turnover of personnel and therefore it was hard to generate a large cadre of reservists. To qualify for a pension, soldiers had to serve 25 years. By contrast, three-year short-service men, who could take opportunities for periodic retraining, were few and far between and, in any case, insufficiently trained to be useful. Often, sickness and civilian employment rendered ex-soldiers unfit for further military service. The result was an army of some experience in mountain warfare, cohesive, with a strong sense of its exclusive identity, but without any notion of formation-level operations or high-intensity European war, and unable to draw on a large pool of trained reservists.

In India, despite all the concerns about the loyalty of Indian subjects in the nineteenth century, there was particular enthusiasm for Britain's cause at the outbreak in 1914. When the Viceroy declared war on India's behalf, unfashionable though it may seem today, there was a sincere response from many Indian leaders and organisations: the All-India Muslim League, Punjab Provincial Congress, the Princely States and many thousands of individuals expressed their loyalty to the British Empire. Offers of money, horses, medics, hospital ships and ambulances were made, and 21 of the 27 princes' Imperial

Service Troops contingents were mobilised. The Nizam of Hyderabad committed his troops to the war effort and gave 60 lakhs of rupees (£400,000). The Maharaja of Mysore gave a further 50 lakhs (£333,000). Enthusiasm and cohesion were not in doubt: The Jodhpur Lancers, for example, were even commanded by their septuagenarian regent maharaja, Major General Sir Pratap Singh.

Four expeditionary forces were mobilised, far more than had been planned for. It was to the credit of the pre-war planners that the Indian Army at least had a scheme for mobilisation and deployment in place when the war broke out, and India had two infantry divisions and one cavalry brigade available for immediate operations.[36] But the requirement to expand this deployment rapidly caused disruption and overwhelmed the depots. The Lahore and Meerut Divisions (Force 'A') were assembled and dispatched urgently to France. Indian Expeditionary Forces B and C, barely at brigade strength, went to East Africa, ostensibly to secure the coast and neutralise the German naval threat to shipping in the Indian Ocean but also to protect the British railways into Kenya, for which there was insufficient manpower for defence.

There were problems from the outset.[37] The call-up occurred in August when most personnel were on leave, and, in an age before information technologies, it took time to make contact with everyone, especially those up in the hills. The depot system, which was supposed to operate as the rear link for deploying units, handling call-ups, reservists, pensions and discharges, was completely overwhelmed and remained chaotic well into 1915. While units made their way to Bombay relatively quickly, the entire force was deficient in artillery and possessed only two machine guns per battalion.[38] Insufficient numbers of troopships meant 30 vessels had to be hurriedly converted. As bewildered sepoys embarked, many of them on a ship for the first time, their officers struggled to contain the rumours about their destination, which varied from guarding the Suez Canal to joining the fighting in Europe. Most thought the greatest risk was that the war would be over before they arrived, but, in the short term, there were more prosaic preoccupations about rations, stores and orders to reorganise from their standard eight companies into the British model of four companies.[39] While the Lahore and Meerut Divisions (Force 'A') assembled, efforts were also made to get back British officers on the reserve list with the Indian Army. Of the 47 available, half were swept up in the corresponding British mobilisation. There were also too few Indian reservists to provide for the 10 per cent of the strength anticipated for battle casualty replacements.

The initial deployments were also a mixed success. It was remarkable that two entire divisions could be transported with most of their equipment so rapidly to the far side of the world and prepared for any operations. Nevertheless, there were still significant gaps in the readiness and the ability to sustain enduring operations in the Indian Corps.[40] Force A had disembarked briefly at Suez before setting off for France, where the first division landed at Marseilles on 26 September. There it was issued with the newer Mark III Lee–Enfield rifle, conducted marches, organised stores, was allocated liaison officers and established a camp. Transport was provided in the form of London butchers' carts, but, apart from the distribution of some greatcoats, the troops wore their light tropical uniforms. There was considerable enthusiasm among the French for the newly arrived Indian troops, and the soldiers experienced a form of culture shock, remarking in their letters on the existence of aircraft, women working in agriculture, strange food and, for Muslim troops, the alleged idolatry of the pork-eating French.

From Marseilles, the Indian Corps was moved by rail to Ypres to relieve the shattered British Second Corps, and their contribution helped stabilise the line at a time when manpower shortages were critical.[41] From the railheads the 129th Baluchis and Wilde's Rifles were transported by bus and rushed into the shallow trenches and ditches to relieve the British cavalry at Wytschaete and Messines. Neither the British cavalry nor the Indian troops, divided into company groups, were supported by sufficient artillery.[42] On 22 October a German thrust was held only with the greatest difficulty, most of the casualties being caused by German shell fire. Trenches were flattened, and reinforcing sepoys were forced to lie in the open to repel a German infantry assault. The Baluchis' machine guns, placed in a prominent farmhouse, took a direct hit. One company was entirely overrun and wiped out but for the sole survivor Khuda Dad Khan. A similar fate befell the Dogra company of Wilde's Rifles; Jemadar Kapur Singh, realising he was the only survivor, shot himself to prevent his capture; Havildar Gagna, having killed five Germans around him, broke his bayonet in the close-quarter action but snatched up a German officer's sword and accounted for more: he was later found, alive, with six wounds.[43] At Neuve Chapelle the village was lost on 28 October when Indian sappers and miners were overwhelmed in another close-quarter battle; all their officers and over 100 of the 300 men available were killed or wounded. After a week's further fighting, some 500 sepoys were killed.

The accounts of the troops indicate the typical problems of these early days of the war. The Poona Horse sowars did not initially take cover in their unfamiliar dismounted role, and they had little training in infantry tactics or trench warfare. Consequently their casualties were severe. Fresh night operations were stalled by the inability to seize the high ground that lay to the east of Neuve Chapelle, by the abysmal autumn weather and by the evident confusion of troops unfamiliar with the environment.[44]

From personal accounts we know that some officers struggled to keep their men in place. Captain 'Roly' Grimshaw (Poona Horse) came across some Gurkhas attempting to seek out Germans in no man's land on their own initiative, while others were clearly shirking in culverts, ditches and ruins. He explained that 'the sight which met the eyes at daybreak was perfectly revolting ... corpses choked the trenches ... fragments of human beings everywhere. Most of the dead seemed to have been bayoneted, but some had their heads blown clean off.'[45]

Between the shelling and sniping, the greatest hazard was the environment itself. None of the men had waterproofs, braziers or 'rugs' (blankets). By November the troops were occupying trenches almost brimful of water. At Festubert two men of the 8th Gurkhas drowned within hours of occupying their 'miniature canals'. On 23 November the Germans broke into the Indian lines and several trenches were lost. Close-quarter fighting over the next 24 hours resulted in some of those positions being recovered, but the cost was high. Sikhs and Pathans were described as having lost turbans, revealing their long and straggling hair, matted with mud. All ranks were terribly filthy and often exhausted. Some Gurkhas discarded their boots, complaining that sore feet were worse inside their footwear. There were other unseen and unexpected enemies: a German mine detonated under the Indian lines killed 200 and induced profound shock.

Under these conditions, it is more understandable that Jemadar Mir Mast and 14 Afridis deserted to the relative comfort of the German lines that winter, that there were higher-than-'average' statistics of self-inflicted wounds among Indian 'other ranks', and that censor reports recorded a lowering of morale.[46] Officer casualties were difficult to replace, but the sheer numbers of losses and the nature of the conditions evidently had their effect too.

By the following spring, the Indian Corps had to some extent recovered from its emergency deployment. New equipment had arrived and much-needed winter clothing along with rifle grenades, Mills bombs, mortars and trench periscopes. Morale improved. Nevertheless, what the Corps lacked was artillery and, without a superior weight of fire support, it was difficult to see how they could retake the objective of Neuve Chapelle, lost to the Germans in October 1914. Since then the village had been prepared extensively for defence, was ringed with wire and its approaches were criss-crossed with water-filled ditches and flooded ground, and the whole area was dominated by German guns on and behind the Aubers Ridge. When the order to retake the village came, all the Allied artillery fire that was available was concentrated into a short bombardment at dawn on 10 March 1915, and the initial assault by the Garhwali Brigade was successful. By 9.30 that morning, the Garhwalis were inside the village, although their British officers, characteristically leading from the front, had suffered heavy casualties and the 2/3rd Gurkhas had lost direction and become separated. The usual problems of communication across the debris of the battlefield delayed the arrival of the Dehra Dun Brigade, which was forced to take up a temporary defensive position along Layes brook, to the west of the village. The Germans counter-attacked, determined to recover their forward strongpoints. This was defeated despite a blizzard of shelling and yet another crop of casualties for the Indian Corps.

Attempts to restart the offensive failed repeatedly. Subsequent attacks in April and May at Festubert and Aubers Ridge were also unsuccessful. Explanations were sought in terms of inadequate artillery support, shell short-ages, and criticism of Indian Army staff work.[47] Senior Indian Army officers had been criticised for valuing seniority over merit, failing to have sufficient numbers put through staff college, and being unfamiliar with large-formation manoeuvres that characterised European warfare. Diversionary operations at Moulin Saint-Pierre by the Indian Corps during the Battle of Loos were marked by a successful assault, but a failure in staff work meant that there were no reserves or supports so that captured ground was enveloped and the lead-ing battalions were compelled to make a fighting retreat.[48] Yet, as elsewhere during the First World War, the relentless mathematics of modern warfare, together with the engineering capabilities of the German Army, was the true cause of failure. During the assault on Aubers Ridge on 6 May, Allied artillery fire had failed to make much impression on German trenches or their well-revetted strongpoints. As the Dehra Dun Brigade rose from the ground some yards ahead of their sodden trenches, following unseasonably heavy rain, the German infantry and machine gunners had a clear field of fire. The German Maxims had been calibrated in advance to fire at just eight inches above the ground, and they scythed down the extended lines with impunity.[49] In one leading company of 6th Jats every man was killed or wounded before they advanced a hundred yards. The 2/2nd Gurkhas lost all their officers and NCOs, but the survivors dashed forward and got to the German trenches, where they were all killed or wounded. Just 20 minutes after the assault had begun, the battlefield was empty, save for handfuls of men sheltering in craters and ditches, and strewn across the ground were the wounded and the dead.

Other divisions on alternative axes were also checked, and a second wave, scheduled to take place on the same front of the Dehra Dun Brigade, was cancelled. Nevertheless, it was determined that the Bareilly Brigade would continue with its attack once the communication trenches had been cleared of the wounded. This second assault got barely 30 yards from its start line before it was cut down. Vaughan's Rifles lost 50 per cent killed and wounded in this advance, and the 41st Dogras lost 401 casualties of a strength of 645, including all its officers. The Garhwal Brigade suffered the same fate on 15 and 16 May, being decimated by the sheer weight of fire. When the action concluded on the 18th, the gains were pitifully small and the landscape was a scene of Dantean desolation.

Allegations of Deteriorating Morale in the Indian Corps

The Indian Corps was not limited to operations at Neuve Chapelle and Aubers Ridge. In April the Germans used poison gas to the north-east of Ypres, and the Lahore Division was thrust into the gap in the line. Due to confusion about the geography, the division attempted to reach what it believed was the original French front line, only to find that the position had long been abandoned, and, as they pressed on to their objective, vaguely defined as 'the enemy trench', they had to storm across a thousand yards of no man's land. The attack, with derisory artillery support, was broken up by German fire.[50] The Ferozepur Brigade was then subjected to a retaliatory gas attack, which, for troops without any respirators or protection, inflicted severe casualties. Some terrified sepoys fled, but others were rallied by junior leaders like Jemadar Mir Dast, who, for his determined resistance, courageous inspiration to others and his insistence on going back out into no man's land to recover wounded comrades, was awarded the Victoria Cross.[51] A handful of survivors under the command of Major Deacon of the Connaughts with survivors of the Manchesters, far in advance of the rest, grimly clung to the mud and drove off German counter-attacks.[52] The division held on, but the gas attack had been another profound shock to the troops.

For some time the deterioration of the Indian Corps had been noted. British regiments in the Army in India had not had the same dislocation over officers, despite similar losses.[53] Some British officers posted to the Indian regiments did not speak the language of the soldiers. Losses in Viceroy's commissioned officers were also severe. Familiar faces, who knew the men well, were often now gone.[54] Moreover, Indian units had to be reinforced with drafts and, although efforts were made to replace class companies with men of the same background, in the confusion of the early months of the war this had not been possible.[55] Despite the larger numbers of reinforcements available by June 1915, the cohesion of the Corps could no longer be guaranteed.[56]

The decision was taken to move the Indian infantry out of France and relocate them in Middle Eastern theatres where communications with India were shorter and, for those from the plains of India at least, the climate was more familiar.[57] In any case, the expansion of the campaigns in the Middle East demanded more manpower, and the Mesopotamian operations came under the direction of the Indian government.[58] The cavalry stayed on and took part in the larger actions of the war on the Somme, although without success, but the unique composition of the Indian Army, while a strength on frontier operations, had suffered severely under the pressures of very heavy losses and such trying conditions in France and Flanders.[59]

By the autumn of 1915 the Indian Army had been through a transformative experience, a crucible of war that no one could have conceived of even twelve months before. From a strategic perspective India was secure and, despite German efforts to ignite unrest through Ghadr subversion and Bengali revolutionaries, the subcontinent did not show signs of unrest. Even on the truculent North West Frontier there was only a brief period of resistance by Mahsuds in 1915, and this was contained by a blockade rather than conventional operations. Territorial battalions from Britain released British and Indian Army units for service overseas, thus maintaining the strength of the garrison.[60] Beyond the frontier, despite the widespread fighting inside Persia, Afghanistan was curiously quiet. In Mesopotamia and East Africa there had been significant defeats and evidence of poor performance, including the lacklustre actions of the Indian cavalry near Ctesiphon, but overall, despite the British authorities' anxiety that there would be widespread disaffection, desertion or even mutiny, the Indian Army remained cohesive.

In France and Flanders there had been a handful of desertions by Muslim soldiers but never to the extent that some British officers had feared, and the cases were usually related to the appalling conditions of the fighting front. Some deterioration of performance was to be expected in subsequent deployments when one considers that the forces being dispatched overseas at short notice were far in excess of what the pre-war planners had prepared for. On the Western Front morale had been an issue, but this is hardly surprising given the casualties and winter conditions in which the sepoys and sowars served. It is surely more remarkable that their spirit of cohesion and the quality of the leadership enabled the Indian Corps to remain intact under such stresses. While most units fought well, making use of frontier warfare training and experience, there were exceptions. The 9th Bhopal Regiment tried to cross no man's land at Neuve Chapelle by crawling under German fire, but their slow rate of movement and exposure led to heavy casualties and there had been no attempt to co-ordinate fire and movement tactics, although the battalion redeemed itself with a fighting withdrawal.[61] By contrast, the 2/3rd Gurkhas utilised the tactics they had learned in clearing sangars at Dargai on the North West Frontier in 1898 to assault buildings in Neuve Chapelle. Their skirmishing tactics enabled them to co-ordinate movements and covering fire, and clear machine-gun posts which would otherwise have pinned down the entire brigade.[62] The verdict on the performance of the Indian Corps is therefore a mixture of success and setback.

It was understandable that, during and after the war, Indian Army officers would emphasise the excellent examples of courage and determination shown by Indian units and their soldiers.[63] Critics would place greater significance on the incidence of self-inflicted wounds to show that Indian troops' morale made them unsuitable for the European theatre. Champions and critics alike had their agendas.[64] In recent years these have been replaced with new historiographical trends. There have been efforts to show that the Indian Army was merely an issue of race and coercion, apparently representing the organising principles of the British Empire. The problem with this interpretation is that it was clearly not the way the soldiers and officers of the Indian Army saw it themselves at the time.[65] They were organised primarily as an army, with a distinct cultural emphasis that could and often did generate fierce loyalty, competitiveness and *esprit de corps*. However, it was an army built around certain assumptions about the character of the war they would be called upon to fight. No one could have foreseen the demands that were to be placed upon it, and we should remember that the Indian Army was pitched hastily into a conflict without the luxury of preparation in order to hold the line in France, replace shattered divisions or secure vulnerable parts of the Empire. Crucially, it had insufficient numbers of qualified young officers or experienced Indian officers to replace the casualties it suffered. Although largely withdrawn from France and Flanders, from 1917 the Indian Army that took the offensive in Palestine, Mesopotamia, and Africa was a significantly different organisation from that in 1914. Better equipped, seasoned, expanded, with better staffs, intelligence, logistics and materiel, it would go on to provide a great contribution to Allied victory in all these theatres.

The Indian Army in the Middle East

The initial mission in Mesopotamia was to provide security for the Persian oilfields and access to the refineries at the head of the Gulf. Expeditionary Force D was successful in neutralising Turkish resistance and, even when outnumbered in the early stages of 1915, won a significant victory at Shaiba, near Basra. To the west, British and Indian forces also defeated the Ottoman attempts to capture the Suez Canal and prevented their efforts to foment unrest in Egypt through the Libyan Sanussi tribes on the western border. These British successes encouraged a counter-offensive into Sinai, a sustained penetration of Mesopotamia up the Tigris, and landings at the Gallipoli Peninsula in April 1915 which, it was thought, would knock the Ottoman Empire out of the war. Although the forces in Sinai were able to defeat the Ottoman offensives, there were logistical and manpower limits on how far the British could penetrate. There was also a great reluctance on the part of the British War Cabinet to divert resources needed for the Western Front and Gallipoli to Egypt or Mesopotamia. Consequently, the attempt to reach Baghdad in late 1915 was a failure. After the pyrrhic victory at Ctesiphon between 22 and 24 November, the Tigris force was driven back to Kut and besieged. Relief attempts, while making some progress, did so at an enormous cost. Some 23,000 casualties were sustained in the effort to rescue the garrison of approximately 10,000. At Gallipoli, the initial attacks ended in stalemate. Among the reinforcements there were the 29th Indian Brigade, consisting of three battalions of Gurkhas and one of Sikhs. During the fighting, much of it at relatively close quarters, approximately 1,700 Indians were killed. The entire force was evacuated by January 1916.

The operations in Mesopotamia, unlike those in Egypt and Gallipoli, came under the direct command of the Indian Army and the government of India, and not the War Office. Some 675,000 Indian soldiers served in the Great War, and the largest contingent was deployed on the Tigris and Euphrates. Their mission became all the more important after the setbacks at Gallipoli and the fall of Kut in the spring of 1916, when more Ottoman divisions were redirected to Mesopotamia. Nevertheless, the government of India was severely criticised for the inadequate logistical arrangements in the Mesopotamian theatre between 1914 and 1916. There was far too much improvisation in supply, medical arrangements and transport. The cultural habits of restricted diets for sepoys worsened the incidence of diseases and led to cases of beriberi and scurvy, both of which were the result of nutritional deficiencies. Nevertheless, it was the high casualties and overwhelmed transport facilities, especially with the shortage of rivercraft, that attracted most attention. At the Battle of Ctesiphon, almost 4,600 out of the 13,756 men in the Tigris force became casualties, but getting the wounded and the sick back to the main base at Basra overwhelmed the system: there were simply not enough doctors, medics, orderlies, ambulances or hospital vessels to treat them all. Several died en route or while waiting for the transport, and boats arrived further south with patients in a shocking condition. The supply system had failed in other respects: Kut had fallen because the garrison had run out of food. The relief force had struggled to mass sufficient forces, including artillery, against the Ottoman defences because of lack of transport and an inadequate supply chain.[66]

In the Middle East, as in other theatres, there was insufficient manpower for all the tasks required. There were only 34,000 pre-war reserves in the Indian Army, and, as the war progressed, when news filtered back of conditions at the front, families became more reluctant to release men for service in the army. The British authorities introduced recruitment bonuses and other incentives, including free rations and uniforms, but still struggled to acquire the numbers they needed, especially at harvest time. There was also a critical shortage of qualified British officers. There were only 40 pre-war reserve officers for the Indian Army.[67] Replacements were not able to speak the relevant languages and lacked experience.

Under these conditions in the Middle East, it is not surprising that there were episodes of unrest in the Indian Army during the war. At Singapore in January 1915, three companies of Pathans mutinied. Seven of the ringleaders were condemned to death and 197 sentenced to transportation.[68] On 23 February 1916, the 15th Lancers mutinied at Basra in Mesopotamia. This Muslim regiment had been recruited entirely from Multan, and their grievance was their concern that they would have to march from Basra against the holy places of Islam, especially Karbala. They asked instead that they be allowed to fight in Europe.[69] Some 429 men were arrested and disarmed, then sentenced to transportation in the Andaman Islands. However, all except the ringleaders were released the following year.

In 1916, dissatisfied with the administration of the government of India during the Mesopotamia campaign, the War Office took control of all military operations in the Middle East. Lieutenant General Sir Stanley Maude, who assumed command in Mesopotamia that summer, overhauled the logistical, supply and transport arrangements. His application of the methods of the Western Front and his manoeuvre south of Baghdad unhinged the Ottoman defences. The Indian Army, which still formed the bulk of the force across the Middle East—13 of the 17 British and Imperial divisions deployed to Palestine and Mesopotamia were Indian—made steady progress thereafter. The capture of Baghdad in March 1917 was a significant achievement for the British war effort, for it made more accessible a number of shrines to Muslims. By 1918, the British were in control of the entirety of Mesopotamia and able to secure the oilfields of Mosul, the city being captured at the time of the armistice with the Ottoman Empire in October.[70]

The Prime Minister, Lloyd George, made a direct appeal to India to provide more men in the crisis of Spring 1918 during the final German offensive on the Western Front. In April, the All-India War Conference, with the Viceroy, pledged to provide half a million more troops that year, of which the Punjab would provide 200,000.[71] The commitment required the dilution of the 'martial races' approach, although the Punjab was still expected to provide a disproportionate number of men. After the war, when it was imperative to reduce costs, the Indian Army provided the garrison forces for Palestine, Transjordan and Mesopotamia. The outbreak of revolts across Iraq in 1920 necessitated the deployment of 85,000 Indian troops.[72] Muslim troops were nevertheless unhappy about the long service away from home and the defeat of the Ottoman Empire. The abolition of the Caliphate in 1922 did little to improve morale.

In 1918, at the armistice, almost a million Indian troops were serving overseas.[73] In the Middle East, the Indian Army had released British Dominion divisions to fight in other theatres, and there had been a decision to 'Indianise' the Egyptian Expeditionary Force in Palestine when the requirement for British manpower on the Western Front became acute in late 1917. Some 60,000 Indian soldiers were killed or died of wounds in the war. Despite a few episodes of unrest, including the mutiny in Singapore in 1915, the majority of the Indian Army had remained cohesive and loyal to the British. This was all the more remarkable when one considers the unexpected and hasty expansion between 1914 and 1917, the acute problems of supply and logistics that had characterised the operations in Mesopotamia, and the widespread efforts at subversion attempted by the Ottomans and the Germans during the war. Nevertheless, in India, there was frustration with wartime inflation, the quota demands for manpower and wartime restrictive regulations. This frustration boiled over into protests in Amritsar in 1919, which ended in severe repression, and fostered a nationalist movement that grew in scale and confidence over the following three decades.

For the soldiers themselves, there was great pride in their achievements, not only in retrospect but also at the time. The Egyptian Expeditionary Force was a composite imperial force, in which Australian, New Zealander, British, Indian and other Asian forces worked to achieve common objectives. After the action at Magdhaba in 1917, when an Ottoman position had been captured, the gunners of the Hong Kong and Singapore Artillery 'came up smiling', the Australians looked favourably on their British counterparts in the Yeomanry, and there were enthusiastic cheers from the Bikaners and Indian Imperial Service Troops for their part in the victory. The incident is a reminder that cohesion can be forged in shared danger and hardship, regardless of ethnicity, background or experience.

African Troops in the East Africa Campaign

Experience of previous colonial campaigning had shown that the African colonies needed troops that were lightly equipped and more mobile than regular infantry battalions, and that were cheaper to administer. The King's African Rifles were not, in fact, under the jurisdiction of the War Office but the Colonial Office. Nevertheless, British officers and NCOs were seconded from the regular army and all tended to be experienced men. At its height, the King's African Rifles had six battalions, but at the outbreak of war three had been disbanded to save money.[74] The remaining units had territorial affiliations to assist recruiting and, again, to keep costs to a minimum. The 1st Battalion was recruited from Nyasaland; the 3rd Battalion from British East Africa (Kenya); and the 4th Battalion from Uganda. The 3rd and 4th Battalions contained a number of Sudanese soldiers and officers, the legacy of previous colonial wars, and the tradition was that the fourth platoon of each company was Sudanese. Each of the battalions was distributed in company-size groups over a wide area, which meant that officers and men developed a sense of self-reliance. The total establishment in 1914 was just 70 British officers, 3 British NCOs and 2,325 Africans. The troops were well armed with Lee–Metford or Lee–Enfield rifles and one Vickers machine gun per company. The 3rd Battalion of the King's African Rifles also possessed one camel-mounted company in the far north.

Northern Rhodesia had no regular military establishment, but it did have, from 1911, the Northern Rhodesia Police, which was organised along military lines. In Southern Rhodesia, the British South Africa Police also followed a military format. These constabularies were also well armed with rifles and machine guns, which, while obsolete by modern standards, were sufficient to overmatch tribal forces. In 1910, the Committee of Imperial Defence had decided that in the event of a major war, these forces would be limited to an internal security role. Constrained budgets did not permit regular military training or anything approaching formation-level concentration. The result was that the companies were competent in small tactical operations, self-contained and mobile, but ill-prepared for larger-scale operations.

The initial operation in East Africa, the landing of Indian forces at Tanga, suffered a severe setback on 4 November 1914. The Indian brigade suffered 800 casualties, and, shocked by the effectiveness of German machine-gun fire, their morale almost collapsed. The defeat placed the British on the defensive for almost a year. After the setback at Tanga, and with all available personnel from West Africa committed to the Cameroons campaign, and the South Africans engaged in operations in German South-West Africa, there were no reserves available to assist in the defence of British East Africa. There were no prospects of further reinforcements from India in the short term either, or additional British personnel from the United Kingdom. Local military officers therefore recommended immediate expansion of the King's African Rifles. The civil administration refused. There was simply too much opposition to the idea of arming large numbers of black personnel. There was also the rejection of a private offer to raise a battalion of Swazis and another of Zulus in South Africa.

The only additional troops available were men of the 25th Royal Fusiliers, a wartime unit made up of former adventurers with some African experience. The only other troops to arrive were a squadron of the 17th Cavalry and the 130th Baluchis from the Indian Army. White settlers from East Africa formed their own small volunteer units, later titled the East African Mounted Rifles and the East African Regiment. White settlers in Uganda also formed their own Uganda Volunteer Rifles and those from Zanzibar created the Zanzibar Volunteer Defence Force. More recruits were available from the East Africa Protectorate Police Battalion, the Arab Rifles (from the coast), a Uganda Police Service Battalion, the Uganda armed levies and the Zanzibar African Rifles (which was derived from the Zanzibar Armed Constabulary). Each of these units was of battalion size and provided with British officers, either from the police or from volunteer settlers. In Nyasaland, white settlers formed a Volunteer Defence Force, while in Northern Rhodesia they formed a similar unit called the Northern Rhodesia Rifles.

In early 1916, the British were able to mount their own offensive, against the advice of the Secretary of State for War, Lord Kitchener. Although the designated commander was Lieutenant General Sir Horace Smith-Dorrien, he soon fell ill and was replaced by Lieutenant General Jan Smuts, the veteran of the South African War.[75] The South Africans provided the critical mass for the offensive. Smuts could bring to the theatre of operations one mounted and two infantry brigades, with an artillery brigade of five batteries. Alongside these white troops there was a Cape Corps battalion made up of men from the Cape Coloured population, paid by the British government, but with white officers from South Africa. By the end of the campaign, some 18,000 Cape Corps personnel had served in East Africa.

The Indian Army provided an additional two infantry battalions, while the South Africans sent two more battalions and field artillery to Rhodesia. The total force available to Smuts in British East Africa was 27,350, with an additional 1,900 in the Uganda Lake Force and, further south, some 2,593 in Northern Rhodesia. The Belgians augmented this force with 12,000 of their personnel. The German adversaries, operating as guerrilla groups, could muster 3,000 Europeans and 11,000 askaris with 2,500 irregular levies. Smuts's plan was to make a series of converging thrusts against the Germans in East Africa in order to prevent them being strong on any one front. The problem was that the German units were more mobile and made use of the broken terrain to slow the British advance and evade the jaws of the British offensive.[76] The German tactics were to engage a force, inflict as many casualties as possible, but withdraw before they were caught. Nevertheless, by the end of 1916, two-thirds of the German territory was in British hands. The chief difficulty in late 1916 was the onset of diseases in the Allied ranks, and the situation was worsened by the German scorched-earth policy which deprived the Allies of local resources. As a result, food, ammunition and equipment had to be carried across the whole theatre of operations. Despite the proven value of local forces, particularly on the German side, there was little enthusiasm from Smuts and the Colonial Office for any expansion of the King's African Rifles. Only the severity of casualties from disease among white personnel compelled the British military authorities to re-establish the 2nd and 5th King's African Rifles in 1916 and double the size of the 2nd, 3rd and 4th Battalions.

In the first half of 1917 the Allies were occupied in trying to track down and neutralise German groups. In this exhausting work, they were assisted by African units from West Africa who had gained their experience in the Cameroons.[77] General A.R. Hoskins, who replaced Smuts as overall commander in January 1917, an officer with a great deal of experience in East Africa, was enthusiastic about the expansion of the King's African Rifles.[78] Before he could implement a full expansion of African troops, he too was replaced, by Van Deventer, a South African officer, in May of that same year. Despite German efforts to break out of their encirclement, by November 1917 their forces were hemmed into the south-west corner of their colony and they enjoyed only minor tactical successes. Just one small contingent remained at large by the end of the war in 1918.

In the final year of the war, most of the South African units had been withdrawn and the Gold Coast Regiment and 2nd Battalion West India Regiment had replaced them.[79] The Nigerian Brigade, made up of four battalions that had served in Cameroons, was deployed in 1917, while the 2nd Rhodesia Native Regiment was amalgamated with the 1st to become the Rhodesian African Rifles.[80] To meet the shortfall in manpower, more Indian Army regiments were deployed, including the 30th Punjabi, 55th Frontier Force Rifles, 75th and 109th Infantry, 127th Baluchis and the 25th Cavalry. The 130th Baluchis and the 5th Light Infantry had mutinied in 1914 and 1915 respectively, and had been sent to Africa, but these men performed without difficulty in their new theatre of operations.

General Hoskins had served as Inspector General of the King's African Rifles before the war. Before his departure, he raised a new 6th King's African Rifles of two battalions from former askaris in German service. While both these battalions were allocated to garrison duty, one of them took part in hunting down German Schutztruppe and acquitted itself well. There was also expansion of the African contingents with a King's African Rifles mounted infantry unit and a signals company. By the end of the war, there were 22 KAR battalions numbering 35,424 men.[81] Other African units also doubled in size, bringing them up to the same strength as units of the Indian or British Army. By contrast, white volunteer units practically ceased to exist by 1917, many of their members being absorbed into other units as officers and NCOs. Arms and munitions also improved for African units as the war progressed. By the end of the conflict the Allied forces were able to support them with aircraft, heavy machine guns, light machine guns and mortars. There had also been an expansion in the so-called Carrier Corps, the porters who were essential in a landscape where horses and mules died quickly from tsetse fly infections.[82] The organisation grew from 7,000 in 1915 to 150,000 in 1917. By the end of the war, approximately 500,000 had served in this role. They fell under the command of the Military Labour Bureau, but when exhausted and malnourished carriers returned to Uganda, there was dismay at the conditions they had endured.

African personnel had played an important part in the protracted campaign in East Africa, as well as elsewhere in the continent. The greatest success was achieved where existing regiments were expanded and absorbed new personnel. The more inexperienced units struggled, as one would expect, until they had become used to the conflict environment and the tactics of the German forces. Despite the reluctance to increase the numbers of armed black personnel, for political reasons, it was the high rates of sickness and the demands for manpower in what was, essentially, a counter-insurgency-style campaign that compelled the British and Imperial authorities to expand African units. KAR casualties numbered 8,225, a rate of 22 per cent, mostly from disease. The King's African Rifles had a reputation for high levels of discipline and the tradition was maintained after the war, but inevitably cost-cutting measures meant that the KAR and other African units were reduced in scale in peacetime. By 1920 they had been reduced to 5,700 men, but, with the outbreak of the Second World War, they would be expanded again in significant numbers.

Chinese Military Labour

In 1895 China suffered a staggering defeat in the Sino-Japanese war. Just five years later, the internal convulsions in the country produced a rebellion by the Society of Harmonious Fists, the 'Boxer' Rebellion, between 1898 and 1901. The revolt compelled European forces to occupy the coastal areas of China, and Beijing fell under their influence, which the Chinese regarded as an unbearable humiliation. Soon after, in 1911, the deeply unpopular Imperial Chinese system was overthrown and China became a republic. The new Chinese government believed that the First World War created an opportunity to re-establish China as a respected nation and to bargain away all forms of foreign occupation. China therefore made an attempt to join the war against Germany in 1914. Ostensibly China would be able to recover Shandong province, which had been in German hands since 1898, but the real value in participating in the war was that China would be represented at any international peace conference. It believed it would be able to throw off its reputation as a weak and decrepit state which had become, to all intents and purposes, a colony of the European powers.

Although the orthodox view among scholars was that China was pulled into the war by outside forces, the historian Xu Guoqi has shown that the

Chinese government itself made a very serious effort to join the war for its own national interests.[83] The problem was that China was already bitterly divided by the time of the outbreak of the First World War. Various national groups, including Sun Yat-sen's nationalist party in the south, faced competition from rival warlords in the centre and north. Nevertheless, China first appealed to the United States to act as its champion and offered to join the war in order to uphold Article II of the Hague Convention of 1907, which condemned aggression against other states, a clear reference to Germany's invasion of Belgium and France. Both Britain and Japan rejected China's attempt to participate in the war, and the Americans agreed to drop any support for China. China then attempted to lobby the United States more directly in the hope it would appeal to Tokyo and London, on the grounds that it must have Shandong province.

The Japanese forestalled this second Chinese bid by seizing part of the Shandong peninsula, having declared war on Germany on 23 August 1914. In January 1915, Japan then issued its Twenty-One Demands to China in an attempt to render the country no more than a protectorate. Neither Britain nor the United States would recognise these demands. In desperation, in late 1915 the Chinese offered the Allies financial assistance and munitions for their war effort, but the major powers realised that China's contribution would inevitably be small, and, once again, Japan objected. Since Japan was already an Allied nation, it was difficult for Britain, France or any other Western power to defy Tokyo. Moreover, there was concern that Japan might be tempted to change sides and support Germany, particularly when the Allies had failed on most fronts in 1915. In order to keep Japan on the Allied side, it was necessary to turn down the Chinese offer.[84]

In 1915, China made a new attempt to join the Allies by offering military personnel. The heavy losses on the Western Front had clearly created a need for manpower, but, other than the British military attaché in Beijing, Lieutenant Colonel David Robertson, there was little enthusiasm for Chinese troops. The War Office believed such a scheme to be unrealistic, and not just because of Japanese objections; the reputation of the Chinese as soldiers was not exemplary in Western eyes. The solution, it was suggested, was to send labourers for military projects instead or, as the Chinese government put it, '*yigong daibing*', 'labourers as soldiers'. The idea was promoted by the Chinese Finance Minister, Liang Shiyi, and was to be facilitated by a private company with which he had connections. The first group of Chinese labourers arrived in France in August 1916, and by the end of 1917 there were about 100,000

Chinese working for the French government.[85] The contract with Paris was renewable for five years and the Chinese were given equal legal status to the French. Their rations were generally good and the work they carried out was regarded as valuable to the war effort.[86]

In 1918, however, the French Foreign Ministry suddenly broke the contract and refused to accept any more Chinese workers. They argued that the quality of the labour was abysmal. This verdict was disputed by some military officers, including Marshal Foch, and by the French embassy in Beijing. Most believed the Chinese had been very useful in military construction and the creation of field fortifications since their arrival. Nevertheless, although those already in France were retained, no new labouring details were accepted.

The British government's own efforts to recruit Chinese fared little better. Chinese labour was a contentious issue because, in 1903, it had been proposed to carry out the reconstruction of South Africa, after the war of 1899–1902, with Chinese workers.[87] Organised labour in Britain feared that cheaper Chinese workers would not only flood the imperial job market but also affect the British economy. However, such were the demands for manpower in the war that Chinese labourers were welcomed for construction, road-making, agricultural labour and factory work.[88] The British offered three-year contracts, but inserted a clause whereby they could discontinue any contract after one year with just six months' notice. Initially, they had trouble recruiting in northern China around Weihaiwei because the British did not use a Chinese front company as the French had done.

There were further problems when the Chinese government created a list of requests in return for its labour on the 23 February 1917. These were to end indemnity payments incurred after the Boxer Rebellion, to permit the Chinese to impose their own tariffs and to have a seat at any international peace conference.[89] The British Foreign Secretary, Arthur Balfour, expected that, for these terms to be met, China would have to join the Allies and participate fully in the war effort. This opportunity came when the United States declared war on Germany in February 1917: China severed relations with the Central Powers in March and entered the war in August 1917, the delay being the result of internal disagreements in China. The Chinese still wanted to send a large military contingent and more labourers, but an acute shipping shortage and the prioritisation of sending American troops to Europe precluded the opportunity. Internal unrest in China nevertheless produced thousands of volunteers for labouring work in Europe. Those that were selected could earn an initial bounty, then $10 a month thereafter. This was far in excess of anything that a worker could obtain in China at the time, and labourers were also given clothing and rations. After passing through medical examinations, the workers were issued with identity tags, hosed with disinfectant, and embarked on the available shipping. The transit across the Indian Ocean via the Suez Canal and through the Mediterranean proved too hazardous to continue for long, not least when German U-boats sank one of the vessels en route. The new route involved crossing the Pacific Ocean, a transit by rail across Canada, and then re-embarkation for the final leg across the Atlantic. When in France, the workers repaired roads, built huts, carried out repairs to vehicles, and dug trenches behind the front line. A number were also employed in food preparation for the troops.[90] But segregation was enforced and the Chinese were, to some extent, 'hidden'. The British banned the Chinese from frequenting cafés and estaminets and they were discouraged from communicating with other Europeans. To ease identification, they wore special uniforms, but they were treated with some disdain.[91] British officers acting as supervisors did not speak Chinese and were generally unsympathetic. Chinese workers could be subjected to a variety of punishments, including shooting *in extremis*. Chinese labourers continued to work on the Western Front until well after the end of the war, and were involved in hazardous battlefield salvage and clearance. Despite these efforts, the Chinese government did not achieve many of its objectives at the peace conference that followed the war. While it did succeed in removing the indemnities imposed by Germany and Austria-Hungary, the disappointment at the failure to gain more in 1919 produced the May Fourth Movement, an anti-imperialist protest led by students and intellectuals in China. The disenchantment with the attempt to co-operate with the Europeans lingered on through the inter-war years and created a legacy of distrust for decades.

Embedded Adviser: T.E. Lawrence

Thomas Edward Lawrence, known as 'Lawrence of Arabia', attracts both critics and aficionados, but there is little doubt that his war service as an adviser to the irregular Arab forces of the Hejaz in the First World War remains an instructive example of how a guerrilla campaign can be orchestrated to serve mutual interests. While his book *Seven Pillars of Wisdom* and its preliminary version 'The Evolution of a Revolt' are well known for their literary value, they are also detailed and often brutally honest guides to the challenges an adviser could face. Lawrence made no secret of his feelings in *Seven Pillars*, although he could obscure the most extreme of his personal failings. During an action against an Ottoman patrol, which became a prolonged and exhausting firefight, for example, he narrated the effects of the heat, his temporary inability to continue skirmishing, his exasperation with the poor marksmanship of the Arabs with him, and then, when one of the fighters launched a premature charge, how, in the excitement of this final assault, he accidentally shot his own camel in the head and was pitched headlong to the ground.[92] Lawrence admitted that Auda, one of the most experienced fighters in his force, had criticised him for seeking some shade during the firefight, and Lawrence had 'spat back' because he was 'angry with everyone and with myself', and wounded the pride of the old fighter with the condemnation of Auda's men: 'They shoot a lot and hit a little.' Auda went 'pale with rage, tore off his headcloth and threw it on the ground beside me' before he 'ran back up the hill like a madman, shouting to the men in his dreadful strained and rustling voice'. It was wounded pride that provoked the final charge, which, by luck, was a success. Lawrence admitted that this action had not been planned or advised, and his comrade was delighted because 'he had confounded me and shown what his tribe could do'.[93]

Lawrence was not an orthodox army officer but he possessed a passion for the Arab world and had a good command of the language. His pre-war experience and knowledge were of immense value. Lawrence had been educated at Oxford in medieval military history and archaeology. He was physically fit, and his interest in medieval fortifications prompted him to make three journeys by bicycle around France in order to study first-hand the architecture of various castles.[94] He was also interested in medieval culture, especially that of the Crusades, and he made several visits to the fortifications of the Near East; these became the subject of his academic thesis.[95] His journeys took him through Lebanon, Syria and Urfa on the Euphrates between June and October 1909, and he made ethnic, administrative, social and cultural observations en route. He noted, for example, that religious observance was in decay in some areas and he developed a low opinion of the Turkish administrators he encountered. After his graduation, in 1910, Lawrence joined the archaeological expedition of David Hogarth, his former tutor at Oxford, and he took part in the excavations at Carcamesh.[96] He also took the opportunity to carry out surveys, including assessments of the progress of the Berlin–Baghdad railway and the opinions or loyalties of the various populations of the Ottoman Empire.[97]

Lawrence developed a strong sense that he was the inheritor of a chivalric tradition, and his writings indicate he felt he was on a personal journey of discovery and often struggling to live up to the idealised values of an earlier epoch. Lawrence desperately wanted to fulfil the virtues of courage, self-sacrifice, redemption, justice and charity. He wanted a 'cause' that would enable him to demonstrate these qualities, and it was no accident that he carried with him a copy of Sir Thomas Malory's *Morte d'Arthur* on the subsequent campaigns of the First World War.[98] He convinced himself that assisting the Arabs towards their liberation fulfilled a deeply held desire to be of value in the world, but in the image of his cultural heroes. He described the Arab forces he accompanied in the language of the Arthurian ideal: 'We were a self-centred army without parade or gesture, devoted to freedom, the second of man's creeds, a purpose so ravenous that it devoured all our strength, a hope so transcendent that our earlier ambitions faded in its glare. As time went by our need to fight for the ideal increased to an unquestioning possession, riding with spur and rein over our doubts.'[99]

Yet Lawrence was also eager to carry out his duty, with modesty and resolution, in order to do his part in serving his country's national interests. He revealed something of his approach to the Arab forces too when he wrote: 'I was sent to these Arabs as a stranger, unable to think their thoughts or subscribe to their beliefs, but charged by duty to lead them forward to develop to the highest any movement of theirs profitable to England in her war. If I could not assume their character, I could at least conceal my own, and pass among them without evident friction, neither a discord nor a critic but an unnoticed influence.'[100]

As an adviser, he struggled with the desire to join in the fight for liberation with the Arabs but, at the same time, ensure that the Arabs' actions complied with British operational and strategic needs. It was the apparent contradiction of these missions that played on Lawrence's mind. He found it hard to reconcile the idea of an independent Arabia with the British requirement to prioritise the interests of their French allies, and Lawrence experienced a personal crisis over the matter in 1916–17. Yet he also struggled with the idealised version of Arab unity he wanted to construct and the hard reality of bitter tribal and national divisions he encountered. Moreover, in fighting techniques he made use of his knowledge of medieval warfare to good effect, but he found more contradictions at the strategic level. Again, his aspirations, based on his academic knowledge, became both an asset and a hindrance. In his advance from the Hejaz northwards, he wrote: 'I felt that one more sight of Syria would put straight the strategic ideas given me by the Crusaders.'[101] Yet by 1918, on leaving Damascus, Lawrence was disillusioned, not only with the Allies' post-war plans, but with the disagreements between Arabs themselves about their future. He wrote: 'it is a pity to go, and it would have been unwise to stay. I feel like a man who has suddenly dropped a heavy load—one's back hurts when one tries to walk straight'.[102]

The idea of British support for the revolt of the Hashemites of the Hejaz had its origins in exploratory talks between the Sharif Hussein of Mecca and the British authorities in Egypt before the war. At that time, when the Ottoman Empire was not yet committed to the Central Powers, Britain did not wish to entertain the suggestion made by Hussein that the Arabs of the Hejaz would be prepared to regard the British as their protectors if they gave assistance and facilitated greater autonomy and eventual independence. When the war broke out and the Ottomans aligned themselves with Berlin and Vienna, the British offered an alliance with the Sharif if he would promise to support the British war effort. In return, Kitchener, as newly appointed Secretary of State for War, was prepared to offer 'independence' to the Arabs of the Hejaz. While ensuring their safety and freedom from the Ottomans, what Kitchener had in mind was a caliphate that was more spiritual in nature, not political.[103] Hussein delayed, knowing that he could not yet guarantee that many Arabs would follow him and that the Ottoman forces in Arabia were strong enough to crush any premature revolt. Moreover, his ambitions were initially unclear. It was only later, once the British had begun to secure their position in Palestine, that Hussein began to consider a role as leader of the entirety of Arabia and, perhaps, of the Muslim world.[104] Far from being a proto-nationalist struggle for the sake of Arabism, this was a bid for dynastic security and an opportunity to replace the secularists in Istanbul with a genuine Caliphate. Hussein believed that the war was opening up the opportunity to attain a long-cherished ideal, but he knew he lacked the means to fulfil it.[105]

In June 1915, Hussein and his sons considered the British offer and the contrasting Ottoman demands to have the Arabs support, unconditionally, the war effort against the Entente powers. Hussein put forward his own terms to both sides, but he was moving towards a preference for co-operation with the British. In the exchange of letters with the authorities at Cairo, known subsequently as the Hussein-McMahon correspondence, the Hashemites revealed their plan for an uprising and claimed to represent 'the whole of the Arab nation'.[106] The British reaction was to dismiss this extensive claim to represent the Arab 'nation', but there was some sympathy for the idea of a revolt which might potentially tie down thousands of Ottoman troops. Sir Henry McMahon, the British High Commissioner in Egypt, therefore offered association with Great Britain and support for a revolution, but he refused to give any backing to a final territorial settlement, which, he perceived, would change as the war progressed. Hussein tried to press the British on the basis this was a claim substantiated not by his clan, the Hashemites, but by the whole Arab people. It was not until October, as British fortunes in the Middle East began to falter, that McMahon would confirm the details of any territorial settlement. He insisted, understandably, that Britain's allies and partners in the Gulf, namely the rulers of Kuwait, Oman, the Arabian coast, the Trucial States, Qatar and Bahrain, were to remain under British supervision because of long-standing treaties. As events turned out, the British were right: the Hashemites were not strong enough to rule Arabia against their rivals in the region.

The chief difficulty for Britain was that it had to acknowledge French aspirations for Syria. In March 1915 a secret wartime pact between the British and French governments to allocate defined spheres of influence across the Middle East once the Ottoman Empire had been defeated was drawn up privately by François Georges-Picot and Sir Mark Sykes. It was not disclosed to Hussein. The agreement was only revealed when Russia collapsed in revolution in 1917 and the new Bolshevik regime published it. By its terms, France was to control southern Turkey, Syria, northern Levant and part of northern Iraq; Britain was to administer the *vilayets* (provinces) and *sanjaks* of Palestine, Jordan and Mesopotamia; for its part Russia would acquire Istanbul and Armenia.[107] The exact boundaries were not determined, and the agreement was a contingency document designed to co-ordinate war aims, but it was later regarded by Arab nationalists as a conspiratorial imperialist agenda and seen as evidence of betrayal. They argued, subsequently, that Britain and France were insincere about an independent national homeland for the Arabs. Sykes and Picot had assiduously set aside the entire interior of their demarcated zones for Arab autonomy, and they discussed this matter with Hussein in 1917.[108] Lawrence's claims that Britain had betrayed the Arabs' aspirations were somewhat disingenuous.

The agreement between the British and Hussein was the signal for the Hashemites to initiate their revolt, although an imminent purge by the Ottoman authorities would have necessitated action in any case. General Hamid Fahreddin 'Fakhri' Pasha had already been sent to assume command in Medina. This effectively replaced the theocratic local government with martial law and was intended to deter revolt. The Ottomans also knew that the Arabs were divided along clan lines and undisciplined in military matters. Although Fakhri possessed only a relatively small garrison, some 11,000 strong, his forces could easily overmatch the Hashemites. Ali, another son of

Hussein, could muster only 1,500 fighters at Medina and with this small force he hoped only to detain the Ottoman troops while his father launched the revolt in Mecca. Ali issued an ultimatum to the garrison commander on 9 June 1916, and the Sharif Hussein announced the outbreak of war between Arabs and Ottomans the next day with a single gunshot from his balcony.

The Ottoman garrison in Mecca numbered only 1,500 and was divided into three locations. While one of these was overwhelmed on the first day of street fighting, the other two used artillery and machine-gun fire to halt the Arab attacks. The result was stalemate, but with the Ottoman advantage in artillery, they could not be dislodged. It took until July for an Egyptian formation, sent by Britain, and some light guns to break down the defences. Eventually, short of water, the garrison capitulated on 9 July 1916. Meanwhile, at Medina, Ali's forces had attempted to seize a railway junction at Muhit but were driven off. Fakhri then counter-attacked with two brigades, pursuing the Arabs southwards and establishing strongpoints along his main communications routes. At Taif, south-west of Mecca, the initial Arab attempt to take the town also ended in failure. The Ottoman troops were determined in their resistance and, even when the Egyptian guns arrived from Mecca, the garrison held out until September. The Arab fighters lacked the heavy weapons necessary to capture towns and rail junctions. Without these in their possession, there was nothing to prevent the arrival of Ottoman reinforcements. Early assessments therefore suggested that the revolt was doomed to failure unless British assistance could be secured urgently.[109] This required the capture of the Red Sea ports, where the Royal Navy could land arms, especially artillery, supplies and munitions.

British intervention undoubtedly saved the revolt. As Lawrence noted, Arab attempts to stand against regular Ottoman troops were futile. In his retrospective study, he assessed the relative value of irregular forces. When the Ottomans began an offensive from Medina to recapture Mecca, some fifty miles from their start point lay a line of hills, and beyond this for a stretch of 70 miles was a coastal plain that ran towards Rabegh. Lawrence wrote:

> Our military advisers had told us that Rabegh was the key of Mecca ... Its defence was therefore of the main importance ... They thought that Bedouin tribesmen would never be of any value in a fixed position, and that therefore an Arab regular force must be formed and trained as soon as possible to undertake this duty ... A personal reconnaissance of the Arab positions, here and in the hills where Feisal was, caused me to modify the views of the experts a little. Faisal had some thousands of men, all armed with rifles, rather casual, distrustful fellows, but very active and cheerful. They were posted in hills and defiles of such natural strength that it

seemed to me very improbable that the Turks could force them, just by their superior numbers ... Accordingly, I reported that the tribesmen (if strengthened by light
machine guns, and regular officers as advisors) should be able to hold up the Turks
indefinitely, while the Arab regular force was being created. As was almost inevitable in view of the general course of military thinking since Napoleon, we all looked
only to the regulars to win the war.[110]

The Arabs were not sent machine guns or advisers, and Lawrence continued: 'The Turks suddenly put my appreciation to the test by beginning their
advance on Mecca. They broke through my impregnable hills in 24 hours, and
came forward from them towards Rabegh slowly. So they proved to us the
second theorem of irregular war—namely, that irregular troops are as unable
to defend a point or line as they are to attack it.'[111]

Lawrence made his deductions from this incident: 'In the emergency it
occurred to me that perhaps the virtue of irregulars lay in depth, not in face,
and that it had been the threat of attack by them upon the Turkish northern
flank which had made the enemy hesitate for so long.' Lawrence advised that
the Arab irregulars move the base of their operations to Wejh, and noted that
this manoeuvre forced the Ottomans to pull back all the way to Medina lest
their flank was threatened.[112]

Lawrence admitted that he was unprepared for the role of military adviser
in that he had no formal training. He therefore fell back on his reading of
military history and to some extent on the philosophy of war. He turned the
dictum that victory depended on 'the destruction of the organised forces of
the enemy' on its head. He wrote: 'and as I thought about it, it dawned on me
that we had won the Hejaz war. We were in occupation of 99% of the Hejaz
... This part of the war was over, so why bother about Medina? ... The Turks
sat in it on the defensive, immobile, eating mules, the transport animals which
were to have moved them to Mecca, but for which there were no pastures in
their now restricted lines.'[113]

Lawrence claimed that the situation compelled him to reconsider strategy
and tactics. He wrote: 'In each I found the same elements, one algebraic, one
biological, a third psychological. The first seemed a pure science, subject to the
laws of mathematics, without humanity.' This element dealt with time, space,
fixed conditions, topography, railways and munitions. Lawrence calculated
that the Ottomans could not defend the 140,000 square miles of Arabia,
particularly if the Arab forces were 'a thing invulnerable, intangible, without
front or back, drifting about like a gas'. He surmised that armies were 'like
plants, immobile as a whole, firm rooted, nourished through long stems to the

head. We [the Arab forces] might be a vapour, blowing where we listed. Our kingdoms lay in each man's mind, and as we wanted nothing material to live on, so perhaps we offered nothing material to the killing.'[114] All this Lawrence called hecastics.

The second element was biological, or bionomics as Lawrence called it.[115] Soldiers must eat and drink, and for Lawrence the Ottomans' materiel was scarce and precious. Consequently his objective was to destroy not the army, but its material support. This included railway lines and bridges, supplies or the enemy's weapons.

Whereas in conventional war Lawrence noted that 'both forces [are] striving to keep in touch to avoid tactical surprise', in guerrilla warfare 'our war should be a war of detachment: we were to contain the enemy by the silent threats of a vast unknown desert, not disclosing ourselves to the moment of attack'. Lawrence placed considerable emphasis on this third element of psychology. He wanted the Ottoman soldiers to fear not only the Arab raiders but also the desert itself. By deterring them from entering the desert, he would ensure mobility for the Arab forces. But the mental preparation of his fighters was also important. Lawrence concluded: 'we had to arrange their minds in order of battle, just as carefully and as formally as other officers arrange their bodies; and not only our own men's minds, though them first; the minds of the enemy, so far as we could reach them; and thirdly, the mind of the nation supporting us behind the firing line, and the mind of a hostile nation waiting the verdict, and the neutrals looking on'. His verdict was that 'the printing press was the greatest weapon in the armoury of the modern commander'.[116]

He also argued that the Arab forces relied on 'speed and time, not hitting power, for these gave strategic strength rather than tactical strength'.[117] He specifically avoided fixed points, and the tactics of his forces were to tip and run, the objective being to avoid prolonged contact with the Ottoman forces.[118] To ensure mobility, Lawrence embraced the Arab preference for camels and horses, and fighters carried no more than a bag of flour to make unleavened bread in the ashes of fires and a pint of drinking water for each man. Water was consumed every other day, but prolifically at wells.[119] Nevertheless, on several occasions, groups of Arab fighters were almost compromised by the destruction of wells or their dependence on grazing for the camels. Moreover, the winter of 1917–18 caused many casualties, some of whom it froze to death. It was rarely possible to repair weapons and there was a limit to how much ammunition or explosive the small teams of Arab fighters could carry.[120] In the latter stages of the campaign the Arab forces with

Lawrence were assisted by aircraft, which included the provision of supplies by the Handley Page bomber.

Lawrence noted that there were other particular difficulties and opportunities in working with local indigenous forces. He wrote: 'The distribution of the raiding parties was unorthodox. It was impossible to mix or combine tribes, since they disliked or distrusted one another. Likewise, we could not use the men of one tribe in the territory of another. In consequence, we aimed at the widest distribution of forces, in order to have the greatest number of raids on hand at once, and we added fluidity to their ordinary speed, by using one district on Monday, another on Tuesday, a third on Wednesday. This much reinforced their natural mobility. It gave us priceless advantages in pursuit, for the force renewed itself with fresh men in every new tribal area, and gave us always our pristine energy. Maximum disorder was in a real sense our equilibrium.'[121]

Since the Arab fighters were all volunteers, any of them could return home whenever they felt so inclined. Lawrence noted: 'Our only contract was honour.' Consequently, 'we had no discipline, in the sense in which it is restrictive, submergence of individuality, the lowest common denominator of men'. Lawrence believed: 'The deeper the discipline, the lower the individual efficiency, and the more sure the performance. It is a deliberate sacrifice of capacity in order to reduce the uncertain element, the bionomic factor, in enlisted humanity.' But Lawrence's critique of discipline reflected more his personal preferences for freedom of action. He made no mention of the value of unison, synchronisation, or the ability to withstand the pressures of war. Even in disciplined armies there is always still room for individual creativity and exhibitions of courage. In stressing the simplicity and individuality of Arab fighters and making claim that 'the efficiency of each man was his personal efficiency', Lawrence elided over the shortcomings of Arab irregular fighters. He admitted that the rebellion must have an unassailable base and he was fortunate that the Ottomans possessed only limited air power to halt his mobile forces. But Lawrence was a persuasive advocate of guerrilla war in the desert. He summed up this style of war in fifty words: 'granted mobility, security (in the form of denying targets to the enemy), time, and doctrine (the idea to convert every subject to friendliness), victory will rest with the insurgents, for the algebraic factors are in the end decisive, and against them perfections of means and spirit struggle quite in vain'.[122]

The subsequent seizure of Jeddah, Yanbu and Rabegh transformed the operational situation. As well as the Egyptian troops and guns, a battalion of 700 Arab regulars, mainly men who had become prisoners of war of the

British in Mesopotamia but agreed to serve now against the Ottomans, landed in the Hejaz. British officers provided the co-ordination which the new operations and logistics required, but the 'footprint' of Europeans was deliberately small so as to avoid offending Muslim sensibilities given the proximity of the holiest places of the faith.[123] Jeddah was under the command of Colonel Cyril Wilson, the former Governor of the Sudan, and Colonel Pierce Joyce assumed control of Rabegh in December. Colonel Stewart Newcombe, a Royal Engineer, and Lawrence took a keen interest in the Hejaz railway as the most operationally important feature of the region, and they planned to disrupt all its traffic with a series of raids.

Lawrence believed that working alongside the local fighters offered the best chance of mutual success. He wrote: 'I urged that the situation seemed full of promise. The main need was skilled assistance; and the campaign should go prosperously if some regular British officers, professionally competent and speaking Arabic, were attached to the Arab leaders as technical advisors, to keep us in proper touch.'[124]

By the autumn, French officers had joined the campaign, focusing largely on the area around Mecca and Medina. The opportunity to 'escort' pilgrims, using Muslim North African troops, offered the chance to establish a French presence in the Arab cause in order to fulfil the aspirations of the Sykes-Picot accord, but the British regarded this as an enterprise in colonial rivalry.[125] Colonel Edouard Brémont was the liaison officer to Hussein and Abdullah, while the Muslim officers of French North African regiments, Colonel Cadi and Captain Ould Raho, worked alongside Arab raiding parties.[126] Captain Rosario Pisani, a French adviser attached to what became the Arab Northern Army, was one of the most successful raiders of all. There was a steady increase in the numbers of regular Arab troops available, some 2,000 strong, and these came under the command of Major Ali al-Masri with the title of the Sharifian Army, but the British and the French did their best to continue to limit the presence of non-Muslims.

The Agayl, who made up the majority of irregular fighters, considered themselves to be inherent warriors, but British assessments of their fighting styles considered them unsuitable for anything other than raids. Without modern weapons or training, they could not be used to assault defended positions. Heavy weapons would also compromise their mobility, which was their chief defence until the Ottomans increased the number of aircraft operating against them. Later in the campaign, it became essential to equip the Arab Northern Army with aircraft, armoured cars and anti-aircraft guns, and to augment their regular and irregular contingents with British Imperial Yeomanry and units of the Indian Army.

To gain legitimacy as the true leaders of the Muslim world, which was perhaps Hussein's real ambition, it was vital to secure Medina as they had done Mecca, and, concurrently, they had to keep open the sea ports on the coast through which came all their essential supplies. At the same time, if the Ottoman line of communication and reinforcement, the Hejaz railway, could be cut, there was a chance they could prevent large Ottoman formations from concentrating against them and perhaps starve the garrison of Medina into submission. Lawrence took a different view. By periodically raiding the line, rather than cutting it off entirely, they effectively bottled up the Ottomans in a strategically useless garrison, unable to operate far from their base, yet constantly consuming much-needed supplies. Lawrence also knew that the Arabs would be unable to capture the heavily defended Medina with the forces at their disposal. Lawrence had to use tact and diplomacy to persuade the Sharif Hussein's son Emir Feisal of this operational reality, but also to consider a more valuable project, namely developing the revolt northwards in order to absorb yet more Ottoman resources. Feisal had his own agenda. Aware that he was unlikely to gain any significant position in the post-war dispensation in the Hejaz, Feisal looked to acquire a Greater Syria as a potential source of future power. It was this factor, and the coincidence of objectives with the British, which drew the forces under his command northwards.

General Murray, the commander in Egypt, believed the Arab Revolt was capable only of drawing a proportion of Ottoman forces into the strategically insignificant Hejaz, and away from the more important theatre of operations in Sinai and Palestine. Murray therefore practised an economy of effort in supporting the Hashemites, and he was certainly not prepared to divide his forces and take on a secondary theatre, especially given his experience of having to suppress the Senussi on Egypt's western borders at the same time as fighting the Ottomans and their Bedouin allies in Sinai. Robertson, as Chief of the Imperial General Staff, was even more trenchant, stating: 'My sole object is to win the war, and we shall not do that in the Hijaz or in the Sudan.'[127]

In fact, in late 1916 British intelligence revealed that their own Arab fighters were hungry and downcast, while the Egyptian gunners sent to their aid were equally disenchanted with such a lost cause. Their chief problem was a lack of progress against the Ottomans around Medina and, worse still, the recovery of the Ottomans in the Hejaz. Fakhri Pasha had built up his forces over the autumn and, in December, he was able to make his first thrust against the Arab fighters at Yanbu. He intended to retake the port and then march down the coast, clearing the guerrillas as he went. Arab contingents could not hold the Ottoman regulars, but just when it seemed the port would fall, the arrival of a Royal Navy flotilla tipped the balance.[128] Air attacks, launched from the ships, and naval gunfire deterred a full-scale assault. Fakhri turned instead against Rabegh, but was again subjected to air attack by the Royal Flying Corps, and while he could defeat Arab fighters sent against him, he could not stop their raids on his supply lines back to Medina. The deciding factor, though, was a new Arab attack towards Wejh, the last Ottoman-controlled port in the Hejaz.

In this operation Feisal led a core of 1,200 Agayl, supported by other clans and factions numbering 7,000. The plan was that while Feisal made a land-ward attack on the port, the Royal Navy would bombard and land 600 regular Arab troops there. On 23 January 1917, the amphibious assault, under Major Charles Vickery, went in, but Feisal and the Arab irregulars did not appear. The port was taken in bitter street fighting by the outnumbered attackers, and the Arab 'northern army' eventually reached the port two days later. The strategic objective was achieved, but it was necessary to attribute the significance of the offensive to the presence of a united Arab force rather than its operational effectiveness.

More effect was being achieved by raids on the Hejaz railway in 1917. The British were eager to ensure Fakhri was prevented from moving a significant proportion of his army northwards against their flank as they pushed into southern Palestine. Raiding parties set out, consisting of small groups led by British, French and Arab regular officers, armed with explosives. These railway attacks served their purpose: the capacity of the Ottomans to launch offensives was hamstrung by a lack of supplies and while new Ottoman sweeps were made in the spring and summer of 1917, there was something of a stalemate: Fakhri could not take back the ports and the Arabs could not capture Medina. Ottoman repair teams did their best to keep the lines open, although more audacious raids targeted trains, bent long sections of track, and demolished bridges. At al-Ula, a strong raiding force, augmented by Egyptian and Indian troops and supported by aircraft, severed the Hejaz line for three days.

The strategic breakthrough was the unexpected Arab capture of Aqaba in July 1917. Its success had seemed unlikely earlier that year. The 'means', the Arab Northern Army, was reduced in strength after the capture of Wejh as southern fighters, far from their homelands, began to leave the force. Fortunately, at the same time, it was being augmented with the handfuls of volunteers from greater Syria, northern Hejaz and the interior, including the clans of Howeitat, Shararat, Bani Atiyah and Rwalla. Unsurprisingly, these men looked to the north, hoping that operations against the Ottomans would be conducted there. The 'ends' were not only the 'liberation' of these lands, or the material wealth within them, but the more ambitious idea of seizing all of Syria and Palestine. The driving force of this plan was the rumour that the French intended to land an expeditionary force in Beirut while the British would hold on to Palestine and southern Arabia. The details of the Sykes-Picot agreement were now public, and it was therefore imperative to take possession of these territories before the British and French could. Nevertheless, Feisal knew that he was dependent on the British, and co-operation was essential to avoid destruction at the hands of the Ottomans. Auda abu Tiya, of the Howeitat, and his adviser, Lawrence, therefore devised a daring plan that would put Feisal in a much stronger position.

Aqaba was the last Red Sea port in Ottoman hands but was strongly defended from the seaward side, making any landing like the one conducted at Wejh far too costly. However, with Arab forces approaching from the rear, there was a chance the port could be taken, opening up a new supply route for the Egyptian Expeditionary Force and, crucially, a reconstituted independent Arab army. Lawrence collaborated with the Arabs to the extent that he misled Colonel Joyce, who commanded operations in the area, suggesting that he was co-ordinating an Arab mission against Ma'an to divert Ottoman attention from the mission of Colonel Newcombe against al-Ula. The contingent that left Wejh with Lawrence was only 17 strong and it intended to cross the al-Houl waterless tracts, travel over 600 miles (1,000 kilometres) and then recruit fighters from among local men en route with generous handouts of gold. The chances of survival were marginal, but, by May 1917, they had started their recruitment campaign in the interior, eventually creating a force of 650 men.

Lawrence then travelled further north into Syria on reconnaissance, raiding rail lines and communicating with the Metawila clans. By July, Lawrence had rejoined the main party and carried out an attack on the Ottoman fort at Fuweilah. Learning of the massacre of local Arabs by the garrison, the fighters gave no quarter. An Ottoman relief operation was halted and the battalion concerned was defeated.[129] Other outposts were captured, often by negotiation rather than fighting. As the Arabs approached Aqaba, new volunteer fighters came forward, which tipped the relative strengths of the two sides.[130] The Ottoman commander, realising he was cut off without hope of relief, offered to surrender the port, and Aqaba was taken on 6 July 1917.

The importance of the action at Aqaba was not the operation, despite the dramatic image of a charge into the port (after, in fact, it had already surrendered), but its strategic effect. Lawrence reported the capture in person to GHQ Cairo, where General Sir Edmund Allenby had just taken command. Allenby agreed to support the Arab force at Aqaba, realising that it could provide a new flank against the Ottoman forces dug in at Gaza, where British forces had already twice failed to break through. The strategic significance of Aqaba was not lost on the Ottomans. Knowing that the Arab clans were often enemies, they offered financial incentives to various groups to abandon the Allies. Inactivity also fuelled the old resentments, and there were disagreements between Feisal and Hussein about the leadership and direction of the revolt. The Ottomans made air attacks against the port, hoping to disrupt any build-up of logistics, which further demoralised the Arab rebels.[131]

The solution to the possible fragmentation of the Arab force was to conduct more raiding against Ottoman lines of communication, and consequently there were more tactical successes against railways. It was clear the strength of the 'revolt' lay in a strategy of guerrilla warfare. By contrast, the momentum towards the liberation of Syria was lost entirely, making it patently clear that, for all its later legendary status and bravado, it was not the Arab Revolt that mattered in this theatre, but the relentless pressure exerted by the Egyptian Expeditionary Force under Allenby.

Allenby had listened patiently to Captain Lawrence's ideas for a general uprising in Syria and the potential of the Arab Northern Army. While committing some resources to support the Arabs, and reinforcing Aqaba against counterattack, Allenby insisted on bringing the Sharifian forces under his own command.[132] Only then, he argued, could he achieve the necessary co-ordination of effort. Appealing to London with the possibilities the joint EEF–Arab forces might open up, he requested two new divisions, reversing the trend whereby formations had constantly been drawn away to other theatres.

At the same time, the Ottomans were also trying to augment their forces by recruiting local Arab irregulars. In particular they appealed for men from the Jordan valley.[133] The initial attempts were a failure, most of the men being too old for active service conditions, and it was far more effective to conscript younger men into the existing regular units. The exception was the Circassians who formed a volunteer cavalry force of two squadrons, which proved valuable in mobile patrolling against the Arab raiders. Karak, a mixed Muslim and Christian community, fielded a volunteer militia. More success was achieved with the generous Ottoman funding of Howeitat, Rwalla, Billi and Bani

Atiyya clansmen. With assurances of more money, generous rationing, and regular artillery and air support, the Ottomans prepared for the recapture of Aqaba using these Arab volunteer formations. Since the Arab forces were abandoning pastoralism or agriculture, and often refused to operate far from their homelands, the fighters had to be paid, usually in gold, to serve on a continuous basis, as the British had already discovered. The considerable sums being expended to secure their support were a point of criticism even among supporters at the Arab Bureau intelligence centre in Cairo.

Fortunately for the British, it was evident from the outset that no regular Ottoman army support was to be provided in the operations against Aqaba: the intention was rather to set off feuds and rivalries among Arabs that would ensure that the Sharif's cause would collapse. When the first Ottoman–Arab attack was made, the Howeitat and Bani men stood by, while the volunteers of Karak drove off the Sharifian outposts and seized livestock and supplies for themselves. No further progress was made and Aqaba was not threatened, but, as intended, divisions had been sown.

The Ottomans continued to court the Arabs back to the Ottoman cause.[134] There was condemnation of the Arab Revolt and the connivance of the British and French in trying to establish an Arab kingdom, under Hussein, across the entire Middle East. In secret correspondence with Feisal, the Ottomans argued that the British intended to make slaves of the Arabs, rendering Mecca and Medina mere protectorates, which would be cut off from the rest of the Middle East and therefore dependent on British supplies of food, fodder and finance.[135] There was an offer of full autonomy within the Ottoman Empire if Feisal now agreed to accept an amnesty. Feisal and Hussein were aware that the Ottomans were insincere, and far from accusing the British of betrayal, Feisal passed on the letters from the Ottomans to the Arab Bureau.[136] Nevertheless, the Hashemites had understood that any British and French occupation of Arab lands would be temporary; in other words, wartime measures necessary for the liberation struggle against the Ottomans. On these terms, they agreed to continue their co-operation. In Cairo, Commander D.G. Hogarth, Lawrence's former mentor and the head of the Arab Bureau, reassured the Sharif Hussein in January 1918 that the British were committed to enabling the Arabs the 'opportunity once again of forming a nation in the world' and that there was no question of subjugation. Hogarth explained that Jewish opinion also had to be considered, as they too sought a homeland in the Near East. The Foreign Office reiterated Hogarth's points and denounced the Ottoman attempt to sow discord, reaffirming the British government's willingness to liberate the Arabs.[137]

Colonel Joyce and Lawrence, now a major, also reassured Feisal at his headquarters that the Ottomans had distorted 'either from ignorance or malice' the original intent of the Sykes-Picot agreement, deliberately omitting, for example, the British commitment to obtain the 'consent of native populations and safeguarding their interests'.[138] Lawrence later wrote that he had disclosed the essence of the Sykes-Picot agreement in 1916 to the Arab leaders and felt a sense of shame. Yet this sentiment may well have come after the war, through his disappointment at the failure of the united Arab cause and the peace settlements.[139]

The chief dilemma for the Hashemites was their complete dependence on the British to sustain them. Reinforced at Aqaba, the Arab Northern Army possessed supporting British armoured cars, aircraft and field artillery with which to renew the offensive. Their original objective was Ma'an, a railway junction held by 6,000 entrenched infantry and mobile cavalry reserves. Lawrence correctly estimated that any assault by Arab forces on this strong position would be a costly failure.

Instead, air raids and attacks on the rail lines to the north and south were launched to force the Ottoman troops onto the defensive. Reconnaissance missions were made along potential routes into Palestine which could provide water for advancing regular troops, and, after several successful minor operations, it was Lawrence who was tasked to sever the Damascus–Medina line in the Yarmuk valley deep behind Ottoman lines.

The mission was a disaster. The line was not cut, his force was scattered, and, although the train of the Ottoman commander of VII Corps was derailed, Lawrence claimed to have been briefly captured, although, if untrue, it might suggest he was trying to compensate for his operational failure.[140] Still, there were sufficient numbers of small successes that otherwise convinced Allenby that the Arab Northern Army could be useful as a flanking formation during his proposed advance into Palestine. At Tafila, an Ottoman force had set out from Kerak to recover an area useful for grain and fodder, but they were enveloped on 25 January 1918 by Arab fighters led by Sharif Nasir, accompanied by Lawrence. The Ottoman brigade, numbering around 1,000 men, was routed and part of the force defected. Although the Ottomans later recovered Tafila, it was lost again in the autumn.[141]

At that point, Lawrence returned to Cairo somewhat disillusioned with the Arab campaign, largely over the wasteful distribution of gold supplied by General Headquarters, but Lieutenant Colonel Alan Dawnay led the new Hejaz Operations Staff to improve co-ordination with the Sharifian army. He explained that the plan was for a wing of the Arab Northern Army, under the Ottoman defector Jafar Pasha al-Askari, to take Ma'an, to cut the railway and all lateral communications, while Allenby's columns advanced on Amman. Lawrence was assigned to raise support amongst the local Bani Sakr clans nearby. Then, in March 1918, heavy rains made all movement arduous and prevented the deployment of field artillery. The Arab attack was called off.

The effort was renewed in the spring, and the Arab Northern Army achieved some success in storming Ma'an railway station on 16–17 April, although subsequent efforts to take the town itself failed and the Ottomans relief force of 3,000 men forced the Arabs back to their start lines. Jafar al-Askari blamed the French artillery under Captain Pisani for failures in fire support. Pisani claimed he had too little ammunition, but the Arabs believed Pisani was under orders not to back the Arabs beyond Ma'an, the boundary of the Hejaz and Syria. The French officer had indeed stated he could not support any operations into Syria, which, of course, his leaders regarded as a future French colony.

Regardless of the gunnery, the Arabs could not, despite four days' fighting, dislodge the Ottoman garrison, and morale amongst the Northern Army began to fail. The setback at Ma'an damaged the image of an invincible progress towards victory, underscoring the importance of actual and continued military success to any strategic narrative. Discredited by being in league with the British and French and their nefarious Sykes-Picot plans, accused of rebellion, criticised by other prominent Arabs, including Ibn Saud, and now militarily seen as ineffective without substantial British backing, the Hashemite cause was at its lowest ebb. The result was that the Arab forces returned to guerrilla warfare and continued their attacks on the railways, in the hope of keeping the revolt alive.

General Allenby made use of the Arab revolt in his preparations for a final offensive at Megiddo, seeing their value not in assaulting fortified towns but in creating deception. With the bulk of the Arab force laying siege to Ma'an, a smaller contingent advanced to within 50 miles of Amman. On 16 September, covered by aircraft of the Royal Air Force, Lawrence's Arab irregulars conducted a series of guerrilla actions against the railway line either side of the railway junction of Daraa. This inspired more local Arab tribes to join the revolt and drew in Ottoman reinforcements to defend the area. On the 17th, the Arab Northern Army made another attack on the line, north of Daraa. The town was finally assaulted by the Arab Northern Army on 26 September, and, joined by the British, they set off immediately towards the

Syrian capital. British and Indian cavalry circled round to cut off Ottoman forces making for Beirut and Homs. By 30 September, the combined British and Arab force was on the edge of Damascus.

The entry to the city was an honour accorded by the British to the Emir Feisal's troops, although the 2nd Australian Light Horse was the first into the city to clear it for operational reasons. The population greeted the Arab army as liberators but turned angry when the Sharif's men started looting. The British entry was more prosaic, but Feisal was treated as a conqueror for a short time before being informed, by Allenby, that the city was under British military occupation.[142] Moreover, instructions had been received that the Arabs were not to administer either Palestine or Lebanon, the latter going to the French authorities. The rest of the former Ottoman dominions were Allenby's responsibility. For those who were critical of this decision by Britain to take responsibility for the security of the Ottoman *vilayets*, it is worth noting that it was the British and Imperial forces that had borne the brunt of the fighting, and it was they who had defeated the Ottoman Army.[143] The Arab contribution had been valuable, but it was not more militarily significant. Lawrence too had made a valuable contribution, and he was certainly disappointed that the Arabs did not acquire the full independence he felt they deserved. These concerns have tended to overshadow the methods by which he had secured the co-operation of the Arab clans he encountered, and therefore the military value of the operations that were conducted.

Lawrence's experience suggests that advisers need to understand war and the specific character of conflict in which their local forces are operating; they need to possess a thorough understanding of the culture and have a mastery of the language; and they need to know the nature, strengths and vulnerabilities of their enemy. Lawrence had a particular mission, but he was able to develop the task and exploit opportunities. He demonstrated that strategic objectives were far more important than tactical successes, although the latter were important in so far as they built confidence in the local forces. Lawrence argued that there was a priority order for successful mentoring, and the first was the mental preparation of the local personnel, inculcating a sense of the mission's importance and cultivating the desire to achieve it. He noted that rival groups had to be kept separate, but this could be turned to an advantage by rotating tasks. He claimed that honour was the most important motivating factor, but in his writings he played down the importance of money: it was in his secret reports that he confessed to his surprise and exasperation about how much gold had to be distributed to keep the Arabs in the fight. His '27

Articles' still have resonance, one hundred years or more after he wrote them. He urged his successors to work within the culture of the local forces; to immerse themselves in the task, the force and the language; to offer advice only from behind or through the local leaders (although he did take command himself at times); and he recommended intensive study of the land, people and situation.

The articles together are important and valuable, but it is number 15 which is the most often quoted and remembered. The injunction not to try to do 'too much with your own hands' resonated strongly with Western personnel sent in the twenty-first century to assist the Iraqi and Afghan forces in their counter-insurgency missions, although it could be argued that this desire not to interfere or cause offence actually prevented a more effective response to the breakdown of security in Libya. In other words, there are times, in stabilisation or advisory missions, when robust intervention, firm control and direct command are the only ways to ensure success. Lawrence's situation was unique and distinct. His advice was designed to be a guide, not a substitute for adaptation and thinking.

Local Forces and Total War

The First World War increased the demand for manpower to an unprecedented degree, and that, in turn, drove the imperative to enlist, or conscript, more indigenous personnel from colonies and allies into the armed forces of the Western powers. Thousands of these recruits ended up on European battlefields, but thousands more served in the theatres of war in Africa, the Middle East and East Asia. The need for more personnel increased the pressure on local communities that had supplied the manpower before the war, even to the extent of facing quotas for men, but it also diversified the sources of supply. As volunteers, young men were attracted, as before, by a combination of the prospects for adventure, higher status and better pay, and some were conscious of the historic significance of this European and world war. Nevertheless, large numbers of men had no choice and were conscripted, and others became forced labourers.

Conditions on the Western Front for those serving the British and French armies are well documented and were frequently hazardous. For men from the climates of tropical Africa and southern Asia, the winter weather, use of poison gas, mine explosions, prolonged artillery fire and heavy casualties had a deteriorating effect on morale. However, those that survived the experience often developed a greater resilience and were seasoned to the conditions. The largest number of African and South Asian troops served in theatres outside Europe, which had their own challenges, including extreme temperatures, lack of water, poor infrastructure, large distances, limited transport, and higher levels of disease and infection. As is well known, more men died from sickness than from combat operations in the war, and the statistics for losses in Mesopotamia, Palestine, Gallipoli and East Africa are particularly high.

As was true before the war, there were anxieties about whether colonial troops would stand against European enemies and a concern that white troops should not be seen to fail in front of colonial personnel. In the war, these concerns proved groundless. British and Indian troops served alongside each other in Mesopotamia, during the siege and relief of Kut; Africans served with Europeans in the efforts to control Kenya and Tanganyika; and West Africans fought alongside French troops on the Chemin des Dames.

The war was also a levelling experience, in which shells and small arms fire showed no distinction between races or classes, and the conditions of trench life were the same for all. Despite episodes of low morale, desertions and ill-discipline, the majority of colonial soldiers performed well. Cohesion and discipline remained generally intact. There was a more significant problem with officer casualties. Those few Europeans who had been selected and trained specifically for command of colonial troops could not be replaced quickly, at least not with the same levels of experience. In the British Indian Army, where a personalised style of command had been deliberately preserved, officer casualties had a particularly detrimental effect. To make matters worse, the colonial officer corps in both Britain and France had far too few staff officers to manage expansion or the higher-formation staff work required. The logistics problems that plagued the Indian Army in Mesopotamia were in large part due to a habit of small and relatively short-lived campaign experiences and insufficient numbers of suitably qualified staff officers. Worse, there were no plans or systems in place for large-scale expansion. The early mobilisation overwhelmed the pre-war arrangements, exhausted supplies and confounded procurement demands.

The First World War was not entirely a question of fighting manpower; it required millions of labourers. China believed the war gave it the opportunity to offer labouring personnel, if not fighting forces, in return for an end to the semi-colonial relationship with the Western powers and Russia. Despite their efforts, the Chinese government was to be bitterly disappointed by the outcome in 1919. But then, it has to be said, very few countries achieved their expectations after the war. And for those who assumed that the war would change the colonial relationships between Europe, Africa, Asia, the Caribbean and the Middle East, they would feel that their hopes were unfulfilled. In the next chapter, we examine the contribution of local Arab forces, the aspirations of their leaders and mentors, and the advisory work of T.E. Lawrence, and why, in each case, there were profound disappointments.

10

LOCAL FORCES IN THE SECOND WORLD WAR

In his outstanding work on the British Empire in the Second World War, Professor Ashley Jackson aptly summed up the kaleidoscope of deployments wrought by the conflict:

> Before the end of the war, the Burmese jungle would hear the voices of men from the Gambia, Somaliland and Northern Rhodesia, the Levant would witness men from the fringes of the Kalahari digging tank traps and constructing military railways, Basotho muleteers would support Allied infantry in Italy, and the flag of the Swazi nation would be paraded victoriously through the streets of Tunis, as world war caused a galaxy of the most unlikely connections to span the globe.[1]

The sheer variety of nationalities, ethnicities and communities, and the plethora of formations, categories of units and scale of movements, were astonishing, and the entire process was not only orchestrated from London, but was compelled to react to—and adapt to—three hostile powers that had long prepared for the conflict. The fact that this great complexity of forces was militarily successful, along with critical allies like the United States, is even more remarkable. Despite widespread criticism from many of its African and Asian subjects, the British could also quietly refer to the absence of violent internal unrest, with the exception of India in the years 1943–4, and they regarded the cohesion of the Empire as a vindication of their achievements and efforts. The victory parade in London in 1946 featured thousands of the men who had made their success possible, drawn from all parts of the Empire. Yet, this crowning moment concealed the deep fissures and immense expectations that had been generated by the war. Men in the ranks of the colonial

273

forces, like their counterparts in the British Army, Royal Navy and Royal Air Force, anticipated that, with the war concluded, all the rhetoric of liberation would be converted into actual self-determination.

In France, a country which had suffered catastrophic defeat in 1940 and years of humiliating occupation, also had to come to terms with the legacy of Vichy, where thousands of Frenchmen had sided with the Nazi occupiers and expressed deep hostility to the Western Allies. To compensate, the narrative of liberation and the resistance was amplified more loudly, but this only served to reinforce the belief in the French colonies that their independence could not be delayed. The return of French colonial officials in Indochina was met with bewilderment as much as anger, but France would demonstrate that it was prepared to fight to retain its colonies.

The United States was in a far stronger position. It had emerged from the war as the pre-eminent global power—more wealthy, more confident and more determined than ever to assert a new international order that would prevent further major wars like that of 1937–45. It possessed, exclusively, the ultimate weapon system in the atomic bomb, and had developed a vast military machine, a huge fleet and a gigantic air force. Its ideology was firmly fixed on the liberation of subject peoples, the establishment of democracy and the free passage of global commerce. It therefore took exception to the relics of the past such as the British and French empires, and it looked with deep concern at the coercive nature of the Soviet Union and its vast military capacity.

At the outbreak of war in 1939, the situation had been so different. In the Middle East, the Indian Ocean, the Caribbean, South Asia, South East Asia and the Pacific, it was Britain that appeared to be the hegemonic global power. That influence relied primarily on the strength of the Royal Navy, supported by the reach and capability of the Royal Air Force, but also on the land power of the British and colonial armies, and a system of finance and commerce that circulated around the world, orchestrated by the nerve centre of London and its satellites in Ottawa, Cape Town, Canberra, Auckland, Cairo, Delhi, Singapore and Hong Kong, among others. Nevertheless, the First World War and the inter-war years had demonstrated how vulnerable the British were, not least to subversion from those who would propagate a liberationist agenda.[2]

Local Force in the Middle East

On the southern tip of the Arabian Peninsula, Aden was an Indian dependency until 1937, but its defence was the responsibility of the RAF since 'air policing' was the cheaper method of maintaining security in the region.[3] The RAF established an Air Command in Aden from 1927, as they had done in Iraq and Transjordan, but Aden became a Crown Colony from 1937 and included Kuria Muria and Perim islands in its jurisdiction. To guard the main airbase at Khormaksar, the British created the Aden Protectorate Levies in 1928. With a strength of 600 men, in wartime it was reinforced by a battalion of the 5th Mahratta Light Infantry. The Aden Protectorate Levies were also doubled in size soon after the war broke out and their duties extended to security of the Arabia hinterland and to Sharjah on the coast of Oman, as well as the islands of Socotra and Masirah. The RAF then established an important base at Masirah while the Navy developed their own installations at Salaya in Oman. These facilities became centres for antisubmarine flying boats as well as land-based aircraft, and search-and-rescue launches.

Aden, which was subjected to Italian bombing raids, was an even more important base to launch operations into East Africa and across the Red Sea, and its forces provided protection for convoys en route to Suez. To the east of Aden, the sultanates of Wahidi, Qa'iti, Kathiri and Mahra, known collectively as the Eastern Aden Protectorate, the British formed the Hadhrami Bedouin Legion in January 1940, which, by 1944, consisted of over 100 regular soldiers and 100 reservists. The Aden Protectorate Levies had also grown to a total strength of 1,800 by 1945. In addition, Aden provided a Pioneer Corps of 2,000 men who came under the command of the Air Ministry. The value of Aden as a port, a launching pad for operations across the region, and a small reservoir of manpower was firmly established by the war, and it was regarded as a strategically vital point in the post-war era too.

The vulnerability of British possession was not limited to southern Arabia. Amman, the capital of Transjordan, was bombed by Vichy aircraft in 1940.[4] The British mobilised the Trans-Jordan Frontier Force, increasing its strength from a small gendarmerie to a competent military force of 8,000 men.[5] The Arab Legion, the Emir's own force commanded by Brigadier Glubb Pasha, also expanded to 5,000 men and was placed under British command for the duration of the war. During the Second World War, the Trans-Jordan Frontier Force comprised three cavalry and two mechanised squadrons, while a 'line of communications' squadron was raised to protect the routes between Haifa and Baghdad. Trans-Jordan also provided support services in the form of repair workshops, hospitals and a training depot. When, in 1941, the British garrison at RAF Habbaniya was attacked by pro-Nazi Iraqis, the Trans-Jordan Frontier Force was on standby to relieve it, although at the last minute it was never dispatched. The force did, however, take part from June 1941 in the Syrian campaign, where it secured routes for supplies along the Haifa–Damascus railway and roads. It was then employed in internal security tasks in Syria to maintain law and order before providing the border security force along the Turkish frontier. Meanwhile, the experienced reconnaissance capabilities of the Arab Legion's Desert Mechanised Force meant that it was selected to lead British troops into Iraq. It pushed along the Euphrates, closed off the Mosul road before moving on to Baghdad. The Arab Legion also provided reconnaissance during the Syrian campaign, particularly in the attack on Palmyra, and afterwards provided internal security during a period of widespread unrest.

There was a more complex relationship between Britain and the population of Palestine. The Jewish Agency, which represented the Jews of Palestine, agreed to co-operate with Britain in the struggle against Nazi Germany, and 136,000 Jewish men registered their willingness to support the war effort.[6] The Jewish Agency took the view that participation in the war would give it the opportunity to mobilise the population and prepare for self-government.[7] There had been considerable anger during the inter-war years because of British restrictions on Jewish immigration, and the agency believed it should take every opportunity to establish the government-in-waiting complete with underground organisations. It already controlled the Haganah, a paramilitary organisation which had been decimated by British intelligence before 1940, but this force was reconstituted with British support. Orde Wingate, who had considerable experience in the African colonies, assisted in the training of groups, including the 'special night squads', that confronted Arab gangs intent on attacking Jewish settlements.[8]

New units, such as Palmach, were established as 'stay behind' forces in the event of invasion.[9] They were subsequently used to gather intelligence and even made a raid on oil refineries in Tripoli. Although the Palmach was officially closed down by the British when the threat of German attack receded, its personnel regrouped in secret and retained as many weapons as possible. The Haganah did its best to acquire weapons and equipment. A breakaway group of the force, the Irgun Zvai Leumi, which had been formed in 1937 to protect Jewish settlements against Arab attacks, began its own campaign of sabotage against the British from May 1939. At the outbreak of the Second World War it had declared a truce, but Abraham Stern, who was dissatisfied with the suspension of anti-British activities, established his own group, or gang, in 1940. The Irgun also returned to violent anti-British activities in

December 1943. The British regarded this as a bitter betrayal, for when British pilots were losing their lives over Germany, it seemed that Jewish volunteers whom they had armed and trained, and taken into their confidence within intelligence and SOE units, were prepared to turn their guns against their own allies.[10] After the war, the misunderstanding deepened still further, and the murder of British service personnel, not least in the callous terrorist attack against off-duty soldiers in the King David Hotel in 1946, which killed 91 men, was regarded as the final act of treachery.

Palestinian Arabs also served in the British war effort. An Arab company of the Royal Pioneer Corps went to France in February 1940, and this group became the nucleus of Number 51 (Middle East) Commando, which fought in East Africa. A total of 4,000 Palestinians served in the Royal Pioneer Corps, and these units were to be found in North Africa, Egypt and Greece. Palestinians also enlisted into the Royal Army Service Corps, Medical Corps, Ordnance Corps, Royal Engineers and support branches of the RAF. Across the Mediterranean, the RAF estimated some 3,000 men had served from Palestine, Cyprus and Malta. Arab and Jewish men also formed companies that were attached to the East Kent Regiment from 1940. The first group, originally just 500 strong, increased to 2,800 men, and was eventually transferred into the Palestine Regiment, which, although designed for guard duty and internal security, was used in the Syrian campaign. A total of 10,000 Jews and 4,000 Arabs served in the British armed forces in this period.

The Jews still hoped for an autonomous Jewish army, but it was not until September 1944 that the British Parliament gave its approval for the formation of a Jewish Brigade group. The War Office was in no hurry to see this formation created because there was every expectation it would become an anti-British movement in the future. Winston Churchill nevertheless gave his support and its 5,500 men served in Italy in the last weeks of the war during the assault on Ravenna. As the war came to an end, the brigade facilitated the illegal immigration of Jews to Palestine and was responsible for a number of atrocities against German civilians and disbanded combatants. By the end of the war, some 30,000 Jews and 12,000 Arabs had served with the British, but the co-operation did not survive long. By 1948, the British tried to hand over Palestine to the new United Nations, and, when this was not accepted, they pulled out, regarding the communal violence between Jews and Arabs as insoluble.

The Islands of the Indian Ocean, Caribbean, Pacific and Atlantic

In the Seychelles, a small Defence Force was raised and placed under the control of the War Office while two companies were formed of Pioneers and an Artisan Works Company. These, along with the Indian Ocean pioneers from Mauritius, were amalgamated with men from Cyprus, Palestine and Africa to form a military labour force in support of the British Eighth Army. Approximately 1,500 men from the Seychelles served in British forces, while a headquarters was established in the islands to co-ordinate the 27th Coastal Battery, Hong Kong and Singapore Royal Artillery, the 3rd Indian Garrison Company and the Diego Garcia Garrison Company.

Bermuda was an important base for the Royal Navy for both the North Atlantic and the West Indies patrols, particularly the convoy system that transited between them. Despite a small population, Bermuda sent some of its manpower into the British forces and also established its own Bermuda Volunteer Rifle Corps. This served in Europe as a company attached to the Royal Lincolnshire Regiment. Meanwhile, the Bermuda Militia infantry and artillery formed the Bermuda contingent of the 1st Caribbean Regiment, and this served in Italy in 1944.

The Caribbean as a whole was the responsibility of the Royal Navy. Inevitably the war produced an increased demand for manpower, so the Colonial Office, in consultation with the War Office, announced in May 1942 the formation of the Caribbean Regiment. The West Indies Regiment had been disbanded in 1926, and as a result there was no regular establishment on which to base the new formation. Shortages in arms and equipment also affected the formation of the Caribbean Regiment adversely, and so the majority of available manpower served in the RAF and Royal Navy, or were shipped to Britain to augment the wartime economy. However, the demand for the creation of security forces for Mediterranean bases prompted the War Office to raise a West Indian battalion in December 1943. Named as the 1st Battalion, the Caribbean Regiment, and trained in America, it finally arrived in Italy in July 1944. Its performance was regarded as very poor, and so it was sent for further training in Gaza in Palestine before being transported to Egypt. As a result, it did not see active service.

The Trinidad Naval Force increased in size to over 1,000 men in response to increasing German U-boat attacks, and men from Trinidad, along with many other Western Indians, served in the Merchant Navy. Recruits were also drawn from across the Caribbean via its central reception centre at Kingston, Jamaica, for a variety of service vacancies. Some 5,500 men, for example, made the transit to Britain to serve as ground staff for the RAF. West Indians also provided aircrew to the Royal Air Force and Royal Canadian Air Force, and, among the 300 that did so, about a third were commissioned as officers. Both Trinidad and Bermuda had flying training schools, while in the Bahamas an Air Service Squadron was established with a strength of 300 men.[11]

Other islands provided their own defence forces. In the Falkland Islands and South Georgia, to augment the presence of the Royal Navy and British reservists, a Falklands Islands Defence Force was established from among the islanders. Although Argentina seized the opportunity presented by the war to take over British bases in the Antarctic, their claims were never upheld, and the British along with Australia, Chile, France, New Zealand and Norway staked out their own claims to the southern continent. However, only the Royal Navy could provide the means to enforce any claims, and the Falklands Islands Defence Force was retained within its territory.

In the Pacific, the Fiji Military Force, with officers drawn from New Zealand, deployed to the Solomon Islands and played their part in the security of the western Pacific against the Japanese. Fijians regarded themselves as a self-reliant martial race, although it should be noted that it was the New Zealand Expeditionary Force that provided the primary defence force of the South Pacific islands.[12] The pre-war Fiji Defence Force, which had been established in 1923, became the Fiji Military Force in December 1942. It consisted of three infantry battalions when it served in the Solomon Islands. In doing so it changed from a part-time territorial to a full-time regular organisation with a heavy artillery regiment, service units and an infantry brigade. By January 1945, it was 6,000 strong, including 590 men from New Zealand. However, some 11,000 Fijians served across the Commonwealth armed forces, providing personnel in roles as diverse as coastal defence artillery and anti-aircraft batteries. One Fijian contingent of 200 men was also known as the 1st Commando Fiji Guerrillas, while a second unit, known as the South Pacific Scouts, which included men from the Solomon Islands and Tonga, took part in the landings on New Georgia in July 1943. The Fijian battalions also saw service in the battle for Bougainville in December 1943 and Fiji provided personnel for a Labour Battalion, which found themselves in the front line.

The Papua Infantry Battalion was raised just before the Japanese attack in February 1942. Initially only 300 men served in the unit, but the force was quickly expanded and was merged with the indigenous 1st New Guinea Infantry Battalion in October 1944 to become the Pacific Islands Regiment. Three more New Guinea battalions were then raised. Throughout the war these indigenous troops acquired a reputation as skilled jungle fighters, feared by the Japanese, and were accorded immense respect by the Australian troops who served with them. By the end of the war, 3,500 Papuans and New Guineans had served in the regiment. The Royal Papuan Constabulary also fought during the war with a strength of over 3,000, and the islands provided medical and service support staff.

In the Solomon Islands, a defence force was hastily established in 1939, and, although it was scheduled for disbandment in February 1942, it was still in existence at the time of the Japanese landings in March 1942. A Solomon Islands Labour Corps was also created under British supervision at the strength of 2,500 men in support of the Americans. The generous pay they received from the United States stood in contrast to the low wages provided by the British, and created significant discontent.

In South East Asia before the war, the only fighting force available was the Burma Rifles, which was organised along the lines of a standard Indian Army regiment. Its role was primarily internal security because it was not envisaged that Burma would ever become a theatre of operations against an external power. In 1940, the Burma Rifles were expanded from four to six battalions and an officer cadet school was established at Maymyo to train British, Burmese and Anglo-Burmese candidates. A seventh battalion was formed from the Civil and Military Police and an eighth from the Burma Frontier Force. The rest of the Burma Frontier Force consisted of five battalions of Burma Military Police, but remained along the border. A ninth Burma Rifles battalion was raised as a training establishment as was the tenth. An 11th and a 12th battalion were established for the security of lines of communication while a 13th and a 14th battalion were raised to protect the local Shan states and provide internal security. The entire formation was known as the 1st Burma Division from July 1941, but they lacked the experience or equipment to match the Japanese invaders. The Burmese formations lacked artillery support or anti-aircraft defence. To make matters worse, many of the communities of Burmese, with a strong dislike of the Burmans, were reluctant to co-operate even though the Chins, Kachins and Karens had formed the basis of the 'martial races' of Burma. The only other forces that could augment the Burma Rifles were the 17th and 7th Indian divisions. At the last minute, the British 7th Armoured Brigade arrived, but these forces were insufficient to turn the tide against the Japanese 15th Army.

There was rather more success in resisting the Japanese among the Malayan People's Anti-Japanese Army, which was supported by the Special Operations

Executive (SOE). Major Freddy Spencer Chapman, an SOE officer, was particularly prominent in facilitating anti-Japanese guerrilla activity, often with Chinese Malays. In 1945, the Malayan People's Anti-Japanese Army numbered 7,000 and came to dominate large parts of the country, but they also provided crucial intelligence and reconnaissance. In 1944, SOE Force 136 created its own country section for Malaya and, by making contact with Ceylon, brought in new agents, radio equipment and munitions. The organisation provided its own propaganda facilities and made anti-Japanese radio broadcasts. Guerrillas were supplied by airdrops provided by the RAF. The system was so successful that new units that specialised in operations deep inside enemy-occupied territory were established, some carrying out missions as far afield as Indochina and Laos.[13]

Ceylon provided an important base for operations across the Indian Ocean region. It also provided its own local military forces numbering 3,500 in 1939 and 26,000 by 1945.[14] The Ceylon Defence Force was expanded rapidly after 1941 when Japanese attacks on the island seemed more likely. It consisted of the Ceylon Light Infantry, with an establishment of five battalions, Ceylon Garrison Artillery and a collection of anti-aircraft units, engineers, pioneers, signallers and coastal artillery as well as transport and medical sections. The Ceylon Garrison Artillery deployed a unit to protect the Seychelles in April 1941. A second detachment was sent to the Cocos–Keeling Islands to protect them from invasion. The Ceylon Railway Engineering Corps operated an armoured train on the island and was staffed by its own indigenous personnel and Anglo-Indian railway staff. The European settlers before the war formed their own Ceylon Planters Rifle Corps, which was itself an amalgamation of the Ceylon Rifle Corps and the Ceylon Mounted Rifles, which had been raised in 1892, but its personnel gradually declined in numbers as its members were sent to India and the Middle East to provide officers for other units. A large number were sent to Dehradun in India for officer training.

A number of Ceylonese served in the British Army in units such as the Royal Army Service Corps, the Royal Artillery, the Royal Engineers and the Royal Pioneer Corps. These men saw service in the Middle East, Sicily, Greece, Italy and France. However, the British were selective about the tasks they performed, and many ended up in light motor transport companies or in clerical tasks because 'of their high standard of education and poor physique'.[15] Men from the Indian Ocean as well as from Hong Kong, Africa and the Caribbean provided personnel for the Royal Navy and the merchant fleet. Ceylon had its own Volunteer Naval Defence Force, which consisted of 1,200 officers and ratings by 1945.[16] They fulfilled a number of maritime tasks, including the protection of Colombo harbour, convoy security for merchant shipping, anti-submarine missions, mines sweeping patrols, and escort duties across the Indian Ocean. They also provided men for search-and-rescue missions, aiding the personnel of those vessels that had been sunk by Japanese air attacks. In 1943, the Royal Navy took over responsibility from the volunteer force and it was retitled the Ceylon Royal Naval Volunteer Reserve. The Royal Navy also established an aircraft training establishment on the island to train personnel for carrier duty in the Eastern Fleet.[17]

African Formations

At the outbreak of war, the forces available to the British in Africa were very modest indeed.[18] The Royal West African Frontier Force (RWAFF) was 4,400 strong; the King's African Rifles (KAR) was 2,900; the Somaliland Camel Corps (SCC) was 600; the Sudan Defence Force (SDF) was 4,500; and the Northern Rhodesia Regiment (NRR) was 430.[19] By 1945, these formations had grown to over half a million strong. The King's African Rifles and Royal West African Frontier Force fought in East Africa, Madagascar and Burma, and provided internal security in Africa itself. In Burma, 120,000 East and West African soldiers were employed against the Japanese, including the 22nd (East Africa) Infantry Brigade. This brigade actually saw service in East Africa, Italian Somaliland, Abyssinia, Madagascar, Ceylon and Burma. To meet the immense labouring demands of the war, the African Pioneer Corps, part of the British Army's Royal Pioneer Corps, employed tens of thousands of men from across the African territories and moved them into the Middle East and southern Europe as part of a 100,000-strong logistics force in support of the Eighth Army.[20] Africans also saw service in the Royal Navy and the Royal Air Force. The Royal Navy Volunteer Reserves formed units in Gambia, Kenya, Tanganyika and Nigeria. Some 3,500 Nigerians served in the Royal Navy and an even larger number in the Merchant Navy. Thousands of West Africans provided the ground staff for British airbases. Many more provided the physical labour to support war industries and the supply of the armed forces during the conflict.

The garrison of British Somaliland was much smaller than the Italian Fascist forces in neighbouring Italian Somaliland and Abyssinia, while French Somaliland was a Vichy-aligned entity. The officers of the Somaliland Camel Corps were dismayed when they learned that the authorities of Middle

Eastern Command did not intend to defend the colony, aiming to evacuate despite the inevitable loss of prestige that would follow. They were even more exasperated by the decision to disband the Camel Corps because this meant abandoning their men. However, in September 1939 the new Commander-in-Chief Middle East, General Sir Archibald Wavell, reversed the decision and five infantry battalions were hastily collected to provide for the colony's defence. Nevertheless, the fall of France and the alignment of Djibouti towards the Vichy regime compelled the evacuation to go ahead. As a result, Italian forces invaded on 4 August 1940 and were opposed by just one British battalion, two Indian, one King's African Rifles and one Northern Rhodesia Regiment, supported by the East African Light Battery and the remaining members of the Somaliland Camel Corps. At this point in the war, the Camel Corps numbered just 14 officers and 400 askaris, but they were augmented by a Nyasaland Rifle Company equipped with Ford motor trucks and by a para-military tribal police force, the Illalos, numbering 1,000 men. After offering token resistance and in order to avoid complete destruction, all these forces were evacuated. Winston Churchill was angry that the colony had been given up at such a low cost in casualties, but Wavell defended his decision on the basis that: 'a big butcher's bill was not necessarily evidence of good tactics'.[21]

In Aden, the Somaliland Camel Corps was reconstituted and efforts were made to raise two companies of Somali irregulars to guard the large numbers of Italian prisoners of war that were accumulating from each of the African theatres of operations. In May 1941, the 26th (East African) Brigade took over responsibility for the blockade of French Somaliland, and they were assisted by local Somali fighters. In May 1942, these auxiliaries, which had increased to a strength of six companies, were formally designated the Somaliland Scouts. The operations were conducted over a wide area, and involved the use of auxiliaries of the Mounted Police and local *arbagnoch*, as well as 'scouts' and 'irregulars' from Northern Kenya, Somalia and Somaliland. These forces joined the combined operations against the Italians and assisted in overrunning all the territory in East Africa that had been occupied. Meanwhile, the Somaliland Camel Corps was converted into an Armoured Car Regiment, but, with the prospect of service overseas, many of the men mutinied at Burao.[22] Among their grievances was their desire not to be treated 'like Africans'. Nevertheless, Somalis were recruited into their own battalions, which were attached to the King's African Rifles brigades that were being formed for service in Burma. The 71st (Somaliland) KAR took part in operations in Burma against the Japanese as part of the 28th (East African) Brigade. The 72nd KAR remained in Kenya and supplied reinforcements.

In West Africa, the War Office took over responsibility from the Colonial Office in June 1940 and established the West Africa Command. This organisation assumed responsibility for recruiting, training, supplying and moving some 200,000 soldiers drawn from across the region. Under its jurisdiction, the Royal West African Frontier Force expanded rapidly. In October 1941, the RWAFF stood at 42,000, but by 1942 it had more than doubled in size to 92,000. Moreover, the RAF and Royal Navy also sought recruits from within West Africa. To meet the demand for officers, many British personnel were joined by men from Southern Rhodesia and even 400 from Poland. Equipment was always in short supply given the rapidity and scale of the expansion. Shortages in shipping and demands from within Europe added to the pressure.

Much of the prejudice that the soldiers of the KAR encountered was racially motivated, but it was also class-based.[23] White officers of the KAR were treated with disdain by other officers who were serving in more prestigious regiments.[24] Among the rank and file, the soldiers sang marching songs about black Americans landing from the air to deliver them from white rule.[25]

The Indian Army in the Second World War

During the Second World War, the Indian Army expanded from 200,000 to more than 2.5 million men without even the imposition of conscription.[26] The conflict nevertheless raised significant questions about its composition and its status. The 'Indianisation' of the officer corps, for example, had begun in the inter-war years, but it was accelerated during the war.[27] Just as significantly, recruitment extended well beyond the groups formally designated as 'martial races'. The rapid expansion raised new concerns about the quality of the troops. Setbacks in the fighting against the Japanese between 1941 and 1943, and the existence of an anti-British Indian National Army (INA), produced considerable anxiety. However, the Indian Army came through all its problems and conducted itself professionally and reliably against a number of enemies in a variety of theatres.

In 1941, the Indian Army had already expanded to 1.5 million men and was organised into more than ten divisions. However, severe equipment shortages meant that few of these divisions were equipped for modern mechanised warfare. The first deployments involved the 5th and 11th Indian Infantry Brigades being sent to Egypt in the defence of Suez, with the 7th Indian Infantry Brigade following soon after. These three brigades formed the nucleus of the

4th Indian Division. This was the first formation to see active service in the war and was among the most accomplished. In this early stage of the conflict the brigades conducted rigorous training in desert warfare prior to their deployment into Libya under the command of General Sir Archibald Wavell. His force of some 31,000 was outnumbered by the Italians by more than two to one but, after three days of intense fighting in December 1940, more than 20,000 Italian prisoners were taken and four Italian divisions were destroyed for a loss of approximately 700 casualties. Following this success, 4th Indian Division was redeployed to Sudan, where it joined the newly arrived 5th Indian Division. By now these formations were mechanised, but their advantages were neutralised by the mountainous nature of the terrain in southern Abyssinia through which they were fighting. The Italians contested the ridges and defiles with determination, but both Indian divisions prevailed and the Italians surrendered in mid-1941.

In March 1941, when the pro-German Iraqi army staged a *coup d'état*, the 20th Indian Brigade of the 10th Indian Division was redirected to Basra where, fortunately, the Iraqi Army showed no signs of resistance. The 10th Division moved on to Baghdad and secured the oilfields around Mosul while the 21st Indian Brigade advanced into western Syria to support British operations there. The 5th Indian Brigade also participated in the capture of Damascus.[28] German agents also attempted to orchestrate the takeover or destruction of the Persian oilfields, so the 8th and 10th Indian Divisions were redeployed from Iraq to secure southern Iran. British forces also occupied Teheran. Two entire divisions were required for internal security duties in the areas of the Middle East that had come under British occupation.

The 4th Indian Division re-formed to take part in operations in North Africa, but in July 1941 Wavell was replaced as Commander-in-Chief Middle East by General Sir Claude Auchinleck, and the British Western Desert Force was renamed the Eighth Army for the forthcoming offensive. The 4th Indian Division took part in the attack against Axis forces in November 1941. The 4/16th Punjabis were involved in close-quarter fighting at Libyan Omar, where they suffered such severe casualties that the assault had to be postponed. The offensive was resumed by the Indian Division along with other Allied forces in late November. Late in the year, the Germans counter-attacked and the 4th Indian Division, along with the rest of the army, was tumbled back towards the Egyptian border. Elements of the 7th Indian Brigade were cut off and had to fight their way back from behind German lines. During the subsequent stalemate in the spring of 1942, the 4th Indian Division was replaced by the 5th, which was, in turn, joined by the 10th. There was severe fighting in May, and by June the British were on their final defence lines west of El Alamein. A series of attacks and counter-attacks followed, but the line held. The 4th Indian Division returned to North Africa while the 5th was retasked to undergo jungle warfare training in order to conduct operations in Burma.

Until this point in the war, most of the training of the Indian Army had been for mechanised warfare in the desert, so it came as a profound shock when the Japanese mounted offensives through the jungles of Burma and Malaya. The 3rd Indian Corps had formed a defensive line in northern Malaya but had found itself outflanked by more fluid Japanese forces. A similar problem confronted forces sent to Burma. Fortunately, those that had escaped the disaster at Singapore were able to bring valuable lessons about jungle fighting to the newly formed divisions. Nevertheless, there was no disguising the crushing defeat of the Allies in this region. Burma Corps, which included the 17th Indian Division, was cut off in Rangoon, having suffered heavy casualties in January 1942. Only reluctantly did they abandon Burma to the Japanese and withdraw into Assam, their retreat covering a distance of 900 miles at the height of the monsoon.

The Japanese, in emulation of the Europeans, made use of colonial troops, encouraging fellow Asians to join their war efforts against the British, Dutch and French empires. The Imperial Japanese Army placed enormous emphasis on physical and mental toughness and aggression, which produced brutal reprisals against civilians or captured military personnel. The Koreans, treated as colonial subjects by the Japanese, played out their own assertion of aggression and toughness through the mistreatment of Allied prisoners of war.

By contrast, the British made a concerted effort to improve the welfare of their Indian troops. Particular attention was paid to maintain morale through radio programmes, army publications, entertainers visiting the fronts and an acknowledgement that, after the war, self-government was only a matter of time. In 1942, there were promises of representative government and Dominion status after the war, but this did not stop the orchestration of the Quit India movement.[29] A widespread civil disobedience campaign was supposed to persuade the British to abandon India, but there were concerns among those in the nationalist movement that many of their supporters favoured violence.[30] Worse, there was anxiety that the British might simply be replaced by the Japanese as an imperial power. Disruptions to the food supply caused acute shortages in some areas. Telephone lines, post offices, courts, revenue offices and even police stations were the targets for attack and arson.

In extreme cases, railway tracks were torn up. At its height, the Quit India campaign required an entire British division to be diverted to Bombay to quash the unrest.

The Viceroy, Lord Linlithgow, informed Churchill that he was 'engaged here in meeting by far the most serious rebellion since that of 1857, the gravity and extent of which we have so far concealed for reasons of military security ... Mob violence remains rampant over large tracts of the countryside and I am by no means confident that we may not see in September a formidable effort to renew this widespread sabotage of our war effort.'[31] Eventually, with the Indian Army and its British units at full stretch, the campaign was brought to manageable levels of violence. The authorities anticipated that the end of the war would mean a return to widespread violence which the Army would be unwilling and perhaps unable to contain. Army Headquarters informed the Military Secretary: 'It is fair to say that, as the war draws to its close ... the general I[nternal] S[ecurity] position is bound to deteriorate, as interested parties begin to prepare (as they are now preparing) for the eventual struggle for power.'[32] In 1945, plans drawn up to deal with political agitation and violence showed that everything depended on the loyalty of the Indian troops, but this could not be taken for granted.[33]

The British focus on improving morale and welfare provision stood in direct contrast to the Japanese instrumentalisation of Indian personnel. The Indian National Army was the brainchild of the extremist Congressman Subhas Bose. With Japanese approval, and having already been rejected by the Nazis, he was granted permission in 1943 to create his own military force made up of prisoners of war. At its height, the INA mustered 430,000 personnel, a not insignificant number, although it couldn't sustain this size throughout the war and many INA subsequently rejoined the British-led war effort. The morale of the INA suffered severely, not only because they were neglected or mistreated by the Japanese, but because they did not receive the warm support from Indians they encountered near the border. Despite all the hardships imposed by the conflict, the overwhelming majority of Indians continued to work for the British. Despite more recent attempts to rewrite the history of the INA and to manufacture the idea that his movement was somehow popular, Bose was a failure. Indeed, many Indian regular soldiers believed the former INA men should be punished as traitors. During the war, they had fought them in Burma and were often unimpressed by either their allegiances or the fighting ability.

In the summer of 1942, the 14th Indian Division was tasked to clear the Arakan region of Burma, and, after a period of jungle warfare training, they embarked upon their mission. By January 1943, they had cleared a portion of the peninsula but then suffered steady losses in what became a war of attrition with the Japanese. A Japanese counter-offensive from mid-March to the end of April drove the British and Indian units back to their start lines, forcing Wavell to conclude that there was 'still a great deal to learn about jungle fighting'.[34] Greater efforts were made to disseminate best practice in tactical training. Severe fighting lay ahead. At the end of 1943 the Indian Army was holding the line around Imphal in Assam. The second effort was made by the 5th and 7th Indian Divisions to recover the Arakan.

Meanwhile, in North Africa, the 4th Indian Division participated in the battle of El Alamein and pursued the Afrika Korps to the Matruh line and beyond. There was particularly bitter fighting around Wadi Akarit, but, soon after, the Germans were driven out of North Africa for good. General Montgomery's verdict was that the 4th Indian Division was among his most experienced and best formations. The Allies moved on, and made their first penetration of Europe from the south. The 8th Indian Division was deployed to Italy to assist and in November 1943 this formation fought its way across the River Trigno. It went on to cross the Sangre River, battled its way through fortified villages, and crossed the Moro River before winter called its advance to a halt. The 4th Indian Division took part in the attempts to take Cassino, which the Germans had turned into a line of almost impregnable positions. The first attacks involving Indian troops were a failure. When the 1/9th Gurkhas succeeded in capturing Hangman's Hill, which the Germans regarded as 'key terrain', they were subjected to intense counter-attacks, but the Allies held on in desperate conditions, which led to a stalemate. In the sustained fighting around Monte Cassino, the division suffered 4,000 casualties.

The final attacks were mounted by Allied forces, which included the 8th Indian Division, and, at last, Cassino was captured. Nevertheless, the campaign was far from over. Yet more fighting was required through the 'tough old gut' of Italy and involved severe combat for the villages and the fortified defensive lines the Germans had constructed. Before the fighting in Italy was concluded, the 4th Indian Division, which had already done so much in the conflict, was redeployed to Greece to intervene in the civil war that had broken out when the Germans withdrew. In April 1945, just weeks before the war ended in Europe, the 8th and 10th Indian Divisions were involved in difficult operations to cross the Senio River. The Germans continued to contest every mile until the very end.

In South East Asia, the fighting was also intense. In February 1944, the Indian formations of the 14th Army were involved in bitter fighting with the Japanese, who intended to drive the British deep into India. Much of the fighting was at close quarters and a number of Indian personnel received the highest decorations for their courage in these savage encounters. The defences of Imphal and Kohima were perhaps the hardest fought of the war. It was not unknown for both British and Indian units to receive an order to hold an area 'to the last man and last round'. Fighting in all-round defence, in box formations, the 14th Army was supplied from the air but it was otherwise self-reliant. By late 1944, Field Marshal William Slim had broken the Japanese forces in northern Burma. In December 1944 his army's counter-offensive began, and the 19th and 20th Indian Divisions were among those that crossed the Chindwin River. The Japanese held their positions determinedly, forcing Slim to manoeuvre his brigades and divisions in and around the Japanese formations. The Japanese also conducted resolute counter-attacks, and the terrain, with its dense vegetation, necessitated more fighting at close quarters. By March 1945, Meiktila was in British hands, but the Japanese continued to contest and counter-attack every advance. By now, the Indian Army had perfected jungle fighting and combined arms operations. When the landscape opened up around Rangoon, Indian units quickly adapted and reverted to a more mobile mechanised warfare. Rangoon was even captured with an amphibious assault on 3 May 1945.

General Sir Claude Auchinleck, who became the Commander-in-Chief of the Indian Army in 1941, and resumed that position between 1943 to 1947, disagreed with the racial prejudices that had determined which groups served in the Indian Army before the war, and who became officers. He immediately began the abolition of a racially selected force. The moves were much appreciated by the Indian personnel themselves.[35] From 1940, Indian officers were recruited on the same basis as the British, and granted exactly the same status, so that they could serve on courts martial, even presiding over British soldiers and officers. Equality in pay took time to catch up, and was not fully resolved until 1945. British officers still remained the majority in the officer corps of the Indian Army but, by 1945, for every four British officers there was at least one Indian. By the end of the war, there were a number of Indian colonels and three brigadiers, many of whom had been decorated for bravery.

With these changes, men who came from communities previously considered as non-martial now joined the Indian Army in large numbers. The transformation of the Indian Army during the Second World War was crucial in creating equality between the British and Indian personnel and did more than anything else to pave the way for Independence. By serving together and sharing the same hardships, by operating their own warships and flying their own combat aircraft, the Indian personnel were entirely trusted by their British commanders. There was close co-operation on the front line too, and by the time the war came to an end there was a strong sense that India was about to inherit nationhood.

The Armée du Levant and the Armée d'Afrique

When France was awarded the Mandate to govern Syria and Lebanon after the First World War, it raised the Syrian Legion. Its title reflected that fact it was a mixed force of infantry and mounted units, but its distinctive characteristic was that it was recruited entirely from minority groups within Syria. As such, it was thought it would show little sympathy for the majority Sunni Arab population. After the Druze Revolt in 1925, the Syrian Legion was reorganised into a new formation known as the Troupes spéciales du Levant (Special Troops of the Levant) augmented by North African soldiers, the Foreign Legion and other African colonial personnel. The force was still otherwise made up of minorities from the Levant, namely the Druze, Circassians, Christians and Alawites. The Troupes spéciales numbered 10,000 local personnel organised into ten battalions of infantry (the majority being Syrian Alawis), four squadrons of cavalry (consisting of Druze, Circassians and other Syrians), three companies of *méharistes* (camel corps), as well as engineers, signallers, and support units. There were also Troupes supplémentaires (the Auxiliaries) made up of nine companies of *chasseurs libanais*, Lebanese light infantry, and twenty-two squadrons of Druze, Circassian and Kurdish mounted infantry. In keeping with French ideas of citizenship within the colonies, and the guarantees of collaboration, two-thirds of the officers of the Troupes spéciales were from the Levant, with an officers' academy at Homs. The arrangement in some ways represented a continuity with the Ottoman era, when minorities could be promoted within the imperial system through officer training academies.

The fall of France in 1940 led to the establishment of Vichy governments in the colonies, and Syria was held by French troops, including the 24th Colonial Infantry Regiment and Foreign Legion. They were accompanied by two battalions of Senegalese, and the composite units were known as the Régiment mixte colonial. The Troupes spéciales were increased to eleven battalions of infantry, made up of three Lebanese *bataillons de chasseurs libanais* and eight Syrian *bataillons de Levant*. For mobility, the Troupes spéciales could draw on 5,000 cavalry, with three squadrons that were motorised. By 1941, there were an additional thirteen battalions of African infantry and the 7,000-strong contingent of North African cavalry including the 4th Tunisian, the 1st Moroccan and the 8th Algerian Spahis. Several of the squadrons had lorries or armoured cars, while the 6th and 7th Chasseurs d'Afrique was mechanised with 90 tanks. The entire force was supported by an air arm consisting of 289 aircraft.

In North Africa, the formations available had initially been sent to assist in the defence of France, but the defeat of 1940 led to a similar reorganisation as in the Levant. At the outbreak of war there had been 42 regiments of Algerian, Tunisian and Moroccan *tirailleurs*, and 13 battalions of African Light Infantry. This was in addition to the largely European 14 regiments of Zouaves and 12 regiments or demi-brigades of the Foreign Legion. After the fall of France, Germany demanded that the forces in Africa were to be reduced to 120,000 men. The French nevertheless managed to conceal 60,000 trained personnel in the role of auxiliary police and labourers.

The Armée d'Afrique was able to join the Allies in the liberation of North Africa in late 1942. Under the command of General Henri Giraud, French and colonial units fought as the French Expeditionary Corps in the Tunisia campaign, in the liberation of Corsica in 1943, and the Italian campaign between 1943 and 1944. In those years, the Armée d'Afrique doubled to 260,000 men, half of whom were North Africans, forming, among other units, the 2nd and 4th Moroccan Infantry Divisions and the 3rd Algerian Infantry Division. There were also three independent legions of Goumiers, reorganised as the Groupement de tabors marocains, as well as batteries of artillery, engineer companies, commando units and armoured squadrons of Spahis.

In the inter-war years in North Africa and Syria there had been regiments of Tonkinese Rifles from French Indochina, and they had seen action in Syria in 1920 and Morocco in 1925–6. Old tensions had remained, however, and elements of 4th Tonkinese Rifles mutinied on 9 February 1930 at Yên Bái, although the unrest was crushed by loyal members of the same regiment. The Tonkinese Rifles went on to assist the French in a series of border skirmishes with Thailand between 1940 and 1941. All six of the Tonkinese and Annamite Rifle regiments were disbanded during the Japanese coup of 9 March 1945 against the French colonial government. Although some units were raised during the Indochina conflict in the 1950s and a commando unit later served in the Algerian War, the majority of Vietnamese were unwilling to serve the French after the war. Most were dismayed to see the French re-establish their colonial authority after the brief British occupation at the end of the conflict. It was not long before that sentiment turned to anger and active resistance.

Local Forces in a Global War

Local forces in Western service in the war were characterised by a unity of effort and considerable loyalty (despite some well-known exceptions), notwithstanding the ferocity of fighting on certain fronts, a significant expansion in numbers that diluted the pool of experienced professionals, and a potentially contradictory cause for which to fight. When the United States championed the liberationist agenda, it might understandably have caused the erosion, if not entire collapse, of the European colonial armies, but indigenous and non-European personnel remained in service, even in the most extreme case of the fall of France. Indeed, cohesion remained during a change of identity, through severe setbacks and defeats, and despite a number of opportunities to abandon the European Allied powers.

Local personnel fulfilled a great variety of roles. Colonial bases across the world proved invaluable to air and maritime forces, and local men provided guards, pioneers, merchant sailors, combat troops, and even Special Operations Executive commandos. The colonial peoples, including the families of service personnel, endured not only the uncertainty of the safety or whereabouts of the troops, but also mounting economic hardship, shortages or other wartime hazards.

The motivations were, in part, some continuities of the past and universal attractions, but there was undoubtedly a sense that wartime service was moving the people and the country concerned towards independence. In India, for example, there was a growing sense that British rule would end. The concessions the British made in political representation were also manifest in the progressive Indianisation of the officer corps. Indian personnel became pilots, took command of British as well as Indian troops, were protected by a penal system that treated Indians and British personnel equally, and could be certain, by 1945, that the British would respect their aspirations for national independence. The war created a profound change in expectation about national independence for colonial peoples, but it did not bring to an end the use of indigenous personnel. Indeed, as the next chapter demonstrates, the wars of decolonisation saw further uses for local and indigenous forces.

11

LOCAL FORCES DURING THE WARS
OF DECOLONISATION

Decolonisation, a complex process driven by the geopolitics of the Super-powers, domestic popular pressure, new agendas in the European states and widespread disaffection among indigenous populations, necessitated the transfer of power to new polities with increasing frequency after 1945.[1] The Europeans made extensive use of local forces in trying to prevent the emergence of independent states, but, periodically, even in the transfer of authority, indigenous military forces were often the basis of state power on independence. Where European states tried to facilitate decolonisation, local forces were designed to build national states in order to keep them free of communism. To be clear, armies were critical in all forms of state-building.

The Europeans found it difficult to abandon local forces they had trained, and many officers felt a sense of betrayal and humiliation. Those who had served in the colonial armies could also face retribution or ostracism. The senior officers of the new, independent national armies regarded themselves as the guardians of the state, and, when civilian politicians seemed intent on pursuing their own, more narrow interests or were guilty of exploiting national divisions, these military personnel felt compelled to intervene in politics, leading to a higher incidence of *coups d'état* in the decades after 1945.

To suppress armed liberationist movements, the Europeans developed or revised doctrines of counter-insurgency. Sir Robert Thompson, who had been a Chindit in the war and then Permanent Secretary for Defence in Malaya during the so-called Emergency, as the author of *Defeating Communist Insurgency* noted that the government 'must have a clear political aim, namely to establish and maintain a free, independent and united country which is politically and economically stable and viable'.[2] He also noted that the priority was to defeat the political subversion of the adversary, not the guerrillas themselves. He spelt out the specific role and variety of local forces: 'The government should formulate long-term political aims, backed by political and economic initiatives; these in turn will be supported by a counter-insurgency plan involving the police, the armed forces and any locally raised militias, home guards and other auxiliary forces.'[3] These were important not least because they compelled commitment from portions of the population towards the government. Their families too were making a choice to support, albeit indirectly, the government. Counter-insurgency is, in essence, the government's contestation for control of the population and, even where local forces had little military value, they still fulfilled an important political purpose.

The French theorists of counter-insurgency in the 1960s, David Galula and Bernard Fall, drew the same conclusions.[4] Amid the measures of *guerre revolutionaire*, with its emphasis on establishing *taches d'huile* (oilspots of security and development that were spread out across the country), *quadrillage* (dividing up the terrain with physical barriers), *ratissage* (combing out insurgents), *regroupement* (relocating populations) or *razzia* (raids), local forces were an important element of the strategy. Galula wrote: 'A victory is not only the destruction in a given area of the insurgent's forces and his political organization. It is that, plus the permanent isolation of the insurgent from the population, isolation not enforced upon the population but maintained by and with the population.' To ensure that 'permanent isolation' invariably required the active participation of men in local defence organisations.

Counter-insurgency is manpower-intensive. In order to establish a persistent presence among the population, in order to ensure their protection against insurgents, various ratios of security forces personnel to the population, or to the numbers of insurgents, were estimated.[5] Numbers were nevertheless a misleading guide if the allegiance of the population swung dramatically behind the insurgency.[6]

Aside from raw numbers of manpower, local forces provided other critical advantages for the governments conducting counter-insurgency. Military operations were usually intelligence-led, and this placed particular importance on indigenous security personnel, including the police. General Frank Kitson noted that 'the problem of defeating the enemy consists very largely of finding him'.[7] Information on the local terrain, the textures of the population, and presence of insurgents played a key role, and, with training, there was the possibility of penetrating insurgent movements with local personnel. Nevertheless, insurgents were also able to infiltrate indigenous security forces and orchestrate ambushes and betrayals.[8] On the other hand, local personnel can assist in the process of reconciliation and conflict termination by persuading members of the community to turn insurgents and reduce levels of violence for the sake of the public in certain areas. During unrest in the Philippines in the 1950s, the Defence Minister, Ramon Magsaysay, encouraged by his American military advisers, rewarded the Hukbalahap guerrillas who voluntarily surrendered by giving them land of their own, and the conduit of the negotiations was local auxiliaries and agents.[9] The British also made extensive use of local forces, or employed men from neighbouring states, known as the Sarawak Rangers, as trackers during operations in densely vegetated terrain in Malaya.[10]

Men were 'enlisted' to act as 'home guard' units in a number of campaigns, their role being to defend their own settlement or protect a portion of a route required by the security forces. They were often armed with their own weapons or with a limited issue of government firearms. This technique was used by the British in Malaya and Kenya, and by the Americans in Vietnam.[11]

The clandestine nature of insurgent groups, and their hit-and-run tactics, increased the temptation to 'fight fire with fire' for government forces. Along with Special Forces, which grew in popularity and importance from the Second World War onwards, there was the opportunity to recruit local men, and especially insurgents that had been captured and 'turned' to act as members of counter-gangs and pseudo-gangs. The historians Geraint Hughes and Chris Tripodi define these as special forms of 'surrogate' forces.[12] Counter-gangs, small teams of no more than twenty men, using the same techniques and moving in the same way as insurgents, were used to conduct reconnaissance, hunt down cells, and even mount ambushes. The Americans raised the Philippines Constabulary in its operations against Filipino rebels in 1901, and these reappeared as the Provincial Reconnaissance Units under the guidance of Special Operational Forces and the Central Intelligence Agency in the Vietnam War between 1968 and 1972.[13] The Philippines Scouts, the majority of whom were Macabebe tribesmen, assisted in the capture of Emilio Aguinaldo, the leader of the nationalist insurgency in March 1901.[14] The British made use of the Special Night Squads, made up of Jewish personnel during the Arab unrest in Palestine in 1936, and replicated the idea as the 'Q

Patrols' of loyalists and ex-EOKA fighters employed during the Cyprus insurgency.[15] The British Army and Special Branch, a specialist wing of the police, made extensive use of counter-gangs in Kenya, many of whom had been members of the Mau Mau insurgent movement, to track and pursue other insurgents.[16] Pseudo-gangs were units that specifically posed as insurgents, and naturally there was some overlap with counter-gangs in operations. Their value was not only in being able to track or get within close proximity of insurgent groups; they could also provoke incidents that could be blamed on the insurgent movement as part of a psychological operation.[17] The Selous Scouts in Rhodesia were effective in posing as an entirely separate force in order to mislead the insurgents.[18] Insurgent leaders regarded the existence of such gangs as a serious threat to their security, and their treatment of captured personnel was often severe. The Cypriot EOKA leader, Colonel George Grivas, claimed that British-inspired Q Patrols were Turkish 'gangsters', and he refused to accept that some of his own people, the Greek Cypriots, were prepared to join the British against him.[19] Suspicions of treachery have been enough to tear apart sections of insurgent movements because their personal security was such a key vulnerability.

As with other irregular formations, governments sacrifice control when such groups are employed. It is difficult to prevent pseudo-groups carrying out their own retribution, and, since the objective of the government must be to undermine the legitimacy of the insurgency and reduce levels of violence, the activities of counter-gangs and pseudo-gangs can be entirely counterproductive. Denunciation of other communities can also lead to counter-insurgent forces being deployed against entirely innocent parties. In Malaya, former insurgents who had joined the British felt they had to act ruthlessly against the remaining insurgents because they, or their families, could expect no quarter if captured by 'Traitor Killing Squads'.[20] Most British theorists of counter-insurgency deplored the idea of such groups, arguing that adherence to the law, crucial to the establishment of legitimacy in the eyes of the population, was an advantage that far outweighed the satisfaction of revenge by counter-gangs against insurgents.

On the other hand, the use of counter-gangs in Kenya produced a more effective suppression of the Mau Mau movement in the Aberdare highlands than the cumbersome sweep operations of the British Army. The counter-gangs accounted for more of the insurgents' casualties than the regulars.[21]

The existence of local auxiliaries and militias, especially in the context of an insurgency, represents the limits of government power. Counter-insurgency theorists argued that irregular auxiliaries were best in spaces beyond the urban centres in the rural peripheries, but not in the heartlands of the insurgency, which should be the responsibility of the regular armed forces.[22] In Vietnam, the authorities had established the Civil Guard (the police force), the Self-Defence Corps (the part-time Specials of the constabulary) and the Republican Youth and Hamlet Militia (home guard for village defence), but these were ground-holding units, and more serious operations were conducted by the military. In Malaya, the scheme was similar, with the police expanding from 11,000 to 30,000 regular and another 30,000 special constables.[23] Thompson noted that the role of the military forces was to clear the insurgents from the populated areas, but to avoid engaging heavy weapons or air power, which would alienate the population. The role of Special Forces, Thompson argued, was solely to make contact with remote ethnic minorities and aboriginal populations, to recruit and organise them into self-defence units. Raising similar auxiliaries in highly populated areas was less desirable because 'such units tend to become independent private armies, owing allegiance less to the government than to some territorial figure, and, as a result, bearing little responsibility for their actions'.[24] Consequently, their guerrilla-versus-guerrilla actions 'fail to restore permanent order to the area [and] they merely create a never-ending situation of civil war'.

The End of the British Indian Army

Within two years of the end of the Second World War, with rising political agitation, the British assessment of the local political administration, which had been placed in their hands, was that co-operation could no longer be expected.[25] More worrying still was the rise of communal violence between Hindus and Muslims, or between minorities. All services, especially the police, were no longer functioning. Wavell concluded: 'These have been diluted during the war; and service traditions have been weakened. Communal or sectional interests are now powerful and loyalty to the government has been undermined ... partly by the knowledge that British control will soon terminate and that the services must look for the prospects to new masters. It is, therefore, no longer possible to rely implicitly upon them to carry out the orders of a British Government. Similar considerations apply to the Army, though, at present in a much less degree.' Wavell warned his colleagues that 'law and order in the country depends almost entirely on the reliability and cohesion of the Indian Army', but 'one cannot expect to maintain indefinitely the integrity of the Army while both the main political parties are preaching communal war and when it is known that the British officers, who alone hold the army together, are leaving soon.'[26]

The Cabinet concluded on 10 December 1946: 'The strength of British forces in India was not great. And the Indian Army, though the Commander in Chief had great personal influence with it, could not fairly be expected to prove a reliable instrument for maintaining public order in conditions tantamount to civil war. One thing was quite certain viz., that we could not put back the clock and introduce a period of firm British rule. Neither the military nor the administrative machine in India was any longer capable of this.'[27] During 1946, the Indian Army staged a military exercise to practise internal security duties, including the use of minimum force, the rules for the use of lethal force, and the anticipated moments to assume martial law and when to relinquish it to civilian authorities. Although it was a long-established practice, civilian administrators seemed unfamiliar with their duties and reluctant to use their powers.[28] At the end of the year, Wavell wrote in his journal on 31 December 1946: 'The loyalty of the Police is doubtful in some of the Provinces, they are tinged with communalism; fortunately, the Indian Army seems unaffected so far, but it can hardly remain so indefinitely, if communal tension continues.'[29]

Wavell was replaced by Lord Louis Mountbatten, but he reached the same conclusions. A timetable for British withdrawal was therefore fixed. The Indian Army was to be divided between the new nations of India and Pakistan, although some units were informed in great haste where they would be going. Transition also some required a degree of continuity, and it was the request of all Indian parties that the British leave British officers within the new armies of India and Pakistan 'to assist in carrying out the division of the army between the new States and building up effective military organisations on a fresh basis'. Furthermore, the Princely States were advised to choose either the new India or Pakistan.

While the Indian Army was tasked to provide security as best it could across the country, in the Punjab, where the worst unrest was anticipated, the Indian government set up the Punjab Boundary Force (PBF) in May 1947. Its personnel were drawn from Hindu, Muslim and Sikh backgrounds, led by Asian and European officers. Daniel Marston, who researched this force, believes that the PBF managed to remain impartial in the majority of cases where communal violence had broken out.[30] There were, admittedly, a few incidents in Lahore and Amritsar, where the violence was at its worst, but, on the whole, soldiers and officers from the different communities remained cohesive and focused on their mission.[31] Many British officers praised the Indian troops for their impartiality and professionalism in the face of severe provocation, including ambushes and attacks by armed police. The press at the time was highly critical of the PBF because it seemed they did nothing to prevent the shocking and large-scale massacres taking place, but such a small force was overwhelmed by the extent of the fighting. Furthermore, Marston argues that the collapse of the police force and civil administration in the province deprived the PBF of the intelligence about the problems and likely conflicts in specific districts. PBF units were therefore often operating 'blind', unable to prevent conflict between the most militant parts of each community, and forced to react, which meant supporting the evacuation of the many refugees. Insufficient manpower meant the troops could not prevent all the violence that developed. The fact that the Punjab had been the preferred recruiting ground of the Indian Army for generations, and especially during the war, meant that a large number of men conducting the killings had military experience.[32] Having to divide the Indian Army at the same time, including the Gurkhas (half of which remained in British service), was felt to be tantamount to betrayal. Auchinleck had informed Mountbatten that the task of dividing up the army would take three years, but it not until June 1947 that a committee for the 'Reconstitution of the Armed Forces of India' was set up, and Mountbatten wanted the division of the army complete by August.[33]

The sense of abandonment of Indian soldiers was particularly difficult for British officers of the Indian Army to bear since it impinged directly on their sense of honour and loyalty. Rupert Mayne, of Mayne's Horse, drove past great columns of refugees passing in opposite directions between Amritsar and Lahore. A former soldier of 4th Indian Division stepped out of the line, stood to attention and explained that he had fought through North Africa and Italy, and then asked for help. Mayne was unable to help him. He replied: 'Your politicians asked for *swaraj* [independence], and this is *swaraj*.'[34] Yet, senior officers were aware that some former soldiers were leading the murder gangs and General Messervy advised that pensioners should be informed their pensions would be stopped if they were found participating in the violence.

Lieutenant J.P. Cross, 1/1st Gurkha Rifles, was angry that his unit had received no instructions on the handover 'until the last minute'. Despite promises that the battalion would transfer into British Army service, it transpired that it would not: 'The Gurkhas could not understand it; nor could we. We were left without positive directions and therefore could give none. Pressures of events obscured the heartbreak, ... there was no properly planned handover to the Indian officers. They never came until after the bitter end. And [referring to the massacres] the end was bitter.' He continued:

> However fine the motive behind the act of pulling out, where men meant more than ciphers and numbers, it hurt. Those who have never served in a tight knit community like a Gurkha battalion can have little idea of the wealth of camaraderie and warmth of human relationship that exists between officers and men. Nothing really made sense and it was a heartless and painful experience ... On parting, tears were shed and the sorrow was genuine and hard to bear ... [I was] indignant at the unseemly haste of having to meet an unrealistic political deadline. We were abandoning our men, we had broken trust and, by God, it hurt.

One officer believed the breaking up of the Indian Army ruined all that had been achieved and gave an equally emotional response: 'to us it was the heartbreak of heartbreaks. We felt it beyond credence. We had united these dozens of different castes, creeds, colours and beliefs under one flag. We had united them under one regimental colour. It took us two hundred years to build that up, and for that to go literally at the stroke of a pen—it was something that one will never get over.'[35] Auchinleck, as Commander-in-Chief in India, wrote: 'All Indian Army officers hated the idea but we did as we were told. They had to be split ... which meant that regiments like my own, half Hindu and half Moslem, were just torn in half—and they wept on each other's shoulders when it happened ... you felt your life's work would be finished when what you had been working at all along was just torn in two pieces.'[36] This feeling that partition was a disaster and 'horrifying' was reinforced by the communal killing and the sense that unification of India, which the British regarded as one of their key achievements, had been destroyed.

Leaving and Staying in Southern Arabia: Aden and Oman, 1967–1976

There were two utterly contrasting British approaches to southern Arabia in the space of a decade, which had very different outcomes for local forces.[37] In the case of Aden and the Federation of South Arabia, the unavoidable verdict was: 'By unilaterally deciding to withdraw our forces from these areas by the end of 1971, the Labour government have broken their promises to the governments and peoples of these areas and are exposing these British interests and the future of Britain's friends to unacceptable risk.'[38] By contrast, in the case of Oman, which had not been a colony but a long-standing partner, Britain made a long-term commitment of forces and money. Moreover, the

British and their Omani allies were not oly successful not only in defeating a communist insurgency, but they won the backing of teams of former insurgents, the firqats, with tact, appropriate development support and robust military support. One of the principal architects of the operations concluded: 'One of the principles of successful handling of a firqat was "coincidence of aims" ... There was absolutely no point in tasking a firqat to do something that they did not wish to do or which would bring no profit to them.'[39] The two cases exemplify the contrasts of decolonisation: on the one hand, abandonment, and on the other, a coincidence of aims, respect for the sovereignty of the partner and an enduring relationship.

This section examines the fate of Arab forces who worked with the British in southern Arabia, where, against the odds, at least in Oman, an enduring partnership was established.[40] While Britain was considering withdrawal from all of its colonial possessions 'east of Suez', security broke down in Aden after 1967, and local security forces mutinied or transferred their allegiance to Marxist revolutionaries. This produced a significant shift in Britain's Middle Eastern policy. By the mid-1970s, the British had established long-term support for the Omani regime, despite another Marxist insurgency there and Britain's apparently comprehensive 'exit' from the Gulf. In contrast to examples that illustrate confusion or failure in local security arrangements between 1967 and 1970, the British actions in Oman suggest a more determined policy was pursued which successfully combined local and British interests.

Nevertheless, the outcomes were not simply determined by policymakers in London. In Aden in 1967–8, local police and portions of the South Arabian Army (SAA) became so unreliable that they made continued British control there impossible. By contrast, British enlistment of a local Dhofari auxiliary force, the Firqat, and the development of the Sultan's Armed Forces (SAF) bolstered the Omani regime. Yet events in southern Arabia were never so simple and the story of betrayal, loyalty or co-operation was not limited to the British and their partners. In Aden, the Marxist National Liberation Front (NLF) betrayed and destroyed its rivals, co-opting the old SAA and police into its new political apparatus, while in Dhofar and Oman the Marxist Popular Front for the Liberation of the Occupied Arabian Gulf (PFLOAG), which initially enjoyed widespread support, lost its credibility among local people, was abandoned by its external sponsors and was resisted successfully by the British and the SAF.

For British soldiers and local administrators, the precipitate withdrawal from Aden produced a strong sense of betrayal and anguish. The Governor (and then High Commissioner) had failed to find a political solution during a period of intense local agitation. Plans for a federation that preserved the power of pro-British sheikhs in the interior, but united the urban elites of Aden, collapsed and was abandoned amid increased rioting, assassination and insurgency. The decision to pull out, rather than let the British troops fight on against the insurgents, meant that power was effectively handed over to the Marxist NLF, who had 'earned the right to rule by a campaign of intimidation and murder, waged mostly against their fellow countrymen and political opponents'.[41] British soldiers were disgusted when it transpired that their allied tribesmen of South Yemen were put on board trucks by NLF men, taken out into the desert, and, within earshot, shot down with 'long bursts of machine gun fire'. Joe Starling, a British soldier present, recalled. 'Our orders were very clear: "It's not our problem, don't get involved."' And he added with poignancy: 'Sometimes it's very difficult to obey orders.'[42] The South Arabian Army, which Britain had trained and partnered, threw in its lot with the Yemeni agitators, and turned its guns on the rival leftist faction. British troops extracted without taking further casualties against this background of intra-Arab murder, but its attempts to leave behind a pro-Western state had failed.

By contrast, the British chose to support the Omani regime in its conflict with communist-inspired insurgents (1970–6). There was a significant commitment of Special Forces, RAF, contract personnel and British 'loan service officers'. Britain, and especially the British Army, remained close to the regime after the conflict, such that Omani officers attended British military establishments continuously for decades. Moreover, many Omani tribal groups, with the exception of many of the Dhofaris, were reconciled with the regime in Muscat, choosing their traditions over Marxism. However, rather than being the successful outcome of a counter-insurgency strategy, the British were in fact fortunate that the momentum of Marxism in this portion of southern Arabia was lost when the sponsors in Egypt and Yemen were forced to reassess their priorities.

The analyses offered of southern Arabia over the last few decades have tended to fall into a number of rather exclusive groupings that don't give much emphasis to local military forces. British work on the period 1916–67 has concentrated on the 'end of empire', with detailed explanations of how and why the British withdrew. In the 1960s and 1970s, there was considerable interest in the successor regimes, and a fascination with Marxist interpretations. One article, for example, sought to explain the fortunes of the Adeni and Southern Arabian Federation elites through the inability of the latter to draw upon the 'commanding heights' of a capitalist economy, without much mention of the tribal divisions that underpinned rivalry between southern Arabian political groups. The failure of the Yemeni government in the 1980s attracted less attention than might have been expected, but after 2003 there was renewed interest in the fortunes of British counter-insurgency in Aden and Oman, and the cluster of these works are of a significantly high quality.[43] It is this interaction of local and metropolitan, and dynamics within local politics, which are so crucial to our understanding of the region. British decision-making over Oman was made partly in response to local events, and partly according to its own agenda, which was, in itself, a reaction to previous failures. Local decision-making also incorporated this dynamic of calculation and reaction.

However, it is equally important to acknowledge the role of local military forces in southern Arabia, to illustrate the relative value of Britain's domestic political considerations, a sense of strategic requirements, and the worth of the local forces themselves, for it was these that drove the process of either abandonment or partnership. Insurgents and local actors responded to changes taking place in southern Arabia, recalibrating their decision to co-operate or resist, and measuring the strength or will of the British and their local military partners. The key point is that the dynamic combinations of British assumptions and miscalculations, and local armed forces and actors, were crucially important to the outcomes in the region.

After 1945, the British could not ignore a developing trend of communist influence and nationalist politics around the globe and particularly throughout the Middle East. Premier Mossadegh had nationalised Anglo-Persian Oil in 1951 and was thought to be a socialist, and the seizure of the refinery of Abadan prompted the opening of a new facility at Aden. Britain was fighting communist insurgency in Malaya. It was confronted in Europe by a vast conventional Soviet and Warsaw Pact army, backed by atomic weapons. Moreover, the Suez Canal was the conduit for a vast proportion of Britain's oil supplies on which its economy depended and its nationalisation by Gamal Abdel Nasser prompted military intervention. The operations of 1956, collusion with Israel, and humiliating climbdown are well documented and need not be narrated here. Our purpose is to examine the effects on Britain's strategic relationship with Arabia, particularly Yemen, Aden and Oman.

Aden had always acted as a link to other parts of the British Empire, latterly as an air base. In 1960, Middle East Command, the headquarters of British military forces in the region, was established in the colony. Aden included a thriving port, a BP oil refinery (from 1954) and barracks that could accommodate a rapid reaction force.[44] The Sultan of Muscat was reinforced from Aden during the Imamate Rebellion in 1954. It had been a port for the strategic reserve during the revolt against the King of Jordan in 1958 and acted a staging post for troops to be deployed by air and sea to Kuwait in 1961 in order to deter an Iraqi attack there. After the Suez Crisis, Aden's value seemed to increase. Sir William Luce, the British Political Resident in the Gulf, remarked in 1961: 'Britain at this moment stands more deeply committed in the Persian Gulf, both politically and militarily, than at any time since the last war, a situation which is in marked contrast with the great contraction of our political and military commitments elsewhere in the world over the last fifteen years.'[45]

Despite the apparent strength of the British position, its influence was steadily declining. The Colonial Office had maintained a policy of pacifying the hinterland, concluding treaties with the local sheikhs, appointing British political officers as advisers, and raising sanctioned tribal forces such as the Aden Protectorate Levies and the Hadrami Bedouin Legion. This advice and support nevertheless increased the dependence of the tribal rulers on the British authorities. The Colonial Office also attempted to reform the traditional tribal councils, the *daulahs*, insisting that development aid to the rulers in the 1950s and 1960s be channelled through them. Saul Kelly notes that far from leaving the interior as an uninterrupted and underdeveloped backwater, this initiative had the unintended effect of undermining the authority and influence of the tribal rulers, and perhaps helped to generate a growing political consciousness.[46] Development aid became a point of contention and was regarded as foreign influence rather than benign benefaction. In 1954, growing unrest in the interior prompted the Colonial Office to scale back its policy of 'support'.

The British believed the traditional rulers of the 24 states making up the Federation would act as a conservative 'brake' on the more vociferous critics in the Aden Trade Unions Congress (ATUC), but they delayed the implementation of the federation plan because of the rejection by the ATUC. The delay was a serious miscalculation. The Sultan of Lahej, in the Western Protectorate, and the South Arabian League, a loose political grouping, looked instead to Nasser and the Yemenis for their future protection. In 1962, after a favourable vote in the Aden legislature, the British government announced that Aden would join the newly created Federation of South Arabia, consisting of 25 autonomous states.[47] There was immediate and noisy opposition on the streets, organised by the ATUC and its political wing, the People's Socialist Party (PSP), which was funded, through Yemen, by Egypt. The vote coincided with the overthrow of the new Imam of Yemen, al-Badr, by a military coup, led by Yemeni General Sallal, again supported by Egypt. Some PSP leaders set off to join the new Yemeni socialist government and to organise further resistance against the British in Aden. Nasser deployed two regular divisions, some 20,000 men, to foster the 'people's struggle' in South Arabia.

In Yemen, the National Liberation Front (NLF), a Marxist-inspired terrorist group, was established and began a campaign of assassination. It also launched a series of random grenade attacks, often by paying inexperienced local youths to attack personnel associated with colonial authority. Nasser and his Egyptian secret service nevertheless preferred the Organisation (later Front) for the Liberation of Occupied South Yemen (FLOSY), a nationalist organisation that was based on the ATUC but eager to mount mass demonstrations that would discredit colonial authority and bring Aden to a standstill. Both groups ran campaigns of terrorism against the British and the Federation partners.[48] An Arab civil war developed in the interior, in which a small contingent of SAS participated, effectively containing Yemeni and Egyptian forces there.

The British plan to govern by consent was nevertheless failing. Subsequently they were to attempt direct rule and then use the 'Indian option', that is, to hand over power as quickly as possible. The dilemma then was who they should transfer power to. Their preference was to ensure that the sheikhs of the interior provided the political stability and the South Arabian Army and police would guarantee security. Neither succeeded. The sheikhs were under increasing pressure from their opponents, internally and externally, and in the final months they would be abandoned.

The revolutionaries achieved considerable success in persuading the Adeni population that there was some momentum to their movements and that, in time, Aden would seem ungovernable. Lord Trevelyan, the last High Commissioner of the Federation of South Arabia and the apologist for British policy in this period, admitted 'the only question of importance was whether the country would hold together or be submerged in anarchy'.[49] In fact, in the 1964 elections, the opposition parties campaigned on the issue of the restrictive franchise and collectively boycotted the actual election. The result was that the Federalists were in power, including the Protectorate-based SAL (South Arabian League), and the rest in opposition. The SAL had established a party in 1950 from a collection of foreign-educated modernisers, but its members were drawn from families from the Sultanate of Lahej. It was a successful party in terms of popular support after 1962, but it failed to deliver the reforms most desired and consequently was eventually outflanked by the more radical NLF.

The NLF promoted a radical reform programme but was founded on the single theme of liberation. It possessed a clear, unambiguous and ideologically committed programme which gave it the initiative from 1965 onwards. The merger of Aden with the Protectorate states almost certainly accelerated political consciousness and the anti-colonial agendas articulated by the NLF. The Yemeni revolutionaries and their Egyptian allies provided the crucial means to sustain a campaign of resistance and political agitation, with Yemen offering a safe haven to anti-colonial dissidents.

In 1964, a conference in London proposed that Aden and the Protectorate should become independent no later than 1968. To reassure the sheikhs of the Federation, Britain would retain a base at Aden and reinforce them when called upon to do so. This would, in fact, never be fulfilled. This announcement that Britain would leave Aden served to encourage the agitators, and convinced them that their tactics of disobedience and resistance were succeeding. The sudden announcement of the abrogation of Britain's control produced a scramble. Although the government expected an improvement in relations with the Arab world when Britain gave up its imperial control, no such sentiment emerged. To its allies, the British were guilty of abandonment and, to its adversaries, the British were weakened and increasingly irrelevant.

With the active encouragement of Egypt and Yemen, there was an attempt at rapprochement between the various rival groupings in southern Arabia in 1966. In January that year, the NLF temporarily joined the front of FLOSY, thus forming a united organisation with the ATUC and the PSP. The alliance lasted a year until Yemeni interests, led by the majority NLF, challenged the Egyptian-preferred ATUC and FLOSY. By January 1967, FLOSY and NLF supporters were at war with each other, waging a campaign of assassination and murder, while maintaining their regular attacks on the British in Aden.

The level of insecurity increased just at the time that the British were trying to complete the process of 'Arabisation' of the local security forces. Brigadier Jack Dye had overall responsibility for the SAA (South Arabian Army), a formation of ten battalions with its own armoured forces, artillery and engineers. From an original contingent of 50 officers and 250 NCOs, the British advisory team numbered just 4 officers and 10 NCOs by early 1967. In the interior, this transformation was accompanied by a handover of responsibility for security. To assist the loyal sheikhs, Dye personally organised their evacuation, and that of their families, to Saudi Arabia. The final withdrawal of British forces from the old Protectorate took place in June 1967.

When it was announced that the date for the British withdrawal from Aden would be brought forward to January 1968, the Federal government protested that they were not yet ready to take responsibility, particularly when the internal security situation was deteriorating so rapidly. The government tried to reassure the Federal elites by arguing that a carrier group would remain offshore in support, before changing the date of exit to 29 November 1967.

The British appointed a new High Commissioner, Sir Humphrey Trevelyan, who, on arrival, announced his intention to end the state of emergency, release political prisoners and invite the two leading movements to participate in a provisional government. NLF and FLOSY rejected the British proposal and instead demanded an immediate British withdrawal, with power handed over to the nationalist representatives. The British chose to ignore the demands, but withdrew the bulk of their forces anyway, urging the remaining loyalist sheikhs to flee for safety.

If the 'agency' of locals was ever in doubt, then events on 20 June 1967 confirmed its importance and, at the same time, underscored the importance of local military forces. The mutiny of a portion of the SAA and the local police on 'Black Tuesday' left 23 British personnel and some 200 Arabs killed. Aaron Edwards rightly notes that it marked the failure of the British policy of Arabisation, which had been attempted all too quickly and without sufficient care.[50] It also encouraged the British political elite to consider that Aden was a lost cause. The irony was that this landmark had been caused not by the sustained resistance of the NLF and FLOSY, even though the mutiny had been inspired by some of those movements' propaganda, but by what soldiers today call an 'insider threat' or a 'green on blue'.

In the last two weeks of their presence, the British recognised the NLF as the new government. The sheikhs were abandoned and the concept of federation with it. Power was to be transferred, with as much dignity as could be salvaged, to the men who had fought them with methods of insurgency and terror. Almost immediately the SAA assisted the NLF to wipe out the remnants of FLOSY and their allies. One British officer described 'an orgy of blood-letting'. Joe Starling recalled hearing the gunfire as the purges were orchestrated and 'found a mass grave being dug up by wild dogs which were feeding on the corpses'.[51]

Trevelyan tried to put a gloss on the departure. He argued that his priority, after the events of 'Black Tuesday', was: 'We could not leave British troops to face the alternative of either being drawn into a civil war with an uncertain outcome or of sitting helplessly and dangerously while the place crumbled around them.'[52] Yet, British forces had frequently been sent in the past to tackle precisely the sort of civil disorder and civil war he was describing. Even more astonishing was Trevelyan's assessment that he did not face a 'strong and coherent nationalist movement'. He concluded that the peaceful transfer of power, from the British perspective, had shown that the 'local boys had made good'. He claimed that 'our withdrawal was the result not of military or political pressure but of our decision, right or wrong, to leave'.[53] This conclusion does not seem to accord at all with the local NLF verdicts. For them, popular pressure, infiltration of the police and sustained resistance had made the colony of Aden ungovernable. Crucially, for Marxists in southern Arabia, they believed they now had momentum and they looked to drive the British out of the region altogether.

Oman and the Dhofar Rebellion

Often the British actions in Aden and Oman in the period 1966–74 are studied in isolation, which is curious when the two crises were so closely connected. The British government's announcement of its intention to withdraw 'east of Suez' by the end of 1971 was the spur for the resolution of old disputes in the Gulf region. However, the threat posed by the Marxist rebellion in Oman's Dhofar province, supported by the same revolutionary forces that had been active in neighbouring Aden, posed a particular challenge to the British government and forced a change of policy from disengagement to reinforcement. While both Labour and Conservative governments wanted to limit their liabilities, they certainly did not want a repetition of the debacle that had marked Britain's withdrawal from Aden.

In essence, for Britain after 1968, the domestic and international situation regarding the Middle East had changed. The sterling bloc crisis of 1967–9 (which necessitated the devaluation of sterling to secure a loan from the International Monetary Fund, a situation produced by the reduction of oil supply from the Gulf during the 1967 war), the energy crisis of 1973, and the advance of communism in Asia and the Middle East were directly related to events in the Arabian Peninsula. Saul Kelly argues that each of these problems was the result of the failure of British governments in the period, who made 'a misjudgement of monumental proportions'.[54]

Yet, at the time, not all were so blind to the new strategic threats. The Foreign Office and Ministry of Defence were especially concerned that the spread of Marxist insurgency into Dhofar from South Yemen could pose a threat to the entire region.[55] The Conservative Party was also concerned that precipitate withdrawal would damage Britain's standing in the world and represent an unacceptable abrogation of its international responsibilities.

Edward Heath and Douglas Hurd, leaders of the Conservative Opposition, made visits to the Gulf region, including Oman, looking for evidence to reverse the Wilson government's 1968 decision of withdrawing from the Gulf or, at the very least, retain some sort of presence there if it proved too problematic to reverse the policy entirely. The Foreign Office was nevertheless lukewarm about giving local elites the idea they could depend entirely on the British and were certainly not eager to attempt another federation in the light of the failure in South Arabia.[56] Moreover, Heath's priority was to get Britain into the EEC in order to reap the benefits of the European common market. To do so meant jettisoning the image of colonialism, even though retaining a security presence in the Gulf could have provided, in Saul Kelly's words, 'an attractive dowry [for] entering into a state of wedded bliss with the European Economic Community'.[57] Nevertheless, the British government was concerned that the UN, in December 1965, had described Oman as a British colonial dependency which, the General Assembly resolved, was preventing the Omani people from exercising their right to self-determination.[58] In July 1970, the Foreign Secretary, Sir Alec Douglas-Home, appointed Sir William Luce, now retired, to examine opinion in the Gulf on a possible reversal of the policy of withdrawal from the Gulf. Luce concluded from his investigation that neither reversal nor postponement was now possible, not least because of expectations raised in Iran.

Instead, Home advocated 'continuing links and assistance' with loan service officers seconded to Gulf allies. He felt that British personnel could act in a training role and facilitate equipment transfers. He felt the local police might be assisted and there could be opportunities to offer support in political reform and development activity.[59] In essence, without treaties and overt garrisons, Britain could support its Gulf partners by other ways and means. Heath addressed the Commons on 1 March 1971 and the date was set for the official withdrawal from the Gulf in December that year. Home's concomitant statement was designed to encourage the Gulf rulers to take responsibility for their own governance but in the sure knowledge that Britain was willing to offer assistance and support in the future without the need for bases or a permanent garrison presence.

The Marxist verdict on unrest in Dhofar was that 'the people of Dhufar [are] waging an armed struggle of liberation against British imperialism and its local agents, the albu-Sa'id dynasty'.[60] It was also asserted that the confrontation was ultimately between an army of the 'wretched of the earth' and the 'goliaths of the era of monopoly capitalism'—the oil corporations. The depth of feeling about the issue was unsurprising. Dhofar, its 38,000 square miles considered the westernmost province of Oman, was the personal fiefdom of the Sultan of Muscat. The 300,000 inhabitants consisted of the Hashemite Sada, who made up a religious and mediating cadre; the settled tribespeople of the plains and coast; and finally the nomadic tribes of the interior, dominated by the Qara and Kathir (Shafi-i) confederations and four other (Ibdali) clans. Most economic activity was subsistence agriculture, but what meagre wealth was generated was exploited in a social stratification of privileges. The Sada, Qara and Kathirs enjoyed the highest standing, but others were styled *da'af* (weak) or slaves. Although the province was annexed by the Sultan of Muscat in 1877–9, with British support, tribal resistance was endless. After a serious revolt in 1896, which required British military assistance, the sultans exploited the tribal feuds, enlisting one clan against another. They also made use of the economic dependence of the interior on the coast: taxation generated resistance, but economic blockades invariably brought the clans to heel.[61]

In 1957, a Dhofari rebellion compelled the Sultan, Said bin Taimur, to evacuate Muscat and establish himself at Salalah, where he implemented a more severe form of governance on the province. Throughout the 1950s, young men had begun to migrate towards the oil industry and other economic opportunities elsewhere in Arabia and the Gulf, but the Sultan was determined to neutralise the development of the province. He deprived the inhabitants of political representation and controlled every aspect of social and economic activity. Even in Salalah there was only one market, which was strictly controlled; there were no hospitals, and just one school which was reserved for the Sultan's family and associates. There was no electricity supply, no veterinary support, and no modern machinery of any kind. All manner of social relations were restricted: smoking, alcohol, bicycles, football, barbers, trousers, shoes and ownership of radios were banned. If villages expressed opposition to these strictures, their wells were dynamited or sealed with concrete. If payments of taxes were withheld, tribal chiefs would be held hostage. Despite attempts to curb migration, young men who were exposed to radical ideas among trade unionists in southern Arabia, especially Aden, drew obvious contrasts with the situation of their families in Dhofar.

In 1964, the Dhofar Benevolence Society and a local branch of the Nasserite Arab Nationalist Movement merged to form the Dhofar Liberation

Front, expressing the desire to liberate the province from British imperialism and Said bin Taimur's tyranny by armed struggle. Despite the union, the two branches had distinct objectives. The Benevolence Society was locally-inspired, separatist and patriotic, and sought 'Dhofar for the Dhofaris' whereas the Arab Nationalists, educated and cosmopolitan, wanted to join a pan-Arab movement to liberate the entire Gulf region. Later that year, Musallam bin Tafl, the leader of the Bait-Kathir, aligned his clan with the DLF and funding was secured from Saudi Arabia, Iraq and the United Arab Republic, a short-lived union between Egypt and Syria. As resistance developed, in June 1965 many of the DLF leaders were rounded up and arrested, forcing the remnants into the mountains. Here, suffering severe deprivation and short of essential munitions, the rebellion was all but extinguished, and yet their attacks persuaded the American John Mickem Company to abandon its operations in the interior, and, in April 1966, the DLF attempted to assassinate Said bin Taimur at a military parade at Rizat Camp along with his Pakistan Army commander.

In 1968, the dying embers of the rebellion were reignited. The triumph of the Marxists in Aden, now styled South Yemen, meant that the neighbouring NLF, which committed itself to support the Dhofaris against imperialism, offered a lifeline to the struggling insurgents. Moreover, the Sultan's draconian measures had generated significant popular disaffection which favoured the revolutionaries. All moderate-sized settlements were ringed with barbed wire; movements into and out of Dhofar were banned; Dhofaris were forbidden to serve in the security forces; and the standard economic blockade was accompanied by a campaign of reprisals.[62] The insurgents grew more committed and restyled themselves as the Popular Front for the Liberation of the Occupied Arabian Gulf (PFLOAG). Its agenda was self-consciously Marxist, and the leadership was now dominated by the more radical members of the former DLF. The Benevolence men were ousted, some of whom became so embittered as to join a counter-revolutionary force later. PFLOAG established a People's Liberation Army (PLA) with commissars to oversee political education, declared itself in favour of the freeing of slaves, the equality of women and common ownership of land, and supported the causes of other liberationist movements in the region, including Palestine.

Sensing the threat, the Sultan's forces had launched a major offensive into the western districts of Dhofar in 1967, hoping to drive a wedge between the NLF in South Yemen and the insurgents. One British officer, on loan service to the Sultan's army, believed that most of the local Qara clans had joined the revolt or at least were sympathetic too it.[63] PFLOAG claimed to control all western districts of Dhofar by August 1969 and they implemented a programme of re-education, including attempts to end the tribal system. Fighting intensified in the central and eastern parts of the province. The Himrin road, guarded by posts of the Sultan's army and nicknamed the 'Red Line' by the insurgents, was the axis of ambush and counter-ambush operations. PFLOAG also infiltrated into the plains, near Salalah, and attempted mortar attacks on the British and SAF bases. In mid-1970, the town of Sadh was overrun. The Prime Minister, Tariq bin Taimur, feared that three-quarters of Dhofar was effectively in insurgent hands. There were calls for direct British intervention, and echoes of support for similar action by Bahrain and Iran.

The SAS assessed the state of the Omani forces against the insurgency in bleak terms. 'The SAF are overstretched and tired .... the methods used by the rebels, so far, are effective and they have seized the initiative and are dominating the *jebal*. There is a feeling of abandonment among the uncommitted *jebali* and the operations by the SAF are hampered by interference from the Sultan, no clear long-term aim, no overall direction and poor intelligence.'[64] Lieutenant Colonel Watts, commanding the SAS, urged the Sultan to reform and develop the province while expanding his armed forces. Initially, Said approved of military expansion, but refused the development aspects of the British proposals.

In June 1970, attacks by insurgents spread from Dhofar to central Oman. On the 12h, the camps of the Sultan's Armed Forces were attacked at Izki and Nizwa.[65] The insurgents styled themselves the National Democratic Front for the Liberation of Oman and the Arabian Gulf (NDFLOAG), the Omani branch of PFLOAG, and they aimed to establish their own Liberation Army in Jabal al-Akhdar. The following month, NDFLOAG cells and caches of Chinese weapons were found at Matrah, Sur and Mutti along the northern coast of Oman.[66] The manifesto of this new movement announced it would 'operate along the same lines as PFLOAG in Dhofar', emphasising its commitment to armed struggle.[67] It appeared that the situation that had occurred in Aden and the Federation was about to be repeated: a protracted rural insurgency in the hinterland, gradually developing into urban guerrilla war and popular disobedience in the cities. The British were concerned that 'another Aden' could occur closer to the vital Gulf oil supplies precisely at the moment when Britain was attempting to withdraw its forces from the area.

Shortly after the election of the new Conservative government in the summer of 1970, the Foreign Secretary, Alec Douglas-Home, stated that the aim was 'to establish a stable political situation' before withdrawal from the Gulf, and recognised that 'even if we withdraw completely by the end of 1971 we would retain major economic interests in the Gulf area'. Nevertheless, he expressed concern about 'a special and potentially embarrassing relationship with Muscat and Oman' because of the unsettled character of the situation there.[68] The Foreign Secretary stated that he was 'considering what contribution we can make by a political and/or military presence'.

At the end of July 1970 Home appointed the ubiquitous Luce as his special representative in the Persian Gulf, a figure well known for his disapproval of withdrawal. Luce had described Labour's decision to leave Aden 'as morally wrong, unwise and unnecessary'.[69] But with gathering criticism in the UN, from Iran and Kuwait, the Conservative government needed to evacuate the Gulf while preserving British interests. Douglas Hurd wrote in his memoirs that 'by the time Ted [Heath] became Prime Minister the withdrawal from the Gulf had gone too far to be reversed'.[70] The solution was to treat Oman as a partner and an ally, to avoid any overt military occupation and to work through the Omani government to ensure a coincidence of interests.[71]

On 23 July 1970, the Sultan of Oman, who had refused to implement much-needed reforms in Dhofar, was deposed in a coup.[72] He was succeeded by his son Qaboos, a reforming personality who had been under arrest in Salalah. It seems Qaboos was able to organise the coup with the assistance of contract officers.[73] While there was no evidence of direct British action in the coup, Britain certainly benefited from the ouster of the old Sultan and the Foreign Office approved of the outcome.[74] The Marxist view was that the British had deliberately engineered the whole thing.[75] Whatever the truth, a significant obstacle to combating a serious insurgency was removed. Qaboos proved far more willing to consider British military assistance to save his western province of Dhofar.

A full-scale British military deployment was out of the question, but further consideration was given to a development of the 'hearts and minds' campaign proposed by the SAS from April 1970, which had enjoyed some success in Dhofar.[76] The SAS commitment eventually consisted of 'a light SAS squadron to operate in detachments training the two SAF battalions stationed in northern Oman' and 'an SAS troop reinforced with interrogators, intelligence collators and a PSYOPs-trained NCO to operate on the Salalah plain gathering intelligence, supervising the training of auxiliary forces by SAF and assisting with the rehabilitation of the inhabitants of the Salalah plain'.[77] There was some hesitation about even this modest force because of the risk of casualties and Britain's reputation: 'were an incident to occur involving casualties, it could lead to parliamentary and public concern'.[78] Further caveats stipulated that the deployment should not become 'open-ended' and that the entire SAS operation should be secret: 'it should be possible since the SAS would be under operational command of CSAF [Commander of the Sultan's Armed Forces], would wear SAF uniform and would be accommodated in SAF camps'.[79]

The British military contribution, although clandestine, was crucial to turning the tide against the insurgents. RAF Salalah's defences were strengthened and more RAF Regiment personnel were deployed. A Royal Artillery team, known as Cracker Battery, used radar to locate precise targets, offering support to the SAF on the plain. A Surgical Team supported British and SAF personnel, improving their morale while a Royal Engineers detachment assisted in development projects for the population. The 65-strong SAS contingent, augmented briefly by a second squadron in mid-1971, expanded their initial role of training leaders within the SAF and its support elements, and began working on surrendered rebels in an attempt to turn them into a local security force. After 1971, an Omani Navy was created, as were technical support services for the SAF. Helicopters, the workhorses of any counter-insurgency, were introduced. The British government also tried to find ways of relieving the Omani government of its cash-flow crisis, not least because the insurgency and defence bills were costing millions. It was estimated that each loan service officer within the SAF cost £5,000 a year. Nevertheless, the fledgling SAF offensive against the Jebel in eastern Dhofar, and interdiction operations closer to the insurgents' lines of supply across the border with South Yemen, were not very effective. Local people simply regarded the Omani troops from the coast as outsiders and they were reluctant to co-operate. A new approach was required.

The Firqat

The solution was for the Special Forces and the British Army Training Teams to recruit Dhofaris into irregular 'firqat' units which could either work alongside or independently of the Sultan's Armed Forces.[80] Major General Tony Jeapes, a former SAS officer, recalled: 'The Firqats' understanding of ground and their speed of manoeuvre were both superior to SAF troops, but when it came to straight military tactics the SAF's discipline won every time. The two forces were complementary; neither could have won the war alone.'[81] Recruited from the tribal Jebalis, they were essentially drawn from the same stock as the personnel of the insurgency, thereby establishing a form of competitive control within the indigenous population.[82] The force was nevertheless small in scale. In June of 1974 there were 16 firqat formations, which numbered up to 1,000 men. A year later, when the insurgency had been contained, there were 18 firqat formations, 'varying in strength from 50 in cleared areas to about 150 in areas known to harbour insurgents', where they operated as a 'kind of tribal police'.[83]

General Jeapes noted that only by ensuring that local, tribal interests were met could there be any chance of operational success. He wrote: 'One of the principles of successful handling of a firqat was "coincidence of aims" ... There was absolutely no point in tasking a firqat to do something that they did not wish to do or which would bring no profit to them; the[y] were not disciplined regulars.'[84]

The raising of each firqat was part of a wider development programme involving well-drilling and medical aid. Jeapes explained the procedure:

> A SAF operation in strength supported by a Firqat secures a position of the Firqat's choice which dominated its tribal area. Military engineers build a track to the position giving road access, followed by an airstrip if possible. A drill is brought down the track followed by a Civil Action Team (who set up a) shop, school, clinic and mosque. SAF thins out to a minimum to provide security. Water is pumped to the surface and into distribution systems prepared by military engineers to offer storage points for humans and troughs for animals. Civilians come in from miles around to talk to the Firqat, SAF and Government representatives. They are told that enemy activity in this area will result in the water being cut off. Civilians move out in surrounding areas and tell the enemy not to interfere with what is obviously a good thing (they also provide intelligence). Enemy, very dependent on the civilians, stops all aggressive action and either goes elsewhere or hides. Tribal area is secure. All SAF are withdrawn.[85]

Despite the apparent ease of this process, at times relations could be strained, not least because the firqats tended to be so undisciplined.[86] Careful selection of those best suited to work with the tribesmen was essential. Training involved ten weeks of intensive Arabic. Not all could manage the delicate balance of observance of local custom, interests, discipline and aggression. Rank meant nothing to the local fighters and unsuitable British personnel, who lost the trust of their firqats, were promptly replaced.[87] The point of collision was often that of the professional and the casual worker: British soldiers valued self-discipline, completion of the task, and self-sacrifice, but the firqats were considered 'undisciplined, untidy and selfish'.[88] Trust was established by demonstrating that there was a common cause to be fought for, and by a low ratio of British personnel: there were never more than 5 soldiers per 100 firqat. Moreover, Jeapes recalls that the experience of living, training and fighting together over long periods created a close bond.[89] The firqats required patience and understanding, but as a result they provided 'an invaluable adjunct to the regular army' as well as 'information on the ground, the people and the enemy which could not have been obtained in any other way'.[90]

The firqats provided security for a particularly small and defined area, but they were most effective when used as intelligence collectors and the means to communicate with insurgents, paving the way for fighters to defect from their Marxist leadership. Defections tended to have a momentum of their own, separate from any other military operations.[91] Nevertheless, there were particular risks. The firqats would rarely fight unless the training teams framed the action in terms of the self-interest of the clan, and voting whether to engage in battle was not uncommon. The intelligence they provided was sometimes misleading, perhaps deliberately or through simple misunderstandings. Far better intelligence was gleaned by the regular SAF and particularly the air force.[92] Attempts to combine firqat groups rarely succeeded either. The mixing of clans led to feuding. Maintaining the distinct identity of each group was preferred by the locals themselves, an important matter when one considers PFLOAG's attempts to eradicate all forms of clan distinction. Accusations that the British practised divide and rule are equally unjustified in this context: local agency asserted itself far more strongly than the impositions of outsiders. Jeapes concluded that without the firqats 'the campaign could never have been brought to a successful conclusion'.[93]

The British were considered to be partners who could offer a better future than the Marxists in both material and spiritual terms. Radio Dhofar was established by the British and used to persuade rebels and loyalists alike that the regime could offer civil aid projects while the Marxists were duplicitous atheists hostile to Islam. Moreover, the British had significant firepower. The Sultan's Air Force, using ex-RAF Strikemasters and loaned RAF personnel, attacked camel caravans which had crossed the border, and gave effective close air support against the insurgents. If there was local opposition in the villages, the threat that the benefits of the regime would be withdrawn was often sufficient to ensure compliance.

By 1975 the rebellion in the Dhofar Province had largely been defeated. A small, 300-strong contingent of the United Arab Emirates had joined the British forces and, after a concerted campaign by the Foreign Office, it was followed by personnel from Saudi Arabia, the Royal Iranian Army, the Royal

Jordanian Army, Pakistan, India and Qatar. The British tried to co-ordinate the various contingents, but the fixed lines of defence tended to be taken up by independent Iranian units, leaving the deeper interior to the British SAS and the firqats.

The Labour Party had returned to power in Britain in 1974 and was under considerable American and domestic pressure, despite the secretive nature of the conflict in Oman, to draw the campaign to a conclusion. The concerns at home included the economic consequences of the energy crisis, pressure to reduce spending in the defence review, and the ideological embarrassment of supporting an undemocratic Gulf state regime three years after the official withdrawal from the region. A gradual transition was therefore designed. Initially, with the reduction of any threat to RAF Salalah, the RAF Regiment was withdrawn in June 1975, three months after the Royal Artillery contingent was pulled out.[94] Plans were also made to close RAF Salalah in favour of the more useful base at RAF Masirah. The Sultan was informed that, despite the draw–down, there would be a 'residual British deterrent presence'. Qaboos felt that this was premature and he persuaded the British to delay until 31 March 1977, after an agreement to pay for the extra costs for the RAF to remain in place. Nevertheless, the Labour government's defence review concluded that both the bases at Salalah and Masirah must be closed.

The process of developing the Omani armed forces was to be continued over a much longer period, and, to offset the problems of costs, it was to be a shared endeavour with other countries. Moreover, military reform occurred in parallel with civil development. Road-building, hospital construction and the improvement of the delivery of goods and services were accompanied by reforms to the central administration and links to local government. Boys' schools were established, for example, initially to provide recruits for the Sultan of Oman's technical support units. Civil policing was introduced to provide security with consensus.[95] The notion of national rebirth under a benign and generous leadership was created to replace the Dhofar–Omani divisions and the history of exploitation under the old sultans. There was considerable emphasis on symbolism and celebrated traditions.[96] British loan service officers and NCOs had been critical of the functioning of the Sultan's armed forces during the insurgency, but there were significant attempts to fulfil an 'Omanisation' from the 1970s. This transition was conducted gradually so that, in 1987, the heads of all three branches of the Omani armed forces were British, either on loan service or serving as contract officers. By the early 1990s, while the commanders were all Omani, they still had British advisers.[97]

It is worth noting that the British personnel who served in Oman, other than the SAS, believed, under oath, they were commanded by the Sultan. While they remained conscious that they were serving British interests indirectly, specifically to defeat a Marxist state on the shores of the Gulf, they felt a commitment to the stabilisation and better prosperity of the people of Oman. The SAS personnel were perhaps more sanguine but were well trained, and willing to operate under local customs and to learn local languages. The relationship has been reciprocated. A high proportion of the officers in the Omani forces are still British. Oman is seen as vital to Western interests given its position at the Straits of Hormuz, and it regards the United Kingdom as an important partner. Omani officers regularly attend British military, air and naval training establishments, such as the Royal Military Academy Sandhurst, the Defence Academy and the Royal College of Defence Studies. There is no question of this being a neo-colonial relationship, but an alliance and a genuine partnership.

PFLOAG had been defeated, but not only by British and Omani counter-insurgency methods or the arrival of, primarily, Emirati, Iranian and Jordanian troops. Fred Halliday, reflecting on articles he had written in the 1970s some twenty years later, concluded that the insurgency had actually suffered from some significant internal problems and the loss of crucial external backing. By the 1980s, PFLOAG had 'withered to a small group of Libya-based émigrés'.[98] The insurgents had been forced into South Yemen, itself put onto the defensive by Saudi Arabia in 1976. South Yemen had also failed to sustain revolutionary changes in North Yemen and suffered from brutal internal convulsions in 1978 and 1986, before entering an ultimately detrimental union with North Yemen in 1990. More broadly, Nasserite Arab nationalism was thrown into disarray by the defeat of Egypt in 1967, and this was underpinned by significant resentment of Egyptian chauvinism throughout southern Arabia. Revolutionary Nasserite nationalism was replaced by the appeal of militaristic versions of Arabism exemplified by Saddam in Iraq. The collapse of Soviet communism in 1990 was only the culmination of the ideological bankruptcy of revolutionary socialism across the Middle East.

Yet, the Cold War had another part to play in the loss of momentum in southern Arabia. In 1956, during the Suez Crisis, the Chinese had made strong condemnations of the British presence in the region. At the National People's Congress in 1965, Zhou Enlai declared China would offer support to 'the people of Arab countries in its struggle against imperialism'.[99] In September that year, Lin Piao published *Long Live the Victory of People's War*, which extolled the virtues and inevitability of victorious peasant armed resistance against the cities of the world. Two months later, the Cultural Revolution was under way in China, a movement that placed particular emphasis on the value of total commitment to armed struggle.

By 1967, the chorus of people's liberation was deafening: 'the entire Arab people will not lay down their arms and, like the heroic Vietnamese people, will fight on unflinching, resolutely and stubbornly until final victory'.[100] The Chinese believed that 'Southern Yemen won its independence because its people persevered in prolonged armed struggle and dealt the British imperialists very severe blows,' but warned: 'The US imperialists and Soviet modern revisionists too will try to get a foothold there'. Consequently China established diplomatic relations with the new republic in January 1968. However, within four years, rivalry with the Soviet Union meant it severed its relationship with the Yemenis.

For Oman, the situation was similar. China had supported the revolt against the British and Sultanate forces in 1957 and it approved of the Marxist leadership of PFLOAG in 1968, but by 1972 it had terminated its support entirely as its policy towards the Middle East underwent a dramatic transformation. When the insurgency had developed in 1969–70, annual delegations of New China News Agency correspondents visited Dhofar, and a PFLOAG party was warmly received in China by Zhou Enlai and the Army Chief of Staff, Yung-sheng.[101] Regular reports on the progress of the insurgency continued until 1972.[102] Then, suddenly, it was Iran that was praised for its intervention in preventing Soviet expansion in the Gulf. Soviet 'social-imperialism' was considered a greater danger to China, and so all movements associated with Moscow, including PFLOAG, were simply ignored.[103] By 1976, China was in talks with the Sultan of Oman himself. By 1973, the combined effects of the termination of China's support, the defeat of Egypt in its war with Israel, and more pressing domestic concerns for Yemen meant the momentum of revolutionary war in southern Arabia began to ebb away. The tide had turned in favour of the Sultan of Oman.

Trevelyan, the last High Commissioner of Aden, had concluded: 'We could not ignore Arab nationalism. It was strongly backed by the Afro-Asian world, which regarded itself as the anti-colonial front, by the communists intent on winning Arab friendship, and, up to a point, by the Americans, mainly for historical and sentimental reasons.'[104] Despite the error of many of his strategic assessments, he had recognised the sheer importance of Arab nationalist and socialist forces. What he seemed less clear about was the ways and means of tackling the challenge strategically.

The far more experienced Sir William Luce had also made it clear that the threat to Britain's interests in Arabia were 'subversion and revolution from Arab nationalist and left-wing elements against the remaining traditional regimes, and their encouragement and exploitation by Russia and possibly by China.' Yet Luce had a clear sense of the practical response to such a threat rather than the counsel of despair. He advocated that, despite the withdrawal scheduled for 1971, Britain ought to act positively to support its regional allies and partners.[105] Luce had argued: 'Although stopping short of full military support, continued assistance in training of local forces, in particular through the continuing secondment of British forces personnel, should be provided.' Luce urged naval visits to reassure and contingency plans to support emergency treaties in times of crisis. From the practical point of view, the British Army in Aden had failed to suppress nationalist and communist movements by resorting only to force or the blunt robustness of 'military aid to the civil power'. A far better response had materialised with the SAS in Dhofar, whose campaign of using local supporters, training programmes for the SAF, and courageous and clandestine operations against the bases of the revolutionaries proved crucial, but which benefited from two important changes within the revolutionary environment: specifically, the decline of external support, and the reconciliation of the tribes of the interior with the Sultanate of Muscat. The British had managed to combine successfully a policy of providing security and much-needed political and economic reform; this was driven home through a consistent message of supporting traditional social relations and Islam against alien and secular Marxism. Material improvement proved a better offer than protracted armed struggle for its own sake.

In their operations, the alignment of British forces and the Omani government with the conservative, Islamic sentiments of the SAF and local people, represented through the Firqat, proved a stronger partnership. Ultimately, the Firqat was more than a security force: it was the means to enable the people of the interior to have a stake in the existing political system, and it compelled a commitment to the Omani regime.

In the post-1971 diplomatic environment, after the withdrawal 'east of Suez', the British emphasised that their relationship with the Sultanate of Oman was a partnership, not colonial control. Oman remained a staunch ally of Britain from the moment it first offered assistance against the Dhofar insurgency. By contrast, in Aden, uncoordinated interventions, like the Colonial Office development programme, merely alienated and undermined the very elites Britain sought to promote.

In summary, the British had failed to implement an effective strategy in Aden and could find no answer to the revolutionary momentum of the nationalist resistance groups, beyond military force. In Oman, the British aligned their interests and methods more effectively to the local elite and also to the sentiments of a conservative population. Here their strategy was more effective, but it was also fortunate that they benefited from a changed situation for revolutionary movements across the region. In the Federation and in Aden, Britain's partners had been abandoned. In Oman, they were supported consistently.

The two cases illustrate vividly the importance and the malleability of legitimacy and the role of local military forces in them. In southern Arabia, legitimacy was imagined, created, internalised and changed, and local military personnel legitimised the rule of colonial authorities, offered the means to preserve the power of favoured elites, and at the same time empowered and legitimised nationalist resistance. The NLF and PFLOAG sought to recruit military personnel in order to mobilise the population and discipline them along ideological lines. Local forces were recruited by the British in Oman for equally instrumentalist reasons, specifically to augment its security forces, but also to justify its conception of acceptable local governance and to fulfil its approach to transition and exit. The Firqat provided a security screen and an air of legitimacy in the interior, where the government's writ was weak; while the SAF was a regular force, representing and enforcing the Sultan's monopoly of power.

The two cases also raise the question of faithfulness and betrayal, specifically who betrayed whom. The orthodox discourse for Aden emphasises British perfidy towards the sheikhs rather than NLF's betrayal of its former leftist allies, the FLOSY, or the transfer of SAA loyalty to the NLF, its former enemies. In the case of Oman, British writers have tended to focus on the winning of the Dhofaris' 'hearts and minds' to a new Sultan, rather than either PFLOAG's betrayal of traditional Dhofari aspirations, or the Marxist view that the sultans turned to the imperialists for assistance against a legitimate, representative movement for political change in Oman. On the other hand, Dhofaris appeared to work in their own self-interest in three ways: one, resisting the Sultan's exploitative policies of the 1960s; two, fighting to maintain their traditional way of life; and, three, embracing the development and military employment opportunities that arose after 1970. As such, we are drawn to the conclusion that, ultimately, the dynamic interaction of metropolitan and competing local agencies, not least over the fate of local military forces, generated the situations that arose in these countries.

Mentoring Montagnards in Vietnam

In countering insurgency, local forces can augment the numbers of armed men available to the government for military tasks but also, from a political point of view, compel a population to make a choice between the legitimate administration or the illegal forces of the revolution. Local forces assist in the collection of intelligence and often its interpretation, they possess the language and cultural skills necessary to communicate the government's ideas to the public and can offset the otherwise antagonistic presence of any foreign interventionist force. They can check the freedom of movement of insurgent groups, break the links between the people and the insurgency, encourage defection from insurgent ranks, and give all groups, including participating minorities, a stake in society.

After the experience of the Korean War (1951–3), the United States believed that to prevent a similar communist invasion of the Republic of South Vietnam, it would need to rapidly expand its regular army, complete with its own enlarged artillery, armoured and infantry divisions, and modern signals and logistics capabilities, as well as a supporting navy and air force. Much work had already been done by the French colonial authorities, but after the defeat of France in 1954, the South Vietnamese forces were in need of reorganisation. In agreeing to provide assistance for South Vietnam, the number of advisers flown into the country by the United States increased dramatically. The result was the reinvigoration of the Army of the Republic of Vietnam (ARVN).

It became clear very quickly that the primary activity of the ARVN was countering the guerrilla forces in the country that were being aided covertly by North Vietnam and its allies. The Vietnamese government drew criticism for using the opportunity of the developing insurgency to attack minority groups, such as the Cao Dai and Hoa Hao. Severe corruption in government and a lack of progress in the conflict caused the *coup d'état* of General Duong Van Minh in 1963, the first of several military interventions in South Vietnam's politics. The military takeover did little to stem the abuses of power or corruption that occurred. However, until the United States committed itself fully to the conflict, the ARVN bore the brunt of the fighting. While there were significant setbacks, during the war the army suffered losses of 254,256 killed, with 40,000 in just one year. Over a million men had become casualties by 1974. Many of the losses resulted from large-scale 'pacification' sweeps of the countryside. These operations were unpopular, morale was invariably low, and many men deserted. Senior ARVN officers were also implicated in drug-trafficking for personal profit, further damaging their authority. On the other hand, some ARVN units fought to the bitter end in 1974–5. The 18th Infantry Division held up the entire North Vietnamese Army advance to Saigon for two weeks without support.

The ARVN could provide rural security for short periods but lacked the numbers to hold every settlement or 'full-time sustained protection at the key village/hamlet level'.[106] The ARVN were also not suitable to defend a location where they were fixed and lost their advantages in mobility. The preference was for local men to be armed to defend their own homes or a paramilitary constabulary. Robert Thompson wrote in 1966: 'So often one heard from good province chiefs in Vietnam … that they would prefer to have two or three extra Civil Guard companies rather than an army battalion [to hold villages].'[107] Holding a settlement, as the British had found in Malaya, was critical to deprive the insurgents of resources from the people and kept the insurgent 'fish' permanently separated from the 'water' of the population. The Americans also recognised that clusters of villages had an importance way beyond their humble appearances, and nicknamed them 'strategic hamlets'.[108]

The insurgents would not expect poorly educated peasants to comprehend the finer points of Marxist–Maoist doctrine, and intimidation was more frequently the means by which the people decided on their allegiance. Promises of assistance might help. The arrival of armed foreigners or a heavy-handed ARVN unit might confirm their alignment. On the other hand, a villager who believed that the ARVN would stay and protect them, and therefore terminate the prospect of being visited by insurgents, was enough to ensure the population would support the government.

Before 1963, Ngo Dinh Diem had raised a Self-Defence Corps, which the Americans equipped.[109] Its successor, the Popular Force, was augmented by the Combined Action Program (CAP) run by the United States Marine Corps between 1965 and 1971, which involved mixed platoons of Marines and Vietnamese villagers. The effectiveness of such groups was variable. CAP platoons were efficient. The Marines committed a mere 4 per cent of its manpower to these formations, but they inflicted up to 33 per cent of the Vietcong's losses during the war each year.[110] Nevertheless, many home guard formations were poorly armed and untrained, and were vulnerable to insurgent attacks, which would swarm to overwhelm the small local defence force.

Regional and Popular Forces (RFs and PFs) were supposed to overlap to cover local area defence.[111] Made up of locally -recruited men, many were volunteers hoping to avoid the ARVN's draft.[112] Their appeal was in their relative cost: they were far cheaper than ARVN units. Village defence cost only 2–4 per cent of the total annual bill of the war.[113] They also released regular forces to conduct operations elsewhere.[114] But the quality varied throughout the conflict and by area. Initially, they were generally:

> poorly trained and equipped, miserably led, and incapable of coping with insurgents; they could scarcely defend themselves, much less the peasantry. Indeed, they proved to be an asset to the insurgents in two respects: they served as a source of weapons; and their brutality, petty thievery, and disorderliness induced innumerable villagers to join in open revolt against the [Government of Vietnam].[115]

The fault lay with the ARVN corps and division commanders, who did not think that local security was worthwhile. Instead, they made use of local auxiliaries in their larger-scale clearance operations.[116] After 1965, the RFs and PFs were placed under the command of locals whose survival depended on being able to keep the insurgents out.[117] The Marines' Combined Action Platoon (CAP) programme therefore bolstered the system at a critical time.[118] The Marines acted like Special Forces in training and commanding the RFs and PFs. Finally, the 1968 Civil Operations and Rural Development Support (CORDS) programme, put the people at the heart of the counter-insurgency campaign, and increased government control throughout Vietnam. It also led to a huge expansion in numbers participating on the government's side: the number of auxiliaries increased from approximately 300,000 in 1967 to 532,000 in 1971.[119]

The CIA established the Civilian Irregular Defense Groups (CIDG) in 1961, aiming to bolster the paramilitary presence among minority groups that were vulnerable to insurgent infiltration.[120] The training teams for the programme were drawn from the American 5th Special Forces Group, the Green Berets, and they focused their effort on area development centres.[121] The villagers were trained for two weeks, but special strike teams, capable of rapid reaction to Vietcong units, known as Mobile Strike Forces or 'Mike Groups', were also established. Their power lay in their mobility and therefore their ability to mass quickly.[122] Their status as minorities, with a long-standing dislike of the Vietnamese, also gave them a strong motivation. The groups were popular and the programme expanded. It certainly conformed to the observation made by Robert Thompson that 'the sole reason for the establishment of Special Forces [is] to make contact with tribes [in marginal areas] and recruit and organise into units for their own defence on the side of the government'. The presence of advisers and the guidance of the Special Operational Forces also heeded Thompson's warning: 'the establishment in the [densely] populated areas of similar groups is not desirable because such units tend to become independent private armies, owing allegiance less to the government than to some territorial local figure, and as a result bearing little responsibility for their actions'.[123]

In the central highlands, the Montagnards, divided into 29 separate tribal groupings, were regarded with contempt by the Vietnamese, who referred to them as *moi* (savages). The North Vietnamese were particularly disliked because it was their policies that had driven many ethnic Vietnamese south into Montagnard lands. The government of Saigon sanctioned the land seizures which only served to reinforce the tribesmen's dislike of the southerners too. These matriarchal groups, which lived in family groups, responded positively to the offer to assist them against outsiders, but the South Vietnamese authorities and the insurgents pursued their own agendas, trying to recruit individuals who would bring entire tribal groups over to their respective sides. The situation mirrored the formation of militias elsewhere including two Vietnamese syncretistic religious sects, the Cao Dai and Hoa Hao, as well as the Binh Xuyen organised-crime syndicate, a group that had been enlisted by the French to fight the Vietminh during the late 1940s.[124]

By August 1962, more than 200 villages were in the CIDG or 'Buon Enao' scheme, which gave the government control of most of the central highlands. Once established, responsibility was handed over to the chief of Darlac province. However, in September 1964, the Montagnards in five of the CIDG bases revolted against the South Vietnamese, ostensibly to assert old rights, but inspired by communist subversion through a pseudo-group and aided by French intelligence, who were eager to assert their influence in a proposed neutral zone between the communist north and the pro-American south. The revolt petered out and the US Special Operational Forces were ordered to extend their role from defence to offensive operations. General William Westmoreland ordered that the irregulars should adopt the mission of 'becoming hunters and finding and destroying the enemy'.[125] This demand and the Montagnards' expertise in gathering intelligence meant that they were soon tasked to act as mobile strike forces, and in May 1966 they were given helicopter transport to increase their mobility. The number of combat platoons increased from 34 to 73 by the end of the year. Nevertheless, there was mounting pressure to regularise these fighting units and enrol them into the ARVN command structure. The LLDB, the South Vietnamese Special Operational Forces, were earmarked to take over from the American advisers, and the transfer took place in mid-1967. The idea was to eventually phase out all Americans by 1971, and then to extend the offensive missions of the Montagnards, but the Tet Offensive, the surprise nationwide assault by the North Vietnamese and Vietcong insurgents, caused the plans to be postponed and then abandoned.

Adviser: Captain Barry Petersen

Captain Barry Petersen was a member of the Australian Army Training Team who, in less than two years, built up a formidable Montagnard force of over a thousand troops, complete with a secure command and administrative structure. The Montagnards succeeded in denying to the Vietcong control of much of the high plateau in the central highlands of Vietnam, which, in turn, guarded the northern approaches to Saigon. Captain Petersen was assisted by just two Australian warrant officers and he was funded by the CIA. In late 1963, Petersen and his team made familiarisation visits to villages in the Montagnard area, making every effort to learn the local languages. Petersen could already speak Malay, which greatly assisted the process of learning the local dialects. He described the locals as 'a strongly built people, with broader shoulders than the Vietnamese and darker skin. They are quick to learn, loyal, as a rule very cheerful, but not afraid to fight courageously.'[126]

There had been a history of antagonism between the Montagnards and the Vietnamese. As recently as 1958, Montagnard demonstrators had been dispersed by force by the Vietnamese Army's 21st Division. Several leaders had been arrested. The willingness to develop their own forces and autonomous political system was therefore strong. Once Petersen had recruited his first 100 men, he realised he was in a politically precarious position as a foreigner in command of a minority group, faced on the one hand by communist insurgents, but equally under threat from the Vietnamese authorities themselves.[127] Petersen's solution was to approach the provincial governor and ask him to become the 'commander-in-chief of the armed propaganda and intelligence teams', in other words, to give him a stake in the force that was being created and make him feel that he was part of its command structure. The province chief already controlled his own Regional Force (RF) unit but was also responsible for the Popular Forces among the villages of the highlands in his area. This left the provincial chief overburdened and extremely busy, but that aided the devolution of command and therefore benefited the freedom of action of the Montagnard forces.

At the beginning, Petersen concentrated on basic training in weapon handling and minor tactics so that his force could handle any skirmish with the

Vietcong. At this stage, 'their basic role was to operate as armed teams throughout the province, disseminating propaganda and collecting intelligence'.[128] However, very quickly, instructions arrived for the force to be expanded to 350, and then upwards still further. The objective was to prevent the North Vietnamese using the trails that ran through the highlands into the south for the infiltration of men, equipment and weapons. The expansion prompted Petersen to consider a regular command, training and logistics structure, and a dedicated training cadre that could handle the new recruits. As a captain, Petersen had not anticipated that he would effectively be in command of a battalion-sized group. To manage the size of the new force, Petersen divided the Montagnards into eight-man teams. Each team was equipped with a light machine gun and two automatic sub-machine guns, while the rest were armed with rifles, a handful of sniper rifles or shotguns. He was careful to train one radio operator and one medical orderly to accompany the teams. Each group was organised according to the geographical location of the villages of the members. Where a group would otherwise be too small, villages were clustered for administrative purposes and teams made up as a composite force. His fighters did not stay overnight in a village but set night ambushes on tracks approaching one or other of villages in their area of responsibility. To avoid becoming a Vietcong target, they would be told not to remain in the same location in two consecutive nights.[129]

Although used principally as reaction forces to defend villages, before long these teams, which became adept at locating insurgent groups, were ordered to more offensive. Petersen noted that the American preference for hundred-man groups made them more vulnerable to ambush, and he preferred to retain the eight-man units, which were more stealthy. He also noted that the insurgents would try to draw large reaction forces into prepared ambushes by making a deliberate attack on a nearby village. Anticipating that the strike force would use the shortest route to relieve a village, the Vietcong could predict which roads would be used and mine them, or, more frequently, they would use the established tactic of attacking the lead and rear vehicles before destroying the rest of the column in a more deliberate fashion. Petersen believed: 'My aim was to keep the Truong Son force a group of small, mobile, hard-hitting and elusive elements which could play the Vietcong at their own game.'[130]

In 1964, some 3,000 Montagnards were involved in a revolt against the South Vietnamese authorities, inflicting a number of casualties, including Americans, although most of the Special Operational Forces personnel caught up in the unrest were taken hostage. The rebels demanded autonomous government, their own flag, their own language in schools and administration, and, crucially, their own officers and NCOs in command of Montagnard troops. Petersen observed that not every American officer worked to restore relations between the Montagnards and the South Vietnamese, which would have been crucial to the war effort. He suspected that some individuals were determined to make their own name by appearing to play a leading role in negotiations, rather than letting the Vietnamese do it, or that they wished to appear 'strong' against one side or the other.[131] A number of Montagnard rebels left the highlands and moved across the indistinct border into Cambodia, where they proclaimed their allegiance to a new autonomy movement, the Front for the Liberation of the Oppressed Races (FULRO). Later it was revealed that the movement was not truly nationalist, but was orchestrated by the Chams (a marginal group in the highlands and mainly located in Cambodia), where it was influenced and largely controlled by the communists.[132] The Communists also appointed local men to try to take control of the Montagnard forces from within. Their tactics included making inflammatory speeches that were anti-Vietnamese among the troops and villagers, but they were weeded out.[133] Petersen also firmly believed that the French secret intelligence service had fostered the revolt.[134] Later, members of the FULRO movement were betrayed by the Khmer Rouge in Cambodia, and, despite appeals to their French sponsors for protection, they were abandoned. Most were murdered. One survivor explained that they had been taken en masse to a soccer field on the northern outskirts of Phnom Penh and made to run backwards and forwards from goalpost to goalpost while the Khmer Rouge shot them down.[135]

In light of the revolt, some American Special Forces bases were closed down, especially when desertions by the Montagnards began to increase. Many of these made their way to the FULRO movement across the border. By contrast, Petersen's own force remained intact and grew in strength. Part of the explanation lies in the clan divisions of Montagnard society. The Americans had recruited their men from the heart of Darlac province and the majority were Rhade and Jarai. A substantial portion of Petersen's men were the M'nong. The cohesion of his own force was also due to its greater military success, its strong sense of identity as Tiger Men, and his leadership style, which emphasised the importance of each individual and encouraged initiative and self-reliance. After his service, Petersen reflected that the advisory mission had been far more likely to succeed than the combat operations that were implemented in Vietnam. The deployment of regular troops was, in his view 'unsuitable to eradicate the communist insurgents'.[136] He believed: 'had we increased our advisory effort rather than committing troops to the field, although it would have placed a strain on our respective regular volunteer armies, it might have attracted less adverse public criticism at home'.[137] However, like most military officers he also took the view that firm commitments had to be honoured: 'I believe it is naive to say that the occupation of another sovereign nation is not our concern. If every nation adopted that attitude, then we might all eventually come under the domination of a more aggressive and powerful nation. If a stand is taken, then it should be maintained at all costs.'[138] After the communist victory in 1975, many of the Montagnards were held as political detainees in 're-education camps', but thousands were killed.

The Harkis of Algeria

General Challe, the newly appointed commander of the French forces in Algeria in 1958, announced that he intended to make greater use of indigenous Algerians to prosecute what was an increasingly unpopular war in France. He stated: 'The best Fellagha hunter is the Frenchman of North African descent'.[139] During the conflict, approximately 20 per cent of Algerian men were conscripted, totalling 100,000.[140] A large number of draftees were rejected on medical grounds, and there was further selection when the French authorities feared betrayals, but conscription was an efficient way of ensuring that large segments of the population were effectively committed to the government. The chief problem was that the families of the men serving were more vulnerable and the FLN, the Algerian nationalist movement, specifically targeted them, hoping to either persuade or intimidate them sufficiently so that the men would desert or defect.

Alongside the conscripts there were also the volunteers. Attracted by the salaries on offer, these part time auxiliaries, known as the Harkis, were hired on a daily basis and disbanded just as readily.[141] The spirit of improvisation had come with the establishment of the rural auxiliary police, the GMPR, at the outbreak of the conflict. The army soon followed with their own version. Raised for patrols in sparsely populated terrain, the men were selected for their local knowledge and their connections with the populations rather than their skills in combat. The hiring system was a method to spread influence and to create the impression that the *goumier* and his family were on the government's side. The Harkis were separate from the GAD, the self-defence groups whose role was to guard their own villages. Most of the men were under the command of local leaders, although periodically they could be brought under direct military command. The system was legalised retrospectively in 1956.[142]

The system worked well enough for it to be expanded after 1957. Initially there were 2,000 Harkis, but by 1960 their numbers had risen to 60,000.[143] Their purpose was also developed into a more formalised role of psychological warfare and counter-insurgency. The assumption was that native men were the best suited to fight against guerrilla fighters.[144] Armed with hunting weapons, which were issued at the start of their employment and withdrawn as soon as a mission was completed, they were asked only to operate in areas they already knew well. The French authorities went to considerable lengths to convey the idea that the Harkis were the inheritors of the ethos of the resistance that had defied the Nazis. Challe encouraged a spirit 'of the maquisards and not one of collaborators'.[145] He even claimed: 'If we build heroes of the Resistance, the population will be on our side.'[146] A handful embraced the concept, but the majority were motivated more by money and opportunity.[147] Among those prepared to endorse the French concept, to the extent that he gave public speeches to his countrymen on the value of service to the government, was Bachaga Boualam. A member of the National Assembly, Boualam was the leader of his own harka and, after the ceasefire, but prior to independence, he led his own more extensive maquis group, funded and supported by the OAS, the French terror group that had developed within a segment of the French Army.[148]

General Challe believed the Harkis were important not only in providing a pro-French presence in the peripheries, but in absorbing men who might otherwise join the FLN and its military wing, the ALN. Yet, even in the eastern areas, such as the Constantinois, where the Harki concentrations were strongest, they did not constitute more than a third of French forces. The Plan Challe involved sweeping the countryside in a process of *ratissage*, but French forces also retained small mobile teams to carry out specific operations, and these too involved the Harkis.

The most dedicated members of the Harkis were those who had abandoned the ALN. These groups operated like the insurgents, and they knew their personnel, their methods and their locations. The motivation was singular: either they had to destroy their former comrades or they and their families would be executed by the ALN. Once screened and interrogated by teams of Military Intelligence, the turned insurgents would be entrusted to form their own harka, using their native language and knowledge of the enemy to great effect. Treachery remained a risk. In 1956, the French believed that they had raised an effective indigenous unit in the Kabyle mountains known as Force K. In fact, Force K was heavily infiltrated by the FLN and subsequently defected after killing several loyalist Algerians.[149] The Harkis sometimes provided vital information for other units to exploit, but their role was widely understood to consist of three elements, 'combat, hunting, intelligence'.[150] For much of the time, however, the French could not entirely trust the information the Harkis provided. The fear of double agents was strong.

The French authorities believed that native Algerians would be more ruthless in the pursuit and killing of the ALN. General de Pouilly, who commanded the western sector, admitted that one harka, Commando George, was 'sometimes a little too vigorous' as it was 'unfortunately adapted to the lore of their co-religionists whom they knew more than anybody else'.[151] It was guilty of the most extreme violence and three-quarters of the force were former insurgents.[152] Officers believed that the Harkis should not be restricted in any way when attacking the ALN.[153] One officer chillingly noted in his diary the *modus operandi* of the force: 'No gunshots: [just the] blade. All former fellagha [and] killers. For sure, I know that whatever they did in the past, it's better to have them with us today, but I don't care, their presence is frightening. Tonight will be atrocious for many: the questioning, the electric generator [for torture], the settling of scores ... robberies, rape, looting ... deaths, just deaths ... [including the] innocent ones.'[154]

There were some well-publicised successes where Harkis assisted in turning other insurgents, but there were also episodes where volunteer Harkis defected to the ALN and took their weapons with them. The ALN also attempted to make use of the Harkis still in French service. They made contact, via their families, putting them under pressure where necessary, and encouraged them to smuggle weapons, provide information or even open the gates of bases to facilitate more daring raids.

Towards the end of the conflict, when it was likely that Algeria would win its independence, there was a hasty and chaotic attempt to establish who would be brought to France. Evidently, the Algerians of European descent were favoured, but only very late was there any consideration of the Harkis. The Harkis were not issued with a formal contract of employment until 1961. Once it became clear there was to be a ceasefire, many of the Harkis began to desert.[155] To stem the flow, the French authorities issued six-month contracts during the transitional period.[156] At the same time there were efforts designed to deter the Harkis from applying to move to France. As a result, about 80 per cent simply left the service. However, as it became clear that independence was imminent and the FLN would take over, anxiety gripped the Harkis and their families. Thousands appealed to their former officers and pleaded for passage to France. Although forbidden, many officers took the risk and paid, from their own funds, for the Harkis to escape retribution.[157] Some 12,000 Harkis and their relatives reached France in 1962.

Those that did not get out of the country were soon subjected to considerable intimidation. Many were forced to give their pensions to the new state. Others were publicly humiliated and ostracised. Some were tortured. Although there are no reliable statistics, most analysts agree that the figure for the numbers killed by the nationalists is somewhere between 10,000 and 30,000. An estimated 80,000 eventually managed to reach France. Confined to camps, the new arrivals did not receive an especially warm welcome. This was a war that had divided French society and which had ended in defeat and humiliation. France wanted to forget. The situation began to change in the 1990s. In 1994, France recognised that a moral debt existed towards the Harkis. In 2001, a Memorial Day was instituted for the force, and a year later Harkis were included in the national war memorial in Paris. In Algeria, the term Harkis became a term of abuse, a shorthand for 'traitor'. Veterans who fled to France are forbidden to return to the homeland and Algerian law denies former Harkis the rights of citizens. Half a century later, the consequences of the use of local labour continues to haunt both countries.

Local Forces at the End of Occupation

The value of local forces, including irregulars, during a counter-insurgency is that their presence is a visible and often powerful indication of the authority of the government, but also an indication that an element of the population has chosen to side with the government. The fact that they often share the same language and culture as the population is a distinct advantage, but they can also act as a route through which insurgents can be encouraged to change sides. Crucially they compel a section of the population to commit themselves to one side or another.

These advantages were denied to South Vietnam in the 1960s because of the corrosive effect of the corruption in government and the instability that followed in a series of *coups d'état* orchestrated by the military. The ARVN senior officers were often implicated in corruption too, which undermined the confidence and competence of the army. The verdict of Robert Thompson, the veteran and author of the Malayan counter-insurgency campaign, was that the population often received better protection from the local auxiliary forces rather than from the cumbersome and less sympathetic or committed regular troops. Self-Defence Corps, the Regional Forces and Popular Forces, and other home guard initiatives, enjoyed some success if they were used in remote areas and peripheries and operated close to their homes, but the attempt to form larger formations for strike operations, the Mike Groups, appeared to founder. The conclusion from the Vietnam War was that local irregular forces should be recruited and used in the area in which they live and with which they are familiar.[158] They had to be recruited, trained and advised by a carefully selected specialist cadre. They could not be used in isolation, but as part of a joint plan of other activities and institutions, with regular military support on hand, the backing of the established law enforcement, the direction of the local government, and the licence to operate from their national government. They needed to be kept in relatively small formations, since large groupings can become militias led by individuals who will assume far too much power, which, in turn, will invariably lead to abuses. They will necessarily be lightly armed, preferably mobile, and conscious of the limits imposed upon their operations. Nevertheless, rewards and benefits always need to be specified and honoured.

The advisory role was a difficult one, and Captain Petersen was clearly an exceptional, resourceful and courageous individual who thrived on the responsibility he was given. Petersen was tasked with raising a large number of personnel in a short period, but he instinctively knew that the most effective forces would be small and would benefit from being created in cadres. The greatest threats to these small home guard units were the ability of the insurgents to mass locally a larger number in order to overwhelm them, or to infiltrate their members and try to erode their allegiances. Petersen countered these with a better early warning system, where villages warned each other and worked together to concentrate their forces if necessary, and by confronting the subversives through a thorough knowledge of the personnel in the force and keeping informed of their concerns and agendas. Identity was also important, and Petersen went to great lengths to ensure that clans remained separate and their sense of place and of pride and individual character were fostered.

In Algeria, there was a long tradition of local men serving in French forces, and the sense of combined identity was strong, not least because of Algeria's status as an integral department of France. From the outset, there was a casual hiring of Harkis and GAD for patrols, guard duty, reconnaissance or ground-holding garrisons, and there was evident value in their ability to gather intelligence, create a picture of local allegiances and promote the government. The pay was generous and, while the Harki units were not the most effective combat forces, they did not need to be: their strategic function was to show the people that the government was in control, had the support of the people and had a physical presence at the tactical level. The Harkis were also a useful way of absorbing manpower that might otherwise support the other side. Nevertheless, the families of the Harkis were vulnerable, and this only increased as the conflict reached its bitter conclusion. The fighting was also characterised by a low-level 'dirty war', in which Harkis, consisting of turned insurgents, waged a murderous struggle with their former comrades. Betrayals became more frequent, and the insurgents established their own forms of pseudo-gangs to access and defeat pro-French forces. Intelligence, counter-intelligence and deception produced a febrile atmosphere, destroyed trust and atomised Algerian society. It was for this reason that, when the war staggered to its conclusion, there was fear of Algerians coming to France, despite their loyalty. The results were a rather shameful mistreatment of those that had served and their families.

During decolonisation, local forces provided the means to assist in the defeat of insurgency. They could compel choice among the population and therefore isolate the insurgents from the people. They could provide the means to enable a colonial power to withdraw and therefore hasten the handover of power. They provided crucial intelligence, could hunt down insurgent groups and threaten their greatest point of vulnerability: their security. But weak local forces could be overwhelmed. They could generate more violence and deepen a civil war. They could encourage retribution and tit-for-tat killings. Moreover, local forces always had their own agency. They could cease to co-operate, as in Aden in 1967, but even the threat of that withdrawal of labour, when combined with weakening political will, mounting losses and a sense of exhaustion, could be enough to induce withdrawal, as in the case of India.

Local military forces, especially the use of militia, represent the boundary or the limit of government power and authority. It is striking that, when confronted by armed resistance, governments sought to turn some of the insurgents or the population to support the government by greater involvement of the population in security and government service. Counter-insurgency is, in part, a struggle for control of the population, its allegiance and its commitment. The government compels choice by a variety of means, and that includes the establishment of local forces, home guards and auxiliary police. The role of trained regulars was to concentrate on pursuing and engaging insurgents, although the proper role for Special Forces, at least in their original tasking, was to work with local forces, particularly training and supporting militias and home guards.

There was considerable controversy over the relative value and ethical limits of counter-gangs, not least because of concerns that adopting clandestine tactics might encourage illegal killings or internments. The activities of Special Night Squads and Q Patrols have attracted criticism ever since. Moreover, the use of such gangs is thought to encourage revenge from insurgents, fuelling violence and disorder. Pseudo-gangs attract similar controversy, in that they depend on deception and could be responsible for illegal killings, but their supporters argued their role was to gain access or make a reconnaissance for regular forces or police to follow up.

The employment of local personnel in security forces during insurgencies and civil wars cannot guarantee allegiance. The potential loss of support from the local armed forces was instrumental in terminating British rule in India and set its timing, despite the excellent work carried out by the diligent and outnumbered Punjab Boundary Force. In Aden, a mutiny also did much to break the confidence of the British government in retaining the colony, and the failure of its federation plan accelerated the withdrawal. Local military forces were effectively handed over to the insurgents and political agitators, especially when it was clear the police had been thoroughly infiltrated. By contrast, the British expanded, developed and enhanced the Omani forces, and committed themselves to a programme of turning insurgents and employing local irregulars to track and defeat the rebels of Dhofar and their confederates across the border in Yemen. It was a scheme that not only achieved some success, reinforced by the arrival of forces from neighbouring states, but also created an enduring link between Britain and Oman through the respective military forces of the two countries.

12

BUILDING THE AFGHAN
AND IRAQI SECURITY FORCES, 2003–2014

The terrorist attacks on the United States on 11 September 2001, which killed thousands of civilians, prompted a more vigorous American counter-terrorism strategy. This involved, as a first priority, the death or capture of the principal architect of the attacks, Osama bin Laden, who had been given a secure base from which to operate by his allies the Taliban of Afghanistan. The American-led coalition of powers that struck against the Taliban and the al-Qaeda terrorist front took control of Afghanistan in a matter of days. The air onslaught was overwhelming, and the first Western ground contingents were able to find partners in the anti-Taliban armed groups known collectively as the 'Northern Alliance'. Al-Qaeda were driven reeling into the comparative safety of the mountainous border with Pakistan, and most of the Taliban collapsed. The Americans were nevertheless eager not to repeat the mistakes of the Soviets and become enmeshed in a protracted and contested nation-building project with the Afghans. They intended to maintain a light footprint, made up largely of Special Forces and CIA operatives, concerned with the hunting down of al-Qaeda. The future of Afghanistan was placed firmly in the hands of the United Nations.

Within a year, the administration of George W. Bush examined the conditions that had given rise to the violent actors like Al-Qaeda and concluded that rogue anti-Western regimes, such as Libya, Iran and Iraq, posed an even more pressing threat. If a relatively small organisation like Al-Qaeda could inflict mass casualty terrorism on the people of the United States, it was reasoned, just imagine what regimes armed with greater arsenals, including weapons of mass destruction (WMD) could do. Saddam Hussein had defied the United Nations for over a decade, despite his defeat in the First Gulf War (1990–1), and there was considerable alarm that his refusal to co-operate with weapons inspectors, his periodic defiance of no-fly zones imposed to protect the Kurdish and Shia populations of Iraq, and the secretive nature of his regime, not to mention his record of invading two sovereign nations and use of chemical weapons against civilians, made Iraq the next priority. When Iraq refused to comply with a new UN resolution and appeared to be attempting to conceal a WMD programme, the decision was taken to remove Saddam by force and to democratise the country. Intelligence assessments, while vague, confirmed the fact that Saddam was despised and feared by neighbouring Arab states and many of his own people. In the atmosphere of '9/11', the Bush administration and its closest coalition partners grew more determined to root out illiberal regimes and conclude the conflicts of the Middle East for good. In 2003, the invasion was an overwhelming success. Once again, within days, resistance had been smashed and the regime of Saddam Hussein brought to an abrupt end.

The immediate difficulty was how to expunge all the Saddam loyalists, the Ba'athists, from the civil administration and the security forces and, at the same time, reconstruct the country after a decade of sanctions and a short but destructive conflict. The priority was given to eradicating the former members of the regime from government and the disbandment of Saddam's army in May 2003, in the belief that a new democratically elected Iraqi authority would quickly rebuild the nation. This turned out to be the single most important error of the entire period of occupation.[1] It flooded the country with unemployed soldiers and police, men trained in handling weapons, angry at their sudden loss of employment and humiliated by the cavalier act of foreign interference. Sunni tribal elders, who had relied on the licence given them by Saddam to run their own affairs and skim off their own profits from corrupt practices, were afraid that the Shia and the Kurds would seek to use the Americans against them. Reaching a compromise over the form and composition of the government took two years. Meanwhile, essential services were in disarray. Anger and anxiety surfaced in the form of an insurgency, fuelled by sectarian fighting, inter-ethnic antagonism and economic hardship. This conflict ecosystem demanded a massive increase in security manpower, and it was then that it dawned on the American administration that they now needed the very army they had just disbanded.

The Iraqi Army of 1990 had been the largest and arguably the most com-bat-seasoned in the Middle East. It had fought a ten-year-long war against Iran along its entire eastern frontier. After a brief early incursion into south-western Iran, it spent most of the war on the defensive. It made extensive use of chemi-cal warfare, and developed a preference for overwhelming firepower to deal with the massed infantry assault of Iranian forces. By 1989, as the war came to an end, it was making significant progress against Iran, leading one contempo-rary American analyst to conclude: 'What won [the war] for them was their superior fighting prowess and greater commitment.'[2]

The Iraqi Army had been schooled in Soviet doctrine, with large-scale defence in depth or combined arms thrusts while on the offensive. The Soviet system had been to concentrate great volumes of artillery fire on specific objectives to destroy static defences and to pour troops along relatively unop-posed axes, the idea being to 'reinforce success'. Soviet doctrine also empha-sised that urban areas were to be neutralised with fire and bypassed where possible. Only very few knew how to conduct insurgency or counter-insur-gency after some experience against Kurdish irregulars in the 1970s; most were more familiar with conventional warfare. The disbandment in 2003 was therefore going to be a steep learning curve for those that took up arms against the new interim government and their American allies. For the Coalition, there was now the problem of how to raise an army from scratch, train it and lead it to success in the midst of a growing and lethal insurgency. In the early years, the Coalition struggled. It was compelled to escalate force by 'surging' more of their own troops in order to create a window of opportunity for the Iraqi security forces to be reconstructed.

It was widely believed, among Coalition troops, that not only did they have to recast their doctrine and tactics to a mode of counter-insurgency, but they had to accelerate the development of the Iraqi forces as their 'ticket home', or, put another way, the faster the Iraqi forces were created and could take over security responsibilities, the quicker would be the draw-down of the Western formations. Political imperatives also had a part to play. Terrorist bombings in Baghdad persuaded the UN to withdraw its personnel. The British govern-ment, anxious that its public were turning rapidly against intervention, espe-cially after a compelling if erroneous narrative from critics that this was 'an illegal war', decided unilaterally to pull its military forces out of its area of responsibility in southern Iraq. In theory it had handed over to the Iraqi secu-rity forces, especially the police, but at the time these were little more than Shiite militiamen controlled by the Jaish al-Mahdi movement.[3] Basra, the second largest city of Iraq and a vital economic hub, therefore fell into the hands of thugs and paramilitary groups from the Badr Corps, the Fodila and the Mahdi army, which, inadvertently, the British military authorities had themselves recruited into the police.[4]

In Afghanistan, the security situation was also getting worse. After the handover to the UN, the Bonn Conference of 2002 established an International Security and Assistance Force (ISAF) and called for the establishment of a provisional government. The new force and the new administration had limited influence in the country and were really confined to the area around Kabul. With the exception of the entirely separate US mission to hunt down Al-Qaeda, known as Operation Enduring Freedom, only Special Operational Forces existed in the hinterlands of Afghanistan. Most armed forces in the country were the tribal militias that had either fought the Taliban in the 1990s or were themselves remnants of the old Taliban and narcotics cartels. The temporary expedient of creating Afghan National Auxiliary Police out of these militias did not enhance security and merely legitimised these illegal armed actors. Worse, it confirmed to Afghans that the men in Kabul had no real power and were entirely dependent on foreigners for money and military support.

Corruption, factionalism and dependence on foreign aid weakened the legitimacy of the government and the security forces it raised in the first few years after the Western intervention. The Afghan National Police (ANP) were riddled with drug abuse, theft, arbitrary abuse of powers, and systematic extortion.[5] Some were guilty of collaboration with the Taliban. The Afghan National Army was dominated by Tajiks, Uzbeks and Hazaras from the north, but were deployed in the Pashtun east and south where its conduct was often excessive and inefficient. There were calls for a return to traditional tribal security forces, such as the *arbakai*.[6] Some American and European academics, such as the Network of Concerned Anthropologists, argued that the use of indigenous militias was a cover for repression by the state against the people of Afghanistan and, at best, would simply condemn the country to decades of civil war.[7]

No Afghan regular army or police had existed since 1992 when the country had collapsed into civil war. Militias had systematically stripped the country of resources, including schools, hospitals and power stations, and citizens developed a survivalist mentality, hoarding whatever resources they could acquire from foreign donors. The United States and its partners tried to work through a centralised government structure, encouraging the Afghan administration to use its responsibilities, but there was frustration with the slow pace of change, rising levels of violence and developing problems of corruption. In 2006, as the Taliban and confederate insurgent groups sought to regain control in the provinces, ISAF was authorised to extend the remit of the government of Afghanistan. While the Western forces provided the hard shell, the idea was to develop the Afghan security forces, and gradually use them to replace ISAF formations. Against a background of worsening insurgency, some thought was given to more local security forces. In Iraq, the Coalition had benefited from the emergence of an anti-al-Qaeda Sunni movement, known as the al-Anbar Awakening or Sons of Iraq programme. Local self-defence groups, eager to drive out the extremists, had co-operated with the Americans, who had themselves changed tactics and redeployed into smaller groups to protect the local population, bringing the new Iraqi security forces detachments with them. There was some hope that a 'surge' in Afghanistan and the fostering of local security might mirror Iraq, but the two cases were quite distinct.[8]

The value of raising large national security forces and police units was less spectacular than an 'awakening' of the people against the insurgents. It was instead the development of a sense of security, delayed by inevitable misunderstandings and setbacks, and beset with difficulties due to the levels of violence, that gradually reassured the population that the government was in control, and degraded the insurgents' support and freedom of action. These regular forces, together and alongside local auxiliaries, did eventually fulfil the doctrinal aspiration expressed in the American field manual on counter-insurgency: 'while home guards are not trained in offensive operations, their constant presence reminds the populace that the H[ost] N[ation] government can provide security. Effective home guards can free police and military forces from stationary guard duties.'[9] Once the population were secured, regular forces could afford to take the fight to their enemies. In Iraq, this was for a time achieved, but in Afghanistan, it proved more difficult because the insurgents were more firmly enmeshed with the population.

In 2014, as Western Coalition forces brought their combat missions to an end in Afghanistan, the Iraqi Army largely collapsed in the face of attack from the Jihadist movement known as Daesh. Elements of the army, exasperated by their own Shia-dominated government, even defected to the Jihadists, taking their armour, munitions and equipment with them. The relative successes and failures of the Western efforts to build local and national security forces are examined here.

The Afghan National Security Forces

The effort to raise, train, equip, field and advise local forces became critical to the success of the stabilisation operations in Iraq and Afghanistan. There were eventually over 350,000 Afghan security forces personnel and 625,000 Iraqi military and police, the result of years of dedicated perseverance, political will and generous funding, and all achieved while both nations were confronted with lethal insurgent operations, widespread intimidation of the civil population (including the families of the security forces), and the corrupt practices of many layers of immature and grasping governance.

In 2001, when the United States led the operation in Afghanistan, there were no plans to build a local security force. In November 2001, just weeks after the intervention, the administration in Washington was already focused on the next phase of its plans for Iraq. The Bonn Conference, a UN-brokered negotiation process, produced an Afghan interim authority, but it was not until the end of December that the UN gave authorisation for the establishment of ISAF. The remit for ISAF was only to provide security in Kabul and start the process of training Afghan security personnel. Real 'security', especially outside the capital, was in the hands of the various leaders and groups that had emerged after the departure of the Taliban. The largest contingents were those of the Shura-i Nazar, the Northern Alliance, but it was unclear if these would be folded into the new forces envisioned at Bonn. There was an aspiration to create a 50,000-strong Afghan National Army with a further 63,000 men in the Afghan National Police, but no resources were allocated by the UN or any other entity for their creation. The following month, in January 2002, at the Tokyo Donors' Conference, it was decided that there would be 'lead nations' in specific fields. Italy was to design the constitution, the United Kingdom was to head up the counter-narcotics question, Germany was to train the police, and the United States would create the Afghan army.[10]

The British, who had responsibility for the security of Kabul, and then the Turks, realised that local security forces were required immediately, and they unilaterally took on the responsibility to train a battalion (kandak) of infantry. At the same time, the US Special Operational Forces had already been creating or mentoring small detachments of Afghan militia around the country, fully expecting that these men could create a degree of security and then be included into the Afghan National Security Forces (ANSF) at a later date. This was the situation throughout most of 2002. It was not until the end of the year that the new Office of Military Cooperation—Afghanistan (OMC-A) was established to design the formations at battalion level.

Several things struck the Americans from the outset. The first was the divided nature of Afghan society. Each community and ethnic group had their own militias, and the sense of difference had been entrenched after years of civil war. The second observation was that the Northern Alliance, which had spent years under Taliban attack, felt a strong sense that this was their victory. They had suffered but prevailed, and they were determined that the Pashtuns, which had dominated the Taliban, would not control the country again. They were determined to build a state which gave them the lion's share, if not exclusive control, of political appointments, economic opportunities and military personnel. It was largely believed, especially among Tajik-Afghans, that, had he lived, Ahmad Shah Massoud would have been either the commander of the Afghan army or, at the very least, Minister of Defence. The northern factions believed there should be a peace dividend that benefited them, and they were determined to use a variety of tactics, including subtle obstruction of the foreigners, to ensure they emerged as the hegemons.

The third factor which was obvious to every person arriving in Afghanistan was that the country was at ground zero as far as institutions and logistical infrastructure were concerned. Training troops was relatively straightforward, but there was no banking system for pay, no barracks, no catering, no sanitation, no transport, no procurement chain, no manufacturing base, and no one with experience in the bureaucracy of personnel management. Military command consisted entirely of personalised charismatic leadership or a ruthless expropriation of resources and its distribution among comrades. There were no training facilities or schools, and levels of illiteracy were among the highest in the world. The new 'ministries' that were established initially occupied semi-ruined buildings or tents, but there were no records and no computers. As one British officer put it: 'In Afghanistan, we are not doing *re*construction; we are doing *construction*.'[11] Most believed that Afghanistan would need between thirty and fifty years to become a functioning country. Cynics said that was too optimistic, by about seventy years.

There were a few that had been trained by the Soviets. Their tactical training was sound, but the Soviets had never encouraged initiative below the divisional level, except in the Special Forces Brigade. At the National Defence College established by the Americans some years later, there was celebration when, one morning, the Afghan commandant decided, entirely on his own initiative, to order all the officer cadets to clean the camp. Although a modest event, the American mentoring personnel present regarded this as a significant breakthrough. At the Army Air Corps training wing in the same period, there was a sense of triumph when Afghan recruits, after several months, managed to parade for training wearing their boots and berets, although the same personnel had not, according to the American staff, quite managed to master their personal hygiene. Stories like this are legion. Yet they were entirely understandable. The difficulty was that the process of training an entire security force from scratch was a culture shock to both sides, Afghans and NATO personnel.

Major General Karl Eikenberry, the first commander of OMC-A, established a training formation called Task Force (TF) Phoenix, which consisted of elements of 10th Mountain Division, logistics teams, some Marines, and a clutch of individuals sent from nine other nations. From the outset this multinational effort, with all the complications of languages and reporting lines, created for itself some bureaucratic hurdles. To tackle the training for the ministries, which lay outside of the field of experience of military personnel, the Americans hired MPRI (Military Professional Resources Inc.). However, while TF Phoenix dispatched its training teams out to Afghan kandaks, and sought to develop a cadre of Afghan trainers, it had to contend with the fact that the British were training the Afghan NCOs and the French were training the officers. The idea was to produce three companies of trained men, then attach the competent NCOs and officers from their respective streams to create the combat-ready kandaks. But it was immediately evident that the American expectations of what NCOs do, based on their own army, were different from the British approach. Similarly, there were problems with the attachment of officers from French training who had not had the opportunity to know either their NCOs or their men. To the Western soldiers it was pretty obvious this was going to go wrong. Yet, when questions were raised, as so often happened throughout the ISAF mission in Afghanistan, somehow the obvious was ignored, bypassed or subsumed in excuses about the need to act swiftly, the budgetary and political constraints imposed from the capitals of the United States and its NATO allies, or the need to avoid offending an influential Afghan, including the new president, Hamid Karzai.

While the embryonic efforts were being made to create the first competent kandaks, in the hinterlands the militias were able to establish their own control. In the south, for example, militia leaders tried to take control of smuggling or narcotics production, which had become the most lucrative commercial activities. There were turf wars and armed clashes. The hope at Tokyo had been that Afghanistan could be demilitarised by taking out of commission thousands of weapons. The Disarmament, Demobilisation and Reintegration Programme (DDR) failed from the beginning. Some communities were disarmed, but that left them vulnerable to the subsequent predations of both militias and 'police' units. Moreover, former Taliban and many Pashtuns refused to countenance the idea of disarmament in the face of the evident threat from the, by now heavily armed and well-funded, Northern Alliance. The only success of DDR was in removing attack helicopters, artillery and armour. The country remained awash with small arms and other munitions.

At the second Bonn conference, or Bonn II, in December 2002, the government of Afghanistan and its donors agreed to increase the numbers of Afghan security personnel to 43,000 combat troops, 21,000 logistics and support staff, a Ministry of Defence, and a personal bodyguard for the President numbering 3,000.[12] Marshal Fahim, the Defence Minister, believed the scale of the force was too small. He called for 250,000 men.[13] As it turned out, even this was far fewer than were eventually established ten years later. By then, there were 350,000 security personnel, not including Western military personnel and civilian security contractors.

In early 2004, it had become clear that the development of Afghan security forces was just not keeping pace with a developing insurgency. The Taliban, encouraged by the remnants of Al-Qaeda and sympathetic personnel inside Pakistan, were able to reorganise. Meeting almost no resistance, they made contact with increasingly disgruntled Pashtuns in the rural areas of the south and east. The Afghans' expectations of 2001–2, which had been absurdly exaggerated and over-optimistic, had not been met. The men of violence whom the Taliban had ejected in the mid-1990s were back in power and the Americans appeared to be backing them. There was no security in the countryside and little sign of improvement in a range of other issues. Kabul was remote and, for most, irrelevant.

OMC-A was doing its best. It established an eight-week training programme for the army, created corps headquarters and tried to work with the ministries. By July 2005, it had produced 24,300 troops, but this was just half of the numbers envisaged by Bonn II and a tenth of the scale envisaged by the Afghan Minister of Defence. When it was clear that eight weeks was far too little to produce anything like competent personnel, the training programme was extended to fourteen weeks. With dedication and urgency, the training teams worked flat out to generate a force of 46,000 by the end of 2007. This effort was costing a large sum. The budget in 2002 was $179 million, but three years later the cost had risen to $2 billion, with an estimate that the bill was likely to rise to $7.2 billion and an annual sustainment cost of $600 million.[14]

The escalating violence in southern and eastern Afghanistan was increasing the demand for more men to be put into the field. This meant that even when the OMC-A (renamed Office of Security Cooperation in 2005) approached its targets, the numbers required of them expanded and the shortages of trainers, which was a constant problem, merely worsened. The new scale required was for 70,000 Afghan Army personnel and 82,000 police. In 2006, the training mission was retitled again, this time to Combined Security Transition Command—Afghanistan, nicknamed 'See-Sticka' to reflect its initials, CSTC-A. The new designation brought with it the tasks of mentoring the ministries as well as the training of soldiers and police. Under this sort of burden and faced with a mounting insurgency, it was not surprising that the metrics were bad: only 2 of the 105 sub-units so far trained, in 2008, were competent in the field, according to the Americans' own audit. Afghans themselves disputed the figure, saying that no units were yet able to function properly. More than half of the units envisaged had not even been formed. Visiting the training establishments on the edge of Kabul, there were impressive numbers undergoing tactical exercises. The rain-drizzled hills were literally swarming with Afghan trainees. Yet, despite all the progress and activity, Afghans interviewed were not optimistic. One Afghan colonel believed that, without the Americans, the Afghan 'army' would simply collapse.[15] Another former Mujahideen commander, serving as a more senior officer and occupying an impressive office and efficient-looking facility outside Kabul, said the same.[16] He explained his experience had been as a guerrilla commander, but this, defending the nation as a regular army, was an entirely alien task. The American and European personnel at CSTC-A exuded the confidence that military professionals need in the face of adversity, and their work was truly impressive and highly professional, but the mission was simply immense.[17]

To list all the problems the training teams faced would occupy an entire volume, but they were all as one would expect in trying to build an army, with no experience to draw upon, without the infrastructure within the state behind it.[18] There were shortages in everything. Even when personnel were issued with blankets, cooking equipment and other tools, they invariably disappeared—sold on to civilians, sometimes to pay for extortions, bribes or for the promotion secured from more senior men. Vehicles could not be maintained because there were not yet the qualified personnel to maintain them. Commanders preferred to hoard transport, munitions, radios and especially supplies as they believed these gave them greater importance and reinforced the status of their rank. These ideas had been the direct result of their experience during the civil war: men with material wealth possessed power. Devolution or distribution represented a diminution of that power. Drug abuse, apathy, an aversion to combat and a lack of interest in any mission or the civilian population were all too common among the rank and file. Many Afghan 'warriors', the optimistic name for individual soldiers', were not trusted by their NCOs and officers. They were seen as cannon fodder by some commanders or a dangerous armed rabble. One Afghan leader, in a distant post in what became Regional Command-East, refused to join a patrol with his men, despite the urgings of the American mentors present. His explanation was that his men did not like him, would not follow him and might even kill him. He had 'purchased' his commission and was more interested in getting back to the relative safety of Kabul, preferably with enough money to pay off the debts he had accrued through the purchase of his rank.

For the Western training mission there was a constant shortage of trainers and mentors. This made the training of Afghan officers and NCOs, crucial to the improvement of the army, a particular problem. One can imagine the reaction when CSTC-A were informed in 2008 that there would be yet another expansion of the ANSF: 80,000 Army personnel and 82,000 police officers were required.[19] Nor were the troops to be just light infantry: there was a requirement for a mechanised brigade, a commando brigade, headquarters and support units, combat engineers, Afghan training units and an air corps. There was growing concern that, in the haste to create a larger army, the quality of the forces would suffer.[20] Finding sufficient trained and reliable leaders was proving problematic.[21]

In late 2009, in order to augment the numbers of training staff, CSTC-A was joined by NATO personnel under the designation NTM-A (NATO Training Mission—Afghanistan). Some 37 nations were represented, further complicating the difficult diplomatic and reporting system. The Americans not only tolerated this, with all the irritations of less co-operative and parochial foreign militaries, but they generously funded the entire operation. They also took on police training and were soon responsible for the development of hospitals, medical personnel, counter-narcotics commandos and the apparatus for paying the soldiers. If this were not enough, they were still negotiating the treacherous and delicate shoals of senior Afghan officers and politicians eager to acquire as much power, influence or funding as they could. Yet, amid all this, you would not find a single American officer who doubted the mission. For all the criticism of the United States and their handling of the conflict in Afghanistan, the men and women who took part in it must rank as the most dedicated, patient and persevering individuals to be found anywhere. They kept at it, day after day, and endured a heart-breaking steady casualty toll with breaking stride. It was a humbling experience to watch them at work.

Advisory work required particular skills. As an example, the Australians who made up half of the 205th Corps Coalition Advisory Team found significant differences in the experience and approaches of the Afghans:

> Many of the senior officers had served in the military forces of the former Democratic Republic of Afghanistan (DRA). Many struggled to survive during the Taliban era and were forced to either flee the country or adopt very low public profiles. The influence of their training by the Soviets and exposure to the Red Army remains considerable and permeates many aspects of their institutional culture. Another group, albeit considerably smaller, consisted of ex-Mujahideen fighters. Many lack formal staff training but this was, to an extent, compensated by their sometimes stronger local knowledge and connections. It was probably more typical to find ex-Mujahideen officers in lower level command and staff appointments. Understandably, the potential for friction between these two particular groups remains considerable. The last distinct group were those officers and senior non-commissioned officers (SNCOs) with no military experience prior to 2001. This group has been influenced greatly by its exposure to ISAF, particularly US, training. By necessity most within this group tend to be more junior in rank.[22]

The mentors noted that there was no initiative or flexibility. Officially no action was undertaken without a formal written order from the Ministry of Defence and those orders could be vague, producing great caution and a variety of excuses. Inaction characterised even the simplest logistical activities. In operational tasks, however, 'the headquarters proved adept at managing short notice and short term crises'. It was noted that there was a 'sense of urgency and commitment to action' which stood in marked contrast with the approach to 'less urgent, but equally challenging issues'.[23] The staff remained 'particularly poor at addressing longer term campaign and institutional development challenges'.

The advisers' verdict was that 'maintaining one's sense of humour is critical', adding that there was a 'requirement for large doses of tact, patience, humility and persistence'. In theory the two forces, Western and Afghan, were complementary in the counter-insurgency effort:

> The ANA has better local situational and cultural awareness, better access to human intelligence sources and a better approach to information operations. On the other hand, ISAF is able to provide sophisticated enablers, such as joint fires, intelligence/surveillance/reconnaissance platforms, medical evacuation assets, and, perhaps more importantly, access to material resources. ISAF officers and soldiers are also able to provide their Afghan partners with an example of contemporary command, staff, leadership and management procedures.[24]

The reality was that many senior officers could not speak the same language as the southern Afghans and had as little knowledge of the area as ISAF staff. The Afghans were frustrated by the haste of Western directions, their own logistics and communications being unable to keep up. The result, because of national pride, was a number of tokenistic actions designed to show ISAF the corps could do some things. At brigade level or below, it was often easier to blame ISAF and claim there was confusion caused by the Westerners. The mentors themselves admitted:

> the biggest challenge as an adviser at the corps level was attempting to adhere to Lawrence's famous saying that 'it is better to let them do it themselves imperfectly than do it yourself perfectly. It is their country, their way, and our time is short'. In a perfect world this guidance is completely valid, but in practice it is very difficult to honour. Advisers are no more immune than other ISAF personnel from the desire to produce tangible results during their short tours.[25]

In 2010, the demands continued to mount. The numbers required in the Afghan National Army (ANA) were set at 171,600 and 134,000 in the ANP (Afghan National Police). Despite the offer of support from NATO, NTM-A was staffed by only half of the personnel needed.[26] Those that were deployed worked at full stretch throughout their tours. There had been frustration with the slower pace of police training compared with the speed of development in the ANA. The problem was once again a shortage of trainers. The American military had very limited numbers of military police, and for a fully functioning law-enforcement capability, the training mission had depended on, initially, the Germans as lead nation for this task. The German programme, while evidently thorough, was just not producing enough personnel. The US State Department was asked to step up the process and they contracted the work to DynCorp. This private company established a two-week course for existing officers and an eight week one for recruits. It didn't take long to realise this was totally inadequate if one required qualified police officers. At best, it was producing men fit for guard duty. There was no literacy training and no follow-on training. After seven years of poor results, ISAF requested that the Department of Defense take over from the State Department, but DynCorp took the US government to the Federal Court and won their suit for breach of contract. One can imagine the reaction among those who were in Afghanistan trying to create an effective police force. It was fascinating to experience DynCorp's 'lobbying' during a visit to NTM-A CSTC-A in 2010, and to observe the resentment from the military and police trainers present.

An equally serious failure involved the European Union. From mid-2007 the EU mission EUPOL was supposed to provide training for senior Afghan police officers from mid-2007, which included those in the ministries of Interior and Justice. The European Union provided less than half of the trainers it had promised and allocated many of the personnel to Provincial Reconstruction Teams. Even when they did offer training, it was clear that there was no tailoring to the specific conditions pertaining to Afghanistan. Typical of the institution, it was overly bureaucratic, inflexible and self-obsessed by its own terms of reference.[27] It remained an irrelevance throughout the campaign. By contrast, the officers of the Italian Carabinieri and French Gendarmerie provided effective, relevant and professional training. Their commitment was impressive and pride in their work was obvious to all. Nevertheless, the real challenge was converting the training into better policing on the ground. Police extortion and abuses were balanced by the sympathy one felt for them given the level of casualties they were taking.[28]

The solution that was found was to temporarily replace the existing uniformed police in districts with the much more professional and reliable Afghan National Civil Order Police (ANCOP). While ANCOP swept in, the local police could be extracted, put through retraining, and then returned. For a while this FDD (Focused District Development) worked, but ANCOP officers were exhausted by the relentless rotations. Moreover, the ANP officers were often guilty of simply cutting a deal with the insurgents, partly to stay alive. British soldiers reported how some ANP were definitely aiding their enemies—giving details of patrols and bases to the insurgents. When the police were left to protect one district centre, as the Americans tried to hand it over, they fled almost immediately. In Helmand, all the officers of a police post near Highway One were found dead one morning. The adjacent police posts claimed to have seen and heard nothing, but British troops believed that the men had been killed by other police officers or through a tip-off to the Taliban by rival officers.

To add to the pressure, President Obama announced that the Western intervention in Afghanistan would be brought to an end, and an 'end date' was set rather than an 'end state'. One British officer explained that his work of assisting the ANA was really only at the beginning, but there was to be a 'conditions-based transition'. When questioned further, he admitted that the only condition was 'time'.[29] The challenge was now not only how to reach the required quantity and quality of ANSF personnel in training terms, but how to prepare them to take over the full responsibility for security in just four years. The plan was to hand over areas in 'tranches', with the first ones being where security incidents were lowest. Gradually, the more violent provinces and districts would be in Afghan hands, but it would buy precious time for inoculation to the conditions the ANSF would face. Later, General John Dunford would amend this policy, handing over more difficult districts to 'stress-test' the ANSF units. If they failed, the Americans would know where to concentrate their remedial training or mentoring efforts.[30]

General William Caldwell, who assumed command of the combined NTM-A CSTC-A in 2009, was clear about his mission but realistic about the problems in his path.[31] Among the more prominent difficulties, aside from those already listed, were the need for retraining of existing personnel, the need for Afghans to take control of the recruiting system, the duplication of leadership training but the continued shortfall in sufficient numbers of competent and reliable Afghan officers, a lack of accountability, the challenges of the logistics chain under Afghan control to guarantee delivery of supplies to the forward bases and units, the attrition rate of casualties, temporary absences and desertions, ghost payrolling, extortion by officers of the policemen or troops under their command, chronic nepotism, and the absence of standardised metrics or evaluation among Afghan ministries.[32] Nevertheless, the training mission had managed to catch up with the target numbers, and had produced 134,000 soldiers and 115,000 police personnel by the end of 2010. Literacy was also being tackled. Some police trainees seemed enthusiastic about this schooling, explaining that they saw it as the route to a better job once they left the service. The inability to read had long been a problem for units in the field, from signals communications to navigation.

The demand for numbers continued to rise through 2011 and 2012. Security personnel had to be found to replace the planned draw-down of Western combat units, scheduled for the end of 2014. Quantity was no longer the most difficult aspect of the mission; it was the quality. There was some concern when the original measure of effectiveness, known as 'capability milestones', was changed to categories such as 'independent with advisers'. Comparison was therefore more difficult, but CM1, the metric for fully capable units that could operate without assistance, which was attached to a number of Afghan kandaks officially, tended to raise ironic laughter from soldiers who worked alongside them.

At the tactical level, it had long been the practice that there were embedded training teams working with Afghan personnel. The British called them OMLTs, Operational Mentor and Liaison Teams, or 'Omelettes' to the troops, while US teams were referred to as MITTs. The Western soldiers who took on these duties often found themselves taking on insurgents in firefights with variable levels of support or co-operation from their Afghan comrades. ISAF companies tried attaching a single Afghan platoon, but it was not uncommon to hear soldiers complain that the Afghans took a backseat or simply went to ground when the shooting started. Afghan soldiers would sometimes fire off as much ammunition as they could at the start of a firefight, so they wouldn't have to carry it back to their patrol base. There were rumours, often unsubstantiated, that Afghan soldiers would show more interest when Taliban prisoners had been captured, because they wanted to take them to one side and shoot them. There were more credible and corroborated accounts of Afghan soldiers looting compounds overrun by Western forces, which was a demoralising experience for the ISAF troops doing all the fighting. Crucially, it totally undermined any effort to win over the hearts and minds of the civilian population.

As 'transition' got under way, ISAF units withdrew from the level of tactical embedded support and began to focus on working with Afghan units at battalion and then brigade level, insisting that Afghan officers carry out the planning and execution of operations, while ISAF provided 'overwatch', that is, to bring in air or heavier fire support and augment the ground 'footprint' if the ANSF found themselves in difficulty. The ISAF commanders referred to MAGs (Military Advisory Groups) or BAGs (Brigade Advisory Groups), and some military units were designated PAGs (Police Advisory Groups), despite the obvious issue here of military personnel trying in some way to train or mentor police officers. Some Afghan officers, at brigade and corps level, didn't really understand the concept. 'Transition' to Afghan officers just meant 'handover'. They were puzzled by the Western presence and found it frustrating when their requests for their own artillery and armour, or Western airstrikes, were not forthcoming. More worrying was the tendency for Afghan commanders to categorise any of their casualties as 'serious' cases in the hope that the ISAF medics would fly in and extract them. There were also concerns about extracting the Western forces and the future of the operating bases they had built. Some Afghan officers showed little interest in holding advanced forward operating bases. Their idea was to ignore some areas altogether and to use firepower to coerce the districts they were interested in.

In 2014, the ISAF and NTM-A mission was concluded and replaced with Operation Resolute Support. CSTC-A was retained but the idea was to provide funding and residual support through the Afghan ministries and not directly to Afghan military or police units. In the final year before the changeover, many Afghan officers and ministry officials responded positively. There were definite successes in terms of independent operations, but many of the old problems remained. To provide an ongoing security force for rapid reinforcement, surveillance and security for Kabul, approximately 12,000 Western personnel remained in Afghanistan, many of them stationed at Bagram Air Base, with contingents at Mazar-i-Sharif, Herat, Kandahar and Jalalabad. The ANSF have, contrary to the expectations of the critics, held their own. Casualties have been heavy. Civilian losses certainly increased. But Kabul, at the time of writing, experienced a reduction in violence. Commercial activity in this rapidly growing city increased. The departure of the Western forces also led to fractures within the insurgent ranks. Inspired by Islamic State in Syria and angry at the lack of progress against the government in Kabul, some former Taliban declared themselves to be affiliates of Daesh under the title Wilayat Khurasan. Fragmentation indicated that the insurgency, which was never as homogeneous as the Taliban claimed, was in trouble.

Irregular Auxiliaries and Militias: Afghan Local Security

After 2002, the Afghan National Security Forces (ANSF) were being fashioned on Western models and founded on the Weberian idea that every state must possess a monopoly of violence. Yet in Afghanistan's history, the central state has been forced to negotiate its position with provincial factions and leaders who possess varying degrees of power, authority and influence over the population. The 'negotiated state' has struggled to obtain consensus and has been dominated by titular Durrani Pahstun dynasts who used coercion to compensate for their lack of legitimacy or permanent presence in rural peripheries. The protracted civil war (1989–2001) indicated that no one faction or leader possessed the ability to assert exclusive control of the country. Even the Taliban (1996–2001) never managed to secure Afghanistan entirely. In short, historically there had not been a monopoly of violence in the hands of the state.

In Afghan history, security was layered and dependent on the tribes and clans. National rulers were aware that tribal affiliation ran deeper and more strongly than loyalty to the state. In part, the Mughal system of awarding land and command of certain strengths of horse and foot (*mansabs*) was used, lending itself to a structure of warlords, who nevertheless acknowledged the titular head of state as the ruler to whom they owed their position. Regiments that served the state from the late nineteenth century were still territorially—that is, locally or regionally—affiliated. Security was provided down at a local level, and communities could provide out-of-area operations in war parties or *lashkars*.

Like the 'minute men' of the American War of Independence, levies could be called out to tackle any local, regional or national threat. Homogeneity between tribes could be established in the face of an external enemy, but tended to lapse the moment that peace was restored, when factionalism and feuding once again broke out. A ruler such as Abdur Rahman was not above inventing a foreign threat in the 1890s in order to generate unity and a pro-regime sentiment. The same technique was used by Mohammad Daoud in the 1970s over 'Pashtunistan' and the 'Pakistan threat'.

The loose nature of the organisations and their relatively short service (they were raised to meet a specific threat and soon disbanded) lent themselves more to irregular harassing operations than trying to hold positions. Interestingly, in the early modern period, Afghan mercenary forces and cavalrymen regarded the acquisition of the spoils of war, that is, looting, to be a natural and appropriate reward for military service and the risk of combat. In the early twentieth century, attempts were made to copy Turkish or Western models of military forces and an air force. The experiment in emulation was moderately successful, but, as often happens, the outward adoption of Western forms of organisation and weaponry did not set down deep roots in terms of ethos, doctrine and practice or lead those forces to adapt to their own circumstances.[33]

In Afghan history, there were several models for the array of military forces. The key characteristics of the system were that security had a territorial organisation which reflected tribal land ownership; it was dependent on 'warlord' leadership, and the process of rewards and patronage was a crucial part of the economic and social structure of the country. Militias could be mobilised rapidly but they could only serve for short periods because of their need to farm, manage property or commerce, or otherwise conduct civilian affairs. Loyalty was to family, section, clan, confederation of tribe, and regional power-brokers, and only rather loosely to a central authority that embodied Islamic and 'Afghan' identity. By contrast, 'regular' units were of variable quality and reliability through a lack of formalised bureaucracy and banking, state accommodation or training facilities. The preferred local mode of war was for irregular resistance, maximising use of terrain and time, but permitting immediate dispersal if events went against them. Despite the myth that Afghans have always been implacably opposed to foreign interventions, there were Afghan-Pashtun irregular forces and levies in British service in the First and Second Anglo-Afghan Wars.[34]

The Afghan government was extremely reluctant to consider the idea of arming local militias, given the experience of the country in the early 1990s when large-scale and predatory formations were not loyal to a local community and acted in an arbitrary fashion. Nevertheless, the concern to create highly centralised state structures was just as alien to the Afghans. The Soviet assumption, that the local administration and security apparatus would simply fall into line with the central direction of Kabul, was wrong. The critical element of Afghan history was not the state, but the local layers of administration. Afghans had a strong desire for autonomy, which is a point of pride, and, given that personal honour was the currency of the Afghan, local security mattered to their sense of honour, or *nang*. General David Petraeus, who took command of ISAF in 2010, announced: 'This is a country in which support of the tribes, of the local communities, for the overall effort is essential.'

Afghans were divided between social class, rural and town dwellers, nomads and sedentary farmers, Sunni and Shia, educated and illiterate, high caste and the poor, and progressive and conservative. However, unifying them is social cohesiveness which includes tribal class, ethnic subgroups, religious sects, locality-based groups, and those united by their own interests. Service together in the Soviet war or, indeed, the civil war of the 1990s and the insurgency could overcome old tribal divisions. Responses to external threats have often permitted temporary alliances between subgroups. However, the concept of *qawm*, a basic sub-national identity based on kinship, residence and sometimes occupation, that Westerners often identify as 'tribe' remained strong. As one Afghan put it: 'We are "united-divided"; we are like the Afghan carpet—made up of many weaves, patterns and colours—but a single thing which is very strong.' In other words, networks and a fabric of bonds are intrinsic elements of tribalised society.

Traditional local security was provided by a number of layers of organisation. The *tsalweshtai* was a guard force, normally composed of forty men, drawn from various subsections of the tribe and appointed by their leadership for some special purpose, such as protecting an isolated valley from raiding gangs. This was more common in the north western portion of Pashtun territory and there was a specific tribal injunction to ensure that no blood feud results if someone was killed by a *tsalweshtai* on duty.[35] The *arbakai* are generally identified as a tribal police force. Appointed men supervised the implementation of the tribal council's decisions. The normal punishment for serious disobedience involved burning down the house of the guilty party, and members of the *arbakai* had immunity within the tribe for the decisions of the elders that they implemented. Anyone daring to harm a member of the *arbakai* was severely punished. The system still flourishes in Paktia. A *chagha* was a group of fighters raised spontaneously within a village when faced by a bandit raid, robbery, livestock rustling and similar offences against the villagers. *Chagha* is also the word for the drum that was used to inform the people of the need to come to the location of the drumbeat, fully armed, and prepared to drive off the offenders, resembling a posse or medieval 'hue and cry'. The *chalweshtai* was a larger force than the *tsalweshtai* and was raised by the tribe from young men who volunteered from each family to implement tribal decisions, which could involve local fighting, a more protracted jihad, or even self-help projects that were needed. As with the *arbakai*, the actions of the *chalweshtai* were sanctioned by the tribe's elders and no retaliation was permitted against the members of this force as it implemented tribal decisions. A *chalweshtai* could be engaged in community projects, such as digging a canal or building a dam, but they are more commonly used in the prevention of crimes on roads that they were assigned to police. These organizations had been utilised in Pakistan's Federally Administered Tribal Areas (FATA) in the effort to restore order, but *chalweshtais* were also raised by aggressive tribes involved in resisting the government.

A *lashkar* was a body of tribesmen of a particular *qawm* that normally gathered in response to a particular threat on a large scale. The use of the term was flexible and could be applied to a dozen men going to attack a nearby village as a result of a family feud, but was also a label used for a force of several thousand used to repel an invasion or resist a government army. Historically, the *lashkars* were used for resistance to the state. In 1929, tribal *lashkars* of the south-east, in Paktia, assisted Nadir Khan (a Barakzai) to overthrow King Habibullah Ghazi. He rewarded them with exemption from compulsory military service and freedom from taxation. In order to hold those traditional *maliks* and khans, the community leaders, from those exempted regions close to the national government, the royal family frequently brought the sons of the tribal elders and leaders to Kabul for education. Some were eventually selected to go on to the Soviet Union for further and higher education. However, Nadir Shah also exercised the traditional rulers' policy of divide and rule, setting tribes against each other, or attempting to break up stronger tribes.

After the collapse of the communist Afghan Army between 1980 and 1982, there were rapid improvements. Discipline was tightened, desertion curtailed and mullahs were incorporated into the army's administration to improve morale. Meanwhile, territorial units were established among tribal chiefs who had been former resistance leaders. These groups were essentially co-opted to regular army formations or given regular unit designations. The men were expected to serve for three years, and were recruited as volunteers. A third of the established strength served at the local depot, while the rest remained at home until called. Tribal leaders selected the local unit commanders.

Attempts to resolve the national Mujahideen insurgency in the 1980s led the communist government to raise militias alongside the Afghan regular army. By 1985–6, large-scale Soviet operations had become rare and the emphasis was on reaching agreement with local tribal leaders. They were encouraged to set up self-defence units.[36] There were, as a result, fewer attacks on government forces in some Pashtun areas in the eastern border regions and elsewhere across the country.

When the Soviet Union withdrew its forces from Afghanistan in early 1989, the militias were expanded and became more important. Following General Tanai's attempted coup in 1990, President Najibullah no longer trusted the Pashtun-dominated army and began to rely upon militias as the sole counterweight to the Mujahideen. In other words, it was the failure of the project to build a regular army that left room for the militias to be strengthened. The largest militias were ethnically based, including Uzbeks of the Jowzjani militia of Abdul Rashid Dostum, the '53rd Infantry Division', and the Ismaili militia led by Sayed Jafar Naderi. These forces were too large to provide local security in an accountable way.[37] Their leaders had their own ambitions, particularly when they could see that, on their own, they could not hold back the Mujahideen.

The Uzbek-Afghan Jowzjani militia became the rapid reaction corps of the country, deploying by air to a succession of troublespots.[38] However, as casualties mounted, the undisciplined Uzbek militia became known as the Gilam-Jam, or 'Rug-Snatchers.' There were many allegations of looting, torture and extra-judicial murder.[39] Dostum's men even destroyed the Kandahar hospital and looted everything in sight. Nevertheless, they continued to fight hard because it was generally held that Pashtun mujahideen fighters would execute their prisoners.

The Ismailis too responded positively to Najibullah's call for a militia because they were a marginalised group. Surrounded by sectarian or ethnic rivals, they were eager to defend themselves in the Kayan valley of Baghlan province. When the Tajiks and Pashtuns near the Salang Tunnel aligned themselves either with Jamiat or with the jihadist Hizbi-i Islami, Sayyed Mansur Naderi of Kaihan, brother of the *pir* (spiritual head) of the Ismailis, organised his community to defend themselves and the road between Kabul and the Soviet border. By 1989, Naderi had 13,000 troops organised in the '80th Division' under the command of his son, Jaffar, and held a place in the local government council.[40]

Effectively, the mistake here was not to raise auxiliaries, but to use the auxiliaries to replace the regular army as the main arm of the state. Moreover, Najibullah's tendency to devolve authority to militia commanders and not local government members of the People's Democratic Party (which was hopelessly divided on factional lines) further empowered the militias. By 1992, there were perhaps as many as 170,000 militia in the 'armed forces', dwarfing the original regular army. This imbalance allowed militia leaders to establish personal fiefdoms in certain areas. Dostum controlled Jowzjan, Balkh, Samangan, Sar-i Pul and, later, Mazar-e Sharif.

Militias were vulnerable to the death of their leaders. To the north of Kabul, the Andarabi militia, led by Juma Khan, emerged because the government needed a force capable of blocking the supply lines of the Mujahideen faction Jamiat. A rival resistance faction, under the command of Gulbuddin Hekmatyar, Ahmad Shah Masood's enemy, was also looking for a way to cut off Jamiat. According to Barnet Rubin: 'There was no ideological component to this adhesion [between Hekmatyr and the Juma Khan militia]. The Andarabis maintained their independence, but they did not fight the government.' Masood captured the Andarab valley briefly and then relinquished it during a Soviet offensive, but, although Juma declared for the government, he was killed in mysterious circumstances and his militia fell apart soon after.[41]

When Soviet funds were suddenly cut off in 1991, the militias had no further reason to support the Afghan government. Their defection literally terminated the state. Subsequently, the militia commanders frequently fought each other because their loyalty was to themselves. When the government of Najibullah collapsed, each militia leader and mujahideen commander took control of different parts of the country in a scramble for power and money. Kandahar and Kabul were subjected to systematic looting and then, in the case of Kabul, months of destructive factional warfare.

The Afghan government and ISAF experimented with local defence forces from 2005. The failure of the Afghan National Auxiliary Police led to a more limited experiment with a local uniformed Afghan Public Protection Programme (AP3) in 2007, which was extended to the Community Defence Force and the Local Defence Initiative (LDI) in 2009, and finally the Village Stability Operations and the Afghan Local Police (ALP) in 2010.

The Afghan Public Protection Programme was an Afghan-led initiative in Wardak province in Regional Command-East, from March 2009, whose mission was to 'enhance security and stability, strengthen community development, and extend the legitimate governance of the GIRoA [Government of the Islamic Republic of Afghanistan] to designated districts in key provinces through community-based security forces'.[42] It comprised local security forces under the authority of the Ministry of the Interior, closely co-ordinated with the ANA, ANP and international forces. The AP3 used the same community leaders, the elders, that the Independent Directorate for Local Governance (IDLG) worked with through the Afghan Social Outreach Programme. The hope was that it would therefore tie together security and development. The community elders, in conjunction with the district councils, selected military-aged men between 25 and 45 to serve as members of their local security forces. Each local AP3 unit focused on securing districts, although the authority of many *shuras* (councils) did not align with government district boundaries. Despite the administrative complications, the aim was to involve the people in keeping their local area clear of insurgents, once ANSF and ISAF had driven the insurgents out in more deliberate operations. The regular forces also had to ensure that they could provide sufficient support so that the AP3 would not be overwhelmed by insurgents.

The government's task was to provide 'both administration and oversight of the effort through the MOI and ANP, respectively, and to develop consensus among the key local leaders so that they will not only support the program, but also provide reliable manpower for it'.[43] The involvement of the Interior Ministry was seen as a means of creating legitimacy for the Afghan government. The American Task Force Catamount with the 2nd Battalion, 87th Infantry Regiment, supported the programme. Captain Marco Lyons, Headquarters Company commander, noted its organic roots: 'The Afghan Public Protection Program is an Afghan requested, initiated, and developed program. It enables respected young men of local communities to become public protectors.' Each member of the new force was vetted by the National Security Directorate (the internal intelligence service). Theoretically, they were to be trained by the Afghan National Police, who in turn were at that time trained by a team of American Special Forces. In reality, it was the Special Forces that trained and mentored them. The AP3 officers were instructed on several topics, including integrity, ethics, use of force, discipline and the law.

The 'Guardians', as they were nicknamed, had been championed by the Afghan Interior Minister, Mohammad Hanif Atmar, who believed the police lacked knowledge of local villages to secure them against insurgents, claiming: 'For security, you must know the community.' He made no mention of the problem of roadside robbery and other abuses by the police, and it seems that AP3 was an attempt by the government to find a solution to the predations of their own security forces. The Guardians received three weeks of training, a uniform, a weapon, and $120 a month from the Interior Ministry, but all of it was paid for by the United States. Pay was problematic: without banking, the Interior Ministry paid the men at regular parades to avoid accumulations of money or men absconding with funds without providing service.

The pilot programme produced some broad lessons. First, community-based security forces needed to be fully supported and vetted by local community leaders; they needed to be overseen in some form by the regular security forces; and like many other security efforts, success was catalysed by linking them to locally based development initiatives. Second, ISAF commanders and Afghan officials at all levels cautioned against a blanket application of a single AP3 model in all areas. Some community-based forces may founder as a result of a community's strong antipathy towards a government. However, governments provide the legal basis of such forces, so they have to be involved, even if it is a distant connection. It is essential that governments retain approval authority over the formation of community-based security forces. There was some concern in Afghanistan that there was a proliferation of 'home-grown' Special Forces: a unit known as the KAU in Uruzgan and the Helmandi Scouts. To establish the correct formula there needs to be, for any given geographic area, a clear definition of the requirement for a local force, with clearly assigned training and oversight roles. The creation and use of local forces must be based on a co-ordinated approach developed by regional and local actors working closely with provincial and district governors. They cannot be imposed, but have to be encouraged. They tended to be less suitable in areas where traditional tribal structures or more cohesive communities have been weakened significantly by displacement, migration and civil war.

There were some successes with local forces. Children in the Jalrez valley reported the location of a roadside improvised explosive device (IED) to Afghan Public Protection Force officers. This enabled ISAF to safely dispose of the device. Lieutenant Tyler Kurth, the programme co-ordination officer, stated: 'I've spoken to local residents in the Jalrez bazaar,' and 'They appreciate that local villagers patrol the area, and they believe the Afghan Public Protection Program will work. The local shop owners in Jalrez think it's a great program, because it enables local residents to provide for their own security while simultaneously defending their communities and their country.' Locals were more alert to changes in the security situation. They look out for strangers. But, unlike the Sons of Iraq in Anbar province, the Guardians were not a fighting force, and they were recruited only after an area was cleared of insurgents. Nevertheless, there was always the possibility that the locals would throw in their lot with whichever side appeared to be in the ascendant, which was a pragmatic response by peoples experienced in survival.[44] The question was therefore whether the search for local security solutions brings a country closer to a political settlement of civil war. If we accept the principle of local forces, what does this mean for governance as it is currently configured? Does it mean a return to a devolved polity, or does encourage vested interests to cling to the existing, centralised state or seek alternative power structures?

The Afghan government, concerned by the development of alternative sources of power that might later side with the insurgents, limited the numbers of local security forces.[45] In 2011, there were just 73 units across the country. However, their very existence suggested that Afghan security was in the process of returning to local control, but with a national structure above it. Regular forces were in a position to move into an area under threat and impose order, but traditionally this required negotiation and compliance with local authorities to make it hold. Afghanistan was always a 'negotiated state'. Security was contingent on local powerbrokers because the central state was weak. Those who provided security forces indicated the limits of state power.

Afghanistan had not resolved the question of cost in its defence and internal security. The size of the ANSF in 2016 was unsustainable from internal revenues and needed donors to continue, but this created dependence and made Afghanistan a client state of the developed world. In 2015, the ANSF cost $4.1 billion. The Afghan government was supposed to find $500 million every year to meet sustainment costs too, but this was at odds with the desire to prioritise development.

Finally, there was the question of turnover in security personnel. Afghanistan needed to recruit 110,000 men every year to maintain a force of 350,000. The plan was always to reduce the size of the ANSF as the insurgency ebbed away. However, after the Western military draw-down, violence had not subsided and actually increased in some areas. If a solution could be found to the insurgency the ANSF could reduce rapidly, but that would also put pressure on the civilian economy, flooding the country with unemployed men. Either way, local security forces remained central to the future of the country.

The Iraq Security Forces

After the disbandment of the Iraqi security forces shortly after the intervention, the Coalition Provisional Authority (CPA) and interim occupation authority, led by General Paul Eaton, was told in May 2003 he had to create a new army. He had a staff of just five officers, no planning guidance and initially no budget. The mission he was given included the demand that the force he created was to be for external defence only and that, because of fears of the Iraqi Army in the past, its logistical capability was to be provided by civilian contractors. No Iraqi army unit would be allowed to operate more than 80 miles from its home base, so there could be no threat to any neighbouring state. No one considered that the Iraqi Security Forces (ISF) might be needed for internal security. The tasking was based entirely on the reputation of the Iraqi Army from the 1980s onwards: an organisation that had invaded the sovereign territory of Iran and Kuwait, threatened and launched missiles against Saudi Arabia and Israel, and tried, in vain, to stem the conventional invasion of Iraq by the US forces and their allies. The emphasis was therefore on limiting the new force.

The Coalition Military Assistance Transition Team was established to create just three motorised divisions, each of 12,000 men, and the period allocated for the process was three years, after which control would be handed back to the Iraqis. Constraints were placed on the composition of the Iraqi Army to reflect the national profile, with 60 per cent Shia, 20 per cent Kurd and 20 per cent Sunni personnel. The troops were to be used for external defence. An immediate flaw in the plan was the lack of any judicial system in the armed forces. There was no punishment for desertion or absence. Men could simply abandon their employment without penalty. There were very few facilities for the army: CMATT had to find every office, training team and interpreter. When the first call was put out for trainers, only four men arrived—two from the United Kingdom and two from Australia. Moreover, there were no experienced senior Iraqi officers to lead the three divisions: all the officers had been members of the Ba'ath Party and had been dismissed.

Despite the authority of the CPA, some Coalition commanders had used their initiative when confronted by a rising tide of insurgent violence. American divisional commanders, who had their work endorsed by the CPA, authorised the raising of the Iraq Civil Defence Corps, a 'National Guard' who received between three days and six weeks of training under the Americans. However, their role varied in each area. Some were co-located with the Coalition's troops, but others were more independent. General Eaton believed that the problem was that he lacked a senior figure in his own army or government who would champion the Iraqi Army reconstruction programme. There were so many competing demands on the American government that this became a serious handicap for the mission.

The gap in trainers was outsourced to Vinnell, a private corporation. With over twenty years' experience in training personnel in the Arab-speaking world, and with progress made in the provision of barracks, bases, catering, maintenance and recruiting centres, the private contractors were an essential addition to the Coalition's efforts. The problem was that Vinnell had conducted its previous work out of a conflict zone. The 1st Battalion of the Iraqi Army they trained suffered such attrition that it was only at 50 per cent of its establishment. The 2nd Battalion, ordered to assist in the urban operations to clear Fallujah in 2004, practically ceased to exist.[46] Training in military skills was not at issue, but the private contractors had not been able to instil the morale and will to fight that were essential to success.

Getting the funding from the Pentagon was also a significant restraint on the development of the Iraqi forces. Every facility had to be built or refurbished from scratch because of widespread looting in 2003–4, but the flow of money determined the speed at which these facilities could be created, trainers recruited, and units formed up. The lack of trainers and interpreters led to misunderstandings. Disputes were a frequent interruption to the programmes.

The CPA was even more dissatisfied with police training, and, to the dismay of CMATT, all police development was placed under their jurisdiction as well. In addition, the American administration at home demanded a tripling of the numbers of Iraqi forces, placing an unprecedented strain on the already understaffed organisation. Recognising the problem, the Americans replaced CMATT with Multi-National Security Transition Command—Iraq (MNSTC-I), authorising it to cover the development of the army, the police and the ministries. Lieutenant General David Petraeus and then General George Casey were to lead the new outfit. In 2004, there were just 30,000 trained police and two infantry battalions. The border guards were 18,000 strong on paper but less than 4,000 of them were armed. Within a year there were plans for some 80 Iraqi infantry battalions, over 100,000 police and 32,000 border guards, which, it was thought, would be sufficient to hand over responsibility for the country to the Iraqis.

To make the transition more effective, General Casey envisioned partnering and mentoring the new Iraqi units, under the command of MNC-I (Multi-National Corps—Iraq), by co-locating them, or by replacing areas of responsibility (AORs) that had Iraqi formations, with American mentors. Despite the increasing levels of violence, the numbers of Iraqi battalions had risen to 98 by January 2006, the equivalent of over 100,000 armed services personnel and 80,000 police officers. Two American combat brigades were withdrawn in the same period.[47] The problem was that the number of civilians being killed and the general lawlessness of the country was now a political issue of international concern. Moreover, the Iraqi Army was weak in several respects. It possessed only one mechanised brigade and its vehicle fleet was from the former Soviet bloc. The units tended to be of exclusive ethnic or sectarian origin, with the Kurds, Shia and Sunni increasingly drawn to protect their own interests. Police collusion with death squads was a frequent accusation and necessitated comprehensive retraining.[48] There was still no judicial system for the punishment of misconduct, and soldiers refused to obey orders whenever it suited them.

The Iraqi armed forces continued to grow. In 2007, the ISF consisted of 194,000 military and 241,000 police personnel. With these forces came the American military 'surge', which poured troops into the most violent districts. More equipment was made available to the ISF, including armoured 'Humvee' personnel carriers. New divisional staffs were created. Fresh Iraqi formations were deployed alongside the Americans and flooded certain areas. When the British withdrew from Basra, no less than 22 Iraqi battalions, supported by American airpower, Special Forces and mentors, recaptured the city.

The Iraqi Army and the Anbar Awakening

The al-Anbar Awakening, involving thousands of Sunnis, angry with the predations and arbitrary violence of extremists of al-Qaeda in Iraq (AQI), was a turning point against the insurgency. In late 2007, some 91,000 former insurgents joined the government's side, known as the Sons of Iraq, leading to co-operation between the Americans and the leaders of the *muqawamah* (resistance). The co-operation led to a significant reduction in violence

Saddam Hussein had cultivated his relations with Sunni tribal groups as part of a strategy to retain power. He understood that, on the peripheries, tribal power was the basis of political authority. In the ancient past, and under the Hashemites, the tribal leaders had considerable autonomy. However, from the 1950s, Sunni tribal power began to decline.[49] The Ba'ath Party reasserted tribal identity and authority, using patronage and encouraging co-operation in return for personal rewards.[50] Saddam Hussein, faced with sanctions, was forced to let local sheikhs develop their own private security forces to police their regions. The reward was 'extra-legal sources of additional revenue from smuggling, government corruption and kickbacks, and even outright extortion and hijacking'.[51] The Anbaris also developed their own rudimentary healthcare, employment and social welfare facilities when the state no longer provided opportunities.[52] The Anbaris were urbanised, and not a rural militia, but there was a great deal of emphasis on personal authority within a patronage hierarchy, enabling sheikhs to control their tribe's activities.[53]

When Saddam Hussein was overthrown in 2003, the system of tribal patronage was thrown into disarray.[54] It did not take long before the Anbaris were engaged in serious fighting against the American-led Coalition. The Sunni decision to boycott the first elections worsened the situation, because the Shia became the dominant element in Iraqi politics and in the composition of the first government.[55]

The CPA decision to dissolve the Iraqi Army and its programme of de-Ba'athification put thousands of men out of work.[56] American errors and heavy-handedness further antagonised the population.[57] The insurgency was dominated by ex-Ba'athists from late 2003.[58] However, Musab al-Zarqawi and al-Qaeda in Iraq soon 'produced mayhem in the hapless country [with] abductions, beheadings and suicide bombings'.[59] AQI was set on creating a Sunni caliphate out of Iraq and looked to recruit the Anbaris, who seemed marginalised and eager to kill Americans. Arab media organisations deliberately or unwittingly spread the call for jihad, which created a steady flow of foreign fighters into Iraq.[60]

The Anbaris were then alienated from AQI. The Jihadists had begun to impose their own interpretation of correct social relations and detribalisation in Anbar. They seized local illegal sources of revenue, depriving the sheikhs of income, including the hijacking of oil trucks, smuggling and local 'taxation'.[61] In one example, Sheikh Sattar al-Rishawi of the Albu Risha tribe, who would go on to found the Awakening Movement, was 'a smuggler and highway robber' who saw his authority and income eroded as AQI took over.[62] AQI also orchestrated forced marriages to build connections with the tribes. They murdered anyone who protested at their actions, and imposed a brutal form of justice based on a ruthless interpretation of Sharia law.[63] Victims of their justice were tortured, beaten and executed in a horrific manner, leading to condemnation from Osama bin Laden himself.

In 2005 a coalition of tribes attempted to drive AQI out of Anbar, while simultaneously fighting the Coalition, but the uprising was defeated by AQI insurgents.[64] To punish the tribes, AQI intensified its campaign of murder and intimidation. Few were eager to make a second attempt against such an onslaught.[65]

Nevertheless, it was clear that the United States was making a better offer. The Americans had not withdrawn and were eager to drive away AQI. They had implemented a systematic policy of reconstruction and development. Their public announcements that they intended to stay until the country was secure had an obvious appeal to those living under the AQI reign of terror. The Western approach to counter-insurgency was only of marginal relevance to the Anbaris, but in June 2006 the American 1st Brigade of 1st Armoured Division, which was engaged in securing Ramadi, the capital of Anbar province, realised that security was dependent not on the government of Baghdad, but on local tribal authority.[66] It was the officers on the ground that made the decision to enable the local tribes and thus take the role of patron that Saddam Hussein had established.[67] Once AQI were being driven out, the tribes reasserted control of the smuggling and other illicit businesses they had once dominated.

The 'key leader engagement' activities were matched with the deployment of smaller and more numerous detachments around the region to control the ground and provide quick-reaction forces to the appearance of AQI. Local fighters located and guided the more heavily-armed American and Iraqi units. The Americans also deployed men to mentor and advise Iraqi units so that they had access to the same fire support. The Military and Police Transition Teams (MiTT and PiTT) shared the same risks as the Iraqis, and set an example of confidence and professionalism, but also helped to deter misconduct or the settling of scores.[68] The presence of the ISF in Anbar also enhanced the prestige of the sheikhs, as they were able to show their people that they could command the support of the coalition.[69]

One incident had been enough to drive these underlying factors into action. On 21 August 2006, AQI murdered and mutilated a sheikh in Ramadi who had refused to give a woman of his tribe over to AQI to be married to one of their fighters.[70] When Sheikh Sattar convened a tribal council on 9 September 2006, announcing the 'Awakening', fifty tribes agreed to fight collectively against AQI.[71] Unlike in 2005, the Americans actively supported the Anbaris against the Jihadists.[72] The Awakening–Coalition alliance was further tested November 2006 when AQI attacked the Albu Soda tribe in an attempt to force them back into the insurgency. The Albu Soda requested Coalition assistance and a combined ISF and Coalition force routed AQI.[73] By January 2007, sensing the direction the conflict was taking, every tribe in the vicinity had joined the Awakening.

The Awakening units, known as Sons of Iraq, formed local security forces, funded by the Coalition, but operating independently. There was a further spin-off. Awakening councils agreed to provide recruits to the ISF. The tribal security forces were divided into Emergency Response Units (ERUs), Auxiliary Police and Neighbourhood Watches. The ERUs conducted operations against AQI under the control of the Iraqi Ministry of the Interior in theory, although in practice they were independent.[74] Auxiliary Police units were recruited in remote villages too isolated to receive Coalition support. They acted as police in the absence of regular, trained constabulary.[75] Neighbourhood Watches were informal groups that provided intelligence and the face of village-level security.[76]

The Anbaris augmented ISF significantly with Sunni recruits. Police recruits were provided cash incentives if they completed training and remained in service for at least 90 days. Army recruitment was more difficult as few were willing to serve in national units away from home, but a territorial arrangement was made.[77] Trained Anbari personnel were simply permitted to operate closer to their own home areas.[78] Few tribal elders wanted their men to serve in a government run by the Shia.[79]

By 2010, the security forces numbered some 625,000, and while there were still problems in logistics, procurement, budgeting and higher-level management, it was a force that could provide continuing internal security. Size, however, could conceal the more fundamental fractures which existed along sectarian lines.

The Anbar Awakening had a significant effect in reducing violence and driving out al-Qaeda. Its councils agreed to support local and national government initiatives too, hoping that they would enjoy the restoration of some balance of power in Iraqi politics. In 2009, the former militias participated in the national elections. There was also a delicate handover of the system of paying the Sons of Iraq, from American to Iraqi government control. However, Sunni anger at Shia domination in government and widespread abusive and corrupt practices meant that sectarian violence never entirely disappeared. The Americans withdrew hoping that the administration of Nouri al-Maliki would improve power-sharing, but it did not.

Worse, the appearance of Islamic State (IS), which was a movement that claimed to want to defeat the Shia, had its own appeal to the Sunni. As a new movement it did not initially resemble al-Qaeda and claimed to want to support Sunnis. But optimism soon turned to disillusionment. Daesh atrocities and murder campaigns proved just as devastating. It seemed that the Anbaris had repeated the mistake of 2004, and, no less paradoxically, the fighters of Islamic State seemed to be repeating precisely the same levels of violence that had alienated the population before.

Mosul, which was the responsibility of two Iraqi divisions, fell when its security forces simply collapsed. Analysts noted that the cause was the long period of deterioration that had occurred under Maliki. Many officers were political appointees. Formations existed on paper, since ghost payrolling by officers intent on profiting from the government, was widespread.

Local Forces in the Global War on Terror

The Western training missions that worked in support of a wider counter-insurgency campaign suffered from a number of problems. The most critical was the constant shortage of trained personnel, with or without a command of local languages. There was often a delay in the release of funds, and yet targets for expansion were frequently increased upwards. There was a constant concern with the quality of recruits being created, an understandable anxiety in a period of such rapid expansion. The development of facilities, logistics, medical installations and casualty evacuation systems, local training teams, pay and leave arrangements, judicial controls and procurement chains was far more complex than simply raising and training battalions. Police training was particular difficult because it takes far longer to train a constabulary than a set of site guards.

Small, locally raised forces were the most useful where they were based on the *tsalweshtai* concept with smaller numbers of men organised for specific purposes, such as defending a village, a valley or a development project that brings benefit directly to them. The error was relying on larger *qawm* affiliations, or allowing the forces to come under the authority of a single commander who could become a 'warlord' and therefore a threat to the state. Paradoxically, where warlord leaders have been the kinsmen of those in power, there have been fewer problems of disloyalty.

The community defence units had to be localised. Tribal organisation is usually more amenable to district control with locally recruited forces, largely because the community can keep the armed men accountable. Any attempt to use them outside their home regions will invariably fail, and many even encourage looting and atrocities against tribal enemies. This is in contrast to regular units which, in internal security missions, are usually deployed outside the areas from which they are recruited. Local rapid reaction forces often come from the same tribe as the village defence forces, and regular troops (not foreign forces) usually provide the heavy weapons and transport that local forces will lack. Support for tribal forces has often been provided by Special Forces advisers capable of co-ordinating fires and air support, as well as medical evacuation and aerial resupply during protracted operations. But local forces cannot be used as 'Special Forces' themselves. They are most effective when limited to local security. In terms of combat engagements, their lack of training usually means they are unable to hold onto an area for long if outnumbered or under serious pressure.

There are opportunities for the post-conflict employment of regular soldiers or militia after a civil war, since local defence constabularies can continue to function in the traditional manner without any specific retraining or large investment. Indeed, such local constabulary forces can be a useful area of employment in providing early warning of a resurgence of violence and creating a security transition phase.

There are significant risks in and many objections to the use of local defence forces in civil conflicts. The most obvious is the risk of arming men who might change sides. Any government preference for selected groups risks stirring rivalries and internal power struggles in regions outside central government control. The perception of special favours to already powerful tribes, including pay and possible arms supplies, could create a backlash from other ethnic groups with their own militiamen and warlords, thus deepening civil conflict.

For Afghanistan, Antonio Giustozzi questioned whether the tribal chiefs would have the will to fight the Taliban as it strengthened and rebuilt its network in the border regions. He stated: 'In the end, I believe it will boil down to bribing people into joining militias. How militarily effective these are going to be remains to be seen.'[80] His assessment was based on the observation that past experiments with community-based forces were failures: the Afghan Auxiliary Police were merely militia men 'owned' by militia commanders, not the government of Afghanistan. Alignment to a government in remote areas beyond the limits of their control invariably invites attack from insurgents. Dozens of pro-government tribal leaders were killed in Afghanistan and the Pakistan border districts by extremists. There is a risk that any effort to raise local units could backfire where tribal forces are seen as fighting on behalf of foreign troops.

There are advantages for states using local militias. Tribal or clan-based societies will have their own tradition of localised security forces, loosely organised and fluid in their operations, which have sometimes been far more successful than 'regular troops'. They have a vested interest in defending a village, a valley or a development project that brings benefit directly to them. They can release state forces from providing fixed-site security or manning local checkpoints, thus allowing them to focus on more serious military and policing tasks. Auxiliaries working with a government might in fact slow, prevent or even reverse the process of insurgent recruitment of marginalised groups. Local security forces can even assist in local governance-building, fostering a 'bottom-up democracy' that is well suited to certain tribal communities, local justice mechanisms and, ultimately, national unity and security.

From a Western perspective, creating the right sort of military force, emphasising either external defence or internal security, was a major difficulty during the interventions in Iraq and Afghanistan. Establishing the right planning horizon, properly financed and supported by qualified trainers, was also a challenge. Unity of effort was disrupted by multinational personnel, complex lines of reporting, national caveats in the deployment of their personnel and their role, and variable levels of funding. There were far too few qualified trainers for the tasks that were set. Frequent changes of personnel, caused by rotations of units on tours, or within training teams, disrupted the continuity of development. Two-year tours would have been far more effective than the six months that some trainers conducted. Different approaches to training caused significant problems, delay and confusion, especially when trying to patch together the elements trained by different nations. Sectarian and other indigenous cultural and social divisions were not acknowledged as Westerners tried to create 'national' forces in their own image, ignoring hundreds of years of experience or the realities of local politics.

The need for clear, functioning and robust judicial systems to govern the personnel of an army and to support the processing of those apprehended by the local police was self-evident but took too long to implement in both Iraq and Afghanistan. Moreover, there was no acknowledgement that local police are often seen as the most predatory in many less-developed countries. Empowering the police, with inadequate training, was a sure way to alienate a population. Ministerial development also lagged far behind the creation of military forces. There remained significant problems in the administration of military and police personnel, as well as in the integration of such forces with the national plans for the economy, the criminal justice system, and even the jurisdiction and powers of the government.

Very often, expectations were wrong. Technological solutions, which are culturally the ones preferred by advanced Western forces, are often inappropriate for countries without the purchasing power and skilled workforce to maintain them. Western troops struggled to get local personnel to conduct duties thought to be essential to discipline and professional efficiency. This created frustration and, occasionally, mutual antagonism. In a few tragic cases, Western personnel were shot by those they had come to assist, although one or two incidents had the hallmarks of gunmen placed by the insurgents. Misunderstanding was not limited to the interface of soldiers. The means by which progress was measured seemed to encourage a conspiracy of optimism and even moderate self-critique was feared because it undermined an agreed 'narrative'. That anxiety exposed the fact that Western military personnel were aware that their missions in Iraq and Afghanistan were unpopular with the public at home and their governments were less than fully committed as a result. To keep the politicians and population content with positive reports was often at odds with ground truth. This simply increased mutual suspicion and made the media even more sceptical.

Quality in local military forces was invariably more important than quantity. While fighting an insurgency or an external foreign power, the training of manpower to the right level is a significant challenge. There is always likely to be a variation in the quality of units, but that is tolerable if roles are differentiated appropriately. Naturally, the training of security forces is far more effective if it can be done before a conflict has broken out—that is, in peacetime.[81]

13

FUTURE CHALLENGES

UPSTREAM ENGAGEMENT AND PRIVATE FORCES

In October 2015, just six months after its commencement, the American 'train and assist' programme for opposition groups in Syria was abandoned. The reasons were clear. Too few men had been recruited, those that had been were too expensive to sustain, and there were few positive results to show for the effort. The failure had not been a military one. In 2011, when the Assad regime began its severe crackdown against opposition groups, the United States had taken some time to approve the distribution of aid, while at the same time agreeing to a more covert programme of delivering military support to the emerging Free Syrian Army resistance. The objective was vague but appeared to be to ensure that there was a viable security force that could assume control as soon as Assad was overthrown and prevent the country from falling into the hands of Jihadists or becoming a failed state racked by civil war. However, anxiety in Congress and the President's office about getting bogged down in 'another Iraq' meant that there were months of indecisive discussion and debate during which time the Syrian resistance was radicalised and the Assad regime received the more active support of Iran, Hezbollah from Lebanon, and Russia. It was not until September 2014 that Congress gave its approval for a 'train and assist' programme, allocating $5 billion for the task. The Department of Defense was given sole authority for the mission and a target of 3,000 fighters for training was established for the first year with provision for a further 5,400 every year thereafter. The planned force was for 15,000 men.

Nevertheless, there were several constraints imposed that limited the effectiveness of the operation. President Obama's counter-terrorism strategy specified the requirement to 'train, build capacity and facilitate partner countries on the front lines'.[1] For the Syrian training mission, the main partners were to be Jordan, Saudi Arabia and Turkey. This was due to the congressional imperative that there were to be no 'boots on the ground', that is, American service personnel were not to conduct training in Syria itself, but through the partner states. The problem was that two of these countries had their own national interests to consider. Saudi Arabia considered itself locked in a proxy war with Iran and there was more sympathy with the Salafi struggle against the Shia and Alawi factions that were represented in the Syrian regime. Turkey too was in a difficult position. It was committed to the overthrow of President Assad but was even more determined to oppose Kurdish groups and prevent them from establishing territorial control. It was alleged that the Turkish intelligence service was initially supplying arms to the radical Jihadists who were fighting the Kurds. Nevertheless, the Turkish authorities changed their position when attacks were made against Turkey itself by Jihadists. Turkey's priority remained the denial of the aspiration for 'Rojava', a continuous Kurdish territorial belt that stretches across the northern borderland of Syria, and the suppression of the Kurdish paramilitaries that operated across the borders of eastern Turkey and northern Iraq.

The United States was just not ready to accept any degree of risk, largely because of the unpopularity of overseas missions in the light of the Iraq and Afghanistan conflicts. There were also several significant delays. The CENTCOM (Central Command) of the US armed forces did not get its facilities up and running for the first batch of trainees until May 2015. The CIA had also been restricted in what it could deliver, and opposition groups complained that the United States was giving almost no assistance at all. Critics commented that you 'couldn't combat barrel bombs', the Assad regime's weapon of choice against neighbourhoods harbouring resistance fighters and their families, 'with baskets of fruit'—a reference to the Obama aid programme.[2] The most telling restriction, however, was the political demand for the vetting of the fighters that were to be enlisted. Each man was subjected to scrutiny to ensure they were not Jihadists and they were made to pledge they would not fight the regime, which the US Congress deemed illegal, only the emerging factions of al-Nusra and the so-called Islamic State of Iraq and the Levant/Syria (ISIL/S), known locally as Daesh. Given the popularity of the Islamic State movement and the *raison d'être* of the resistance against Assad, the demand was astonishing. It was not surprising that very few agreed to join the American initiative.

In 2011, the United States, France and the United Kingdom intervened militarily in Libya, initially to prevent a wholesale destruction of rebel groups by the regime of Colonel Mu'ammer Gaddafi. There was a great deal of optimism that the 'Arab Spring' uprisings across North Africa and the Near East that year would produce democratisation and perhaps create more liberal societies where the interventions of 2001 and 2003 in Afghanistan and Iraq had not. Within months, the combination of local militias and Western air power had created such momentum that the Gaddafi regime collapsed.[3] Gaddafi himself was captured while trying to escape and executed by the rebels. In the aftermath, as militia groups tried to assert control of their own fiefdoms, there were considerable difficulties in the creation of an interim or representative government. Regionalism and clan politics were strong, but it was the power of the militias which stood in the way of the re-establishment of a state. Security deteriorated amid the political impasse.

By 2013, the country was clearly in a state of collapse. To break the deadlock, the United States attempted to train a portion of the militia in the hope they could later be persuaded to form part of the state security apparatus. An attack on the training facilities in August that year prompted the Western allies to consider another method for training a regular force. The United Kingdom government, which had just announced a new strategy of defence engagement which involved new combined departmental work and a shared budget to 'build stability overseas' (known as BSOS), decided it would extract almost 400 men from Libya and bring them to Britain to train out of the conflict zone. Approaches to regional allies, such as Jordan, had been rejected. The trainees that were therefore flown to the United Kingdom were to be the nucleus of a regular army, known as the General Purpose Force (GPF). Once trained, the idea was to return them to Libya where they would act as a cadre for the expansion of a larger army, which would, it was hoped, persuade the militias to disarm and demobilise.[4]

The training commenced as planned, but only after long delays. Nevertheless, the British Army unit tasked to conduct the training was given very little notice of its role and spent most of its time taking over and refurbishing the camp that would receive the Libyans. Language and cultural training had not been prepared even though the unit was designated to concentrate its attention on North Africa, part of a scheme whereby British regiments were allocated parts of the world to become more familiar with, in anticipation of future deployments. The original plan was for training to be conducted over 24 weeks, starting on 10 June 2014, but the programme was first suspended in July and then again in August. The recruits argued that their pay was insufficient, but their deeper concern was the worsening situation in Libya, and creeping doubt that they would have a long-term job or even survival when returned. The morale and discipline of the Libyan GPF deteriorated, and in October a group absconded from the camp they regarded as a prison and carried out a series of violent sexual assaults against British women and one man in Cambridge. The UK National Security Council decided to terminate the programme immediately and by 7 November the Libyans had been returned to their home country.

The breakdown of governance and security in Libya was clearly an important factor in the state of mind of the Libyan recruits: they felt abandoned and irrelevant as events developed. The Western efforts to stabilise the country were too slow, remote and impractical to succeed.[5] Without a significant presence on the ground, there was no way to control the militias or, indeed, the growing numbers of Jihadist extremists that saw Libya as the next safe haven for their own operations against the West.

During the training there had been friction between the British trainers and the recruits. The Libyan officers were appalled that they had to train alongside the soldiers and found it incomprehensible that the British officers always ate after their men had been fed, as a mark of the ethos of humility and service in leadership, since, in their own culture, prestige and privilege dictated that the officers were served first. Fortunately, the arrival of Jordanian instructors smoothed over some of the misunderstanding, proving once again that regional or local knowledge was essential to success. Nevertheless, there were still objections to 'debriefs' in which recruits were encouraged to self-criticise and find faults or areas for improvement. While an important professionalising tool in British military culture, it was considered an affront, a loss of face and a humiliation to the Libyans. Classroom teaching was also unappealing to the recruits, and greater success was achieved with practical, 'hands-on' training.

James Chandler notes that there was little consideration for the morale of the Libyans in terms of public relations or explanation of the cause.[6] By contrast, the reform of the Lebanese Army had been accompanied by a media campaign which emphasised the link between the army and society: the military were portrayed as the means to achieve greater security and protection of the public. In Libya, and among the recruits, this was absent. The result was disillusionment and greater distance between the Libyan trainees and the experience of the Libyan people. The interim Libyan government was beset with problems, despite elections, and power in the country remained in the hands of the militia. The West had attempted to build stability without making a full ground troops and resources commitment, in an effort not to repeat the 'mistake' of Iraq and Afghanistan. But all it had managed to do was prove that, without commitment, there was even less chance of success. Nevertheless, the preferred political interpretation was that the problem was trying to deliver stability when the fighting was already under way. The assumption was, therefore, that stabilisation, including 'security sector reform' and 'security force assistance', should be delivered before a conflict, which was styled as 'upstream engagement' or, in the curious military image-laden jargon, as 'intervention left of bang'.

As with the United States, the United Kingdom's National Security Strategy therefore posited that its defence would be in part dependent on the ability to 'build stability overseas', resolving conflicts 'upstream' through assistance to fragile states. 'We will focus on those fragile and conflict-affected countries or regions where the risks are high, our interests are most at stake and where we know we can have an impact.'[7] In April 2013 the Defence Engagement Strategy was published, illustrating how a variety of government agencies would work together using a single 'conflict pool' fund to build stability. The intention was to align defence, diplomacy and development to produce co-ordinated activity that would create benign Western 'influence' and prevent safe havens for international terrorism. In Sierra Leone, Nigeria and Kenya, 'defence engagement' seemed to have had positive effects and there was some enthusiasm for the strategy in the British Army as it withdrew from Afghanistan in 2014. Nevertheless, successful cases were the result of very specific contexts which may not be transferred easily to different regions. Moreover, the rather mixed success of building the Iraqi and Afghan national armies suggests that some caution in the application of the strategy was required.

Historically, Europeans favoured the concepts of a mass 'nation in arms', citizen army and smaller professional forces, but the abeyance of war in Europe after 1945, increasingly sophisticated technology and the market-led character of Western defence meant the preferred model by the early twenty-first century was for professional armed forces. Using these professionals in partnering and mentoring local forces, created in the image of the West, became not only a way of stabilising weakened or fragile states, but also the method for augmenting and replacing Western military manpower. In an ideal situation, the West envisaged using its air supremacy to protect local militias and regulars, trained by Western troops, as the method to defeat non-state adversaries. Local forces would then protect stabilised states, while Western military forces, which were best suited to rapid expeditionary operations, could be withdrawn. If counter-insurgency, as used in the period 2002–14, was a process of shape, clear, hold and build, then the new approach was to strike, clear, train and hand over.

In the past, the collision of local and Western ideas of governance, and the clash of cultural norms against the changes resulting from foreign intervention, caused considerable distortion as well as development in the societies the Europeans had encountered. Yet in the 2010s there were confident predictions about the value of using indigenous or proxy forces which did not take full account of the problems or the consequences. Moreover, the West was misreading ideas of future conflict, based on their preferences, assumptions and what they thought was acceptable. They were attempting to find convenient, cheap, proxy forces, while potentially undermining the very objective of stabilisation that raising local security forces could imply. Moreover, in attempting to 'template' the use of Western air power and local forces, governments risked an inappropriate solution to an entirely unique problem, which made stabilisation even less likely. It also threatened to preclude the idea that, on occasions, stability is not desirable at all, as in the case of violent and powerful dictatorships exercising arbitrary governance over their own populations.

Foreign military interventions have often underscored the fact that, before deployment on expeditionary warfare or missions designed to stabilise fragile states, what is required is a comprehensive study of each country and its region, a greater effort to understand the dynamics and the aspirations of the people, and the fulfilment of political and economic agendas that do not alienate but assist them. Solutions need to be carefully tailored to the requirements of each country. In Afghanistan, the objective was to establish institutions, on the Western model but this threatened every vested interest. Moreover, a sense of ethnic difference and mutual suspicion had been reinforced by the experience of thirty years of civil war. Looking back, many military officers lament that attempts to build stability in Afghanistan were derailed by a failure to study the country in depth and an effort to assert systems which the Afghans were not equipped or willing to accept.

The idea of using local forces and perhaps training and developing them *before* their states faced a crisis (like those in Afghanistan, Iraq, Libya or Syria) had much appeal. The development of indigenous forces reduced the need for a 'large footprint' of Western military personnel and the associated costs. The absence of Western casualties and the associated costs, would appeal to the voting public, and the lower profile of such forces would attract less negative media attention. The assistance offered by Western military and security forces could represent 'upstream influence' and build capable forces which would, serve the West's interests. A small and timely commitment could also satisfy the political leadership, who are always eager to reduce expenditure. NATO countries, where legal and constitutional constraints constrain deployments to combat operations outside Europe could also find 'advise and assist' missions to make local forces more acceptable politically. Making commitments to states not actually at war or plagued by domestic insurgency helped the Western governments envisage a way to avoid the unpopular risks of protracted insurgency.

The advantages of developing armies outside the West, carries particular requirements for success and intrinsic constraints which are not always fully appreciated. In the development of their own security forces, restricting where and to whom assistance could be given can be anticipated. This 'agency' of local governments might not accord with Western interests, particularly if non-Western governments wanted to train selected factions for their own political purposes, sought to emphasize robust draconian internal security, or refused to accept international supervision in the treatment of their own populations. To train any local force, such as Libyan national army requires a long-term programme, but this fundamental fact is often at odds with the political desire for a short-term planning horizons, political agendas and other political commitments.

Armies and Stabilisation

It is often assumed that threats to Western interests often come from failing or failed states which are environments for the growth of international terrorism. These threats are part of a wider panorama of menace. The US National Intelligence Council's *Global Trends 2025* report suggested: 'owing to the rise of emerging powers, a globalizing economy, an historic transfer of relative wealth and economic power from West to East, and the growing influence of non-state actors, the international system—as constructed following the Second World War—will be almost unrecognizable by 2025'. Apocalyptic assessments of the future, dominated by terrorism but including mass contamination, pandemic, famine and flood, have been accompanied by bleak but assertive predictions about the demise not only of the international system and the rise of 'ungoverned spaces'.[9] Constructivist international relations theory posits that the neo-realist military instrument is obsolete and the future is best served by humanitarian interventionism under 'R2P' (the UN imperative to enforce a 'Responsibility to Protect') and internationalist organisations. Confident predictions about the end of 'security maximisation' and war as policy options for states nevertheless seem premature.

Western states seem to have sustained their appetite for military operations, sometimes under the very guise of 'humanitarian intervention' in the pursuit of their national interests. While the West is quick to condemn the emergence of a 'new' nexus of organised crime, terrorism and insurgency, it is worth noting that leading states preside over an international system that serves their interests. Those that do not benefit from this system seek to change it, expressing anger and frustration, protesting, arming and adapting themselves against foreign occupation, internal state failure or gross official corruption. Worse, leading powers, like Russia, have chosen deliberately to destabilise some states, like Ukraine, or wage an unrestricted military campaign in support of their proxy partner, in Russia's case the Syrian regime, without regard for international humanitarian law.

But war is not waged purely for national or state interests.[10] Noting the importance of civil war, Jeremy Black has pointed out that armed forces are invariably there to control populations, thus maintaining the state and its economic system. Black suggests that, in the future, increasing resource competition, urbanisation and population growth will jeopardise the stability of many states and confront the West with many more scenarios like Afghanistan, Somalia or Libya. There is likely to be a proliferation of non-state belligerents, that, like such movements in the past, are unlikely to accept the norms of war and measures of restraint imposed by the dominating powers. Moreover, the indigenous security forces the West is keen to build may be deployed with increasing frequency against their own populations.

Western attempts to stabilise faltering bureaucratic states have proved problematic when confronted with older, clan-based systems of governance. Given the costs and complexities in trying to impose the 'stabilisation' of bureaucratic states over clan-based polities in recent conflicts, consideration has been given to the alternatives. There is a return to an emphasis on air power, manifest in the form of drone strikes, a policy of counter-terrorism instead of counter-insurgency, and a new policy of 'upstream engagement' or 'defence diplomacy' where faltering states can be assisted and supported to prevent their failure.[11] Western powers are concerned that failed states are havens of terrorism or generate warlordism or paramilitarism which, in turn, create and sustain humanitarian disasters. The distribution of aid money, the sharing of intelligence, the sale of arms and equipment, and the deployment of training teams to support local military forces and their auxiliaries are the manifestations of these concerns in Western policy.

Nevertheless, stabilisation and building capacity are conducted in the image of the Western states themselves. Too often, policies reflect the idealistic aspirations of Western governments which take insufficient notice of local agendas. Where the European states established a monopoly of violence, sovereignty and legal authority, many less developed countries possess competing and contested notions of political economy. Groups, clans, classes and urban–rural interests may dispute even the fundamentals of the Western political model. In some countries, the objective of a faction may be to gain exclusive control and prevent pluralism. The armed forces may have a critical role to play in enforcing this exclusivity.

Conversely, the landscape of power and authority is diverse and can be the source of civil unrest for decades. States enduring civil unrest or war find that Western intervention alters a balance dynamically. It is important to stress the importance of understanding the position and view of the indigenous populations, the organic and historic nature of the 'human terrain', and the perspective of those the West designate and essentialise as the 'enemy'.[12] This is not just the product of the 'cultural turn' in scholarly studies, but an observation of how states function, how Western military operations proceed, and how they are opposed. Western states may establish local military forces, but this can, in fact, encourage local resistance to an empowered central government. It can just as easily empower the 'wrong' sort of power, with devastating results for the population. States are not just institutions that simply impose themselves with their own policies intact, but they are mirrored by non-state groups which also have policies and agendas of their own. Just as states at war utilise labour, resources, work and ideas to mobilise, assert and legitimise, so too do non-state actors, sometimes using their own channels of funding, systems of patronage and tools for popular mobilisation.

Equally, where Western militaries might emphasise uniformity and discipline in the host nation forces, believing that these characterise all efficient armies, local forces might prioritise cultural norms over 'efficiency'. They may seek military service as the means to acquire power, wealth and status, even when they use the language of honour codes. Western military professionals speak of altruism, obedience to international laws and loyalty to the state, but it is not always certain that this is the way such values are interpreted by local forces. Protests, passive resistance and subversion were traditionally more common than mutiny and were perhaps as frequent as the episodes of fighting together alongside foreigners. Patrick Hennessey noted in Afghanistan that the frequent, six-monthly turnover of mentors broke the relationships that were formed with their mentees. He described a 'collective grump' in the Afghan soldiers as new mentors arrived: 'Suddenly, the ANA started showing off and being almost pointedly ill-disciplined in an effort to live down to the [incoming unit's] worst expectations. It made me wonder whether the worst we had seen ... hadn't perhaps been similarly exaggerated, part of a pantomime, the only way the powerless *kandak* could register its displeasure.'[13]

The idea of stabilising states by recruiting and training state security forces, or, perhaps, training rebel armed groups to overthrow another malign state that sponsors terrorism, offers many opportunities for Western states, but it also imposes constraints. Men, and sometimes women, enlist for a variety of reasons which we might broadly characterise as 'push' factors (such as poverty or local threats) and 'pull' factors (allegiances, opportunism, socio-economic or cultural advancement, or a route to survival). These individual factors are often interpreted through a Western concept, that there is a collective citizenly obligation to serve the greater good of the state and its people. Since the late eighteenth century, service in an army has been seen in the West as the means to develop state cohesion, even if the historical reality was rather different.[14] European empires were also willing to incorporate men of fighting age from troublesome territories adjacent to their possessions in order to absorb and neutralise the threat.

There are nevertheless international and local expectations to be fulfilled. International organisations are uncertain about how to distinguish support between factions in a civil war.[15] Equally, there is often confusion over how to carry out disarmament of armed groups. In Afghanistan there were two efforts to disarm and demobilise combatants under the direction of the Disarmament, Demobilization and Reintegration (DDR) and Disbandment of Illegal Armed Groups (DIAG) initiatives. DDR disarmed some 60,000 former combatants between 2003 and 2009, though there were accusations of corruption. DIAG, which aimed to disband all illegal armed groups by 2007, simply failed. By 2009, fewer than 400 armed groups, calculated at five or more people operating outside the law, were disbanded, even though conservative estimates suggested there were 3,000 illegal armed groups in total.[16]

Attempts to disarm local armed groups were difficult in a country where possession of a firearm was considered historically to be a point of honour. Disarming a man constituted a direct threat to his social standing. While some indigenous people wished to seize the opportunity of regular paid employment from Westerners, others resented what they perceived as neo-colonial attitudes. Where some poorly educated men embrace the basic training in combat and survival skills offered by Western training teams, those with responsibility are eager for organisational and logistical support. Many Afghan senior officers have expressed a desire for heavy weapons, transport and armoured vehicles alongside the basic infantry training which has dominated the Western training mission in Afghanistan. While levels of training and support need to be appropriate and calculated to meet the specific needs of any force, which includes the weapons and equipment levels they already possess, they also value technical assistance, which, in many cases, they lack.

Critics, like Roger McGinty, argue that stabilisation missions are a means to legitimise Western hegemony, normalise the use of military forces in peace-building efforts, and protect certain interests. He writes:

> There can be no doubting that international actions have helped topple despots and have introduced significant socio-political change in a number of societies. Yet such change is bounded by essentially conservative parameters that reinforce international order, the primacy of state sovereignty, and the dominance of the market economy ... International financial institution strictures to pare back the state, trim welfare, keep inflation low and open (usually fragile) economies to outside competition are rarely empowering. Indeed, international stabilization programs are often a diet of compliance and discipline.[17]

Nevertheless, Western military training missions do not seem to be evidence of any conspiracy of neo-colonialism, but rather an attempt to exercise 'influence' or facilitate a proxy strategy. This process is not necessarily malign or cynical. There can sometimes be local opportunities in the building of armies which can create mutual benefits. Local rituals and beliefs can be reinforced, creating pride, a vested interest and stability. Combining regional and national identities can, for example, develop a sense of civic pride. In all armies, promotions, rewards and honours can motivate individuals. Power and responsibility can be developed through careful mentoring. There are foreign concepts and expectations against which local forces will fail, particularly if literacy levels are lower, but appropriate levels of training, equipment and procedures can be invaluable. Security, provided by trusted and impartial but local forces, can have a significantly positive effect for vulnerable populations, protecting access to economic centres and routes and providing the basis for sustainable peace and stability. In essence, there are both risks and benefits in building local military capacity to stabilise states.

Private Security and the Privatisation of War

In the early twenty-first century there was a significant increase in the number of private military contractors operating in armed conflicts. Their champions saw them as a natural, inexpensive and useful adjunct to state forces and Coalition troops, but critics feared that the contractor was a new manifestation of the older and sinister problem of the mercenary.

Mercenary forces developed a grim reputation from the 1960s in Africa, and there were some moments of scandal in international affairs when private forces appeared to be either interfering in politics or, in the case of Iraq, operating outside the law.[18] One eyewitness in Baghdad in 2006–7 noted that private security contractors belonging to Blackwater would regularly open fire on every suspected threat once outside the green zone with small arms or heavier weapons in their protection of their clients and themselves.[19] Certain companies developed such a shocking reputation that they were eventually ejected from Iraq. Nevertheless, companies can quickly change their identity and recommence business, and they will claim to be operating under the jurisdiction of governments and states, which are legally constituted. The criticisms of private security contractors are that they do not adhere to laws and regulations, they readily violate human rights or rules of engagement, and they are difficult to hold to account.[20] Moreover, their claim to be cheaper than state forces was disputed. There were concerns in Iraq and Afghanistan that there was too little competitiveness in the bidding process for contracts and that their supervision was inadequate.

The criticisms of private contractors are not limited to their conduct in high-risk environments but extend to their very existence. Armies, navies and air forces are sanctioned by the laws that govern states, and therefore they are accountable to their populations and to the international system. While not a fool-proof safeguard, it means that soldiers, sailors, airmen and marines are ultimately responsible to the law and owe their allegiance to the people they serve. By contrast, private contractors owe allegiance to their shareholders and to the company. They work not for any sacred causes but for profit. While that company may be subject to laws, recent cases involving social media and internet companies' refusal to disclose data to governments in order to track terrorists reveal that private companies have mechanisms for evading the usual sanctions of states, including taxation, regulation and legal jurisdiction.

Contractors also lack staying power. They will be dictated by their company's directives to make a profit. If the contracts are ending or are no longer lucrative, there will be no incentive for a contractor to stay on. If the currency of regular armed forces is honour, for the contractor it is, and can only be, money. Some contractors could expect to earn ten times the equivalent rates of pay of American military personnel.[21] Moreover, if regulation is deepened, a private security company may deem the legal environment too hostile and limiting to be worthwhile precisely at the moment they are needed or when a state has become somewhat dependent on them.[22]

On the other hand, contractors have had an appeal to governments for a number of reasons, and the private security companies have had to do much to clear up their reputation. Towards the end of the American intervention in Iraq, Washington was able to claim that it had diminished the risk to its own personnel and reduced its 'footprint', as the gap was filled by large numbers of private contractors. As one analyst noted, in Vietnam there had been one contractor for every one hundred soldiers; by the end of the intervention in Iraq, the proportion was one contractor for every 1.5 soldiers.[23] While the levels of training and competence of some of these individuals were variable, there was at least an imperative on the companies to act in a more ethical way towards the Iraqis.

Private contractors represent a means to escape rising costs of standing armies, in that temporary militarised personnel can be hired and then fired.[24] Specialist personnel could also be hired on this basis, although there is no sound argument why this cannot be done by the government directly, with all the safeguards for the employee and the employer, rather than the 'middleman' of a private security business.[25] One analyst argues that private companies could represent a strategic edge for the United States in future conflict, but the inevitable consequence would be to add to the erosion of international restrictions on armed conflict.[26]

The problems therefore remain. One former British officer in command of contingents of private security personnel drawn from a variety of national backgrounds in Iraq was plagued by strikes.[27] The security contractors were invariably demanding higher pay because of alleged risks. The moral issues aside, the question of pay does at the very least indicate an older established fact about military forces, and that is their assessment of their own market value. If personnel regard themselves as undervalued, they will leave the service. There has often been concern among senior military personnel about the difficulty of attracting and retaining the best talent, especially in the most specialised fields. Contractors have the potential to accelerate that corrosive effect.

For states there are perhaps advantages in using private military contractors precisely because they are less concerned with the rules of engagement or laws of armed conflict; in other words, they can act more ruthlessly. They thus represent a form of paramilitarism. It is this ability to act on private judgements without being public agents that alarms the critics. Moreover, contractors can be motivated to use violence on the basis of a financial contract, and not in a 'just' manner involving public duty and altruism, and the values of *jus ad bellum*, of proportionality, last resort and right intention. Ironically, privately employed contractors can more easily reject the terms and conditions of service they don't like, which is a position denied to volunteer state personnel or conscripts. This makes them even less reliable and dependable.

Private security companies insist that the majority of their work is benign and non-violent, obedient to the laws and rules of engagement of whichever state force they are accompanying, and motivated by the desire to assist, protect and stabilise. They are keen to make distinctions between private military companies (which prioritise logistics) and private security contractors, although the differences can be blurred.[28] Ultimately we must judge on the performance of such entities, and, to be clear, the arguments of benign benefit are not supported by the evidence in the last few decades.

Local Forces and Stabilisation

During the conflict in Syria which began in 2011, some of the Western states looked favourably upon the idea of arming and perhaps training what was initially known as the Free Syrian Army and the Kurdish factions with their minority allies. The rise of extremist Jihadist groups, some of whom were opposed to the resistance and some of whom were integral to it, caused the West to hesitate. Russia, which regarded Syria as its last strategically important ally in the Middle East, chose to back the Syrian regime when Assad's forces appeared to be close to collapse. In 2015, efforts were made to try to co-ordinate Western and Russian air forces operating over Syrian air space, but the fundamental contradiction about which actors they were supporting on the ground found its logic in a breakdown in diplomatic relations in 2016. In Syria, Kurdish fighters, which had made steady progress under an American air umbrella, were halted by Turkish intervention, which the United States, as a NATO ally of Turkey, felt obliged to support. Meanwhile, the Islamic State fighters, which had made significant territorial gains in 2014–15, found themselves under increasing military pressure in Iraq and from Western air attacks. The so-called moderate opposition was also checked and then driven back by a reinvigorated Syrian Army, backed by Russian air power. Local forces were being accompanied by the air power of rival nations, and the war dragged on. Paradoxically, a similar conflict, also involving external air forces and local ground units, was played out in Yemen at the same time.

In Libya, many believed the model of Western air power in support of local militias had been successful, but the failure to build a viable political system or a national army condemned the country to further instability and violence. Local militias had become, as many had anticipated, a power unto themselves. On occasions, there had been some successes, and this underlined the point that the contexts were different and therefore a single 'model' was inappropriate. The French armed forces had been successful in their operations in Mali precisely because they had not depended on local forces, but had led the operations with their own troops on the ground. They handed over security responsibility once areas had been cleared and secured. But stabilisation requires more than military intervention, air supremacy and elections. It requires the building of institutions, public consent, and a viable local security apparatus.

The fashion for training local military forces is commendable but has to be tailored to be a success. Where foreign forces are involved, there are principles of mentoring, partnering and training local forces which ought to be promoted. First and foremost, the planning and conduct of training and development must genuinely be a joint, equitable and partnered effort. Western forces have to understand their charges in order to motivate them, and it is essential that local forces be given a clear imperative to train and fight. Wherever possible, local solutions must be applied, framed within cultural points of reference and tolerated if they collide with Western norms. Local leaders must be selected and developed, progressively testing their abilities, and inculcating appropriate values of meritocracy, personal and professional development, or obedience to civil authority and the law. Pairing commanders of the same rank is vital to avoid any loss of status for the indigenous officers. Trainers must emphasise the importance of setting long-terms goals and assisting local forces to realise them in stages in order to develop confidence. Nevertheless, all training requires flexibility, not least to manage local problems in logistics, military setbacks and co-ordination.

Training is the way to build not only capability but also allegiances. Officer training should emphasise the fundamental importance of loyalty to civil authority and the laws of war, and is well served by developing skills 'two-up', that is, getting each rank familiar with the duties of the two ranks above them in order to emphasise responsibility. Mentors and trainers need to possess considerable tact, patience and humility, knowing how and when to intervene and when to remain in reserve. Clearly, high-order language skills are essential, but so is a deeper knowledge of customs, traditional recruiting patterns, power relationships and other aspects of so-called human terrain. Trainers themselves need to be familiar with theories and methods of personal development alongside their own professional military skills. Above all, they would need a clear understanding of the overall mission and some faith in their devolved responsibilities.

Private contractors seem to appear with more frequency in security matters, but their uses remain limited. The primary concerns about their profit motive, their ethical standards and priorities, their accountability, and their potential to erode state forces' missions continue to cause doubts about their utility. Are they inevitable, and can they be valuable? The questions remain unanswered.

It is worth considering further what underpins the desire for 'upstream engagement', a phrase used to describe Western inputs to influence and prevent 'state failure'. While seemingly a plausible concept and one worthy of the popular humanitarian agenda, it is too often a reassuring semantic phrase that perhaps masks the reality of the West's difficulties in tackling civil war and insurgency in the Global South. Raising local forces requires time and investment. Relatively benign base areas are needed and newly formed units have to be tested, inoculated and trained progressively. Furthermore, they require more than the outward trappings of close-quarter combat training so favoured by Western militaries, and they need more profound development than the provision of precise or heavy weapons. National armies require a deeper immersion in national values and must reflect the society from which they are drawn. To avoid becoming a threat to their state and societies, brigands preying on their own people or those of neighbouring states, and to avoid the assumption that it is only they who can provide order and security for their country, they need to embrace an ethos of civil primacy, the desire to protect the population, and their representative institutions. These ethics are not easily imported, but must be established from within their own cultural terms of reference. In the history of many national and colonial armies, loyalty and allegiance were as important as combat-effectiveness.

The recruitment of local forces for stabilisation, both proxy actors and regular units, will always raise the question of consequences. It is unclear whether the real intent of Western forces and their governments is to spread democracy, fulfil national interests or create a stable global order. The Western powers hope to achieve all three, but not all would be attractive to their partners and allies. Nor is it entirely clear to whom Western-led training missions are acceptable: do they serve Western interests or local ones? What is the likelihood that a force raised and trained by the West will inflict casualties on the civilian population or pursue its own agenda against its rivals? Critics of Western missions in Iraq, Afghanistan and Libya point to human rights abuses, insider attacks, higher civilian casualties, the potential fuelling of internal conflict, and the consequent undermining of the mission of stabilisation. As always, a coherent and well-considered, long-term strategic analysis is required, but there are some inherent risks. Therefore, what may appear, initially, as limited liability and upstream engagement for greater influence may turn out to be a downstream entanglement for which smaller Western forces, trained in high-intensity conventional operations, are ill equipped. Investing in indigenous forces cannot simply be a cheaper alternative in the fulfilment of national strategy, if only for the reason that the consequences of getting it wrong could be very costly indeed.

14

CONCLUSION

'Okay, so I get what this book is about, but does it show me how to actually, like, do it; you know, at our level?'

Anonymous Corporal, 22 SAS, 2016

This volume has been an attempt to broaden the criteria by which local military forces in foreign service have been assessed. Moving beyond a typology, the factors which have influenced performance in combat, which is the ultimate purpose of an army, have been clustered in order to assist comparisons and to measure effects across time and space. The numerous case examples, which are illustrative and not exhaustive, allow us to assess external influences on performance alongside the internal factors, that is, those cohesive elements which are generated from within individuals and units. This approach challenges the preferred agendas of some scholars, who seek to argue that a particular element can be prioritised, as well as the more instrumentalist approach of military professionals. Whether this book could be of any practical use, as the NCO of the British Special Forces who asked me the question above wondered, must be judged by others.

It is hoped that its value lies in a clearer theoretical approach. The combined conceptual and historical methods used in this volume illustrate that circumstances were just as influential as the continuities in training and discipline, and in any of the other individual elements. On the other hand, in order to assist comparison, this volume has ranged across the globe and through

391

time, applying a wide set of criteria to each case. To make the comparisons more manageable, the emphasis has been on the United States, France and the United Kingdom and their interactions with a number of regions.

As a reminder, the criteria for assessment included the initial motivation on recruitment, status, terms and conditions of service, the size of force, loyalty and reliability, training and experience, cohesion, discipline, resilience, the compulsion to change and the survival of relics. It has also considered technologies with which the local forces were equipped, the tactics they preferred, leadership and command, the condition of civil–military relations, the common use of the force, cultural influences and their manifestations, the socio-economic background and quality of officers and men, the prevailing political system, their state stabilisation role and view of internal security, and the prevalence of war and their exposure to it. This is a far more comprehensive list than can be found in standard typologies, but is itself only a simple theoretical model for the purposes of clarity, understanding and comparison.

In assessing the results, it is clear that the impact of each criterion can vary enormously and create a dynamic effect. Thus the arrival of a new and more effective leader can transform unpromising military personnel, producing a virtuous enhancement in performance, cohesion, morale and resilience. Equally, while periodic exposure to conflict and casualties can create a seasoned force, it can just as easily cause a steady deterioration in performance. The idea of the more detailed criteria is only to bring us closer to the assessments of change, difference and the specificities of each case.

Indigenous Personnel in European Forces before 1945

The employment of local forces across the period covered by this study the context was very different compared with the twenty-first century, and the values, legal jurisdiction, sovereignty and agency of all parties changed considerably over time. In the colonial era before 1945, Europeans established their own legal systems, enlisted a selection of men according to their own preferences and prejudices, and placed European officers in command. European regiments were stationed alongside local forces to supervise them, and most kept the most advanced weapon systems out of their hands; the British, for example, took the precaution of depriving Indian units of field artillery between 1858 and 1939. There were, however, strong incentives to use local forces: they were abundant and cheap, they absorbed labour that would otherwise pose a security threat to the European colonies, and they conferred a degree of legitimacy on the imperial project, opening up a strong link with local populations and making their families dependent on the continuation of colonial rule.

The motivation for local personnel to enlist was often considerable. Although we have only fragmentary records for the experience of enlistment and service, it is possible to reconstruct the main factors that drove the process. When previous polities were shattered by European intervention, men with military backgrounds would seek employment to maintain their status, and the new colonial authorities invariably offered a regular income at much better rates than could be procured elsewhere. It was the certainty and regularity of pay that appealed to many of the men in Madras and Bengal in the mid-1700s. Relics of previous epochs survived too. There were slave soldiers in the West Indies, maintained under the threat of severe punishments but also with the understanding that their lot was far better than those in hard labour, such as plantation work. There was the promise of liberation at the end of one's service, and also the benefits of money to spend in peacetime garrisons and the chance of other 'spoils of war' while serving.

For those indigenous peoples that allied or partnered with the British and French in North America, there was the prospect that, protected by a major power, their lands would be inviolate and their way of life secure. There was the potential for looting and enhancement of warrior status, two important avenues for the fulfilment of the rites of passage into manhood.

The system did not always function. Men could become dissatisfied to the point of violence with bad leadership, reductions in pay and allowances, infringements of privileges, affronts to cultural icons, or misuse in terms of their role. Desertion, mutiny and murder of European officers were relatively common. The Indian Mutiny was the most severe outbreak of unrest in the nineteenth century, not least because the British had placed so many local men under arms. It was the result of a multitude of problems which had been brewing for years, but money, insults, draconian punishments, neglect and a reduced British garrison were the most important. The 'greased cartridges' affair was just the final exasperating affront to a disgruntled army.

On the other hand, the Indian Army survived as an institution, partly through mutual necessity, but also because much of it remained free of the unrest that had beset the troops of the Bengal Army. Indian troops on operations in Persia in the year of the Mutiny showed no sign of disaffection and in 1860, just two years after the fighting in India, the sepoys performed without issues in China. The British were also able to draw on new pools of labour, especially from the Punjab and the peripheries of India, which established a precedent for recruitment that would last almost until the end of the Raj. Men of the Punjab, Nepal and the mountainous north-west had long believed themselves to be a distinctly 'warrior' caste and the British encouraged their beliefs. The 'martial races' theory, based in part on experience and observation, and partly on a self-reinforcing sense of identity, was not limited to South Asia and was applied in one form or another across the colonised world.

Of the great variety of types and categories that the Europeans employed, such as scouts, levies, home guards, auxiliaries, pioneers, paramilitary police, irregular cavalry, mountain gunners, camel corps, muleteers and infantrymen, those who were fully trained regulars performed best. Irregulars were retained if they possessed certain skills or knowledge, such as command of the indigenous languages or fighting prowess in mountain, desert or jungle warfare. Discipline, a robust legal system that endorsed a range of punishments, efficient systems of supply, increasingly advanced weaponry relative to local polities, and regularity in pay all reinforced the system that produced regular troops. It also generated, over time, a sense of professional pride that set soldiers apart from civilians.

The sheer variety of forces employed by Europeans naturally created a significant variation in performance. Many factors could determine how well indigenous forces fought, how cohesive they were and what they could endure. Some elements have a universal application. Where men feel that they have been part of an exclusive selection, after rigorous training or some initiation ceremony, they feel a strong sense of needing to live up to the elite status they have acquired. There may be a powerful desire to acquire rewards, such as promotion. Men who volunteered to be the 'forlorn hope', the first to storm a breach in an enemy's defences, which therefore implied a greater chance of death, often did so because, if they survived, immediate promotion was very likely. Indigenous men might also perform more effectively on the basis of better nutrition, because of some attachment to a charismatic leader, or through the determination to fulfil a status based on religion or identity. European officers were expected to show example, which mutually reinforced the desire of followers and leaders to excel. Motivation to enlist was distinct from battlefield performance, and historical analyses have frequently shown how the specific cohesive nature of experienced military personnel, and an enhanced professionalism, were far more important than the factors which induced men to enlist. Moreover, prosaic material benefits, like pay and conditions, or remote sentiments towards family, community or institution, couldn't make men brave in the immediate stress of combat. In the close-quarter battles that characterised warfare before 1900, it was the timeless factors of honour, protection of comrades, and a determination to fulfil a mission that mattered most.

There was considerable value for Europeans in raising and utilising local forces. Until medical advances could guarantee survival, indigenous troops were essential in tropical garrisons because of high death rates. They were often more acclimatised, a crucial factor in rapid expeditions made into remote and high mountainous regions. Local forces could augment much-needed manpower on large-scale operations or provide garrisons. Sometimes indigenous personnel were motivated by the opportunity to inflict retribution against long-standing enemies, and the frequent accusation that the Europeans imposed a system of 'divide and rule' to govern their colonies might also have to acknowledge that locals themselves were invariably eager to use the licence the Europeans offered them to settle old scores. The Sikhs enlisted readily in 1857 to inflict revenge against Hindus, whom they despised for their part in the destruction of the Sikh Kingdom a decade earlier. There was antagonism between the black soldiers of the Ceylon regiments and the Kandyans, mutual contempt between Sikh soldiers and Pashtuns in the fighting along the North West Frontier in the 1890s, and fear and loathing between the Afrikaners and armed Barolong at Mafeking in 1900. Racial prejudice was even more pronounced among Chinese confronted by Indian sepoys or other foreign contingents.

Methods of recruitment and retention in the period before 1945 relied a great deal on being able to tap into the social structures of local communities. Broadly speaking, those with existing strong hierarchical systems were more amenable to military service, while democratised ones, like the Coorgs or the Pashtuns of South Asia, were not. The relative homogeneity of communities seems to have been less critical, since men from both strongly cohesive and more atomised social groups featured in colonial forces. The Europeans themselves had a preference for less-educated, rural men, perceiving them to be more biddable, loyal, conservative and physically robust. Hierarchical ties were more resilient in the countryside compared with urban inhabitants, and so it was thought that allegiances could be more easily transferred.

Leadership appears to have been another area where results were variable. Some armies opted for a proportion of indigenous leaders to lead local forces, but many units were commanded by Europeans. Much depended on the degree of allegiance and military effectiveness that an existing force could offer the Europeans. Yet the Europeans might also seek to replace the local leadership entirely, creating their own units in the European style, and relying on a combination of higher incomes, training, cohesion through professionalism, and some degree of cultural concession, such as dress, rituals, fighting styles and rewards.

There were myriad problems with local forces. Misunderstandings based on language and cultural differences were common, which made the appointment of men with the vernacular language skills crucial, either the European officers and NCOs or, in many cases, men selected from the ranks and promoted as 'native' officers. Men who regarded themselves as warriors might cause difficulties because of their expectations regarding battlefield tactics, the treatment of prisoners, women or property, or the peacetime tasks they would or would not perform. Manual labour was not considered appropriate by certain castes or classes of men, which limited their versatility as pioneers or in the excavation of field defences, construction work or the carriage of supplies. There was often anxiety about the use of indigenous personnel in internal security duties, and Europeans usually endeavoured to deploy their troops outside the area in which they were recruited to prevent the risk of fraternisation. Desertion and wastage through sickness were a constant headache and more significant in less well-trained or cohesive forces, and changing sides could not be ruled out in certain conflicts in which allegiances could be easily divided.

Assessments of Units before 1945

Regarding the types prevalent in the period before 1945, this volume has examined across a range of categories in order to make a comparative assessment. 'Untrained personnel' is to some extent a misleading starting point since many groups that the Europeans encountered had some inherent experience of violence or self-defence, and many possessed fighting skills which, while not those of regular troops, were equal or superior to them in certain environments. Nevertheless, men in the category of 'untrained' were not expected to stand and defend for long, or to press home an attack in order to destroy an enemy at close quarters. Terrified porters employed by the British in the Zulu War, for example, fled when there was a prospect of facing the discipline impis. On the other hand, local men without formal training employed on the North West Frontier as *khassadars* to protect British political officers considered it a point of personal honour to defend the foreigner with their life. Arab Bedouin fighters who fought for the Sharif of Mecca but were accompanied by British and French officers as advisers and their leaders were notoriously unreliable. They would occasionally refuse battle, break off an engagement when it suited them, take leave to return to their families when they chose to, act with excessive violence towards prisoners, and quarrel with rival clans regardless of a higher-priority mission. In many ways, the Sharifian forces were closer to the category of local levies than 'untrained' personnel. Levies tended to be hired for very short periods, sometimes mere days, and were armed with their own weapons, possessed their own transport, if any, and were invariably led by their own commanders.

Militia or irregular cavalry might have undergone minimal training, possess some issued armaments and even wear the uniforms of their European supervising powers. They usually remained plagued by the sort of problems that characterised the untrained or hired forces described above.

'Scouts' was a term used to describe something beyond a mere local guide or reconnaissance group, and could suggest a highly motivated and disciplined band such as the Guides Cavalry. Moreover, unlike militia which might be limited in use to guarding specific sites or lines of communication, scouts implied a more mobile and offensive capability. The overlap becomes more problematic when considering the next category of inexperienced regulars, which could be described as units whose training is incomplete or in other ways below standard. The level of proficiency would be low and the category might also encompass units that, having mutinied or suffered significant casualties, had to be reconstituted with almost entirely new personnel.

The more effective categories of experienced regulars and veteran regulars represent those whose training, discipline, cohesion and other variables were of a standard that, when in the field, they could be relied upon to perform their duties, take casualties, endure a high level of hardship and yet remain combat-effective, cohesive and able to complete their allotted tasks. Of course, the conditions of war could reduce the effectiveness of any units to the point where it would fail these tests, but the description is used here in order to establish only the characteristics of the category. Experienced veteran units that had been subjected to relentless attrition or suffered losses in combat, for example, might actually become less effective through an unwillingness to go through the crucible again compared with inexperienced but enthusiastic personnel.

Among the most effective and consistently highly-motivated category would be officers and elite forces, whose status, skills, ethos and expectations tended to produce the standards for a unit's performance. As the old maxim has it: 'there are no good or bad regiments, only good or bad officers'. There were certainly plenty of examples of both. The British cavalry officers Hodson,

Nicholson and Chamberlain, who led Sikh, Punjabi, Pashtun and Rajput personnel during the first half of the nineteenth century, or Gordon in China commanded almost cult-like allegiance from their men. By contrast, many officers of the West India and Ceylon regiments fell far short of the standards expected. Careful selection was a crucial element in their subsequent performance. Battlefield success could create a sense of awe and future good fortune that surrounded particular leaders, but others were ruthlessly exploitative and had expectations of their men that could not be fulfilled, such as General Mangin and *le force noir* on the killing fields of the Chemin des Dames.

Mercenaries remain a problematic category, which might be found anywhere along the spectrum. There is no guarantee they are either the most effective or the least useful; they can be as motivated and courageous as any other type of force, and examples such as the Foreign Legions of France or Spain point to their exceptionalism.

Local Forces post-1945

Local forces played an important role during the process of decolonisation, sometimes hastening the end of the colonial empires, and sometimes delaying it. There were examples in which local forces certainly made the process of exit more violent, but, in other cases, the existence of local military forces ensured a peaceful transition to a new state, since the independent government inherited a Western-trained and competent army, air force, coastal defence force or navy. In military operations, local troops could provide intelligence and counter-insurgency units and act as a physical symbol of government power. Nevertheless, weak local forces could be overwhelmed, they could erode confidence if their allegiances began to change, and they could generate violence against the population that could create the conditions for a civil war. It is striking that much of the literature on the withdrawal of European colonial control has focused on national liberation movements or the actions of the Westerners, but this has rather overshadowed the importance of local military personnel.

In this volume, it is clear that local militias represent the boundary of state power and jurisdiction. Where governments lack manpower and face armed resistance, they have had to turn to the population for support through enrolment in forces that can contribute to state security. Counter-insurgency campaigns demand that the people commit to the government, part of a process of re-establishing a weakened social contract, and the most dedicated element of that commitment can be found in local military forces, including home guards and militia, for it is here that the public demonstrate their willingness to accept a greater degree of risk to defend their interests and, by default in some cases, align themselves with the existing political order. Regular law-enforcement units and armed forces are usually insufficient in number to control all routes, populated areas and strategic points, but the raising of local forces, while diluting the Weberian norm of a monopoly of force, which defines the power of the state, provides a practical instrument to augment state power.

The controversy of irregular forces in government service concerns the inability to guarantee their control or professional conduct. As some of the examples in this volume illustrate, the nature of insurgency or civil war tends to encourage violence between civilians, not least because laws of armed conflict and civil laws are infringed, and attacks are invariably delivered by personnel not wearing uniforms or carrying arms openly. Once they have been subjected to ambushes, indiscriminate bomb attacks, assassinations and terrorism against civilians, there is inevitably a great risk that both local and regular forces will step across the normal legal and ethical thresholds to exact revenge and inflict reprisals. Less well-trained and disciplined forces are more likely to take such action, but organised and state-sanctioned activity can also accelerate the descent into illegality and barbarism on both sides. Countergangs, state terror and betrayals escalate all too easily. It hardly needs to be restated, but evidently one answer to an insurgency is to use all means to achieve a political settlement, re-establish a social contract, and, by definition, take the heat out of the conflict by restoring normal policing, creating conflict-free districts and searching for political agreement. Nevertheless, historical examples also suggest a less encouraging solution can be just as effective, and that is the wholesale destruction or defeat of the insurgency by the greater militarisation and surveillance of society by the government, and the enlistment on a large scale of local security forces.

The participation of populations in local military forces, even those that receive regular training, is no guarantee of government victory. The most common problem is the corrosive effect of corruption, but any form of political instability can rapidly undermine attempts to provide security. In Vietnam, a series of *coups d'état*, orchestrated by the military, and the damaging corrupt practices of senior officers, corroded the confidence and competence of the army. On the other hand, officers like Robert Thompson and Barry Petersen recognised that the population often received better protection from local auxiliary forces than regular troops. Self-Defence Corps, the Regional Forces and Popular Forces, and other home guard initiatives, were successful when they operated in rural peripheries, close to their homes, under the protection of rapid reaction forces or government airpower, and when they were committed to support the government. Attempts to form larger militias, with indifference towards the government and weakened responsibility towards the local population, too often became liabilities. Successful militias were small in number, localised, and could not be used in isolation; they had to be an integral part of a joint plan of other activities and institutions, with regular military reinforcement when required, the backing of the established law-enforcement agencies, and the licence to operate from their national government. Rewards and benefits needed to be specified and honoured, but there had to be a plan for their subsequent demobilisation. It was unfortunate that, in Vietnam, the aspiration of the Montagnards for greater autonomy was never fulfilled and latent antagonism with the ethnic Vietnamese increased as a result.

The period after 1945 offers many examples of advisory work by Western powers, and unfortunately it has not been possible to include more cases, such as the CORDS programme in Vietnam, the successful British training mission in Sierra Leone after 2000, and French advice and assist activities in West Africa. These need to be the focus of study for other scholars and professionals. Nevertheless, the handful of cases offered in this volume suggest that the advisory role was a difficult one, conferring immense responsibility and increased risk on the personnel involved.

The best practice of advisory work probably also lies beyond the scope of this book. Nevertheless, it is evident from the cases that appear in the period after 1945 that a high standard of cultural awareness and command of the local languages were essential. Advisers had to spend considerable lengths of time with their mentees in order to build knowledge, trust and mutual respect. Advisers had to fight alongside the local forces. They had to possess a high degree of tactical skill and technical proficiency, but also knowledge of information warfare, psychological operations and adroit judgement of men, especially their collective behaviour or individual traits. This awareness enabled them to develop, in conjunction with local forces, early warning systems, the ability to confront subversives, and anticipate the shifting moods of the population. Identity, a sense of territoriality and esteem appear to have been important, acting as a form of currency far more valuable at times than hard cash. An accomplished peace negotiator explained that offering money to gain co-operation could be seen as an affront to some groups, and merely trying to increase the amount deepens the insult. As he put it: 'If I offered you money to buy your wife, you'd be offended; if I offered to double the amount, you'd probably put a bullet in my head.'[1]

Advisers and mentors found it easier to assist local forces where there was a long-standing tradition. In Algeria, the French had employed local men for decades and there was a sense of shared identity. The Harkis and GAD local units, encouraged by short-term contracts and generous pay, were not the most effective combat forces, but their role was to show the people that the government was in control, absorbed manpower that might otherwise support the insurgency, and provided a mechanism for gathering intelligence. However, the Harkis, like many irregular units, jeopardised the government's need to adhere to the law. Their murderous struggle with the insurgents embittered the conflict and made finding a favourable political solution less likely. The lesson is clear: local forces have to be carefully controlled and supervised in counter-insurgencies and civil wars, lest they escalate the violence, generate insecurity, and undermine efforts to assert government hegemony in the minds of the population.

In the Western training missions in the Iraq and Afghanistan campaigns, there were insufficient numbers of qualified personnel, with or without a command of local languages. There were often delays in the release of funds and in the required organisations, although the targets for expansion were frequently increased. There were debates about what types of forces were needed, and in Iraq the early decision to simply disband the entire Iraqi Army, in order to fulfil a political agenda, was the single most important factor in fuelling an insurgency. There was a constant concern with the quality of forces, here and in Afghanistan, given the conflicting allegiances of the population and, in the case of Iraq, an increasingly sectarian national government. Training organisations had to consider not just the recruitment and development of personnel, but also the facilities, logistics, medical installations and casualty evacuation systems, pay and leave arrangements, criminal justice processes and institutions, ministerial oversight and procurement chains. Police training suffered from a lack of available advisers and trainers, and private contractors failed to fill the gap to the required standards.

The urgent need for security and the difficulty of raising security forces in sufficient numbers during a worsening insurgency meant that the Western authorities looked more favourably on local community defence units. The decision of the Anbari sheikhs to reject al-Qaeda and reach out to the Americans and the government in Baghdad was of strategic significance in the Iraq conflict. What emerged in Anbar and in much of southern and eastern Afghanistan was that tribal organisation was more amenable to district control with local forces, where the community could keep any armed men accountable, but, in order to ensure the state gained some control, local units required the licence of the national authorities. Control could be ensured through pay, arms and equipment, as well as legal status, representing a contractual relationship between the state and its peripheries. The support of heavy weapons, air power and transport came from regular units, ideally provided by the national government rather than foreigners, although that was not always possible. Western Special Forces advisers proved very effective in training local units but also in co-ordinating fires and air support, as well as medical evacuation and aerial resupply. But local forces were most effective when limited to local security, though all local forces have been a vital component in the security transition from Western intervention to national control.

There are plenty of objections to the use of local irregular defence forces in civil conflicts. There is a frequent concern that such forces can change sides, a common feature of civil wars. Selected groups can be empowered by being armed, leading to power struggles, which can generate rivalry from those that perceive themselves disenfranchised. Part of the reason for the sudden breakdown of the Iraqi Army in 2014 was the imbalance in the national government and special privileges granted to Shia factions.

It was difficult to achieve unity of effort in training missions in Afghanistan because of the decision to make it a multinational endeavour, while in Iraq budgetary complications, a small training team and a changing strategy caused significant problems. The fact these efforts took place against a background of worsening violence and growing domestic criticism did not make them any easier. American commanders privately expressed their frustrations about complex lines of reporting, national caveats from European personnel, and variable levels of funding. Public criticisms, or at least those leaked by the media, led to dismissals, which made honest appraisals and therefore any solutions much more difficult. Different approaches to training across NATO and Coalition partners imposed delays and confusion, and attempts to create 'national' forces in their own image took too little account of local expectations, norms and procedures. A frequent admission one heard was that Coalition trainers tended to use PowerPoint for everything, but reverted to pens and paper or verbal briefings when they realised these just got better results from local commanders and their personnel.

The conflicts in Iraq, Afghanistan and Libya highlighted the need to develop police forces at a different rate than military personnel. Moreover, the need for functioning judicial systems for the local forces and to process insurgent prisoners and criminals took much longer to implement and, in the case of Libya, it failed to materialise. In much of the developing world, police officers do not meet the standards expected in the West: there are many examples where vehicle checkpoints, ostensibly for security, are the means by which the police acquire funds through 'shakedowns' and extortion. Empowering such an inadequately trained force reinforced local perceptions that their governments could not be trusted. Furthermore, the administration of military and police personnel suffered from degrees of nepotism in promotion, cronyism and financial corruption.

Western trainers and mentors found it difficult to tackle this corruption, even where it self-evidently threatened discipline and professional efficiency. Reporting up the chain of command of local forces, the default option, created no changes, as senior officers were often the source of the problem. Exposing corrupt commanders was almost impossible because of a local conspiracy of silence. Once again, there were local expectations that their rank should confer upon them a range of privileges, including additional financial rewards and allowances. This remained a constant source of friction and generated cynicism among many Western soldiers.

Partnering and Mentoring

The objective of partnering and mentoring is to create local security forces that are self-sustaining, effective and accountable. The purpose of military forces is to protect the population and the state, but therein lies an inherent risk when indigenous personnel are trained, mentored and made more effective: there may be a greater temptation to use their power to exert influence over the population, acquire material resources, or seize political authority for themselves. Partnering, mentoring and training local forces therefore need a long-term approach, in which relationships can be developed and the ethos of a responsible armed force, in the service of the state and the people, can be inculcated. It requires a significant shift in mindset among Western forces. In the difficult days of countering the insurgency in Afghanistan, General David Petraeus stated: 'We must do things dramatically differently—even uncomfortably differently—to change how we operate and how we think.' He continued: 'Our every action must reflect this change of mindset: how we traverse the country, how we use force, and how we partner with the Afghans.'[2]

It is clear that the development of an army, navy or air force, or a police service, must balance the needs for combat-ready units with service support. The functioning of services and logistics requires as much training as combat forces and, in some cases, it requires more time, education and resources. Crucially there must be justice processes integrated throughout the entire system, governing the conduct of individual riflemen up to the acquisition of contracts and goods within the ministries. In preparing a force, the behaviour and discipline are as important as 'mass' and numbers.

The long term approach also assists in planning for the demobilisation of large forces that are swollen by internal unrest or a war. Soldiers, sailors and airmen at the end of their period in the services need civilian skills to minimise the disruption to the economy. This can be achieved relatively easily by training soldiers in basic vehicle mechanics, motorcycle maintenance, improvised repair, construction tasks, problem-solving activities, and planning exercises. Literacy and computing skills are particularly valuable. These additional benefits made military service more appealing to the troops and potential future recruits. Demobilising personnel will avoid flooding the economy with unskilled and unemployed labour. Instead they will contribute to national wealth and recovery.

Planning for partnering and mentoring is important, although inevitably time is always a limited resource. It is critical that the nature of the problem is identified correctly. During the intervention in Iraq, it was thought that the country needed a small and carefully harnessed army because of its aggression over the previous two decades. Yet the priority was an internal security force that could manage the developing insurgency and, crucially, a force that could be neutral in a lethal sectarian conflict. The partnering forces need to understand the local actors' motivations, their situation and their environment. There can be varying degrees of willingness to actually accept mentors and trainers. Developing an understanding may take weeks or months.

Internal solutions will be, as T.E. Lawrence identified, superior in the long run. Internal considerations will dominate in the capabilities that can be built and sustained, in the level of service support that local troops can expect, and in the level of education. These will influence the type and complexity of equipment that can be introduced, the capacity of the procurement system, and the pace at which infrastructure can be developed, cadres of local trainers formed and units generated. There must be assessments of the relationship between the armed services and the population, and the degree of mutual trust and support between the officers and their civilian leadership. In terms of co-ordination, it is clearly better to have a single headquarters, even if multinational contributions are to be made, than a plethora of independent and overlapping commands. Assessing the targets and metrics, with a long-term plan, is vital. Civilian interference and frequent changes in targets should be avoided. Timelines must be realistic.

There should also be a preference for talent rather than rank, and there must be constraints placed on the tokenistic presence preferred by willing allies. Only if capable and competent teams are provided should offers of support be accepted, although invariably those nations donating funding will expect to have some influence on how their money is spent. Specialists will be needed too. Expertise in, for example, borders, immigration and customs will be vital if developing a border force. Maritime specialisms will be needed for a littoral coastguard or navy. Legal experts are essential to all force development.

The personnel for training teams and mentoring tasks must be selected with care. Not every soldier is suited to the work. Those who have been mentors, historically and more recently, have reiterated again and again the same traits that are required: patience, tolerance, good humour, social skills, confidence, empathy and the ability to endure long periods of discomfort. Professional knowledge is vital, but the ability to convey it is an advanced skill. Instilling competition is highly effective, but fear is often counterproductive. Training is a device that not only teaches skills; it is a mechanism for developing values and allegiance too. It creates cohesion. It can also develop responsibility, particularly if troops are taught to manage affairs 'two-up', that is, the tasks of not only their immediate commander, but the one above that as well. Training will establish standards, and loyalty can be developed through certificates, badges, clothing or insignia.

'Basic' training is well established in armed forces, but there may be some adjustments in situations where a country has experienced a civil war, not least in establishing new standards such as rules of engagement (ROE), managing influential local leaders and former commanders, and ensuring equity in the allocation of training, equipment and logistics. Training packages will always have to be tailored to local needs, and may not involve 'basic' or low-level training at all.

A great deal of support may be needed at the corps level and in the interface with civilian ministries and political leadership. Here, planning and systems management are far more important. Mentors may need to concentrate on long-term demographic projections to assess recruitment patterns, have an understanding of governance and economics to assist and advise on procurement, or develop a grasp of the histories of an area to understand and advise on the integration of antagonised local factions. These are a far cry from most Western military manuals and doctrines, which concentrate only on low-level military training. At the time of writing, it is hard to find, for example, a single example of how an indigenous military force would integrate drone surveillance into its own doctrine and how this would align with national expectations; and advice on how to establish a pay structure, pensions model or procurement system is equally nonexistent even though these might be of strategic significance.

There are differences in military culture, which are derived from historical experience, long-standing social and economic situations, and even the political economy. Trainers and mentors must develop a sense of the local military norms, usually by visits and familiarisation, since reliance on interpreters is likely to lead to misunderstanding. Obviously, command of the language is a significant advantage. But understanding must go beyond military culture and into the national psyche, the historical experience, the political economy and the sense of national (or subnational) identity.

Recruitment of local forces has been relatively easy across the developing world because of the economic conditions and high unemployment that prevail. Nevertheless, poor countries tend to have a far higher number of unsuitable recruits on medical grounds. Selection will involve assessments of motivation as much as physical condition, but, as was so often found in the past, those with previous experience, including former enemy combatants or 'turned' guerrillas, could become excellent material in government service if properly handled. Equally there would need to be a robust policy and system in place to handle the contentious problem of former war criminals, past abuses, corrupt government ministers and other issues concerned with national reconciliation.

The mentoring role is never static, since its purpose is to move the local force progressively towards fully independent operation. There will be an evolution. To assist in the transition, mentors require a single scheme, which all can work towards, but which is sufficiently flexible that it can be accelerated or slowed as required. Trainers in multinational missions need to guard against introducing their own schemes and systems. Embedded personnel, which are essential at the beginning, will gradually be phased out and operate in a reserve capacity, providing supervision. A frequent debriefing period with local forces' officers or NCOs, conducted in private, can be valuable to assess progress and 'coach' the leaders. Progressive testing will assist in the selection of junior commanders and specialists, such as signallers and electrical engineers.

When building a force from scratch, such as after a civil war, most trainers agree that it can take up to four times longer than the training package for

Western personnel.[3] During training, a cadre of local trainers can be developed, and these will gradually take over from any mentoring teams. The 'politics' of these appointments should be anticipated. One mentor explained that an academy regimental sergeant major candidate at a national officers' training facility, who was an exceptional individual, was passed over by the local elites in favour of a political appointee who was, to all intents and purposes, incompetent. The solution was to permit the new appointee his post, but strip it of any real power, and the better candidate was therefore effectively in the command appointment, if without the title or status, for which he was more suited.[4]

The Performance of Local Forces in Combat

Using local forces in combat operations in their own territories has obvious advantages, not least reassurance for the population that it is their own military personnel, not foreigners, who can ensure security. Local personnel are more likely to understand the nuances of the environment and gather local human intelligence. Nevertheless, care in inoculating a new indigenous unit to combat is essential. Historically, trainers and mentors have noted that local forces needed to be given a series of small operational successes, by selecting relatively easy targets and missions, in order to build confidence and inure them to the shock of battle. An early setback could shatter confidence and lead to a permanent setback in morale and motivation. Embedded Training and Advisory Teams (ETATs) were valuable in providing continuous advice and support, especially in the delivery of fires and provision of transport and medical evacuation facilities. The presence of the advisers maintained confidence in the early stages, but a gradual reduction in numbers and a more rearward position as the unit became more experienced were found to work in Iraq. Mentors need not outstay their welcome and a formal handover can itself be used to establish trust. On the other hand, the idea of loan service personnel or a long term embedded adviser can provide continuity and enhance the sense among indigenous personnel that they have not been forgotten, and help will be on hand if things go wrong.[5]

There will be great variation in the combat readiness and performance of local forces. The British and Americans developed a simple 'traffic light' system to assess performance, with red as indicating the need for considerable support or even remedial training, orange as developing, and green as fully functional and independent. Mentoring support and other assets could be applied as necessary, even within brigades and divisions that were otherwise deemed as 'trained'. It was here that levels of command were most important. Trying to use captains from Western armies as mentors to local colonels or generals was an obvious error, but the shortages of trainers during the operations in Iraq and Afghanistan made this a more common problem than one would expect. In the nineteenth century, this problem would have been averted by creating a local rank for the adviser, as in the case of Major Charles Gordon who was considered a general of the Chinese forces, although in that period the Western officers were often in full command.

During the Western interventions in Iraq and Afghanistan, the reliability of trained local forces was an issue that required the appropriate combat deployment. Less reliable or inexperienced units could be used to hold flanks, guard installations and lines of communication, or patrol areas that were considered relatively benign. As their experience grew, they could be used to provide the simple tasks of fire support and ground holding while more complex tasks remained with the Coalition. Gradually, all the functions of operations were handed over, but by then the local leaders and their troops had gained valuable experience and had not suffered serious setbacks along the way.

There were two areas that, as counter-insurgency operations, required careful handling.[6] One was the sharing of intelligence and the other was joint command and control. Intelligence was passed on progressively as the local forces proved themselves. A fully shared system could not be introduced straight away because of the risk to operational security. In terms of joint planning, Western forces were reluctant to allow local commanders the ability to direct Western troops and assets, but eventually a fully integrated and joint command was evolved so that neither side would act without sharing the decision. Problems remained in the provision of logistics and other assets, but pragmatism dictated the solution. If local forces required an air strike to cover a manoeuvre, it was delivered; if they required extraction because the troops were fatigued, this might or might not be made available. Developing their own systems was the preference, and it was interesting to note that the Afghan Army was eager to acquire artillery where it lacked air power in order to maintain its firepower.

The purpose of mentoring is to create local security forces that are sufficiently self-reliant, professional and competent to be able to deal with any internal security problem in a manner that meets the international requirements of legal, restrained and humane approach. Moreover, where a large external threat exists, the partnering country or countries are there to provide a guarantee to meet this liability until their partnership has developed the security forces to enable them to be self-reliant against external threats.

The effectiveness of the method of operating must be constantly reassessed. Mistakes are inevitable. The important point is to recover from them and adjust. In Kenya, the first year of the campaign against the Mau Mau did not create the conditions for the restoration of order because the indigenous Kikuyu-led police committed abuses without appropriate supervision.[7] By contrast, in the Dhofar Campaign, the British adjusted their approach and made use of the relative strengths of local forces, the regulars of the SAF and the firqat irregulars of the Jebel. British Special Forces advisers developed a five front plan for the campaign.[8] These were to identify insurgents through localised intelligence; to convey the government's plans down to the local level; to provide security for their own territories; to distribute medical aid to the people; and to provide veterinary services for the cattle on which the population depended. Dhofar needed economic development. The insights that led to this appropriate campaign plan were based on the direct observations of British troops embedded with the population and on the expertise of the British loan service officers, and local forces were used in the implementation of that plan.

There have been cases where the intervention forces did not have overall authority and were subject to the demands of the host nation government. In Oman, the British officers were clear that 'we were not fighting a British war. It was Oman's and Sultan Qaboos's war and he engaged the services of officers and servicemen from other countries, primarily from Britain, but also from Jordan, Iran, India and Pakistan.'[9] Each of these contingents had to conform to the national government's plan, but British advisers were active in helping to shape the direction of the effort.

Good mentors and advisers who understand their mission and their partners are invaluable. Not everyone is a good mentor, and selection is essential. Those who are tasked must be prepared well, and must be deployed long enough to ensure sufficient continuity in the delivery of their support. As an example, British officers in Oman on 'loan service', seconded to the Sultan's armed forces, usually spent two years in their appointment. These officers also spent 42 weeks conducting language training before they even reached the region.[10] They were nearly all single and were selected on the basis of their prior experience as commanders. Many of them were junior in rank and they were not all 'orthodox', but the criteria for their selection were entirely based on their suitability to work with local forces with professionalism and tact. Some of the most successful trainers and leaders of local forces have been considered 'mavericks' in the sense that they have shown a willingness to take risks and use their initiative. On the other hand, those same officers had to know how to remain loyal to the overall objectives and not be tempted to 'go native'. Although T.E. Lawrence was right to emphasise when not to interfere with local methods of operating with his injunction 'it is better to let them do it imperfectly, rather than do it perfectly ourselves, for it is their country', which did not mean an abrogation of responsibility or the adviser giving up on a mission to professionalise training.[11] Standards can still be maintained or insisted upon. They should just be tailored and adapted to the operating environment and the norms of the country.

It was striking that, during the British and American pre-deployment training for Iraq and Afghanistan, there were increasing amounts of time allocated to 'cultural awareness'. An Afghan adviser on a British Army training exercise explained how impressed he was at the progress being made: 'when I first came here, no-one knew even how to greet me', he said, 'but now, every soldier will say *salaam ul'aleikum*', and he gestured with his hand across his heart and made a slight bow to indicate the polite form of the greeting. He said that far more officers and men had learned some Pashto and Dari, avoided the use of their left hand, and averted their gaze from women. These details, while seemingly minor, had impressed those they worked with. Even when there were continual mistakes, many Afghans seemed to appreciate that the Westerners were at least trying not to cause offence.

Cultural knowledge is a far more demanding undertaking than 'awareness'. It implies a rich understanding of the language, customs and details, and can usually be acquired only after long immersion in a country. In the Dhofar campaign, the Sultan himself explained to his British partners that giving a gift implied an obligation on the receiver, as much as it meant a blessing upon the giver. His adviser recalled: 'The Sultan was prepared to pay but turned down my suggestion that the tribe should act first, and then be paid or rewarded. 'Give them the money now', he said, 'and don't mention what it is for. They will know that by accepting the cash they have made a commitment. When I tell them what that commitment is they will express surprise and argue like mad, but they will do it.'[12]

Despite cultural differences, there are elements of motivation and morale common to local troops, namely money, family or extended clan, the status of the individual and the regiment, the availability and quality of food, access to sex, variations in security, adherence to faith and personal honour. British Gurkha soldiers refer to the 'five Ps': *pariwar* (family), *paltan* (regiment), *paisa* (money), *piet* (stomach) and *putiley* (literally butterflies, but a reference to women). Afghan Pashtuns believed that conflict stemmed from the issues that mattered most, namely *nang* (honour), *zar* (gold), *zan* (women) and *zamin* (land), and a soldier with each of these would be content. Many cultures regard personal honour as sacrosanct to the point where sacrifice would be necessary to preserve it, and yet the emergence of an existential threat can galvanise even apparently pacific cultures. One is reminded of the enduring importance of Thucydides' observation about the drivers of war: 'It was the course of events which first compelled us to increase our power to its present extent: fear of Persia was our chief motive, though afterwards we thought, too, of our own honour and our own interest.'

Personal honour could be used by Western forces to ensure compliance in very practical ways. To avoid desertions during periods of leave, each cohort was informed that they would only be allowed to go once all of the first group had returned. Collective and personal honour ensured that the troops came back, or the perpetrators would suffer the ignominy of ostracism at home.[13] Nevertheless, the attraction of pay, and the chance that it might be terminated for good, could also be a strong motivation.

Mentoring teams in Iraq and Afghanistan found that frequent rotations of advisers interrupted training and development, and, in some cases, entirely undermined it. Mentors and advisers need to be in place for twelve months and preferably longer. There should always be sufficient overlap, perhaps one month, between teams, during which the newcomers understudy the existing group, discuss individual mentees and examine the rate of progress in training.

Developing effective local officers and NCOs is essential for success, but this is often the most challenging task because it takes a lot longer to create an officer corps and effective NCOs who are able to enforce their authority with confidence. Once again, military cultures matter. In the United States Army, or the Turkish Army, for example, NCOs have far greater responsibility as junior commanders than the British equivalents, but British NCOs have a tradition of being more executive and highly effective in small-team responsibilities. To overcome the cultural gaps, mentors need to have knowledgeable indigenous leaders with them who fulfil the role of cultural guardianship and can offer candid advice to help the mentors avoid giving unwitting offence, to explain how to adjust a training programme and adapt to the norms expected by the trainees, at least initially. In the attempt to train the Libyan General Purpose Force, there were misunderstandings when the training teams tried to apply a British model without adjustments. It would have been far better, for example, to train the officers separately, even where they were doing the same type of training as the soldiers. Similarly, NCOs will require their own cadres and programmes.

Alongside the selection of a local leader or cultural adviser, it is a recommendation to develop informal methods for the better understanding of soldiers' concerns. Brigadier Rigden, a British officer with considerable experience in this field, urged the appointment of a selected and competent indigenous soldier to be a trainee radio operator within the training or mentoring team, who could pass on insights directly to the Western training commander. The role might equally be a driver, medic or a local training NCO, as long as it enabled a clear and direct passage of communication through everyday working.

The creation of armies has always required that recruits pass through a process of initiation, where their identities are transformed. A number of well-established techniques are used, including drill, combat training, physical fitness programmes, dress codes and even haircuts. Who could forget the French Foreign Legion's insistence that new recruits have their hair removed completely in a style known as *boule à zero*. Whatever programme is adopted, individual recruits have to be inducted properly into the unit or formation that they are joining. During training, recruits need to be reminded, at frequent intervals, of the purpose and cause for which they are preparing. Morale can easily decline under the relentless pressure of basic training, but a sense of mission, welfare measures, the opportunity for sports and socialization, and any form of training that enhances bonding and cohesion can overcome even the most downhearted. When they are deprived of all the usual creature comforts of civilian life, it is remarkable to observe recruits or officer cadets spontaneously burst into song together. The effect is as impressive as it is extraordinary, and seems to reach into the primeval spirit of a warrior culture.

This brings us to the training itself. Training is the single most important aspect of creating an army and follows a number of principles. The first is that it must be relevant. It should also be progressive, building skills in small increments for individuals, pairs and small teams, and gradually working up into larger formations. The progression in stages allows for the development of confidence, time for remedial action, and the practice of exercises which can gradually apply pressure, of time or discomfort, in order to simulate operational and combat conditions. The iterative development of skills also offers the opportunity to gradually inoculate and desensitise troops to the stresses of war, but also equip them with life-saving techniques, which, in turn, further develop confidence. The classic tools of training are the use of competitions, the introduction of realistic scenarios or settings, repetition, and the completion of certain skills at speed. Recruits are often brought to a high standard of proficiency in weapon handling for example, by challenging shooting competitions and by that old favourite, field stripping and reassembly of a weapon blindfolded or at night.

Training indigenous forces requires a high standard of language skills among the trainers, mentors and advisers. Local personnel should be allowed to make mistakes during training, and some armies expect to have injuries where training is realistic. The learning process can be positive when mistakes are made, as long as they are handled in such a way that men are not humiliated. Everyone appreciates constructive criticism and the opportunity to set right a mistake. A bit of verbal coercion is necessary to engender urgency, focus attention and apply pressure, but there needs to be individual development too. Recruits who endure constant verbal abuse and physical hardship without relief will underperform. Training requires rewards and incentives. Men respond well to brief and modest concessions, such as a little time off, when the tempo of work is high. But trainees also need a progressive hierarchy of awards, ranging from badges to medals. The more difficult these are to earn, the harder trainees will work to get them. Icons, rituals and other forms of veneration and honour code can combine the generation of cohesion with the reward of playing a leading part in such events.

Trainees are measured against operational standards. In Afghanistan, there were some successes among counter-narcotics forces, some units of police, commando units, pilots, and combat engineers. There were also some failures. A number of infantry battalions never reached an acceptable standard of efficiency or effectiveness, and weaknesses remained across the spectrum of leadership, within the Ministry of Defence and all the way down to the kandaks (battalions). All units require some fundamental competency in shooting and combat proficiency, the ability to manoeuvre tactically, control fires, and ensure the efficient flow of logistics. They must also possess a level of professional conduct (such as obedience to the law). Beyond this, local forces need specialists, as drivers, signallers, IT operatives, repair teams, medics, engineers and, of course, competent, courageous and dedicated leaders.

Training programmes for local forces will always need to be tailored to the situation, but there may be common requirements. As a framework, there may be certain lines of development. The first will be in command and leadership. From the outset, Western trainers and mentors will need to start the process of developing not only junior leaders, but also senior officers possibly up to the two-star level. Consideration needs to be given to courses, curricula and facilities, as well as the content. Specialist civilians are almost certain to be needed, especially in the advisory work at the senior officer and ministerial level.

The next area is operations and training, and that requires the development of headquarters and staff work, at the tactical as well as the operational level. Mentors and advisers will look to enhance existing planning, the execution of operations, and the 'lessons learning' process. The training programmes need to accommodate any operational developments with a rapid feedback loop. Training would need to be adapted, updated and adjusted on a regular basis, and here the rotation out of the line of experienced personnel, and their appointment for a period of local training officers, are essential.

Continuation training for those who have already completely basic phases will also be valuable, and specialist courses can be developed for those who have shown the greatest aptitude in the initial recruit programmes. A range of skills can be developed. There needs to be particular attention to fire control, reconnaissance skills, the introduction of heavy weapons, and more operationally relevant skills such as vehicle control, covert patrolling, prisoner handling and other tasks.

The next area of generic development would be in the individual personnel and units. This would involve the establishment of functioning medical support including evacuation and treatment of casualties; professional standards in adherence to the law of armed conflict or specific rules of engagement, and knowledge of the Geneva Convention and other areas of personal accountability; the development of pay systems and the fair allocation of leave or rotations; and there may be a requirement to enhance survival skills against improvised explosive devices, mines or ambush. There may need to be consideration of how to engage the local population too, to ensure there is public understanding of the local forces' role and ethos, public appearances through parades and open days, sports fixtures and media appearances.

The final area, but one of the most important, is in service support and logistics. Local forces need to be guided through the development of requisition and procurement processes, the stewardship of property and the accountability for all valuable equipment or munitions. There would invariably be a need to develop repair and maintenance processes, not least because the quality of vehicle fleets and scarcity of equipment are likely to be a common problem. Trainers and mentors need to adjust their expectations in this regard, while looking to make appropriate enhancements. Offering a high-end piece of equipment or specialised vehicle to an army without the education, technical skills or infrastructure to sustain these items will consign the donations to

CONCLUSION

redundancy within a relatively short period of time. It is far better to supply and develop the tools with which they are already familiar. Improvisation is highly likely. Trainers must be resourceful and creative.

The research questions that were posed at the start of this volume began with the issue of why men enlist, co-operate and remain in foreign armies, and through a variety of historical examples, we have examined the relative importance of the 'push' and 'pull' factors for individual men from indigenous communities. Some were common to all men and women, but there were specific cultural, economic and strategic considerations too. This book shows that forces are ideally structured as regulars, unless they possess some special skill or attribute or, indeed, the more powerful partner is not yet in a position to assert itself fully over local, auxiliary or irregular forces. Some local forces managed transformation and other situational changes very well, but others did not. In some cases, culture, morale, leadership, environment and the character of the conflict could play a part in the ability to accommodate change and development. In all the cases we have considered, morale and cohesion were critical, and the fact that local men had enlisted under foreign, alien leadership made this an area of particular attention. The quality of leadership, and officers' treatment of their men, were the most important of all. Even local troops of variable or low quality could be successful under an effective leader or adviser, if conditions remained broadly favourable.

Raising local forces requires time and investment, but one of the research questions was: how long? The answer was invariably 'longer'. A firm and long-lasting relationship was vital for trust.

The advantages of indigenous forces lie in their ability to augment other armies, the intelligence they can gather more readily from a local population, and their corresponding ability to discriminate between adversaries and the innocent. Their knowledge of terrain and the political environment can be valuable. They can be used to hold onto terrain won by others, but their background gives them a greater empathy and possibly more acceptance among the people in those areas. Their existence can help build a stake in a society or the political order, and they can tie local populations to their national government, thereby building a more resilient and accountable structure of governance. From a more Machiavellian perspective, the subsidies and payments made to local forces can create dependence on a central authority and ensure compliance, and this itself might be an essential requirement in the conditions of civil war.

There are a number of drawbacks in the use of indigenous forces. Reliability is a frequent problem for governments and intervention forces, and there is a

415

natural concern that local forces, especially if largely untrained, can start to exert control of certain areas for their own self-interest. Criminal elements may believe local forces give them a licence to act as they please, and they may fight to protect illegal activities such as smuggling or narcotics production. They may decide to protect their own allies or favour particular sections of society over others. They may abuse subsidies and payments, using them to fuel a conflict which they have an interest in sustaining. The development of pseudo-gangs and counter-gangs can perpetuate conflict and deepen antagonism between sectarian, ethnic or political groups. Local forces, depending on their level of training, armaments and equipment, may not be able to withstand an enemy on their own and their dependence may make the restitution of sovereignty more problematic. Successful and powerful local military forces can be tempted to see themselves as the sole guardians of the state or constitution, to the extent that they are prepared to seize political power for themselves.

Partnering can be a challenging task. While it may offer the chance to continue training and development, and to inculcate values of accountability and loyalty to a government and people, it is a process fraught with difficulty. In an ideal world it would ensure smooth co-operation, joint planning and the sharing of vital intelligence, but in reality partner relationships are constantly shifting. Pooling risks, rewards and resources can be an aspiration, but invariably there is friction. Vehicles, equipment and even munitions can be scarce or of a low standard. Some local troops will lack a regularised system of pay, leave and even uniforms, let alone body armour, heavy weapons or functioning communications. It can be, for example, a disquieting experience to accompany nervous, half-trained and poorly armed African troops, as they tramp along in wellies or flip-flops, faced by larger numbers of well-concealed and ruthless guerrillas, without air support, any chance of casualty evacuation or even a decent radio. Such is the reality of many local forces in the Global South.

Local cultures may expect military command to be allocated to select groups, for personal advancement and wealth, or as political rewards. Ethnic, religious or sectarian, and historical grievances and cultural differences can hamper the development of a local force, unless such fundamental divisions are turned into virtues through unit identities, differentiated roles or territorial deployment. Leadership can be crucial to the success or failure of local forces, and officers can serve as the guardians of a culture of professionalism, act as the ethical guides of an army, and set the standards of the force.

Local forces will always have agency. It is the local personnel who will confer legitimacy on intervention projects and on local communities by embracing participation in military forces. They can gain for themselves recognition, status and improvements within a society, which are important considerations for many minorities. Local forces can retain their autonomy in action and may not be entirely subsumed into regular security forces, but the historical record suggests that states will try to ensure that they possess a monopoly of violence; local forces that lie on the edge of, or even outside the jurisdiction of the state, are an indication of the limits of state power, but trust between government and locals on this boundary of power is often tenuous. Therefore local leaders matter a great deal. Their influence, sense of autonomy and orchestration of forces can be the basis of a social and political contract between a central state and its peripheries, or it can mean the breakdown of state power.

It seems likely that, in the future, more powerful polities will continue to utilise local, indigenous personnel to augment and enhance security in certain parts of the world. These may be employed in the pursuit of terrorists or in the suppression of insurgency. It is likely they will also be fostered as proxies for other states to pursue their national interests, recruiting auxiliaries as guerrillas, saboteurs and intelligence operatives. In a hybridised conflict environment, states make use of local fighters to legitimise a narrative, to establish a claim or to 'spoil' a political process.

Leading states will continue to seek cheap and abundant manpower to help them achieve their strategic ends, which, given the demographics of the twenty-first century, would seem to be a promising possibility for them. As the nature of global manufacturing changes through greater automation, the demand for skilled technicians, repair teams and security forces looks likely to increase. Indeed, as millions face unemployment and hardship, there may be a greater willingness to absorb larger numbers in security tasks. In urban areas in the early part of this century, there has been a growth in gated communities, where private security contractors are employed as patrols and guards, and this trend looks likely to continue, perhaps across entire regions.

As always, there will be a focus on how private militarised security forces will operate. Their loyalty may not always be to their clients, but to their shareholders and their profit margins. Their endurance may be determined by the cash flow rather than environmental conditions. They may impose significant conditions and limits on their service, refusing to operate if the security environment deteriorates unless higher premiums are paid. To these limits and expense, the question will be whether private security represents value for money, especially when state forces traditionally served for less, with greater motivation and in more flexible conditions. On the other hand, the evolution of private security forces may just be another iteration in the commodification of military labour that began millennia ago.

Military forces so often reflect the societies from which they are drawn, and attitudes towards leadership, accountability, cost and casualties are invariably to be found there. Any assessment of the future employment of local forces must therefore encompass a study of the society and political economy we are likely to inherit. A thorough understanding, through intense study and direct personal experience, of the generic behaviour and psychology of men and women in conflict, tailored to and qualified by the specific culture and situation of local forces, may ensure that these personnel remain true to their salt.

APPENDIX

THE TWENTY-SEVEN ARTICLES

T.E. Lawrence's advisory notes were published in the *Arab Bulletin* on 20 August 1917 and are reproduced here in full, not least because, without the usual abridgements, they reveal the greater complexity and nuance of the advisory task he faced.[1] He wrote:

The following notes have been expressed in commandment form for greater clarity and to save words. They are, however, only my personal conclusions, arrived at gradually while I worked in the Hejaz and now put on paper as stalking horses for beginners in the Arab armies. They are meant to apply only to Bedu; townspeople or Syrians require totally different treatment. They are of course not suitable to any other person's need, or applicable unchanged in any particular situation. Handling Hejaz Arabs is an art, not a science, with exceptions and no obvious rules. At the same time we have a great chance there; the Sherif trusts us, and has given us the position (towards his Government) which the Germans wanted to win in Turkey. If we are tactful, we can at once retain his goodwill and carry out our job, but to succeed we have got to put into it all the interest and skill we possess.

1. Go easy for the first few weeks. A bad start is difficult to atone for, and the Arabs form their judgments on externals that we ignore. When you have reached the inner circle in a tribe, you can do as you please with yourself and them.

2. Learn all you can about your Ashraf and Bedu. Get to know their families, clans and tribes, friends and enemies, wells, hills and roads. Do all this by listening and by indirect inquiry. Do not ask questions. Get to speak their

419

dialect of Arabic, not yours. Until you can understand their allusions, avoid getting deep into conversation or you will drop bricks. Be a little stiff at first.

3. In matters of business deal only with the commander of the army, column, or party in which you serve. Never give orders to anyone at all, and reserve your directions or advice for the C.O., however great the temptation (for efficiency's sake) of dealing with his underlings. Your place is advisory, and your advice is due to the commander alone. Let him see that this is your conception of your duty, and that his is to be the sole executive of your joint plans.

4. Win and keep the confidence of your leader. Strengthen his prestige at your expense before others when you can. Never refuse or quash schemes he may put forward; but ensure that they are put forward in the first instance privately to you. Always approve them, and after praise modify them insensibly, causing the suggestions to come from him, until they are in accord with your own opinion. When you attain this point, hold him to it, keep a tight grip of his ideas, and push them forward as firmly as possible, but secretly, so that no one but himself (and he not too clearly) is aware of your pressure.

5. Remain in touch with your leader as constantly and unobtrusively as you can. Live with him, that at meal times and at audiences you may be naturally with him in his tent. Formal visits to give advice are not so good as the constant dropping of ideas in casual talk. When stranger sheikhs come in for the first time to swear allegiance and offer service, clear out of the tent. If their first impression is of foreigners in the confidence of the Sherif, it will do the Arab cause much harm.

6. Be shy of too close relations with the subordinates of the expedition. Continual intercourse with them will make it impossible for you to avoid going behind or beyond the instructions that the Arab C.O. has given them on your advice, and in so disclosing the weakness of his position you altogether destroy your own.

7. Treat the sub-chiefs of your force quite easily and lightly. In this way you hold yourself above their level. Treat the leader, if a Sherif, with respect. He will return your manner and you and he will then be alike, and above the rest. Precedence is a serious matter among the Arabs, and you must attain it.

8. Your ideal position is when you are present and not noticed. Do not be too intimate, too prominent, or too earnest. Avoid being identified too long or

too often with any tribal sheikh, even if C.O. of the expedition. To do your work you must be above jealousies, and you lose prestige if you are associated with a tribe or clan, and its inevitable feuds. Sherifs are above all blood-feuds and local rivalries, and form the only principle of unity among the Arabs. Let your name therefore be coupled always with a Sherif's, and share his attitude towards the tribes. When the moment comes for action put yourself publicly under his orders. The Bedu will then follow suit.

9. Magnify and develop the growing conception of the Sherifs as the natural aristocracy of the Arabs. Intertribal jealousies make it impossible for any sheikh to attain a commanding position, and the only hope of union in nomad Arabs is that the Ashraf be universally acknowledged as the ruling class. Sherifs are half-townsmen, half-nomad, in manner and life, and have the instinct of command. Mere merit and money would be insufficient to obtain such recognition; but the Arab reverence for pedigree and the Prophet gives hope for the ultimate success of the Ashraf.

10. Call your Sherif 'Sidi' in public and in private. Call other people by their ordinary names, without title. In intimate conversation call a Sheikh 'Abu Annad', 'Akhu Alia' or some similar by-name.

11. The foreigner and Christian is not a popular person in Arabia. However friendly and informal the treatment of yourself may be, remember always that your foundations are very sandy ones. Wave a Sherif in front of you like a banner and hide your own mind and person. If you succeed, you will have hundreds of miles of country and thousands of men under your orders, and for this it is worth bartering the outward show.

12. Cling tight to your sense of humour. You will need it every day. A dry irony is the most useful type, and repartee of a personal and not too broad character will double your influence with the chiefs. Reproof, if wrapped up in some smiling form, will carry further and last longer than the most violent speech. The power of mimicry or parody is valuable, but use it sparingly, for wit is more dignified than humour. Do not cause a laugh at a Sherif except among Sherifs.

13. Never lay hands on an Arab; you degrade yourself. You may think the resultant obvious increase of outward respect a gain to you, but what you have really done is to build a wall between you and their inner selves. It is difficult to keep quiet when everything is being done wrong, but the less you lose your temper the greater your advantage. Also then you will not go mad yourself.

14. While very difficult to drive, the Bedu are easy to lead, if you have the patience to bear with them. The less apparent your interferences the more your influence. They are willing to follow your advice and do what you wish, but they do not mean you or anyone else to be aware of that. It is only after the end of all annoyances that you find at bottom their real fund of goodwill.

15. Do not try to do too much with your own hands. Better the Arabs do it tolerably than that you do it perfectly. It is their war, and you are to help them, not to win it for them. Actually, also, under the very odd conditions of Arabia, your practical work will not be as good as, perhaps, you think it is.

16. If you can, without being too lavish, forestall presents to yourself. A well-placed gift is often most effective in winning over a suspicious sheikh. Never receive a present without giving a liberal return, but you may delay this return (while letting its ultimate certainty be known) if you require a particular service from the giver. Do not let them ask you for things, since their greed will then make them look upon you only as a cow to milk.

17. Wear an Arab headcloth when with a tribe. Bedu have a malignant prejudice against the hat, and believe that our persistence in wearing it (due probably to British obstinacy of dictation) is founded on some immoral or irreligious principle. A thick headcloth forms a good protection against the sun, and if you wear a hat your best Arab friends will be ashamed of you in public.

18. Disguise is not advisable. Except in special areas, let it be clearly known that you are a British officer and a Christian. At the same time, if you can wear Arab kit when with the tribes, you will acquire their trust and intimacy to a degree impossible in uniform. It is, however, dangerous and difficult. They make no special allowances for you when you dress like them. Breaches of etiquette not charged against a foreigner are not condoned to you in Arab clothes. You will be like an actor in a foreign theatre, playing a part day and night for months, without rest, and for an anxious stake. Complete success, which is when the Arabs forget your strangeness and speak naturally before you, counting you as one of themselves, is perhaps only attainable in character: while half-success (all that most of us will strive for; the other costs too much) is easier to win in British things, and you yourself will last longer, physically and mentally, in the comfort that they mean. Also then the Turks will not hang you, when you are caught.

19. If you wear Arab things, wear the best. Clothes are significant among the tribes, and you must wear the appropriate, and appear at ease in them. Dress like a Sherif, if they agree to it.

20. If you wear Arab things at all, go the whole way. Leave your English friends and customs on the coast, and fall back on Arab habits entirely. It is possible, starting thus level with them, for the European to beat the Arabs at their own game, for we have stronger motives for our action, and put more heart into it than they. If you can surpass them, you have taken an immense stride toward complete success, but the strain of living and thinking in a foreign and half-understood language, the savage food, strange clothes, and stranger ways, with the complete loss of privacy and quiet, and the impossibility of ever relaxing your watchful imitation of the others for months on end, provide such an added stress to the ordinary difficulties of dealing with the Bedu, the climate, and the Turks, that this road should not be chosen without serious thought.

21. Religious discussions will be frequent. Say what you like about your own side, and avoid criticism of theirs, unless you know that the point is external, when you may score heavily by proving it so. With the Bedu, Islam is so all-pervading an element that there is little religiosity, little fervour, and no regard for externals. Do not think from their conduct that they are careless. Their conviction of the truth of their faith, and its share in every act and thought and principle of their daily life is so intimate and intense as to be unconscious, unless roused by opposition. Their religion is as much a part of nature to them as is sleep or food.

22. Do not try to trade on what you know of fighting. The Hejaz confounds ordinary tactics. Learn the Bedu principles of war as thoroughly and as quickly as you can, for till you know them your advice will be no good to the Sherif. Unnumbered generations of tribal raids have taught them more about some parts of the business than we will ever know. In familiar conditions they fight well, but strange events cause panic. Keep your unit small. Their raiding parties are usually from one hundred to two hundred men, and if you take a crowd they only get confused. Also their sheikhs, while admirable company commanders, are too 'set' to learn to handle the equivalents of battalions or regiments. Don't attempt unusual things, unless they appeal to the sporting instinct Bedu have so strongly, unless success is obvious. If the objective is a good one (booty) they will attack like fiends, they are splendid scouts, their mobility gives you the advantage that will win this local war, they make proper use of their knowledge of the country (don't

take tribesmen to places they do not know), and the gazelle-hunters, who form a proportion of the better men, are great shots at visible targets. A sheikh from one tribe cannot give orders to men from another; a Sherif is necessary to command a mixed tribal force. If there is plunder in prospect, and the odds are at all equal, you will win. Do not waste Bedu attacking trenches (they will not stand casualties) or in trying to defend a position, for they cannot sit still without slacking. The more unorthodox and Arab your proceedings, the more likely you are to have the Turks cold, for they lack initiative and expect you to. Don't play for safety.

23. The open reason that Bedu give you for action or inaction may be true, but always there will be better reasons left for you to divine. You must find these inner reasons (they will be denied, but are none the less in operation) before shaping your arguments for one course or other. Allusion is more effective than logical exposition: they dislike concise expression. Their minds work just as ours do, but on different premises. There is nothing unreasonable, incomprehensible, or inscrutable in the Arab. Experience of them, and knowledge of their prejudices will enable you to foresee their attitude and possible course of action in nearly every case.

24. Do not mix Bedu and Syrians, or trained men and tribesmen. You will get work out of neither, for they hate each other. I have never seen a successful combined operation, but many failures. In particular, ex-officers of the Turkish army, however Arab in feelings and blood and language, are hopeless with Bedu. They are narrow minded in tactics, unable to adjust themselves to irregular warfare, clumsy in Arab etiquette, swollen-headed to the extent of being incapable of politeness to a tribesman for more than a few minutes, impatient, and, usually, helpless without their troops on the road and in action. Your orders (if you were unwise enough to give any) would be more readily obeyed by Beduins than those of any Mohammedan Syrian officer. Arab townsmen and Arab tribesmen regard each other mutually as poor relations, and poor relations are much more objectionable than poor strangers.

25. In spite of ordinary Arab example, avoid too free talk about women. It is as difficult a subject as religion, and their standards are so unlike our own that a remark, harmless in English, may appear as unrestrained to them, as some of their statements would look to us, if translated literally.

26. Be as careful of your servants as of yourself. If you want a sophisticated one you will probably have to take an Egyptian, or a Sudani, and unless you are very lucky he will undo on trek much of the good you so labori-

ously effect. Arabs will cook rice and make coffee for you, and leave you if required to do unmanly work like cleaning boots or washing. They are only really possible if you are in Arab kit. A slave brought up in the Hejaz is the best servant, but there are rules against British subjects owning them, so they have to be lent to you. In any case, take with you an Ageyli or two when you go up country. They are the most efficient couriers in Arabia, and understand camels.

27. The beginning and ending of the secret of handling Arabs is unremitting study of them. Keep always on your guard; never say an unnecessary thing: watch yourself and your companions all the time: hear all that passes, search out what is going on beneath the surface, read their characters, discover their tastes and their weaknesses and keep everything you find out to yourself. Bury yourself in Arab circles, have no interests and no ideas except the work in hand, so that your brain is saturated with one thing only, and you realize your part deeply enough to avoid the little slips that would counteract the painful work of weeks. Your success will be proportioned to the amount of mental effort you devote to it.

NOTES

PREFACE

1. Austin Long, 'The Anbar Awakening', *Survival*, 50/2 (2008), 67–94, 'For Us and Sunni Allies, a Turning Point', *Washington Post*, 30/09/08, http://www.washingtonpost.com/wp-dyn/content/story/2008/09/30/ST2008093000905.html.
2. 'Afghan Surge Continues', *Foreign Policy*, 16/12/08, http://blog.foreignpolicy.com/node/10575 and 'U.S. Military to Launch Pilot Program to Recruit New Local Afghan Militias', USNews.com, http://www.usnews.com/articles/news/iraq/2008/12/16/us-military-to-launch-pilot-program-to-recruit-new-local-afghan-militias.html, accessed December 2008; Stathis N. Kalyvas *The Logic of Violence in Civil War* (Cambridge: Cambridge University Press, 2006); see also Antonio Giustozzi, 'The Afghan National Army: Unwarranted Hope?', *RUSI Journal*, 154, 6 (December 2009), 36–42.
3. Andrew Hubbard, 'Plague and Paradox: Militias in Iraq', *Small Wars and Insurgencies*, 18, 3 (2007), 345–362.
4. R.M. Cassidy, 'The Long Small War: Indigenous Forces for Counterinsurgency', *Parameters*, 36, 2 (Summer 2006), 47–62.
5. David Anderson and David Killingray, *Policing and Decolonization: Nationalism, Politics and the Police, 1917–65* (Manchester: Manchester University Press, 1992).
6. Ian Beckett's *Modern Insurgencies and Counter-Insurgencies* (Routledge 2001), in *Survival*, 43, 4 (2001).
7. Huw Bennett, 'The Other Side of the COIN: Minimum and Exemplary Force in British Army Counterinsurgency in Kenya', *Small Wars and Insurgencies*, 18, 4 (2007), 638–639.
8. Mark Moyar, *Phoenix and the Birds of Prey: Counterinsurgency and Counterterrorism in Vietnam* (Lincoln, NE: University of Nebraska Press 2007).
9. See, for example, Kevin O'Brien, 'Special Forces for Counter-Revolutionary Warfare. The South African Case', in *Small Wars and Insurgencies*, 12, 2 (2001); Prem Mahadevan, 'Counter Terrorism in the Indian Punjab; Assessing the "Cat" System', *Faultlines*, 18 (2007).

10. This issue was recognised by Ronald Robinson in 'Non-European Foundations of European Imperialism: Sketch for a Theory of Collaboration', in R. Owen and B. Sutcliffe (eds.), *Studies in the Theory of Imperialism* (London: Longman, 1972), 117–142.

1. INTRODUCTION: PARTNERING WITH INDIGENOUS FORCES

1. Mary Kaldor, *New and Old Wars: Organised Violence in a Global Era* (Stanford University Press, 2nd edn, 2007).
2. Hew Strachan, 'The Changing Character of War', S.T. Lee Distinguished Annual Lecture, 15 January 2010.
3. David Kilcullen, *Accidental Guerrilla: Fighting Small Wars in the Midst of a Big One* (London: Hurst and Co., 2011).
4. David Galula, *Counterinsurgency Warfare: Theory and Practice* (1965; repr., New York: Praeger, 2006).
5. Sir Robert Thompson, *Defeating Communist Insurgency* (London: Chatto and Windus, 1966).
6. Kaldor, *New and Old Wars*.
7. Strachan, 'The Changing Character of War'.
8. Author's interview, 2012, name withheld under Chatham House Rule.
9. Antonio Giustozzi and Artemy Kalinovsky, with Paul Robinson, Bob Spencer, and Alfia Sorokina, *Missionaries of Modernity: Advisory Missions and the Struggle for Hegemony in Afghanistan and Beyond* (London: Hurst, 2016), pp. 313–329.
10. T.E. Lawrence, 'The Evolution of a Revolt', *Army Quarterly and Defence Journal* (October 1920), p. 8.
11. Nick Ritchie, 'Rethinking Security: A Critical Analysis of the Strategic Defence and Security Review', *International Affairs* (2011).
12. Stathis Kalyvas, *The Logic of Violence in Civil War* (New York: Cambridge University Press, 2006).
13. Michael Roberts, 'The Military Revolution, 1560–1660', in Michael Roberts (ed.), *Essays in Swedish History* (London: Weidenfeld and Nicolson, 1967), p. 12.
14. Geoffrey Parker, 'The "Military Revolution", 1560–1660: A Myth?', *Journal of Military History*, 48, 2 (1976), pp. 195–214.
15. For a more comprehensive examination of labelling theory, see David Mazta, *Delinquency and Drift* (London: Transaction Publishers, 1990).
16. David Omissi, *The Sepoy and the Raj* (London: Macmillan, 1994), p. 67; David Killingray, 'Guardians of Empire', in David Killingray and David Omissi (eds), *Guardians of Empire* (Manchester: Manchester University Press, 1999), p. 15.
17. Tarak Barkawi, *Soldiers of Empire*, forthcoming.
18. Karine Varley, 'Contesting Concepts of the Nation in Arms: French Memories of the War of 1870–1 in Dijon', *European History Quarterly*, 36, 4 (October 2006), pp. 548–573.

19. Ashley Jackson, on behalf of Afghan Civil Society Forum (ACSF), Afghan Peace and Democracy Act (APDA), Association for the Defence of Women's Rights (ADWR), Cooperation Centre for Afghanistan (CCA), Education Training Centre for Poor Women and Girls of Afghanistan (ECW), Oxfam GB, Organization for Human Welfare (OHW), Sanayee Development Organization (SDO) and The Liaison Office (TLO), *The Costs of War: The Afghan Experience of Conflict, 1978–2009* (November 2009).

20. John A. Lynn, 'The Evolution of Army Style in the Modern West, 800–2000', *International History Review*, XVIII, 3 (1996), pp. 505–756.

21. See, for example, Russell F. Weigley, 'The "American Way of War" Revisited', *Journal of Military History*, 66, 2 (April 2002), pp. 501–533; Victor David Hanson, *The Soul of Battle: From Ancient Times to the Present Day* (New York: Free Press, 1999).

22. *Dead Birds*, directed by Robert Garner, Peabody Museum of Cambridge, CRM Films, 1962, cited in Randall Collins, *Violence: A Micro-Sociological Survey* (Princeton: Princeton University Press, 2009).

23. Lynn, 'The Evolution of Army Style', p. 509.

24. David Ralston, *Importing the European Army* (Chicago, 1990).

25. See Charles Kirke's excellent study of the British Army in *Red Coat, Green Machine: Continuity in Change in the British Army 1700 to 2000* (London: Continuum, 2011).

26. Lynn, 'The Evolution of Army Style', p. 510.

27. See, for example, Ardant du Picq, *Battle Studies* (repr. 2012).

28. For a full discussion of this issue, and its redefinition, see Anthony King, *The Combat Soldier: Infantry Tactics and Cohesion in the Twentieth and Twenty-First Centuries* (Oxford: Oxford University Press, 2013), pp. 27ff.

29. See King, *The Combat Soldier*.

30. Robert Graves, *Goodbye to All That* (London: Jonathan Cape, 1929), p. 157.

31. See James McPherson, *For Cause and Comrades: Why Men Fought in the Civil War* (Oxford: Oxford University Press, 1997).

32. Julius Caesar, *Commentarii de Bello Gallico*, IV, 25.

33. Collins, *Violence*, pp. 83ff; Ardant du Picq (1903), pp. 88–89, cited in ibid.

34. Edward A. Shils and Morris Janowitz, 'Cohesion and Disintegration in the Wehrmacht in WWII', *Public Opinion Quarterly*, 12, 2 (Summer 1948), pp. 280–315.

35. Samuel A. Stouffer, *Studies in Social Psychology in the Second World War* (Princeton: Princeton University Press, 1949).

36. Hew Strachan, 'Training, Morale & Modern War', *Journal of Contemporary History*, 41, 2 (April 2006), pp. 211–227, accessed online 16/2/2011, http://www.jstor.org/stable/30036383, p. 212.

37. Vejeune D. Gota, 'The Aftermath of War: PTSD, Social Support and Alcohol Consumption in Lithuania', Paper delivered at the 'Afghanistan, the Cold War and the End of the Soviet Union' conference, Hamburg, 14–16 March 2013.

38. Ben Shephard, *A War of Nerves: Soldiers and Psychiatrists, 1914–1994* (Cambridge: Harvard University Press, 2001).
39. John Keegan and Richard Holmes, *Soldiers* (London: Hamish Hamilton, 1985), p. 46.
40. Anthony King, 'The Word of Command: Communication and Cohesion in the Military', *Armed Forces and Society*, 32 (2005), pp. 1–20.
41. Stephen D. Wesbrook, 'The Potential for Military Disintegration', in Sam Sarkesian, *Combat Effectiveness: Cohesion, Stress and the Volunteer Military* (Beverly Hills and London: PUBLISHER, 1980), pp. 247–252.
42. William Ian Miller, *The Mystery of Courage* (Cambridge: Harvard University Press, 2000), p. 131.
43. Keegan and Holmes, *Soldiers*, p. 56.
44. John Crawfurd, 'China and the Chinese', *Journal of the Royal United Services Institution*, I (1858).
45. Taxonomies of culture are broadly defined in terms of cultural influences, cultural variations and cultural manifestations. Each of these consists of further subdivisions with a military relevance, such as history, the veneration of iconic leaders, the prevalence of oaths and rituals, or the relationships between officers and men. Clifford Geertz, *The Interpretation of Cultures* (New York: Basic Books, 1973).

2. RAISING ARMIES: NORTH AMERICAN AND SOUTH ASIAN PERSONNEL IN BRITISH, AMERICAN AND FRENCH SERVICE, 1746–1783

1. South Asian labour was not confined to filling the ranks of the Europeans' armies as a great number of local civilians and camp followers were vital to the functioning of the logistical chain. However, this aspect of employment remains outside the scope of this chapter.
2. Edward Said, *Orientalism* (New York: Pantheon, 1978); Ranajit Guha and Gayatri Spivak, *Selected Subaltern Studies* (New York: OUP, 1989); Gayatri Spivak, 'Can the Subaltern Speak?', in Cary Nelson and Lawrence Grossberg (eds), *Marxism and the Interpretations of Culture* (London and New York: Palgrave, 1988), pp. 271–313.
3. David Washbrook, 'Orients and Occidents: Colonial Discourse Theory and the Historiography of the British Empire', in Robin Winks (ed.), *The Oxford History of the British Empire*, vol. 5: *Historiography* (Oxford: OUP, 1999).
4. The causes of the war were complex and included anger over the 1747 expedition against Memeskia 'Old Briton' and his pro-British Piankashaw tribesmen. The execution of the chief and the driving out of British traders prompted counter-claims and desultory conflict for several years.
5. F. Anderson, *Crucible of War: The Seven Years' War and the Fate of Empire in British North America, 1754–63* (New York: Alfred Knopf, 2000), pp. 102–103.

6. Joseph T. Glattenhaar and James Kirby Martin, *Forgotten Allies: The Oneida Indians and the American Revolution* (New York: Hill and Wang, 2006).
7. Richard M. Ketchum, *Saratoga: Turning Point of America's Revolutionary War* (New York: Henry Holt, 1997), pp. 276–277.
8. Philip Mason, *A Matter of Honour: An Account of the Indian Army, Its Officers and Men* (London: Jonathan Cape, 1974), pp. 29–38.
9. Channa Wickremesekera, *European Success and Indian Failure in the SEC: A Military Analysis* (Monash Asia Institute, 1998). See also Channa Wickremesekera, *Best Black Troops in the World: British Perceptions and the Making of the Sepoys* (New Delhi: Manohar, 2003).
10. Gerald Bryant, *The East India Company and Its Army, 1600–1778* (London: University of London, 1975).
11. Mason, p. 30.
12. Bruce Lenman, *Britain's Colonial Wars, 1688–1783* (London: Pearson, 2001), p. 88.
13. Mason, *A Matter of Honour*, p. 30.
14. Arthur Gilbert, 'Recruitment and Reform in the East India Company Army, 1760–1800', *Journal of British Studies*, 15, 1 (1975), p. 91.
15. In analysing the numbers sick in Clive's return of 1757, we find that, for the British, 16 officers out of 70 were sick, representing 22% of their strength. There were 176 Other Ranks (ORs) out of 1,219 (including 25 out of 257 topasses), representing 14%. For the sepoys, 53 out of 1,914 were sick, representing just 3% of their strength. Average sick rates in 1790s for the Company Army as a whole were 17% and the death rate was 5%. WO 17 1742 and 1743, National Archives, Kew.
16. R. Orme, *Historical Fragments of the Mughal Empire* (London, 1805; repr., 1974).
17. See, for example, Maj. Stainford to K. Kyd, 9 March and 17 March 1779, P/18/47, India Office Records (IOR).
18. Ghulam Hussein Khan, *Seir Mutaquerin* (Review of Modern Times), (repr., 1975).
19. John Prebble, *Mutiny: Highland Regiments in Revolt, 1743–1804* (London: Penguin, 1977); Colin C. Galloway, *White People, Indians and Highlanders: Tribal Peoples and Colonial Encounters in Scotland and America* (Oxford: OUP, 2008).
20. Warren Hastings, Collections of Essays, Add. 29234, Hastings Papers.
21. Cornwallis to the Bishop of Salisbury, 1788, Cornwallis Papers, PRO 30/11/187, National Archives, Kew.
22. James Laver, *British Military Uniforms* (London: Penguin, 1948); Samuel Hutton, 'The Life of an Old Soldier', cited in Roy Palmer (ed.), *The Rambling Soldier* (Harmondsworth: Penguin, 1977), pp. 15–17.
23. G. Penny, *The Traditions of Perth* (1836), pp. 60–61.
24. The figures we have for the 1770s suggest that the lowest price was one guinea per man (1776), but in wartime (1777) this rose to five or six guineas per man. India Office Records, Committee of Shipping Report B92, 3 December 1776.

25. Letter by 'A.B.', *Public Advertiser*, 12 March 1771.
26. A.J. Farrington, L/Mil/9/85, IOR.
27. Despatches to Bengal, 25 March 1757, IOR.
28. Despatches to Bengal, 1759, IOR.
29. Gilbert, 'Recruitment and Reform', p. 98.
30. *London Evening Post*, 16–18 April 1771.
31. See *Colonel Brownrigg's Inspection Records*, 1792, WO 113/15, National Archives, Kew.
32. Court of Directors Letter to Bengal, enc. Cornwallis to Directors, 15 December 1790, L/Mil/Misc./127, IOR.
33. A fascinating contrast can be made with the Royal Navy's patterns of recruitment in the late eighteenth century. New Research by Jeremiah Dancy suggests that 'pressed men' constituted on average no more than 10 per cent of the crews since ships required skilled labour. The decline of crimping coincides with the disfavour towards impressments in the Senior Service. Jeremiah Dancy, 'British naval manpower during the French Revolutionary Wars, 1793–1802' (DPhil, Oxford University, 2012).
34. Cited in Lenman, *Britain's Colonial Wars*, p. 106.
35. Mason, *Matter of Honour*, p. 38.
36. Cornwallis to Dundas, 16 November 1787, Home Misc. Series, vol. 85, IOR.
37. Mason, *Matter of Honour*, p. 63.
38. Lenman, *Britain's Colonial Wars*, p. 100.
39. Mason, *Matter of Honour*, p. 66.
40. Mason, *Matter of Honour*, p. 40.
41. Stewart Gordon, *The New Cambridge History of India: The Marathas, 1600–1818* (Cambridge: CUP, 1993).
42. Lenman, *Britain's Colonial Wars*, p. 96.
43. Letters by Clive, 6 February 1757 ff, 1962-10-142, National Army Museum, London (NAM).

3. THE MERCENARY MOTIVE, CONTRACTS AND MUTINY

1. Richard Holmes, *Firing Line* (London: Penguin, 1985).
2. When a British officer was captured, castrated and flayed—his skin being pegged out nearby—his Indian troops were ordered to beat a wounded Pathan prisoner. Arthur Swinson, *North West Frontier* (London: Hutchinson, 1967), p. 378.
3. Lieutenant-General Sir Henry Daly, lecture, 27 June 1884, Royal United Services Institution, p. 920.
4. T.A. Heathcote, *The Indian Army: The Garrison of British Imperial India, 1822–1922* (London: David and Charles, 1974), p. 158.
5. Cited in Heathcote, *The Indian Army*, p. 160.
6. See William Francis Finlason, 'Martial Law' (Bristol Selected Pamphlets, 1872),

14207/X10–425–117–3, University of Bristol Library; Lauren Benton, *Law and Colonial Cultures: Legal Regimes in World History, 1400–1900* (Cambridge: Cambridge University Press, 2002).

7. 'The Government of Subject Races', *Edinburgh Review*, 207, 423 (January 1908), p. 2.

8. It is noteworthy that the colonial authorities were frequently reactive to events, see Burroughs, 'Imperial Institutions and the Government of Empire', in Andrew Porter (ed.), The Oxford History of the British Empire, III: The Nineteenth Century. (Oxford: Oxford University Press, 1999)', pp. 170–171.

9. Lady MacGregor (ed.), *The Life and Opinions of Major-General Charles Metcalfe MacGregor* (Edinburgh: William Blackwood and Sons, 1888), II, p. 107. See, for example, Secret, no. 194, dated 24 August 1880, in A.W. Moore, *Narrative of Events in Afghanistan from August 1878 to December 1880, and Connected Correspondence* (in continuation of memorandum dated 30 August 1878), Political and Secret Dept, India Office, 31 December 1880, L/PS/20/Memo5/17, IOR.

10. Ronald Hyam, *Britain's Imperial Century, 1815–1914: A Study in Empire and Expansion* (2nd edn, London: PUBLISHER, 1993), p. 310; Burroughs, 'Imperial Institutions', p. 177.

11. W.M. Hogben, 'British Civil-Military Relations on the North West Frontier of India', in A. Preston and P. Dennis (eds.), *Swords and Covenants: Essays in Honour of the Royal Military College of Canada, 1876–1976* (London: Croom Helm, 1977), p. 129.

12. A.J. Stockwell, 'Power, Authority and Freedom', in Peter Marshall (ed.), *The British Empire* (Cambridge: Cambridge University Press, 1996), pp. 163–164. H. Beattie, 'Negotiations with the Tribes in Waziristan, 1849–1914: The British Experience', *Journal of Imperial and Commonwealth History*, 39, 4 (2011), p. 571; and K. Hack, 'Between Terror and Talking: The Place of "Negotiation" in Colonial Conflict', *Journal of Imperial and Commonwealth History*, 39, 4 (2011), pp. 539–549.

13. John Keegan, *A History of Warfare* (London: Hutchinson, 1993), p. 32.

14. Sir John Kaye, *The Indian Mutiny* (London: WH Allen, 3rd edn, 1864), vol. 1, p. 162.

15. Kaye, *A History of the Sepoy War in India*, vol. 1, p. 163.

16. Ibid., p. 177.

17. Ibid., pp. 185–186.

18. Ibid., p. 189.

19. Ibid., p. 194.

20. Ibid., p. 196.

21. Ibid., p. 198 n110.

22. Niall Ferguson, *Empire: How Britain Made the Modern World* (London: Allen Lane, 2003), p. 146.

23. Kaye, *A History of the Sepoy War in India*, vol. 1, pp. 202–211.

24. Ibid., pp. 216–217.
25. Ibid., p. 218.
26. Ibid., p. 221.
27. The army had grown significantly since the turn of the century, but the number of Europeans declined to approximately 12 per cent of the total in 1857. See Philip Mason, *A Matter of Honour: An Account of the Indian Army, Its Officers and Men* (London: Jonathan Cape, 1974), p. 140; W.J. Wilson, *A History of the Madras Army from 1746 to 1826* (Madras, 1888).
28. Raymond Callahan, *The East India Company and Army Reform 1783–1798* (Cambridge, MA: Harvard University Press, 1972); Peter Stanley, *The White Mutiny: British Military Culture in India, 1825–75* (London: Hurst, 1998); Byron Farwell, *Queen Victoria's Little Wars* (London: Allen Lane, 1973), p. 135.
29. Mason, *A Matter of Honour*, p. 247.
30. A.L. Menezes, *Fidelity and Honour: The Indian Army from the Seventeenth Century to the Twenty-First Century* (New Delhi: Penguin, 1993; repr., Oxford University Press, 1999).
31. Anon., 'A Resident of the North West Provinces of India' (London, 1858), p. 34: contrast this with Charles Grant, *Observations on the State of Society among the Asiatic Subjects of Great Britain, particularly with Respect to Morals and the Means of Improving It, written in the Year 1792* (privately printed), p. 220, cited in Michael Edwardes, *Red Year: The Indian Rebellion of 1857* (London: Sphere, 1975), p. 22.
32. The *Delhi Gazette* of 2 February 1842 and 20 June 1842 reported that Muslim sermons called for the defeat of the British.
33. Sir Francis Tuker, *Yellow Scarf* (London: J.M. Dent, 1961), p. 124.
34. Captain L.J. Trotter, *The Life of Hodson of Hodson's Horse* (London, 1906), p. 80, cited in V.G. Kiernan, *Colonial Empires and Armies, 1815–1960* (Stroud: Sutton, 1998), p. 47.
35. Saul David, *The Indian Mutiny, 1857* (London: Viking, 2002), p. 37.
36. Robert Montgomery, Punjab Administration Report, 1857–8, in *Selections from the Public Correspondence of the Administration of the Affairs of the Punjab* (Lahore, 1859), p. 190, in Montgomery Papers, MSS Eur D1019/3, IOR.
37. C.A. Bayly, *Empire and Information: Intelligence Gathering and Social Communication in India, 1780–1870* (Cambridge: Cambridge University Press, 1996), pp. 322–323.
38. Lawrence James, *Raj: The Making and Unmaking of British India* (London, 1997), p. 236.
39. James, *Raj*, p. 236.
40. E.A. Reade, Acting Lieutenant Governor of the North West Provinces, to John Kaye, 10 March 1864, Reade Papers, MSS Eur E124, 223, IOR.
41. Mark Thornhill, *The Personal Adventures and Experiences of a Magistrate during the Rise, Progress and Suppression of the Indian Mutiny* (London, 1884), p. 3; David, *Mutiny*, pp. 65–66.

42. T. Rice-Holmes, *History of the Indian Mutiny* (London, 1904), p. 90; Sir John Kaye, *History of the Sepoy War*, vol. 1, pp. 632–639; Sir Syed Ahmed Khan, *An Essay on the Causes of the Indian Revolt* (Calcutta, 1860), p. 3.
43. James, *Raj*, p. 265.
44. Ferguson, *Empire*, p. 150.
45. Casualties by the end of the action at Delhi were, of the original 490, some 327 killed and wounded, and 8 of the 9 officers killed. The final officer was wounded in the final assault on the city.
46. Letters of Emma Ewart, MSS Eur B 267, IOR.
47. Home Miscellaneous Series 725, pp. 390–1, IOR.
48. Thornhill, *Adventures*, pp. 10, 20, 68 and 71.
49. Home Miscellaneous Series 725, pp. 615–16, IOR.
50. M. Gubbins, *An Account of the Mutinies in the Oudh and the Siege of the Lucknow Residency* (London, 1858), pp. 102–103; Correspondence of Lieutenant Colonel Herbert Bruce, Add Mss 44,003, p. 113, British Library.
51. Sir John Kaye, *History of the Indian Mutiny of 1857–8*, edited by Colonel G.B. Malleson (London, 1864), vol. 6, pp. 168–169.
52. *Mutiny Correspondence*, vol. 1 (Lahore, 1911), p. 193.
53. Kiernan, *Colonial Empires and Armies*, p. 49.
54. Charles Edward Callwell, *Small Wars: Their Principles and Practice* (London: HMSO, 1899), p. 72; Robert Johnson, 'General Roberts, the Occupation of Kabul and the Problems of Transition, 1879–1880', *War in History*, 20, 3 (July 2013).
55. Callwell, *Small Wars*, p. 209.
56. Ronald Hyam, *Britain's Imperial Century, 1815–1914* (2nd edn, London: PUBLISHER, 1993), p. 306.

4. DISCIPLINE AND PUNISHMENT

1. David Omissi, *Sepoy and the Raj* (London: Macmillan, 1994), p. 4.
2. Report of the Peel Commission, Appendix 55, Memo by Canning, L/Mil/7/120, British Library.
3. Lord Roberts, as Commander-in-Chief, returned to the idea in 1890, asking the military member of the Viceroy's Council whether or not 'Zulus or some other good fighting men in Africa' could be enlisted to fill the gaps in the Madras and Bombay armies where 'it would be wise not to have too many Punjab and frontier men in our ranks'. Roberts Papers 100–7/CXXXVIII, National Army Museum, London.
4. Omissi, *Sepoy and the Raj*, p. 9.
5. Note by Colonel Newmarch, 30 April 1890, L/Mil/7/2203.
6. Roberts, *Forty-One Years in India* (London: Macmillan, 1898), p. 00.
7. Omissi, *Sepoy and the Raj*, p. 12.

8. Roberts to Arbuthnot, 6 April 1889, Roberts Papers 100–6/CCCLXXXIV, National Army Museum.

9. Roberts to Viceroy, 18 May 1890, Roberts Papers, 99–1/LXXXIX, National Army Museum.

10. Government of India to Secretary of State for India, 24 June 1881, L/Mil/7/5445, British Library.

11. Omissi, *Sepoy and the Raj*, p. 15.

12. General Frederick Haines, Commander-in-Chief India, Minute, 22 March 1880, L/Mil/7/5445, British Library.

13. Government of India Advance Despatch, 27 August 1920, cited in Omissi, *Sepoy and the Raj*, p. 11.

14. Kaushik Roy, *Brown Warriors of the Raj* (New Delhi: Manohar, 2008), p. 85; W.B. Cunningham, *Dogras* (Government of India, 1932), p. 57; Omissi, *Sepoys and the Raj*, p. 31; Stephen P. Cohen, *Indian Army: Its Contribution to the Development of a Nation* (2nd edn, Oxford: Oxford University Press, 2001), p. 51.

15. Omissi, *Sepoys and the Raj*, p. 28; Cunningham, *Dogras*, p. 96.

16. Cunningham, *Dogras*, pp. 89–90.

17. Philip Mason, *A Matter of Honour: An Account of the Indian Army, Its Officers and Men* (London: Jonathan Cape, 1974), pp. 352–354.

18. Omissi, *Sepoy and the Raj*, p. 35; General Staff, Strategical Survey of India and Burma, 1911, War Office WO 106/154, National Archives, Kew.

19. Omissi, *Sepoy and the Raj*, p. 37.

20. Tony Gould, *Imperial Warriors* (London: Granta, 1999), p. 120.

21. Henry Edward Fane, *Five Years in India* (London, 1842), vol. 1, p. 194.

22. Government of India Report, *East India: Army System*, n.d., pp. 30–33, cited in Gould, *Imperial Warriors*, pp. 122–123.

23. T.A. Heathcote, *The Indian Army: The Garrison of British Imperial India, 1822–1922* (Newton Abbott: David & Charles, 1974), p. 93.

24. Roberts to the Duke of Cambridge, 9 July 1884, Roberts Papers, 7101/23/97, National Army Museum.

25. V.G. Kiernan, *Colonial Army and Empires* (Stroud: Sutton, 1998), p. 43.

26. Kaushik Roy, 'Logistics and the Construction of Loyalty: The Welfare Mechanism in the Indian Army, 1859–1913', in Partha Sarathi Gupta and Anirudh Deshpande (eds.), *The British Raj and Its Indian Armed Forces, 1857–1939* (New Delhi: Oxford University Press, 2002), p. 110.

27. Omissi, *Sepoy and the Raj*, p. 235.

28. Gould, *Imperial Warriors*, p. 134.

29. Douglas Peers, 'Sepoys, Soldiers and the Lash: Caste and Army Discipline in India, 1820–1850', *Journal of Imperial and Commonwealth History*, 23, 2 (1995), pp. 211–247.

30. Letter no. 810, 10 March 1835, C.H. Philips (ed.), *The Correspondence of Lord*

William Cavendish Bentinck: Governor General of India, 1828–1835, vol. 2 (1832–1835), (Oxford: Oxford University Press, 1977), pp. 1448–1449.

31. Letter no. 802, 16 February 1835, *Correspondence of Lord William Cavendish Bentinck*, pp. 1427–1431.

32. *Papers Concerned with the Reorganisation of the Army in India, Supplementary to the Report of the Army Commission* (London, 1859), House of Commons, Session 2, C. 2541; Papers Received from Sir John Lawrence, Brigadier General Neville Chamberlain and Lieutenant Colonel Herbert B. Edwardes, no. 1, p. 20; Papers Received from H.B.E. Frere, Commissioner of Sind, no. 2, p. 58; Papers Received from Brigadier J. Christie, no. 28, p. 311.

33. *Papers Concerned with the Reorganisation of the Army*, House of Commons, C. 2541. Letter, Bartle Frere to Lieutenant Colonel Durand, 6 November 1858, p. 61.

34. *Papers Concerned with the Reorganisation of the Army*, House of Commons, C. 2541, p. 58.

35. Kaushik Roy, *Brown Warriors of the Raj: Recruitment and the Mechanics of Command in the Sepoy Army, 1859–1913* (New Delhi: Manohar, 2008), p. 228.

36. *Papers Concerned with the Reorganisation of the Army*, House of Commons, C. 2541, pp. 54–55.

37. *Papers Concerned with the Reorganisation of the Army*, House of Commons, C. 2541, pp. 38 and 311.

38. E.E. Steiner, 'Separating the Soldier from the Citizen: Ideology and Criticism of Corporal Punishment in the British Army, 1790–1815', *Social History*, 8, 1 (1983), p. 25.

39. Major General S.F. Whittingham to Lord Bentinck, no. 740, 24 June 1834, in C.H. Philips, *The Correspondence of Lord William Cavendish Bentinck*, p. 1311.

40. Peers, 'Sepoys, Soldiers and the Lash', p. 212.

41. *Papers Concerned with the Reorganisation of the Army*, House of Commons, C. 2541, pp. 33–34; Roy, *Brown Warriors of the Raj*, pp. 229–230.

42. Circular to Officers Commanding Divisions, Districts, Brigades, Regiments of Indian Cavalry and Infantry: Summary Trials, Memorandum, Adjutant General's Office, no. 26/N, 15 March 1864, Adjutant General's Circulars, Vol. IV., Office of the Adjutant General B. Crown Period, series 2, Military Department, National Archives of India, Delhi.

43. Confidential Circular, 16 May 1865, Adjutant General's Circulars, vol. 5, cited in Roy, *Brown Warriors of the Raj*, p. 231.

44. Roy, *Brown Warriors of the Raj*, p. 244.

45. *Army Regulations, India*, vol. 2: *Regulations and Orders for the Army* (1913), p. 2.

46. Confidential Circular, to Officers Commanding Divisions and Districts, Adjutant General's Office, 17 February 1865, Adjutant General's Circular, vol. 5, cited in Roy, *Brown Warriors of the Raj*, p. 237.

47. *Papers Concerned with the Reorganisation of the Army*, House of Commons, C. 2541, pp. 21 and 34.

48. *Papers Concerned with the Reorganisation of the Army*, House of Commons, C. 2541, p. 30.

49. Roy, *Brown Warriors of the Raj*, p. 240.

50. *Papers Concerned with the Reorganisation of the Army*, House of Commons, C. 2541, pp. 56 and 58.

51. *Army Regulations India*, p. 10; *Proceedings of the Summary Courts Martial*, no. 374, 15 April 1895, General Order by the Commander-in-Chief India, cited in Roy, *Brown Warriors of the Raj*, p. 256.

52. David Killingray, 'The Rod of Empire: The Debate over Corporal Punishment in the British African Colonial Forces, 1888–1946', *Journal of African History*, 35 (1994), p. 201.

53. Killingray, 'The Rod of Empire', p. 211.

54. Killingray, 'The Rod of Empire', p. 205.

55. CO 96/197/3064, 31 December 1888, National Archives, Kew.

56. Armitage to Officer Commanding Gold Coast Regiment at Lome, 27 August 1914, ADM56/I/59, National Archives of Ghana, Accra, cited in Killingray, 'The Rod of Empire', p. 207.

57. I.F. Nicolson, *The Administration of Nigeria: Men, Methods and Myths* (Oxford: Oxford University Press, 1969), p. 112; Killingray, 'The Rod of Empire', p. 208.

58. W032/4349 cited in David Killingray, 'The Mutiny of the West African Regiment in the Gold Coast, 1901', *International Journal of African Historical Studies*, 16 (1983), pp. 441–454.

59. Minute by Beattie, 2 July 1917, CO 445/39/31551, National Archives, Kew.

60. Lt. Col. H.B. Potter to Colonial Secretary, 14 December 1917, enclosure in Clifford to Long, 15 Dec. 1917, CO 445/39/1833, National Archives, Kew.

61. General Nosworthy to War Office, 22 April 1944, CO 820/52/34197, National Archives, Kew.

62. Reserves Minister to Secretary of State at the Colonial Office, 7 July 1944, and CO Meeting, 12 July 1944, CO 820/52/34197, National Archives, Kew.

63. Ashley Jackson, *Distant Drums: The Role of Colonies in British Imperial Warfare* (Brighton: Sussex Academic Press, 2010), p. 203.

64. Jackson, *Distant Drums*, p. 207.

65. Jackson, *Distant Drums*, p. 209.

66. 3960, Sound Archive, Imperial War Museum, cited in Jackson, *Distant Drums*, p. 209.

67. Jackson, *Distant Drums*, p. 212.

68. War Diary, 1 MR, Quarterly Morale Report, WO 169/18285, National Archives, Kew.

69. Jackson, *Distant Drums*, p. 220.

5. SLAVE SOLDIERS OF THE AMERICAS

1. Secretary at War, out letters, 16 October 1795, p. 33, WO 4/338, National Archives, Kew.
2. Returns of Recruits purchased for the 2nd West India Regiment, WO 40/20; Establishing Black Regiments in the West Indies, WO 40/22 (1805A), National Archives, Kew.
3. Adam Williamson to the Duke of Portland, Port au Prince, 6 July 1795, p. 428, WO 1/61, National Archives, Kew.
4. Letter to Major General Simcoe, 25 November 1796, pp. 445–6, WO 1/65, National Archives, Kew.
5. Return of Troops on Jamaica, 8 June 1807, WO 137/119, National Archives, Kew.[6] A.D.G., 'On the Utility and Economy of the West India Regiments', *United Services Journal*, 2 (London, 1833), p. 493.
7. Letter from Belcarres, Jamaica, 18 November 1799, WO 137/103, pp. 87–8, National Archives, Kew.
8. Letter to Sir Ralph Abercrombie, September 1796, WO 1/65, p. 278, National Archives, Kew.
9. J.F. Maurice, *The Diary of Sir John Moore*, vol. 1 (London: Edward Arnold, 1904), pp. 231 and 235.
10. A.D.G., 'Utility and Economy', p. 495.
11. Brian Dyde, *The Empty Sleeve: The Story of the West India Regiments of the British Army* (St John's, Antigua: Hansib Caribbean, 1997), p. 34.
12. Letter to Major General Simcoe, 25 November 1796, p. 446, WO 1/65, National Archives, Kew.
13. Colonel J.E. Caulfield, *100 Years' History of the 2nd West India Regiment 1795 to 1898: 50th or the Queen's Own Regiment* (London: Naval and Military Press, 2005), pp. 10–15.
14. Letter to Secretary of State, Colonial Office, Jamaica, 13 April 1799, p. 338, WO 137/101, National Archives, Kew.
15. Caulfield, *100 Years' History of the 2nd West India Regiment*, p. 20.
16. R.N. Buckley, *The Napoleonic War Journal of Captain Thomas Henry Browne, 1807–1816* (Stroud: Army Records Society, 1987), p. 143.
17. Caulfield, *100 Years' History of the 2nd West India Regiment*, p. 29.
18. Proceedings of General Court Martial, March 1799, WO 71/182, National Archives, Kew.
19. Governor Sir James Cockburn, Government House Bermuda, letter no. 22, 23 August 1815, p. 24, CO 37/73, National Archives, Kew.
20. Major Kinsman, Headquarters 3rd Battalion, Royal and Colonial Marines, to Cockburn, 10 August 1815, pp. 58–9, CO 37/73, National Archives, Kew.
21. Proceedings of General Court Martial, March 1799, WO 71/182, National Archives, Kew.

22. Balcarres, letter, Jamaica, 1 December 1798, p. 49, CO 137/101, Proceedings of General Court Martial, March 1799, WO 71/182, National Archives, Kew.
23. Buckley, *The Napoleonic War Journal of Captain Thomas Henry Browne*, p. 114.
24. Return of the Jamaica Militia, 18 March 1796, p. 274, CO 137/96, National Archives, Kew.
25. Edward Braithwaite, *The Development of Creole Society in Jamaica, 1770–1820* (Oxford: Clarendon Press, 1972), p. 106.
26. Court Martial, Grenada, 5–30 November 1796, WO 71/181, National Archives, Kew.
27. Buckley, *The Napoleonic War Journal of Captain Thomas Henry Browne*, pp. 111–117.
28. Letter, Downing Street, 29 February 1812, p. 58, CO 137/134, National Archives, Kew.
29. Dyde, *The Empty Sleeve*, p. 24.
30. Dyde, *The Empty Sleeve*.
31. Dyde, *The Empty Sleeve*, p. 106.
32. Dyde, *The Empty Sleeve*, p. 37.
33. Dyde, *The Empty Sleeve*, pp. 37–38.
34. Caulfield, *100 Years' History of the 2nd West India Regiment*, pp. 28–30.
35. Port au Prince, 25 October 1796, p. 377, WO 1/65, National Archives, Kew.
36. Port au Prince, 27 January 1796, WO 1/65, National Archives, Kew.
37. Extracts from the Letters and Memorials addressed to W. Malouet, St Domingo, January to March 1795, p. 165, WO 1/61, National Archives, Kew.
38. Extracts from the Letters and Memorials addressed to W. Malouet, p. 161, WO 1/61.
39. See, for example, General Order, Adjutant General Barbados, 4 September 1802, CO 318/20.
40. R.N. Buckley, *Slaves in Red Coats: The British West India Regiments, 1795–1815* (New Haven, CT: Yale University Press, 1979), pp. 145–147.
41. Dyde, *The Empty Sleeve*, p. 56.
42. Dyde, *The Empty Sleeve*, p. 79.
43. Proceedings of a Court Martial held in Barbados, July 1799, WO 71/184, National Archives, Kew.
44. See WO 71/178 to WO 71/185, National Archives, Kew.
45. Dyde, *The Empty Sleeve*, p. 99.
46. Dyde, *The Empty Sleeve*.
47. Dyde, *The Empty Sleeve*, p. 100.
48. Dyde, *The Empty Sleeve*, p. 37; Buckley, *Slaves in Red Coats*, p. 112.
49. Caulfield, *100 Years' History of the 2nd West India Regiment*, p. 14.
50. Adam Williamson to Whitehall, 9 August 1795, p. 597, WO 1/61, National Archives, Kew.

51. Buckley, *Slaves in Red Coats*, p. 109.
52. Dyde, *The Empty Sleeve*, p. 113.
53. Dyde, *The Empty Sleeve*, p. 24.
54. Dyde, *The Empty Sleeve*, pp. 51–55.
55. Buckley, *Slaves in Red Coats*, p. 118.
56. Braithwaite, *The Development of Creole Society in Jamaica*, p. 300.
57. Braithwaite, *The Development of Creole Society in Jamaica*, p. 301.
58. Dyde, *The Empty Sleeve*, p. 31.
59. Dyde, *The Empty Sleeve*, p. 43.
60. Letter dated 6 November 1798, CO 318/16, National Archives, Kew.
61. Letter dated 20 January 1797, Jamaica, pp. 408–10, CO 4/338, National Archives, Kew.
62. See WO 43/108, National Archives, Kew.
63. Maurice, *The Diary of Sir John Moore*, vol. 1, p. 257.
64. Letter Adam Williamson to Whitehall, 9 August 1795, p. 597, WO 1/61, National Archives, Kew.
65. Braithwaite, *The Development of Creole Society in Jamaica*, p. 160.
66. Dyde, *The Empty Sleeve*, p. 45.
67. Christopher Hibbert (ed.), *The Recollections of Rifleman Harris* (London: Weidenfeld and Nicholson, 1996), p. 114.
68. Braithwaite, *The Development of Creole Society in Jamaica*, p. 28.
69. Maurice, *The Diary of Sir John Moore*, vol. 1, p. 224.
70. Maurice, *The Diary of Sir John Moore*, vol. 1, p. 219.
71. Downing Street to Lieutenant General Cook, 5 August 1807, p. 99, CO 137/119, National Archives, Kew.
72. Dyde, *The Empty Sleeve*, p. 25.
73. 'The Negro as a Soldier in the War of the Rebellion', in *Selected Letters and Papers of N.P. Hallowell* (Peterborough, N.H: Richard R. Smith and Co., 1896), p. 34. I am grateful to Professor Natalie Zemon Davies for access to this material.
74. *Selected Letters and Papers of N.P. Hallowell*, p. 40.
75. M1801, Compiled Service Records of Soldiers who served in the 55th Massachusetts Infantry (Colored), RG 94, National Archives and Records Administration (NARA), Washington DC.
76. *Selected Letters and Papers of N.P. Hallowell*, pp. 44–45.
77. *Selected Letters and Papers of N.P. Hallowell*, pp. 45–46.
78. *Selected Letters and Papers of N.P. Hallowell*, p. 48.
79. Colonel William P. Hardeman, letter, 30 July 1864, Compiled Service Records, Records of the Adjutant General's Office, 1780s–1917, RG 94, NARA.
80. Douglas Porch, *Wars of Empire* (London: Cassell, 2000), p. 135.
81. Porch, *Wars of Empire*, p. 141.

6. ARMIES OF EMPIRE

1. H. Marshall, *Military Miscellany* (London, 1846), pp. 77–78.

2. W.O., Cost of Principal Wars, 1857–1899, confidential print, 1902, National Army Museum, London.

3. W.O., *Military Report on British Somaliland* (London, 1925), p. 23.

4. F. Wakeman, *Strangers at the Gate: Social Disorder in South China, 1839–1861* (Berkeley: University of California Press, 1966), p. 56.

5. A.S. Kanya-Forster, *The Conquest of Western Sudan: A Study in French Military Imperialism* (Cambridge: Cambridge University Press, 1969), p. 272.

6. Major General E. Upton, *The Armies of Asia and Europe* (New York, 1878), p. 302.

7. Colonel G.B. Malleson, *The Indian Mutiny of 1857* (4th edn, London, 1892), p. 410.

8. Private J.P. Swindlehurst, Lancashire Fusiliers, Diary, 1919–1921, 4 November 1919, Document Collection, 10415, Imperial War Museum, London.

9. Major D.H. Cole, *Imperial Military Geography* (9th edn, London, 1937), p. 378.

10. Cole, *Imperial Military Geography*.

11. Sir C. Crosthwaite, *The Pacification of Burma* (London, 1912), cited in V.G. Kiernan, *Colonial Empires and Armies, 1815–1960* (Stroud: Sutton, 1998), p. 55.

12. J-J. E. Roy (ed.), *Quinze ans de sejour à Java: Souvenirs d'un ancient officier* (Tours, 1861), pp. 319–321.

13. Callwell, *Small Wars*, p. 443.

14. Kiernan, *Colonial Empires*, p. 152.

15. D. Jardine, *The Mad Mullah of Somaliland* (London, 1923), pp. 84–86.

16. Kiernan, *Colonial Empires*, p. 153.

17. *Natal Witness*, 30 January 1879, cited in Kiernan, *Colonial Empires*, p. 156.

18. Captain W.R. King, *Campaigning in Kaffirland, 1851–1852* (London, 1853), p. 283.

19. Kiernan, *Colonial Empires*, p. 156

20. Kiernan, *Colonial Empires*, p. 156.

21. Major Broadfoot, 'British Bullets and the Peace Conference', *Blackwood's Magazine* (September 1899).

22. P. Magnus, *Kitchener: Portrait of an Imperialist* (London: John Murray, 1958), p. 143.

23. J.W. Sherer, *Havelock's March on Cawnpore 1857: A Civilian's Notes* (London, 1910), p. 125.

24. M.E. Yapp, *Strategies of British India: Britain, Iran and Afghanistan, 1758–1850* (Oxford: Oxford University Press, 1980), p. 549.

25. E. Sanderson, *Africa in the Nineteenth Century* (London, 1898), pp. 152–153.

26. James Lunt (ed.), *Sita Ram: From Sepoy to Subedar* (1873; repr., London, 1970), p. 73; C.A. Bayly, *Empire and Information: Intelligence Gathering and Social*

Communication in India, 1780–1870 (Cambridge: Cambridge University Press, 1996), pp. 87–88.

27. J.G.A. Baird (ed.), *The Private Letters of the Marquess of Dalhousie* (1858; repr., Edinburgh, 1910), p. 414.
28. Cited in T.A. Heathcote, *The Afghan Wars* (Oxford: Osprey, 1980), p. 72.
29. Callwell, *Small Wars*, p. 82.
30. Callwell, *Small Wars*, pp. 74, 148.
31. Kiernan, *Colonial Empires and Armies*, p. 160.
32. Kiernan, *Colonial Empires and Armies*, p. 161.
33. D.G.E. Hall, *A History of South East Asia* (London: PUBLISHER, 1955), p. 567.
34. King, *Campaigning in Kaffirland*, p. 266.
35. F.W. Hirst et al., *Liberalism and the Empire* (London, 1900), p. 146.
36. Kevin Linch, *Britain and Wellington's Army: Recruitment, Society and Tradition, 1807–1815* (Basingstoke: Palgrave, 2011).
37. A. Swinson and D. Scott (eds.), *The Memoirs of Private Waterfield* (London, 1968), p. 107 cited in Kiernan, *Colonial Empires*, p. 26.
38. C.M. MacGregor, *Official History*, pp. 194–225. FULL DETAILS
39. Frederick Roberts, *Forty-One Years*, p. 418. FULL DETAILS
40. Tony Gould, *Imperial Warriors: Britain and the Gurkhas* (London: Granta, 1999), p. 32.
41. Gould, *Imperial Warriors*, p. 46.
42. Edward Thompson, *The Making of the Indian Princes* (PLACE: PUBLISHER, DATE), pp. 188–189.
43. *Bengal Military Consultations*, vol. 57, no. 35, Dehra Dun, 29 Dec. 1829, India Office Records, British Library (IOR).
44. Gould, *Imperial Warriors*, p. 59.
45. Gould, *Imperial Warriors*, p. 95.
46. Hon. W.G. Osbourne, *The Court and the Camp of Runjeet Singh* (London, 1840), pp. 107–108.
47. H.A. Oldfield, *Sketches from Nipal* (London, 1880), pp. 29–30; Gould, *Imperial Warriors*, pp. 101–102.
48. Colonel Ramsay, cited in Gould, *Imperial Warriors*, p. 104.
49. Leo Rose, *Nepal: Strategy for Survival* (Berkeley, CA: PUBLISHER, 1971), p. 133.
50. B.H. Hodgson, 'Origin and Classification of the Military Tribes of Nepal' in *Essays on the Languages, Literature and Religion of Nepal and Tibet* (London, 1874), p. 40.
51. Bishop Reginald Heber, *Narrative of a Journey through the Upper Provinces of India* (London, 1843), vol. 1, p. 273.
52. Cited in Gould, *Imperial Warriors*, p. 109.
53. Captain F.B. Doveton, *Reminiscences of the Burmese War, in 1824–5–6* (London, 1852), p. 22.

54. Sir Alfred Lyall, *The Rise and Expansion of British Dominion in Asia* (London, 1894; 5th edn, 1910), pp. 323–324; Captain L.J. Trotter, *The Life of Hodson of Hodson's Horse* (London, 1901), pp. 21–23.

55. J. Ryder, *Four Years' Service in India, by a Private Soldier* (Leicester, 1853), pp. 127–130; Kiernan, *Colonial Empires*, p. 42.

56. Ryder, *Four Years' Service in India*, p. 173.

57. K.M.L. Saxena, *The Military System of India, 1859–1900* (New Delhi: PUBLISHER, 1974), pp. 268–269.

58. A.K. Slessor, 'Why and How the Afridis Rose', [*Colburn's*] *United Services Magazine*, 20 (1899–1900), pp. 388–400.

59. Colonel H.C. Wylly, *From the Black Mountain to Waziristan* (London: Macmillan, 1912), p. 314. Of the 2,000 Afridis employed within the Indian Army, some had deserted, prompting the authorities to deploy the remainder away from the theatre of operations. Nevertheless, the majority remained in service and some fought at Malakand despite the entreaties of the Pashtun fighters that they should desert.

60. It was rumoured that 80,000 rifles had been sold by the Amir of Afghanistan to the tribesmen.

61. Wylly, *From the Black Mountain to Waziristan*, p. 384.

62. Captain H.L. Nevill, *Campaigns on the North West Frontier* (London, 1912; repr., Nashville, TN: Battery Press, n.d.), pp. 267–268.

63. Nevill, *Campaigns on the North West Frontier*, p. 273.

64. Nevill, *Campaigns on the North West Frontier*, p. 268.

65. 'The Pioneer', cited in Nevill, *Campaigns on the North West Frontier*, p. 269.

66. Nevill, *Campaigns on the North West Frontier*, p. 270.

67. David Omissi, *The Sepoy and the Raj* (London, 1994), pp. 10–29.

68. T.A. Heathcote, *The Indian Army: The Garrison of British Imperial India, 1822–1922* (London: David and Charles, 1974), p. 103.

69. Eric St J. Lawson, Commissioner of Police, Siam, 20 February 1905, External A, May 1905, nos. 175–177, National Archives of India, New Delhi.

70. Commissioner Central Africa to Commander-in-Chief India, 8 August 1892, Military B Programmes, May 1893, nos. 2107–46, National Archives of India, New Delhi.

71. Emily Innes, *The Chersoese with the Gilding Off* (1885; repr., Kuala Lumpur, 1974), vol. 2, p. 74.

72. See Halford Mackinder's remarks in Peter Hansen, 'Classical Boundaries: National Identities and British Mountaineering on the Frontiers of Europe and the Empire, 1868 to 1940', *Journal of Imperial and Commonwealth History*, 24 (1996), p. 56; 'Report on the Administration of the Eastern Portion of British Central Africa from 1891 to 1894', *Parliamentary Papers* 1894, vol. 57, p. 779; 'Report on the Uganda Protectorate', 10 July 1901, *Parliamentary Papers*, vol. 48, p. 577.

73. National Archives of India, Police, June 1890, nos. 1–18 and 126–38; R. Rodd to H.M. Durand, 3 September 1893, National Archives of India, Foreign Sec. E, January 1894, no. 480–86.

74. Note, Military Departments by E.H.H.C. of 24 April 1891, Foreign External B, May 1891, nos. 46–47, National Archives of India.

75. Government of India to Secretary of State for India, 12 March 1889, National Archives of India, Military Programmes, March 1889, nos. 2215–19; Secretary of State to Viceroy, 23 April 1891, Foreign External B, May 1891, nos. 46–47.

76. Governor General to Secretary of State, 23 June 1890, Military Programmes, July 1890, nos. 144–57.

77. H.H. Johnston to Commander-in-Chief India, 8 July 1892, Military B Programmes, May 1893, no. 2107–2146; Lieutenant Colonel H. Moyse-Bartlett, *The King's African Rifles* (Aldershot, 1956), pp. 17–23; Roland Oliver, *Sir Harry Johnston and the Scramble for Africa* (London: Chatto & Windus, 1957).

78. H.H. Johnston to Foreign Secretary, 10 November 1894, Revenue and Agriculture (Emigration), February 1895, no. 8, National Archives of India.

79. Government of India to Secretary of State, 27 October 1898, Military A Programmes, December 1898, no. 1314, National Archives of India.

80. Its first commanding officer was from the Indian Army, Lieutenant Colonel W.H. Manning, who had come to Africa with the Sikhs contingent in 1893.

81. Note by Curzon, 25 February 1903, Military B Programme, April 1903, no. 1512–16, National Archives of India.

82. [D.A. Sandford], *Leaves from the Journal of a Subaltern during the Campaign in Punjaub, September 1848 to March 1849* (Edinburgh, 1849), pp. 109, 119.

83. Doveton, *Reminiscences of the Burmese War*, pp. 86–7; W.F.B. Laurie, *The Second Burmese War: A Narrative of the Operations at Rangoon in 1852* (London, 1853), pp. 79 and 122.

84. Surgeon C. Pine, Diaries, 28 May 1842, 31 July 1840, National Army Museum, London.

7. IMPERIAL ARMIES IN AFRICA

1. Peter Warwick, *Black People and the South African War, 1899–1902* (Cambridge: Cambridge University Press, 1983).

2. Brian Willan, 'Blacks in the Siege', in Iain R. Smith (ed.), *The Siege of Mafeking* (Johannesburg: Brenthurst Press, 2001), vol. 2, p. 287.

3. S. Plaatje, *Native Life in South Africa* (London, 1916), p. 239; Willan, 'Blacks in the Siege', p. 293.

4. Willan, 'Blacks in the Siege', p. 294.

5. Willan, 'Blacks in the Siege', p. 296.

6. F. Pretorious, *Life on Commando during the Anglo-Boer War, 1899–1902* (Cape Town: Tafelberg, 1999), p. 269; Willan, 'Blacks in the Siege', p. 302.

7. E. Ross, *Diary of the Siege of Mafeking*, ed. Brian Willan (Cape Town, 1980), 17 January 1900; Willan, 'Blacks in the Siege', p. 305.

8. Plaatje, *Native Life*, pp. 246–247.

9. Willan, 'Blacks in the Siege', p. 310.

10. Baden-Powell, Staff Diary, 8 February 1900, cited in T. Jeal, *Baden-Powell* (London: Hutchinson, 1989), p. 266.

11. Willan, 'Blacks in the Siege', p. 315.

12. Charles Bell's Intelligence Report, 20 May 1900, cited in Willan, 'Blacks in the Siege', p. 320.

13. Its alternative title was Troupes de marine, a name it adopted formerly after 1961.

14. Anthony Clayton, *France, Soldiers and Africa* (London: Brassey's Defence Publishers, 1988); CEHD (Centre d'Etudes d'Histoire de la Défense), *Les Troupes de marine dans l'armée de terre: Un siècle d'histoire (1900–2000)* (Paris: Lavauzelle, 2001).

15. Robert Hure, *L'Armée d'Afrique: 1830–1962* (Paris: Charles-Lavauzelle, 1977).

16. Shelby Cullom Davis, *Reservoirs of Men: A History of the Black Troops of French West Africa* (Westport, CN: Negro Universities Press, 1970).

17. H.M. Walmsley, *Sketches of Algeria during the Kabyle War* (London, 1858), pp. 31 and 51.

18. V.G. Kiernan, *Colonial Empires and Armies, 1815–1960* (Stroud: Sutton, 1998), p. 101.

19. A. Mounier-Kuhn, *Les Services de santé militaires français pendant la conquête du Tonkin et de l'Annam, 1882–1896* (Vicennes: Services Historique de la Marine, 2005).

20. For links between the approaches in Indo-China and Madagascar, see Michael Finch, *A Progressive Occupation? The Gallieni-Lyautey Method and Colonial Pacification in Tonkin and Madagascar, 1885–1900* (Oxford: Oxford University Press, DATE).

21. W.A. Wills and L.T. Collingridge (eds.), *The Downfall of Lobengula* (London, 1894), p. 26.

22. A.S. Kanya-Forster, *The Conquest of Western Sudan: A Study in French Military Imperialism* (Cambridge: Cambridge University Press, 1969), p. 248.

23. G.W. Steevens, *With Kitchener to Khartoum* (Edinburgh: William Blackwood and Sons, 1898), p. 150.

24. Steevens, *With Kitchener to Khartoum*, p. 150.

25. Steevens, *With Kitchener to Khartoum*, p. 276.

26. Steevens, *With Kitchener to Khartoum*, pp. 280–2882.

27. Steevens, *With Kitchener to Khartoum*, pp. 295–296.

28. Admiralty War Staff, (Naval) Intelligence Division, *A Handbook of German East Africa* (January 1916), pp. 200 and 203.

8. IRREGULARS AND ADVISERS IN COLONIAL SERVICE

1. Bishop Heber, cited in K. Roy, 'Military Synthesis in South Asia: Armies, Warfare and Indian Society, c.1740–1849,' *Journal of Military History*, 69, 3 (July 2005), p. 687.
2. Philip Mason, *A Matter of Honour: An Account of the Indian Army, its Officers and Its Men* (London: Jonathan Cape, 1974), p. 317.
3. Mason, *A Matter of Honour*, p. 321.
4. Mason, *A Matter of Honour*, p. 321.
5. Mason, *A Matter of Honour*, p. 322.
6. Lieutenant General Sir Henry Daly, lecture, 27 June 1884, Royal United Services Institution, p. 908.
7. Daly, lecture, 27 June 1884, Royal United Services Institution, p. 909.
8. Daly, lecture, 27 June 1884, Royal United Services Institution, p. 909.
9. Daly, lecture, 27 June 1884, Royal United Services Institution, p. 911.
10. Daly, lecture, 27 June 1884, Royal United Services Institution, p. 920.
11. Stuart Sampson, 'The Journals of Lt.-Col. John Pennycuick', in Rob Johnson (ed.), *The British Indian Army: Virtue and Necessity* (Cambridge: Cambridge Scholars Publishers, 2014), p. 19.
12. Robert Johnson, *The Afghan Way of War* (London: Hurst, 2011).
13. T.A. Heathcote, *The Indian Army: The Garrison of British Imperial India, 1822–1922* (London: David and Charles, 1974), p. 114.
14. Roy, 'Military Synthesis in South Asia', p. 656.
15. The Nizam of Hyderabad offered a portion of his revenues to the government of India, an example which was promptly followed by other state rulers.
16. Tony McClenaghan, 'The Imperial Service Troops Scheme in the Nineteenth and Twentieth Centuries', in Johnson, *The British Indian Army*, p. 94.
17. Letter from Secretary to the Government of India to the Chief Commissioner of Mysore, Fort William, 15 January 1878, India Office Records, British Library (IOR).
18. Roberts to Chesney, 4 December 1890, 100–7/CXXXVIII, Roberts Papers, National Army Museum, London.
19. McClenaghan, 'The Imperial Service Troops Scheme', p. 97.
20. McClenaghan, 'The Imperial Service Troops Scheme', p. 98.
21. McClenaghan, 'The Imperial Service Troops Scheme', p. 100.
22. Peter Hopkirk, *The Great Game* (Oxford: Oxford University Press, 1990), p. 41.
23. See Lieutenant General William Montieth, *Kars and Ezeroum, with the Campaigns of Prince Paskiewich in 1823 and 1829, and an Account of the Conquests of Russia beyond the Caucasus* (London, 1856).
24. Douglas Porch, *Wars of Empire* (London: Cassell, 2000).
25. Charles Chenevix Trench, *Charley Gordon: An Eminent Victorian Reassessed* (London: Allen Lane, 1978), pp. 25ff.

26. Gordon's correspondence with his family, British Library, Add. MSS 52389, leaves 387–8.

27. Trench, *Charley Gordon*, p. 34.

28. Trench, *Charley Gordon*, p. 34.

29. Trench, *Charley Gordon*, p. 34.

30. Trench, *Charley Gordon*, p. 39.

31. Add. MSS 52386, leaves 37–42, British Library; FO 17/393 and 396, National Archives, Kew.

32. Trench, *Charley Gordon*, p. 42.

33. Add. MSS 52389, leaves 393, British Library.

9. COLONIAL ARMIES AND IRREGULARS IN THE FIRST WORLD WAR, 1914–1918

1. General Staff of the German Army, *The German War Book, being the Usages of War on Land*, ed. and trans. J.H. Morgan (London, 1915), pp. 66–67.

2. Frederich von Bernhardi, *Germany and the Next War* (1911; English edn, London, 1918), pp. 90, 146; S.P. Davis, *Reservoirs of Men: A History of Black Troops of French Africa* (Chambéry, 1934), ch. 4.

3. Volker Berghahn, *Germany and the Approach of War* (Leamington: Berg, 1985), p. 143.

4. V. Rothwell, 'The British Government and Japanese Military Assistance, 1914–1918', *History* (February, 1971), pp. 39–43.

5. V.G. Kiernan, *Colonial Empires and Armies* (Stroud: Sutton, 1998), p. 184.

6. J.C. Wedgwood, Lord Barleston, Papers, letter, 29 September 1916, Documents collection, 16598, Imperial War Museum, London.

7. J. D. Hargreaves, *The End of Colonial Rule in West Africa* (London: Historical Association, 1976), p. 14.

8. M. Crowder, *Revolt in Bussa*: A Story of British 'native administration' in Nigerian Borgu, 1902–1935 (London: Faber and Faber, 1973), pp. 114–15, 146–149.

9. Commandant F. Ingold, *Les Troupes noirs au combat* (Paris: Berger-Levrault, 1940), pp. 97–98.

10. Kiernan, *Colonial Empires and Armies*, p. 185.

11. Major General Sir Richard Ewart (then Deputy Director General Supply and Transport in the Indian Army), notebook of memoirs, Documents, 683, p. 91, Imperial War Museum.

12. Major General H.V. Lewis, letters, 26 October 1914 and 29 June 1915, Documents, 2531, Imperial War Museum; Philip Mason, *A Matter of Honour: An Account of the Indian Army, Its Officers and Men* (London: Jonathan Cape, 1974), p. 413.

13. Lieutenant Colonel K.H. Henderson, Papers, memoir, pp. 117–20, Documents, 10942, Imperial War Museum.

14. Kiernan, *Colonial Empires and Armies*, p. 186.

15. Lewis, letter, 1 Sept 1914, Documents, 2531, Imperial War Museum.
16. Robert Johnson, *The Great War and the Middle East* (Oxford: Oxford University Press, 2016), ch. 2.
17. Court of Enquiry Report, A.H. Dickinson, Officer Cadet of the Straits Settlement Police, Documents, 9749, Imperial War Museum.
18. Major E.A. Brown, 'Narrative of the Singapore Mutiny, 1915', Documents, 11392, ch. 5; Dickinson, Testimony to Court of Enquiry, pp. 15–16, Documents, 9749, Imperial War Museum.
19. Brigadier General (Sir) Edward Northey, War Diary, pp. 243, 279, Documents, 9796, Imperial War Museum.
20. Northey, pp. 68–69, Documents, 9796, Imperial War Museum.
21. Lewis, scrapbook, undated press cutting [1916]; Northey, war diary, pp. 96 and 128, Documents, 9796, Imperial War Museum.
22. Lewis, 2 April 1916, 10 May 1916 and 26 December 1916, letters, Documents, 2531, Imperial War Museum.
23. Lewis, scrapbook, undated press cutting [1916], Documents, 2531, Imperial War Museum.
24. Cited in Kiernan, *Colonial Empires and Armies*, p. 189.
25. Kiernan, *Colonial Empires and Armies*, p. 145.
26. Redistribution of the Army in India, 1904, Committee of Imperial Defence 58-D, CAB 6/2, National Archives, Kew.
27. Caste Returns, 1 January 1904, L/Mil/7/17084, India Office Records, British Library, London (IOR).
28. George Morton-Jack, *The Indian Army on the Western Front: India's Expeditionary Force to France and Belgium in the First World War* (Cambridge: Cambridge University Press, 2014), p. 3.
29. Auchinleck served with the 62nd Punjabis and was decorated for his dedication and courage in actions at Suez, the Hanna, Kut, and in northern Mesopotamia between 1915 and 1919. Charles Allen, *Plain Tales from the Raj* (London: Penguin, 1975), pp. 239–240.
30. There were two examinations, with further training in specialist languages as required.
31. Incidentally, Auchinleck succeeded; Montgomery failed. Charles Chenevix Trench, *The Indian Army and the King's Enemies, 1900–1947* (London: Thames and Hudson, 1988), p. 25.
32. David Omissi, *The Sepoy and the Raj: The Politics of the Indian Army, 1860–1940* (London: Macmillan, 1994). For a contemporary view, see George MacMunn, *The Martial Races of India* (London: Sampson Low, 1933).
33. Francis Ingall, *The Last of the Bengal Lancers* (London: Leo Cooper, 1988), p. 5.
34. The 129th Baluchis, for example, despite the title, contained no Baluchis but was made up of Pashtuns, Mahsuds and Punjabis. In Wilde's Rifles, there were companies consisting of Dogras, Pathans, Punjabis and Sikhs.

35. The most significant losses of the frontier wars occurred in the 1897–8 Pathan Rising. On the Tirah expedition, some 287 were killed and a further 853 were wounded, but this was exceptional. Captain H.L. Nevill, *Campaigns on the North West Frontier* (London, 1912), p. 301.
36. A further five cavalry brigades could be deployed with sufficient notice. Indian Expeditionary Force A, War Diary, Simla, October 1914, p. 136, L/Mil/17/5/3088, IOR.
37. Robert Johnson, "'I Shall Die Arms in Hand, Wearing the Warriors' Clothes": Mobilisation and Initial Operations of the Indian Army in France and Flanders', *British Journal for Military History*, 2, 3 (February 2016).
38. Sir Moore Creagh, the former CiCI, had demanded modern arms and equipment to fulfil Kitchener's planned expeditionary force capabilities but the government and his successor as CiCI deferred the decision on grounds of cost. Even after six months of war the government of India remained on a peacetime footing with regard to military expenditure.
39. Reorganisation, 1861–1936, L/Mil/7/120, IOR.
40. Logistics, for example, had to fit into a British Army system, with which the Indian Army was unfamiliar. H. Alexander, *On Two Fronts, Being the Adventures of an Indian Mule Corps in France and Gallipoli* (New York: Dutton, 1917), p. 42.
41. Indian Corps war diary (October–December 1914), WO 95/1090, National Archives, Kew.
42. J. Willcocks, *With the Indians in France* (London: Constable, 1920), ch. 20.
43. The Battalion had deployed with 11 British officers and 729 Indian other ranks; three days later, 5 officers and 274 Indians returned: a casualty rate of 63 per cent.
44. Morton-Jack, *Indian Army on the Western Front*, p. 15. He lists the authors endorsing the suffering caused by the climate.
45. Captain R. Grimshaw, *Indian Cavalry Officer, 1914–15* (London, 1986), cited in Trench, *Indian Army*, p. 35.
46. J. Greenhut, "'Sahib and Sepoy': An Enquiry into the Relationship between British Officers and Native Soldiers of the British Indian Army', *Military Affairs*, 48 (1984), pp. 16–17; 'Nominal roll of Indian prisoners of war suspected of having deserted to the enemy or to have given information or to have otherwise assisted the enemy after capture', List A, secret, L/Mil/17/5/2403, IOR.
47. The latter is strongly refuted by Gordon Corrigan, *Sepoys in the Trenches: The Indian Corps on the Western Front, 1914–15* (Stroud: Spellmount, 2006), pp. 168 and 247. See Nikolas Gardner, *Trial by Fire: Command and the British Expeditionary Force in 1914* (Westport, CT: Praeger, 2003), pp. 177–182.
48. John Buchan, *A History of the Great War* (New York: Houghton Mifflin, 1923), vol. 1, pp. 150–149.
49. Corrigan, *Sepoys in the Trenches*, pp. 204–207.
50. Willcocks, *With the Indians in France*, pp. 266–267.

51. Mir Dast was awarded the VC and was, ironically, the brother of the deserter, who allegedly received an Iron Cross.
52. Corrigan, *Sepoys in the Trenches*, pp. 189–190.
53. Morton-Jack, *Indian Army on the Western Front*, p. 168.
54. Morton-Jack, *Indian Army on the Western Front*, p. 185.
55. John Merewhether and Sir Frederick Smith, *The Indian Corps in France* (London: John Murray, 1919), pp. 462–489; Morton-Jack, *Indian Army on the Western Front*, pp. 19 and 162–165.
56. Merewhether and Smith, *The Indian Corps in France*, p. 463; Morton-Jack, *Indian Army on the Western Front*, p. 18.
57. George Morton-Jack refutes the idea that the Indian Corps was withdrawn because of suffering from the northern European climate or operational underperformance. See, *Indian Army on the Western Front*, p. 157.
58. Morton-Jack, *Indian Army on the Western Front*, p. 154.
59. Robin Prior and Trevor Wilson, *The Somme* (New Haven: Yale University Press, 2005), p. 139.
60. Although, it should be noted, that the regular contingent was down to 15,000 men, too few to garrison 300 million in the event of a major insurrection.
61. Corrigan, *Sepoys in the Trenches*, p. 71.
62. Morton-Jack, *Indian Army on the Western Front*, p. 231.
63. Willcocks, *With the Indians in France*, p. 9.
64. See Morton-Jack, *The Indian Army on the Western Front*, p. 13; Merewhether and Smith, *The Indian Corps in France*, pp. vii, chs. 2 and 14.
65. See 'Introduction' in Rob Johnson (ed.), *The Indian Army: Virtue and Necessity* (Cambridge: Cambridge Scholars Press, 2014).
66. David Omissi, 'The Indian Army in the First World War, 1914–1918', in Dan Marston and Chandar S. Sundaram (eds.), *A Military History of India and South Asia: From the East India Company to the Nuclear Era*, (Bloomington, IN: Indiana University Press, 2007), p. 81.
67. F.J. Moberly, *The Campaign in Mesopotamia, 1914–1918* (London: HMSO, 1923), vol. 1, p. 63.
68. Viceroy to Kitchener, 29 January 1915, Kitchener Papers, 30/57/69, National Archives, Kew.
69. Memorandum by Kirkpatrick, 6 May 1916, WO 106/5443, National Archives, Kew.
70. Peter Sluggett, *Britain in Iraq, 1914–1932* (London, 1976), pp. 9–14; Hew Strachan, *The First World War: A New Illustrated History* (London: Simon and Schuster, 2003), p. 316.
71. M. O'Dwyer, *India As I Knew It, 1885–1925* (London: Constable, 1925), p. 225.
72. Radcliffe, memorandum, 'The Situation in Mesopotamia', 7 December 1920, CP 2275, CAB 24/116, National Archives, Kew.

73. R. Holland, 'The British Empire and the Great War, 1914–1918', in Judith M. Brown and W.R. Louis (eds.), *The Oxford History of the British Empire*, vol. 4: *The Twentieth Century* (Oxford: Oxford University Press, 1999), p. 117.

74. Malcolm Page, *The King's African Rifles: A History* (London: Pen and Sword, 2011), p. 9.

75. Page, *The King's African Rifles*, p. 34.

76. C. Holdern, *Military Operations in East Africa, 1914–1916* (London: HMSO, 1941).

77. A. Haywood and F.A.S. Clarke, *A History of the RWAFF* (Aldershot: Gale and Polden, 1964).

78. Page, *The King's African Rifles*, p. 36; see also Lieutenant Colonel H. Moyse-Bartlett, *The King's African Rifles* (Aldershot: Gale and Polden, 1956).

79. Sir Hugh Clifford, *The Gold Coast Regiment in the East African Campaign* (London: John Murray, 1920).

80. See Christopher Owen, *The Rhodesian African Rifles* (London: Leo Cooper, 1970).

81. Page, *The King's African Rifles*, pp. 42 and 49.

82. Page, *The King's African Rifles*, p. 41.

83. Xu Guoqi, *China and the Great War: China's Pursuit of a New National Identity and Internationalization* (Cambridge: Cambridge University Press, 2005), p. 74.

84. FO 350/13, 23 December 1915, National Archives, Kew.

85. FO 371/3682/1259, War Office Report, National Archives, Kew.

86. WO 106/33/44, October 1916, National Archives, Kew.

87. Tu T. Huynh, 'From Demand for Asiatic Labor to Importation of Indentured Chinese Labor: Race Identity in the Recruitment of Unskilled Labor for South Africa's Gold Mining Industry, 1903–1910', *Journal of Chinese Overseas*, 4, 1 (May 2008), pp. 51–68.

88. WO 106/33, 7 June 1915, National Archives, Kew.

89. FO 405/222, 23 February 1917, National Archives, Kew.

90. Michael Summerskill, *China on the Western Front: Britain's Chinese Workforce in the First World War* (Cambridge: Cambridge University Press, 1982), pp. 81–92, 118.

91. FO 371/3682/8785, confidential, 18 September 1919, National Archives, Kew.

92. T.E. Lawrence, *Seven Pillars of Wisdom* (London: Jonathan Cape, 1935), pp. 292–294.

93. Lawrence, *Seven Pillars*, p. 295.

94. Jeremy Wilson, *Lawrence of Arabia* (New York: Atheneum, 1990), pp. 34–40, 45–52, 68.

95. M.D. Allen, *The Medievalism of Lawrence of Arabia* (University Park, PA.: Pennsylvania State University Press, 1991), pp. 29–33; John E. Mack, *The Prince of Our Disorder: The Life of T.E. Lawrence* (Boston: Little, Brown, 1976), pp. 53–55.

96. Lawrence, *Seven Pillars*, p. 58.

97. Robin Bidwell (ed.), *The Diary Kept by T.E. Lawrence While Travelling in Arabia during 1911* (Reading: Garnet, 1993), pp. 6, 9–10.

98. Lawrence, *Seven Pillars*, pp. 111 and 485; Mack, *The Prince of Our Disorder*, p. 44.

99. Lawrence, *Seven Pillars*, p. 29.

100. Lawrence, *Seven Pillars*, p. 30.

101. Lawrence, *Seven Pillars*, p. 282.

102. Lawrence, letter to Major Scott, 15 October 1918, cited in Wilson, *Lawrence of Arabia*, p. 572.

103. Donald M. McKale, *War by Revolution Germany and Great Britain in the Middle East in the era of World War I*, p. 75. (Kent: Kent State University Press, 1998)

104. Efraim Karsh and Inari Karsh, 'Myth in the Desert, or Not the Great Arab Revolt', *Middle Eastern Studies*, 33, 2 (April 1997), pp. 267–312.

105. Zeine N. Zeine, *The Emergence of Arab Nationalism: With a Background Study of Arab-Turkish Relations in the Near East* (1958; 3rd edn, Delmar, NY: Caravan, 1976), pp. 106–109 and 116; William Oschenwald, 'Ironic Origins: Arab Nationalism in the Hijaz, 1882–1914' in Rashid Khalidi et al. (eds.), *The Origins of Arab Nationalism* (New York: Columbia University Press, 1991), pp. 189–196; David Fromkin, *A Peace to End All Peace: The Fall of the Ottoman Empire and the Creation of the Modern Middle East* (New York: Avon, 1989), p. 221; Himmet Umunc, 'In Pursuit of a Futile Fantasy: A Critique of T.E. Lawrence and the Arab Revolt', Paper presented to the 15th Turkish History Congress, 11–15 September 2006, Ankara. I am most grateful to Professor Umunc for permission to cite his paper.

106. J.C. Hurewitz (ed.), *The Middle East and North Africa in World Politics: A Documentary Record* (New Haven, CT: Yale University Press, 1979), vol. 2, pp. 46–56.

107. Hurewitz, *The Middle East and North Africa in World Politics*, vol. 2, pp. 60–64.

108. Correspondence between Sir Henry McMahon and the Sharif of Mecca, July 1915–March 1916, Cmd 5957 (London, 1939), p. 3; Elie Kedourie, *In the Anglo-Arab Labyrinth: The McMahon–Husayn Correspondence and Its Interpretations, 1914–1939* (Cambridge: Cambridge University Press, 1976), Wingate to Balfour, 25 December 1917, FO 371/3395/12077, National Archives, Kew. See also Karsh and Karsh, 'Myth in the Desert, or Not the Great Arab Revolt', pp. 289–290; Ali Allawi, *Faisal I of Iraq* (New Haven, CT: Yale University Press, 2014), pp. 138–141.

109. This was certainly the view of the Arab Bureau in Cairo. 'Note on the Conference at Ismailia', 12 September 1916, FO 882/4, National Archives, Kew.

110. T.E. Lawrence, 'The Evolution of a Revolt', *Army Quarterly and Defence Journal* (October 1920), pp. 2–3.

111. Lawrence, 'The Evolution of a Revolt', p. 3.

112. Lawrence, 'The Evolution of a Revolt', p. 4.

113. Lawrence, 'The Evolution of a Revolt', p. 6.

114. Lawrence, 'The Evolution of a Revolt', p. 8.

115. Lawrence, 'The Evolution of a Revolt', p. 9.

116. Lawrence, 'The Evolution of a Revolt', p. 11.

117. Lawrence, 'The Evolution of a Revolt', p. 13.

118. Lawrence, 'The Evolution of a Revolt', p. 15.

119. Lawrence, 'The Evolution of a Revolt', p. 15.

120. Lawrence, 'The Evolution of a Revolt', p. 17.

121. Lawrence, 'The Evolution of a Revolt', p. 19.

122. Lawrence, 'The Evolution of a Revolt', p. 22.

123. Eliezer Tauber, *The Arab Movements in World War I* (London: Frank Cass, 1993), pp. 102–117; Rogan, *Fall of the Ottomans*, p. 302.

124. Lawrence, *Seven Pillars*, p. 113.

125. Edouard Brémont, *Le Hedjaz dans la Guerre Mondiale* (Paris: Payot, 1931), p. 35; James Barr, *Setting the Desert on Fire: T.E. Lawrence and Britain's Secret War in Arabia, 1916–1918* (London: Bloomsbury, 2006), p. 47.

126. Robin Bidwell, 'The Brémond Mission in the Hijaz, 1916–17: A Study in Inter-Allied Co-operation', in Robin Bidwell and Rex Smith (eds.), *Arabian and Islamic Studies* (London: Longman, 1983), pp. 182–195.

127. Robertson to Murray, 16 October 1916, Add 52463, British Library.

128. The near collapse of the Arab force appears in Lawrence, *Seven Pillars of Wisdom*, pp. 116–132. Inactivity also affected Feisal: 'With the Northern Army', Secret Despatches from Arabia, 15 February 1917, cited in Malcom Brown, *T.E. Lawrence in War and Peace* (London: Greenhill, 2005), p. 99.

129. Details of the actions are in Lawrence, *Seven Pillars*, pp. 294–302.

130. The Ottoman garrison was only 600 strong. See G. McMunn and Cyril Falls, *Military Operations, Egypt and Palestine* (London: HMSO, 1928), vol. 1, p. 240.

131. Johnson, *The Great War and the Middle East*.

132. Barr, *Setting the Desert on Fire*, p. 166.

133. Rogan, *Fall of the Ottomans*, p. 339.

134. Barr, *Setting the Desert on Fire*, p. 210.

135. Djemal to Feisal, November 1917, FO 686/38, National Archives, Kew.

136. Scott Anderson, *Lawrence in Arabia: War, Deceit, Imperial Folly and the Making of the Modern Middle East* (London: Atlantic, 2013), pp. 270–272.

137. Barr, *Setting the Desert on Fire*, p. 217.

138. E.H.T. Robinson, *Lawrence the Rebel* (London: Lincolns-Prager, 1946), p. 119.

139. Lawrence, *Seven Pillars*, p. 326; 'Arabia-Hejaz', Intelligence Report, 24 July 1917, cited in Malcolm Brown, *T.E. Lawrence in War and Peace* (London: Greenhill, 2005), p. 200.

140. Lawrence claimed to have been betrayed by an Ottoman agent of Moroccan descent, Abd el-Kadir. See Phillip Knightley and Colin Simpson, *The Secret Lives of Lawrence of Arabia* (London: Nelson, 1969), p. 83.

141. Barr, *Setting the Desert on Fire*, pp. 225–257.

142. Wilson, *Lawrence of Arabia*, pp. 566–567.

143. Lloyd George to M. Pichon, Quai d'Orsay, 30 October 1918, F120–21; I.C./84, Lloyd George Papers, National Archives, Kew.

10. LOCAL FORCES IN THE SECOND WORLD WAR

1. Ashley Jackson, *The British Empire and the Second World War* (London: Hambledon Continuum, 2006), p. 182. See also Ashley Jackson, *Distant Drums: The Role of Colonies in British Imperial Warfare* (Eastbourne: Sussex Academic Press, 2010).

2. Foreign Office, Abyssinian Revolt: Obstruction from Local Authorities, 11 July 1940, HS3/5, National Archives, Kew.

3. Cliff Lord and David Birtles, *The Armed Forces of Aden, 1839–1967* (Solihull: Helion, 2000), p. 57; David Omissi, *Air Power and Colonial Control* (Manchester: Manchester University Press, 1990).

4. Jackson, *The British Empire and the Second World War*, p. 143.

5. James Lunt, *Imperial Sunset: Frontier Soldiering in the 20th Century* (London: Macdonald Futura, 1981), pp. 52–53.

6. Yoav Gelber, *Jewish Palestinian Volunteering in the British Army during the Second World War*, 4 vols. (Jerusalem: Yad Izhak Ben-Zvi, 1979–1984); my thanks to Jacob Stoil for this reference and the material in Hebrew from Steven Wagner. See also Jackson, *The British Empire and the Second World War*, p. 139.

7. See Jacob Stoil, 'Indigenous Forces in the Middle East and Africa' (DPhil thesis, University of Oxford, 2016), and 'Structures of Cooperation and Conflict: Local Forces in Mandatory Palestine during the Second World War', *Ex Historia*, 5 (2013), pp. 136ff.

8. Jackson, *The British Empire and the Second World War*, p. 140.

9. Cypher Telegram from HC Palestine to Secretary of State for Colonies, 1 April 1942, Defence—Local Defence Forces, 1942, CO 733/448/15, National Archives, Kew.

10. Martin Thomas, *Empires of Intelligence: Security Services and Colonial Disorder after 1914* (London: University of California Press, 2008), p. 254; M.R.D. Foot, *Resistance: An Analysis of European Resistance to Nazism 1940–1945* (London: Eyre Methuen, 1976), p. 163.

11. Jackson, *The British Empire and the Second World War*, p. 84.

12. Asesela Ravuvu, *Fijians at War, 1939–45* (PLACE: University of the South Pacific, 1988); R.A. Howlett, *The History of the Fijian Military Forces, 1939–1945* (Suva: PUBLISHER, 1948).

13. Andrew Gilchrist, *Bangkok Top Secret: Force 136 at War* (London: Hutchinson, 1960); F.S. Chapman, *The Jungle Is Neutral* (London: Chatto & Windus, 1949); Jackson, *The British Empire and the Second World War*, p. 434.

14. Jackson, *The British Empire and the Second World War*, p. 316.

15. Jackson, *The British Empire and the Second World War*, p. 318.

16. Peter Beauchamp, 'Some Account of Ceylon's "Wavy-Navy" between 1939 and 1945', *Indian Navy Association Journal* (1993).

17. Jackson, *The British Empire and the Second World War*, p. 319.

18. David Killingray, *Fighting for Britain: African Soldiers in the Second World War* (Woodbridge, Surrey: James Currey, 2010).

19. F.A.S. Clarke and A. Haywood, *The History of the Royal West African Frontier Force* (Aldershot: PUBLISHER, 1964).

20. E.R. Elliott, *Royal Pioneers, 1945–1993* (Hanley Swan, S.P.A., 1993); E.H. Rhodes-Wood, *War History of the Royal Pioneer Corps, 1939–1945* (Aldershot, 1960).

21. Ronald Lewin, *The Chief: Field Marshal Lord Wavell, Commander in Chief and Viceroy, 1919–1947* (London: Hutchinson, 1980), p. 25; Jackson, *The British Empire and the Second World War*, p. 211.

22. Jackson, *The British Empire and the Second World War*, p. 212.

23. See David Killingray and David Omissi (eds.), *Guardians of Empire: The Armed Forces of the Colonial Powers c.1700–1964* (Manchester: Manchester University Press, 1990).

24. W. Lloyd-Jones, *KAR: The Origins and Activities of the King's African Rifles* (London, 1926), p. 106; V.G. Kiernan, *Colonial Empires and Amies* (Stroud: Sutton, 1998), p. 207.

25. George A. Shepperson, 'America through Africa and Asia', *Journal of American Studies*, 14, 1 (April 1980), pp. 52–53.

26. 'The Indian Army and the Second World War: A Force Transformed', in Daniel P. Marston and Chandar S. Sundaram (eds.), *A Military History of India and South Asia: From the East India Company to the Nuclear Age* (Bloomington, IN: Indiana University Press, 2007), p. 102.

27. Indianisation of the officer corps produced nearly 16,000 Indian officers by 1945.

28. *PAIFORCE: The Official History of the Persia and Iraq Command, 1941–1946* (London, 1948); Marston and Sundaram, *A Military History of India and South Asia*, p. 105.

29. Gandhi, 'Quit India' movement and disturbances: calendars of events, narratives, reports and other information compiled in India to assist Secretary of State in replying to Parliamentary Questions (Sept. 1942–April 1943), L/PJ/8/627, Coll. 117/C27/Q Pt 2, India Office Records, British Library (IOR).

30. An assessment of the unrest by Congress was intercepted by Military Intelligence. See WO 208/819A, 25C, National Archives, Kew.

31. N.M. Mansergh, E.W.R. Lumby and P. Moon (eds.), *Constitutional Relations*

between Britain and India: The Transfer of Power: 1942–47 (London: Allen and Unwin, 1970), vol. 2, pp. 853–854.

32. GHQ (India) to the Military Secretary, India Office, Most Secret, 20 Dec. 1942, L/WS/1/1337, IOR.

33. Defence HQ Outline Plan, Operation Asylum, Most Secret, 9 Dec. 1945, L/WS/2/65, IOR; Chiefs of Staff Committee, Indian Army, 'Subversive attempts on the loyalty of the Indian Army', Secret, 10 May 1943, L/WS/1/707, IOR.

34. Daniel P. Marston, *Phoenix from the Ashes: The Indian Army in the Burma Campaign* (London: Praeger, 2003), pp. 86–91.

35. Auchinleck Papers, 23 April 1945, University of Manchester.

11. LOCAL FORCES DURING THE WARS OF DECOLONISATION

1. In the considerable literature on decolonisation and its driving forces, see especially John Darwin, *Britain and Decolonization: The Retreat from Empire in the Post-War World* (London: Macmillan, 1987).

2. Robert Thompson, *Defeating Communist Insurgency* (1966; repr., St Petersburg, FL: Hailer, 2005), p. 51.

3. Thompson, *Defeating Communist Insurgency*.

4. David Galula, *Counter-Insurgency Warfare: Theory and Practice* (1964; repr., New York: Praeger, 2006).

5. Thompson, *Defeating Communist Insurgency*, p. 109.

6. David Kilcullen, *The Accidental Guerrilla: Fighting Small Wars in the Midst of a Big One* (London: Hurst, 2009), p. 181; See, for example, Panagiotis Dimitrakis, 'British Intelligence and the Cyprus Insurgency, 1955–1959', *International Journal of Intelligence and Counterintelligence*, 21, 2 (2008), pp. 375–394.

7. Frank Kitson, *Low Intensity Operations* (2nd edn, London: Faber and Faber, 1991), pp. 95–96.

8. During the Palestinian unrest in 1936, British officials realised that Arab and Jewish constables in the police could not be trusted to act against insurgents within their own communities and some colluded with them. See, for example, G.D.G. Hayman, War Office, to F.G. Lee, Colonial Office, Memorandum, 14 February 1939, WO 106/5720, National Archives, Kew.

9. Anthony James Joes, 'Counterinsurgency in the Philippines 1898–1954', in Daniel P. Marston and Carter Malkasian (eds.), *Counterinsurgency in Modern Warfare* (London: Osprey 2007), p. 51.

10. Edgar O'Ballance, *Malaya: The Communist Insurgent War, 1948–1960* (London: Faber and Faber, 1966), p. 133.

11. David Anderson, 'Surrogates of the State: Collaboration and Atrocity in Kenya's Mau Mau War', in George Kassimeris (ed.), *The Barbarisation of Warfare* (London: Hurst, 2006), pp. 159–174.

12. Geraint Hughes and Christian Tripodi, 'Anatomy of a Surrogate: Historical Precedents and Implications for Contemporary Counter-Insurgency and Counter-Terrorism', *Small Wars and Insurgencies*, 20, 1 (March 2009), pp. 1–35.

13. John J. Tierney Jr, *Chasing Ghosts: Unconventional Warfare in American History* (Washington DC: Potomac Books, 2007), pp. 128–129.

14. Tierney, *Chasing Ghosts*, pp. 137–139; Robert M. Cassidy, 'The Long Small War: Indigenous Forces for Counterinsurgency', *Parameters*, 36, 2 (Summer 2006), pp. 47–62.

15. Simon Anglim, 'Orde Wingate and the Special Night Squads: A Feasible Policy for Counter-Terrorism?', *Contemporary Security Policy*, 28, 1 (2007), pp. 28–41.

16. Dimitrakos, 'Cyprus Insurgency', p. 388; Frank Kitson, *Gangs and Counter-Gangs* (London: Barrie and Rockliff, 1960).

17. Hughes and Tripodi, 'Anatomy of a Surrogate', p. 5.

18. Ron Reid-Daly, *Pamwe Chete: The Legend of the Selous Scouts* (Blairgowrie: Covos Day Books, 2000).

19. General George Grivas, *Guerrilla Warfare and EOKA's Struggle* (London: Longman, 1964), p. 42.

20. O'Ballance, *Malaya*, p. 126.

21. David Anderson, *Histories of the Hanged: The Dirty War in Kenya and the End of Empire* (London: Weidenfeld and Nicholson, 2005), pp. 257–269 and 284–290.

22. Thompson, *Defeating Communist Insurgency*, pp. 104–105.

23. Thompson, *Defeating Communist Insurgency*, p. 103.

24. Thompson, *Defeating Communist Insurgency*, p. 108.

25. See Robert Johnson, 'Decolonisation in India and Pakistan', in Robert Johnson and Timothy Clack (eds.), *At the End of Military Intervention: Historical, Theoretical and Applied Approaches to Transition, Handover and Withdrawal* (Oxford: Oxford University Press, 2014).

26. Similar views were expressed by General Tucker, see M.D. Wainwright, 'Keeping the Peace in India, 1946–7: The Role of Lt General Sir Francis Tuker in Eastern Command', in C.H. Philips and M.D. Wainwright (eds.), *The Partition of India: Policies and Perspectives, 1935–1947* (London: George Allen and Unwin, 1970).

27. 'India: Constitutional Position, Cabinet Conclusions', 10 Dec. 1946, CAB 128/8, National Archives (TNA).

28. Rob Johnson, 'Military Aid to the Civil Power: The Army in India and Internal Security', in Alan Jefferies and Patrick Rose (eds.), *The Indian Army, 1939–1947* (London: Ashgate, 2012).

29. Penderel Moon (ed.), *Wavell: The Viceroy's Journal* (Oxford: Oxford University Press, 1973), p. 402.

30. Daniel Marston, 'The Indian Army, Partition and the Punjab Boundary Force, 1945–47', *War in History* 16, 4 (November 2009), pp. 469–505.

31. Urvashi Butalia, *The Other Side of Silence: Voices from the Partition of India* (London: Viking, 2000); Yasmin Khan, *The Great Partition: The Making of India and Pakistan* (Yale University Press, 2007); Ian Talbot, *Divided Cities: Partition and Its Aftermath in Lahore and Amritsar, 1947–1957* (New York: Oxford University Press, 2007).

32. Robin Jeffrey, 'The Punjab Boundary Force and the Problem of Order, August 1947', *Modern Asian Studies*, 8 (1974); S. Aiyar, 'August Anarchy: The Partition Massacres in Punjab, 1947', *South Asia*, 18 (1995).

33. Marston, 'The Indian Army, Partition, and the Punjab Boundary Force', p. 485.

34. Charles Allen, *Plain Tales from the Raj* (London: Penguin, 1975), p. 257.

35. Allen, *Plain Tales*, p. 252.

36. Allen, *Plain Tales*, p. 252.

37. A version of this section appeared as Robert Johnson, 'Out of Arabia: The Fate of Omani Forces Allied with the British, 1967–76', *International History Review* (2016). I am indebted to Professor David Anderson for his critical observations on the article.

38. Conservative Party Manifesto, in J.B. Kelly, *Arabia, the Gulf and the West* (New York: Basic Books, 1980), pp. 78–79.

39. General Jeapes, cited in G. Hughes, 'A "Model Campaign": The Counter-Insurgency War in Dhofar, Oman, 1965–1975', *Journal of Strategic Studies*, 32, 2 (2009), p. 283.

40. For broader contextual works, see Cassidy, 'The Long Small War', pp. 47–62; Erik-Jan Zuercher (ed.), *Fighting for a Living: A Comparative History of Military Labour 1500–2000* (Amsterdam: Amsterdam University Press, 2014); Will Clegg, 'Irregular Forces in Counterinsurgency Warfare', *Security Challenges*, 5, 3 (Spring 2009), pp. 1–25.

41. Cited in Robin Neillands, *Fighting Retreat: The British Empire, 1947–97* (London: Hodder and Stoughton, 1996), p. 403.

42. Neillands, *Fighting Retreat*, p. 403.

43. Among the very best works are James Worrall's various studies on the political context of the British involvement in Dhofar, Clive Jones on military intelligence, and Spencer Mawby's research on the various groupings of southern Arabia, which offers the opportunity to assess both local and British intentions and actions together. See James Worrall, 'Britain's Last Bastion in Arabia: The End of the Dhofar War: The Labour Government and the Withdrawal from RAF Salalah and Masirah, 1974–1977', in Tore T. Petersen (ed.), *Challenging Retrenchment in the Middle East* (Rostra Series, Trondheim: Tapir Academic Press, 2010); Clive Jones, 'Military Intelligence and the War in Dhofar: An Appraisal', *Small Wars and Insurgencies*, 25, 3 (2014), pp. 628–646; Spencer Mawby, 'Orientalism and the Failure of British Policy in the Middle East: The Case of Aden', *History: The Journal of the Historical Association*, 95, 319 (2010), pp. 332–353.

44. Gillian King, *Imperial Outpost Aden: Its Place in British Strategic Policy* (Oxford: Oxford University Press, 1964).

45. Sir William Luce to Earl of Home, no. 98, 22 November 1961, FO 371/98323, National Archives, Kew.

46. Saul Kelly, 'Vanishing Act: Britain's Abandonment of Aden and Retreat from the Gulf', in Robert Johnson and Timothy Clack (eds.), *At the End of Military Intervention* (Oxford: Oxford University Press, 2014).

47. HMG, *Treaty of Friendship and Protection between the United Kingdom of Great Britain and Northern Ireland and the Federation of South Arabia and Supplementary Treaty providing for the accession of Aden to the Federation, September 1964* (London: HMSO, 1964), Cmd. 2451. The title of the Federation of Arab Emirates of the South was changed to the Federation of South Arabia on 3 May 1962.

48. Neillands, *Fighting Retreat*, p. 378; Aaron Edwards, *Mad Mitch's Tribal Law: Aden and the End of Empire* (Edinburgh: Mainstream, 2014).

49. J.B. Kelly, 'Recollections and Reflections of a British Diplomat', Review of Lord Trevelyan's *The Middle East in Revolution* (London: Macmillan, 1970) in *Middle East Studies*, 3 (October 1973), p. 368.

50. Aaron Edwards, '"A Graveyard for the British"? Tactics, Military Operations and the Paucity of Strategy in Aden, 1964–67', in Johnson and Clack, *At the End of Military Intervention*.

51. Joe Starling, cited in Neillands, *Fighting Retreat*, p. 403.

52. Trevelyan, cited by Kelly, 'Recollections and Reflections of a British Diplomat', p. 368.

53. Trevelyan, cited in Kelly, 'Recollections and Reflections of a British Diplomat', p. 370.

54. Saul Kelly, 'Vanishing Act', in Johnson and Clack, *At the End of Military Intervention*.

55. D.J. McCarthy (Head, Arabian Department) to Sir S. Crawford, Doc. 60, FCO 8/979, National Archives, Kew.

56. D.J. McCarthy (Head, Arabian Department), Doc. 70, June 1970, FCO 8/979, National Archives, Kew.

57. Kelly, 'Vanishing Act', in Johnson and Clack, *At the End of Military Intervention*.

58. Fawaz Trabulsi, 'The Liberation of Dhuffar', Address to Arab-American students, Boston University, 30 October 1971, reproduced in *Pakistan Forum*, 3, 2 (November 1972), p. 8.

59. Sir Alec Douglas Home, *Hansard*, 1 March 1971.

60. Trabulsi, 'The Liberation of Dhuffar', p. 8.

61. J.E. Peterson, *Oman's Insurgencies: The Sultanate's Struggle for Supremacy* (London: Saqi Books, 2007).

62. These appear to have included the destruction of livestock, wells and the public display of insurgents killed during operations. Trabulsi, 'Liberation of Dhuffar', p. 12.

63. Captain C.F. Hepworth, cited in Trabulsi, 'Liberation of Dhuffar', p. 12.
64. Doc. 72, An Outline Plan to Restore the Situation in Dhofar Using Special Air Service Regiment Troops, 7 April 1970 FCO 8/1437, National Archives, Kew.
65. Ian Skeet, *Oman: Politics and Development* (Basingstoke: Palgrave Macmillan, 1992), p. 38; Kelly, *Arabia, the Gulf and the West*, p. 141.
66. Skeet, *Oman: Politics and Development*, p. 38.
67. Kelly, *Arabia, the Gulf and the West*, p. 141.
68. CAB 148/101, Foreign Policy Issues, 29 June 1970, National Archives, Kew.
69. Kelly, *Arabia, the Gulf and the West*, p. 81.
70. Douglas Hurd, *Memoirs* (London: Abacus, 2003), p. 200.
71. Oman was never a colony. An agreement was first made in 1646 with the Honourable East India Company which was developed into a full commercial treaty in 1798, with subsequent agreements to abolish the slave trade (1839, 1844); restrictions on Oman's ability to sell without British approval territory (1891) or make oil concessions (1923); and the granting of extraterritorial rights to British citizens (1939). All were superseded by a Treaty of Friendship, Commerce and Navigation in 1951. In 1958, an Exchange of Letters gave approval for the British to retrain and indeed lead the SAF.
72. The *wali* of Dhofar, Sheikh Breik, had demanded the Sultan step down, but in the ensuing firefight, Sultan Said was wounded and evacuated by the RAF to Bahrain and then to London.
73. Telegram no. 46, 26 July 1970, FCO 8/1425, National Archives, Kew; John Townsend, *Oman: The Making of the Modern State* (London: Croom Helm, 1977), pp. 74–75. See also James Worrall, 'Transitioning in and out of COIN: Efficiency, Legitimacy and Power in Oman', in Johnson and Clack (eds.) *At the End of Military Intervention*.
74. Telegram no. 46, 26 July 1970, FCO 8/1425, National Archives, Kew.
75. Farrukh Dhondy, 'Britain's Gulf War', *Economic and Political Weekly*, 7, 29 (July 1972), p. 1351.
76. Doc. 72, An Outline Plan to Restore the Situation in Dhofar Using Special Air Service Regiment Troops, 7 April 1970, FCO 8/1437, National Archives, Kew.
77. Visit of the Military Secretary to the Sultan of Muscat and Oman, 'Flag E', 12 October 1970, DEFE 25/186, Folio no. 21, National Archives, Kew.
78. Note, Baker (MOD) to Hall (FCO), 17 August 1970, DEFE 25/186, National Archives, Kew.
79. Note, Douglas-Home to Secretary of State for Defence, SAS Assistance to the Sultanate of Oman, 4 September 1970, DEFE 25/186, National Archives, Kew.
80. Walter Ladwig III, 'Supporting Allies in Counterinsurgency: Britain and the Dhofar Rebellion', *Small Wars and Insurgencies*, 19, 1 (March 2008), p. 62.
81. Colonel Tony Jeapes, *SAS: Operation Oman* (London: William Kimber, 1980), p. 11.

82. The Jebalis were a mountainous people who, unlike most Omanis, were not ethnically Arab. They were believed to be of 'Ethiopian' descent, spoke their own language similar to Aramaic and, in 1974, numbered around 10,000. See D.L. Price, 'Oman: Insurgency and Development', *Conflict Studies*, 53 (1975), p. 1.
83. Price, 'Oman: Insurgency and Development', p. 11.
84. Jeapes, *SAS*, p. 100.
85. Jeapes, *SAS*.
86. Hughes, 'A "Model Campaign" Reappraised', p. 283.
87. Ian Gardener, *In the Service of the Sultan: A First Hand Account of the Dhofar Insurgency* (Barnsley: Pen and Sword, 2006), pp. 26, 49–57, 57; Jeapes, *SAS*, pp. 100 and 230; Ranulph Fiennes, *Where Soldiers Fear to Tread*, (London: Hodder and Stoughton, 1975), p. 62; Ladwig, 'Supporting Allies in Counterinsurgency', pp. 73–5.
88. Jeapes, *SAS*, p. 230.
89. Jeapes, *SAS*, p. 130.
90. Jeapes, *SAS*, p. 231.
91. Jeapes, *SAS*, p. 83.
92. Jones, 'Military Intelligence and the War in Dhofar', p. 636.
93. Jeapes, *SAS*.
94. Worrall, 'Britain's Last Bastion in Arabia', pp. 165–166.
95. James Worrall, 'Policing Oman: From the Oman Gendarmerie to the Royal Oman Police, Britain's Role in the Creation of Internal Security Structures', Unpublished Cconference paper, 2009.
96. Dawn Chatty, 'Rituals of Royalty and the Elaboration of Ceremony in Oman: View from the Edge', *International Journal of Middle East Studies*, 41 (2009), pp. 39–58.
97. See Alan Hoskins, *A Contract Officer in the Oman* (Tunbridge Wells: Costello, 1988).
98. Fred Halliday, 'Arabia without Sultans Revisited', *Middle East Report*, 204 (July–September 1997), p. 28.
99. Nigel Disney, 'China and the Middle East', *MERIP Report*, 63 (December 1977), p. 7.
100. *Peking Review*, 24 (1967).
101. *Peking Review*, 15 (1970).
102. 'Dhofar: Victories in National Revolutionary War', *Peking Review*, 4 (1972); 'Dhofar Area: Revolutionary Armed Struggle Enters Its Eighth Year', *Peking Review*, 25 (1972).
103. 'Scramble for Hegemony: Soviet Expansion in West Asia, *Peking Review*, 39 (1976).
104. Trevelyan, cited in Kelly, 'Recollections and Reflections of a British Diplomat', p. 363.

105. CAB 148/102, DOP (70), Meeting 44, Cabinet, Note by Secretary of State for Foreign and Commonwealth Affairs: Policy in the Persian Gulf, 8 December 1970, National Archive, Kew.

106. R.W. Kromer, *Impact of Pacification on Insurgency in South Vietnam* (Santa Monica, CA: RAND Corporation, 1970), p. 5.

107. Robert Thompson, *Defeating Communist Insurgency* (London: Chatto & Windus, 1966), pp. 106–108.

108. Francis West, *The Village* (Madison: University of Wisconsin Press, 1985), p. 191.

109. David Kaiser, *American Tragedy* (Cambridge, MA: Harvard University Press, 2000), p. 152; Neil Sheehan, *A Bright Shining Lie* (London: Pan Books, 1990), pp. 183–184 and 308.

110. Mark Moyar, *Phoenix and the Birds of Prey. Counterinsurgency and Counterterrorism in Vietnam* (Lincoln, NE: University of Nebraska Press, 2007), pp. 159–160. Anthony James Joes, *Resisting Rebellion: The History and Politics of Counterinsurgency* (Lexington, KY: University Press of Kentucky, 2006), pp. 114–116; Cassidy, 'The Long Small War', p. 57.

111. Andrew F. Krepinevich, *The Army and Vietnam* (Baltimore: Johns Hopkins University Press, 1988), p. 218.

112. Krepinevich, *The Army and Vietnam*, p. 5.

113. Krepinevich, *The Army and Vietnam*, p. 219.

114. Krepinevich, *The Army and Vietnam*, p. 219.

115. *Pentagon Papers: The Defense Department of the Unites States' Decision-Making on Vietnam*, Senator Gravel Edition, vol. 1 (Boston: Beacon Press, 1971), p. 314, cited in Will Clegg, 'Irregular Forces in Counterinsurgency Warfare', p. 14.

116. Krepinevich, *The Army and Vietnam*, p. 219.

117. Kromer, *Impact of Pacification on Insurgency in South Vietnam*, p. 6.

118. Cassidy, 'The Long Small War', p. 57.

119. Krepinevich, *The Army and Vietnam*, p. 220.

120. Eugene G. Piasecki, 'Civilian Irregular Defense Group: The First Years, 1961–1967', first published in Veritas, The Journal of U.S. Army Special Operations, http://smallwarsjournal.com/documents/cidgprogram.pdf, accessed September 2016.

121. Colonel Francis Kelly, *Vietnam Studies: U.S. Army Special Forces* (Washington DC: Department of the Army, 1989), p. 6.

122. Christopher Ives, *US Special Forces and Counterinsurgency in Vietnam* (London: Routledge, 2007).

123. Thompson, *Defeating Communist Insurgency*, pp. 108–109.

124. Jacques Dalloz, *The War in Indochina, 1945–54* (Dublin: Gill and Macmillan, 1990), pp. 109–111.

125. Kelly, *Vietnam Studies*, p. 77.

126. Barry Petersen, *Tiger Men: An Australian Soldier's Secret War in Vietnam* (London: Sidgwick and Jackson, 1988), p. 43.

127. Petersen, *Tiger Men*, p. 49.
128. Petersen, *Tiger Men*, p. 50.
129. Petersen, *Tiger Men*, p. 52.
130. Petersen, *Tiger Men*, p. 61.
131. Petersen, *Tiger Men*, pp. 82–83.
132. Petersen, *Tiger Men*, p. 84.
133. Petersen, *Tiger Men*, pp. 87–89.
134. Petersen, *Tiger Men*, p. 91.
135. Petersen, *Tiger Men*, p. 95.
136. Petersen, *Tiger Men*, p. 238.
137. Petersen, *Tiger Men*, p. 238.
138. Petersen, *Tiger Men*, p. 239.
139. Annex to the Directive no. 1, 28 December 1958, SHD 1H 2942, Service Historique de la Défense, Vincennes, Paris.
140. Stéphanie Chauvin, 'Des appelés pas comme les autres? Les conscrits "français de souche nord-africaine" pendant la guerre d'Algérie', *Vingtième Siècle: Revue d'Histoire*, 48, 4 (1995).
141. Tom Charbit, *Les Harkis* (Paris: La Découverte, 2006); Yoav Gortzak, 'Using Indigenous Forces in Counterinsurgency Operations: The French in Algeria, 1954–1962', *Journal of Strategic Studies*, 32, 2 (April 2009), pp. 307–333.
142. François-Xavier Hautreux, 'L'Emploi des harkis dans la guerre d'Algérie: Essai de périodisation', *Vingtième Siècle: Revue d'Histoire*, 90, 2 (2006).
143. SHD 1H 1391/3, Vincennes, Paris.
144. 'Les Meilleures troupes de contre-guérilla sont à base d'autochtones', in 'Guérilla et contre guérilla en Algérie', fiche du 3ᵉ Bureau de l'état-major de la Xᵉ région militaire, October 1955, SHD, 1H 1809/2, Vincennes, Paris.
145. Briefing to the commanding officers of military zones and sectors, CAA, 26 October 1959, SHD, 1H 2750/1, Vincennes, Paris.
146. Briefing to the commanding officers of military zones and sectors, CAA, 26 October 1959, SHD, 1H 2750/1, Vincennes, Paris.
147. Charles-Robert Ageron, 'Les Supplétifs algériens dans l'armée française pendant la guerre d'Algérie', *Vingtième Siècle: Revue d'Histoire*, 48, 4 (1995).
148. After the war, he fled to France with dozens of his men and their families. He wrote several books including Bachaga Saïd Boualam, *Mon pays la France* (Paris: France Empire, 1962).
149. Alastair Horne, *A Savage War of Peace: Algeria, 1954–1962*, (New York: The Viking Press, 1978), pp. 255–257.
150. Instruction issued by General Crépin, 20 September 1960, SHD, 1H 2772/3, Vincennes, Paris.
151. Letter from General de Pouilly to the Commander-in-Chief, 27 February 1961, SHD, 1H 1240/8, Vincennes, Paris.

152. Report from the Officer commanding the Saïda sector, 25 May 1962, SHD, 1H 2028/3, Vincennes, Paris.
153. Internal memo from General Gambiez, 21 July 1960, SHD, 1H 3087/1, Vincennes, Paris.
154. Alain Maillard de La Morandais's diary, 26 July 1960, published in part in Alain Maillard de La Morandais, *L'Honneur est sauf* (Paris: Le Seuil, 1990). I am indebted to Professor Raphaelle Branche for this and related references.
155. Charles-Robert Ageron, 'Le Drame des harkis en 1962', *Vingtième siècle: Revue d'Histoire*, 42, 2 (1994).
156. Information note from the Ministry of the Military Forces to the Commanding Officers of Army Corps in Algeria to 'éclairer les destinataires dans l'action qu'ils devront mener, dès l'annonce du cessez le feu, auprès de leurs subordonnés', 8 March 1962, SHD, 1H 2467/6, Vincennes, Paris.
157. See François Meyer, *Pour l'honneur, avec les harkis: De 1958 à nos jours* (Tours: CLD, 2005).
158. Clegg, 'Irregular Forces in Counterinsurgency Warfare', p. 2.

12. BUILDING THE AFGHAN AND IRAQI SECURITY FORCES, 2003–2014

1. Ibrahim al-Marashi and Sammy Salama, *Iraq's Armed Forces: An Analytical History* (Abingdon: Routledge, 2008), pp. 201–205; Ahmed Hashim, *Insurgency and Counter-Insurgency in Iraq* (London: Hurst, 2006), pp. 92–99.
2. Stephen Pelletiere and Douglas V. Johnson III, *Lessons Learned: The Iran–Iraq War* (US Army War College: Strategic Studies Institute, 1991), Appendix A, pp. 83ff.
3. James K. Wither, 'Basra's Not Belfast: The British Army, "Small Wars", and Iraq', *Small Wars and Insurgencies*, 20, 3 (2009), pp. 611–635.
4. Michael Knights and E. Williams, *The Calm before the Storm: The British Experience in Southern Iraq* (Washington DC: Washington Institute for Near East Policy, Policy Focus Paper no. 66, 2007).
5. Brian Brady, 'Drugs and Desertion: How the UK Really Rates Afghan Police', *Independent on Sunday*, 28 March 2010; 'Get out of the Way', *The Economist*, 13 February 2010.
6. Seth G. Jones, 'Community Defense in Afghanistan', *Joint Forces Quarterly*, 57, 2 (2010), pp. 9–15.
7. The NCA expressed the concern that Western counter-insurgency in Afghanistan could incite Taliban attacks on villagers and it deeply opposed the idea of 'human terrain teams' which appeared to use anthropologists not to gather neutral scientific data but to manipulate the people. See http://sites.google.com/site/concerneanthropologists/faq. What the NCA did not acknowledge was the consequences of not using human data or the large number of deaths being inflicted by the Taliban upon the population.

8. Mohamed Osman Tariq, *Tribal Security System in Southeast Afghanistan* (Crisis States Research Centre, London School of Economics and Political Science: Occasional Paper no. 7, 2008); Joshua Foust, 'Tribe and Prejudice: America's "New Hope" in Afghanistan', *The National*, 11 February 2010, online at http://www.thenational.ae/apps/pbcs.dll/article?AID=/20100211/REVIEW/702119988/1008.

9. Field Manual Counterinsurgency FM3–24, p. 212.

10. Tim Bird and Alex Marshall, *Afghanistan: How the West Lost Its Way* (New Haven: Yale University Press, 2011), p. 119.

11. Interview with the author, name withheld, September 2003.

12. Government Accountability Office, *Afghanistan Security* (Washington DC: GAO, 2005), p. 6.

13. Bird and Marshall, *Afghanistan: How the West Lost Its Way*, p. 114.

14. Government Accountability Office, *Afghanistan Security*, p. 3.

15. Author interview, name withheld, KMTC, 2010.

16. Author interview, name withheld, NMC, 2011.

17. North Atlantic Treaty Organisation (NATO), *Progress in Afghanistan*, Bucharest Summit, 2–4 April 2008 (Brussels, 2008), p. 8, www.isaf.nato.int/pdf/progress_afghanistan_2008.pdf.

18. See Antonio Giustozzi and Atemy Kalinovsky, *Missionaries of Modernity: Advisory Missions and the Struggle for Hegemony in Afghanistan and Beyond* (London: Hurst, 2016), ch. 9.

19. In September 2008, the Joint Commission and Monitoring Board, co-chaired by the Afghan government and the United Nations, agreed to increase the total strength of the ANA to 122,000 personnel with a 12,000-strong training element. See http://www.nato.int/isaf/docu/epub/pdf/placemat.html, accessed 22 October 2009; Department of Defense, *Progress toward Security and Stability in Afghanistan: January 2009 Report to Congress in Accordance with the 2008 National Defense Authorization Act* (Section 1230, Public Law 110–181), (January 2009), p. 33.

20. Metrics for measuring performance, the capability milestones, at SIGAR, Special Inspector General for Afghan Reconstruction, *Quarterly Report to Congress, July 30, 2009*, p. 55. For ANP, see p. 54.

21. Author's interviews at NTM—A CSTC—A, Kabul, 5 March 2010, conducted under Chatham House rules.

22. Lieutenant Colonel Gavin Keating, '"Living in the Twilight Zone": Advising the Afghan National Army at the Corps Level', *Australian Army Journal*, 8, 3 (Summer 2011), p. 3.

23. Keating, 'Living in the Twilight Zone', p. 5.

24. Keating, 'Living in the Twilight Zone', p. 6.

25. Keating, 'Living in the Twilight Zone', p. 7.

26. Special Inspector General for Afghan Reconstruction (SIGAR), *Actions Needed*

to Improve the Reliability of Afghan Security Force Assessments (Arlington, VA: SIGAR, 29 June 2010), p. 2, at www.sigar.mil/pdf/audits/2010–06–29audit-10–11.pdf.

27. Michelle Hughes, 'The Afghan National Police in 2015 and Beyond', US Institute of Peace (USIP), (Washington DC, May 2014), p. 2, at www.usip.org/sites/default/files/SR346_The_Afghan_National_Police_in_2015_and_beyond.pdf.

28. Robert M. Perito, 'Afghanistan's Police: The Weak Link in Security Sector Reform', United States Institute of Peace Special Report, US Institute of Peace (USIP), (Washington DC, August 2008), p. 1, at www.usip.org/sites/default/files/Afghanistan_Police.pdf.

29. Interview with the author, name withheld, July 2010.

30. Author's interview with General Dunford, June 2016.

31. Public briefing at the Royal United Services Institute, London, 2009.

32. Statement of Lieutenant General William Caldwell IV to the Committee of Oversight and Government Reform Subcommittee on National Security, Homeland Defense and Foreign Operations, 12 September 2012, pp. 2–3 at http://oversight.house.gov/wp-content/uploads/2012/09/Caldwell-Testimony.pdf.

33. David B. Ralston, *Importing the European Army: The Introduction of European Military Techniques and Institutions into the Extra-European World, 1600–914* (Chicago: University of Chicago Press, 1990), pp. 173–180.

34. Robert Johnson, *The Afghan Way of War: Cultural and Pragmatism; A Critical History* (London: Hurst, 2011); Brian Robson, *Road to Kabul: The Second Afghan War, 1879–81* (London: Arms and Armour Press, 1986), pp. 59–61.

35. See *Journal of the Royal Central Asian Society*, 19 (1932) for an explanation of the *tsalweshtai* system.

36. Soviet General Staff, *The Soviet-Afghan War*, ed. Lester Grau (Lawrence, KS: University Press of Kansas, 2002), p. 27.

37. Rizwan Hussein, *Pakistan and the Emergence of Islamic Militancy in Afghanistan* (London: Ashgate, 2005), p. 150.

38. Ahmad Rashid, *Taliban: Oil and the New Great Game in Central Asia* (New Haven: Yale University Press, 2001), p. 56.

39. Antonio Giustozzi, *Koran, Kalashnikov and Laptop: The Rise of the Neo-Taliban Insurgency in Afghanistan* (London: Hurst, 2007), p. 12.

40. Angelo Rasanayagam, *Afghanistan* (London: I.B. Tauris, 2005), p. 130; Barnett R. Rubin, *The Fragmentation of Afghanistan* (New Haven, CN: Yale University Press, 2002), pp. 159–160.

41. Rubin, *The Fragmentation of Afghanistan*, p. 160.

42. DOD (June 2009).

43. Anthony H. Cordesman, *Winning in Afghanistan: Creating Effective Afghan Security Forces; Working Draft Revised December 9, 2008* (Washington DC: Center for Strategic and International Studies [CSIS], December 9, 2008), p. 91.

44. Antonio Giustozzi, *War, Politics and Society in Afghanistan, 1978–1992* (Washington DC: Georgetown University Press, 2000), p. 218.
45. Daniel Glickstein and Michael Spangler, 'Reforming the Afghan Security Forces', *Parameters*, 44, 3 (2014), p. 101.
46. In April 2004, the US government decided to hand over responsibility for the security of the city entirely to Iraq's 'Fallujah Brigade', but this force, officered in part with former Ba'athists and Republican Guard, showed no loyalty to the new interim authority in Baghdad. It disintegrated and, in some cases, defected to the insurgents. In the subsequent fighting to recover the city, some insurgents made use of captured Iraqi National Guard uniforms to try to infiltrate Marine formations. Richard S. Lowry, *New Dawn: The Battles for Fallujah* (New York: Savas Beatie, 2010), p. 182.
47. DOD, *Measuring Stability and Security in Iraq* (Washington DC: DOD, February 2006), p. 27 at www.defense.gob/home/features/Iraq_Reports/docs/2006–02-Report.pdf.
48. Robert M. Perito, 'The Iraqi Federal Police: US Police Building under Fire' (US Institute of Peace, June 2006), pp. 4–5 at www.usip.org/sites/default/files/SR291_The_Iraqi_Federal_Police.pdf.
49. Austin Long, 'The Anbar Awakening', *Survival*, 50, 2 (April–May 2008), p. 69.
50. Long, 'The Anbar Awakening', p. 71.
51. Hashim, *Insurgency and Counter-Insurgency in Iraq*, p. 75.
52. Hashim, *Insurgency and Counter-Insurgency in Iraq*, p. 74.
53. Carter Malkasian and Jerry Meyerle, *How Is Afghanistan Different from Al Anbar?* (Center for Naval Analysis, February 2009), p. 6.
54. Hashim, *Insurgency and Counter-Insurgency in Iraq*, p. 106.
55. Hashim, *Insurgency and Counter-Insurgency in Iraq*, p. 47.
56. Anthony H. Cordesman, *Iraq's Insurgency and the Road to Civil Conflict* (London: Center for Strategic and International Studies [CSIS], 2008), vol. 1, p. 47.
57. Hashim, *Insurgency and Counter-Insurgency in Iraq*, p. 107.
58. Cordesman, *Iraq's Insurgency and the Road to Civil Conflict*, vol. 1, p. 27.
59. Hashim, *Insurgency and Counter-Insurgency in Iraq*, p. 144.
60. Joseph Felter and Brian Fishman, 'Al-Qaeda's Foreign Fighters in Iraq: A First Look at the Sinjar Records' (Combating Terrorism Center, U.S. Military Academy at West Point), at http://www.ctc.usma.edu/harmony/pdf/CTCForeignFighter.19.Dec07.pdf.
61. Matthew M. McCreary, 'Military Awakening: Clear, Hold, Build and the Development of Awakening Councils and Iraqi Police', *Infantry*, 97, 4 (July–August 2008), p. 32; Malkasian and Meyerle, *How Is Afghanistan Different from Al Anbar?*, p. 15.
62. Long, 'The Anbar Awakening', p. 80.
63. James Scott Linville, 'Captain Patriquin, Candidate Obama and the Anbar

Awakening', *Standpoint Magazine Online*, http://www.standpointmag.co.uk/obama-patriquin, accessed 28 November 2008.

64. Neil Smith and Sean MacFarland, 'Anbar Awakes: The Tipping Point', *Military Review* (March–April 2008), p. 42.

65. Long, 'The Anbar Awakening', p. 79.

66. Smith and MacFarland, 'Anbar Awakes: The Tipping Point', p. 41.

67. Long, 'The Anbar Awakening', p. 81.

68. McCreary, 'Military Awakening: Clear, Hold, Build and the Development of Awakening Councils and Iraqi Police', p. 33.

69. McCreary, 'Military Awakening', p. 34.

70. David Kilcullen, 'Anatomy of a Tribal Revolt', *Small Wars Journal* (August 2009) at http://smallwarsjournal.com/blog/anatomy-of-a-tribal-revolt, accessed September 2016.

71. Smith and MacFarland, 'Anbar Awakes: The Tipping Point', p. 47.

72. McCreary, 'Military Awakening: Clear, Hold, Build and the Development of Awakening Councils and Iraqi Police', p. 32.

73. 1ˢᵗ Brigade, 1ˢᵗ Armored Division, U.S. Army. *Operation Iraqi Freedom after Action Report January 2006–February 2007*, p. 67.

74. 1ˢᵗ Brigade, 1ˢᵗ Armored Division, U.S. Army, *Operation Iraqi Freedom after Action Report January 2006–February 2007*, p. 92.

75. *Operation Iraqi Freedom*, p. 93.

76. *Operation Iraqi Freedom*, p. 93.

77. *Operation Iraqi Freedom*, p. 90.

78. Martin LeBlanc, 'Anbar Awakening, Continuing to Deny AQI Safe Haven', *USMC News*, 7 March (2007), http://www.usmc.mil/units/marforpac/imef/1stmardiv/pages/MAR28.aspx.

79. DOD, *Measuring Stability and Security in Iraq*, p. 31.

80. Fisnak Arbashi, 'Petraeus: Afghan Tribes Needed to Fight Militants', Associated Press, 6 November 2008.

81. Giustozzi and Kalinovsky, *Missionaries of Modernity*, pp. 343–354.

13. FUTURE CHALLENGES: UPSTREAM ENGAGEMENT AND PRIVATE FORCES

1. Department of Defense, 'Counter-Terorism Partnerships Fund, FY2016' at http://comptroller.defense.gov/Portals/45/Documents/defbudget/fy2016/FY2016_CTPF_J-Book.pdf.

2. Tara McKelvey, 'Arming Syrian rebels: Where the US Went Wrong', 10 October 2015, at http://www.bbc.co.uk/news/magazine-33997408.

3. I. Daalder and J.G. Starridis, 'NATO's Victory in Libya', *Foreign Affairs*, 91, 2 (2012), pp. 2–7.

4. James Chandler, 'UK International Defence Engagement Strategy: Lessons from Bassingbourn', Chatham House Research Paper, April 2016, p. 4.
5. The UK Stabilisation Unit only began to consider the comprehensive package of support Libya would need at the end of 2013 after the Prime Minister's intentions were clarified in June that year.
6. Chandler, 'UK International Defence Engagement Strategy'.
7. United Kingdom, *National Security Strategy*, 2011.
8. Nick Ritchie, 'Rethinking Security: A Critical Analysis of the Strategic Defence and Security Review', *International Affairs* (2011).
9. James Putzel and Jonathan Di John, *Meeting the Challenge of Crisis States* (Crisis States Research Centre Report, LSE, 2012).
10. Steven Metz and Philip Cuccia, 'Defining War for the 21st Century', 2010, SSI Annual Strategy Conference Report, p. 15.
11. State 'failure' is a contested idea: while there is widespread recognition of social, economic or political indicators of an executive's ability to govern, William Easterly and Laura Freschi argue that it has no coherent definition and is used to justify Western intervention. William Easterly and Laura Freschi 'Top 5 reasons why "failed state" is a failed concept', AidWatch, 13 January 2010, http://aidwatchers.com/2010/01/top-5-reasons-why-%E2%80%9Cfailed-state%E2%80%9D-is-a-failed-concept/, accessed 25 March 2013.
12. Anatol Lieven, *Pakistan: A Hard Country* (London, Allen Lane: 2011), pp. 19–21.
13. Patrick Hennessey, *Kandak: Fighting with Afghans* (London: Allen Lane, 2012), p. 122.
14. Karine Varley, 'Contesting Concepts of the Nation in Arms: French Memories of the War of 1870–1 in Dijon', *European History Quarterly*, 36, 4 (October 2006), pp. 548–573.
15. *Cedric de Coning,* 'Understanding Peacebuilding as Essentially Local', *Stability: International Journal of Security and Development*, 2, 1 (2013), p. 6, doi: http://dx.doi.org/10.5334/sta.as, accessed May 2013. See also R. MacGinty, 'Against Stabilization', *International Journal of Security and Development*, 1, 1 (2012), pp. 20–30, doi: http://dx.doi.org/10.5334/sta.ab, which illustrates the failure to embrace local needs for the sake of international agendas.
16. International Crisis Group, 'Afghanistan: Getting Disarmament Back on Track', International Crisis Group Asia Briefing no. 35 (February 23, 2003), at http://www.crisisgroup.org/home/index.cfm?id=3290&l=1, accessed May 2013.
17. Roger McGinty, 'Transitions and Hybrid Political Orders', in Robert Johnson and Timothy Clack (eds.), *Tactical Transitions: Historical, Theoretical and Applied Approaches to Stabilisation and Drawdown* (Oxford: Oxford University Press, 2014).
18. Examples included Executive Outcomes, Brown & Root Services, and MPRI. The United Nations banned mercenaries in Article 47 of the International Protocol

(1977); P.W. Singer, *Corporate Warriors: The Rise of the Privatised Military Industry* (New York: PUBLISHER, 2008), pp. 102–105, 109, 117.

19. J. Scahill, *Blackwater: The Rise of the World's Most Powerful Mercenary Army* (New York: Cornell University Press, 2008).

20. Theoretically, from 2007, the United States could court-martial a contractor but the amendment to the Code of Military Justice had not been invoked or tested. For the backgrounds of many contractors, see Singer, *Corporate Warriors*, pp. 76–7, 221 and Scahill, *Blackwater*, pp. 246–265.

21. Singer, *Corporate Warriors*, p. 74.

22. S. Chesterman and C. Lehnardt (eds.), *From Mercenaries to Market: The Rise and Regulation of Private Military Companies* (New York: PUBLISHER, 2007).

23. J.J. Carafano, *Private Sector, Public Wars: Contractors in Combat; Afghanistan, Iraq and Future Conflicts* (Westport: PUBLISHER, 2008), p. 38.

24. Carafano, *Private Sector, Public Wars*, p. 100.

25. D.D. Avant, *The Market for Force: The Consequences of Privatising Security* (New York: PUBLISHER, 2005), p. 19.

26. Carafano, *Private Sector, Public Wars*, p. 12.

27. Name withheld. Interview with the author, Oxford, 2014.

28. Singer, *Corporate Warriors*, pp. 89–90; Scahill, *Blackwater*, pp. 21–22.

14. CONCLUSION

1. Author's interview conducted under the Chatham House Rule, March 2016.

2. General David Petraeus, Commander ISAF.

3. Interviews with the author, June 2010—July 2011. My gratitude to Col. Alex Alderson (Ret.) for his insights.

4. Interview with the author, name withheld, November 2014.

5. Interviews with Brigadier Richard Iron, 2014.

6. *Army Field Manual*, vol. 1, part 10 (January 2010), section 10–11.

7. Ashley Jackson, 'British Counterinsurgency in History: A Useful Precedent?', *British Army Review*, 139 (Spring 2006), p. 16.

8. Thomas R. Mockaitis, *British Counter-Insurgency in the Post-Imperial Era* (Manchester: Manchester University Press, 1995), p. 74. The plan was formulated by Lieutenant Colonel (later General) Johnny Watts of 22 SAS.

9. John Akehurst, *We Won a War: The Campaign in Oman 1965–1975* (Salisbury: Michael Russell, 1982), p. 8.

10. Brigadier Ian Gardiner, *In the Service of the Sultan: A First-Hand Account of the Dhofar Insurgency* (London: Pen and Sword, 2006).

11. Colonel T.E. Lawrence, '27 Articles', 1917, Article 15: 'Do not try to do too much with your own hands. Better the Arabs do it tolerably than you do it perfectly. It is their war, and you are there to help them, not to win it for them. Actually, also,

under the very peculiar conditions of Arabia, your practical work will not be as good as, perhaps, you think it is.'

12. Akehurst, *We Won a War*, p. 8.

13. Major (Ret.) Gerald Davies MBE, 6GR and RGR, Company Commander in Dhofar, 1975 and 1976, interviewed by Brigadier Ian Rigden in 2010. I am most grateful to Brigadier Rigden for permission to use this example.

APPENDIX: THE TWENTY-SEVEN ARTICLES

1. Lawrence's manuscript, FO 882/7, folios 93–97.1 Lawrence's manuscript, FO 882/7, folios 93–97.

BIBLIOGRAPHY

Archive Material

United Nations

United Nations Assistance Mission in Afghanistan (UNAMA), *Annual Report on Protection of Civilians in Armed Conflict, 2009* (New York: January 2010).

United States' Government

Department of Defense, *Measuring Stability and Security in Iraq* (Washington DC: DOD, February 2006).

Department of Defense, *Progress toward Security and Stability in Afghanistan January 2009 Report to Congress in Accordance with the 2008 National Defense Authorization Act* (Section 1230, Public Law 110–181) (January 2009).

Statement of Lieutenant General William Caldwell IV to the Committee of Oversight and Government Reform Subcommittee on National Security, Homeland Defense and Foreign Operations, 12 September 2012.

Government Accountability Office, *Afghanistan Security* (Washington DC: GAO, 2005).

SIGAR, Special Inspector General for Afghan Reconstruction, Quarterly Reports to Congress.

National Archives and Records Administration (NARA), Washington DC

M1801 Compiled Service Records of soldiers who served in the 55th Massachusetts Infantry (Colored), Records of the Adjutant General's Office, 1780s–1917, RG 94.

North Atlantic Treaty Organisation

North Atlantic Treaty Organisation (NATO), *Progress in Afghanistan*: Bucharest Summit, 2–4 April 2008 (Brussels, 2008), www.isaf.nato.int/pdf/progress_afghanistan_2008.pdf.

Joint Commission and Monitoring Board, NATO/ISAF (September 2008): http://www.nato.int/isaf/docu/epub/pdf/placemat.html.

Parliamentary Papers, United Kingdom

National Security Strategy, 2011.

Strategic Defence and Security Review, 2010 and *2015.*

Papers Concerned with the Reorganisation of the Army in India, Supplementary to the Report of the Army Commission (London, 1859), House of Commons, Session 2, C. 2541.

Report on the Administration of the Eastern Portion of British Central Africa from 1891 to 1894, Parliamentary Papers 1894, vol. 57.

Report on the Uganda Protectorate, Parliamentary Papers, 1901, Vol. 48.

The National Archives, Kew, London

Cabinet Records, CAB.

Colonial Office Records, CO.

Foreign Office Records, FO.

War Office Records, WO.

Records of the Ministry of Defence, DEFE.

India Office Records, the British Library, London

Political and Secret Files, P/, L/PS/.

Military Department Records, L/Mil/7—20.

India Office, War Staff Papers, L/WS

Home Miscellaneous Series, L, Home Correspondence.

Public and Judicial Department Files, L/PJ.

India: Crown Representative: Political Department Indian States Records 1880–1947, R/1.

India: Crown Representative: Indian States Residencies Records, R/2.

Nepal: Kathmandu Residency Records, R/5.

Gulf States: Records of the Bushire, Bahrain, Kuwait, Muscat and Trucial States Agencies, R/15.

Aden: Records of the Administration in Aden, R/20.

Mutiny Correspondence, I (Lahore, 1911).

Army Regulations, India, vol. II: Regulations and Orders for the Army (1913).

Vincennes, Paris

Service Historique de la Defense, SHD.

BIBLIOGRAPHY

National Archives of India, Delhi

Office of the Adjutant General B. Crown Period, series 2, Military Department.
Military B Programmes.
Police Series.
Foreign External A Series.
Foreign External B Series.
Revenue and Agriculture (Emigration).

Private Papers

National Archives, Kew, London

Cornwallis Papers, PRO 30/11.
Kitchener Papers, PRO 30/57.
Lloyd George Papers, LG.

The British Library, London

Warren Hastings, Add MSS 29234.
Montgomery Papers, MSS Eur D1019.
Reade Papers, MSS Eur E124.
Emma Ewart, MSS Eur B 267.
Herbert Bruce, Add MSS 44003.
Charles Gordon, Add MSS 52389.

The National Army Museum, London

Robert Clive.
Frederick Sleigh Roberts.
Surgeon C. Pine, Diaries.

The Imperial War Museum, London

A.H. Dickinson, Documents Collection, 9749.
Sir Richard Ewart, Documents Collection, 683.
K.H. Henderson, Documents Collection, 10942.
H.V. Lewis, Documents Collection, 2531.
Sir Edward Northey, Documents Collection, 9796.
J.P. Swindlehurst, Document Collection, 10415.
J.C. Wedgwood, Lord Barleston, Documents Collection, 16598.
Sir Archibald Murray, Documents Collection, 7180.

BIBLIOGRAPHY

Bodleian Library

T.E. Lawrence Papers.

John Rylands Library, University of Manchester

Auchinleck Papers.

Published Works

A.D.G., 'On the Utility and Economy of the West India Regiments', *United Services Journal*, 2 (London, 1833).

Ageron, Charles-Robert, 'Le Drame des harkis en 1962', *Vingtième Siècle: Revue d'Histoire*, 42, 2 (1994).

Ageron, Charles-Robert, 'Les Supplétifs algériens dans l'armée française pendant la guerre d'Algérie', *Vingtième Siècle: Revue d'Histoire*, 48, 4 (1995).

Ahmed Khan, Syed, *An Essay on the Causes of the Indian Revolt* (Calcutta, 1860).

Akehurst, John, *We Won a War: The Campaign in Oman 1965–1975* (Salisbury: Michael Russell, 1982).

Alexander, H., *On Two Fronts, Being the Adventures of an Indian Mule Corps in France and Gallipoli* (New York: Dutton, 1917).

Allawi, Ali, *Faisal I of Iraq* (New Haven CT: Yale University Press, 2014).

Allen, Charles, *Plain Tales from the Raj* (London: André Deutsch and Penguin, 1975).

Allen, M.D., *The Medievalism of Lawrence of Arabia* (University Park, PA: Pennsylvania State University Press, 1991).

Anderson, David, *Histories of the Hanged: The Dirty War in Kenya and the End of Empire* (London: Weidenfeld and Nicholson, 2005).

Anderson, David, 'Surrogates of the State: Collaboration and Atrocity in Kenya's Mau Mau War', in George Kassimeris (ed.), *The Barbarisation of Warfare* (London: Hurst, 2006): 159–174.

Anderson, David, and David Killingray, *Policing and Decolonization: Nationalism, Politics and the Police, 1917–65* (Manchester University Press 1992).

Anderson, A., *Poems Chiefly Written in India* (London, 1809).

Anderson, F., *Crucible of War: The Seven Years War and the Fate of Empire in British North America, 1754–63* (New York: Alfred Knopf, 2000).

Anderson, Scott, *Lawrence in Arabia: War, Deceit, Imperial Folly and the Making of the Modern Middle East* (London: Atlantic, 2013).

Anglim, Simon, 'Orde Wingate and the Special Night Squads: A Feasible Policy for Counter-Terrorism?', *Contemporary Security Policy*, 28, 1 (2007), 28–41.

Annesley, George, Viscount Valentia, *Voyages and Travels to India, Ceylon, the Red Sea, Abyssinia, and Egypt, in the Years 1802, 1803, 1804, 1805, and 1806* (London: W. Bulmer, 1809).

Baird, J.G.A. (ed.), *The Private Letters of the Marquess of Dalhousie* (1858; repr., Edinburgh, 1910).

Barr, James, *Setting the Desert on Fire: T.E. Lawrence and Britain's Secret War in Arabia, 1916–1918* (London: Bloomsbury, 2006).

Bayly, C.A., *Empire and Information: Intelligence Gathering and Social Communication in India, 1780–1870* (Cambridge: Cambridge University Press, 1996).

Beattie, H., 'Negotiations with the Tribes in Waziristan, 1849–1914: The British Experience', *Journal of Imperial and Commonwealth History*, 39, 4 (2011).

Beckett Ian, *Modern Insurgencies and Counter-Insurgencies* (London: Routledge, 2001).

Bennett, Huw, 'The Other Side of the COIN: Minimum and Exemplary Force in British Army Counterinsurgency in Kenya', *Small Wars and Insurgencies*, 18, 4 (2007), 638–639.

Berghahn, Volker, *Germany and the Approach of War* (Leamington: Berg, 1985).

Bernhardi, Frederick von, *Germany and the Next War* (1911; English edn, London, 1918).

Benton, Lauren, *Law and Colonial Cultures: Legal Regimes in World History, 1400–1900* (Cambridge: Cambridge University Press, 2002).

Bidwell, Robin (ed.), *The Diary Kept by T.E. Lawrence While Travelling in Arabia during 1911* (Reading: Garnet, 1993).

Bidwell, Robin, 'The Brémond Mission in the Hijaz, 1916–17: A Study in Inter-Allied Co-operation', in Robin Bidwell and Rex Smith (eds.), *Arabian and Islamic Studies* (London: Longman, 1983).

Bird, Tim, and Alex Marshall, *Afghanistan: How the West Lost Its Way* (New Haven: Yale University Press, 2011).

Boualam, Bachaga Saïd, *Mon pays la France* (Paris: France Empire, 1962).

Braithwaite, Edward, *The Development of Creole Society in Jamaica, 1770–1820* (Oxford: Clarendon Press, 1972).

Brémont, Edouard, *Le Hedjaz dans la Guerre Mondiale* (Paris: Payot, 1931).

Brohier, R.L., *Discovering Ceylon* (Cleveland, OH: Lake House Investments, 1973).

Brown, Malcom, *T.E. Lawrence in War and Peace* (London: Greenhill, 2005).

Bryant, Gerald, *The East India Company and Its Army, 1600–1778* (London: University of London, 1975).

Buchan, John, *A History of the Great War*, vol. 1 (New York: Houghton Mifflin, 1923).

Buckley, R.N., *The Napoleonic War Journal of Captain Thomas Henry Browne, 1807–1816* (Stroud: Army Records Society, 1987).

Bujra, A.S., 'Urban Elites and Colonialism: The Nationalist Elites of Aden and South Arabia', *Middle Eastern Studies*, 6, 2 (May 1970).

Bussche, L. de, *Letters on Ceylon: Particularly Relative to the Kingdom of Kandy* (repr., PLACE: Palala Press, 2015).

Callahan, Raymond, *The East India Company and Army Reform 1783–1798* (Cambridge, MA: Harvard University Press, 1972).

Callwell, Charles Edward, *Small Wars: Their Principles and Practice* (London: HMSO, 1899).

Campbell, Lt. Col. James, *Excursions, Adventures, and Field-Sports in Ceylon. Its Commercial and Military Importance, and Numerous Advantages to the British Emigrant*, 2 vols. (London: T. and W. Boone, 1843).

Cassidy, R.M., 'The Long Small War: Indigenous Forces for Counterinsurgency', *Parameters*, 36, 2 (Summer 2006), 47–62.

Caulfield, Colonel J.E., *100 Years' History of the 2nd West India Regiment 1795 to 1898: 50th or the Queen's Own Regiment* (London: Naval and Military Press, 2005).

CEHD (Centre d'Etudes d'Histoire de la Défense), *Les Troupes de marine dans l'armée de terre: Un siècle d'histoire (1900–2000)* (Paris: Lavauzelle, 2001).

Chapman, F.S., *The Jungle Is Neutral* (London: Hutchinson, 1949).

Chatty, Dawn, 'Rituals of Royalty and the Elaboration of Ceremony in Oman: View from the Edge', *International Journal of Middle East Studies*, 41 (2009).

Charbit, Tom, *Les Harkis* (Paris: La Découverte, 2006).

Clarke, F.A.S., and A. Haywood, *The History of the Royal West African Frontier Force* (Aldershot: Gale & Polden, 1964).

Chauvin, Stéphanie, 'Des appelés pas comme les autres? Les conscrits "français de souche nord-africaine" pendant la guerre d'Algérie', *Vingtième Siècle: Revue d'Histoire*, 48, 4 (1995).

Clayton, Anthony, *France, Soldiers and Africa* (London: Brassey's Defence Publishers, 1988).

Clegg, Will, 'Irregular Forces in Counterinsurgency Warfare', *Security Challenges*, 5, 3 (Spring 2009), 1–25.

Clifford, Sir Hugh, *The Gold Coast Regiment in the East African Campaign* (London: John Murray, 1920).

Cohen, Stephen P., *The Indian Army: Its Contribution to the Development of a Nation* (2nd edn, Oxford: Oxford University Press, 2001).

Cole, Major D.H., *Imperial Military Geography* (1924; 9th edn, London, 1937).

Collins, Randall, *Violence: A Micro-Sociological Survey* (Princeton, NJ: Princeton University Press, 2009).

Cordesman, Anthony H., *Iraq's Insurgency and the Road to Civil Conflict*, vol. 1 (Washington DC: Center for Strategic and International Studies [CSIS], 2008).

Cordesman, Anthony H., *Winning in Afghanistan: Creating Effective Afghan Security Forces: Working Draft Revised December 9, 2008* (Washington DC: Center for Strategic and International Studies [CSIS], 2008).

Cordesman, Anthony H., 'Shaping Afghan National Security Forces: What It Will Take to Implement President Obama's New Strategy' (Washington DC: Center for Strategic and Internal Studies [CSIS], 2009).

Cordiner, James, *A Description of Ceylon*, 2 vols. (London: Longman, 1807).

Corm, G., 'The War System: Militia Hegemony and Reestablishment of the State', in

D. Collings (ed.), *Peace for Lebanon? From War to Reconstruction* (Boulder, CO: Lynne Rienner, 1994), 215–230.

Corrigan, Gordon, *Sepoys in the Trenches: The Indian Corps on the Western Front, 1914–15* (Stroud: Spellmount, 2006).

Crawfurd, John, 'China and the Chinese', *Journal of the Royal United Services Institution*, 1 (1858).

Cross, J.P., and Field Marshal Sir John Chapple, *Gurkhas at War* (London: Greenhill, 2007).

Crowder, M., *Revolt in Bussa* (London: PUBLISHER, 1973).

Cunningham, W.B., *Dogras* (Government of India, 1932).

Dalloz, Jacques, *The War in Indochina, 1945–54* (Dublin: Gill and Macmillan, 1990).

David, Saul, *The Indian Mutiny, 1857* (London: Hutchinson, 2002).

Davis, Shelby Cullom, *Reservoirs of Men: A History of the Black Troops of French West Africa* (Westport, CN: Negro Universities Press, 1970).

Davis, S.P., *Reservoirs of Men: A History of Black Troops of French Africa* (Chambéry, 1934).

Darwin, John, *Britain and Decolonization: The Retreat from Empire in the Post-war World* (London: Macmillan, 1987).

Dimitrakis, Panagiotis, 'British Intelligence and the Cyprus Insurgency, 1955–1959', *International Journal of Intelligence and Counterintelligence*, 21, 2 (2008).

Disney, Nigel, 'China and the Middle East', *MERIP Report*, 63 (Dec. 1977).

Dodge, T., and S. Simon, *Iraq at the Crossroads: State and Society in the Shadow of Regime Change* (London: Routledge, 2005).

Doveton, Captain F.B., *Reminiscences of the Burmese War, in 1824–5–6* (London, 1852).

Dyde, Brian, *The Empty Sleeve: The Story of the West India Regiments of the British Army* (St John's, Antigua: Hansib Caribbean, 1997).

Edwards, Aaron, *Mad Mitch's Tribal Law: Aden and the End of Empire* (Edinburgh: Mainstream, 2014).

Edwards, Aaron, '"A Graveyard for the British"? Tactics, Military Operations and the Paucity of Strategy in Aden, 1964–67', in Johnson and Clack, *At the End of Military Intervention* (Oxford: Oxford University Press, 2014).

Edwardes, Michael, *Red Year: The Indian Rebellion of 1857* (London: Sphere, 1975).

Elliott, E.R., *Royal Pioneers, 1945–1993* (PLACE: Hanley Swan, 1993).

Fane, Henry Edward, *Five Years in India* (London, 1842).

Farrar, Major M.L. (ed.), *The Diary of Colour-Sarjeant George Calladine, 19th Foot, 1793–1837* (London: Eden Fisher and Co., 1922).

Farwell, Byron, *Queen Victoria's Little Wars* (London: Allen Lane, 1973).

Felter, Joseph, and Brian Fishman, 'Al Qaeda's Foreign Fighters in Iraq: A First Look at the Sinjar Records' (Combating Terrorism Center, US Military Academy at West Point, 2007).

Ferguson, Niall, *Empire* (London: Allen Lane, 2003).

Finlason, William Francis, 'Martial Law' (Bristol Selected Pamphlets, 1872), 14207/ X10–425–117–3, University of Bristol Library.

Foot, M.R.D., *Resistance: An Analysis of European Resistance to Nazism 1940–1945* (London: Eyre Methuen, 1976).

Fromkin, David, *A Peace to End All Peace: The Fall of the Ottoman Empire and the Creation of the Modern Middle East* (New York: Avon, 1989).

Galbraith, J.S., 'The "Turbulent Frontier" as a Factor in British Expansion', *Comparative Studies in Society and History*, 11 (1959–60), 151–168.

Galloway, Colin C., *White People, Indians and Highlanders: Tribal Peoples and Colonial Encounters in Scotland and America* (Oxford: Oxford University Press, 2008).

Galula, David, *Counterinsurgency Warfare: Theory and Practice* (1965; repr., Westport, CT: Praeger, 2006).

Galula, David, with Bruce Hoffman, *Pacification in Algeria, 1956–1958* (New York: RAND, 2006).

Gardener, Ian, *In the Service of the Sultan: A First Hand Account of the Dhofar Insurgency* (Barnsley: Pen and Sword, 2006).

Gardner, Nikolas, *Trial by Fire: Command and the British Expeditionary Force in 1914* (Westport, CT: Praeger, 2003).

Geertz, Clifford, *The Interpretation of Cultures* (New York: Basic Books, 1973).

Gelber, Yoav, *Jewish Palestinian Volunteering in the British Army during the Second World War*, vols. 1–4 (Jerusalem: Yad Izhak Ben-Zvi, 1979–1984).

General Staff of the German Army, *The German War Book, being the Usages of War on Land*, edited and translated by J.H. Morgan (London, 1915).

Gilbert, Arthur, 'Recruitment and Reform in the East India Company Army, 1760–1800', *Journal of British Studies*, 15, 1 (1975).

Gilchrist, Andrew, *Bangkok Top Secret: Force 136 at War* (London: PUBLISHER, 1960).

Giustozzi, Antonio, 'The Afghan National Army: Unwarranted Hope?', *RUSI Journal*, 154, 6 (December 2009), 36–42.

Giustozzi, Antonio, *Koran, Kalashnikov and Laptop: The Rise of the Neo-Taliban Insurgency in Afghanistan* (London: Hurst, 2007).

Giustozzi, Antonio, *War, Politics and Society in Afghanistan, 1978–1992* (Washington DC: Georgetown University Press, 2000).

Giustozzi, Antonio, and Atemy Kalinovsky, *Missionaries of Modernity: Advisory Missions and the Struggle for Hegemony in Afghanistan and Beyond* (London: Hurst, 2016).

Glattenhaar, Joseph T., and James Kirby Martin, *Forgotten Allies: The Oneida Indians and the American Revolution* (New York: Hill and Wang, 2006).

Glickstein, Daniel, and Michael Spangler, 'Reforming the Afghan Security Forces', *Parameters*, 44, 3 (2014).

Gordon, Stewart, *The New Cambridge History of India: The Marathas, 1600–1818* (Cambridge: Cambridge University Press, 1993).

Gortzak, Yoav, 'Using Indigenous Forces in Counterinsurgency Operations: The French in Algeria, 1954–1962', *Journal of Strategic Studies*, 32, 2 (April 2009), 307–333.

Gould, Tony *Imperial Warriors: Britain and the Gurkhas* (London: Granta, 1999).

Grau, Lester (ed.), Soviet General Staff, *The Soviet–Afghan War* (Lawrence, KS: University Press of Kansas, 2002).

Graves, Robert, *Goodbye to All That* (London: Jonathan Cape, 1929).

Greenhut, J., '"Sahib and Sepoy" An Enquiry into the Relationship between British Officers and Native Soldiers of the British Indian Army', *Military Affairs*, 48 (1984).

Grivas, General George, *Guerrilla Warfare and EOKA's Struggle* (London: Longman, 1964).

Gubbins, M., *An Account of the Mutinies in the Oudh and the Siege of the Lucknow Residency* (London, 1858).

Guha, Ranajit, *Elementary Aspects of Peasant Insurgency in Colonial India* (New Delhi: PUBLISHER, 1983).

Guha, Ranajit, and Gayatri Spivak, *Selected Subaltern Studies* (New York: Oxford University Press, 1989).

Guoqi, Xu, *China and the Great War: China's Pursuit of a New National Identity and Internationalization* (Cambridge: Cambridge University Press, 2005).

Gupta, Partha Sarathi, and Anirudh Deshpande (eds.), *The British Raj and its Indian Armed Forces, 1857–1939* (New Delhi: PUBLISHER, 2002).

Hack, K., 'Between Terror and Talking: The Place of "Negotiation" in Colonial Conflict', *Journal of Imperial and Commonwealth History* 39, 4 (2011), 539–549.

Hall, D.G.E., *A History of South East Asia* (London: PUBLISHER, 1955).

Hallowell, N.P., *Selected Letters and Papers of N.P. Hallowell* (Peterborough, N.H: Richard R. Smith and Co., 1896).

Halliday, Fred, 'Arabia without Sultans Revisited', *Middle East Report*, 204 (July–September 1997).

Hansen, Peter, 'Classical Boundaries: National Identities and British Mountaineering on the Frontiers of Europe and the Empire, 1868 to 1940', *Journal of Imperial and Commonwealth History*, 24 (1996).

Hanson, Victor David, *The Soul of Battle: From Ancient Times to the Present Day* (New York: Free Press, 1999).

Hargreaves, J.D., *The End of Colonial Rule in West Africa* (London: Historical Association, 1976).

Hashim, Ahmed, *Insurgency and Counter-Insurgency in Iraq* (London: Hurst, 2006).

Hautreux, François-Xavier, 'L'Emploi des harkis dans la guerre d'Algérie: Essai de périodisation', *Vingtième Siècle: Revue d'Histoire*, 90, 2 (2006).

Haywood, A., and F.A.S. Clarke, *A History of the RWAFF* (Aldershot: Gale and Polden, 1964).

Heathcote, T.A., *The Afghan Wars* (Oxford: Osprey, 1980).

Heathcote, T.A., *The Indian Army: The Garrison of British Imperial India, 1822–1922* (London: David and Charles, 1974).

Heber, Bishop Reginald, *Narrative of a Journey through the Upper Provinces of India* (London, 1843).

Hennessey, Patrick, *Kandak: Fighting with Afghans* (London: Allen Lane, 2012).

Hibbert, Christopher (ed.), *The Recollections of Rifleman Harris* (London: Weidenfeld and Nicholson, 1996).

Hirst, F.W., G. Murray and J.L. Hammond, *Liberalism and the Empire* (London, 1900).

Hodgson, B.H., 'Origin and Classification of the Military Tribes of Nepal', in *Essays on the Languages, Literature and Religion of Nepal and Tibet* (London, 1874).

Holdern, C., *Military Operations in East Africa, 1914–1916* (London: HMSO, 1941).

Holland, R., 'The British Empire and the Great War, 1914–1918', in Judith M. Brown and W.R. Louis (eds.), *The Oxford History of the British Empire*, vol. 4: *The Twentieth Century* (Oxford: Oxford University Press, 1999).

Holmes, Richard, *Firing Line* (London: Penguin, 1985).

Hopkirk, Peter, *The Great Game* (Oxford: Oxford University Press, 1990).

Horne, Alastair, *A Savage War of Peace: Algeria, 1954–1962* (New York: Viking Press, 1978).

Hoskins, Alan, *A Contract Officer in the Oman* (Tunbridge Wells: Costello, 1988).

Howlett, R.A., *The History of the Fijian Military Forces, 1939–1945* (Suva, 1948).

Hubbard, Andrew, 'Plague and Paradox: Militias in Iraq', *Small Wars and Insurgencies*, 18, 3 (2007), 345–362.

Hughes, G., 'A "Model Campaign": The Counter-Insurgency War in Dhofar, Oman, 1965–1975,' *Journal of Strategic Studies*, 32, 2 (2009).

Hughes, Geraint, and Christian Tripodi, 'Anatomy of a Surrogate: Historical Precedents and Implications for Contemporary Counter-Insurgency and Counter-Terrorism', *Small Wars and Insurgencies*, 20, 1 (March 2009), 1–35.

Hughes, Michelle, 'The Afghan National Police in 2015 and Beyond', US Institute of Peace (USIP) (Washington DC, May 2014).

Hurd, Douglas, *Memoirs* (London: Abacus, 2003).

Hure, Robert, *L'Armée d'Afrique: 1830–1962* (Paris: Charles-Lavauzelle, 1977).

Hurewitz, J.C. (ed.), *The Middle East and North Africa in World Politics: A Documentary Record* (New Haven, CT: Yale University Press, 1979).

Hussein, Rizwan, *Pakistan and the Emergence of Islamic Militancy in Afghanistan* (Aldershot: Ashgate, 2005).

Hussainmiya, B.A., *Orang Rejimen: The Malays of the Ceylon Rifle Regiment* (Bangi, 1990).

Huynh, Tu T., 'From Demand for Asiatic Labor to Importation of Indentured

Chinese Labor: Race Identity in the Recruitment of Unskilled Labor for South Africa's Gold Mining Industry, 1903–1910', *Journal of Chinese Overseas*, 4, 1 (May 2008), 51–68.

Hyam, Ronald, *Britain's Imperial Century, 1815–1914: A Study in Empire and Expansion* (2nd edn, Basingstoke: Macmillan, 1993).

Ingold, Commandant F., *Les Troupes noir au combat* (Paris: Berger-Levrault, 1940).

Innes, Emily, *The Chersoese with the Gilding Off*, 2 vols. (1885; repr., Kuala Lumpur, 1974).

International Crisis Group, 'Afghanistan: Getting Disarmament Back on Track', International Crisis Group Asia Briefing no. 35 (23 February 2003).

Ives, Christopher, *US Special Forces and Counterinsurgency in Vietnam* (London: Routledge, 2007).

Jackson, Ashley, *The British Empire and the Second World War* (London: Hambledon Continuum, 2006).

Jackson, Ashley, *Distant Drums: The Role of Colonies in British Imperial Warfare* (Brighton: Sussex Academic Press, 2010).

James, Lawrence, *Raj: The Making and Unmaking of British India* (London: Little, Brown and Co., 1997).

Jardine, D., *The Mad Mullah of Somaliland* (London, 1923).

Jeal, T., *Baden-Powell* (London: Hutchinson, 1989).

Jeapes, Colonel Tony, *SAS: Operation Oman* (London: William Kimber, 1980).

Jefferies, Alan, and Patrick Rose (eds.), *The Indian Army, 1939–1947* (London: Ashgate, 2012).

Jeffrey, Robin, 'The Punjab Boundary Force and the Problem of Order, August 1947', *Modern Asian Studies*, 8 (1974).

Joes, Anthony James, 'Counterinsurgency in the Philippines 1898–1954', in Daniel P. Marston and Carter Malkasian (eds.), *Counterinsurgency in Modern Warfare* (London: Osprey, 2007).

Joes, Anthony James, *Resisting Rebellion. The History and Politics of Counterinsurgency* (Lexington, KY: University Press of Kentucky, 2006).

Johnson, Robert, *The Afghan Way of War* (London: Hurst, 2011).

Johnson, Robert, 'Decolonisation in India and Pakistan', in Robert Johnson and Timothy Clack (eds.), *At the End of Military Intervention: Historical, Theoretical and Applied Approaches to Transition, Handover and Withdrawal* (Oxford: Oxford University Press, 2014).

Johnson, Robert, 'General Roberts, the Occupation of Kabul and the Problems of Transition, 1879–1880', *War in History*, 20, 3 (July 2013).

Johnson, Robert, '"I Shall Die Arms in Hand, Wearing the Warriors' Clothes": Mobilisation and Initial Operations of the Indian Army in France and Flanders', *British Journal for Military History*, 2, 3 (February 2016).

Johnson, Rob (ed.), *The British Indian Army: Virtue and Necessity* (Cambridge: Cambridge Scholars Publishers, 2014).

BIBLIOGRAPHY

Johnson, Robert, *The Great War and the Middle East* (Oxford: Oxford University Press, 2016).

Johnson, Robert, 'Out of Arabia: The Fate of Omani Forces Allied with the British, 1967–76', *International History Review* (2016).

Johnson, Robert, and Timothy Clack (eds.), *Tactical Transitions: Historical, Theoretical and Applied Approaches to Stabilisation and Drawdown* (Oxford: Oxford University Press, 2014).

Johnston, Arthur, *Narrative of the Operations of a Detachment in an Expedition to Candy, in the Island of Ceylon* (London: C. and R. Baldwin, 1810).

Jones, Clive, 'Military Intelligence and the War in Dhofar: An Appraisal', *Small Wars and Insurgencies*, 25, 3 (2014), 628–646.

Jones, Seth G., 'Community Defense in Afghanistan', *Joint Forces Quarterly*, 57, 2 (2010), 9–15.

Kaiser, David, *American Tragedy* (Cambridge, MA: Harvard University Press, 2000).

Kaldor, Mary, *New and Old Wars: Organized Violence in a Global Era* (2nd edn, Cambridge: Polity Press, 2006).

Kalyvas, Stathis N., *The Logic of Violence in Civil War* (Cambridge: Cambridge University Press, 2006).

Kanya-Forster, A.S., *The Conquest of Western Sudan: A Study in French Military Imperialism* (Cambridge: Cambridge University Press, 1969).

Karsh, Efraim, and Inari Karsh, 'Myth in the Desert, or Not the Great Arab Revolt', *Middle Eastern Studies*, 33, 2 (April 1997), 267–312.

Kaye, Sir John, *The Indian Mutiny*, 6 vols. (London, 1864).

Keating, Lieutenant Colonel Gavin, '"Living in the Twilight Zone": Advising the Afghan National Army at the Corps Level', *Australian Army Journal*, 8, 3 (Summer 2011).

Kedourie, Elie, *In the Anglo-Arab Labyrinth: The McMahon–Husayn Correspondence and Its Interpretations, 1914–1939* (Cambridge: Cambridge University Press, 1976).

Keegan, John, *A History of Warfare* (London: Hutchinson, 1993).

Keegan, John, and Richard Holmes, *Soldiers: A History of Men in Battle* (London: Hamish Hamilton, 1985).

Kelly, Colonel Francis, *Vietnam Studies: U.S. Army Special Forces* (Washington DC: Department of the Army, 1989).

Kelly, J.B., *Arabia, the Gulf and the West* (New York: Basic Books, 1980).

Kelly, J.B., 'Recollections and Reflections of a British Diplomat', Review of Lord Treveleyan's *The Middle East in Revolution* (London: Macmillan, 1970) in *Middle East Studies*, 3 (October 1973).

Kelly, Saul, 'Vanishing Act: Britain's Abandonment of Aden and Retreat from the Gulf', in Robert Johnson and Timothy Clack (eds.), *At the End of Military Intervention* (Oxford: Oxford University Press, 2014).

Ketchum, Richard M., *Saratoga: Turning Point of America's Revolutionary War* (New York: Henry Holt, 1997).

Khalidi, Rashid, Lisa Anderson, Muhammad Muslih and Reeva S. Simon (eds.), *The Origins of Arab Nationalism* (New York: Columbia University Press, 1991).

Kiernan, V.G., *Colonial Empires and Armies, 1815–1960* (Stroud: Sutton, 1998).

Kilcullen, David, *Accidental Guerrilla: Fighting Small Wars in the Midst of a Big One* (London: Hurst and, 2011).

Kilcullen, David, 'Anatomy of a Tribal Revolt', *Small Wars Journal* (August 2009).

Killingray, David, *Fighting for Britain: African Soldiers in the Second World War* (Woodbridge, Surrey: James Currey, 2010).

Killingray, David, 'The Mutiny of the West African Regiment in the Gold Coast, 1901', *International Journal of African Historical Studies*, 16 (1983), 441–454.

Killingray, David, 'The Rod of Empire: The Debate over Corporal Punishment in the British African Colonial Forces, 1888–1946', *Journal of African History*, 35 (1994).

Killingray, David, and David Omissi (eds.), *Guardians of Empire: The Armed Forces of the Colonial Powers c. 1700–1964* (Manchester: Manchester University Press, 1990).

King, Anthony, *The Combat Soldier: Infantry Tactics and Cohesion in the Twentieth and Twenty-First Centuries* (Oxford: Oxford University Press, 2013).

King, Anthony, 'The Word of Command: Communication and Cohesion in the Military', *Armed Forces and Society* 32 (2005), 1–20.

King, Gillian, *Imperial Outpost Aden: Its Place in British Strategic Policy* (Oxford: Oxford University Press, 1964).

King, Captain W.R., *Campaigning in Kaffirland, 1851–1852* (London, 1853).

Kitson, Frank, *Gangs and Counter-Gangs* (London: Barrie and Rockliff, 1960).

Kitson, Frank, *Low Intensity Operations* (2nd edn, London: Faber and Faber, 1991).

Knightley, Phillip, and Colin Simpson, *The Secret Lives of Lawrence of Arabia* (London: Nelson, 1969).

Knights, Michael, and E. Williams, *The Calm before the Storm: The British Experience in Southern Iraq* (Washington DC: Washington Institute for Near East Policy, Policy Focus Paper No. 66, 2007).

Krepinevich, Andrew F., *The Army and Vietnam* (Baltimore: Johns Hopkins University Press, 1988).

Kromer, R.W., *Impact of Pacification on Insurgency in South Vietnam* (Santa Monica, CA: RAND Corporation, 1970).

Ladwig, Walter, III, 'Supporting Allies in Counterinsurgency: Britain and the Dhofar Rebellion', *Small Wars and Insurgencies*, 19, 1 (March 2008).

Ladwig, Walter, III, *The Trouble with Allies in Counterinsurgency: US Intervention in the Philippines, Vietnam, and El Salvador* (Cambridge: Cambridge University Press, 2017).

La Morandais, Alain Maillard de, *L'Honneur est sauf* (Paris: Le Seuil, 1990).

BIBLIOGRAPHY

Laurie, W.F.B., *The Second Burmese War: A Narrative of the Operations at Rangoon in 1852* (London, 1853).

Laver, James, *British Military Uniforms* (London: Penguin, 1948).

Lawrence, T.E., 'The Evolution of a Revolt', *Army Quarterly and Defence Journal* (October 1920).

Lawrence, T.E., *Seven Pillars of Wisdom* (London: Jonathan Cape, 1935).

Lenman, Bruce, *Britain's Colonial Wars, 1688–1783* (London: Pearson, 2001).

Lewin, Ronald, *The Chief: Field Marshal Lord Wavell, Commander in Chief and Viceroy, 1919–1947* (London: PUBLISHER, 1980).

Lieven, Anatol, *Pakistan: A Hard Country* (London: Allen Lane, 2011).

Linch, Kevin, *Britain and Wellington's Army: Recruitment, Society and Tradition, 1807–1815* (Basingstoke: Palgrave, 2011).

Lloyd-Jones, W., *KAR: The Origins and Activities of the King's African Rifles* (London, 1926).

Long, Austin, 'The Anbar Awakening', *Survival*, 50, 2 (2008), 67–94.

Lord, Cliff, and David Birtles, *The Armed Forces of Aden, 1839–1967* (Solihull: Helion, 2000).

Lowry, Richard S., *New Dawn: The Battles for Fallujah* (New York: Savas Beatie, 2010).

Lunt, James (ed.), *From Sepoy to Subedar: Being the Life and Adventures of Subedar Sita Ram, a Native Officer of the Bengal Army, Written and Related by Himself* (London: Military Book Society, 1970).

Lunt, James, *Imperial Sunset: Frontier Soldiering in the 20th Century* (London: Macdonald Futura, 1981).

Lyall, Sir Alfred, *The Rise and Expansion of British Dominion in Asia* (1894; 5th edn, London, 1910).

Lynn, John A., *Battle: A History of Combat and Culture from Ancient Greece to Modern America* (Boulder, CO: Westview Press, 2003).

Lynn, John A., 'The Evolution of Army Style in the Modern West, 800–2000', *International History Review*, 18, 3 (1996), 505–756.

MacGinty, R., 'Against Stabilization', *International Journal of Security and Development*, 1, 1 (2012), 20–30.

MacGregor, Lady (ed.), *The Life and Opinions of Major-General Charles Metcalfe MacGregor* (Edinburgh: William Blackwood and Sons, 1888).

Mack, John E., *The Prince of Our Disorder: The Life of T.E. Lawrence* (Boston: Little, Brown and Company, 1976).

Magnus, P., *Kitchener: Portrait of an Imperialist* (London: John Murray, 1958).

Malkasian, Carter, and Jerry Meyerle, *How Is Afghanistan Different from Al Anbar?* (Center for Naval Analysis, February 2009).

Malleson, Colonel G.B., *The Indian Mutiny of 1857* (4th edn, London, 1892).

Marashi, Ibrahim al-, and Sammy Salama, *Iraq's Armed Forces: An Analytical History* (Abingdon: Routledge, 2008).

Marshall, H., *Military Miscellany* (London, 1846).

Marston, Daniel, 'The Indian Army, Partition and the Punjab Boundary Force, 1945–47', *War in History*, 16, 4 (November 2009), 469–505.

Marston, Daniel P., *Phoenix from the Ashes: The Indian Army in the Burma Campaign* (London: Praeger, 2003).

Marston, Dan, and Chandar S. Sundaram (eds.), *A Military History of India and South Asia: From the East India Company to the Nuclear Era* (Bloomington, IN: Indiana University Press, 2007).

Mason, Philip, *A Matter of Honour: An Account of the Indian Army, Its Officers and Men* (London: Jonathan Cape, 1974).

Maurice, J.F., *The Diary of Sir John Moore*, 2 vols. (London: Edward Arnold, 1904).

Mawby, Spencer, 'Orientalism and the Failure of British Policy in the Middle East: The Case of Aden', *History: The Journal of the Historical Association*, 95, 319 (2010), 332–353.

McClenaghan, Tony, 'The Imperial Service Troops Scheme in the Nineteenth and Twentieth Centuries', in Rob Johnson (ed.), *The British Indian Army: Virtue and Necessity* (Cambridge: Cambridge Scholars Press, 2014).

McCreary, Matthew M., 'Military Awakening: Clear, Hold, Build and the Development of Awakening Councils and Iraqi Police', *Infantry*, 97, 4 (July–August 2008).

McMunn, George, and Cyril Falls, *Military Operations, Egypt and Palestine*, vol. 1 (London: HMSO, 1928).

McPherson, James, *For Cause and Comrades: Why Men Fought in the Civil War* (Oxford: Oxford University Press, 1997).

Merewhether, John, and Sir Frederick Smith, *The Indian Corps in France* (London: John Murray, 1919).

Meyer, François, *Pour l'honneur, avec les harkis: De 1958 à nos jours* (Tours: CLD, 2005).

Miller, William Ian, *The Mystery of Courage* (Cambridge, MA: Harvard University Press, 2000).

Moberly, F.J., *The Campaign in Mesopotamia, 1914–1918*, vol. 1 (London: HMSO, 1923).

Mockaitis, Thomas R., *British Counter-Insurgency in the Post-Imperial Era* (Manchester: Manchester University Press, 1995).

Mohamed Osman Tariq, 'Tribal Security System in Southeast Afghanistan' (Crisis States Research Centre, London School of Economics and Political Science: Occasional Paper No. 7, 2008).

Montieth, Lieutenant General William, *Kars and Ezeroum, with the campaigns of Prince Paskiewich in 1823 and 1829, and an account of the conquests of Russia beyond the Caucasus* (London, 1856).

Moon, Penderel (ed.), *Wavell: The Viceroy's Journal* (Oxford: Oxford University Press, 1973).

Morton-Jack, George, *The Indian Army on the Western Front: India's Expeditionary Force to France and Belgium in the First World War* (Cambridge: Cambridge University Press, 2014).

Mounier-Kuhn, A., *Les Services de santé militaires français pendant la conquête du Tonkin et de l'Annam, 1882–1896* (Paris: PUBLISHER, 2005).

Mowle, Thomas S., 'Iraq's militia problem', *Survival*, 48, 3 (2006), 41–58.

Moyar, Mark, *Phoenix and the Birds of Prey: Counterinsurgency and Counterterrorism in Vietnam* (Lincoln, NE: University of Nebraska Press 2007).

Moyse-Bartlett, Lieutenant-Colonel H., *The King's African Rifles* (Aldershot: Gale and Polden, 1956).

Neillands, Robin, *Fighting Retreat: The British Empire, 1947–97* (London: Hodder and Stoughton, 1996).

Nevill, Captain H.L., *Campaigns on the North West Frontier* (London, 1912; repr., Nashville, TN: Battery Press, n.d.).

Nicolson, I.F., *The Administration of Nigeria: Men, Methods and Myths* (Oxford: Oxford University Press, 1969).

O'Ballance, Edgar, *Malaya: The Communist Insurgent War, 1948–1960* (London: Faber and Faber, 1966).

O'Dwyer, M., *India as I Knew It, 1885–1925* (London, 1925).

Oldfield, H.A., *Sketches from Nipal* (London, 1880).

Oliver, Roland, *Sir Harry Johnston and the Scramble for Africa* (London: Chatto & Windus, 1957).

Omissi, David, *Air Power and Colonial Control* (Manchester: Manchester University Press, 1990).

Omissi, David, *The Sepoy and the Raj: The Politics of the Indian Army, 1860–1940* (London: Macmillan, 1994).

Orme, R., *Historical Fragments of the Mughal Empire* (London, 1805; repr., New Delhi: Associated Publishing House, 1974).

Osbourne, Hon. W.G., *The Court and the Camp of Runjeet Singh* (London, 1840).

Owen, Christopher, *The Rhodesian African Rifles* (London: Leo Cooper, 1970).

Page, Malcolm, *The King's African Rifles: A History* (London: Pen and Sword, 2011).

PAIFORCE: The Official History of the Persia and Iraq Command, 1941–1946 (London: HMSO, 1948).

Parker, John, *The Gurkhas: The Inside Story of the World's Most Feared Fighters* (London: Headline, 2005).

Peers, Douglas, 'Sepoys, Soldiers and the Lash: Race, Caste and Army Discipline in India, 1820–1850', *Journal of Imperial and Commonwealth History*, 23, 2 (1995), 211–247.

Pelletiere, Stephen, and Douglas V. Johnson III, *Lessons Learned: The Iran–Iraq War* (US Army War College: Strategic Studies Institute, 1991).

Percival, Robert, *An Account of the Island of Ceylon Containing Its History Geography*

Natural History with the Manners and Customs of Its Various Inhabitants (London: Baldwin, 1805).

Perito, Robert M., 'The Iraqi Federal Police: US Police Building under Fire' (US Institute of Peace, June 2006).

Perito, Robert M., 'Afghanistan's Police: The Weak Link in Security Sector Reform' (United States Institute of Peace Special Report, August 2008).

Petersen, Barry, *Tiger Men: An Australian Soldier's Secret War in Vietnam* (London: Sidgwick and Jackson, 1988).

Peterson, J.E., *Oman's Insurgencies: The Sultanate's Struggle for Supremacy* (London: Saqi Books, 2007).

Philips, C.H. (ed.), *The Correspondence of Lord William Cavendish Bentinck: Governor General of India*, 2 vols. (Oxford: Oxford University Press, 1977).

Philips, C.H., and M.D. Wainwright (eds.), *The Partition of India: Policies and Perspectives, 1935–1947* (London: George Allen and Unwin, 1970).

Piasecki, Eugene G., 'Civilian Irregular Defense Group: The First Years, 1961–1967', first published in *Veritas, Journal of U.S. Army Special Operations*, http://smallwarsjournal.com/documents/cidgprogram.pdf.

Plaatje, S., *Native Life in South Africa* (London, 1916).

Porch, Douglas, *Wars of Empire* (London: Cassell, 2000).

Powell, Geoffrey, *The Kandyan Wars: The British Army in Ceylon, 1803–1818* (London: Leo Cooper, 1973).

Prebble, John, *Mutiny: Highland Regiments in Revolt, 1743–1804* (London: Penguin, 1977).

Preston, A., and P. Dennis (eds.), *Swords and Covenants: Essays in Honour of the Royal Military College of Canada, 1876–1976* (London: Croom Helm, 1977).

Pretorius, F., *Life on Commando during the Anglo-Boer War, 1899–1902* (Cape Town: Tafelberg, 1999).

Price, D.L., 'Oman: Insurgency and Development', *Conflict Studies*, 53 (1975).

Prior, Robin, and Trevor Wilson, *The Somme* (New Haven: Yale University Press, 2005).

Putzel, James, and Jonathan Di John, 'Meeting the Challenge of Crisis States' (Crisis States Research Centre Report, LSE, 2012).

Ralston, David, *Importing the European Army* (Chicago: University of Chicago Press, 1990).

Rasanayagam, Angelo, *Afghanistan* (London: I.B. Tauris, 2005).

Rashid, Ahmed, *Taliban: Oil and the New Great Game in Central Asia* (New Haven: Yale University Press, 2001).

Ravuvu, Asesela, *Fijians at War, 1939–45* (PLACE: University of the South Pacific, 1988).

Reid-Daly, Ron, *Pamwe Chete: The Legend of the Selous Scouts* (Blairgowrie: Covos Day Books, 2000).

Rhodes-Wood, E.H., *War History of the Royal Pioneer Corps, 1939–1945* (Aldershot: PUBLISHER, 1960).

Rice-Holmes, T., *History of the Indian Mutiny* (London, 1904).

Ritchie, Nick, 'Rethinking Security: A Critical Analysis of the Strategic Defence and Security Review', *International Affairs* (2011).

Roberts, Lord Frederick, *Forty-One Years in India* (London: Macmillan, DATE).

Robinson, E.H.T., *Lawrence the Rebel* (London: Lincolns-Prager, 1946).

Robinson, G., 'The Battle for Iraq: Islamic Insurgencies in Comparative Perspective', *Third World Quarterly*, 28, 2 (2007), 267–273.

Robinson, Ronald, 'Non-European Foundations of European Imperialism: Sketch for a Theory of Collaboration', in Roger Owen and Bob Sutcliffe (eds.), *Studies in the Theory of Imperialism* (London: PUBLISHER, 1972).

Robson, Brian, *Road to Kabul: The Second Afghan War, 1879–81* (London: Arms and Armour Press, 1986).

Rogan, Eugene, *The Fall of the Ottomans* (New York: Basic Books, 2015).

Rose, Leo, *Nepal: Strategy for Survival* (Berkeley, CA: University of California Press, 1971).

Ross, E., *Diary of the Siege of Mafeking* (Cape Town: Van Riebeeck Society, 1980).

Rothwell, V., 'The British Government and Japanese Military Assistance, 1914–1918', *History* (February 1971), 39–43.

Roy, J.-J. E. (ed.), *Quinze ans de sejour à Java: Souvenirs d'un ancient officier* (Tours, 1861).

Roy, Kaushik, *Brown Warriors of the Raj: Recruitment and the Mechanics of Command in the Sepoy Army 1859–1913* (New Delhi: Manohar, 2008).

Roy, Kaushik, 'Military Synthesis in South Asia: Armies, Warfare and Indian Society, c. 1740–1849', *Journal of Military History*, 69, 3 (July 2005).

Rubin, Barnett R., *The Fragmentation of Afghanistan* (New Haven: Yale University Press, 2002).

Rubin, Barry, 'The Military in Contemporary Middle East Politics' *Middle East Review of International Affairs*, 5, 1 (2001).

Ryder, J., *Four Years' Service in India, by a Private Soldier* (Leicester, 1853).

Said, Edward, *Orientalism* (New York: Pantheon, 1978);.

Sampson, Stuart, 'The Journals of Lt-Col John Pennycuick', in Rob Johnson (ed.), *The British Indian Army: Virtue and Necessity* (Cambridge: Cambridge Scholars Publishers, 2014).

Sanderson, E., *Africa in the Nineteenth Century* (London, 1898).

[Sandford, D.A.], *Leaves from the Journal of a Subaltern during the Campaign in Punjaub, September 1848 to March 1849* (Edinburgh, 1849).

Saxena, K.M.L., *The Military System of India, 1859–1900* (New Delhi: Reliance Publications, 1974).

Sheehan, Neil, *A Bright Shining Lie* (London: Pan Books, 1990).

Shephard, Ben, *A War of Nerves: Soldiers and Psychiatrists, 1914–1994* (Cambridge, MA: Harvard University Press, 2001).

Shepperson, George A., 'America through Africa and Asia', *Journal of American Studies*, 14, 1 (April 1980).

Sherer, J.W., *Havelock's March on Cawnpore 1857: A Civilian's Notes* (London, 1910).

Shils, Edward A., and Morris Janowitz, 'Cohesion and Disintegration in the Wehrmacht in WWII', *Public Opinion Quarterly*, 12, 2 (Summer 1948), 280–315.

Skeet, Ian, *Oman: Politics and Development* (Basingstoke: Palgrave Macmillan, 1992).

Skinner, Major Thomas, *Fifty Years in Ceylon: An Autobiography* (London: W.H. Allen, 1891).

Sluglett, Peter, *Britain in Iraq, 1914–1932* (London: Ithaca, 1976).

Smith, Neil, and Sean MacFarland, 'Anbar Awakens: The Tipping Point', *Military Review* (March–April 2008).

Sondhaus, Lawrence, *Strategic Culture and Ways of War* (London: Routledge, 2006).

Speirenburg, Pieter, 'Faces of Violence: Homicide Trends and Cultural Meanings', *Journal of Social History*, 17 (1994), 701–716.

Spivak, Gayatri, 'Can the Subaltern Speak?' in Cary Nelson and Lawrence Grossberg (eds.), *Marxism and the Interpretations of Culture* (London and New York: Palgrave, 1988), 271–313.

Stanley, Peter, *The White Mutiny: British Military Culture in India, 1825–75* (London: Hurst and Company, 1998).

Steevens, G.W., *With Kitchener to Khartoum* (Edinburgh: William Blackwood and Sons, 1898).

Steiner, E.E., 'Separating the Soldier from the Citizen: Ideology and Criticism of Corporal Punishment in the British Army, 1790–1815', *Social History*, 8, 1 (1983).

Stoil, Jacob, 'Structures of Cooperation and Conflict: Local Forces in Mandatory Palestine during the Second World War', *Ex Historia*, 5 (2013).

Stouffer, Samuel A., *Studies in Social Psychology in the Second World War* (Princeton: Princeton University Press, 1949).

Stockwell, A.J., 'Power, Authority and Freedom', in Peter Marshall (ed.), *The British Empire* (Cambridge: Cambridge University Press, 1996), 163–164.

Strachan, Hew, *The First World War: A New Illustrated History* (London: PUBLISHER, 2003).

Strachan, Hew, 'Training, Morale and Modern War', *Journal of Contemporary History*, 41, 2 (April 2006), 211–227.

Swinson, Arthur, *North West Frontier* (London: Hutchinson, 1967).

Tauber, Eliezer, *The Arab Movements in World War I* (London: Frank Cass, 1993).

Thomas, Martin, *Empires of Intelligence: Security Services and Colonial Disorder after 1914* (London: University of California Press, 2008).

Thompson, Edward, *The Making of the Indian Princes* (Oxford: Oxford university Press, 1943).

BIBLIOGRAPHY

Thompson, Sir Robert, *Defeating Communist Insurgency* (London: Chatto and Windus, 1966).

Thornhill, Mark, *The Personal Adventures and Experiences of a Magistrate during the Rise, Progress and Suppression of the Indian Mutiny* (London, 1884).

Tierney, John J., *Chasing Ghosts: Unconventional Warfare in American History* (Washington DC: Potomac Books, 2007).

Townsend, John, *Oman: The Making of the Modern State* (London: Croom Helm, 1977).

Trabulsi, Fawaz, 'The Liberation of Dhuffar', address to Arab–American students, Boston University, 30 October 1971, reproduced in *Pakistan Forum*, 3, 2 (November 1972).

Trench, Charles Chenevix, *Charley Gordon: An Eminent Victorian Reassessed* (London: Allen Lane, 1978).

Trench, Charles Chenevix, *The Indian Army and the King's Enemies, 1900–1947* (London: Thames and Hudson, 1988).

Trotter, Captain L.J., *The Life of Hodson of Hodson's Horse* (London, 1906).

Tuker, Sir Francis, *Yellow Scarf* (London: J.M. Dent, 1961).

Ucko, David, and Robert Egnell, *Counterinsurgency in Crisis: Britain and the Challenges of Modern Warfare* (New York: Columbia University Press, 2013).

Upton, Major General E., *The Armies of Asia and Europe* (New York, 1878).

Varley, Karine, 'Contesting Concepts of the Nation in Arms: French Memories of the War of 1870–1 in Dijon', *European History Quarterly*, 36, 4 (October 2006), 548–573.

Wakeman, F., *Strangers at the Gate: Social Disorder in South China, 1839–1861* (Berkeley, CA: University of California Press, 1966).

Walmsley, H.M., *Sketches of Algeria during the Kabyle War* (London, 1858).

Warwick, Peter, *Black People and the South African War, 1899–1902* (Cambridge: Cambridge University Press, 1983).

Washbrook, David, 'Orients and Occidents: Colonial Discourse Theory and the Historiography of the British Empire', in Robin Winks (ed.), *The Oxford History of the British Empire*, vol. 5: *Historiography* (Oxford: Oxford University Press, 1999).

Weatherford, Stephen, 'Measuring Political Legitimacy', *American Political Science Review*, 86, 1 (DATE), 149–166.

Weigley, Russell F., 'The "American Way of War" Revisited', *Journal of Military History*, 66, 2 (April 2002), 501–533.

Wesbrook, Stephen D., 'The Potential for Military Disintegration', in Sam Sarkesian (ed.), *Combat Effectiveness: Cohesion, Stress and the Volunteer Military* (Beverly Hills: SAGE Publications, 1980), 247–252.

Wickremesekera, Channa, *Best Black Troops in the World: British Perceptions and the Making of the Sepoys* (New Delhi: Manohar, 2003).

Wickremesekera, Channa, *European Success and Indian Failure in the SEC: A Military Analysis* (PLACE: Monash Asia Institute, 1998).

Willan, Brian, 'Blacks in the Siege', in Iain R. Smith (ed.), *The Siege of Mafeking*, vol. 2 (Johannesburg: Brenthurst Press, 2001).

Willcocks, J., *With the Indians in France* (London: Constable, 1920).

Wills, W.A., and L.T. Collingridge (eds.), *The Downfall of Lobengula* (London, 1894).

Wilson, Jeremy, *Lawrence of Arabia* (New York: Atheneum, 1990).

Wilson, W.J., *A History of the Madras Army from 1746 to 1826* (Madras, 1888).

Winegard, Timothy, *Indigenous Peoples of the British Dominions and the First World War* (Cambridge: Cambridge University Press, 2014).

Wither, James K., 'Basra's not Belfast: The British Army, "Small Wars", and Iraq', *Small Wars and Insurgencies*, 20, 3 (2009), 611–635.

Worrall, James, 'Britain's Last Bastion in Arabia: The End of the Dhofar War, the Labour Government and the Withdrawal from RAF Salalah and Masirah, 1974–1977', in Tore T. Petersen (ed.), *Challenging Retrenchment in the Middle East* (Rostra Series, Trondheim: Tapir Academic Press, 2010).

Worrall, James, 'Transitioning in and out of COIN: Efficiency, Legitimacy and Power in Oman', in Robert Johnson and Timothy Clack (eds.), *At the End of Military Intervention* (Oxford: Oxford University Press, 2014).

Wylly, Colonel H.C., *From the Black Mountain to Waziristan* (London: Macmillan, 1912).

Yapp, M.E., *Strategies of British India: Britain, Iran and Afghanistan, 1758–1850* (Oxford: Oxford University Press, 1980).

Younossi, O., P. Thruelsen, J. Vaccaro, J. Sollinger and B. Grady, *The Long March* (PLACE: RAND, 2009).

Zeine, Zeine N., *The Emergence of Arab Nationalism: With a Background Study of Arab–Turkish Relations in the Near East* (1958; 3rd edn, Delmar, NY: Caravan, 1976).

Zuercher, Erik-Jan (ed.) *Fighting for a Living: A Comparative History of Military Labour 1500–2000* (Amsterdam: Amsterdam University Press, 2014).

INDEX

Abadan, Iran, 303

Abbas Mirza, Crown Prince of Persia, 215, 216

Abenaki, 44

Abyssinia, 97, 146, 282, 285

Account of the War in India (Cambridge), 64

Adbur Rahman Khan, Amir of Afghanistan, 163, 354

Aden, xii, 20, 274–5, 283, 300–308, 312, 313, 320, 321

Aden Protectorate Levies, 275, 304

Aden Trade Unions Congress (ATUC), 304–5, 306

advise and assist missions, 6, 379, 400

Afghan Local Police (ALP), 358

Afghan National Army (ANA), xi, 340, 342, 343–53, 359, 377, 382

Afghan National Auxiliary Police (ANAP), 340, 358, 369

Afghan National Civil Order Police (ANCOP), 350

Afghan National Police (ANP), 340, 342, 346, 347, 349–50, 352, 359

Afghan Public Protection Programme (AP3), 358, 359–61

Afghan Social Outreach Programme, 359

Afghanistan
Anglo-Afghan War, First (1839–42), 79, 151–2, 203, 207, 208
Anglo-Afghan War, Second (1878–80), 72, 97–8, 104–5, 147, 153, 189
arbakai, 340, 355
chagha, 356
chalweshtai, 356
Christie's visit (1810), 215
Civil War (1989–2001), 353, 357–8
Durrani Empire (1747–1826), 353
First World War (1914–18), 239
irregular forces, 353–61
lashkars, 354, 356
Operation Resolute Support (2014–), 352
qawm, 17, 355, 356, 368
Soviet War (1979–89), xii, 337, 343, 348, 355, 356–7
Taliban Emirate (1996–2001), 353
tribes, 353–6, 368
tsalweshtai, 355, 368
Wilayat Khurasan (2015–), 353
Afghanistan War (2001–14), ix–xi, xiii, 2–3, 6–11, 19, 20, 38, 269, 337, 340–61, 378, 380
Afghan Local Police (ALP), 358